D1556970

The Ultimate Rogov's Guide
to Israeli Wines

Daniel Rogov

THE ULTIMATE ROGOV'S GUIDE TO ISRAELI WINES

The Toby Press

The Ultimate Rogov's Guide
to Israeli Wines
Eighth Annual Edition
The Toby Press LLC

POB 8531, New Milford, CT 06776-8531, USA
& POB 4044, Jerusalem 91040, Israel

www.tobypress.com

ISBN 978-161-329-0194, *hardcover*

A CIP catalogue record for this title is
available from the British Library.

Typeset in Chaparral by KPS

TABLE OF CONTENTS

FOREWORD

André Tchelistcheff, perhaps the most influential of California winemakers, was referred to by three generations of those who followed his path as "maestro," his words and teachings held dear by them. One of Tchelistcheff's often-quoted axioms is: "In a good year, don't worry about the wine. God made the wine for you. In a bad year, pray to God that your winemaker knows how to make wine."

Although Israel only rarely suffers from catastrophic vintage years, the harvests of 2009 and 2010 were difficult in many ways, the weather playing nasty tricks and in some cases extending the harvest for a month or more beyond its normal duration and in other cases demanding early harvest to save the grapes from rot or over-ripeness. In Tchelistcheff's terms, these were winemakers' years, and those who are well founded in both intuition and knowledge have produced some very fine wines indeed. The best wines of these two years are two or more years away from release, but barrel tastings have shown that we will find only a few wines capable of anything more than medium-term cellaring. It has also shown that winemakers relying on integrity will have down-graded many of their grapes. That is to say, those grapes that in a better year might have been destined for top-of-the-line wines will now go into wines a step-down in status and that is indeed the honorable thing to do.

Even more important than the past two vintage years, Israel continues to produce wines that challenge many of the best that can be found in North America and Europe. Looking back, when I first arrived in Israel, nearly thirty-five years ago, the wine situation in the country was fairly abysmal. A great number of wines were indeed being produced but the vast majority of those were wines intended for Kiddush and other blessings. Most were red, sweet and coarse, and not a few of those had more of a resemblance to cough medicine than to fine wine. Being charitable, there were few acceptable wines, none that might be considered excellent and quite a few that were out-and-out horrid.

The times they have indeed a'changed, and since the release of the first wines from the Golan Heights Winery in 1984, it has become ever increasingly apparent that Israel is now a legitimate contender on the international wine scene. Carmel, the oldest and still-largest winery in the country, celebrated its 120th harvest in 2010, and two medium-sized wineries, Dalton and Galil Mountain, celebrated their 10th anniversaries. As the Golan Heights Winery continues to produce world-class wines, so do Carmel, Dalton and Galil Mountain. No less important, an increasing number of other large, medium and small wineries, some of those scoffed at by wine lovers even a decade ago, have joined Israel's wine revolution and are producing wines that are worthy of the attention of even the most sophisticated of wine lovers.

Today, Israeli wines continue to receive highly positive reviews not only in Israel but abroad. Whereas a mere decade ago, no serious wine critic in Europe or America would have considered reviewing Israeli wines, today they are reviewed on a regular basis by the most serious critics in many of the most prestigious journals. More important, many wineries have continued to demonstrate increases in quality not only in their most prestigious wines but in those wines meant for inexpensive, everyday consumption. From the point of view of consumers, although the per capita consumption of wine did not increase in Israel, there is a growing awareness within the country that wine can be an integral part of a cultured and civilized lifestyle.

Indeed, as is the case in all wine-producing countries, not all wineries are producing good wines. There is no question, however, that the number of fine wines available is on the increase. The days when Israel was producing primarily sweet red wines for sacramental purposes are long gone, and today Israel is acknowledged as a serious wine producer. Wines are being made from highly prized grape varieties at more than two hundred wineries scattered all over the country, from the Upper Galilee and the Golan Heights to the Judean Hills and the Negev Desert. The construction of state-of-the-art wineries, the ongoing import and cultivation of good vine stock from California, France and Australia, and the enthusiasm and knowledge of young, well-trained winemakers who are not afraid to experiment with new wine varieties and blends has yielded an abundance of quality wines that can compete comfortably with many of the fine wines of the New and Old Worlds.

The purpose of this book is to provide readers with extensive knowledge about the wineries and wines of Israel, and to serve as a convenient guide for selecting and storing local wines. The introduction supplies the reader with the necessary historical and geographical background, while the major part of the guide is devoted to the wines, offering tasting notes and scores for wines that are now on the shelves or scheduled to appear within the next six to nine months, as well as wines that are still stored in the cellars of wine lovers.

How to Use the Guide

Wineries are arranged in the book by alphabetical order, and in the few cases where wineries may be known by more than one name, especially outside of Israel, readers will find the alternative names listed in the index. Following a brief description of the location, history and production of each winery are the reviews, ranging from the top-level series to the lower. Each series is arrayed from red wines to whites, followed by sparkling and dessert wines. These are further divided into grape varieties such as Cabernet Sauvignon, Merlot, etc. Each variety is arranged according to vintage years, from the most current release to the most mature available or still likely to be found in a fine wine cellar. Each review concludes with a Score and a suggested drinking window.

Key to Symbols and Scores

THE WINERIES

- ***** A WORLD-CLASS WINERY, REGULARLY PRODUCING EXCELLENT WINES
- **** CONSISTENTLY PRODUCING HIGH-QUALITY WINES
- *** SOLID AND RELIABLE PRODUCER WITH AT LEAST SOME GOOD WINES
- ** ADEQUATE
- * HARD TO RECOMMEND

The ratings of wineries that have been releasing wines for less than three years should be considered as tentative, much depending on the consistency of future releases.

SCORES FOR INDIVIDUAL WINES

In recent months, after a great deal of personal reflection as well as consultation with several colleagues whose opinions I value, I have concluded that with nearly every wine- producing region of the world now giving us wines that improve in quality on a regular basis, the time has come to somewhat revise not my scores, but the meanings of those scores.

As an example: In the past a wine scoring 75–79 points might have been considered average in quality. Today, with world-wide improvement, the "average"-quality rating will now include wines that earn scores between 80–84 while wines scoring 75–79 are now best categorized as mediocre.

Following is what will be my "adjusted" scoring system from this date on.

95–100	Truly Great Wines, My Highest Recommendation
90–94	Exceptional in Every Way, Highly Recommended
85–89	Good to Very Good and Recommended
80–84	Average and Not Exciting, Recommended Primarily as Entry-Level Wines
75–79	Mediocre and At Least Somewhat Faulted, Not Recommended

| 70–74 | Drinkable But with a Major Fault and Not Recommended |
| Under 70 | Seriously Faulted and Most Definitely Not Recommended |

As always, I remind my readers that scores are merely a shorthand way of noting a critic's overall impression of the quality of a wine. While a Score may thus give some clues as to quality it says nothing about whether one individual or another will enjoy the wine. A Score is nothing more than two digits, and once in a while three, at the end of a tasting note. Insights into the style and personality of a wine are found not in the Score but in the tasting note. It is also important to be aware that different critics may well perceive the same wines in different ways and it falls on those who read wine criticism to determine which critic or critics give them the best direction for their own tastes.

Special Note about Tentative Scores

The scores of wines tasted only from the barrel – that is to say, well before release and sometimes even before final blends have been made – are scored within a range and noted as *tentative*. Wines attaining such scores will be retasted and updated in future editions.

DRINKING WINDOWS

A drinking window is the suggested period during which the wine is at its very best. The notation "best 2014–2018," for example, indicates that the wine needs further cellaring before it comes to its peak and will then cellar comfortably through 2018. "Drink now–2015" indicates that although the wine is drinking well now it will continue to cellar nicely until 2015. "Drink now" indicates that the wine is drinking well now but can be held for another year or so. "Drink up" suggests that the wine is at or past its peak and should not be cellared any longer. "Drink from release" refers to wines that are not yet on the market. Some will appear within the coming nine months and others may appear only in two to three years. Such wines were tasted either from bottles as advance tastings or from barrels.

KOSHER WINES

That there is no contradiction between making fine wine and the laws of kashrut is made apparent in the introduction to this guide. Within the guide, the reviews of all wines that have received a kashrut certificate from a recognized rabbinic authority are followed by the symbol K.

Introduction

The History of Wine in Israel

Ancient Times

The history of wine in the Land of Israel is as old as the history of the people who have inhabited that land over the centuries. As early as five thousand years ago people cultivated vines and made, stored and shipped wines. The first mention of wine in the Bible is in a reference to Noah, who is said to have planted the first vineyard and to have become intoxicated when he drank the wine (Genesis 9:20–21). Another well-known reference concerns the spies sent by Moses to explore the Land of Canaan. They returned after their mission with a cluster of grapes said to have been so large and heavy that it had to be borne on a carrying frame (Numbers 13:23). The vine is also mentioned as one of the blessings of the good land promised to the children of Israel (Deuteronomy 8:8).

Much of the process of winemaking has remained consistent throughout this time. Already in the Bible, we find a list of the necessary steps to care for a vineyard:

> My beloved had a vineyard in a very fruitful hill;
> And he dug it; and cleared it of stones,
> And planted it with the choicest vine,
> And built a tower in the midst of it,
> And also hewed out a vat therein;
> And he looked that it should bring forth grapes.
> He broke the ground, cleared it of stone and
>   planted it with choice vines.
> He built a watchtower inside it,
> He even hewed a wine press inside it.
>
> *(Isaiah 5:1–2)*

Vintners in ancient times knew as we do today that locating vineyards at higher altitudes, where there are greater temperature changes between night and day, would cause the fruit to ripen more slowly, adding to the sweetness of the fruit and its ability to produce fine wines. Two ways of growing vines were known: in one the vines were allowed to grow along the ground; in the other they were trained upward on trellises (Ezekiel 17:6–8). It was widely accepted then as today that vines cultivated by the second method almost always produce superior grapes.

Remains of ancient wine presses may be found today in all parts of Israel, from the Galilee to Jerusalem and the Negev Desert. In nearly every part of Israel, archaeologists have discovered hundreds of jars for the storage and transportation of wine. Many of these amphorae list in detail where and by whom the wine was made, as well as the year of the vintage, indicating that even in antiquity the source of the grapes and the quality of the harvest were considered important.

It is known today that even during the Bronze Age, Egyptian Pharaohs enjoyed wines that were shipped from Canaan. The growing of grapes and the production of wine was a major agricultural endeavor during the periods of the First and Second Temples, and the kings of Judah and Israel were said to have owned large vineyards as well as vast stores of wine. The vineyards and stores of King David in particular were so numerous that he is said to have appointed two officials, one to be in charge of the vineyards, and the other to be in charge of storage (I Chronicles 27:27).

In biblical times the harvest was a celebratory period as well as a period of courtship. The treading of the grapes was done most often on a *gat* or an *arevah*, the *gat* being a small, generally square, pressing floor that had been cut into bedrock, and the *arevah* a smaller treading surface that could be moved from vineyard to vineyard. From either of these the must (that is to say, the fresh and as yet unfermented grape juice) ran into a *yekev*, which was a vat for collecting the must as it flowed from the treading floor through a hole carved in the stone. When natural bedrock was unavailable, an earthen treading surface lined with mosaics was used.

In several areas, caves or large cisterns carved from natural bedrock have been found, which would have served two purposes – first for storing the grapes until they were pressed, and then, because they were cool and dark, for storing the wine while it fermented and then aged in clay jugs.

Once fermentation had been completed, the wines were stored in pottery vessels which were sealed with wood, stone or clay stoppers. For purposes of shipping, the stoppers were wrapped in cloth and coated with clay. Since new clay vessels tend to absorb as much as 20 percent of the wines stored in them, it became common practice to store better wines in older jars. A major development, during the third century BCE, was the discovery that stoppers made from cork were an effective way to seal amphorae.

As much as these wines were prized, it must be understood that they were very different from wines as we know them today. They were often so intense and coarse that they needed a fair amount of "adjustment" before they were considered drinkable. To improve the bouquet, the Romans were known to add spices and scents to their wines. To make the wine sweeter, they added a syrup made by heating grape juice in lead containers for a long period over a low flame. To improve flavors and hide faults it was customary to add honey, pepper, chalk, gypsum, lime, resin, herbs and even seawater.

In the time of the First and Second Temples, wine was widely consumed by the local populace, but the very best wines were set aside for libations in the Temple. The Bible specifies the different types of offerings – a quarter of a *hin* (one *hin* was the equivalent of about 5.7 liters or 1.5 gallons) of wine when offering a sheep; a third of a *hin* for a ram; and half a *hin* for an animal from the herd, such as a cow (Numbers 15:5). In addition, people were required to give tithes of new wine to the Temple (Deuteronomy 12:17). Wines were so central to the culture during that period that those who planted vineyards were exempt from military service, and illustrations of grapes, grape leaves, amphorae and drinking vessels were often used as symbols on seals and coins as well as for decorations on the friezes of buildings.

After the destruction of the Second Temple, wine was

integrated into all religious ceremonies including *brit milah* (circumcision), weddings, the Sabbath and high holidays. It is especially central in the Passover *Seder*, where it is customary to drink four glasses of wine.

During the late Roman and Byzantine periods, running from the fourth to the sixth century, the wine industry shifted from Judea to the southern part of the land, where the port towns of Ashkelon and Gaza became centers of wine trading. The wines produced in the area were so coveted by the Romans that they shipped them to their legions throughout the Mediterranean and North Africa, and Christian pilgrims brought them back to Europe.

The Moslem conquest of the Holy Land in the seventh century put an end to this prosperous industry. The Moslem rulers banned the drinking of alcohol and as a result the flourishing local wine industry almost ceased to exist. The only wines allowed were the small amounts that Christians and Jews required for sacramental purposes. Throughout the twelfth and thirteenth centuries, the Crusaders made sporadic attempts to revive the wine industry in the Holy Land, but these were short-lived, as it was easier to ship wines from Europe. It was only with the renewal of Jewish settlement in the nineteenth century that the local winemaking industry was reestablished.

Modern Times

The Jewish philanthropist Sir Moses Montefiore, who visited the Holy Land numerous times in the nineteenth century, encouraged the Jews living there to work the land and re-plant vines. One person who heeded his call was Rabbi Itzhak Schorr, who founded a new winery in Jerusalem in 1848. Rabbi Abraham Teperberg followed suit, founding the Efrat winery in 1870 in the old city of Jerusalem. In addition, he also opened an agricultural school in Mikveh Israel, not far from Jaffa. This school was financed and run by *Alliance Israélite Universelle*, a Jewish organization based in France that aimed at training Jewish settlers in agricultural work. The school was the first to plant European grape varieties, and had a winery as well as large wine cellars. Many of its graduates became vine growers.

An important boost to the local industry came about when Baron Edmond de Rothschild, the owner of the famed Chateau Lafite in Bordeaux, agreed to come to the help of the Jewish colonies, and financed the planting of the first vineyards near Rishon Letzion, on the coastal plain. Rothschild hoped that the Holy Land would serve as the source of kosher wines for Jews the world over, and that the wine industry would provide a solid economic basis for the new Jewish communities. He brought in experts from Europe and imported grape varieties from the south of France including Alicante Bouchet, Clairette, Carignan, Grenache, Muscat and Semillon. He also funded the first wineries of the new Jewish settlements – first the Rishon Letzion Winery in 1882, then the Zichron Ya'akov winery in the Mount Carmel area in 1890 – thus marking the beginning of the modern wine industry in the Land of Israel. Unfortunately, not all ran smoothly. The first harvests were lost to heat and in 1890–1891 the land was overrun by phylloxera, a plague of aphid-like insects that destroyed all of the vines. The vineyards were dug up and replanted with vines grafted onto phylloxera-resistant root stocks.

In 1906 Rothschild helped to set up a cooperative of grape growers that managed the two wineries, and in 1957 his heirs sold their share to the cooperative. It took the name Carmel Mizrachi, and continued to be the dominant factor in the local wine industry until the early 1980s.

However, Rothschild's dream that viticulture would provide a major source of income for the region was shattered with the advent of three major events which virtually eliminated the fledgling industry's three largest potential markets: the Russian Revolution, the enactment of Prohibition in the United States, and the banning of imported wines to Egypt. Many vineyards had to be uprooted. While several new wineries opened in the following decades, including Segal, Eliaz and Stock, for the most part they and Carmel continued to produce wines largely destined for sacramental purposes. Records from 1948 testifying to the annual consumption of a mere 3.9 liters of wine per person demonstrate that wine had not yet become part of the culture of life in Israel.

The Israeli Wine Revolution

In 1972, Professor Cornelius Ough of the Department of Viticulture and Oenology at the University of California at Davis visited Israel and suggested that the soil and climate of the Golan Heights would prove ideal for the raising of grapes. In 1976 the first vines were planted in the Golan, and in 1983 the then-newly-established Golan Heights Winery released its first wines. Almost overnight it became apparent that Israel was capable of producing wines of world-class quality. During the early 1980s the Israeli wine industry endured an economic crisis, but the revolution had begun and there was no turning back.

Unfettered by outdated winemaking traditions or by a large stagnant corporate structure, the young winery imported excellent vine stock from California, built a state-of-the-art winery, and added to this the enthusiasm and expertise of young American winemakers who had been trained at the University of California at Davis. Equally important, the Golan winery began to encourage vineyard owners to improve the quality of their grapes and, in the American tradition, paid bonuses for grapes with high sugar and acid content, while rejecting substandard grapes. The winery was also the first to realize that wines made from Grenache, Semillon, Petite Sirah and Carignan grapes would not put them on the world wine map, and focused on planting and making wines from Cabernet Sauvignon, Merlot, Sauvignon Blanc, Chardonnay, White Riesling, Gewurztraminer and other noble grape varieties.

The Golan wines were a success from the beginning, not only within Israel but abroad. This success had a great impact on other Israeli wineries, which have made major steps in improving the quality of their wines. There are now five major wineries, twelve medium-sized wineries and a host of small wineries in the country, many of which are producing wines that are of high quality, and several producing wines good enough to interest connoisseurs all over the world.

The Current and Future State of Wine Production in Israel

Accurate data about the local wine industry is difficult to come by due to lack of coordination between the Israeli Wine Institute, the Ministry of Agriculture, the Export Institute and the Grape Growers Association. When wineries submit their production and export figures, for example, they make no distinction between exports of table wines, sacramental wines, grape juice and even brandy and liqueurs. It is estimated that today Israel produces about thirty-six million bottles of table wine a year, an amount representing continued growth of five to ten percent annually over the past five years. Approximately forty-eight thousand dunams (twelve thousand acres) of land are currently under grape cultivation, an increase of fifty-five percent in cultivated land area since 1995. Moreover, the development of vineyards is once again on the rise, and several of the medium-sized wineries are planting vineyards that are intended to double or triple their production. Approximately sixty percent of the table wines produced today are dry reds, while as recently as 1995 production was seventy percent whites and only thirty percent reds.

Following an extended period in which the imagination of the wine-drinking public within Israel was captured by boutique wineries and *garagistes*, the years 2003–2008 might be regarded as the years of the larger wineries. On the other hand, 2009 through 2011 saw a balancing phenomenon, for whereas well over 90% of the better wines in the country are produced by the larger wineries, it is once again the wines of the small and often newer small wineries with which Israelis and those abroad have "fallen in love." In 2003, the Golan Heights Winery released the country's first varietal wines made from Sangiovese, Pinot Noir and Gamay grapes, as well as the country's first single-vineyard organically grown Chardonnay. Under its Yarden label, the winery also produced the country's first Semillon-botrytis wine. During that same year, Carmel released the first wines from its new boutique winery Yatir, and has continued to give us exciting single-vineyard Cabernet Sauvignon, Syrah and Chardonnay wines. Barkan introduced the country's first Pinotage wine. During 2005, Recanati released the country's first wine made from Barbera grapes and several of the medium-sized wineries gave us the country's first Zinfandel wines. Smaller wineries, on the other hand, especially those focused on unusual varietal wines or equally unusual blends, have no less captured the palates of the more wine-sophisticated among consumers both in Israel and abroad.

Although the Golan Heights Winery, with its Katzrin, Rom, Yarden, Gamla and Golan series, remains the obvious quality leader among the large wineries in the country, a great deal of excitement continues to be generated by Clos de Gat, Tabor, Yatir, Pelter, Vitkin, Lewinsohn and Sea Horse, and the mid- and upper-level series of Carmel. Three other large wineries, Binyamina, Teperberg (until recently known as Efrat) and Zion, have now joined the ranks of those wineries on the way up. Each of these wineries, now with well-trained winemakers aboard, are in the process of modernizing their equipment, gaining better control over their vineyards and producing several series of wines that are successfully capturing the attention of sophisticated wine drinkers.

People Are Asking:
What About Wine Competitions?

As is fairly well known to my regular readers, I am only rarely enthusiastic about prizes awarded at wine competitions. Simply stated, at too many competitions all one has to do to win a prize is to enter their wines, pay a fee and walk away with one or more awards.

Of the many wine competitions held annually, two that I consider to have great credibility are the Vinitaly International Wine Competition and the Decanter World Wine Awards, both of which are fully professional and which give awards sparingly and only to those wines deserving of recognition. In 2011, Israeli wineries attained phenomenal success and international recognition at both of those.

As one sign of the seriousness of the Vinitaly competition, in the year 2011, there were 3,720 wines entered in the competition from 30 countries. Only 71 medals were awarded. Of those, two of the grand gold medals were awarded to the Golan Heights Winery (one for the winery's 2008 Heightswine and another for the 2009 Odem Vineyard Chardonnay). Even more impressive, the winery was honored by being declared "the best wine producer in the world."

That title may be somewhat of an exaggeration but it is no exaggeration at all to say that of the thousands of wines in the competition, those of the Golan Heights Winery proved to be the very best. The winery has won grand gold medals at this competition in the past (2004 and 2006), but this is the very first time that any Israeli winery has won what might well be considered "best winery of the competition" and that is no small achievement.

Equally credible is the annual competition of the highly respected *Decanter* magazine in which wines from the entire world are entered. At that event the Carmel Winery stood well above the crowd by winning the highest awards for best Regional and International wines. The Carmel wine that took the greatest honors was their 2006 Kayoumi Vineyard Shiraz.

More than that, this was the very first time that an Israeli winery won the Decanter International Trophy.

There is no question but that both the Golan Heights Winery and Carmel deserve whatever compliments come their way. Even more significantly, these awards reflect positively on the huge advancements continuously being made in the Israeli wine industry. Such recognition goes a long way in bringing Israeli wines to the awareness of an ever-increasing audience of wine consumers.

The Phenomenon of the Boutique Wineries

In recent years, the country has seen a dramatic growth in boutique wineries, *garagistes*, micro-wineries and artisanal producers, each striving, but not all succeeding, to create world-class wines. Such wineries, producing anywhere from under one thousand to one hundred thousand bottles annually, can remain highly personalized affairs, the winemakers having full control over their vineyards, knowing precisely what wine is in what barrel at any given moment and what style they want their wines to reflect. The label of a boutique winery does not, however, guarantee quality. At the top end of the range, a handful of small wineries founded by competent men and women, several of them well-trained professionals, are producing some of the very best wines in the country. At the bottom end are numerous wineries founded by hobbyists who produce wines that are barely acceptable. It is largely the wineries at the lower end of this spectrum that are now closing. Despite this, boutique wineries continue to open at a surprisingly rapid pace, as if to demonstrate that optimism knows no bounds.

Grape-Growing Regions

The ideal areas for the cultivation of wine grapes lie in the two strips between 30–50 degrees north and south of the equator. Israel, which is located on the southern side of that strip in the Northern Hemisphere, is thus ideally situated. Considering Israel's specific climate, it is important to note that the vine can thrive in many different types of soil, as well as in regions that receive little rainfall.

Although the land area of Israel is a mere 7,992 square miles (which is five percent of the land area of California), like many wine-growing regions that have a long north-south axis (Italy, Chile or California, for example), the country has a large variety of microclimates. In the north, snow falls in winter and conditions are comparable to those of Bordeaux and the Northern Rhone Valley of France, yet within a few hours' drive one arrives at the Negev Desert, where the climate is similar to that of North Africa.

The country is divided into five vine-growing regions, the names of which are generally accepted by the European community and appear on all labels of varietal wines that are designated for sale both locally and abroad. Each region is divided into sub-regions, encompassing specific valleys, mountains or other locales. Although various governmental and quasi-governmental agencies are considering implementing a more stringent *appellation controlee* system, the major regions today remain as follows:

GALILEE: Located in the northern part of the country, this area extends to the Lebanese border and incorporates the Golan Heights. It is the region most suited for viticulture in Israel. The high altitude, cool breezes, marked day and night temperature changes and rich, well-drained soils make the area ideal for the cultivation of a large variety of grapes. The area is divided into four sub-regions: the Upper Galilee, the Lower Galilee, Tabor and the Golan Heights. Some of the wineries located here are the Golan Heights Winery, Galil Mountain, Chateau Golan, Dalton, Saslove and Tabor. Development of new vineyards continues apace in the area, many of these owned by wineries located in other parts of the country.

SHOMRON (SAMARIA): Located near the Mediterranean coast south of Haifa, it includes the Carmel Mountain Range and the vineyards surrounding the towns of Zichron Ya'akov and Binyamina. This region remains the largest grape-growing area in the country. The area has medium-heavy soils and a Mediterranean climate, with warm summers and humid winters. Wineries in the area include Margalit, Tishbi, Binyamina and the Zichron Ya'akov branch of Carmel, all relying at least in part on grapes grown in other areas for their better wines.

SHIMSHON (SAMSON): Located between the foothills of the Jerusalem Mountains and the Mediterranean coast, this region encompasses the central plains, including the area around Rishon Letzion and Rehovot. Although the area boasts many vineyards, the limestone, clay and loamy soils and the coastal Mediterranean climate of warm, humid summers and mild winters do not offer ideal conditions for the cultivation of fine varieties, and many of the wineries in the area rely on grapes from other parts of the country. Among the wineries located here are Carmel, Barkan, Karmei Yosef, and Soreq.

JERUSALEM MOUNTAINS: Sometimes referred to as the Judean Hills, this region surrounding the city of Jerusalem offers a variety of soil conditions and a cool Mediterranean climate due to its relatively high altitude. For many years the region served as home primarily to wineries that specialized in sweet sacramental wines, but about a decade ago it became clear that this area could prove excellent for raising noble varieties. The area underwent strenuous revitalization with the major planting of sophisticated vineyards and the opening of several medium-sized and an increasing number of small wineries. More than twenty-five wineries are found in the area, including Castel, Clos de Gat, Sea Horse, Flam, Ella Valley Vineyards, Mony, Tzora and Teperberg. It is clear that a true *route de vins* is developing in this region.

NEGEV: Ten years ago, few would have thought this semi-arid desert region appropriate for growing grapes, but now, sophisticated computerized drip-irrigation systems have made it possible to grow high quality grapes here, including among others Merlot, Cabernet Sauvignon and Chardonnay. The region is divided into two sub-areas: Ramat Arad, which

Vineyard in the Galilee on the Lebanese Border

is situated 600–700 meters above sea level and has impressive night-day temperature changes, where results with noble varieties have been excellent; and the Southern Negev, a lower, more arid area where sandy to loamy soils and very hot and dry summers offer a special challenge to grape growers. Carmel was the first to plant extensive vineyards at Ramat Arad. More recently, Barkan has begun wide-ranging development of vineyards at Mitzpe Ramon in the heart of the Negev. Among the wineries found here, some rely entirely on desert-raised grapes. Others that draw as well on grapes from other areas are Yatir, Asif and Sde Boker.

Grape Varieties in Israel

The last two decades have seen a major upheaval in the vineyards of Israel. Prior to 1985 the grapes planted were largely Carignan, Petite Sirah and Grenache for red and rosé wines, and Semillon, Emerald Riesling and French Colombard for whites. The wineries focused on light, white and often sweet wines, and only a handful of noble varieties were to be found in the country. The scene shifted dramatically with the development of vineyards planted with noble varieties, first on the Golan Heights, then in the Upper Galilee. Today, from the Negev Desert to the northernmost parts of the country, the focus is on many of those varieties that have proven themselves throughout the world.

ROGOV'S
GUIDE
TO
ISRAELI
WINES

■ **Wine Regions**
Vineyard Areas

Galilee
   Upper Galilee
   Lower Galilee
   Golan Heights

Shomron
   Mt. Carmel
   Sharon

Samson
   Dan
   Adulam
   Latrun

Jerusalem Mountains
   Beit-El
   Jerusalem
   Southern Jerusalem Mountains

Negev
   Northern Negev Hills
   Central Negev

Unlike many of the wine-growing regions, especially in Europe, Israel does not have any indigenous grapes that might be considered appropriate for making wine. The closest the country came to having its own grape was the introduction of the Argaman grape, a cross between Souzao and Carignan grapes. Widely planted in the early 1980s, that experiment proved a fiasco: although the grape yielded wines deep in color, they lacked flavor, depth or body.

White Wine Grapes

CHARDONNAY: The grape that produces the great dry white wines of Burgundy and is indispensable to the production of Champagne. The most popular white wine grape in the world today, producing wines that can be oaked or unoaked, and range in flavors from flinty minerals to citrus, pineapple, tropical fruits and grapefruit, and in texture from minerally crisp to creamy.

CHENIN BLANC: Originating in France's central Loire Valley, a grape capable of producing long-lived wines with honeyed notes. Until recently used in Israel to produce ordinary, semi-dry wines but now being shown by several small wineries to produce exciting dry and sweet wines.

COLOMBARD: Known in Israel as French Colombard and producing mostly thin and acidic wines.

EMERALD RIESLING: A cross between the Muscadelle and Riesling grapes developed in California primarily for growth in warm climates, the grape produces mostly semi-dry wines of little interest to sophisticated wine consumers.

GEWURZTRAMINER: This grape originated in Germany, came to its glory in Alsace and has now been transplanted to many parts of the world. Capable of producing aromatic dry and sweet wines that are often typified by their softness and spiciness, as well as distinctive aromas and flavors of litchis and rose petals.

MUSCAT: There are many varieties of Muscat, the two most often found in Israel being the Muscat of Alexandria and Muscat Canelli, both of which are capable of producing wines that range from the dry to the sweet and are almost always typified by their perfumed aromas.

RIESLING: Sometimes known as Johannisberg Riesling, sometimes as White Riesling and sometimes simply as Riesling, this noble German variety has the potential to produce wines, that although light in body and low in alcohol, are highly flavored and capable of long aging. Typified by aromas and flavors of flowers, minerals and lime, and when aged, sometimes taking on a tempting petrol-like aroma. Not to be confused with the definitely inferior Emerald Riesling grape.

SAUVIGNON BLANC: At its best in the Loire Valley and Bordeaux for producing dry white wines, this successful transplant to Israel is capable of producing refreshing, sophisticated and distinctively aromatic and grassy wines, often best consumed in their youth.

SEMILLON: Although this native French grape was used for many years in Israel to produce largely uninteresting semi-dry white wines, its susceptibility to noble rot is now being used to advantage to produce sweet dessert wines with the distinctive bouquet and flavors of melon, fig and citrus. Several small wineries have recently begun producing interesting dry whites from this grape.

TRAMINETTE: A not overly exciting hybrid, a derivative of the Gewurztraminer grape, developed primarily for use in cold-weather New York State and Canadian climates.

VIOGNIER: The most recent white wine transplant to Israel, this grape produces the fascinating Condrieu wines of France's Rhone Valley. Capable of producing aromatic but crisply dry whites and full-bodied whites, some of which have long aging potential.

Red Wine Grapes

ARGAMAN: An Israeli-inspired cross between Souzao and Carignan grapes. Although Segal has produced several Argaman wines of interest the grape is possibly best categorized as the great local wine failure, in general producing wines of little interest. Many of the vineyards that were planted with this grape continue to be uprooted to make room for more serious varieties.

BARBERA: From Italy's Piedmont region, this grape has the potential for producing wines that, although light and fruity, are capable of great charm. Some fine rosé wines are now appearing from Barbera.

CABERNET FRANC: Less intense and softer than Cabernet Sauvignon, most often destined to be blended with Merlot and Cabernet Sauvignon, but even on its own capable of producing dramatically good, leafy, fruity and aromatic reds. A grape with very good potential in Israel.

CABERNET SAUVIGNON: The most noble variety of Bordeaux, capable of producing superb wines, often blended with smaller amounts of Merlot and Cabernet Franc. The best wines from this grape are rich in color and tannins, and have complex aromas and depth of flavors, those often typified by blackcurrants, spices and cedarwood. At their best, intriguing and complex wines that profit from cellaring.

CARIGNAN: An old-timer on the Israeli scene, for many years this originally Spanish grape produced largely dull and charmless wines. In recent years, however, several wineries have demonstrated that old-vine Carignan grapes, especially those in fields that have been unwatered for many years, are producing interesting and high-quality wines.

GAMAY: The well-known grape of France's Beaujolais region, this fairly recent introduction to Israel is capable of producing light- to medium-bodied wines of fragrance and charm, intended primarily for drinking in their youth. Alas, a grape to which the Israeli public has not taken kindly and probably destined more for "nouveau"-style wines than anything else.

GRENACHE: Although this grape has traditionally done well in France's Rhone Valley and Spain, for many years it did not yield sophisticated kosher wines, most being somewhat pale, overripe and sweet in nature. Today, however, there is a growing movement relying on old, often untended vines and to cut back on the yield of the grapes, the result being sometimes concentrated and intense wines of long cellaring potential. An increasing number of fine varietal wines are now appearing based on this grape.

MALBEC: Well known in France's Bordeaux, the Loire and Cahors, and the specialty grape of Argentina, this grape is capable of producing dense, rich, tannic and spicy wines that are remarkably dark in color.

MERLOT: Softer, more supple and often less tannic than Cabernet Sauvignon – with which it is often blended – but capable of producing voluptuous, opulent, plummy wines of great interest. A grape that has proven popular on its own as it produces wines that are often easier to drink and are approachable earlier than wines made from Cabernet Sauvignon.

MOURVÈDRE (ALSO KNOWN AS MATARÓ, OR MONAS-TRELL): A grape with a long and noble history, probably introduced to the Catalonia region of Spain by the Phoenicians about 500 BCE. Thrives in Mediterranean climes, where it is capable of making both fine rosé wines as well as full-bodied, deeply colored, tannic reds. A fine blending agent, especially with Grenache.

NEBBIOLO: The grape from which the Barolo and Barbaresco wines of Italy's Piedmont region are made. Still largely experimental in Israel but with the potential for producing perfumed, fruity and intense wines that are full-bodied, high in tannins, acidity and color, and have the potential for long-term cellaring.

PETIT VERDOT: Planted only in small quantities and used in Israel as it is in Bordeaux, primarily for blending with other noble varieties to add acidity and balance. Capable on its own of producing a long-lived and tannic wine when ripe.

PETITE SIRAH: Related only peripherally to the great Syrah grape, this grape is, at its best, capable of producing dark, tannic and well-balanced wines of great appeal and sophistication. This potential is being realized far more frequently within Israel, especially when the grapes come from older vineyards.

PINOT NOIR: A relatively recent transplant to Israel, this grape, which is responsible for the great reds of Burgundy, is making a very good initial showing. At its best the grape is capable of producing smooth, rich and intricate wines of exquisite qualities, with flavors of cherries, wild berries and violets, which as they age take on aromas and flavors of chocolate and game meat. Also used in Israel, as in the Champagne region of France, to blend with Chardonnay to make sparkling wines.

PINOTAGE: A South African cross between Pinot Noir and Cinsault, capable of being flavorful and powerful, yet soft and full, with a pleasing sweet finish and a lightly spicy overlay. Still to prove its full potential locally.

SANGIOVESE: Italy's most frequently planted variety, found in the simplest Chianti and most complex Brunello di Montalcino wines, this is another grape recently introduced to Israel, showing fine early results with wines that are lively, fruity and full of charm.

SYRAH: Some believe that this grape originated in ancient Persia and was brought to France by the Romans, while others speculate that it is indigenous to France. Syrah found its first glory in France's northern Rhone Valley, and then in Australia (where it is known as Shiraz). Capable of producing deep royal-purple, tannic wines that are full-bodied enough to be thought of as dense and powerful, but with excellent balance and complex aromas and flavors of plums, berries, currants, black pepper and chocolate. Results from this grape have been exciting, and plantings are increasing dramatically.

TEMPRANILLO: The staple grape of Spain's Rioja area, with recent plantings in Israel, this is a grape with the potential for producing long-lived, complex and sophisticated wines typified by aromas and flavors of black fruits, leather, tobacco and spices.

TINTA CÃO: A Portuguese variety, traditionally one of the grapes used in the production of Port. A difficult grape to raise but one showing promise in Israel for use in making non-reinforced and reinforced sweet wines. As a varietal wine can show sweet plums, figs, chocolate and spices along with notes of tobacco and roasted nuts. Probably destined largely to be blended with Touriga Nacional.

TOURIGA NACIONAL: One of the more recent varieties to be introduced to Israel, this is Portugal's finest grape, used not only in the production of Port but increasingly for dry red wines. Showing great promise on the Golan Heights.

ZINFANDEL: Zinfandel (the Italian variety of which is known as Primitivo) is not exactly new in Israel, but until recently the vines that had been planted were capable of producing only mediocre semi-dry blush wines. What is new are recently planted high-quality vines from California that offer the potential for producing full-bodied to massive wines, moderately to highly alcoholic, with generous tannins and the kind of warm berry flavors that typify these wines at their best.

Vintage Reports: 1976–2010

The first formal vintage tables appeared in the 1820s and since then wine lovers have relied on them to help make their buying and drinking decisions. As popular as they are, however, it is important to remember that because all vintage tables involve generalizations, there are no firm facts to be found in them. In a sense, these charts are meant to give an overall picture and perhaps to supply clues about which wines to consider buying or drinking. In making one's decisions it is wise to remember that the quality of wines of any vintage year and in any region can vary enormously between wineries. Also worth keeping in mind is that vintage reports and tables such as those that follow are based on what most people consider "quality wines" and not those made for everyday drinking and thus not intended for aging. More than this, estimates of drinkability are based on wines that have been shipped and stored under ideal conditions. Equally important, whether one enjoys drinking wines when they are young, in their adolescence, during their early adulthood or when they become fully mature is much a matter of personal taste.

Following are short reports on the last five vintage years, these followed by a listing of the years of interest going back to 1976. Vintage years are rated on a scale of 20–100, and these numerical values can be interpreted as follows:

100 = Extraordinary
90 = Exceptional
80 = Excellent
70 = Very Good
60 = Good but Not Exciting
50 = Average but with Many Faulted Wines
40 = Mediocre/Not Recommended
30 = Poor/Not Recommended
20 = Truly Bad/Not Recommended

The following symbols are used to indicate drinking windows (Predictions of drinking windows are based on ideal storage since the wine was released.):

C   = Worthy of Cellaring
D/C = Drink or Cellar
D   = Drink Now or in the Next Year or So
D– = Past Its Prime but Probably Still Drinkable
SA = Well Beyond Its Prime and Probably Undrinkable

The Last Five Years

2010 VINTAGE RATING 88

A second difficult year in a row, many grapes coming to ripeness very early and others very late. More than that, a small and difficult harvest because of the weather. Good wines from those winemakers who truly know how to make wine.

2009 VINTAGE RATING 87

An odd and somewhat difficult year, grapes attaining a certain level of ripeness and then pausing in their development, coming to readiness of a sudden. Some fine wines but few for long-term cellaring. Israel's year of Merlot.

2008 VINTAGE RATING 92

An exceptional year for both reds and whites, advance and barrel tasting revealing rich, ripe qualities and often age-worthy wines. C

2007 VINTAGE RATING 86

The second not at all exciting vintage in a row, reflecting an especially dry winter and spring. Probably best from high altitudes where night-day temperatures were most dramatic and probably better for whites than reds. D/C

2006 VINTAGE RATING 86

An especially dry winter, a cold rainy April and then rains during mid-harvest in October (five times the seasonal norm) led to an extended harvest lasting from August to November, yielding a surprisingly small crop. Probably better for reds than whites, this was not an exciting year and many of the top-of-the line series and single-vineyard releases will not be released from this vintage. D/C

Somewhat Older Vintages

2005	90	D/C
2004	88	D/C
2003	90	D/C
2002	82	D
2001	85	D
2000	89	D/C
1999	86	D
1998	85	D
1997	90	D/C
1996	82	D-
1995	90	SA
1994	84	SA
1993	92	D
1992	85	SA
1991	82	SA
1990	91	D
1989	90	SA
1988	85	SA
1987	78	SA
1986	76	SA
1985	90	SA
1984	86	SA
1983	55	SA

1982	55	SA
1979	92	SA
1976	92	SA

Questions of Kashrut

For many years, wines that were kosher had a justifiably bad name, those in the United States being made largely from Concord grapes, which are far from capable of making fine wine, and many of those from Israel following the perceived need for kosher wines to be red, sweet, coarse and without any sign of sophistication. The truth is that those wines were not so much consumed by knowledgeable wine lovers as they were used for sacramental purposes. Such wines are still made but are today perceived largely as oddities. With kosher wines now being made from the most noble grape varieties in state-of-the-art wineries by talented winemakers, there need be no contradiction whatsoever between the laws of kashrut and the production of fine wine.

Some Israeli Wines Are Kosher, Others Are Not

A look at the current Israeli wine scene indicates that the wines of every large winery and the majority of medium-sized wineries in Israel are kosher, but those of the smaller wineries are often not.

For many years, all of the wines produced in Israel were kosher, with the exception of those made in Christian monasteries. The reasons for this were and still are twofold. The first reason relates to the fact that a large proportion of the Israeli population, even among the non-observant, consume only foods and beverages that are kosher. The second, also with a clear economic basis, is that only kosher products can enter the large supermarket chains in the country. Because the majority of wines produced in the country continue to be purchased in supermarkets, no large winery can give up that considerable sales potential. In addition, kashrut is maintained because many of the wineries continue to target their export sales largely toward Jewish consumers worldwide.

The wines of several medium-sized producers and many

of the boutique wineries have a somewhat different goal in mind – that of producing upper-end wines that are targeted toward higher-end and not necessarily kashrut-observant wine consumers both in Israel and abroad. The production of kosher wines, which more than anything adds the need for additional staff (for example, rabbinical supervisors), as well as fees to the rabbinical authorities, can add prohibitively to the costs and the eventual retail price of wines, especially for small wineries.

Whatever the oenological pluses and minuses of kashrut, an increasing number of small wineries are switching over to kashrut in order to reach larger markets.

What Makes an Israeli Wine Kosher?

In order for an Israeli wine to be certified as kosher, several requirements must be met. As can easily be seen, none of these requirements has a negative impact on the quality of the wine being produced and several are widely acknowledged to be sound agricultural practices even by producers of non-kosher wines.

1. According to the practice known as *orla*, the grapes of new vines cannot be used for winemaking until the fourth year after planting.

2. No other fruits or vegetables may be grown in between the rows of vines (*kalai hakerem*).

3. After the first harvest, the fields must lie fallow every seventh year. Each of these sabbatical years is known as *shnat shmita*.

4. From the onset of the harvest only kosher tools and storage facilities may be used in the winemaking process, and all of the winemaking equipment must be cleaned to be certain that no foreign objects remain in the equipment or vats.

5. From the moment the grapes reach the winery, only Sabbath-observant Jews are allowed to come in contact with the wine. Because many of the winemakers in the country are not Sabbath observant, this means that they cannot personally handle the equipment or the wine as it is being made and are assisted in several of

their more technical tasks by Orthodox assistants and kashrut supervisors (*mashgichim*).

6. All of the materials (e.g., yeasts) used in the production and clarification of the wines must be certified as kosher.

7. A symbolic amount of wine, representing the tithe (*truma vema'aser*) once paid to the Temple in Jerusalem, must be poured away from the tanks or barrels in which the wine is being made.

The Question of Wines That Are Mevushal

Some observant Jews demand that their wines be pasteurized (*mevushal*), especially in restaurants and at catered events, where there is the possibility that a non-Jew may handle the wine. This tradition dates to ancient times, when wine was used by pagans for idolatrous worship: the Israelites used to boil their wines, thus changing the chemical composition of the wine so that it was considered unfit for pagan worship. Wines that are *mevushal* have the advantage that they can be opened and poured by non-Jews or Jews who are not Sabbath observant.

Today, *mevushal* wines are no longer boiled. After the grapes are crushed, the common practice is to rapidly raise the temperature of the liquids to 176–194 degrees Fahrenheit (80–90 Celsius) in special flash pasteurizing units, hold it there for under a minute and then return the temperature, equally rapidly, to 60 degrees Fahrenheit (15 Celsius).

There is no question that modern technology has reduced the impact of these processes on the quality of the wine, but most winemakers and consumers remain in agreement that, with very few exceptions, wines that have been pasteurized lose many of their essential essences, often being incapable of developing in the bottle and quite often imparting a "cooked" sensation to the nose and palate. It is important to note that since 2008 the best wines of Israeli wineries have not been *mevushal* for local consumption but often undergo that process for wines destined for export.

Some wines are produced in both regular and *mevushal* versions, the *mevushal* editions destined for the export market or for the highly observant within Israel. Because it is almost impossible for anyone outside of the wineries to keep track of and taste all of those wines, no attempt is made within this book to report on such "double bottlings."

Simply stated, a wine that is *mevushal* is no more or less kosher than a wine that is not, and none of the better wines of Israel today fall into this category. Those who are concerned with such issues will find the information they require on either the front or rear labels of wines produced in the country.

A Few Lists

In the 13th century, King Henry III of England declared that bakers who shortchanged customers could be punished by losing one of their hands to an axe. In fear of such punishment, bakers started the policy of giving 13 rolls, cookies or cakes for the price of 12, thereby making it known that they were not thieves. Thus, according to popular (but almost certainly mistaken) belief was born the origin of the term "baker's dozen."

Leaving the realities of the origin of the term to historians and linguists, instead of the usual ten wineries, on each of the lists that follows are a baker's dozen in each category, in this case reflecting continuous improvements in the Israeli wine industry.

A Baker's Dozen of the Best Wine Producers

1. Golan Heights Winery (Katzrin, Yarden, Gamla)
2. Margalit
3. Yatir
4. Castel
5. Clos de Gat
6. Flam
7. Chateau Golan
8. Pelter
9. Carmel (Limited Edition, Mediterranean, Single Vineyard)
10. Sea Horse
11. Recanati
12. Tzora
13. Vitkin

A Baker's Dozen of Up-and-Coming Producers (in alphabetical order)

Asif
Assaf
Avidan
Barkan/Segal
Binyamina
Gvaot
Lewinsohn
Na'aman
Odem Mountain
Psagot
Shvo
Tabor
Teperberg

A Baker's Dozen of Value Producers

1. Galil Mountain
2. Tabor
3. Dalton
4. Golan Heights Winery (Gamla, Golan)
5. Recanati
6. Saslove
7. Barkan
8. Tishbi
9. Teperberg
10. Carmel (Appellation)
11. Segal
12. Tzora
13. Chillag

The Best Wines Released in the Last Twelve Months

In earlier editions of this book, the list of best wines released in the year preceding publication was limited to ten wines. This year, for the third year running, I have departed from that rule, for with thirty-six wines earning 93 or more points it would be unfair to readers to omit any of these truly excellent wines. In each Score category wineries are listed in alphabetical order.

EARNING 95 POINTS

Golan Heights Winery, Rom, Yarden, 2007 (K)

Margalit, Cabernet Sauvignon, Special Reserve, 2009

EARNING 94 POINTS

Clos de Gat, Ayalon Valley, 2007

Clos de Gat, Chardonnay, 2009

Golan Heights Winery, Syrah, Yonatan Vineyard, Yarden, 2007 (K)

Flam, Cabernet Sauvignon, Reserve, 2008

Margalit, Cabernet Sauvignon, 2009

Pelter, Cabernet Sauvignon, T-Selection, 2008

EARNING 93 POINTS

Binyamina, The Cave, Old Vine Cabernet Sauvignon, 2007 (K)

Bustan, Cabernet Sauvignon, 2006 (K)

Bustan, Merlot, 2006 (K)

Carmel, Limited Edition, 2008

Carmel, Mediterranean, 2008

Carmel, Cabernet Sauvignon, Single Vineyard, Kayoumi, Upper Galilee, 2008

Carmel, Shiraz, Single Vineyard, Kayoumi, Upper Galilee, 2008

Carmel, Single Vineyard, Gewurztraminer, Late Harvest, Sha'al, Golan, 2009

Chateau Golan, Touriga Nacional, Royal Reserve, 2008

Chateau Golan, Og, 2008

Clos de Gat, Syrah, Har'el, 2009

Ella Valley Vineyards, Syrah, 2008 (K)

Golan Heights Winery, Merlot, Kela Vineyard, Yarden, 2008 (K)

Golan Heights Winery, Syrah, Avital Slopes Vineyard, Yarden, 2007 (K)

Golan Heights Winery, Syrah, Tel Phares Vineyard, Yarden, 2008 (K)

Golan Heights Winery, Cabernet Sauvignon, Yarden, 2008 (K)

Golan Heights Winery, Cabernet Sauvignon, El Rom Vineyard, Yarden, 2007 (K)

Lewinsohn, Rouge, Garage de Papa, 2009

Lewinsohn, Blanc, Garage de Papa, 2009
Margalit, Cabernet Franc, 2009
Margalit, Enigma, 2009
Pelter, "I", 2008
Recanati, Special Reserve, 2007 (K)
Recanati, Special Reserve, White, 2009 (K)
Recanati, Carignan, Reserve, Kerem Ba'al, 2009 (K)
Saslove, Cabernet Sauvignon, Reserved, 2008
Tabor, Mes'cha, 2006 (K)

The Best Wines As Reported in the 2011 Edition of This Book

EARNING 96 POINTS
Golan Heights Winery, Rom, Yarden, 2006 (K)

EARNING 95 POINTS
Margalit, Cabernet Sauvignon, Special Reserve, 2008

EARNING 94 POINTS
Clos de Gat, Cabernet Sauvignon, Har'el, 2008
Clos de Gat, Merlot, Har'el, 2008
Clos de Gat, Ayalon Valley, 2006
Golan Heights Winery, Chardonnay, Odem Organic
    Vineyard, Yarden, 2008 (K)
Golan Heights Winery, Syrah, Ortal Vineyard, Yarden, 2004 (K)
Golan Heights Winery, Syrah, Yonatan Vineyard, Yarden,
    2007 (K)
Golan Heights Winery, Cabernet Sauvignon, El Rom
    Vineyard, Yarden, 2004 (K)
Margalit, Enigma, Special Reserve, 2007
Margalit, Cabernet Franc, 2008

EARNING 93 POINTS
Carmel, Shiraz, Single Vineyard, Kayoumi, Upper Galilee,
    2008 (K)
Carmel, Cabernet Sauvignon, Single Vineyard, Kayoumi,
    Upper Galilee, 2008 (K)

Carmel, Mediterranean, 2007 (K)
Carmel, Limited Edition, Upper Galilee, 2007 (K)
Carmel, Gewurztraminer, Late Harvest, Single Vineyard,
    Sha'al, Golan, 2009 (K)
Castel, Chardonnay "C", Blanc du Castel, 2008 (K)
Castel, Grand Vin Castel, 2008 (K)
Castel, Petit Castel, 2008 (K)
Clos de Gat, Syrah, Har'el, 2008
Dalton Matatia, 2006 (K)
Flam, Cabernet Sauvignon, Reserve, 2008
Golan Heights Winery, Katzrin, 2007 (K)
Golan Heights Winery, Syrah, Ortal Vineyard, Yarden,
    2007 (K)
Golan Heights Winery, Cabernet Sauvignon, El Rom
    Vineyard, Yarden, 2007 (K)
Margalit, Cabernet Sauvignon, 2008
Pelter, Petit Verdot, T-Selection, 2008
Pelter, Cabernet Sauvignon, T-Selection, 2006
Recanati, Special Reserve, 2006 (K)
Yatir, Yatir Forest, 2007 (K)
Yatir, Shiraz, 2007 (K)

People Are Asking: What About New Stars?

The past year has been a good one for local wineries in that five have moved up from their ratings of 4 to 5 stars. The wineries are (in alphabetical order): Bustan, Recanati, Sea Horse, Tzora and Vitkin.

Seven wineries moved from 3 to 4 stars. Those are: Barkan, Meishar, Savion, Shiloh, The Cave, Vortman and Ye'arim.

Drinking Habits

Within Israel

Since the founding of the state in 1948 and until 1997, annual Israeli wine consumption held steady at about 3.9 liters per capita. Although there is some debate about precisely how much wine is being consumed by Israelis, recent years have seen a major increase, and consumption now stands at about 7 liters annually. This figure puts Israelis far behind the French and Italians, who consume 56 and 49 liters respectively, or even the Australians who consume 20 liters per year. It is also interesting that recent studies show that in Israel there is no significant correlation between wine consumption and either alcoholism or automobile accidents.

The increase in local consumption reflects of course the increasing quality of local wines. However, it also reflects the fact that more and more Israelis are traveling abroad and dining in fine restaurants where wine is an integral part of the meal. Today, many Israelis are touring the fine wineries of Bordeaux, Tuscany and the Napa Valley, and even though such wine appreciation is still limited to the upwardly mobile segment of the population, more and more people now order wine to accompany their meal in a fine restaurant.

In addition to showing a growing appreciation of wine in general, Israelis are moving in several directions that can be seen in many other countries as well. Consumption is shifting from semi-dry to dry wines, from whites to reds, from light to heavier wines and most importantly, there is a movement toward buying higher quality wines. Twenty-five years ago, more than eighty percent of the wines produced in the country were sweet. Today, more than eighty percent of the wines produced are dry.

Israelis also continue to increase their consumption of imported wines, and the better wine shops of the country stock wines from every region of France, Italy, Australia, New Zealand, California, Washington State, Spain, Portugal, Germany, Austria, Chile and Argentina. Some members of the local wine industry perceive this phenomenon as having a negative impact on the local industry. Others, perhaps with a greater sense of foresight, realize that imported wines pose a challenge to the local wine industry to continue to improve the quality of its products.

A Potential Problem

Even though Israelis are now consuming a bit more wine, the population has come to a watershed and from all projections there seems to be no further increase on the near horizon with regard to wine drinking habits. With large and small wineries developing new vineyards at an unprecedented pace, the question must be asked: "Precisely who is going to be drinking all of the wine that will start coming on line in another three to four years?" Simply stated, if local consumption and exports hold constant, the industry may be facing a major crisis.

Sacramental versus "Wine Culture"

Within Israel, as in nearly every country with a Jewish population, some continue to drink wine entirely for sacramental purposes – as, for example, for the Kiddush blessing that opens the two main meals of the Sabbath and holidays. An increasing number have realized that any kosher wine is appropriate for such purposes, but others hold to the perceived tradition that such wines should be red, thick and sweet. Although such wines hold no interest for sophisticated wine drinkers, several of the large wineries continue to produce Kiddush wines and there are wineries that focus entirely on these consumers.

Within the "Jewish World"

Nearly all of the better wine stores of the major cities of North America, the United Kingdom and France have at least a small section devoted to kosher wines, and in recent years the wines of Israel, both kosher and not kosher, have taken a more prominent place on those shelves alongside wines from California, France, Spain, Australia, Chile and Argentina. The reception of Israeli wines is gradually getting warmer: they are now being reviewed more regularly in magazines devoted to wine as well as in the weekly wine columns of many critics, and are appearing on the menus of an increasing number of prestigious restaurants.

The Wineries and Their Wines

For many years it was possible to group Israeli wine producers into one of two broad categories – large and small wineries. The last fifteen years have seen dramatic changes, for during that time seven new medium-sized producers have appeared on the local scene, several of the wineries that could be categorized as boutiques have expanded their production, and although some boutique wineries have closed, a host of small wineries continues to open. Within each category there are wineries that produce excellent and often exciting wines.

The wines reviewed in this guide include only those I have tasted – wines already on the market, wines due to be released within the next several months, or those still in the cellars or homes of wine lovers. Also listed are barrel tastings, some being those of wines scheduled to be released only in another two to three years. Not included in the guide are wineries that produce wines primarily for sacramental purposes, as those wines hold no interest for wine consumers at large. Nor, with only a few exceptions, does the guide rate the wines of those wineries producing under 3,000 bottles annually. Ratings for wineries (1–5 stars) are based on current status. For wineries that have been releasing wines for less than three years, ratings should be considered as tentative, as those ratings might move up or down in the next editions of this guide, much depending on the consistency of future releases.

Those seeking reviews of more mature wines not listed herein are referred to earlier editions of this book. If that is not possible, inquiries may be addressed to the author at rogov@tobypress.com.

People Are Asking:
Why Does This Book Get "Fatter" Every Year?

The first edition of this guide, printed in 2005, contained a mere 278 pages. This 2012 edition contains over 700 pages. People want to know why the book increases in size on an annual basis.

Two major factors will help in explaining this:

1. An increasing number of boutique wineries open every year and including those obviously calls for additional pages.
2. Even more important, reflecting ongoing progress in the local wine industry, many wineries are now producing quality wines that show far longer drinking windows and this guide strives to review all of the wines that may still be on sale or are still stored in people's homes.

It is the author's opinion, however, that the book, like Kansas City (in the Rodgers and Hammerstein musical *Oklahoma*) has "gone about as far as it can go," and future editions will not continue to grow in size, the plan being to eliminate from the text any of those wines that are so far beyond their peak that they are no longer worthy of consideration.

Abaya ✳✳✳

Founded in 2006 by Yossi Yodfat in Kfar Clil, not far from Mivtsar Yechiam (the Fortress built at Yechiam by the Crusaders) in the Western Galilee, the winery relies largely on Sangiovese, Cabernet Sauvignon, Syrah, Petit Verdot and Carignan grapes. The winery has a deep commitment to both organic and biodynamic principles, and although some sulfites are used in the winemaking process, those stay within limits internationally accepted by organic methodology. Current production is about 4,500 bottles annually.

ABAYA, SANGIOVESE, HIDE & SEEK, 2006: Lightly oaked, blended with 3% of Cabernet Sauvignon, ruby toward garnet in color and showing soft tannins and the barest hint of spicy wood. Opens to show traditional plum, cherry and wild berry fruits, those with a hint of mocha coming in on the moderately long finish. Not so much a Tuscan Sangiovese but a distinctly Mediterranean one. Not overly complex but a charmer. Drink up. Score 87.

ABAYA, ART, 2008: A blend of Cabernet Sauvignon, Syrah, Carignan and Petit Verdot (51%, 25%, 20% and 4% respectively). Developed in new French oak for 12 months, medium- to full-bodied, a round, soft and mouth-filling wine showing an appealing array of black fruits, purple plums along with notes of Oriental spices and tobacco. Let this one develop a bit longer and it will also reveal the notes of dark, minted chocolate that are waiting to blossom forth. Drink now–2014. Score 90.

ABAYA, LE ROUGE, 2008: A medium- to full-bodied, deeply aromatic blend of 56% Cabernet Sauvignon, 40% Carignan and 4% Petit Verdot. Deep garnet and generously aromatic, medium- to full-bodied. Reflecting its oak-aging with soft, gently caressing tannins and a comfortable level of oak, opens in the glass to reveal a generous array of currants, blackberries and wild berries on a background of white pepper, freshly cut Mediterranean herbs and on the finish, a kiss of licorice. Drink now–2013. Score 89.

ABAYA, MOON-A, 2008: Aged in new French oak for 12 months, a medium-, perhaps medium- to full-bodied, blend of Syrah, Cabernet Sauvignon and Petit Verdot (50%, 47% and 3% respectively). Deep garnet, with tannins and oak that make themselves felt in a genteel manner, on first attack a clear note of cigar tobacco, that parting to make way for purple plums, blackcurrants and espresso coffee. On the long finish a note of freshly roasted herbs. Drink now–2014. Score 90.

ABAYA, MOON-A, 2007: A blend of Carignan, Cabernet Sauvignon and Syrah (50%, 45% and 5% respectively). Reflecting its 12 months in *barriques* with notes of sweet and spicy wood and with moderately firm tannins, opens to show an appealing array of blackberries, blueberries and cassis, those on a background that hints nicely of bittersweet chocolate. Round and generous. Drink now. Score 87.

ABAYA, MIDSUMMER EVE, 2007: Medium- to full-bodied, a blend of 50% Carignan, 45% Syrah and 5% Cabernet Sauvignon. With gently mouth-coating tannins and hints of spicy wood, opens to reveal aromas and flavors of blueberries and blackberries, those accompanied by notes of freshly turned earth, roasted herbs and on the finish a distinct note of cigar tobacco. Just enough complexity to grab the attention. Drink up. Score 88.

Achziv ⋆⋆

Founded in 2005 by the Guberman family, with Mark Guberman as the winemaker, and located on Kibbutz Gesher
Haziv, not far from the city of Nahariya
in the Western Galilee, this small winery
produces red wines from Cabernet Sauvignon, Syrah and Merlot grapes. Current production is about 2,000 bottles
annually.

ACHZIV, CABERNET SAUVIGNON, 2007: Blended with 10% Merlot,
oak-aged for 12 months, an unfiltered wine with its once-firm tannins
now integrating nicely. Medium-bodied, with spicy wood and currants
on first attack, those yielding comfortably to aromas and what seems
at one moment to be eucalyptus, the next mint and yet the next licorice. Soft, round and generous, lingering nicely on the palate. Drink
now. Score 87.

ACHZIV, CABERNET SAUVIGNON, 2006: Blended with 15% Merlot,
full-bodied, firmly tannic and reflecting its 12 months in French oak
with a light smoky overlay. Opens to reveal traditional blackcurrant
and blackberry fruits, those leading to a moderately long finish with
an appealing hint of dark chocolate. Drink now. Score 86.

ACHZIV, CABERNET SAUVIGNON, 2005: Garnet toward purple,
medium- to full-bodied, with soft tannins, a round and generous wine.
Blended with 12% Merlot, showing spices and vanilla from the wood and
an array of currant, berry and purple plum fruits. Drink up. Score 85.

ACHZIV, MERLOT, 2007: A bit of bottle variation here, some bottles
opening with a medicinal aroma but that blowing off within minutes
after pouring. Garnet to royal purple in color, blended with 11% Cabernet Sauvignon, medium- to full-bodied, showing wild berry, cassis
and blackberry fruits on a gentle background of earthy minerals. Soft
tannins and a gentle wood influence lead to a long finish. Drink now.
Score 87.

ACHZIV, MERLOT, 2006: Dark royal purple in color, an oak-aged
blend of 85% Merlot and 15% Cabernet Sauvignon, showing blackberry,
chocolate and citrus peel, those somewhat marred by rough-edged tannins and a high level of acidity. Drink now. Score 84.

Adir ✳✳✳

Founded by the Rosenberg and Ashkenazi families in 2003 with a first release of 1,000 bottles, winemaker Avi Rosenberg is now producing about 50,000 bottles annually. Located in the Upper Galilee on the slopes of Mount Admon, the winery sources Cabernet Sauvignon, Merlot, Shiraz, Cabernet Franc and Chardonnay from its own vineyards at Moshav Kerem Ben Zimra and other choice locations in the Upper Galilee. Now with full control over its vineyards and an increasing level of confidence on the part of the winemaker both in the vineyards and the winery, Adir is most definitely a winery "on the way up."

Plato

ADIR, PLATO, 2009: A tentative blend at this tasting of 91% Cabernet Sauvignon and 9% Shiraz. Deep garnet with a royal purple robe, full-bodied, reflecting its 15 months in oak with gently caressing tannins and a note of black pepper. Generous black fruits here, those with overlays of mocha and tobacco. The best to date from the winery, promising to be long and elegant. Best from mid-2012–2016, perhaps longer. Tentative Score 90–92. K

ADIR, PLATO, 2007: An oak-aged blend, Cabernet Sauvignon with about 8% of Shiraz, showing medium- to full-bodied, with tannins that seem to have become more chunky since the wine was released. On the nose and palate red berries, cassis and blackberries on a lightly spicy background. Sliding past its peak. Drink up. Score 87. K

ADIR, PLATO, 2005: A blend of 92% Cabernet Sauvignon and 8% Syrah, aged for 12 months in older oak and then an additional 12 months in new oak. Dark garnet, showing a bit of clearing at the rim, full-bodied, with tannins that continue to be quite firm and a good deal of sweet cedarwood that has never fully integrated, but does open on the palate to show appealing raspberry, red currant and vanilla notes. Showing age. Drink up. Score 83. K

Reserve

RESERVE, SHIRAZ, 2009: Oak-aged for 15 months, super-dark garnet in color, medium- to full-bodied with a rich red fruit nose and gently caressing tannins. On first attack raspberries and red currants, those parting to make way for notes of saddle leather and fresh Mediterranean herbs. A bit acidic on the finish at this stage but with balance and structure that bode well for the future. Best from mid-2012–2015. Tentative Score 88–90. K

Adir

ADIR, CABERNET SAUVIGNON, 2010: Tasted from components, promising to be full-bodied and muscular but holding those muscles back in the name of elegance. A fruity attack of raspberries and red currants, those parting to make way for blackberries and lightly roasted Mediterranean herbs, all showing signs of coming together as a coherent whole. Drink from release–2016, perhaps longer. Tentative Score 89–91. K

ADIR, CABERNET SAUVIGNON, 2009: Made entirely from Cabernet Sauvignon grapes from the vineyards of Kerem Ben Zimra. Well extracted, super-dark garnet in color, medium- to full-bodied with gently gripping tannins and an array of currants, crushed blackberries and earthy minerals. Somewhat acidic when first poured but that levels off nicely as the wine develops in the glass. Drink now–2013. Score 88. K

ADIR, CABERNET SAUVIGNON, 2008: Opens with a nose of fresh sawdust and spices, those parting to make way for a generous array of cassis, raspberries and roasted herbs. Dark, full-bodied and concentrated. Drink now. Score 87. K

ADIR, CABERNET SAUVIGNON, 2007: Made entirely of Cabernet Sauvignon grapes, oak-aged in mostly French oak for 12 months. Dark garnet and aromatic on the nose, opens in the glass to show generous blackberry, currant and purple plums, those supported by cedarwood and spicy notes. Drink up. Score 88. K

ADIR, MERLOT, 2007: A blend of 86% Merlot and 14% Cabernet Sauvignon aged for 12 months in some new, some second- and third-year *barriques*. Dark, almost impenetrably garnet in color, a deeply extracted medium- to full-bodied wine with gripping tannins and spicy wood in good proportion with black fruits, those on a background of freshly cured tobacco and dried herbs. Technically correct but perhaps best described as "a wine without faults" – in other words, fails to excite. Drink now. Score 86. K

ADIR, SHIRAZ, 2009: Reflecting its development in oak for 12 months with aromas of spicy cedar and a note of vanilla. Medium- to full-bodied, with soft tannins, a ripe wine showing crushed berries, cassis and notes of dark chocolate. On the moderately long finish appealing hints of saddle leather and Mediterranean herbs. Drink now–2015. Score 89. K

ADIR, SHIRAZ, 2008: Full-bodied, with generous, gently gripping tannins. On first attack red berries and plums, those yielding to notes of blackberries and citrus peel on a background of leather. Tannins and spicy notes rise on the finish. Drink now–2016. Score 90. K

ADIR, CABERNET SAUVIGNON-SHIRAZ-MERLOT, 2007: Dark ruby toward garnet in color, medium- to full-bodied, with soft tannins and a gentle influence of spicy oak, opens to show appealing red berry, cassis and spicy notes. Not long but round and generous. Drink now. Score 88. K

ADIR, CHARDONNAY, 2010: Light gold in color, reflecting an intentionally light hand with new French oak, opens in the glass to reveal grapefruit and lime fruits on a background that hints nicely of flinty minerals. Drink now. Score 87. K

Agmon ✸✸✸

Founded by Adi Mizrachi and Itzhik Elman on Kibbutz Ma'arit, not far from Hadera in Northern Israel, this boutique winery is producing about 7,000 bottles annually and plans to grow to production of 15,000–20,000 bottles.

AGMON, CABERNET SAUVIGNON, 2008: Made entirely from Cabernet Sauvignon grapes, oak-aged for 18 months, garnet toward royal purple, and showing aromas and flavors of black currants, wild berries and spices. Medium- to full-bodied with just enough complexity to grab the attention. Drink now. Score 86.

AGMON, CABERNET SAUVIGNON, 2007: Garnet to royal purple, medium- to full-bodied, reflecting its 24 months in oak with chunky tannins and generous smoky wood giving the wine a rustic feel. On the nose and palate currants and wild berries, those on a background of earthy minerals. Drink now. Score 86.

AGMON, MERLOT, 2008: Medium-dark garnet to royal purple, oak-aged for 18 months, showing gently gripping tannins and appealing notes of vanilla and spices on the nose. Medium- to full-bodied, opens in the glass to reveal aromas and flavors of currants, blueberries and blackberries. Round and generous. Drink now–2014. Score 87.

Agur ✳✳✳

Set on Moshav Agur in the Judean plains, this boutique winery, owned by winemaker Shuki Yashuv and a Spanish partner, has grown from releasing 1,800 bottles in the 2000 vintage to between 25,000–30,000 in the 2008 and 2009 vintages. The winery has its own vineyards on the moshav and also draws on grapes from the Ella Valley, those including Cabernet Sauvignon, Merlot, Cabernet Franc and Petit Verdot. Grapes from each vineyard are fermented separately, some in stainless steel vats, others in new and used *barriques*. The winery releases four wines annually, Special Reserve, Kessem, Agur and Special Edition, and those have been kosher from the 2007 vintage.

Special Reserve

SPECIAL RESERVE, 2009: A blend of Cabernet Sauvignon Merlot, Cabernet Franc and a bit of Petit Verdot. Almost impenetrably dark garnet in color, a rich and concentrated wine, its firm tannins holding the wine back at the moment but those simply waiting to integrate. On the nose and palate blackcurrants, wild red and black berries, notes of bittersweet chocolate, green olives and tobacco. Drink now–2015. Score 89. K

SPECIAL RESERVE, 2008: Opens with a bit of bottle stink, but that blows off quickly to reveal a nose of freshly cut herbs and eucalyptus. Oak-aged for 18 months, a full-bodied blend of Cabernet Sauvignon, Merlot, Cabernet Franc and Petit Verdot (50%, 35%, 10% and 5% respectively), revealing red currants and raspberries on a background of earthy minerals. Drink now–2013. Score 89. K

Special
Reserve
2007
Judean Hills

Ⓚ P

SPECIAL RESERVE, 2007: Dark, almost impenetrable garnet, full-bodied, with wood and tannins in fine balance with fruits and acidity. A blend of Cabernet Sauvignon, Merlot, Cabernet Franc and Petit Verdot (50%, 35%, 10% and 5% respectively). On the nose and palate black- and blueberries, currants, licorice and notes of earthy minerals. The best ever from Agur but needs a bit of time to round out and for the elements to come together. Drink now–2014. Score 90. K

SPECIAL RESERVE, 2006: A medium- to full-bodied blend of 60% Cabernet Sauvignon, 35% Merlot and 5% Cabernet Franc, with firm tannins and generously spicy wood integrating nicely to show appealing blackberry, black cherry and sweet herbs on the nose and palate. Long and generous but showing first signs of age. Drink up. Score 88.

Kessem

KESSEM, 2009: Dark garnet, full-bodied, with still-firm tannins waiting to settle down but already showing good balance and promise for the future. Developed for about nine months in well-used barrels, with generous currant and blackberry fruits supported by notes of dark chocolate and roasted herbs. Drink now–2014. Score 88. K

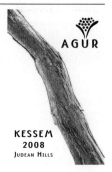

KESSEM, 2008: A medium- to full-bodied, garnet toward royal purple blend of Cabernet Sauvignon, Merlot, Petit Verdot and Cabernet Franc (65%, 20%, 10% and 5% respectively), each variety fermented separately and then developed in oak for six months before final blending. Dark garnet, with surprisingly firm tannins for such short oak-aging but those yielding in the glass to allow blackberry, black cherry and currant notes to be nicely felt. On the moderately long finish a hint of Oriental spices. Drink now. Score 89. K

KESSEM, 2007: Medium- to full-bodied, youthful royal purple in color, a blend of Cabernet Sauvignon, Merlot, Petit Verdot and Cabernet Franc (40%, 30%, 20% and 10% respectively). Oak-aged for six months, a soft, round wine with hints of vanilla and spices on the nose and an array of wild berry, currant and earth-mineral flavors. Drink up. Score 87. K

Agur

AGUR, EPI EUNOPA PONTON, 2006: On the chance that your Homeric Greek or your knowledge of James Joyce is not fully up to date, *epi oinopa ponton* translates to "the wine-dark sea" and this reflects winemaker Shuki Yashuv's thoughts on this wine. Fair enough, for the wine is indeed dark, almost impenetrable garnet in color. A limited release (300 bottles) of 60% Merlot, 30% Cabernet Sauvignon and 10% Cabernet Franc, an aromatic, concentrated and full-bodied wine opening with raspberries and cranberries, those yielding in the glass to blackcurrants, blackberries and notes of licorice, black olives and Mediterranean herbs. Oak-aged for thirty months, with the wood in fine balance with tannins and fruits, lingers long and comfortably on the palate. Drink now–2014. Score 91.

AGUR, ROSA, 2010: Somewhere between cherry red and salmon pink, medium-bodied, with appealing raspberries, cherries and watermelon aromas and flavors. A fun, easy-to-drink wine. Drink now. Score 87. K

AGUR, ROSA, 2009: A blend of 60% Cabernet Franc and 40% Cabernet Sauvignon, a rosé made by the *saignée* method, showing bright cherry red, medium-bodied and revealing aromas and flavors of raspberries and red currants. Said on the label to be half-dry, but to the palate completely dry. Generous alcohol for a rosé (the label says 13.5%) but with no sign of heat whatever, a wine to be served and enjoyed well chilled. Drink up. Score 88. K

AGUR, BLANCA, 2009: A somewhat unusual but quite successful blend of 55% Viognier and 45% Johannisberg Riesling, the grapes intentionally harvested early in order to maintain a quite moderate 11.5% alcohol content. Light, bright gold, with a floral nose on which the Riesling dominates and even shows a light oily note traditional to the variety. Medium-bodied, and on the nose and palate fine citrus, apple and green melon fruits. This wine sits and then lingers nicely on the palate. Has the potential for some age and as it develops in the bottle will become somewhat darker and heavier in body with the Riesling notes rising. Drink now–2014. Score 89. K

Special Edition

SPECIAL EDITION, CABERNET SAUVIGNON-MERLOT-CABERNET FRANC, 2009: A Bordeaux blend of 50% Cabernet Sauvignon, 30% Merlot and 20% Cabernet Franc. Medium- to full-bodied with gentle notes of spicy cedarwood and chewy, somewhat chunky tannins that give the wine an appealing rustic note. On the nose and palate blackberries, currants and blueberries, those supported nicely by notes of earthy minerals and, on the moderately long finish, a hint of minted chocolate. Drink now–2014. Score 88. K

Alexander ★★★

Located on Moshav Beit Yitzhak in the Sharon region, the winery, founded in 1996 by Yoram Shalom, receives grapes largely from contract vineyards over which it has full control at Kerem Ben Zimra in the Upper Galilee. Primary output to date has been of Cabernet Sauvignon, Merlot, Chardonnay and Sauvignon Blanc and now coming on line are Syrah and Grenache.

Initial releases from the 2002 vintage were of 12,000 bottles. With the 2006 vintage the winery switched over to kashrut and current production is about 60,000 bottles annually. In addition to producing two top-of-the-line series, Alexander the Great and Alexander Reserve, the winery also currently releases wines in four other series, Liza, Sandro, Gasto and Gaston. The winery also produces private- label wines for several restaurants.

Alexander the Great

ALEXANDER THE GREAT, CABERNET SAUVIGNON, 2007: Dark, almost impenetrable garnet in color, full-bodied, concentrated and intense. On first attack dried figs and orange peel, those yielding to traditional Cabernet currant and berry notes, all with a sweet chocolate overlay. Drink now–2014. Score 88. K

ALEXANDER THE GREAT, CABERNET SAUVIGNON, 2006: Blended with 5% Merlot, dark garnet toward royal purple, full-bodied and with still-firm tannins and reflecting its development in *barriques* for 15 months with generous spicy wood, those in fine balance and needing only time to integrate. On the nose and palate blackcurrant, blackberry and dark chocolate notes, all leading to a long, mouth-filling finish. Drink now. Score 89. K

ALEXANDER THE GREAT, CABERNET SAUVIGNON, 2005: A blend of 95% Cabernet Sauvignon and 5% Merlot. Made from grapes from

26-year-old vines, this medium- to full-bodied dark-garnet-red wine shows soft tannins, spicy wood and a tempting array of mineral, black fruit, herbal and chocolate aromas. On the long finish, cloves and a hint of iodine. Drink now–2013. Score 90.

ALEXANDER THE GREAT, CABERNET SAUVIGNON, GRAND RE-SERVE, 2004: A blend of 80% Cabernet Sauvignon and 10% each of Merlot and Shiraz. Reflecting its 48 months in new oak *barriques* (24 months in new oak and then transferred again for another 24 months to new oak) with far too generous smoky and vanilla overlays and gripping tannins, those yielding slowly in the glass to reveal moderate levels of plums, blackberries and currants, all with overlays of mocha and herbs. More powerful and intense than elegant, a distinctly overly oaky wine. Drink now. Score 86.

ALEXANDER THE GREAT, CABERNET SAUVIGNON, 2004: Full-bodied and reflecting the *barriques* in which it developed with firm, near-sweet tannins and hints of spicy wood. Generous and long with a complex array of currant, herbal and mineral aromas and flavors. Drink up. Score 90.

Reserve

RESERVE, CABERNET SAUVIGNON, 2007: Deep garnet in color, reflecting its aging in French and American oak for 18 months with gently gripping tannins. Full-bodied, opening in the glass to reveal aromas and flavors of wild berries, currants and blackberries, those supported nicely by notes of tobacco leaf, black pepper and vanilla. Drink now–2014. Score 89. K

RESERVE, MERLOT, 2007: Dark garnet toward royal purple, with generous oak and still-gripping tannins that need time to settle in. Opens in the glass to reveal appealing black and red berries, cassis and notes of minted chocolate. Drink now–2014. Score 89. K

RESERVE, MERLOT, 2006: Dark garnet, full-bodied, reflecting 18 months in French and American oak with firmly gripping tannins and generous notes of spicy wood. On the nose and palate currants, wild berries and licorice, leading to a medium-long finish on which tannins and a note of bittersweet chocolate rise. Drink now–2014. Score 88. K

RESERVE, SHIRAZ, 2008: Blended with 5% Cabernet Sauvignon, full-bodied, reflecting its 24 months in new oak with intense tannins, those parting slowly and not quite fully to make way for aromas and flavors of purple plums, black cherries, earthy minerals and saddle leather. Drink now–2014. Score 88. K

RESERVE, GASTO, 2007: Aged in American and French oak for 24 months, an almost impenetrably dark garnet blend of 40% Cabernet Sauvignon and 30% each of Merlot and Shiraz. Full-bodied, with generous spicy oak and firm tannins now starting to integrate. Opens to reveal aromas and flavors of purple plums, blackberries and black cherries, those supported by notes of vanilla and spices, with a strong note of black pepper on the finish. Drink now. Score 88. K

Alexander

ALEXANDER, CABERNET SAUVIGNON, 2005: Medium- to full-bodied, dark ruby in color, with soft tannins; showing vanilla and spices from the casks in which it aged. On the nose and palate, rich blackcurrant and blackberry fruits along with hints of earthiness. Drink up. Score 88.

ALEXANDER, MERLOT, 2005: Deep royal purple, with firm but nicely integrating tannins. Hints of spicy wood and tobacco balanced nicely by a generous array of black plum, raspberry, cassis and chocolate aromas and flavors. Drink up. Score 89.

ALEXANDER, SYRAH, 2006: Dark garnet, full-bodied, with gripping tannins and spicy wood parting slowly to reveal currant, plum and citrus peel notes, those complemented by overlays of roasted herbs and leather. Drink now. Score 87. K

ALEXANDER, SYRAH, 2005: Dark royal purple, full-bodied, with deep but remarkably soft tannins. Hints of smoky wood, freshly turned earth and spices on a background of black fruits and, on the finish, light smoked meat. Drink up. Score 89.

ALEXANDER, ROSÉ, 2009: Made from Petit Verdot grapes, light- to medium-bodied, with tutti-frutti bubble gum aromas and flavors. Not complex, but good acidity keeps the wine refreshing. Drink up. Score 84. K

ALEXANDER, CHARDONNAY, LIZA, 2009: Medium- to full-bodied, with a creamy texture and reflecting its 18 months of oak-aging with generous overlays of vanilla and spicy wood, those somewhat holding back the citrus, pear and floral aromas. Drink up. Score 85. K

ALEXANDER, CHARDONNAY, LIZA, 2008: Light gold in color, medium-bodied, with good balancing acidity and notes of spices to highlight grapefruit, lime and pear fruits. Drink up. Score 86. K

Sandro

SANDRO, 2009: A Bordeaux blend, medium- to full-bodied, showing spicy oak and lightly chunky tannins. Opens in the glass to reveal appealing berry, currant and raspberry aromas and flavors, those on a background of roasted herbs. Drink now–2013. Score 86. K

SANDRO, 2008: Cabernet Sauvignon, Merlot, Petit Verdot, Shiraz (60%, 20% 10%, 6%) to which, in accordance with latest fashion, 4% of white Sauvignon Blanc grapes were blended. Medium- to full-bodied, reflecting its 13 months in *barriques* with spicy wood and lightly gripping tannins, opens to show wild berry and blackcurrant fruits on a background of earthy minerals. Drink now–2014. Score 88. K

SANDRO, 2007: Deep garnet toward royal purple, medium- to full-bodied, reflecting its 14 months in French and American *barriques* with firm tannins and notes of spicy cedarwood. Nothing odd about blending Cabernet Sauvignon and Merlot (70% and 26% each) but somewhat unusual in that the wine was also blended with 4% Sauvignon Blanc. On the nose and palate blackberry, cassis and raspberry notes, those on a background of earthy minerals and Mediterranean herbs. Drink now. Score 87. K

SANDRO, 2006: Dark ruby, medium- to full-bodied, a blend of Merlot, Cabernet Sauvignon and Sauvignon Blanc (70%, 25% and 5%, respectively). Reflecting 14 months in oak, dusty wood and soft, gently gripping tannins, those parting to show appealing currant, berry and orange peel notes. Drink up. Score 87. K

Gaston

GASTON, CABERNET SAUVIGNON-MERLOT-SHIRAZ, 2006: Developed in French and American oak for 18 months, medium- to full-bodied, a blend of 76% Merlot and 12% each Grenache and Syrah. With soft tannins and notes of spicy oak, opens to reveal aromas and flavors of blackcurrants, blackberries and red plums on a lightly piquant background. Drink now–2014. Score 88. K

GASTON, GMS, 2005: A blend of 76% Merlot and 12% each of Grenache and Syrah. Dark garnet, medium- to full-bodied, aged in *barriques* for 12 months. On first attack generous wood on both nose and palate, but that recedes nicely to reveal currant, wild berry and plum fruits on a just-spicy-enough background. Well balanced and long. Drink up. Score 88.

Aligote **

Established by Tsvika Fante and located on Moshav Gan Yoshiya on the central Coastal Plain, the first wines released by this winery were 800 bottles from the 2002 harvest. Production is currently 4,000 bottles annually.

ALIGOTE, CABERNET SAUVIGNON, RESERVE, 2007: Dark royal purple, medium-bodied, with generous spicy wood and firm tannins that seem not to want to settle in and tend to hide the currants, black fruits and Mediterranean herbs that struggle to make themselves felt, Drink now. Score 85.

ALIGOTE, CABERNET SAUVIGNON, 2006: Garnet toward royal purple, medium- to full bodied, with gripping tannins that yield slowly in the glass. Currant and blackberry fruits, those overlaid by spicy wood and notes of Mediterranean herbs. Drink now. Score 85.

ALIGOTE, CABERNET SAUVIGNON, 2005: Traditional Cabernet aromas and flavors of blackberries and currants, those matched nicely by hints of green olives, spices and espresso coffee. Drink up. Score 84.

ALIGOTE, MERLOT, 2008: Garnet with a rim of royal purple, medium- to full-bodied with soft tannins. Opens in the glass to reveal an appealing array of blackberries and purple plums, those on a background of earthy minerals. Drink now–2013. Score 86.

ALIGOTE, MERLOT, 2007: Dark ruby toward garnet, full-bodied, with gently mouth-coating tannins, opening to show generous red and black cherries, wild berries and red plums on the nose and palate. Drink now. Score 86.

ALIGOTE, MERLOT, 2006: Dark garnet, medium-bodied, with somewhat chunky country-style tannins. Opens to show appealing blackberry, black cherry and spices, with oak and tannins rising on the finish. Drink now. Score 84.

ALIGOTE, MERLOT, 2005: Dark ruby toward garnet, medium-bodied, with soft tannins. Generous cherry, berry and spice flavors with a hint of sandalwood on the finish. Drink up. Score 84.

ALIGOTE, SHIRAZ, 2007: Garnet toward royal purple, medium- to full-bodied with still-firm tannins needing a bit of time to settle down. Opens to reveal blackberry, currant and red plum fruits, those supported by notes of earthy minerals and freshly roasted herbs. Best to date from the winery. Drink now. Score 88.

ALIGOTE, CABERNET FRANC, 2007: Deep and concentrated, with chunky country-style tannins opening in the glass to reveal dried currants, sage, minerals and smoky oak. Powerful, failing to show finesse. Perhaps better with a bit of bottle time. Drink now–2014. Score 86.

ALIGOTE, SANGIOVESE, 2005: Ruby toward purple, medium-bodied, with appealing black cherry, blackberry and spicy aromas and flavors. Not complex but a good quaffer. Drink now. Score 84.

Alon **

Founded in 2003 and located on Moshav Alonei Aba, north of Haifa, this small winery produced about 5,000 bottles from the 2006 vintage and 3,500 from the 2007. Winemaker Chaim Cachala makes wines primarily from Cabernet Sauvignon, Tempranillo, Cabernet Franc, Carignan, Petit
Verdot and Petite Sirah grapes, those predominantly from the Galilee and Jezreel Valley.

ALON, CABERNET SAUVIGNON, 2006: Medium-bodied with gently gripping tannins, this oak-aged red shows appealing red currant and cherry fruits, those with hints of chocolate and licorice. Drink now. Score 84.

ALON, CABERNET SAUVIGNON, 2005: Deep royal purple, medium- to full-bodied, with soft, near-sweet tannins and spicy wood integrating nicely to show appealing black fruits on a background of Mediterranean herbs. Mouth-filling and moderately long. Drink up. Score 85.

ALON, CARIGNAN, 2005: Dark garnet and aromatic, this medium-bodied blend of 86% Carignan and 7% each of Tempranillo and Cabernet Sauvignon shows soft tannins that are settling in nicely with berry, black cherry and currant fruits. Hints of chocolate and licorice on the finish. Drink up. Score 82.

ALON, CABERNET FRANC, 2006: Deep ruby toward garnet, medium- to full-bodied, with silky smooth tannins and gentle spicy wood opening to show raspberry, cassis and light herbal aromas and flavors. Drink now. Score 85.

ALON, PETIT VERDOT, 2006: Dark garnet, medium-bodied, with good varietal character showing cassis, tobacco and herbal notes. Not complex but fresh and crisp. Drink now. Score 84.

ALON, PETIT VERDOT, 2005: An oak-aged blend of 88% Petit Verdot and 12% Tempranillo. Royal purple, light- to medium-bodied, with soft tannins and somewhat generous smoke as it first opens, that yields to reveal berry and cherry fruits together with a hint of licorice. Drink up. Score 84.

ALON, TEMPRANILLO, 2005: Blended with 15% Petite Sirah, this ruby toward garnet, medium-bodied red shows soft tannins, gentle spiciness and appealing plum and herbal notes. Drink now. Score 85.

ALON, PETITE SIRAH, 2005: A pleasant little country-style wine, coarse and tannic but opening to reveal generous red plum and blueberry fruits. Drink up. Score 84.

Alona ✳✳✳

Founded in 2001 by the Azoulay and Rabau families on Givat Nili, not far from the city of Zichron Ya'akov, the vineyards of this small winery are spread on the slopes above Nachal Taninim, and contain Cabernet Sauvignon and Merlot grapes. The winery's flagship wine is entitled Kedem. Current production is about 9,000 bottles annually.

Kedem

ALONA, KEDEM, 2008: Full-bodied and generously tannic blend of one-third each Merlot, Cabernet Sauvignon and Carignan. Developed in French and American oak for 12 months. With the tannins integrating nicely now, opens in the glass to reveal red and blackcurrant fruits, those on a background of graphite, pepper and tobacco with appealing notes of freshly turned earth on the finish. Drink now. Score 90.

Reserve

RESERVE. CABERNET SAUVIGNON, 2006: Oak-aged in barriques for 16 months, showing dark garnet, full-bodied and with generous wood and firm, somewhat chunky tannins starting to integrate with blackcurrant and wild berry fruits, those on a background of licorice and lightly bitter herbs. Drink now. Score 85.

Alona

ALONA, CABERNET SAUVIGNON, 2009: A medium- to full-bodied blend of 85% Cabernet Sauvignon and 7.5% each of Cabernet Franc and Merlot. Reflecting its oak-aging for 12 months with gently gripping tannins and notes of vanilla, opens in the glass to reveal currant, blackberry and crushed wild berries, those on a background of earthy minerals. Drink now–2013. Score 86.

ALONA, CABERNET SAUVIGNON, 2008: Garnet toward royal purple, medium- to full-bodied, reflecting its oak-aging with spicy and vanilla notes. Opens to reveal traditional currant and blackberry fruits, those complemented by notes of grilled herbs. Generous. Drink now. Score 88.

ALONA, CABERNET SAUVIGNON, 2007: Dark garnet, full-bodied, with firm tannins and spicy oak in fine balance with fruits and acidity. On the nose and palate blackcurrants, wild berries and citrus peel, those complemented nicely by notes of Mediterranean herbs and green olives. Drink now–2013. Score 89.

ALONA, CABERNET SAUVIGNON, 2006: Dark and brooding, full-bodied and concentrated, with firm tannins and spicy wood yielding to show currants, berries and notes of Mediterranean herbs. Drink now. Score 86.

ALONA, CABERNET SAUVIGNON, 2005: Dark garnet, full-bodied, with caressing soft tannins and spicy oak, those in good balance with fresh blackberry and currant aromas and flavors. On the finish a touch of cedar. Showing first signs of aging. Drink up. Score 88.

ALONA, MERLOT, 2009: A medium- to full-bodied blend of 85% Merlot, and 7.5% each of Cabernet Sauvignon and Cabernet Franc. On the nose and palate garrigue and earthy minerals together with black fruits and a too generous note of mouth-puckering acidity. Drink up. Score 85.

ALONA, MERLOT, 2008: Oak-aged for 12 months, dark garnet, full-bodied, with gently caressing tannins. On the nose and palate wild berries, purple plums and cassis, those supported nicely by notes of bittersweet chocolate and Mediterranean herbs. Drink now. Score 89.

ALONA, MERLOT, 2005: Deep garnet toward royal purple, medium- to full-bodied, with appealing aromas and flavors of spicy plums and currants. Graceful and elegant, but not for further cellaring. up. Score 90.

ALONA, SHIRAZ, 2009: Garnet toward royal purple, medium- to full-bodied, reflecting its 12 months in French and American oak with gently mouth-coating tannins and notes of spices. Opens in the glass to show aromas and flavors of blackberries, raspberries and roasted herbs. Drink now–2013. Score 86.

ALONA, CABERNET FRANC, 2009: A medium- to full-bodied blend of 85% Cabernet Franc and 7.5% each of Cabernet Sauvignon and Merlot. On the nose and palate, black fruits and an overlay of green peppers, chunky tannins and distinct hint of Brett give the wine a distinctly rustic note. Drink now. Score 83.

ALONA, CABERNET SAUVIGNON-MERLOT, 2005: Medium- to full-bodied, with soft tannins and showing an appealing array of berry and cherry fruits on a lightly spicy background. Lacks complexity but a good quaffer. Drink up. Score 86.

ALONA, AGOL, 2009: A blend of 50% Merlot and equal parts each of Cabernet Sauvignon, Cabernet Franc and Shiraz. Showing tannins that are soft but chunky, a medium-bodied, country-style wine with aromas and flavors of cassis, blackberries and raspberries, all on a lightly spicy background. Not complex but a pleasant entry-level wine. Drink now. Score 86.

ALONA, ROSÉ, 2009: Made entirely from Merlot grapes, rose-petal pink toward orange in color, medium-bodied, with a bare hint of tannins to highlight its cherry-berry and watermelon rind flavors. Drink up. Score 86.

Amona ★★★

Located on the mountainous settlement of Amona, overlooking the village of Ofra, this boutique winery was founded by Yehoyada Nizri and Avicai Boaron, with Nizri serving as the winemaker. The winery draws grapes from the Binyamin mountain vineyards. Production is currently about 13,000 bottles annually.

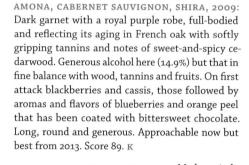

AMONA, CABERNET SAUVIGNON, SHIRA, 2009: Dark garnet with a royal purple robe, full-bodied and reflecting its aging in French oak with softly gripping tannins and notes of sweet-and-spicy cedarwood. Generous alcohol here (14.9%) but that in fine balance with wood, tannins and fruits. On first attack blackberries and cassis, those followed by aromas and flavors of blueberries and orange peel that has been coated with bittersweet chocolate. Long, round and generous. Approachable now but best from 2013. Score 89. K

AMONA, MERLOT, AVIGAIL, 2009: Made entirely from Merlot grapes, showing garnet toward royal purple, and reflecting its development in French oak with somewhat chunky tannins that give the wine a rustic note. On the nose and palate blackcurrants and blackberries, those supported comfortably by notes of roasted herbs and brown spices, all leading to a moderately long finish. Approachable and enjoyable now but best from 2013. Score 88. K

AMONA, DANIEL, 2008: A full-bodied blend of 80% Cabernet Sauvignon, 10% Petit Verdot and 5% each of Merlot and Cabernet Franc. Dark garnet with a rim of royal purple, another high-alcohol wine (14.8%), reflecting its development in oak with still-gripping tannins and aromas and flavors of spicy oak. On the nose and palate blackberries, currants and wild berries, those making way for hints of roasted herbs and freshly hung cigar tobacco. A bit coarse and showing some alcoholic heat on the palate at this stage but with the promise to show more smoothly in the near future. Best from 2013. Score 87. K

AMONA, GIDEON, 2009: A blend of 65% Cabernet Sauvignon and 35% Merlot. Opens with a Port-like nose, that perhaps indicating a bit of early oxidation, going on to reveal itself as a medium- to full-bodied red with primarily red fruits, those unfortunately with a distinct medicinal overlay that make it difficult to find the fruits. Drink now. Score 78. K

Amphorae **

Set in the green and luxuriant mouth of a long-dormant volcano on the western slopes of Mount Carmel, the winery was founded in 2000, and with Gil Shatzberg as winemaker quickly emerged as one of the most promising and interesting wineries in the country. Under Shatzberg's leadership the winery released wines in four series, the top-of-the-line Amphorae Reserve, the regular Amphorae releases, the wines in the Rhyton series and those labeled Med.Red or Med. Blend. The first three series are age-worthy, and the Med.Red and Med.Blend wines were meant for youthful consumption. In early 2008, the talented Shatzberg left Amphorae and took on the role of senior winemaker at the Recanati winery. Despite that, the wines released in what one might think of as "the Shatzberg era" will continue to be noted in this book so long as they are still drinking well and quite a few of them continue to drink very well indeed.

All of which is only the beginning of the story, for the current status of Amphorae is somewhat convoluted. For several months after Shatzberg left, Amphorae was run largely by his assistant winemaker and was then purchased by a group led by David Bar-Ilan of the Keshet winery, a winery that did not come to fruition and did not release any wines. Bar-Ilan, who was working with Arkadi Papikian as a consultant, sold nearly all of the equipment in the existing Amphorae winery, installed his own equipment and undertook major renovations. Not too long after that the winery changed hands again and was taken over by major investor Vladimir Dubov. Papikian became the senior winemaker and a partner in the winery.

Among Amphorae's now-stated goals is the production of wines of extraordinary quality that will compete with the best of the world. The three wines now being released are from the 2006 vintages and are in a new series entitled Unica, that label being used to represent the flagship wines of the winery. Although these wines were made by David Bar-Ilan during his days at Keshet, they carry the Amphorae label. As well as I can understand, the word *unica* derives from Spanish and can be taken to mean either "unique" or "extraordinary." Current and near-future releases are estimated at between 50,000–60,000 bottles annually. The winery is currently working toward rebranding and will be changing the names of their wines.

Unica

UNICA, CABERNET SAUVIGNON, 2008: Dark garnet, full-bodied, with generous sweet and spicy wood and firm, near-biting tannins, opening slowly to reveal traditional Cabernet blackberry and blackcurrant fruits, those complemented by notes of cigar tobacco. Muscular and with a note of alcoholic heat on the finish. Drink from release. Tentative Score 85–87.

UNICA, CABERNET SAUVIGNON, 2006: Made entirely from Cabernet Sauvignon grapes from the Psagot and Manara vineyards and aged for 28 months in French wood barrels of 300 and 500 liters. Full-bodied, deeply extracted and with firm tannins that seem not to want to settle down. Dark garnet, showing blackberries and spicy oak on the nose, and on the palate generous ripe blackcurrants and blackberries, the fruits coming under the influence of a perhaps too heavy hand with the oak and an alcohol content of 15.3% that leaves a too hot note on the finish. Not an elegant wine but one that will appeal to those who like their wines muscular and intense. Drink now. Score 86.

UNICA, SYRAH-MERLOT-CABERNET SAUVIGNON, 2008: Abundant spicy wood, firm tannins and alcohol that adds a simultaneously hot and sweet note. Showing appealing red fruits and spices but the elements not yet integrated. Perhaps better with time. Drink from release. Tentative Score 84–86.

UNICA, SYRAH-MERLOT-CABERNET SAUVIGNON, 2006: A blend of 45% Syrah, 35% Merlot and 20% Cabernet Sauvignon, developed for 28 months in 300 and 500 liter French oak, the grapes from Kfar Yuval. Dark ruby toward garnet, opens with a medicinal hit on the nose, that passing fairly quickly, unlike the almost searing tannins and generous wood that linger and tend to dominate the black fruits and saddle leather that are here. A true blockbuster. Drink now. Score 85.

UNICA, MERLOT-BARBERA, 2008: Deep, dark and concentrated with generous fruits and spicy wood on the nose. Opens to reveal an appealing flavor array of raspberries, cassis and sweet cedar, those with hints of ginger and cigar tobacco. Drink from release. Tentative Score 85–87.

UNICA, MERLOT-BARBERA, 2006: Dark garnet, remarkably full-bodied and tannic considering the blend (83% Merlot and 17% Barbera). A wine that seems to have gone wrong somewhere along the way, showing abundance of too-gripping tannins, alcoholic heat, sweet cedar, sawdust and herbal notes all of which tend to hide the fruits that struggle to make themselves felt. Drink now. Score 85.

AMPHORAE, MED ROSÉ, 2010: A deep pink blend of rosé blend of Cabernet Sauvignon, Merlot and Syrah. On the nose and palate raspberries, peaches and peach pits, those supported by good balancing acidity and a hint of roasted herbs. Drink now. Score 87.

AMPHORAE
Med Rosé
2010
SPECIAL EDITION

Please note that the following Amphorae wines were made prior to the change in ownership of the winery.

Amphorae Reserve

Cabernet Sauvignon 2001 Amphoraevineyard

AMPHORAE, CABERNET SAUVIGNON, RESERVE, 2005: Showing dark, full-bodied and soft, gently mouth-coating tannins, those yielding on the nose and palate to reveal generous black fruits. The potential is here for true elegance and great length. Drink now. Score 92.

AMPHORAE, RESERVE, 2003: A blend of Cabernet Sauvignon, Merlot and Cabernet Franc (70%, 15% and 15% respectively). Generously but not offensively oaked, dark garnet to royal purple, deeply aromatic and full-bodied, with caressing tannins. On the nose and palate an elegant array of currant, blackberry, blueberry, cedar and herbs with hints of cola on the long, generous finish. Drink now–2014. Score 93.

AMPHORAE, CABERNET SAUVIGNON, RESERVE, 2000: Deep garnet-red, remarkably rich, complex and aromatic. Excellent balance, with tiers of currant, plum, Mediterranean herbs and sweet oak coming to a long finish. A wine worthy of cellaring. Drink now–2014. Score 93.

Amphorae

AMPHORAE, CABERNET SAUVIGNON, 2006: Medium- to full-bodied, with soft tannins and gentle wood, a supple and velvety wine offering blackcurrant, blackberry and raspberry fruits, those supported nicely by hints of tobacco and anise. Tightly wound, but with time will show complexity and elegance. Drink now–2013. Score 90.

AMPHORAE, CABERNET SAUVIGNON, 2005: Dark garnet, full-bodied with generous smoky and dusty oak on first attack, that happily settling down as the wine sits in the glass. A deep garnet blend of 90% Cabernet Sauvignon with 5% each of Syrah and Cabernet Franc, showing fine balance between wood, soft tannins and aromas, and flavors of spicy plums, currants and espresso coffee. A long mineral and sage-rich finish. Drink up. Score 90.

AMPHORAE, MERLOT, ORGANIC, 2006: From the organic vineyard at Makura Ranch, this dark ruby-red and deeply aromatic wine is made entirely according to organic principles. Medium- to full-bodied, showing still-gripping tannins and a fine balance and structure that bode well for the future. On the nose and palate, near-sweet black cherries, blackberries and currant fruits, those showing appealing hints of spices and spring flowers. Plush, open-textured and long. Drink now. Score 91.

AMPHORAE, MERLOT, 2005: Dark garnet, medium- to full-bodied, with its once-chewy tannins now settling down nicely and matched comfortably by spicy wood, all in fine balance with currant and black cherry fruits, those supported by hints of chocolate and licorice, and, on the long finish, a hint of sweet cedar. Tight, focused, rich and long. Drink now. Score 91.

AMPHORAE, SYRAH, 2006: Developed in French oak and showing notes of appealing dusty wood. Medium- to full-bodied, opening with traditional Syrah spices, black pepper, leather and earthy minerals, those yielding nicely to blackberry, boysenberry and plums. Long and elegant, with tannins and fruits rising simultaneously on the finish. Drink now. Score 90.

AMPHORAE, SYRAH, 2005: A full-bodied, aromatic and generous wine showing soft, caressing tannins and generous peppery plum, wild berry, exotic spices and hints of roasted meat and earthy minerals. Round, ripe and long with notes of citrus peel and vanilla on the long finish. Drink now–2014. Score 92.

AMPHORAE, SYRAH, 2004: Full-bodied, with firm and well-structured tannins integrating nicely and showing a core of leather, spicy wood and earthiness that highlight rich currant, wild berry, anise and lightly beefy flavors. On the long, elegant finish, generous hints of espresso coffee, violets and toffee. Drink now. Score 91.

AMPHORAE, CABERNET FRANC, 2004: Deep garnet with bright raspberry and plum flavors, this dark, rich and plush wine shows thick, earthy tannins and gamey currant and cedarwood aromas and flavors. Perhaps not elegant but certainly powerful and complex. Drink now. Score 90.

Rhyton

Rhyton Red 2001 Amphoraevineyard

AMPHORAE, RHYTON, 2006: Garnet toward royal purple, a blend of Cabernet Sauvignon, Syrah and Merlot with the Cabernet dominating. At this early stage showing a bit flabby, the tannins soft, the fruits holding back, and spicy and chocolate notes dominating. Past its peak. Drink up. Score 86.

Amram's ✷✷

Founded in 2001 on Moshav Ramot Naftaly in the Upper Galilee by grape grower Amram Azulai and his son Ohad, the team has vineyards of Cabernet, Merlot, Shiraz and Sangiovese grapes in Emek Kadesh. Production from 2004 was 2,800 bottles and current releases are of about 6,000 bottles annually. The winery releases three series – the *barrique*-aged Premium and Breisheit (literally, "Genesis") and Ramot Naftaly, the wines of which are made in large glass containers together with oak chips. Dramatic changes from tasting to tasting in several of the wines tasted lead one to believe that multiple bottlings may have been made.

Premium

PREMIUM, CABERNET SAUVIGNON, 2009: Made entirely from Cabernet Sauvignon grapes, aged for 12 months in new oak and then transferred to three-year-old more neutral oak for an additional year. Rusty garnet in color, medium- to full-bodied, with a black fruit and vanilla nose, opens in the glass to reveal blackcurrants, black cherries and notes of minted chocolate. On the long finish a hint of green olives. Drink now. Score 88.

PREMIUM, CABERNET SAUVIGNON, 2008: Oak-aged for 18 months (12 months in new *barriques* and then for six months longer in three-year-old oak), showing super-dark garnet, full-bodied, with generous soft tannins and notes of spicy oak. Opens with a spicy nose, goes on to reveal traditional Cabernet Sauvignon aromas and flavors of blackberries and blackcurrants, those complemented by notes of Oriental spices. Long and round. Drink now–2014, perhaps longer. The winery's best to date. Score 89.

PREMIUM, CABERNET SAUVIGNON, 2007: Aged in *barriques* for 18 months, showing generous but soft tannins and a gentle overlay of spicy oak. Opens to show appealing currant and berry flavors, those supported nicely by notes of licorice and tar. Drink up. Score 87.

Breisheit

BREISHEIT, CABERNET SAUVIGNON, 2010: Blended with 5% Cabernet Franc, destined for oak-aging for 18 months, showing medium garnet, medium-bodied and with soft tannins. Just starting to take on the impact of the wood, a soft and round wine, unfortunately one-dimensional. Perhaps better with a bit of time. Drink from release. Tentative Score 84–86.

BREISHEIT, CABERNET SAUVIGNON, 2009: Dusty garnet in color, with chunky, country-style tannins and generous acidity. Shows purple plums and crushed blackberries, those marred by a note of Brett that seems on the ascendant. Drink from release. Tentative Score 82–84.

BREISHEIT, CABERNET SAUVIGNON, 2008: A blend of 93% Cabernet Sauvignon, 5% Cabernet Franc and 2% Merlot. Medium- to full-bodied, with its once too generous wood and chunky tannins now integrated well, opens to reveal blackberry, currant and spicy notes all lingering nicely with a note of bittersweet chocolate rising on the finish. Drink now–2013. Score 86.

BREISHEIT, CABERNET SAUVIGNON, 2007: Garnet with a hint of adobe brick, medium- to full-bodied, opening with spicy cedar notes and soft tannins, those going on to show currants, blackberries and a note of bittersweet chocolate. Round and soft, a good entry-level wine. Sliding past its peak. Drink up. Score 84.

BREISHEIT, MERLOT, 2010: Medium-dark garnet, medium- to full-bodied with soft tannins and just the right notes of spicy oak. On the nose and palate red and black currants, raspberries and red plums, all lingering nicely. Not a complex wine but a good choice with small cuts of beef or lamb. Drink from release–2013. Tentative Score 85–87.

BREISHEIT, MERLOT, 2009: Oak-aged for 12 months in primarily new *barriques*, showing garnet with a hint of adobe brick in the color. Medium- to full-bodied (leaning to the full) with an unwanted hint of Brett and too many earthy, loamy notes that tend to conceal the black fruits that are hiding here. Drink up. Score 79.

BREISHEIT MERLOT, 2007: Garnet toward royal purple, medium- to full-bodied, reflecting 12 months oak-aging with gently gripping tannins and notes of spicy wood. On the nose and palate blackberries, black cherries and hints of Oriental spices. Drink up. Score 85.

BREISHEIT, MERLOT-CABERNET SAUVIGNON, 2008: Royal purple, medium-bodied, with soft tannins, gentle hints of wood and generous wild- berry fruits. Not complex but promising to be a good quaffer. Drink up. Score 84.

Harai Naftaly (Naftaly Mountains)

HARAI NAFTALY, CABERNET SAUVIGNON, 2009: Developed with oak chips for 12 months, showing dark garnet and medium- toward full-bodied with soft tannins and notes of spicy oak. On the nose and palate black fruits, those complemented by flavors of tobacco leaf and bitter herbs. Drink from release. Tentative Score 84–86.

HARAI NAFTALY, MERLOT, 2009: Developing with oak chips, showing garnet toward royal purple, medium-bodied and with soft tannins to highlight aromas and flavors of raspberries, green-gage plums and notes of milk chocolate Drink from release. Tentative Score 84–86.

HARAI NAFTALY, MERLOT, 2007: Deep garnet, medium- to full-bodied, with gently gripping tannins and notes of spicy wood. Generous black fruits on the nose and palate, those complemented by hints of tobacco and earthy minerals. Drink up. Score 86.

HARAI NAFTALY, CABERNET SAUVIGNON-SHIRAZ, 2010: A medium- to full-bodied blend of 83% Cabernet Sauvignon and 17% Shiraz, those fermented together. Deep royal purple, with soft tannins, light notes of smoky oak and good balancing acidity. On the nose and palate plums, crushed raspberries and a note of white pepper. Promising to be a fine quaffer. Drink from release. Tentative Score 84–86.

HARAI NAFTALY, CABERNET SAUVIGNON-SHIRAZ, 2007: Garnet toward royal purple, medium-bodied, with somewhat chunky tannins and too-heavy notes of spicy oak that hide the black fruits that are trying to make themselves felt. Drink up. Score 79.

HARAI NAFTALY, MERLOT-CABERNET SAUVIGNON, 2008: Firm and ripe, with notes of spicy oak, a medium-bodied blend of 60% Merlot and 40% Cabernet Sauvignon. Chunky tannins give the wine a rustic nature, showing rather muted black fruits and a somewhat too- generous bitter note that rises from mid-palate on. Drink now. Score 84.

HARAI NAFTALY, CABERNET SAUVIGNON-MERLOT-SHIRAZ, 2008: A medium-bodied blend of Cabernet Sauvignon, Merlot and Shiraz (65%, 22% and 13% respectively). Dusty garnet in color, with black fruits and a too-bitter finish. Drink up. Score 82.

HARAI NAFTALY, CABERNET SAUVIGNON-MERLOT-SANGIOVESE, 2009: A blend of Cabernet Sauvignon, Merlot and Sangiovese (50%, 35% and 15% respectively). Dark garnet, reflecting its seven months in new oak with notes of vanilla, spices and smoke. Medium- to full-bodied, with soft tannins highlighting red fruits, cassis and a generous hint of chocolate. Drink now. Score 87.

Anatot **

Founded in 1998 by Aharon Helfgot and
Arnon Erez, the winery is located in Anatot,
a community north of Jerusalem, and draws
on grapes primarily from vineyards in the
Lachish and Shiloh regions. Current annual
production is 17,500 oak-aged bottles from
Cabernet Sauvignon, Shiraz and Merlot
grapes. Wines are produced in four series,
Alpha, Shani, Anatot, and Notera.

Alpha

ALPHA, 2006: A blend of 60% Shiraz and 40% Merlot, oak-aged for
24 months, showing full-bodied, with generous wood and somewhat
chunky country-style tannins. On the nose and palate blackberries,
blueberries and ripe plums on a background of Oriental spices and
saddle leather. Drink up. Score 85.

ALPHA, MERLOT-SHIRAZ, 2005: Oak-aged for 18 months, medium- to
full-bodied, with generous wood and gripping tannins that part slowly
to reveal berries and plums on a lightly spicy background. Drink up.
Score 82.

Anatot

ANATOT, CABERNET SAUVIGNON, 2006: Garnet toward royal purple,
medium- to full-bodied, with soft tannins, smoky oak and an appealing
array of wild berry, cassis and citrus peel all on a lightly spicy background. Drink now. Score 85.

ANATOT, SHIRAZ, 2005: Deep royal purple in color, medium-bodied,
with soft tannins and spicy wood integrating nicely. Aromas and flavors of plums, berries and hints of tar and licorice. Drink up. Score 84.

ANATOT, SANGIOVESE, 2007: Ruby toward garnet, medium-bodied
with soft tannins and appealing cherry, berry and chocolate aromas
and flavors. Round and fruity with a hint of licorice on the finish. Drink
now. Score 85.

Aneva ★★★

Founded by Ido and Maya Meyrav on Kibbutz Yiron in the Upper Galilee and currently drawing on Cabernet Sauvignon, Merlot and Petit Verdot grapes from the region, the winery released 1,500 bottles from the 2006 and 2007 vintages and 2,000 from 2008. Projected releases from the 2009 vintage are for 4,000 bottles.

ANEVA, MERLOT, 2006: Dark garnet toward royal purple, full-bodied with still-muscular tannins needing a bit more time to settle down but already showing good balance and structure. An unfiltered wine, showing a clean black fruit nose and opening on the palate with black-currants, ripe berries and an appealing overlay of spicy oak. Long and generous. Drink now–2013. Score 89.

ANEVA, SHIRAZ, HERMITAGE, 2006: Made entirely from Shiraz grapes, oak-aged for 20 months, opening nicely in the glass to reveal aromas and flavors of blackberries, citrus peel, white pepper and chocolate and, on the long finish, a hint of eucalyptus sneaking in quietly. Drink now. Score 89.

ANEVA, PINOT NOIR, 2006: Made entirely from Pinot Noir grapes, the wine rather generously oaked after 22 months in *barriques* and therefore a bit more full-bodied and oaky than one might hope for from this variety. Although lacking varietal typicity, an interesting wine, with a nose of black fruits and earthy minerals, opening in the glass to reveal wild berry and blackcurrant fruits, those complemented by notes of minted chocolate and, on the moderately long finish, a lead-pencil hint. Drink now. Score 87.

ANEVA, 2008: A blend of 70% Cabernet Sauvignon and 30% Merlot, oak-aged for eight months, medium-bodied, with soft tannins integrating nicely and showing appealing currant, wild berry and orange peel notes. Not complex but soft, round and easy to drink. Drink up. Score 85.

Argov Winery ✶✶

Located on Moshav Aviel south of Haifa and between Bin-yamina and Givat Ada. Founded by Amir Argov, currently producing about 3,500 bottles annually from Cabernet Sauvignon, Merlot, Shiraz, Petite Sirah, Petit Verdot and Cabernet Franc grapes largely from the winery's own vineyards.

ARGOV, CABERNET SAUVIGNON, 2007: Made in a quasi-*ripasso* method, that is to say by passing the must over older lees, medium-to full-bodied with blackberry, raspberry and notes of cassis liqueur. Soft, round and drinking nicely. Drink now. Score 85.

ARGOV, CABERNET SAUVIGNON, 2006: Light, not completely clear garnet in color, with soft tannins, a medium-bodied wine that opens in the glass to reveal blackberry and currant fruits, those complemented by notes of roasted herbs and cigar tobacco. Drink now. Score 85.

ARGOV, MERLOT, 2007: Garnet toward royal purple, medium-bodied, with soft tannins, opening to show appealing blackberry and blueberry fruits, those supported nicely by hints of roasted herbs. Drink now. Score 85.

ARGOV, MERLOT, 2004: Garnet in color, showing clearing at the rim and a hint of browning. Soft and round, with a somewhat tired berry-cherry personality and an unwanted hint of bitterness on the finish. Drink up. Score 79.

Arza **

Owned by a branch of the Shor family, the Arza winery was founded in 1847 and until recently produced primarily Kiddush wines destined for the ultra-orthodox market. Despite producing several million bottles of wine annually, these wines had little if any interest for sophisticated wine consumers. What has changed is that with French-born and California-trained Philippe Lichtenstein now serving as senior winemaker, Arza is in the process of making major changes in a move to appeal to an increasingly sophisticated audience.

The winery relies primarily on Merlot, Cabernet Sauvignon, Petit Verdot, Carignan, Argaman, Emerald Riesling, Muscat and French Colombard grapes, those sourced from various vineyards. It should be noted that many of the Arza wines will continue to be in the "Kiddush wine" category. For the present moment, production of the new table wines will be of several hundred thousand bottles annually.

ARZA, CABERNET SAUVIGNON, CHARISMA, 2010: Garnet toward royal purple, light- to medium-bodied, with soft, almost unfelt tannins and straightforward aromas and flavors of blackberries, blueberries and purple plums. A good entry-level wine. Drink now. Score 85. K

ARZA, CABERNET SAUVIGNON, 2009: Dark, almost impenetrable garnet in color. Medium- to full-bodied with softly caressing tannins and spicy wood integrating nicely and opening to show wild berry, blackcurrant and purple plums on a background of dark chocolate and green olives. Long and generous. Drink now–2014. Score 87. K

ARZA, CABERNET SAUVIGNON, CHARISMA, 2008: Dark garnet toward royal purple, showing soft tannins and traditional Cabernet fruits. On the nose and palate blackcurrants, blackberries and a note of kirsch liqueur, all on a light peppery and minted background. Drink up. Score 86. K

ARZA, MERLOT, CHARISMA, 2008: Garnet in color, medium- to full-bodied, with somewhat stinging tannins perhaps to settle in, perhaps not, and dusty wood notes from the use of oak chips. Opens to show generous red fruits on a light pepper background. Drink up. Score 82. K

ARZA, SHIRAZ, CHARISMA, 2009: Developed in three–four-year-old French and new American barriques. Garnet toward royal purple, medium- to full-bodied, softly tannic, with a clean, aromatic nose and opening to reveal red plum and cassis fruits, those showing light hints of saddle leather and earthy minerals. Drink now–2013, perhaps longer. Score 87. K

ARZA, HALLEL, 2009: A half-dry red wine, a blend of Carignan, Argaman and Merlot (53%, 30% and 17% respectively). Garnet in color, medium-bodied, with soft tannins, a soft, round wine showing primarily raspberry and strawberry fruits, with the sweetness of the wine set off by good balancing acidity. A good transition for those making their way from sweet to dry wines. Drink up. Score 83. K

ARZA, BLENDED RED, CADENZA, 2009: A dry blend of Carignan, Argaman and Merlot, medium-bodied, with soft tannins. Ruby toward garnet, with a clean, fruity nose. Light- to medium-bodied with a bare hint of oak, showing appealing red berry and cassis fruits. Finishes with a gentle note of red licorice. Drink up. Score 83. K

ARZA, SAUVIGNON BLANC, CHARISMA, 2010: Light golden straw in color, medium-bodied and crisply dry with an appealing array of citrus, tropical and summer fruits. Lively and refreshing. Drink now. Score 85. K

ARZA, MUSCAT, HALLEL, N.V.: Made entirely from Muscat grapes, a distinctly floral and generously fruity white wine, which, despite its categorization as semi-sweet, is so fully sweet that one almost feels sugar grinding between the teeth. One-dimensional and without charm. Drink up. Score 72. K

ARZA, MUSKAT, CADENZA, 2009: Semi-sweet, golden straw in color, with the clean floral aromas associated with the Muscat grape, the sweetness modified nicely by lively acidity. On the nose and palate pineapple and citrus peel notes. An entry-level quaffer. Drink up. Score 84. K

Asif ✶✶✶

Founded in 2006 and now located in the industrial area of Arad on the border between the Negev and Judean deserts, Asif has a double role, the first in making their own wines and the second as a service winery producing wines for other small wineries that do not have their own physical plants. The winery is entirely kosher, and under the supervision of owner-winemaker Ya'akov Oryah is currently producing between 20,000–25,000 bottles annually under its own label and another 15,000–20,000 at least in part for other "wineries," those including Galai, Tura, Kerem Livni, Gavriel and Kfir.

Asif is currently producing wine in three series: Adam v'Adama, Chevlei Aretz and Resheet, the first two being age-worthy, and the third, a popularly priced release destined for early drinking.

Adam v'Adama

ADAM V'ADAMA, CABERNET FRANC, 2008: Oak-aged for ten months in second- and third-year oak, blended with 10% Petit Verdot, showing dark garnet with soft, near-sweet tannins that caress gently. Supple and lively, with raspberry, black cherry and pomegranate aromas and flavors on a background of licorice and freshly hung tobacco, all of which lead to a long and generous finish. Drink now–2014. Score 90. K

ADAM V'ADAMA, TIFFERET, N.V.: Call this one "weird" if you like, but one has to admit that it is weird in a most pleasant manner. A blend of 49% Cabernet Sauvignon from the 2006 vintage (that lightly fortified), 33% Shiraz from the 2008 vintage and 18% Zinfandel from the 2009 vintage, all from extremely low-yield vineyards. Impenetrably dark garnet, opens with a Port-like nose and goes on to reveal ripe raspberry, cherry and plum fruits, those on a background of molasses, espresso and bittersweet chocolate. Thick chewy tannins that go on and on to a long and powerful finish. "Weird" enough that all I can do is guess at a drinking window, from release–2018. Score 90. K

ADAM V'ADAMA, ORANGE WINE, 2010: Another of the winemaker's experiments, and showing quite successful. Israel's first "orange wine," a type made largely in Friuli-Venezia Giulia in Italy, by allowing for long skin contact and maceration of white grapes, giving the wine its color and even a hint of tannins. Medium-, perhaps medium- to full-bodied, showing aromas and flavors of Meyer lemons (a cross between lemons and mandarin oranges), papaya, star fruit, stony minerals and spices, all lingering nicely. Drink from release. Tentative Score 90–92. K

ADAM V'ADAMA, VIOGNIER, 2008: Deep gold with orange and green tints, developed partly on its lees and with 30% in oak. Smooth and round, off-dry but with fine balancing acidity to keep it lively, opening to show aromas and flavors of pears and litchi fruits on a creamy background that hints nicely of white pepper. Long and generous. Drink now. Score 90. K

ADAM V'ADAMA, SEMILLON, 2010: Still in its infancy (and five years from release) already showing deep golden and packed with aromas and flavors, those including apricots, pineapple, honey and vanilla along with a hint of toasted marshmallows on the long finish. Delicious now and promising to develop very nicely before its release. Tentative Score 89–91. K

ADAM V'ADAMA, SEMILLON, 2009: Think of this as an experimental wine, made from intentionally early-harvested grapes and unoaked at this stage. Shows crisp acidity and medium body on a well-balanced frame, and at this stage showing ripe and concentrated with aromas and flavors of tangerines, nectarines, orange blossoms and spices, all starting to come together as a rich and coherent whole. Destined for release only in another 4–5 years when it will show long and fine. Tentative Score 89–91. K

Chevlei Aretz

CHEVLEI ARETZ, ASIF RED, 2010: Dark garnet, full-bodied, with its firm, lip- and cheek-coating tannins now starting to settle in nicely, opens with a distinctly red-fruit nose. A blend of Cabernet Sauvignon, Syrah, Petite Sirah and Merlot (42%, 35%, 20% and 3% respectively). Opens slowly in the glass at this stage to show a generous array of purple plums, black currants and black cherries, those supported comfortably by notes of spices and bitter herbs, all coming together as a coherent whole. Promises very nicely for the future. Drink from release–2015, perhaps longer. Tentative Score 89–91. K

CHEVLEI ARETZ, ASIF RED, 2008: Another of the winery's ever-changing blend this year of 57% Merlot, 26% Cabernet Sauvignon, 12% Petit Verdot and 5% Cabernet Franc. Dark garnet, medium- to full-bodied (leaning to the full), reflecting its development in oak with gently gripping tannins. On the nose and palate blackcurrants, red and black cherries and roasted herbs, all lingering nicely, with tannins and fruits rising on the finish. Drink from release–2014. Score 88. K

CHEVLEI ARETZ, ASIF RED, 2007: Super-dark garnet in color, with red and black fruits on the nose, a medium- to full-bodied, gently tannic blend of 85% Cabernet Sauvignon, 12% Merlot and 3% Syrah. A distinctly red-fruit nose yields in the glass to aromas and flavors of blackcurrants, black cherries and crushed berries, those on a background of freshly picked Mediterranean herbs and tobacco, all with an appealing hint of green almonds. Drink now–2013. Score 87. K

CHEVLEI ARETZ, AVANT GARDE, 2010: A blend that changes a bit from year to year, this year of 25% Gewurztraminer, 20% each of Sauvignon Blanc, Chardonnay and Viognier with 15% of Semillon. Light bright gold in color, opens with a light sulfur stink that blows off quickly to reveal citrus, litchi and tropical fruits. Lacks complexity but round and generous. Drink from release–2014. Score 87. K

CHEVLEI ARETZ, AVANT GARDE, 2009: Light gold in color, with citrus and summer fruits on the nose. A medium-bodied blend of 30% each Sauvignon Blanc and Gewurztraminer, 21% Chardonnay, 12% Viognier and 7% Semillon, opening in the glass to show aromas and flavors of tangerine, grapefruit and star fruit on a background that hints of citrus peel. On the long finish appealing notes of bitter almonds. Drink now–2014. Score 89. K

CHEVLEI ARETZ, CLASSIQUE, 2010: 70% Semillon and 30% Sauvignon Blanc, 20% of which was developed in new oak. Medium-bodied, light shining gold in color, with a floral and fruit-packed nose, opens in the glass to reveal aromas and flavors of lemon and lime, those yielding to citrus peel, exotic spices and notes of kiwis and nectarines. Lively, pleasant and just complex enough to take the attention. Drink from release–2014. Score 89. K

CHEVLEI ARETZ, CLASSIQUE, 2009: Semillon and Sauvignon Blanc (69% and 31% respectively), aged partly in new French oak for four months, showing generous acidity on a medium-bodied frame. On the nose and palate pineapple, white peaches and peach pits on a background that barely hints of spicy oak. Easy to drink and with just enough complexity to grab the attention. Drink now–2013. Score 88. K

CHEVLEI ARETZ, ROSÉ, 2009: A blend of 62% Barbera, 22% Mourvedre and 16% Syrah, the grapes kept in contact for a fairly extended period, giving the wine a deep ruby toward garnet color, far darker than one normally finds in a rosé wine. What surprises is that despite its medium-body, dark color and hint of tannins, the nose and palate perceive this as a true rosé in every way. Crisply dry, with good balancing acidity, on first attack black cherries and wild berries, those yielding to notes of blueberries and raspberries. Delicious and, largely because of the cognitive dissonance caused by the color, body and tannic hint, fascinating. Drink now–2013. Score 90. K

CHEVLEI ARETZ, CHARDONNAY, 2010: Light gold with a green tint, medium-, perhaps medium- to full-bodied, a lively and concentrated wine opening to reveal aromas and flavors of Anjou pears and Granny Smith apples, those followed by notes of nectarines and melon. A wine that seems to open in enchanting layers, all lingering nicely. Drink from release–2014. Score 90. K

CHEVLEI ARETZ, CHARDONNAY, 2009: Unoaked Chardonnay, medium bodied, opening slowly in the glass to reveal notes of lemon and lime on nose and then blossoming to reveal flavors of honeydew melon, pears and roasted almonds, all lingering nicely. Simultaneously lively, refreshing and complex. Drink now–2013. Score 90. K

CHEVLEI ARETZ, CHARDONNAY, 2008: Made entirely from Chardonnay grapes, light golden straw in color with orange reflections. Intentionally unoaked, showing medium-bodied and lively with appealing pear, citrus and citrus peel on a near-creamy background, all lingering nicely. Drink now. Score 88. K

CHEVLEI ARETZ, VIOGNIER, 2010: Unoaked, as is the case with many of the Asif white wines, showing glistening gold with green tints. On the nose and palate, mango and nectarine fruits, those complemented nicely by notes of orange marmalade, vanilla and candied lemon zest. Fine balance between finesse and power, all leading to a long mineral-rich finish Drink from release–2015. Score 90. K

CHEVLEI ARETZ, VIOGNIER, 2009: Unoaked, showing light gold in color, with aromas of peaches and citrus, opening in the glass to reveal flavors of mango, pineapple and almonds on an appealing background of earthy minerals. Drink now. Score 88. K

CHEVLEI ARETZ, CHENIN BLANC, 2010: Light bright golden straw in color, medium bodied, with citrus and tropical fruits on the nose. Opens to reveal green gage plums, white peaches, Jonathan apples and notes of honeysuckle. On the long finish an enchanting hint of chamomile. Impressive even though at this stage of its development, perhaps a bit too acidic. No fear, however, for the balance is here and that acidity will settle down given the appropriate time. Best from mid-2012–2015. Score 90. K

CHEVLEI ARETZ, WHITE BLEND, 2009: Pale golden straw in color, a blend of 64% Sauvignon Blanc, 28% Gewurztraminer and 8% Viognier. Light- to medium-bodied, with aromas and flavors of green apples and pears. A summertime quaffer. Drink now. Score 85. K

CHEVLEI ARETZ, WHITE BLEND, 2008: A somewhat unlikely blend of Sauvignon Blanc, Gewurztraminer and Viognier (64%, 28% and 8% respectively) in which, alas, the varietal traits of each of the grapes is lost. Despite that, a pleasant blend, showing medium-bodied, with lively acidity to highlight aromas and flavors of summer fruits, grapefruit, spices and floral notes. Creamy and round. Drink now. Score 86. K

Resheet

RESHEET, MERLOT, 2008: Dark garnet, medium- to full bodied, a blend of 85% Merlot, 10% Cabernet Franc and 5% Cabernet Sauvignon. Opens with ripe red plums on the nose, goes on to reveal aromas and flavors of cassis, wild berries and tobacco, all on a background of near-sweet, gently gripping tannins. Round and generous. Drink now or in the next year or so. Score 88. K

RESHEET, SYRAH, 2008: Blended with 5% Cabernet Sauvignon, dark garnet with a royal purple rim, showing medium- to full-bodied with gently gripping tannins and generous (perhaps a bit too generous) acidity, opens in the glass to show red plums, cassis and herbal notes, all lingering nicely. Not overly complex but a very pleasant quaffer. Drink now or in the next year or so. Score 88. K

RASHIT, NEGEV RED, 2010: A Bordeaux blend this year of 83% Merlot, 15% Cabernet Sauvignon and 2% Cabernet Franc. Almost impenetrably dark garnet, full-bodied, with generous acidity and lightly gripping tannins. With a nose replete with spicy black fruits, opens in the glass to show black cherry, blackberry and cassis fruits on a background that hints of citrus peel and roasted herbs. Drink from release–2014. Score 88. K

RESHEET, NEGEV RED, 2009: A blend of six grapes (the kind I think of at times as a blend of "everything in the kitchen sink"), those including Cabernet Sauvignon, Petit Verdot, Mourvedre, Cabernet Franc and Malbec in varying percentages. Considering the potpourri blend, a perhaps surprising success, showing dark garnet, medium- to full-bodied and reflecting its 12 months in oak with generously gripping tannins and abundant black fruits, among those blackcurrants, black cherries, blackberries, those on a lightly spicy and herbal background and, on the moderately long finish, a note of bittersweet chocolate. Drink from release–2013, perhaps longer. Score 89. K

RESHEET, ART NOUVEAU, 2010: Deep gold with green and orange tints, a medium-bodied blend of Chardonnay, Semillon, Sauvignon Blanc and Viognier (35%, 30%, 20% and 15% respectively). Unoaked, with fine balancing acidity to highlight aromas and flavors of white peaches, nectarines and citrus peel. Lively and complex. Drink from release–2014. Score 89. K

RESHEET, ART NOUVEAU, 2009: Deep shining gold in color, an unoaked dry white blend of 35% Chardonnay, 25% Viognier and 20% each of, Sauvignon Blanc and Semillon. Opens with a nose rich in summer fruits, goes on to reflect those with peaches, nectarines and citrus on the palate, the fruits supported by light hints of spices that linger through to the long and generous finish. Drink now–2013. Score 89. K

RESHEET, WHITE DESSERT WINE, 2009: Yet another of the winemaker's experiments, a blend of Gewurztraminer, Viognier, Semillon and French Colombard, fermentation stopped by adding enough alcohol to bring the wine to a 13.5% alcohol level. Bright shining gold, medium-bodied, with its moderate sweetness set off by crisp acidity. On the nose and palate, apricots, nectarines and honeyed peaches, all coming together nicely. A fun and easy-to-drink dessert wine. Drink now–2013. Score 88. K

Assaf ✴✴✴✴

Founded in 2004 by Assaf Kedem, the winery is located in the village of Kidmat Tzvi on the Golan Heights. Draws on its own vineyards, those containing Cabernet Sauvignon, Cabernet Franc, Shiraz, Zinfandel, Pinotage and Sauvignon Blanc grapes. Production from the 2007 vintage was 25,000 bottles and anticipated production from the 2010 harvest is 40,000 bottles. Wines are bottled in a reserve and a regular series. The same wines sometimes bottled under the Lili label are intended entirely for export.

Reserve

RESERVE, CABERNET SAUVIGNON, 2008: Oak-aged for 20 months and blended with 11% Cabernet Franc, full-bodied, with gentle wood influence and its once-firm tannins now integrating nicely and showing fine balance and structure. On first attack blackberries and purple plums, those yielding to blackcurrants and wild berries, all on a lightly spicy and tobacco-rich background. Long and generous. Drink now–2016, perhaps longer. Score 92.

RESERVE, CABERNET SAUVIGNON, 2007: Dark garnet, full-bodied with gently gripping, almost plush tannins, blended with 7% Cabernet Franc and showing generous currant and cherry fruits, those supported nicely by hints of spicy wood, eucalyptus and bittersweet chocolate. Drink now–2013, perhaps longer. Score 91.

RESERVE, CABERNET SAUVIGNON, 2006: Oak-aged for 14 months, a blend of 93% Cabernet Sauvignon and 7% Cabernet Franc. Dark garnet toward royal purple, full-bodied and with fine balance and structure that bode well for the future. On the nose and palate hints of sweet cedar followed by blackcurrant, purple plum and blackberry fruits, those supported nicely by hints of minted dark chocolate. Drink now–2013. Score 90.

RESERVE, CABERNET SAUVIGNON, 2005: Dark garnet, medium- to full-bodied, with still-gripping tannins and generous wood waiting to integrate, but showing fine balance and structure. On the nose and palate black and red berries and blackcurrants supported nicely by spicy tobacco and hints of chocolate. Long and generous. Drink now. Score 90.

RESERVE, CABERNET SAUVIGNON, 2004: Garnet toward deep purple, medium- to full-bodied, this blend of 85% Cabernet Sauvignon and 15% Cabernet Franc was aged in partly French, partly American *barriques* for 12 months. Good balance between mouth-coating tannins, vanilla-tinged spicy oak and acidity. On the palate wild berries, red currants and a light but appealing mineral hint, all lingering nicely. Drink up. Score 90.

RESERVE, SHIRAZ, CAESARIA, 2009: Deep garnet toward royal purple, full-bodied, with soft tannins and a gentle overlay of spicy oak. On the nose and palate purple plums, raspberries and cassis, those complemented by hints of freshly tanned leather and stony minerals. Generous and long. Drink now–2016, perhaps longer. Score 89.

RESERVE, SHIRAZ, CAESARIA, 2007: Still young but already showing broad and generous, with generous blackberry, currant and licorice flavors, those with overlays of tar and smoke. Finely tuned balance between wood, tannins and acidity, all leading to a super-long finish. Drink now–2013. Score 90.

RESERVE, SHIRAZ, CAESARIA, 2006: Medium- to full-bodied, ripe, round, soft and generous with blackberry, licorice and mocha notes coming together with hints of smoke and pepper. Oak-aged for 14 months. What cannot help but fascinate is a distinct hint of apricot here. Long, generous and elegant. Drink now–2013. Score 91.

Assaf

ASSAF, CABERNET SAUVIGNON, SILVER, 2008: A blend of grapes selected from four vineyards, showing dark ruby toward garnet. Oak-aged for 11 months, showing medium- to full-bodied, soft and round, with aromas and flavors of black fruits and freshly roasted herbs. On the long finish an appealing hint of licorice. Drink now–2014. Score 90.

ASSAF, CABERNET SAUVIGNON, 2007: Medium- to full-bodied, reflecting its 11 months in oak with gentle notes of sweet cedar and vanilla and soft, well-integrated tannins. On the nose and palate red and black berries and cassis, those complemented nicely by notes of minted chocolate. On the long, mouth-filling finish a hint of red licorice. Drink now–2013. Score 91.

ASSAF, CABERNET SAUVIGNON, 2006: Oak-aged for eight months, dark purple in color, with still-firm tannins, and showing fine balance and structure that bode well for the future. On the nose and palate currants, blackberries, vanilla, dusky herbs and a generously meaty overlay that rises on the long finish. Drink now–2013. Score 90.

ASSAF, CABERNET SAUVIGNON, 2005: Blended with 7% of Cabernet Franc, this medium- to full-bodied, softly tannic, dark garnet toward royal purple wine shows fine balance and structure. Seductive, rich and supple, with lush raspberry, blackberry and currant fruits supported nicely by vanilla and, on the long finish, the tannins rising again. Drink up. Score 90.

ASSAF, SHIRAZ, CAESARIA, 2008: Oak-aged for 20 months but showing a gentle influence of the wood, a full-bodied, round and soft wine, with a generous array of plum, wild berry and raspberry fruits, those supported nicely by notes of saddle leather and earthy minerals. Generous and elegant. Drink now–2017. Score 90.

ASSAF, SHIRAZ, CAESARIA, 2007: Medium- to full-bodied, reflecting its oak-aging for 15 months with notes of spices and cinnamon, a soft-round wine. Opens in the glass to reveal aromas and flavors of purple plums, raspberries and wild berries and, on the long finish, a note of eucalyptus. Blended with 3% Cabernet Sauvignon, a long, concentrated and elegant wine. Drink now–2014. Score 91.

ASSAF, SHIRAZ, 2006: Blended with 3% Cabernet Sauvignon and oak-aged for 14 months, showing a distinctly Shiraz nose of spicy wood, plums and blackberries, all with a hint of saddle leather. Dark garnet toward royal purple, with just the right notes of spicy wood and fine balance between still-firm tannins and fruits. Concentrated and intense but with a distinct touch of elegance and a long finish. Drink now. Score 90.

ASSAF, PINOTAGE, 2007: Made from intentionally early-harvested grapes and developed in used oak barrels. Dark garnet toward royal purple in color, showing blackberry and plum fruits, those supported by generous hints of toast and cedarwood. On the long smooth finish an appealing mineral note. Lively and fresh with just enough complexity to grab our attention. Drink up. Score 89.

ASSAF, 4 SEASONS, 2008: 83% Pinotage, that fleshed out with Cabernet Sauvignon, Cabernet Franc and Shiraz. Oak-aged for 11 months, medium- to full-bodied, with silky tannins and highlights of spicy cedarwood. On the nose and palate an appealing array of wild berry, cassis and fig notes, those supported by hints of black licorice. Drink now–2014. Score 90.

ASSAF, 4 SEASONS, 2007: A blend of Pinotage, Syrah, Cabernet Sauvignon and Cabernet Franc and, as unlikely as that sounds, a fine combination, indeed unusual for Israel but not uncommon in South Africa. Reflecting its seven months in oak with light spices and soft, gently caressing tannins, a medium- to full-bodied and round wine, with generous blueberry, fig and licorice notes coming together nicely and lingering comfortably on the palate with a hint of cedarwood rising on the finish. Drink now. Score 89.

ASSAF, SAUVIGNON BLANC, 2009: Light gold in color, medium-bodied, with appealing citrus and tropical fruits on a background of minerals and a tantalizing note of cinnamon. Elegant and long. Drink up. Score 91.

ASSAF, SAUVIGNON BLANC, 2008: Light golden straw in color, medium-bodied, with fine balance between acidity and fruits, a lively but complex and elegant wine showing tropical and citrus fruits on a background of freshly cut grass. Drink up. Score 90.

ASSAF, SAUVIGNON BLANC, 2007: Developed for three months in 400 liter casks, this deep golden wine shows earthy, mineral and vanilla aromas and flavors that come together very nicely with citrus, pear and melon fruits. Creamy and intense enough that you might describe this white wine as tannic. Drink up. Score 90.

Avidan ✶✶✶✶

Founded in 2000 by Shlomo and Tsina Avidan with Tsina as the winemaker, this boutique winery is located on Kibbutz Eyal in the Sharon region and relies on Chardonnay, Shiraz, Cabernet Sauvignon, Pinot Noir, Grenache, Mourvedre, Carignan, Petite Sirah and Merlot grapes selected from various vineyards in the Jerusalem Mountains, and is currently producing about 30,000 bottles annually. With major expansion and modernization now completed, wines are released in several series – the age-worthy Premium and Reserve wines and the varietal Avidan, and the Blend des Noirs and Petite Soleil, meant for earlier consumption. A relatively new series, "Fringe," is so named because the blends are both playful and unusual.

Premium

PREMIUM, MERLOT, 2006: Oak-aged for ten months and blended with a small amount of Grenache, with somewhat stinging tannins that seem to not want to integrate. Opens slowly to show black cherry, plum, nutty and spicy aromas on a light mineral background. Drink up. Score 87.

PREMIUM, GRENACHE, 2009: Light garnet in color, medium-bodied, with soft tannins and a gentle wood influence, showing good concentration for the vintage. On the nose and palate rhubarb, cherry and spice flavors, those lingering nicely. Bright, silky and appealing. Drink from release. Tentative Score 87–89.

PREMIUM, GRENACHE, 2008: Ruby toward garnet, medium- to full-bodied, with gentle tannins and a light hand with the oak, but perhaps a bit too much acidity here. Opens in the glass to reveal wild berry and sour cherry fruits, those on a lightly spicy background. Perhaps better with time. Drink now. Score 85.

PREMIUM, GRENACHE, 2007: Medium-dark garnet in color, made from 30-year-old low-yield vines, showing fine concentration and intensity. Medium- to full-bodied (perhaps leaning toward the full), with gently caressing tannins showing black cherry, wild berry, blueberry and peppery aromas and flavors. Drink now. Score 88.

PREMIUM, GRENACHE, 2006: Rich and concentrated, medium- to full-bodied, with soft tannins integrating nicely and reflecting its ten months in *barriques* with gently spicy oak. On the nose and palate a generous and intriguing array of aromas and flavors, among those currants, blackberries and plums, nutmeg, sage and vanilla, and ending with the tannins and oak rising on the finish together with hints of grilled beef and cloves. Drink up. Score 90.

Reserve

RESERVE, CABERNET SAUVIGNON, 2008: Super-dark garnet, full-bodied and reflecting its 24 months in oak with generous wood and gripping tannins, those needing only a bit of time to integrate. Expressive and concentrated but destined to show grace and elegance. On the nose and palate black fruits, roasted herbs, licorice and earthy minerals. On the long finish, wild berries and a note of citrus peel. Best 2013–2018. Score 92.

RESERVE, CABERNET SAUVIGNON, 2007: Reflecting its 24 months in oak with surprisingly gentle notes of spicy oak and still-firm tannins, those integrating nicely. Dark garnet, with crushed berries and hints of pepper on the nose, opens in the glass to show blackcurrants, pepper and tobacco, with a tantalizing hint of bitter almonds that comes in on the long finish. Drink now–2017. Score 90.

RESERVE, CABERNET SAUVIGNON, 2006: A blend of 85% Cabernet Sauvignon and 15% Merlot. Deep royal purple, medium- to full-bodied, with soft, mouth-coating tannins and generous black fruits supported by earthy minerals. Oak-aged for 24 months and showing generous spicy wood, along with intriguing tobacco and chocolate aromas and flavors with the fruits rising on the long finish. Drink now. Score 89.

RESERVE, CABERNET SAUVIGNON, 2005: Oak-aged for 24 months and blended with 15% Merlot, dark garnet, full-bodied and showing generous oak and firm tannins, those in fine balance with blackberry, blackcurrant and citrus peel fruits, all with peppery and anise overtones leading to a long, generous finish. A fine wine, but for those who like their reds on the muscular side. Drink now. Score 91.

RESERVE, MERLOT, 2007: Deep, youthful royal purple in color, full-bodied, with gently mouth-coating tannins and notes of spicy cedarwood, opens to show generous currant, wild berry and purple plum fruits, those complemented by notes of earthy minerals. Drink now– 2014. Score 89.

RESERVE, SHIRAZ, 2008: Deep garnet with a purple robe, with notes of spicy cedar and black fruits on the nose. Firm and dense, with currant, blackberry and mineral notes on first attack, those yielding in the glass to hints of cigar tobacco and saddle leather. Long and mouth-filling. Drink now–2018. Score 91.

RESERVE, SHIRAZ, 2007: Almost impenetrably dark garnet in color, with notes of licorice, chocolate and purple plums on the nose. Opens in the glass to reveal black cherry and blackcurrant fruits, those on a background of tobacco and sage. Destined always to be full-bodied and chewy but at the same time polished, long and generous. Drink now–2017.

RESERVE, SHIRAZ, 2006: Made entirely from Shiraz grapes, aged for 16 months in American and French *barriques*, dark garnet to royal purple in color, full-bodied, with soft, gently caressing tannins, opens with a burst of chocolate and leather. Develops in the glass to reveal aromas and flavors of blackberries, red cherries and peppermint, those leading to a long and supple finish. Bright and effusive at this stage and will show greater complexity as it continues to develop. Drink now–2014. Score 91.

RESERVE, SHIRAZ, 2005: Made from an Australian clone but with a distinctly Rhone nose and palate. Developed for 16 months in French oak, it shows a generous mouthful of blackberry, blueberry, plum and cherry fruits, those overlaid nicely by hints of leather, earth and Oriental spices that go on to a long finish. Drink up. Score 90.

Fringe

FRINGE, PINOT NOIR, 2009: Medium-dark garnet, medium- to full-bodied, perhaps with a few more muscles than one expects of Pinot Noir, but don't hold that against the wine because on the nose and palate it is indeed Pinot Noir. In fact, a rather classy Pinot Noir. On the nose strawberries, raspberries and spices, and opening in the glass to show blackberries and a hint of minerals. On the long finish an appealing note of sage. Complex and vibrant. Best from 2013–2018. Tentative Score 90–92.

FRINGE, GRENACHE, 2007: An unusual but successful blend of 85% Carignan, 10% Tempranillo and 5% Petite Sirah. Medium- to full-bodied, soft and open-textured, reflecting its 16 months in *barriques* with soft tannins and a gentle note of spicy wood. On the nose and palate plum, wild berry and notes of spices that linger nicely. Drink now. Score 90.

FRINGE, GRENACHE-MOURVEDRE, 2007: 60% Grenache and 40% Mourvedre, those reflecting oak-aging for 16 months. An aromatic red-fruit nose, opens to show medium- to full-bodied, with generous red fruits and abundant spices, those parting to make way for aromas and flavors of cherries, tar and black pepper. On the long finish with tannins rising, a gentle hint of game meat. A distinctly Rhone or Australian blend but with an absolutely Mediterranean persona. Drink now–2016. Score 90.

FRINGE, FULL WINE, 2009: Deep garnet toward royal purple, a blend of 60% Cabernet Sauvignon and 40% old-vine Petite Sirah. Dark enough to be considered impenetrable, with a nose rich in black fruits, opens to show medium- to full-bodied (leaning to the full). On the nose and palate an appealing array of blackcurrants, crushed berries and roasted herbs all leading to a long and generous finish. Best from 2013–2017, perhaps longer. Score 89.

FRINGE, FULL WINE, 2008: Super-dark garnet, medium- to full-bodied, with its once-firm tannins integrating nicely. A blend of 60% Cabernet Sauvignon and 40% Petite Sirah, oak-aged for 12 months. On the nose spicy oak and freshly turned earth, those integrating well and opening in the glass with generous notes of blackberries, currants and pepper. On the notably long finish an appealing hint of tar. Drink now–2015. Score 91.

FRINGE, PRIO, 2008: Dark garnet with a surprising hint of adobe brick in color, a full-bodied blend of Carignan, Grenache, Cabernet Sauvignon and Merlot. On the nose notes of spicy cedarwood and tar, those parting to make way for aromas and flavors of currants, blackberries, cigar tobacco and licorice, with the fruits and tannins rising on the finish. A wine to capture not only the palate but the imagination. Some will love it. Others will not. Me, I loved it. Drink now–2016, perhaps longer. Score 90.

FRINGE, PRIO, 2007: The name inspired by a visit to Spain's Priorat region. Dark garnet toward royal purple, full-bodied, with soft, gently caressing tannins, a blend of 40% Carignan, 30% Grenache and 15% each of Cabernet Sauvignon and Merlot. Oak-aged for 24 months but showing gentle spicy cedarwood influences. On first attack blackberries, those followed by cassis and purple plums, all set on a background of truffles and baking chocolate. As this one develops look as well for notes of saddle leather and espresso coffee. Drink now–2017. Score 90.

FRINGE, PETIT ROSÉ, 2010: Pale salmon pink in color, a blend of Grenache, Syrah and Cabernet Sauvignon. Medium-bodied, not so much a "lively" rosé as a complex one, even with a hint of tannins to highlight aromas and flavors of peaches, peach pits and freshly cut herbs, with a hint of sweetness that creeps in on the surprisingly long finish. Perhaps at its very best with a platter of goats and sheep cheeses, bread and butter. Drink now. Score 89.

FRINGE, PETIT ROSÉ, 2009: Deep rose-petal-pink toward salmon-colored, a blend of Pinot Noir, Grenache and Carignan. Opens with a tutti-frutti, almost bubble-gum nose but that passes quickly and with a smile to reveal a light- to medium-bodied, lively and crisp rosé with hints of light tannins to complement strawberry, cranberry and blueberry notes. As good a bet with fish and seafood as with 350 gram hamburgers. Drink up. Score 88.

FRINGE, MORE, 2006: Made by the recioto method – drying the grapes on mats before pressing them. A blend of Shiraz, Grenache and Merlot grapes, showing notes of dried currants and prunes, those on a full-bodied background that is rich, dense and silky. With the generous level of sweetness traditional to recioto wines, delicious, opulent and harmonious with fresh fruit notes that linger on and on. Drink now–2015. Score 92.

Avidan

AVIDAN, CABERNET SAUVIGNON, 2005: Showing firm tannins well balanced by spicy wood, herbaceousness and currant and plum fruits. Firm but near-elegant. Drink up. Score 87.

AVIDAN, MERLOT, 2009: Deep garnet with orange and purple reflections, showing a rich red fruit and floral nose. Full-bodied, with gripping tannins only now starting to settle down and opening to reveal generous red fruits, spices and Mediterranean herbs, those on a background that hints at one moment of bittersweet chocolate and at another of mocha. Drink now–2014. Score 89.

AVIDAN, SHIRAZ, 2008: Impenetrably dark royal purple in color, full-bodied, with generous tannins and a moderate hand with spicy wood, those integrating nicely now to show peppery plum, mint, licorice and leathery notes. Destined to be a gentle blockbuster but needs time for its elements to come together. Drink from release. Score 89.

AVIDAN, SHIRAZ, 2007: Developed in American oak, full-bodied, with firm tannins and moderately generous wood and alcohol that make themselves clearly felt. Opens with a somewhat medicinal aroma but that blows off quickly to reveal plum, wild berry, licorice and leathery notes. Drink now. Score 86.

AVIDAN, SHIRAZ, 2006: Dark garnet, medium- to full-bodied, oak-aged for 16 months, showing chunky tannins and skimpy plum and berry fruits. Lacks complexity or depth. Drink up. Score 85.

AVIDAN, PINOT NOIR, 2008: Tight and concentrated, darker, more full-bodied and more tannic than one expects from a Pinot Noir. On the nose and palate dried berries and currants, mint and sage and a bit heavy on its herbal presence. Not at all a typical Pinot but will surely have its fans. Drink now–2014. Score 88.

AVIDAN, CARIGNAN, 2008: A juicy, easy-drinking style showing black fruits, currants, boysenberries and chocolate, all with a modest touch of spicy oak and with tannins that are silky smooth. Drink now. Score 88.

AVIDAN, PETIT VERDOT, 2008: Deep garnet in color, with near-sweet, gently gripping tannins and an appealing overlay of spicy oak parting to reveal fresh and dried currants, black cherries and citrus peel notes, all coming together as a long, generous and coherent whole. Drink now–2014. Score 89.

AVIDAN, PETITE SIRAH, 2008: Super-dark garnet, full-bodied, concentrated and even muscular, with "stick-to-the-lips" tannins but showing its intensity in ways that are discrete. On the nose black fruits, smoke and a hint of white pepper. Opening in the glass to reveal aromas and flavors of both blackberries and raspberries, those complemented nicely by notes of sweet cedar. Long and generous with a hint of bitter-orange peel on the finish. Complex, focused and mouth-filling. Drink now–2016. Score 92.

AVIDAN, PETITE SIRAH, 2007: Dark garnet toward royal purple, full-bodied with still-firm tannins and generous wood waiting to integrate but already showing fine balance and structure. On the nose and palate white pepper and wild berries, those matched nicely by cedarwood, spices and, from mid-palate on, blackberry. Quasi-muscular but lovely and long. Drink now–2014. Score 90.

AVIDAN, GRENACHE-MOURVEDRE, 2009: A blend of 60% Grenache and 40% Mourvedre. Dark garnet, full-bodied with soft tannins integrating nicely showing raspberry, cherry and floral notes. Has the potential to be a polished and subtle wine. Drink from release–2014. Tentative Score 89–91.

AVIDAN, RUBY, N.V.: A brandy-reinforced red wine, one of the few worthwhile red dessert wines made in Israel today. Dark ruby in color, rich and complex, loaded with spices, walnut, nutmeg and espresso coffee on raspberry and cassis fruits. Smooth, well balanced, with no syrupy sensation. Drink from release. Tentative Score 88–90.

AVIDAN, GOLD, N.V.: A white dessert wine based on Chardonnay grapes, and reinforced with brandy to a 17% alcohol level. Generous maple-syrup sweetness set off by spices, orange peel and an appealing floral hint that lingers nicely. Not complex but enjoyable. Drink from release. Tentative Score 86–88.

Blend des Noirs

BLEND DES NOIRS, TAGADOM, SPECIAL EDITION, 2008: Another of Avidan's perhaps odd but quite successful blends, this one of Petite Sirah, Cabernet Sauvignon, Shiraz and Merlot (35%, 30%, 20% and 15% respectively). Dark, almost impenetrable garnet toward royal purple, with soft tannins and a gentle wood influence. Opens in the glass to reveal generous purple plum, black cherry and cassis fruits, those on a background that hints at one moment of licorice and at another of minted chocolate. Drink now–2013, perhaps longer. Score 90.

BLEND DES NOIRS, TAGADOM (RED LABEL), 2007: Oak-aged for 12 months, this medium-bodied blend of Petite Sirah, Cabernet Sauvignon and Shiraz (45%, 35% and 20% respectively), shows super-dark garnet in color. Opens with a fresh, black fruit nose, and goes on in the glass to reveal currants and raspberries, those supported by hints of mint, licorice and espresso coffee. Soft and gently mouth-coating tannins rise comfortably on the finish. Drink now. Score 88.

BLEND DES NOIRS, TAGADOM (RED LABEL), 2006: Aged in French and American oak for ten months, a blend of Shiraz, Cabernet

Sauvignon and Petite Sirah (45%, 35% and 20% respectively). Medium- to full-bodied, with chunky, somewhat coarse tannins, showing straightforward berry and currant notes. A pleasant country-style wine. Drink up. Score 85.

BLEND DES NOIRS, TAGKATOM (ORANGE LABEL), 2009: A blend that varies from year to year depending on the winemaker's whims, this one of 60% Grenache, 20% Argaman and 20% Petite Sirah. Deep garnet with an equally deep royal purple robe, full-bodied, with soft near-sweet tannins and notes of spicy oak. Opens in the glass to show plums, blackberries and currant fruits, those set off by finely tuned acidity and, on the finish, hints of roasted herbs. Drink now–2015. Score 89.

BLEND DES NOIRS, TAGKATOM (ORANGE LABEL), 2008: A blend this year of 40% Cabernet Sauvignon, 35% Merlot and 25% Grenache, those oak-aged for 12 months. Dark garnet with orange reflections, showing medium- to full-bodied (leaning to the full), with soft, gently caressing tannins and notes of spicy wood, complementing and not at all hiding currant, wild berry, and plum fruits, all on a lightly earthy-mineral background. Drink now–2014. Score 90.

BLEND DES NOIRS, TAGKATOM (ORANGE LABEL), 2007: Medium-dark garnet in color, medium- to full-bodied, showing spicy oak and somewhat sharp and stinging tannins at this stage of its development. Beneath the tannins lightly peppery currant and black cherry fruits. Give this one a bit of time for the tannins to settle down. A blend of 45% Cabernet Sauvignon, 30% Merlot and 25% Grenache, oak-aged for 12 months. Drink now. Score 87.

BLEND DES NOIRS, TAGKATOM (ORANGE LABEL), 2006: Garnet toward royal purple, an oak-aged blend of Cabernet Sauvignon, Cabernet Franc and Merlot. Medium- to full-bodied, with ripe blackberry and cassis fruits, those opening to show notes of orange peel and chocolate. Drink up. Score 86.

BLEND DES NOIRS, TAGSEGOL (PURPLE LABEL), 2009: A full-bodied, deep-garnet blend (possibly to be labeled as TagBordeaux), Cabernet Sauvignon, Merlot, Petite Verdot and Petite Sirah (80%, 7%, 7% and 6% respectively). A nose rich with spicy red fruits, opens in the glass to reveal currants, crushed berries and tobacco, all on a gently pronounced background of spicy oak. Finishes with tannins and raspberries rising nicely. Best from 2013–2017. Tentative Score 89–91.

BLEND DES NOIRS, TAGSEGOL (PURPLE LABEL), 2008: A super-dark garnet blend of Merlot, Shiraz, Petite Sirah and Carignan (40%, 25%, 20% and 15% respectively), those aged in mostly second- and third-year French and American oak for 12 months. On the nose black fruits, opening in the glass to show medium- to full-bodied with gentle notes of spicy oak, soft, gently gripping tannins and black currants, wild berries, plums and citrus peel, those yielding on the long finish to flavors of licorice and black olives. Drink now– 2015. Score 90.

BLEND DES NOIRS, TAGSEGOL (PURPLE LABEL), 2007: An identical blend to the 2008 wine (reviewed above), showing dark garnet toward royal purple, with generous wild berries on the nose and opening in the glass to show medium- to full-bodied, with its youthfully firm tannins now integrating nicely. On the nose and palate currant and black cherry fruits on a spicy oak background, all coming to a long finish on which the tannins and fruits rise together. Drink now–2013. Score 89.

BLEND DES NOIRS, PURPLE, 2006: A blend of 40% Cabernet Sauvignon, 35% Merlot and 25% Shiraz. Developed in oak for ten months, garnet toward youthful royal purple, medium- to full-bodied with near-sweet tannins in fine balance with spicy wood. On the nose and palate a generous array of berry, currant and plum fruits, those with hints of espresso and leather. Drink now. Score 87.

Petite Soleil

PETITE SOLEIL, CHARDONNAY, 2008: Not very aromatic, but showing fat and creamy with pear and fig notes matched nicely by notes of Oriental spices and earthy minerals. You may like it or you may hate it, but it will make you think. Drink up. Score 87.

Bar *

Established in 2002 by Ilan Bar in the town of Binyamina in the Sharon area and drawing largely on grapes from the surrounding vineyards, this family-owned winery produces Cabernet Sauvignon, Merlot, Carignan, Sauvignon Blanc and Chardonnay wines as well as Jonathan Red, a blend of Merlot and Cabernet. The winery is currently producing about 3,000 bottles annually.

BAR, CABERNET SAUVIGNON, 2006: Garnet in color, medium-bodied, with spicy and vanilla-rich wood and chunky, country-style tannins. On the nose and palate berries, currants and spices. Lacks complexity. Drink up. Score 84.

BAR, CABERNET SAUVIGNON, 2005: Ruby toward garnet, medium-bodied, with gripping tannins and spicy wood opening to reveal not overly generous red and black berry fruits, this wine is somewhat one-dimensional. Past its peak. Drink up. Score 82.

BAR, CABERNET SAUVIGNON, 2004: Dark ruby, medium-bodied, with generous smoky wood and firm tannins hiding the black fruits that struggle to make themselves felt. Drink up. Score 83.

BAR, JONATHAN RED, 2005: Medium-bodied, garnet in color, with chunky, country-style tannins. On the nose and palate berries, black cherries and hints of spices. Showing age. Drink up. Score 84.

BAR, JONATHAN RED, 2004: A country-style, medium-bodied blend of Merlot and Cabernet Sauvignon with chunky tannins and spicy cedar. Aromas and flavors of wild berries, cassis liqueur and herbaceousness. Showing age. Drink up. Score 83.

Baram **

Located on Kibbutz Baram in the Upper Galilee, this small winery released its first wines from the 2004 vintage. Winery-owned vineyards contain Cabernet Sauvignon and Merlot grapes. First release was of 1,800 bottles, increasing to 5,500 bottles from the 2008 vintage.

BARAM, CABERNET SAUVIGNON, 2007: Light, almost pale ruby in color, medium-bodied, with barely felt tannins, showing aromas and flavors of black fruits and spices. A simple but pleasant quaffer. Drink now. Score 84.

BARAM, CABERNET SAUVIGNON, 2006: Medium- to full-bodied, with chunky, country-style tannins and generous smoky wood somewhat hiding the black fruits that are underneath. Drink up. Score 84.

BARAM, CABERNET SAUVIGNON, 2005: Dark garnet toward royal purple, medium-bodied, with gripping tannins and spicy wood integrating nicely and revealing berry, black cherry and fresh herbal aromas and flavors. Drink up. Score 86.

BARAM, MERLOT, 2008: Dark garnet, medium- to full-bodied with soft tannins and showing straightforward berry, cherry and currant notes. A good quaffer. Drink now. Score 86.

BARAM, MERLOT, 2007: Dark ruby toward garnet, developed in oak for 12 months, showing medium-bodied, with soft tannins and appealing wild berry and currant notes. Not complex but round and easy to drink. Drink now. Score 85.

BARAM, BARAM FOREST, 2007: A medium-bodied blend of 67% Cabernet Sauvignon and 33% Merlot, oak-aged for 15 months, showing somewhat chunky country-style tannins. Opens in the glass to reveal a basic berry–black cherry personality. An easy-going quaffer. Drink now. Score 83.

BARAM, CABERNET SAUVIGNON-MERLOT, 2006: An oak-aged blend of ⅔ Cabernet Sauvignon and ⅓ Merlot. Medium-bodied, with softly caressing tannins, appealing hints of spices and vanilla from the oak and showing generous black fruits. Round and moderately long. Drink up. Score 85.

Bar Giora **

Located on Moshav Bar Giora in the Judean Hills, the winery was founded in 2003, originally as a hobby. Partners Shlomo Aviton and Aviel Schneider are now producing about 4,000 bottles annually. The winery produces red wines only, those based on Cabernet Sauvignon, Merlot, Cabernet Franc, Petit Verdot and Shiraz grapes, with Pinot Noir soon to come on line.

BAR GIORA, CABERNET SAUVIGNON, 2006: Dark garnet, medium- to full-bodied, reflecting its 18 months in *barriques* with firm tannins only now starting to settle in and notes of vanilla and spicy oak. On the nose and palate red and black berries and, from mid-palate on, notes of blackberries. Moderately long with the wood and tannins rising on the finish. Drink up. Score 88.

BAR GIORA, SHIRAZ, 2005: Firm tannins and generous dusty wood dominate at first but those part in the glass to allow the entry of black fruits and spices. Deep garnet, with notes of saddle leather and herbaceousness on the moderately long finish. Sliding past its peak. Drink up. Score 86.

BAR GIORA, PINOT NOIR, 2008: Blended with 5% of Petit Verdot, oak-aged in French *barriques* for 18 months, the wine shows medium- to full-bodied, generously tannic and reflecting a rather heavy hand with the oak. On the nose and palate, dried berries along with notes of mint, sage and bay leaf. A savory if not complex wine and not adequately reflecting the traits of Pinot Noir. Drink now. Score 84.

BAR GIORA, CABERNET FRANC, 2005: Dark garnet, with firm tannins and generous wood that seem not to want to settle down. With a firm, almost chewy texture and distinctly green and earthy notes throughout, opens somewhat to reveal blackberry and currant fruits. Somehow never seems to come fully together. Starting to show age. Drink up. Score 84.

BAR GIORA, PETIT VERDOT, 2007: Gently gripping tannins on a medium- to full-bodied background showing generous near-sweet cedarwood and opening to reveal red berries and cassis. Developed for 18 months in second-year barrels together with oak chips. Medium-dark garnet, medium-bodied, with soft tannins parting to reveal ripe currant and blueberry fruits, those overlaid with notes of sage and white pepper. Not a green note to be found here but do look for atypical but appealing notes of green olives. Long and generous with tannins rising on the finish. Drink now. Score 86.

BAR GIORA, JEHUDA, 2008: A medium-bodied blend of 65% Cabernet Sauvignon, 20% Merlot and 15% Petite Sirah. Oak-aged for 18 months, showing chunky tannins and aromas and flavors of black fruits. A rustic wine with not too many complexities and decidedly at its best with food. Drink now. Score 84.

BAR GIORA, MERLOT-SHIRAZ, 2007: A blend of 80% Merlot and 20% Shiraz, aged in *barriques* for 18 months, and showing a moderate (12.8%) alcohol content along with notes of spicy wood. Soft tannins and generous wild berry and cassis notes, those hinting of earthy minerals, come together as a not overly complex but quite pleasant wine. Drink now. Score 86.

BAR GIORA, BLENDED RED, LISA, 2007: Oak-aged for 18 months, a blend of 65% Petit Verdot, 20% Merlot and 15% Cabernet Sauvignon. Medium- to full-bodied, with chunky country-style tannins and reflecting its time in used oak *barriques* with vanilla and smoke, those parting to reveal plum, wild berry, currant and tobacco flavors, the tannins rising on the finish. Drink up. Score 87.

Barkai **

Headed by winemaker Ettai Barkai, the winery is located on Moshav Roglit in the Ella Valley at the foothills of the Jerusalem Mountains, and relies on Cabernet Sauvignon, Merlot and Shiraz grapes from its own vineyards. Production for 2002 and 2003 was under 1,000 bottles annually. The winery is currently producing about 4,000 bottles annually. A new winery is currently being constructed with a capacity for 10,000 bottles annually.

BARKAI, CABERNET SAUVIGNON-MERLOT, 2006: Medium-bodied, with gently mouth-coating tannins and showing appealing wild berry, black cherry and spicy wood. Drink now. Score 84.

BARKAI, CABERNET SAUVIGNON-MERLOT 2005: Garnet toward royal purple, medium-bodied, with soft tannins. On the nose and palate berries, cherries and sweet cedarwood. Drink up. Score 84.

BARKAI, CABERNET SAUVIGNON-MERLOT, 2004: Deep ruby toward garnet, medium-bodied with generous near-sweet tannins and flavors and aromas of sur-ripe berries, cherries and cassis. Showing age. Drink up. Score 84.

Barkan ✳✳✳✳

Founded in 1990 by Shmuel Boxer and Ya'ir Lerner with the buyout of the former wine and liqueur producer, Stock, the winery was first located in the industrial area of Barkan, not far from Kfar Saba on the Trans-Samaria Highway. In 1999 Barkan began planting extensive vineyards in Kibbutz Hulda, on the central plain near the town of Rehovot, where it now has a state-of-the-art winery. From mid-2008, the full operations of the winery have been at Hulda. Under the supervision of senior winemaker Ed Salzberg, and winemakers Yotam Sharon and Irit Boxer, the first of whom studied in California, the second in France, and the third in Australia, this is now the second-largest winery in Israel, with current production of about eight million bottles.

Barkan, whose main ownership is now in the hands of the soft-drink company Tempo, has a current investment exceeding $20 million, and includes the winery, the adjoining vineyards (1,500 dunams owned jointly by the winery and the kibbutz, making this the largest single vineyard in the country), the new barrel room now completed and a visitors' center well under construction. Barkan is also the parent company of Segal Wines.

The winery releases varietal wines in four series: Superieur, Reserve (of which the Altitude wines may be considered a sub-label), Classic and Domaine. The winery also produces several private label wines including those in the Derekh Eretz series for the Wine Route (Derekh HaYain) chain of shops. In addition, the winery is currently developing a vineyard of 150 dunams (75 acres) at Mitzpe Ramon in the Negev Desert, and will release wines from there under the label Negev Project.

Superieur

SUPERIEUR, CABERNET SAUVIGNON, 2008: Dark, almost impenetrable garnet, full-bodied and intense, with teeth-numbing tannins at this time, those just starting to settle in with smoky wood and black fruits. On first attack blackberry and blackcurrant fruits, those yielding in the glass to notes of baking chocolate and espresso coffee and, on the long, long finish an appealing hint of red licorice. Drink now–2016, perhaps longer. Score 92. K

SUPERIEUR, CABERNET SAUVIGNON, 2007: Full-bodied, dark garnet in color, somewhat reserved on first pouring but opens nicely in the glass to reveal a nose with gentle black fruits and vanilla-tinted wood. On the palate a fine array of black fruits, those matched nicely by hints of mocha and bittersweet chocolate. Long and generous. Drink now–2015. Score 91. K

SUPERIEUR, CABERNET SAUVIGNON, 2006: A full-bodied blend of 90% Cabernet Sauvignon and 10% Merlot aged for 18 months in primarily new French *barriques*.
Dark ruby toward garnet, opens with generous oak and firm tannins, those subsiding in the glass and opening to reveal a light note of vanilla from the wood and then traditional Cabernet blackcurrants and blackberries, those along with notes of blueberries and mint and at what one moment seems to be a hint of lead pencils and another a cigar box note. Well crafted. Drink now–2013. Score 90. K

SUPERIEUR, CABERNET SAUVIGNON, 2003: Dark, almost impenetrable royal purple in color, firm and concentrated, this is one of the best ever from Barkan. Full-bodied, with gently mouth-coating tannins and a judicious hand with spicy oak, shows intense aromas and flavors of blackcurrants, blackberries and black cherries, those complemented by hints of dates, sage and near-sweet cedarwood. A long finish bursting with minerals and black fruits. Showing signs of age. Drink up. Score 91. K

SUPERIEUR, MERLOT, 2008: Still a tentative blend but already showing fine promise. Almost impenetrably dark garnet in color, full-bodied, with black fruits and a light note of sawdust on the nose, showing gently gripping tannins and a tempting array of cassis, wild berries and dark chocolate on the nose and palate. Long and generous. Destined for elegance. Drink now–2016. Score 91. K

SUPERIEUR, MERLOT, 2004: Medium- to full-bodied, with soft tannins integrating nicely; showing smoky blackberry, berry, black cherry and cassis fruits, those on a light background of red peppers and vanilla, all leading to a long, smooth, mouth-filling finish. Drink up. Score 87. K

SUPERIEUR, SHIRAZ, 2006: Super-dark garnet, medium- to full-bodied, a soft, round wine with silky tannins integrating nicely and showing a generous array of raspberries, red-currant and chocolate aromas and flavors, those opening to reveal gentle notes of smoked sawdust and eucalyptus. Tannins and light leathery notes rise on the long, mouth-filling finish. Well crafted. Drink now–2013. Score 91. K

SUPERIEUR, PINOTAGE, 2007: Full-bodied, a meaty and herbal wine with near-sweet, gently gripping tannins and spicy wood parting to reveal plums, currants and dried figs, those supported nicely by notes of sweet herbs. Long and generous, with tannins and fruits rising on the finish. Drink now. Score 88. K

Reserve

RESERVE, CABERNET SAUVIGNON, 2008: A medium- to full-bodied blend of 88% Cabernet Sauvignon and 12% Merlot. Reflects its 16 months in oak with round, gently gripping tannins and notes of spicy cedarwood. On the nose and palate black fruits and a hint of unsweetened cocoa. Not complex but an easy-to-drink wine. Drink now. Score 86. K

RESERVE, CABERNET SAUVIGNON, 2007: Dark and ripe, medium- to full-bodied, reflecting its 20 months in *barriques* with light notes of spices and vanilla and now-well-integrating tannins. On the nose and palate black cherry, currants and a light smoky note, the intensity rising on the finish. Drink now. Score 88. K

RESERVE, CABERNET SAUVIGNON, 2006: Garnet-red, medium- to full-bodied, developing in French and American oak and showing near-sweet tannins opening to reveal raspberry, currant and earthy minerals leading to a medium-long finish. Drink up. Score 87. K

RESERVE, CABERNET SAUVIGNON, 2005: Reflecting 20 months in American, French and Hungarian *barriques* with a generous overlay of spicy wood, showing mouth-coating tannins and with a relatively high alcohol content (15.5%), one might expect this full-bodied red to be somewhat overpowering. Happily, however, the elements come together nicely, opening to show a solid base of blackcurrants and black and red berries, those with appealing bittersweet notes that linger nicely on the finish. Drink up. Score 88. K

RESERVE, MERLOT, 2008: Dark garnet toward royal purple, medium- to full-bodied, with soft tannins, a blend of 88% Merlot, 8% Shiraz and 4% Pinotage. Reflecting 14 months in 50% new and 1-year-old French and American *barriques,* with soft tannins and light notes of spicy wood, opens in the glass to reveal appealing blackberry, black cherry and currant fruits, those matched nicely by notes of earthy minerals and a hint of licorice. Drink now–2013. Score 87. K

RESERVE, MERLOT, 2007: Opens with a floral and fruit-rich nose, goes on to reflect its 14 months in oak with light spicy wood and soft tannins to support generous raspberry and red currant fruits, those complemented by notes of spices, dark chocolate and finally, on the long finish, cigar tobacco. Drink now. Score 89. K

RESERVE, MERLOT, 2006: Dark garnet, medium- to full-bodied, with soft, near-sweet tannins and hints of spicy wood from the 14 months it spent in new French *barriques*. Opens to show blackberries and purple plums, those parting in the glass to make way for red fruits, cassis and notes of citrus peel. On the finish hints of what at one moment seem like mint, at the next of licorice. Generous and appealing. Drink now. Score 88. K

RESERVE, MERLOT, 2005: Aged in oak for 14 months, dark garnet, medium- to full-bodied, with gripping tannins on first attack which yield in the glass to reveal good balance between gentle wood and cassis, red plum and wild berry fruits complemented by hints of pepper, vanilla and chocolate. Lingers nicely on the palate. Drink up. Score 87. K

RESERVE, SHIRAZ, 2008: Deep garnet, opens with an earthy, somewhat funky nose, but that blows off quickly to reveal blackberry and black cherry fruits on a background of saddle leather, dark chocolate and roasted herbs. Drink now–2014. Score 90. K

RESERVE, SHIRAZ, 2007: Oak-aged for 14 months, deep garnet in color, medium- to full-bodied, with silky tannins and hints of spicy wood integrating nicely, opens to show wild berry, plum and peppery notes and, on the moderately long finish, a note of licorice. Drink now. Score 88. K

RESERVE, SHIRAZ, 2006: Deep and youthful garnet toward royal purple in color, reflecting its year in French and American *barriques* with appealing spicy notes. A full-bodied wine, with still-gripping tannins and a tempting note of bitter herbs that runs through. Blended with 4% each of Cabernet Sauvignon and Petit Verdot, opens to show appealing red berry and cherry fruits, those complemented by hints of white pepper and licorice. Drink now. Score 88. K

RESERVE, SHIRAZ, 2005: Oak-aged for 14 months, medium- to full-bodied, dark garnet, firm, and faithful to the Shiraz variety, this red shows oak-accented berry, cherry and licorice flavors backed up by light hints of leather and mint. Lingers nicely. Drink up. Score 88. K

RESERVE, PETIT VERDOT, 2008: Developed for 18 months in one-year-old barrels, a medium- to full-bodied blend of 88% Petit Verdot, 8% Cabernet Sauvignon and 4% Merlot. On the nose and palate toasty oak and bittersweet cocoa, those parting in the glass to reveal currants, blackberries and figs, an appealing note of toasted rye bread rising on the finish. Drink now or in the next year or so. Score 87. K

RESERVE, PINOTAGE, 2008: Blended with 8% Shiraz, showing dark cherry- red toward garnet, full-bodied and reflecting its 12 months in barriques with soft tannins and notes of spicy wood. On the nose and palate blackberries, purple plums and hints of vanilla and sweet herbs. Needs food to show at its best. Drink now. Score 89. K

RESERVE, PINOTAGE, 2007: Oak-aged for 12 months, dark garnet and concentrated, with purple plum and blackberry notes along with sweet and spicy notes that run through this medium- to full-bodied and gently tannic wine. Drink up. Score 87. K

RESERVE, PINOTAGE, 2006: Dark garnet with orange reflections, its once- gripping tannins now integrated nicely and parting to show generous berry, black cherry, purple plum and cassis flavors, those supported by notes of earthy minerals and tobacco. Hints of cloves and cinnamon rise on the moderately long finish. Drink up. Score 87. K

RESERVE, PINOTAGE, 2005: Garnet toward purple, now showing medium- to full-bodied, with soft, near-sweet tannins and reflecting its 12 months in oak with generous spicy wood. Opens to show straight-forward berry, cherry and plum fruits on a lightly spicy background. Showing better than at earlier tastings but not meant for further cellaring. Drink up. Score 87. K

RESERVE, CARIGNAN, 2007: Made from grapes harvested from 25-year-old vines, super-dark royal purple in color, medium- to full-bodied, and reflecting its ten months in oak with soft, gently gripping tannins and sweet and spicy cedarwood. On the nose and palate blackberries, wild berries and purple plums, those supported nicely by hints of bittersweet chocolate. Blended with 8% Cabernet Franc, finishes long and generous with appealing mineral notes. Drink now. Score 88. K

RESERVE, TEMPRANILLO, 2005: Dark ruby in color, with firm tannins now softening and integrating nicely and showing an appealing array of plum, cherry, licorice and tobacco aromas and flavors, all reflecting 16 months in oak with sweet cedarwood. Past its peak. Drink up. Score 88. K

RESERVE, CHARDONNAY, 2009: Light gold, slightly muted when first poured but opening in the glass to show green apple, pear and green almond notes. Medium-bodied, with an appealing hint of bitterness on the finish. Drink now. Score 88. K

RESERVE, CHARDONNAY, 2008: Golden straw in color, with a light wood influence and fine acidity that highlight flavors and aromas of citrus, mango and pineapple on a lightly peppery background. Round, refreshing and complex enough to grab the attention. Drink up. Score 85. K

RESERVE, CHARDONNAY, 2007: Showing light spicy and vanilla notes from the oak in which it was aged for a short while, lively golden in color and showing an appealing array of tropical fruits and red grapefruit. Bright and zesty. Drink up. Score 86. K

RESERVE, SAUVIGNON BLANC, 2009: Bright light gold in color, medium-bodied, with fruits muted at first but opening nicely in the glass to reveal appealing citrus, grassy and herbal notes all with a tantalizing hint of celery seed. Drink now. Score 89. K

RESERVE, SAUVIGNON BLANC, 2008: Unoaked, crisp and lively, a medium-bodied white showing citrus, tropical fruits and an appealing light grassy note. Drink up. Score 87. K

Altitude

Released regularly since 2003, each of the wines in this mini-series is made entirely from Cabernet Sauvignon grapes, those fermented and oaked in similar manners, the major difference between them being reflected in the altitude, micro-climate and soil conditions of the vineyards.

ALTITUDE, CABERNET SAUVIGNON, 412, 2008: Dark royal purple toward garnet with generous wood on the nose and still-firm, near-sweet tannins showing all signs of integrating nicely. Opens in the glass to reveal blackberries, wild berries and currants, those well supported by notes of cinnamon and black pepper. Spicy and forward at this stage. Drink now–2016. Score 90. K

ALTITUDE, CABERNET SAUVIGNON, 412, 2007: Garnet with a royal purple robe, made entirely from Cabernet Sauvignon grapes primarily from the Avnei-Eitan vineyard on the southern Golan Heights and developed largely in new French oak for 14 months. Medium- to full-bodied, in the direction of full, with soft tannins integrating nicely and a moderate reflection of spicy cedarwood from the barriques in which it aged, opens to show a fine array of blackcurrant, blackberry and blueberry fruits, those on a lightly spicy background that calls to mind mint and tobacco. Coherent, long and quietly elegant. Drink now–2015. Score 90. K

ALTITUDE, CABERNET SAUVIGNON, 412, 2006: Made primarily from grapes from the Avnei-Eitan vineyard on the Golan Heights, with 10% of the grapes from the Dishon vineyard, oak-aged in French and American oak for 14 months, a medium- to full-bodied red, with gripping tannins and spicy wood in good proportion to blackberry and currant fruits. Faulted only in that it becomes a bit astringent on the finish. Drink now. Score 87. K

ALTITUDE, CABERNET SAUVIGNON, 412, 2005: Dark garnet in color, medium- to full-bodied, with soft, near-sweet tannins and reflecting its 14 months in oak with spicy wood. On the nose and palate red plums, berries and currants, those with hints of chocolate and tobacco on the finish. Drink up. Score 88. K

ALTITUDE, CABERNET SAUVIGNON, 624, 2008: Dark garnet toward royal purple, with generous soft tannins and gentle notes of spicy wood. On first attack raspberries and chocolate, those followed by notes of blackberries and black cherries. Look as well for flavors of black olives on the generous mouth-filling finish. Drink now–2016. Score 91. K

ALTITUDE, CABERNET SAUVIGNON, 624, 2007: Super-dark garnet, full-bodied, with gripping tannins and spicy wood showing all signs of integrating nicely. On the nose and palate, black fruits "all the way" – that is to say, blackcurrants, blackberries and black cherries, those on a background of dark chocolate and, on the long finish, a note of roasted herbs coming in nicely. Drink now–2015. Score 90. K

ALTITUDE, CABERNET SAUVIGNON, 624, 2006: Made entirely from Cabernet Sauvignon grapes harvested in the Upper Galilee's Alma vineyard. Developed in mostly new French oak *barriques* for 14 months, showing full-bodied, with soft tannins coming together nicely with cedarwood notes to show off a generous array of currant, wild berry and orange peel fruits, those supported nicely by notes of mocha and, on the long finish, a hint of black licorice. Drink now. Score 89. K

ALTITUDE, CABERNET SAUVIGNON, 624, 2005: Deep, almost impenetrable garnet in color, medium- to full-bodied, its once-gripping tannins now settled in nicely with notes of spicy oak and fruits. Black and red currants here, those matched nicely by notes of exotic near-sweet spices and, on the long and generous finish, a note of bitter-citrus peel. Drink now. Score 89. K

ALTITUDE, CABERNET SAUVIGNON, 720, 2008: Dark, almost impenetrable garnet, with appealing notes of saddle leather and black fruits on the nose. Full-bodied, concentrated and intense at this early stage, firm tannins and spicy wood just starting to settle in but already showing fine balance and structure that bode well for the future. Opens in the glass to reveal a generous array of cassis, cherries and raspberries, those yielding to notes of blackcurrants, mocha and freshly cut herbs. Long and generous. Drink now–2016. Score 91. K

ALTITUDE, CABERNET SAUVIGNON, 720, 2007: Deep garnet toward royal purple, full-bodied, with gently gripping tannins and spicy wood integrating nicely. A distinctly black fruit nose and on the palate red cherries, raspberries and currants, those supported comfortably by notes of exotic spices and a tantalizing hint of smoked meat. Rich and concentrated. Drink now–2015. Score 91. K

ALTITUDE, CABERNET SAUVIGNON, 720, 2005: Opens with a smoky, spicy nose, and goes on to deliver appealing plum, blackberry and currant fruits, those overlaid with Oriental spices. Soft, caressing tannins and gentle wood add to the complexity of the wine. Look as well for a tantalizing hint of earthy bitterness that comes in on the long finish. Drink now. Score 91. K

Classic

CLASSIC, CABERNET SAUVIGNON, GALILEE, 2010: Garnet toward royal purple, medium-bodied with soft tannins and pleasant but straightforward black fruits. Not complex but an acceptable quaffer. Drink now. Score 85. K

CLASSIC, CABERNET SAUVIGNON, GALILEE, 2009: Dark garnet, medium-bodied, with gently gripping tannins. Opens to show blackcurrants, blackberry and blueberry fruits on a lightly spicy background. Drink now. Score 85. K

CLASSIC, CABERNET SAUVIGNON, 2008: Dark garnet, medium- to full-bodied, with firm, somewhat coarse tannins but those settling down in the glass to reveal wild berry, cassis and black cherry fruits on an earthy-mineral background. Drink up. Score 84. K

CLASSIC, CABERNET SAUVIGNON, 2007: Medium-bodied, with soft tannins and traditional blackcurrant and blackberry fruits. Sliding past its peak. Drink up. Score 85. K

CLASSIC, MERLOT, 2010: Medium-bodied with gently gripping tannins and straightforward currant and black cherry fruits. A pleasant quaffer. Drink now. Score 84.

CLASSIC, MERLOT, GALIL, 2009: A thoroughly internationalized Merlot, that is to say with no clue whatever as to where the grapes originated. Dark cherry red, medium-bodied, with soft tannins and basic black fruits and a hint of tobacco on the finish. An acceptable entry-level wine. Drink now. Score 83. K

CLASSIC, MERLOT, 2007: Medium-bodied, soft, round and showing a basic cherry-berry personality. A good entry-level wine. Drink now. Score 84. K

CLASSIC, SHIRAZ, DAN, 2010: Cherry red toward royal purple, medium-bodied with gently gripping tannins. On the nose and palate crushed berries, plums and a hint of freshly tanned leather. Drink now. Score 84. K

CLASSIC, SHIRAZ, 2009: Light garnet, medium-bodied, with soft tannins and showing a basic berry-cherry personality. An entry-level wine. Drink now. Score 84. K

CLASSIC, SHIRAZ, 2007: Made entirely from Shiraz grapes, unoaked, showing medium-bodied with soft tannins and opening to show raspberries, red currants and cherry notes, those with a light overlay of white chocolate. Drink up. Score 84. K

CLASSIC, SHIRAZ, 2006: Royal purple in color, medium-bodied, with soft, gently mouth-coating tannins and good acidity to keep it lively. Few varietal traits here, but appealing black and red fruits on a lightly spicy background make this a good quaffer. Sliding past its peak. Drink up. Score 85. K

CLASSIC, PINOT NOIR, NEGEV, 2010: A pleasant enough little wine but you might never guess that it was made from Pinot Noir grapes. Cherry red, medium-bodied, with soft tannins and a basic berry-black cherry personality. An entry-level choice. Drink now. Score 84. K

CLASSIC, PINOT NOIR, 2009: Dark cherry red in color, light- to medium- bodied, with appealing wild berry, cassis and earthy-mineral notes. Nothing complex but a good entry-level quaffer. Drink up. Score 85. K

CLASSIC, PINOTAGE, 2009: Ruby toward garnet in color, medium-bodied, with chunky tannins parting to reveal generous red fruits and notes of freshly turned earth. A simple but pleasant country-style wine. Drink up. Score 84. K

CLASSIC, PINOTAGE, 2007: Dark garnet toward royal purple, with near-sweet tannins and opening to show plum, currant jelly, eucalyptus and smoky notes. Showing age. Drink up. Score 87. K

CLASSIC, ROSÉ, 2009: Made from Shiraz grapes, showing salmon pink in color, a dry but somewhat flat rosé wine, showing minimal berry and cherry fruits and without the character to make it interesting or the acidity to give it liveliness. Drink up. Score 78. K

CLASSIC, CHARDONNAY, 2010: Light gold, medium-bodied, a simple little white that might have been made from any variety whatever. Aromas and flavors of peaches and pears on a light and perhaps unwanted bitter background. Drink now. Score 82. K

CLASSIC, CHARDONNAY, 2009: Light gold, medium-bodied, with straightforward citrus and tropical fruits. Drink up. Score 83. K

CLASSIC, SAUVIGNON BLANC, 2010: Light golden straw in color, light- to medium-bodied, a somewhat flabby wine with muted aromas and flavors that might be summer fruits or citrus. Drink up. Score 80. K

CLASSIC, EMERALD RIESLING, 2009: The color of damp straw, light- to medium-bodied, a half-dry wine that happily avoids being overly sweet but whose fruits are so muted that they defy description. Drink up. Score 78. K

Domaine

DOMAINE, CABERNET SAUVIGNON, 2008: Light, with soft tannins and simple but pleasant berry, black cherry and currant fruits. Drink up. Score 80. K

DOMAINE, MERLOT, 2008: Dark ruby toward garnet, with light herbal overtones highlighting berry and black cherry fruits. An entry-level wine. Drink up. Score 82. K

DOMAINE, SHIRAZ, 2008: Dark garnet, medium-bodied, with soft tannins and showing plum, wild berry and leathery notes. Drink up. Score 84. K

DOMAINE, PETITE SIRAH, 2008: Garnet toward purple, medium-bodied, a simple country-style wine with blackberry, blueberry and spicy notes. Drink up. Score 84. K

Derekh Eretz

DEREKH ERETZ, CABERNET SAUVIGNON, 2008: Ruby toward garnet in color, medium-bodied, an unoaked red with soft tannins and cherry, berry and currant fruits on a somewhat generously acidic background. At its best served lightly chilled. Drink up. Score 84. K

DEREKH ERETZ, MERLOT, 2008: Medium-bodied, unoaked and showing gently caressing tannins and on the nose and palate raspberries and wild berries, those on a lightly earthy background. Nothing complex here but a good quaffer. Drink up. Score 84. K

DEREKH ERETZ, EMERALD RIESLING, 2008: Traditional for half-dry Emerald Riesling, showing floral aromas and flavors of summer fruits and honeydew melon, those on a sweet, almost dried-fruit background. Fine for what it is considering the variety. A wine for people who like this kind of wine. Drink up. Score 80. K

Bashan ✶✶✶

Founded by Uri Rapp and Emmanuel Dassa, the winery is located on Moshav Avnei Eitan on the southern Golan Heights and produces the country's only kosher organic wines, those from grapes raised in its own vineyards. The first releases were from the 2004 vintage, and to date are based entirely on Cabernet Sauvignon and Merlot grapes. Production for 2007 was of 11,000 bottles, for 2008, 8,500 bottles and for 2009, 18,000 bottles. Tentative plans are to grow to production of 50,000–100,000 bottles.

BASHAN, CABERNET SAUVIGNON, 2008: Medium- to full-bodied with silky smooth tannins and notes of sweet cedarwood. On the nose and palate traditional blackcurrant, blackberry and citrus peel notes, those showing a gentle minted-chocolate note. Drink now–2013. Score 87. K

BASHAN, CABERNET SAUVIGNON, EITAN, 2007: Oak-aged for 18 months in new and used *barriques*, showing dark garnet and with soft tannins integrating well with notes of spicy wood. On the nose and palate blackcurrant and red and black berries supported nicely by a tantalizing hint of cigar tobacco. Drink now–2013. Score 88. K

BASHAN, CABERNET SAUVIGNON, EITAN, 2006: Dark royal purple and firmly tannic but showing fine balance and structure that bode well for the future. Well focused, with currant and plum fruits highlighted by mineral and herbal notes and, on the moderately long finish, a hint of toasty oak. Drink now. Score 86. K

BASHAN, CABERNET SAUVIGNON, EITAN, 2005: Medium- to full-bodied, this organic wine shows good balance between sweet oak, generous yeasts and, on the nose and palate, appealing ripe and spicy black fruits. Drink up. Score 88. K

BASHAN, MERLOT, EITAN, 2008: A component tasting, showing full-bodied, with still-firm tannins waiting to integrate but already showing a gentle touch of sweet-and-spicy oak and opening to show blueberry, blackberry and black cherry fruits. Drink now–2013. Score 88. K

BASHAN, MERLOT, EITAN, 2007: Blended with 11% Cabernet Sauvignon, and oak-aged for 18 months. Dark garnet, full-bodied, with a deep berry-rich nose and opening to show red plum, cassis and blueberry fruits. With gently gripping tannins, soft, round and comfortably long. Drink now. Score 89. K

BASHAN, MERLOT, EITAN, 2006: Garnet toward royal purple, medium-bodied, with soft tannins. Showing generous berry, black cherry and milk chocolate aromas and flavors. A caressing, if not long, finish. Drink now. Score 86. K

BASHAN, CABERNET SAUVIGNON-MERLOT, NAVE, 2008: Dark garnet toward royal purple, medium- to full-bodied with firm tannins waiting to settle down and integrate but already showing fine balance and structure. Opens to show generous black fruits on a lightly spicy-herbal background. Drink now. Score 87. K

BASHAN, CABERNET SAUVIGNON-MERLOT, NAVE, 2007: A medium- to full-bodied blend of 85% Merlot and 15% Cabernet Sauvignon. Reflecting 14 months in oak, showing spices, soft tannins and a note of near-sweet cedarwood. Opens on the palate to reveal a soft, round wine with wild berries, black cherries and blackcurrants supported nicely by a hint of red licorice. Lingers nicely. Drink now. Score 88. K

BASHAN, CABERNET SAUVIGNON-MERLOT, NAVE, 2005: A dark garnet, medium- to full-bodied blend of 70% Cabernet Sauvignon and 30% Merlot that spent 14 months in oak. Opens with a light bottle stink, but that passes quickly to reveal a clean, well-balanced wine with soft tannins and appealing currant, berry and eucalyptus aromas and flavors. Not complex but quite appealing. Drink up. Score 86. K

Bazelet Hagolan ✶✶✶

Founded in 1998 on Moshav Kidmat Tzvi in the Golan Heights, the first facility of this winery was located in a cowshed and initial production from that vintage year was 1,800 bottles. Today, under the auspices of Yoav Levy, the winery is producing about 55,000 bottles annually, half of those from grapes grown in its own vineyards on the Golan Heights.

Until 2005 the winery released only Cabernet Sauvignon wines. The winery's first Merlot was released from the 2006 vintage. The wines are in two series: Reserve and Bazelet Hagolan (known sometimes as "Bronze"), the first aged in oak for about 20 months, the second for 8–10 months. Production has been kosher since the 2004 vintage.

Reserve

RESERVE, CABERNET SAUVIGNON, 2008: Reflecting its 20 months in oak with generous spicy and vanilla rich wood, that in good balance with soft, gently caressing tannins. On the nose and palate blackberries, purple plums, licorice and, on the medium-long finish, a note of black olives. Drink now–2013. Score 87. K

RESERVE, CABERNET SAUVIGNON, 2007: Dark royal purple, full-bodied, reflecting its 20 months in oak with generous sweet cedarwood notes and soft tannins. Opens to show generous very ripe, almost jammy blackberry, raspberry and currant fruits. Blended with 10% Merlot, the wood and a sweet overlay dominate. Drink now. Score 84. K

RESERVE, CABERNET SAUVIGNON, 2006: Now mature but showing considerably better than ever before. Deep garnet toward royal purple, full-bodied, aromatic and with once-firm tannins now integrated nicely with wood and fruits. On the nose and palate a hint of Brett but that nicely complementing blackberry, currant and citrus peel notes. On the long, lightly spicy finish a generous note of freshly ground coffee. Drink now. Score 90. K

RESERVE, CABERNET SAUVIGNON, 2005: Aged in oak casks for 20 months, full-bodied, rich, ripe, smooth, generous and well balanced with currant, berry and plum flavors coming together with near-sweet tannins and tempting smoky oak lingering nicely. On the moderately long finish a hint of bitter baking chocolate. Drink up. Score 88. K

RESERVE, MERLOT, 2007: Blended with 10% Cabernet Sauvignon, medium- to full-bodied, reflecting its 20 months in oak with soft tannins and generous spicy wood. Showing forward currant and wild- berry fruits. Easy drinking but somewhat one-dimensional and showing a bit of heat on the finish. Drink now. Score 84. K

RESERVE, MERLOT, 2006: The winery's first Merlot release. Medium- to full-bodied, deep garnet, with soft, gently mouth-coating tannins integrating nicely with spicy cedar notes. Opens to reveal appealing berry, black cherry and cassis fruits on a background of earthy minerals. Long and satisfying. Drink now. Score 88. K

Bazelet Hagolan (Bronze)

BAZELET HAGOLAN, CABERNET SAUVIGNON, 2009: Dark garnet, reflecting its eight months in *barriques* with a gentle hint of spicy oak and soft, gently gripping tannins. On the nose and palate traditional blackcurrant, blackberry and bittersweet chocolate notes. Only medium-long but round and appealing. Drink now–2013. Score 87. K

BAZELET HAGOLAN, CABERNET SAUVIGNON 2008: Medium- to full-bodied, dark garnet in color, and with a Port-like nose that calls to mind premature oxidation. On the palate sur-ripe purple plum and wild berry fruits adding to a not-necessary sensation of sweetness. Drink up. Score 83. K

BAZELET HAGOLAN, CABERNET SAUVIGNON, 2007: Oak-aged for eight months, dark garnet toward royal purple, medium- to full-bodied with soft, gently caressing tannins and notes of sweet cedarwood in fine balance with blackcurrant and blackberry fruits. Opens in the glass to reveal blueberries, earthy minerals and a note of freshly roasted Mediterranean herbs. Drink now. Score 87. K

BAZELET HAGOLAN, CABERNET SAUVIGNON, 2006: Medium- to full-bodied, with chunky country-style tannins and a hint of sweet cedarwood that runs throughout. Opens to show traditional Cabernet currant and blackberry fruits, those matched by hints of light earthiness and sweet herbs. Drink up. Score 87. ᴋ

BAZELET HAGOLAN, MERLOT, 2008: Oak-aged for eight months in new French and American *barriques*, deep garnet in color, with somewhat chunky tannins, perhaps too-abundant acidity and spicy oak notes. Medium-bodied, showing aromas and flavors of currants, wild berries and roasted herbs. Drink now. Score 85. ᴋ

BAZELET HAGOLAN, MERLOT, 2006: Garnet toward royal purple, medium- to full-bodied, with near-sweet tannins and spicy oak highlighting plum and currant fruits. In the background, light toasty bread and smoked meat. A 15% alcohol content gives a fairly hot finish. Drink up. Score 85. ᴋ

BAZELET HAGOLAN, CHUSHNIA, 2006: As far as I can figure it out "chushnia" translates to sensuality. Whatever, a limited-edition blend (all in all of 628 bottles) of equal parts of Cabernet Sauvignon and Merlot, those oak-aged in new French *barriques* for 20 months. Dark garnet, medium- to full-bodied. Beware the tannins as the wine is first poured as they are almost searing, but give the wine time to open and those soften comfortably to show good balance and a mélange of red and black fruits. A hint of sweetness comes in from mid-palate and lingers on the finish. Drink now–2014. Score 89. ᴋ

Beit-El ✴

Established by California-trained wine-maker Hillel Manne in 2001 and located in Beit-El, north of Jerusalem, this small winery has been producing Cabernet Sauvignon and Merlot wines from its own vineyards. The winery is currently producing about 8,000 bottles annually, nearly all of those destined for export to the United States.

BEIT-EL, CABERNET SAUVIGNON, 2008: Dark garnet, a full-bodied wine with somewhat stinging tannins and a generous overlay of spicy oak that tends to hide the black fruits that lurk here. Drink now. Score 79. K

BEIT-EL, CABERNET SAUVIGNON, 2007: Medium- to full-bodied, a country-style wine with chunky tannins and spicy oak, opens to reveal blackcurrant and plum fruits. Not complex but easy to drink. Score 84. K

BEIT-EL, CABERNET SAUVIGNON, 2006: Full-bodied enough to be thought thick, with searing tannins and spices hiding stewed plum fruits. Score 70. K

BEIT-EL, CABERNET SAUVIGNON, 2005: Medium-bodied, with chunky country-style tannins and aromas and flavors of cooked fruits on a sweet, alcoholic and coarse background. Score 65. K

BEIT-EL, MERLOT, 2008: Dark garnet, medium-bodied, with firm tannins and spicy oak. On the nose and palate black fruits, those overpowered by a far too noticeable level of Brett. Drink up. Score 72. K

BEIT-EL, MERLOT, 2007: Dark ruby toward garnet in color, medium-bodied with chunky, country-style tannins. Opens to show perhaps too-generous overlays of spicy oak and vanilla that tend to hide plum and black cherry fruits, those leading to a sweet-and-sour finish. Drink up. Score 76. K

BEIT-EL, MERLOT, 2005: Medium-bodied, showing signs of oxidation despite its youth, and with stewed, sweet fruits on the palate. Drink up. Score 70. K

Benhaim ✳✳✳

Founded in 1997 on Moshav Kfar Azar in the Sharon region, this family-owned winery is currently producing about 35,000 bottles annually from Cabernet Sauvignon, Merlot, Cabernet Franc, Petite Sirah, Chardonnay and Muscat grapes largely from its own vineyards. Under development are vineyards with Shiraz and Traminette, and the winery also produces a Port-style wine.

With vineyards now planted on the eastern slopes of Mount Meron in the Upper Galilee, the winery is planning to expand its production to 50,000 bottles. Wines are released in three series – Grande Reserve, Reserve and Tradition – and have been kosher since the 2001 vintage.

Grande Reserve

GRANDE RESERVE, CABERNET SAUVIGNON, 2006: A Bordeaux blend, reflecting generous oak-age with firm tannins and notes of vanilla and spices. On the nose and palate blackberries, blackcurrants and generous earthy-herbal overtones. On the finish, notes of tobacco and coriander. Drink now. Score 87. K

GRANDE RESERVE, CABERNET SAUVIGNON, 2005: Oak-aged for 28 months, a blend of 85% Cabernet Sauvignon, 8% Cabernet Franc and 7% Petite Sirah. Dark garnet toward royal purple, showing generous toasty wood and firm tannins that yield in the glass to reveal appealing blackberry, currant and citrus peel notes, those on a background of dark chocolate and cigar tobacco. Finishes full, long and round. Drink now. Score 88. K

GRANDE RESERVE, CABERNET SAUVIGNON, 2003: Reflecting more than two years in new oak with full-body, generous spicy and dusty wood, and firm tannins that tend to overpower the fruits. Given time in the glass, the wine opens to reveal currant, purple plum and chocolate, the wood rising again on the finish. Past its peak. Drink up. Score 84. K

Reserve

RESERVE, CABERNET SAUVIGNON, 2007: Potentially the best wine yet from the winery. Deep garnet toward royal purple, full-bodied, with youthful and still-firm tannins and generous but not at all overwhelming wood just starting on the road to integration. Opens to reveal aromas and flavors of raspberries, cherries, currants and mint, those turning to dark fruits and spices on what promises to be a velvety texture. Drink from release. Tentative Score 89–91. K

RESERVE, CABERNET SAUVIGNON, 2006: Garnet toward brick brown in color, medium- to full-bodied, with the aromas and flavors fleshed out by Cabernet Franc and Petite Sirah. Aged in *barriques* for 23 months, shows soft tannins and abundant spicy and dusty oak, those parting to make way for currants, berries and plums, those on a background of green olives. Drink now. Score 87. K

RESERVE, CABERNET SAUVIGNON, 2005: Dark garnet, medium- to full-bodied, a blend of Cabernet Sauvignon, Merlot and Petite Sirah (90%, 7% and 3% respectively). Tannins now showing more firmly than at an earlier tasting, in fact almost lip searing, and with generous dusty and spicy oak from its 20–24 months in oak. As the wine opens it shows spicy blackcurrant and berry fruits on a background of saddle leather. Drink up. Score 85. K

RESERVE, MERLOT, 2006: Garnet with a hint of adobe, medium- to full-bodied (leaning to the full), a blend of 85% Merlot and equal parts of Cabernet Franc and Syrah. Oak-aged for 28 months, with a somewhat funky nose but opening in the glass to show currant, wild berry and citrus peel notes. Opens and closes with a marked earthy note. Drink now. Score 85. K

RESERVE, MERLOT, 2005: Reflecting its oak-aging in new American and French *barriques* for 20 months with generous cedarwood, spicy and vanilla overtones. Dark garnet in color, full-bodied, with firm tannins that part slowly to reveal black fruits and notes of freshly picked herbs. Drink now. Score 85. K

Tradition

TRADITION, CABERNET SAUVIGNON, 2008: A garnet toward adobe-brick-colored blend of 85% Cabernet Sauvignon, that fleshed out with Cabernet Franc and Petite Sirah. Oak-aged for 13 months, medium- to full-bodied, with gently gripping tannins, opens in the glass to reveal blackberry and black cherry fruits. Marred somewhat by a strong herbal overlay. Drink now. Score 85. K

TRADITION, CABERNET SAUVIGNON, 2006: Garnet toward dark purple, medium-bodied, with firm tannins and spicy wood. Opens to show wild berries, currants and notes of tobacco. Drink up. Score 85. K

THE WINERIES AND THEIR WINES

TRADITION, CABERNET SAUVIGNON, 2005: Dark garnet, medium- to full-bodied with soft, mouth-coating tannins and spicy wood. On the nose and palate currant, berry and exotic spices. Showing age. Drink up. Score 83. κ

TRADITION, MERLOT, 2006: Medium-bodied, with soft, mouth-coating tannins and spicy wood. Youthful royal purple in color, opens on the palate to show generous wild berries, spices and a hint of chocolate. Drink now. Score 85. κ

TRADITION, MERLOT, 2005: Garnet toward ruby, medium-bodied, and reflecting its 18 months in oak with firm tannins and generous sweet and spicy cedarwood. Blended with about 10% of Cabernet Franc, opens to reveal blackberry and black cherry fruits, those complemented by a hint of chocolate that lingers nicely on the medium-long finish. Drink up. Score 85. κ

TRADITION, CHARDONNAY, 2008: Light gold, medium-bodied and unoaked, with pineapple and tropical fruits on a lightly spicy background. Drink up. Score 82. κ

TRADITION, CHARDONNAY, 2007: Golden straw in color, an unoaked medium-bodied wine with clean and crisp aromas and flavors of lemon and grapefruit. Not complex but a good entry-level white. Drink up. Score 84. κ

TRADITION, MUSCAT, DEMI-SEC, 2008: With heather and rose petals on the nose, and citrus and tropical fruits on the palate. Lacks the balancing acidity to keep it lively. Drink up. Score 78. κ

TRADITION, MUSCAT, DEMI-SEC, 2007: Unoaked and generously floral on the nose, but with its citrus and tropical fruits carrying an unwanted overlay of what appears to be Brett, that giving the wine a muddled persona. Drink up. Score 78. κ

TRADITION, MOSCATELLE, 2007: Light golden straw in color, a wine that boasts sweet rosewater, violets and vanilla on the nose and not much in the way of fruits. Drink up. Score 78. κ

Benhaim

BENHAIM, LA PETITE SIRA, 2005: Not a typographical error, the *sira* in question being a small boat, reflecting the family's love of sailing. A blend of 50% Merlot, 40% Petite Sirah and 10% Shiraz. Medium- to full-bodied, reflecting its 14 months in oak with black fruits on a lightly spicy background. Drink up. Score 84. K

BENHAIM, LA PETITE SIRA, 2004: A blend of 60% Petite Sirah and 40% Merlot, aged in oak for 12 months. Super-dark garnet, medium-bodied, showing silky tannins and generous black fruit. Drink up. Score 83. K

BENHAIM, VIN NEUF ROUGE, 2008: Ruby-red, a light-bodied blend of 75% Cabernet Sauvignon and 25% Merlot, that with carbon dioxide added to give the wine a light sparkle. With aromas and flavors of raspberries, strawberries and red plums, more of a "shpritz" than a serious wine. Fun for those who enjoy this kind of thing. Drink up. Score 80. K

BENHAIM, ROSÉ, VIN JEUNE, 2007: A blend of 90% Merlot and 10% Cabernet Franc, those with short skin contact, opens with what seems to be dusty wood on the nose, that going on to a too generously acidic background. Muddled berry and red cherry notes here. Drink up. Score 70. K

BENHAIM, CHARDONNAY, VIN JEUNE, 2007: A super-young unoaked release, with no label and meant for light, easy drinking. Alas, too much like a blend of lemon and pineapple juice, to which has been added an artificial sweetener. Drink up. Score 72. K

Ben Hanna ✳✳✳

Located on Moshav Gefen, on the plains between Beit Shemesh and Kiryat Malachi, and receiving Cabernet Sauvignon, Merlot, Grenache, Petit Verdot, Cabernet Franc,
Viognier and Argaman grapes from the Judean Mountains,
this winery is the venture of Shlomi Zadok. The winery's first
release was of 2,500 bottles. Most recent production was for
about 6,000 bottles. The winery is currently not producing
but planning on later revival.

BEN HANNA, CABERNET SAUVIGNON, 2006: Developed in French
oak *barriques*, this medium- to full-bodied wine opens with surprisingly
soft tannins but those build nicely together with spicy oak as the wine
sits on the palate. Traditional Cabernet blackberry and currant fruits
unfolding to reveal hints of mocha and cigar tobacco that linger on the
long, fruity finish. Drink now. Score 89.

BEN HANNA, CABERNET SAUVIGNON, SHALEM, 2005: A blend of
Cabernet Sauvignon, Cabernet Franc and Merlot (80%, 15% and 5%
respectively), aged in French oak *barriques* for 21 months and showing
soft, round and aromatic. On the nose and palate raspberry and red
currant fruits on a background of herbs and mint. Long and generous.
Drink up. Score 89.

BEN HANNA, CABERNET SAUVIGNON, 2005: Dark royal purple,
full-bodied, with soft tannins integrating nicely and showing fine balance between spicy wood, acidity and fruits. On the nose and palate
blackcurrants, blackberries, a hint of green olives and, on the long finish,
fine spices. Drink up. Score 89.

BEN HANNA, MERLOT, 2007: Deep garnet, medium- to full-bodied with soft, gently mouth-coating tannins and appealing notes of spicy oak. Shows a generous array of blackberry, black cherry and blueberry fruits, those complemented by hints of Oriental spices. Drink now–2013. Score 90.

BEN HANNA, MERLOT, 2006: Garnet-red with purple reflections and, in accordance with the winemaker's philosophy, soft and round. On the nose and palate black cherries and wild berries. Easy to drink but with just the right touch of complexity. Drink now. Score 86.

BEN HANNA, CABERNET FRANC, 2006: Medium- to full-bodied, with velvety smooth tannins and appealing floral-scented plum, blueberry and currant fruits on a gentle background of spicy wood and just the barest hint of Brett to add charm. Drink now. Score 89.

BEN HANNA, CABERNET FRANC, LA MARIÉE, 2005: Broad, dense and concentrated, yet caressing and not at all heavy. Opens with generous raspberries and dried currants highlighted by gentle black and red chili peppers. Moves on to plum and floral aromas and flavors with soft tannins rising on the long, spicy and fruit-rich finish. Best yet from the winery. Drink up. Score 91.

BEN HANNA, PETIT VERDOT, 2006: Deep garnet toward royal purple, this full-bodied, oak-aged red shows plush and supple, with currant, blackberry, cola, vanilla and black pepper aromas and flavors, those in fine balance with spicy wood and nicely integrating tannins, all leading to a near-sweet finish. Drink now–2013. Score 91.

BEN HANNA, PETIT VERDOT, LA MARIÉE, 2005: Reflecting 12 months in French oak with gently mouth-coating tannins and hints of spices and vanilla, this medium- to full-bodied wine shows ripe, rich and supple. Dark purple, with generous cherry and currant fruits and, on the long finish, a tantalizing hint of green olives. Drink now. Score 90.

BEN HANNA, PETIT VERDOT, SINGLE HUMPED, 2005: Medium- to full-bodied with silky smooth tannins, this round and well-balanced wine is show-ing plum and raspberry fruits, those highlighted nicely by generous acidity and a light gamey touch on the long generous finish. Starting to show age. Drink up. Score 90.

BEN HANNA, SHALEM, 2006: Dark ruby toward garnet, this oak-aged blend of 70% Cabernet Sauvignon, 20% Merlot and 10% Cabernet Sauvi-gnon shows medium- to full-bodied, with soft tannins and gently spicy wood. On the nose and palate blackberry, currant and blueberries, those on a background of espresso coffee and chocolate. Drink up. Score 88.

BEN HANNA, MEDITERRANEO, 2005: Deep, brooding garnet in color, full-bodied, with still-firm tannins and generous spicy wood waiting to settle down, but showing fine balance and simply needing a bit of time. A blend of Grenache, Petit Verdot, Syrah and Cabernet Franc (50%, 33%, 12% and 5% respectively), aged in French oak for 22 months, opening to show a generous mouthful of black cherry, dried raspberries, eucalyptus and cinnamon. Drink up. Score 91.

Ben-Shushan *

Established by agronomist Yuval Ben-Shushan on Kibbutz Bror Hail in the northern Negev Desert, this winery released its first wine from the vintage of 1998. Desert-raised grapes include Cabernet Sauvignon and Merlot, and other grapes are drawn from the area of Kerem Ben Zimra in the Galilee. The winery produces wines in three series, Kfar Shamai, Har'el and Avdat. Production is currently about 10,000 bottles annually.

Kfar Shamai

KFAR SHAMAI, CABERNET SAUVIGNON, 2007: Dark ruby toward garnet, medium- to full-bodied, showing good balance between wood, tannins and fruits. On the nose and palate wild berries, currants and dark chocolate and, on the moderately long finish, an appealing hint of licorice. Drink up. Score 84.

KFAR SHAMAI, CABERNET SAUVIGNON, 2006: Medium- to full-bodied, with chunky tannins giving the wine a rustic personality. On the nose and palate currant, blackberry and plum fruits, those marred somewhat by a far too high level of volatile acidity. Drink up. Score 80.

KFAR SHAMAI, CABERNET SAUVIGNON, 2005: Aged in French and American oak *barriques* for 16 months, showing generous dusty wood and chunky tannins. Opens to show skimpy black fruits on an acidic and medicinal background. Showing signs of premature aging. Drink up. Score 75.

KFAR SHAMAI, MERLOT, 2007: Garnet toward purple, reflecting its 14 months in oak with notes of spices and vanilla. Somewhat biting tannins tend to hold back the black fruits and mineral notes that lurk underneath. Drink up. Score 82.

KFAR SHAMAI, SHIRAZ, 2007: Dark garnet, full-bodied, with firm and chunky, country-style tannins that add a somewhat coarse note. Opens in the glass to show black fruits on an earthy-mineral background. Drink now. Score 80.

KFAR SHAMAI, CABERNET SAUVIGNON-MERLOT, 2005: A blend of equal parts of Cabernet Sauvignon and Merlot, oak-aged for 14 months. Dark garnet, medium- to full-bodied, with soft, near-sweet tannins and showing sur-ripe raspberry and red plum fruits on a background of freshly turned earth and tobacco. Past its peak. Drink up. Score 81.

Avdat

AVDAT, CABERNET SAUVIGNON, 2008: Garnet toward royal purple, showing medium- to full-bodied with chunky country-style tannins and a rather generous hand with smoky and herbal oak. On the nose and palate black fruits and an abundance of tobacco and herbs. Drink now. Score 83.

AVDAT, CABERNET SAUVIGNON, 2007: Dark garnet in color, reflecting its 18 months in oak with spicy and smoky notes. Opens in the glass to reveal wild berry and black cherry fruits. Somewhat one-dimensional but an acceptable quaffer. Drink up. Score 81.

AVDAT, MERLOT, 2008: Garnet toward royal purple, medium- to full-bodied with soft, gently gripping tannins and notes of spicy cedar on the nose. Opens to show a not-complex but appealing personality of cherries and wild berries, those on a background of earthy minerals. Drink now. Score 84.

Ben-Zimra ✦✦✦

Founded by vintner Yossi Ashkenazi on Moshav Ben Zimra in the Upper Galilee, with Assaf Kedem now serving as the winemaker, this boutique winery has been producing two wines, a reserve and a regular edition of Cabernet Sauvignon since 2003. Wines have shown steady growth in quality from year to year. The winery's vineyards, near the moshav at 870 meters above sea level, are among the best in Israel. Current production is about 14,000 bottles annually, and the winery is planning on growing to a capacity of 20,000 bottles.

Reserve

RESERVE, CABERNET SAUVIGNON, 2008: Deep, almost inky garnet in color, full-bodied, and still firmly tannic but already showing balance and structure that bode well for the future. On the nose and palate traditional blackcurrant and blackberry fruits, those complemented by light hints of green olives and dark chocolate, all leading to a long, mouth-filling finish. The best from the winery to date. Drink now–2013. Score 88.

RESERVE, CABERNET SAUVIGNON, 2007: Oak-aged for about 14 months, dark and deep, medium- to full-bodied with good concentration. Somewhat rustic with a touch of heat on the finish, but showing appealing currant, black cherry and berry fruits with hints of anise and spring flowers. Drink now. Score 87.

RESERVE, CABERNET SAUVIGNON, 2006: Blended with 10% Merlot, not complex but smooth and round. Medium- to full-bodied, well balanced with currant, plum and black cherry fruits and a generous spicy overlay from the oak in which it aged for 14 months. Turns dry and picks up a strong cedarwood note on the finish. Drink up. Score 85.

RESERVE, CABERNET SAUVIGNON, 2005: Opens with a bit of bottle stink but that blows away quickly and then opens to show dark garnet toward royal purple, full-bodied, with firm tannins just starting to settle down, and reflecting its 14 months in *barriques* with spicy wood. Shows an appealing array of currants, blackberries and eucalyptus, those marred somewhat by a high (15.2%) alcohol level that adds an unwanted sweet note and leads to a hot finish. Past its peak. Drink up. Score 84.

Ben-Zimra

BEN-ZIMRA, CABERNET SAUVIGNON, 2008: Ruby toward garnet, medium-bodied, with soft tannins and showing raspberry, cherry and cassis, those supported by hints of green olives, with the tannins rising on the medium-long finish. Drink now. Score 88.

BEN-ZIMRA, CABERNET SAUVIGNON, 2007: Dark and deep, medium- to full-bodied with good concentration. Oak-aged for nine months, somewhat rustic with a touch of heat on the finish, but showing currant, cherry and berry fruits with hints of anise and spring flowers. Simple but pleasant. Drink up. Score 84.

BEN-ZIMRA, CABERNET SAUVIGNON, 2006: Made entirely from Cabernet Sauvignon grapes, oak-aged in new *barriques* for nine months, a straightforward and fruity wine marred somewhat by a too-generous bitter aftertaste. Drink up. Score 84.

BEN-ZIMRA, CABERNET SAUVIGNON, 2005: Dark garnet, medium- to full-bodied, with soft, mouth-coating tannins, reflecting its ten months in oak with gentle spices and a hint of smoke. Slow to open but when it does shows appealing berry, currant and black cherry fruits. Moderately long. Drink up. Score 85.

Binyamina ★★★★

First established in 1952 as Eliaz Wineries, the winery is located in the town of Binyamina at the foothills of the Carmel Mountains. In 1994 a group of investors bought out and renamed the outdated winery, replacing the existing management. They continued to introduce modern technology and equipment, and in recent years, thanks to increasing quality control in the vineyards and fine winemaking practices, the wines have improved dramatically and are making major steps forward in the realm of quality. In 2008 the winery changed hands again, and the new owners are making major investments in the physical plant, equipment and vineyards. Developments in all areas are rapidly bringing the winery to state-of-the-art status, and the winery now has a full-time agronomist working in the field. Equally important, a significant number of the Binyamina wines now attain excellence.

Under the supervision of senior winemaker Sasson Ben-Aharon and winemaker Assaf Paz, the winery is now the fourth largest in the country and produces about 2.6 million bottles annually from a large variety of grapes, those from vineyards in nearly every part of the country.

The winery releases several series: Avnei Hachoshen (English-language labels use the title "The Chosen"), Reserve, Yogev, Tiltan, Bin and Teva, their basic series originally known as Binyamina. In Hebrew, *Avnei Hachoshen* refers to the precious stones that adorned the vest of the high priest in the days of the Temple; *Yogev* is the Biblical term for a farmer, in this case a clear bow to the grape-growers; *Tiltan* is the Hebrew name for clover, a plant that has three distinct leaves on every branch (the logic being that these wines are blends of three different vintage years); and *Teva* means nature.

Avnei Hachoshen

For those not familiar with the Hebrew language, the different stones in the series are: Sapir = Sapphire; Odem = Ruby; Yashfeh = Jasper; Tarshish = Aquamarine; Shoham = Onyx; Leshem = Opal; and Ya'alom= Diamond.

AVNEI HACHOSHEN, CABERNET SAUVIGNON, TARSHISH, 2008: Cabernet Sauvignon from two Golan Heights vineyards (Tel Fares and Kidmat Tzvi). Dark garnet toward youthful royal purple, full-bodied and with fine balance between still-gripping tannins, smoky oak and fruits. On the nose and palate traditional Cabernet aromas and flavors of blackcurrants and blackberries, those complemented nicely by notes of minted chocolate. Drink now–2017. Score 90. K

AVNEI HACHOSHEN, CABERNET SAUVIGNON, TARSHISH, 2007: Made entirely from Cabernet Sauvignon grapes from vineyards on the Golan, dark garnet toward royal purple, full-bodied, with its youthful and still-firm tannins now settling in. Opens in the glass to show an appealing array of blackberry and cassis, those complemented nicely by notes of minted chocolate. Long and generous, will show even greater elegance if you let this one cellar for another year or so. Drink now–2014, perhaps longer. Score 90. K

AVNEI HACHOSHEN, CABERNET SAUVIGNON, TARSHISH, 2006: Almost impenetrably dark garnet in color, full-bodied and concentrated, with spicy wood and firm tannins in fine balance, showing rich and well structured. If ever there has been a wine that was "black fruits all the way," this is that wine – opening to show blackcurrant, blackberry, black cherry and deep earthy overtones, those matched nicely by notes of black pepper and star anise. From mid-palate on an appealing hint of what seems to be mint at one moment, eucalyptus at another. Long, generous and mouth-filling. Drink now–2014. Score 91. K

AVNEI HACHOSHEN, CABERNET SAUVIGNON, TARSHISH, 2005: Dark garnet with purple and orange reflections, and aged in new French oak for 16 months. Opens with super-soft tannins, those firming as the wine develops in the glass, medium-bodied, with appealing currant and red plums on the nose and palate, backed up by a hint of sweet herbs on the moderately long finish. Drink now. Score 89. K

AVNEI HACHOSHEN, CABERNET SAUVIGNON, TARSHISH, 2004: Full-bodied, with spicy, vanilla-rich wood and near-sweet tannins in good balance with blackcurrant, wild berries and minerals, all leading to a long and appealing spicy finish. Drink up. Score 88. K

AVNEI HACHOSHEN, SYRAH, ODEM, 2008: Blended with a small percentage of Viognier, dark garnet, a big full-bodied wine, rich and tannic with generous but not at all overpowering oak. On the nose and palate a fine array of raspberries, plums and chocolate and, from mid-palate, rising notes of saddle leather and dark chocolate, all lingering nicely. Drink now–2016. Score 91. K

AVNEI HACHOSHEN, SYRAH, ODEM, 2007: Blended with a small amount of Viognier, showing deep garnet, reflecting its development in French oak with hints of spicy cedarwood and soft, gently mouth-coating tannins. Full-bodied, soft, round and both spicy and juicy, with a generous array of blueberries, blackberries, black cherries and a mélange of fresh herbal and minty notes that lead to a long finish. Drink now–2013. Score 90. K

AVNEI HACHOSHEN, SYRAH, ODEM, 2006: Blended with 2–3% of Viognier, dark, dense and concentrated, with fine balance and structure. Reflecting 18 months in new French oak, firm tannins are comfortably integrating with spicy wood to show black and red berries, cherries and licorice flavors, all lingering on a long fruity finish. Give this one another year and it will show an appealing saddle-leather overtone. Drink now–2013. Score 90. K

AVNEI HACHOSHEN, SYRAH, ODEM, 2005: Blended with 2–3% of Viognier, intensely dark garnet in color, medium- to full-bodied, with generous near-sweet tannins and smoky oak integrating nicely. Shows red berries, cherries and red plums along with hints of leather and meatiness. Long and generous. Drink up. Score 88. K

AVNEI HACHOSHEN, SYRAH, ODEM, 2004: With 15 months in oak, showing medium- to full-bodied, soft, well-integrated tannins and light herbal-earthy aromas and flavors complemented nicely by plum, berry and cassis fruits. Hints of tobacco and chocolate on the finish. Showing signs of age. Drink up. Score 85. K

AVNEI HACHOSHEN, CABERNET SAUVIGNON-SYRAH-PETIT VER-DOT, YA'ALOM, 2008: A blend this year of 50% Cabernet Sauvignon, 40% Syrah and 10% Petit Verdot. Deep, intense garnet in color, with a nose rich with purple plums and spices. Gripping tannins and generous wood in fine balance with fruits and needing a bit of time to integrate at this stage, but showing fine promise for the future. On the nose and palate currants, wild berries and plums, those on a background of cedarwood and oak resin, the last turning to a note of tar on the long finish. Drink now–2018. Score 91. K

AVNEI HACHOSHEN, CABERNET SAUVIGNON-SYRAH-PETIT VERDOT, YA'ALOM, 2007: An identical blend to the 2006 release – 50% Cabernet Sauvignon, 30% Syrah and 20% Petit Verdot, those developed in new French oak for 20 months. Full-bodied, with still-gripping tannins and generous sweet and spicy cedarwood waiting to settle down but showing fine balance that bodes well for the future. On first attack red currants and ripe plums, those yielding gently to black fruits, all sitting comfortably on a light peppery background. Long and generous. Drink now–2016. Score 91. K

AVNEI HACHOSHEN, CABERNET SAUVIGNON-SYRAH-PETIT VERDOT, YA'ALOM, 2006: Almost impenetrably dark ruby-garnet in color, a Bordeaux blend of 50% Cabernet Sauvignon from two vineyards, 30% Syrah and 20% Petit Verdot. Developed in new French *barriques* for 20 months, at this stage still showing gripping tannins and generous sweet-and-spicy cedarwood notes, those in fine balance and with the kind of structure that bodes well for future integration and development. Shows meaty and herbal overtones, those parting to reveal a generous array of red and blackcurrants and red plums on a peppery and earthy-mineral background. Long and generous. Drink now–2015. Score 92. K

AVNEI HACHOSHEN, CABERNET SAUVIGNON-SHIRAZ-MERLOT, SAPIR, 2008: A blend of 35% Cabernet Sauvignon, 45% Shiraz and 20% Merlot. Dark garnet toward royal purple, a full-bodied and intense wine with soft tannins and a gentle layer of near-sweet cedarwood. Muscular and ripe but all in fine balance. On the nose and palate blackberries, cassis and blueberries, those yielding to notes of black cherries and espresso coffee. Long and generous with tannins and fruits rising on the finish. Drink now–2015. Score 90. K

AVNEI HACHOSHEN, CABERNET SAUVIGNON-SHIRAZ-MERLOT, SAPIR, 2007: Dark garnet, full-bodied and concentrated, showing spicy cedarwood and soft tannins integrating nicely. On the palate blackberries, plums and blueberries, those with a tempting illusion of sweetness on first attack but that receding as the wine opens and shows black cherries and hints of tobacco and *garrigue*. Long and generous. Drink now–2015. Score 90 K

AVNEI HACHOSHEN, CABERNET SAUVIGNON-SHIRAZ-MERLOT, SAPIR, 2006: A blend of 40% Cabernet Sauvignon, 35% Shiraz and 25%

Merlot. Medium- to full-bodied with fine concentration, reflecting its 14 months in new French oak *barriques* with notes of spicy cedarwood and vanilla. On first attack blueberries and chocolate, those leading to blackcurrants, black cherries and a note of cigar tobacco. Complex and long. Drink now. Score 90. K

AVNEI HACHOSHEN, CABERNET SAUVIGNON-SHIRAZ-MERLOT, SAPIR, 2005: A blend of 40% Cabernet Sauvignon, 35% Shiraz and 25% Merlot. Oak-aged for 15 months, showing dark ruby toward garnet, opening with licorice and mint on the nose and palate, those going to bittersweet chocolate and Mediterranean herbs and then to red plums, cassis and spicy notes. Drink up. Score 87. K

AVNEI HACHOSHEN, CHARDONNAY, SHOHAM, 2009: Deep glistening gold, reflecting its ten months' development in oak with generous but well-balanced notes of vanilla-rich wood. On first attack gooseberries and citrus pith, those followed by aromas and flavors of white peaches, Anjou pears and pink grapefruit. Not so much a lively wine as a complex one, deep enough to match nicely with veal or chicken stews. Drink now–2013. Score 90. K

AVNEI HACHOSHEN, CHARDONNAY, SHOHAM, 2008: Developed partly in 225 liter *barriques* and partly in 300 liter barrels. Light golden in color, combining earthy and flinty minerals that complement citrus, white peach and melon aromas and flavors. Promising elegance. Drink now. Score 89. K

AVNEI HACHOSHEN, CHARDONNAY, SHOHAM, 2007: Gold with orange tints, developed *sur lie* for 12–14 months in oak, showing a generous but gentle wood influence and fine balancing acidity. Opens in the glass to show generous peach, pear and citrus fruits all on a light mineral background. Drink up. Score 89. K

AVNEI HACHOSHEN, CHARDONNAY-SAUVIGNON BLANC-VIOGNIER, YASHFEH, 2009: A medium-bodied blend of Chardonnay, Sauvignon Blanc and Viognier (50%, 30% and 20% respectively). Aged in new and old oak for six months, shows a complex nose on which butternuts and ripe pears, those continuing to the glass and opening to reveal notes of honeydew melon and citrus peel. Finishes generously with a near-buttery texture. Drink now–2013. Score 89. K

AVNEI HACHOSHEN, CHARDONNAY-SAUVIGNON BLANC-VIOGNIER, YASHFEH, 2008: Crisply dry, aromatic and generous, with spicy and mineral-rich citrus flavors. Medium-bodied, with fine balancing acidity and a long, snappy finish. Drink now. Score 89. K

AVNEI HACHOSHEN, CHARDONNAY-SAUVIGNON BLANC-VIOGNIER, YASHFEH, 2007: A blend of Chardonnay, Sauvignon Blanc and Viognier (40%, 35% and 25% respectively), gently oak-aged, showing crisply dry with fine balancing acidity and a near-creamy texture. On the nose and palate peach, melon, citrus and light spicy notes leading to a long, refreshing and tantalizing note of sweetness on the finish. Drink up. Score 89. K

Reserve

RESERVE, CABERNET SAUVIGNON, 2009: An aromatic Cabernet, showing mint and chocolate on the nose, both carrying over to the palate on which one will find traditional blackcurrants and blackberries, those complemented by an appealing tarry note. Full-bodied and round with soft tannins integrating nicely. Drink from release–2014. Tentative Score 87–89. K

RESERVE, CABERNET SAUVIGNON, 2008: There are muscles to this deep-garnet, medium- to full-bodied wine but they restrain themselves nicely, with gently gripping tannins in fine balance with spicy oak, fruits and acidity. On the nose and palate blackcurrant, blackberry and plum fruits, those on a background of fresh herbs and exotic spices. On the finish hints of espresso and licorice. Drink now–2014. Score 91. K

RESERVE, CABERNET SAUVIGNON, 2007: Dark garnet, full-bodied, with firm tannins and spicy wood settling in now and opening to show varietally pure blackcurrant, blackberry and spicy notes, those lingering nicely with a hint of chocolate on the finish. Drink now–2014. Score 89. K

RESERVE, CABERNET SAUVIGNON, 2006: Dark garnet in color, deeply aromatic and showing full body and generous but comfortably yielding tannins, those in fine balance with fruits, wood and acidity. Reflecting oak-aging for 18 months with spicy overtones, and opening in the glass to reveal blackberry, currant and purple plum fruits, those supported nicely by hints of black pepper. Medium- toward full-bodied, mouth-filling and long. Drink now. Score 91. K

RESERVE, CABERNET SAUVIGNON, 2005: Medium- to full-bodied, with soft tannins integrating nicely with spicy and lightly smoky wood, those yielding to generous red berries, cassis and spices. Lacks complexity but easy to drink. Drink up. Score 87. K

RESERVE, MERLOT, 2009: Deep royal purple toward garnet, deep and concentrated, full-bodied and with still-firm tannins and spicy wood integrating nicely. On the nose and palate blackberries, plums and wild berries, those supported by notes of espresso coffee, cedarwood and sage. On the long finish a note of dark chocolate. Drink now–2016. Score 88. K

RESERVE, MERLOT, 2008: Oak-aged for 14 months, showing medium- to full-bodied, with soft, gently gripping tannins and light spicy wood, opens in the glass to show generous black fruits, those set off nicely by notes of mocha. Round and generous. Drink now. Score 89. K

RESERVE, MERLOT, 2007: Deep garnet, medium- to full-bodied, with near-sweet tannins and notes of spicy oak, those in fine balance with fruits and acidity. Opens with raspberry and cherry fruits, those yielding to cassis and wild berry notes, all on a background of roasted herbs and freshly turned earth. Drink now. Score 89 K

RESERVE, MERLOT, 2006: Merlot with a unique and charming personality. Full-bodied, reflecting its 14 months in oak with notes of vanilla and spices as well as a cigar-box note that runs through. On the nose and palate opens with strawberries and raspberries, those yielding comfortably to blackberries and currants, all with a generous peppery note that lingers nicely on the long finish. Give this one some time to develop in the bottle and it will show some licorice and smoked meat aromas and flavors as well. One of the best ever from Binyamina. Drink now. Score 92. K

RESERVE, MERLOT, 2005: Dark garnet, medium- to full-bodied, reflecting its development in French oak barrels with hints of spicy wood and generous near-sweet tannins. On the nose and palate raspberry, strawberry and vanilla, those supported nicely by herbal and spicy notes. Drink up. Score 88. K

RESERVE, SHIRAZ, 2009: Garnet with violet hues and deeply aromatic. Full-bodied, with gently gripping tannins showing aromas and flavors of red and purple plums, near-jammy wild berries and, to add complexity, notes of saddle leather, smoked goose breast and spices. This one will round out nicely as it develops. Drink now–2016. Score 89. K

RESERVE, SHIRAZ, 2008: Blended with 2% Viognier, medium- to full-bodied, showing fine concentration. Soft tannins and a gentle wood influence make way for aromas and flavors of plums, wild berries and smoked meat. Rich and long with an appealing note of tar on the finish. Drink now–2013. Score 90. K

RESERVE, SHIRAZ, 2007: Garnet toward royal purple, medium-bodied but with good concentration. With soft tannins and a gentle wood influence, a smooth, round wine loaded with blackberry and plum fruits, those highlighted by notes of tar and licorice. Drink now–2015. Score 90. K

RESERVE, SHIRAZ, 2006: Developed for 12 months in French and American oak, a full-bodied, dark garnet, aromatic Shiraz blended, as seems to be the wont these days, with 2% of white Viognier grapes, the small amount of which adds both liveliness and flavor. On the nose and palate light notes of smoky wood to match black and red berries, cherries and spices, the tannins coating the mouth gently and then lingering on the generously fruity finish. Drink now. Score 90. K

RESERVE, CARIGNAN, 2009: The first varietal Carignan released in the winery's Reserve series and a fine effort indeed. Full-bodied, showing dark garnet in color, with soft tannins and gentle influences of smoky wood giving the wine a persona that is simultaneously outgoing and subdued. On the nose and palate plums, blueberries and spices yielding in the glass to berry-cherry flavors and, on the generous finish, a touch of espresso coffee. Drink now–2015. Score 90. K

RESERVE, ZINFANDEL, 2009: Medium-dark ruby in color, medium- to full-bodied, with silky tannins that caress comfortably. Opens to reveal blackberries, purple plums, licorice and black olive aromas and flavors. From mid-palate on shows appealing notes of huckleberries and black pepper. As good a match to fine steaks or chops as to stews (what comes to mind are French cassoulet and Spanish cocido). Very nice indeed. Drink now–2014. Score 89. K

RESERVE, ZINFANDEL, 2008: Dark royal purple, opening with a sweet and floral California Zinfandel nose but then moving on to also show aromas of berries and cherries. Made from 14-year-old vines, developed in 300 liter American oak hogsheads, those selected for their extra-fine grain to let the wood remain in fine balance with the fruits. Ripe and rich, with generous blackberry, peppery and sage notes, those followed by a tempting note of licorice that rises on the long finish. Drink now–2014. Score 90. K

RESERVE, ZINFANDEL, 2007: Opens with California muscles but those settle down quickly in the glass to reveal a Zinfandel faithful to its variety. Developed in American and French oak for 14 months, with a moderate 14% alcohol content and gently caressing tannins, opens in the glass to reveal wild berry, blackcurrant, raspberry and peppery notes, those matched by notes of chocolate and an appealing hint of dusty wood that rises on the finish. Well done. Drink now. Score 89. K

RESERVE, CHARDONNAY, 2010: Developed in French oak, with one-third of the wine having undergone malolactic fermentation. Light gold with a green tint, with finely tuned acidity to highlight aromas and flavors of pears, melon and citrus peel, those on a mineral-rich background. Drink now–2013. Score 88. K

RESERVE, CHARDONNAY, UNOAKED, 2010: Fresh, fruity and aromatic, medium-bodied, with good balancing acidity to highlight aromas and flavors of white peaches, pineapple and citrus. Not a lively wine but one that will match very nicely with grilled fish, seafood or veal schnitzels. Drink now. Score 87. K

RESERVE, CHARDONNAY, UNOAKED, 2009: Light gold with green tints. A combination on the nose and palate of flinty minerals, tropical fruits, citrus and pears, those followed by hints of lime that linger nicely. Crisp and refreshing but with just enough complexity to grab the attention. Drink up. Score 89. K

RESERVE, CHARDONNAY, 2008: With 70% of the wine developed in 300 liter oak barrels (hogsheads) for eight months and the remainder in stainless steel, a round and polished wine with pear, grapefruit and floral aromas on a mineral-rich background. Generous and long with a lively finish. Drink up. Score 88. K

RESERVE, SAUVIGNON BLANC, 2010: Light golden straw, medium-bodied, with fine acidity to highlight notes of citrus, pineapple and tropical fruits all with a hint of a freshly mown lawn. Drink now. Score 88. K

RESERVE, SAUVIGNON BLANC, 2009: Pale wet straw in color, fully faithful to the variety, opening with notes of grapefruit and lime, those accompanied by notes of stony minerals and, yes, even the traditional hints of cat's pee and asparagus. Aromatic and long. Drink up. Score 89. K

RESERVE, GEWURZTRAMINER, LATE HARVEST, CLUSTER SELECT, 2009: With 20% of the grapes impacted on by botrytis, full-bodied and nearly thick in texture, with an appealing light note of botrytis funk to highlight aromas and flavors of honeyed dried apricots. Low in alcohol (9%) and with fine balancing acidity to keep the wine lively, a tempting dessert wine. Drink now–2016, perhaps longer. Score 92. K

RESERVE, GEWURZTRAMINER, LATE HARVEST, CLUSTER SELECT, 2008: Light gold in color, showing deep Gewurztraminer aromas and flavors of litchis and rose petals. To those add the charm of tangerines and passion fruit. A concentrated and intense dessert wine with just the vaguest hint of botrytis (a small number of the grapes were impacted upon by this noblest of rots), those hints possibly to rise nicely as the wine develops in the bottle. Drink now–2013, perhaps longer. Score 93. K

RESERVE, GEWURZTRAMINER, 2010: True to its variety, opening with a gently floral and spicy nose, a medium-bodied, off-dry white opening on the palate to reveal traditional litchi and rose-petal aromas and flavors, those complemented nicely by notes of citrus, citrus peel and stony minerals, all with a light flinty overlay. Fine balancing acidity keeps the wine simultaneously mouth-filling and lively. Drink now–2013. Score 87. K

RESERVE, GEWURZTRAMINER, 2009: Lithe and refreshing with fine acidity balanced well with grapefruit, floral and spice flavors that are both lively and complex at the same time. Off-dry but with mouthwatering acidity that stands up nicely to the fruits and spices here. Long and generous and will go not only with Asian and North African dishes but on its own as an aperitif. Drink now. Score 90. K

Yogev

YOGEV, CABERNET SAUVIGNON, 2009: Dark garnet with a royal purple robe, medium- to full-bodied with soft tannins and the barest hint of spicy oak, those parting to make way for aromas and flavors of blackcurrants and ripe berries. On the moderately long finish appealing hints of spices. Not complex but a fine match to small cuts of beef, or lamb. Drink now. Score 86. K

YOGEV, CABERNET SAUVIGNON, 2008: Medium- to full-bodied, dark garnet and showing lightly smoky oak that comes together nicely with currant and berry fruits, those complemented by notes of espresso coffee and spices. Drink now. Score 86. K

YOGEV, CABERNET SAUVIGNON-MERLOT, 2009: A blend of equal parts of Cabernet Sauvignon and Merlot. Dark ruby toward garnet, medium- to full-bodied with gently gripping tannins and a light note of spicy oak. A red fruit nose makes itself felt nicely and, on first attack, blueberries and blackberries, those followed by red currants, spices and on the finish an appealing note of licorice. Round and well-balanced. Drink now–2013. Score 87. K

YOGEV, CABERNET SAUVIGNON-MERLOT, 2008: A blend of equal parts of Cabernet Sauvignon and Merlot, showing medium-bodied with soft tannins and basic plum, cherry and berry fruits. Not complex but easy to drink. Drink now. Score 85. K

YOGEV, CABERNET SAUVIGNON-MERLOT, 2006: Medium-bodied, with light oak influences and firm tannins. Opens to reveal currant, berry, and black cherry fruits. Not complex but a good quaffer. Drink up. Score 85. K

YOGEV, CABERNET SAUVIGNON-SHIRAZ, 2009: A blend of 50% each of Cabernet Sauvignon and Shiraz. Full-bodied, with gently gripping tannins and just the right note of spicy oak, opening to reveal currant and blackberry fruits, those supported nicely by hints of saddle leather and spices. Fruits and tannins rise on a moderately long finish. Drink now–2013. Score 87. K

YOGEV, CABERNET SAUVIGNON-SHIRAZ, 2008: Dark garnet toward royal purple, medium-bodied, with somewhat gripping tannins that soften somewhat in the glass and then rise again on the finish. Hints of spicy wood complement black fruits on a background of roasted herbs and tobacco. Drink now. Score 85. K

YOGEV, CABERNET SAUVIGNON-SHIRAZ, 2007: Reflecting its six months in oak with light spicy and vanilla overtones, a medium- to full-bodied wine with soft tannins and appealing berry, black cherry and cassis fruits highlighted nicely by a light peppery overtone. Drink up. Score 87. K

YOGEV, CABERNET SAUVIGNON-ZINFANDEL, 2008: Ruby toward garnet, medium-bodied, with soft tannins and appealing black fruits on the nose and palate. A blend of equal parts of Cabernet Sauvignon and Zinfandel. A good quaffer. Drink now. Score 85. K

YOGEV, CABERNET SAUVIGNON-PETIT VERDOT, 2009: Oak-aged for about six months in second- and third-year *barriques* to intentionally impart only a gentle feel of the impact of the wood. A blend of 80% Cabernet Sauvignon and 20% Petit Verdot showing medium- to full-bodied, with soft tannins, the jammy notes I found earlier now receding nicely. Drink now–2013. Score 86. K

YOGEV, CABERNET SAUVIGNON-PETIT VERDOT, 2008: A blend of 80% Cabernet Sauvignon and 20% Petit Verdot. Medium- to full-bodied, with gently gripping tannins and cedarwood aromas and flavors parting to reveal purple plums, blackcurrants and notes of dark chocolate. Drink now. Score 86. K

YOGEV, CABERNET SAUVIGNON-PETIT VERDOT, 2007: A blend of 80% Cabernet and 20% Petit Verdot. Medium- to full-bodied with chunky tannins, a pleasant but not complex country-style wine with black fruits, spices and spicy oak notes. Drink now. Score 86. K

YOGEV, CABERNET SAUVIGNON-PETIT VERDOT, 2006: A medium-bodied, softly tannic blend of 80% Cabernet Sauvignon and 20% Petit Verdot, opening on the palate to reveal gentle spicy wood and blackberry and currant fruits, those complemented by a light herbal note. Round and moderately long. Drink up. Score 87. K

YOGEV, ROSÉ, 2010: Cherry red in color, a medium-bodied blend of 60% Malbec and 40% Carignan. On the nose and palate red berries, black cherries and strawberries. Lacks the acidity that might have made it more lively. Drink now. Score 85. K

YOGEV, ROSÉ, 2009: A blend of 60% Malbec and 40% Carignan. Light cherry-red in color, light- to medium-bodied, with an abundance of cherry, dried berry and watermelon rind fruits. Look as well for hints of chanterelle mushrooms and spices that linger nicely on the palate. Calls to mind the wines of Coteaux de Provence. Drink up. Score 88. K

YOGEV, SAUVIGNON BLANC-CHARDONNAY, 2010: An unoaked blend of 70% Sauvignon Blanc and 30% Chardonnay, light gold in color, medium-bodied, showing lively aromas and flavors of pineapple, mango and citrus fruits, and from mid-palate on a tempting note of bitter almonds. Fresh and refreshing, with just enough complexity to grab the attention. Drink now. Score 87. K

YOGEV, SAUVIGNON BLANC-CHARDONNAY, 2009: An unoaked blend of 70% Sauvignon Blanc and 30% Chardonnay. Pale golden straw in color, with fresh acidity in fine balance with fruits. On the nose and palate citrus and citrus peel, mango and an appealing hint of freshly cut grass. Drink up. Score 87. K

YOGEV, AROMATIC BLEND, 2010: An off-dry blend of 45% French Colombard, 40% Muscat and 15% Gewurztraminer. Even though the Gewurztraminer is in a minority here its aromas and flavors dominate nicely. Opens with a floral and spicy nose, goes on to reveal aromas and flavors of citrus, litchis and rosewater, all on a background that hints at one moment of white pepper and at the next of crushed juniper berries. As good an aperitif as it is a dessert wine. Drink now. Score 86. K

YOGEV, AROMATIC BLEND, 2009: An off-dry blend of French Colombard, Gewurztraminer and Muscat (45%, 40% and 15% respectively), aromatic is certainly the ideal descriptor for this wine, which opens with a floral, citrus and dried litchi nose and then goes on to reveal flavors of grapes and candied citrus peel. Calls to mind an orange Creamsicle but a bit more acidity would have helped. Drink now. Score 85. K

Tiltan

TILTAN, N.V. 2005–2006–2007: Wines from the 2005, 2006 and 2007 vintages, each developed separately in oak before final blending. Opens with rich chocolate notes on the nose, those carrying over to the palate along with ripe black fruits, licorice and an appealing hint of earthy herbaceousness. Full-bodied, with a long finish. Drink now–2014. Score 90. K

TILTAN, N.V.: A blend not of different grape varieties but of Cabernet Sauvignon grapes from three different vintage years, in this case from 2004, 2005 and 2006. Developed in *barriques* for 18 months, showing generous but not offensive sweet cedarwood and moderately gripping tannins that yield nicely to show blackberry, blackcurrant and orange peel notes, all on a light background of green olives and eucalyptus. Drink up. Score 88. K

TILTAN, N.V.: Made from Cabernet Sauvignon grapes harvested in the 2003, 2004 and 2005 harvests, each developed in wood for a different period of time. Full-bodied, with soft, caressing tannins and a moderate hand with peppery wood, the wine opens on the palate to reveal currants, black cherries and herbal aromas and flavors, all of which are concentrated but not heavy. Finishes with generous tannins and an appealing hint of sage. Drink up. Score 90. K

Bin

BIN, CABERNET SAUVIGNON, 2009: Dark cherry toward garnet, medium-bodied, with soft tannins and clean, fresh black-fruit aromas. Opens in the glass to reveal blackberries, wild berries and cassis notes. Not at all complex but easy and pleasant to drink. Drink up. Score 85. K

BIN, MERLOT, 2009: Cherry red toward garnet, medium-bodied and with soft tannins, a round and gentle wine showing appealing blackberry and cassis notes. Easy to drink, a fine entry-level wine. Drink up. Score 86. K

BIN, CHARDONNAY, 2010: An unoaked Chardonnay, light gold in color, light- to medium-bodied, with lively apple, pineapple, citrus and citrus- peel notes on a background that hints of kiwis. A fine entry-level quaffer. Drink up. Score 85. K

Teva

TEVA, CABERNET SAUVIGNON, 2009: Garnet to royal purple in color, medium-bodied, with soft tannins and a hint of smoky wood, those parting to reveal generous blackberry, cassis and light peppery notes. Drink now. Score 88. K

TEVA, CABERNET SAUVIGNON, 2008: With just a bit of Merlot blended in, dark ruby toward garnet, medium-bodied, with gently caressing tannins and opening to show red currants, plums and raspberry notes. Not complex but appealing. Drink now. Score 86. K

TEVA, MERLOT, 2007: Developed in stainless steel vats with oak staves, deep royal purple, with fine extraction of color and noted but gentle tannins and a light smoky wood influence. Flavors of blackberries, currants and *garrigue* come together nicely. Medium- to full-bodied, truly reflecting the variety and lingering nicely on the palate. Not overly complex but delicious. Drink up. Score 87. K

TEVA, SHIRAZ, 2009: Garnet in color, medium-bodied, with soft tannins showing true to the variety with appealing purple plum and wild- berry fruits, those on a background that hints of fresh herbs and cigar tobacco. Drink now. Score 85. K

TEVA, SHIRAZ, 2008: Dark cherry-red, medium-bodied, with silky tannins, a round wine with easy-to-take red cherries and berries on the nose and palate. Round, soft and easy to drink. Drink now. Score 86. K

TEVA, SHIRAZ, 2007: Ruby toward garnet, medium-bodied, with soft tannins and generous plum and wild berry fruits. Soft and round, a good entry-level wine. Drink up. Score 85. K

TEVA, PINOTAGE, 2009: Deep garnet, medium-, perhaps medium- to full-bodied, with gently gripping tannins and generous black fruits on the nose. Opens in the glass to reveal aromas and flavors of purple plums, wild berries and a gentle hint of roasted herbs and saddle leather. Drink now. Score 87. K

TEVA, PINOTAGE, 2007: Medium-bodied, dark and youthful, royal purple in color at this stage, and showing a generous core of blackberry, wild berry and cherry fruits, those on a background of firm but ripe tannins. Drink up. Score 86. K

TEVA, TEMPRANILLO, 2007: Dark royal purple, with near-sweet tannins, a soft, round red with aromas and flavors of blackberries, vanilla, toast and minerals. A thoroughly modern Tempranillo. Drink up. Score 86. K

TEVA, SHIRAZ-MERLOT, 2009: Dark royal purple, medium-bodied, with soft, gently caressing tannins and a bare hint of spicy woody, an easy-to-drink, soft and round wine happily true to the variety. Look for aromas and flavors of black- and wild berries, saddle leather and earthy minerals that add an appealing Mediterranean touch. Drink now. Score 87. K

TEVA, CHARDONNAY, 2009: Unoaked and without having undergone malolactic fermentation, light gold in color, crisp, clean and refreshing, with appealing but not at all exaggerated citrus and tropical fruits. Not a complex wine but a very refreshing charmer. Drink up. Score 86. K

TEVA, EMERALD RIESLING, 2010: Deep, almost burnished gold in color, medium-bodied, moderately sweet with pineapple, green almonds and mint on the nose and palate. An entry-level quaffer. Drink now. Score 84. K

TEVA, MUSCAT, 2010: Off-dry, opens with a generously floral nose, goes on to reveal aromas and flavors of citrus, pineapple and ripe pears. A pleasant little quaffer. Drink now. Score 84. K

TEVA, MUSCAT, 2009: The color of light straw, as floral as Muscat can be, an off-dry wine with good balancing acidity and showing apricot, mango and tangerine notes. Not complex but a good entry-level quaffer. Drink up. Score 85. K

TEVA, MOSCATO, 2010: Much in the style of Moscato d'Asti, sweet but with just enough balancing acidity to keep it lively, very lightly frizzante, with aromas and flavors of tropical fruits and candied apples. Drink up. Score 84. K

TEVA, MOSCATO, 2009: A plump, off-dry white with just a bit of shpritz (call that lightly *frizzante* if you will), with floral and spicy notes to highlight tropical fruits, ripe apricots and lemon-lime flavors. Enough lively acidity to keep the wine going. Drink up. Score 86. K

Birya ✶✶

Founded by Moshe Porat in the community of Birya near the town of Safed in the Galilee, the winery draws on grapes from Ramot Naftaly in the Upper Galilee, and released its first wines from the 2003 vintage. Production for the 2005 vintage was 4,000 bottles. Because of damage during the Israel-Hezbollah war during the summer of 2006, no wines were produced from that vintage and wines since then have not been available for tasting.

BIRYA, CABERNET SAUVIGNON, 2005: Dark ruby toward garnet, this medium- to full-bodied wine shows soft tannins and generous currant, blackberry and mint on the nose and palate. On the moderately long finish a hint of fresh herbs. Drink up. Score 85. K

BIRYA, CABERNET SAUVIGNON, 2004: Deep garnet toward royal purple in color, medium- to full-bodied, with soft tannins integrating nicely with wood and fruits. Aromas and flavors of blackcurrants and berries on a light herbal background. Drink up. Score 84. K

BIRYA, CABERNET SAUVIGNON, PORAT WINE, 2003: Medium- to full-bodied with firm but well-integrating tannins and traditional Cabernet fruits of blackcurrants and berries with hints of herbs and spices on the finish. Drink up. Score 85. K

BIRYA, MERLOT, 2005: Generous blackberry, purple plum and black cherry fruits on a medium-bodied, softly tannic frame. A good quaffer. Drink up. Score 85. K

Bustan ✭✭✭✭✭

Founded in 1994 by Ya'akov Fogler, this micro-winery situated on Moshav Sharei Tikva in the Shomron region draws Cabernet Sauvignon, Merlot and Syrah grapes from the Jerusalem and Judean Mountains, and produces about 3,000 bottles annually. The winery has earned a good name for its distinctly French-style wines, which have had a formal kashrut certificate since 1999.

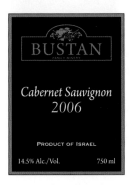

BUSTAN, CABERNET SAUVIGNON, 2006: Deep garnet in color, a dense, rich and concentrated wine, reflecting its 22 months in oak with full body and firm tannins that seem almost to melt in the mouth. On the nose and palate currants, sage and mineral aromas and flavors, those unfolding in the glass to reveal tantalizing hints of anise and earthy minerals. As a food match, consider the best roast of beef you can find. Drink now–2018. Score 93. K

BUSTAN, CABERNET SAUVIGNON, 2005: Deep, almost inky garnet in color, full-bodied, with intensity and concentration. Generous but remarkably soft tannins and spicy wood meld comfortably into the background to highlight traditional Cabernet aromas and flavors of blackcurrants, blackberries and spices, those with appealing overlays of minted chocolate and earthy minerals. On the long finish an appealing hint of near-sweet cedar. Drink now–2015. Score 92. K

BUSTAN, CABERNET SAUVIGNON, 2004: A concentrated wine, dark royal purple in color and full-bodied, with soft, well-integrated, mouth-coating tannins along with aromas and flavors of blackcurrants, blackberries, plums and spices, all with notes of chocolate, minerals and spicy cedarwood. Long and generous. Drink now–2014. Score 91. K

BUSTAN, CABERNET SAUVIGNON, 2003: Dark ruby to garnet, medium-bodied, with soft tannins integrating well and with generous but not overwhelming spicy oak. Spicy currant and berry fruits along with chocolate and tobacco on the powerful but elegant finish. Drink now. Score 90. K

BUSTAN, MERLOT, 2006: A luxuriant and rich wine, dark garnet toward royal purple in color, reflecting its 22 months in oak with notes of vanilla and cinnamon and soft, supple tannins that caress rather than "grab." On the nose and palate a generous array of plums, black cherries, currants, mocha and toasty oak, all lingering comfortably on a remarkably long finish on which tannins and spices rise nicely. A supple and generous wine, perhaps best matched with large or small cuts of lamb or mutton. Drink now–2016. Score 93. K

BUSTAN, MERLOT, 2005: Full-bodied, with deep, near-sweet and gently mouth-coating tannins, a muscular but simultaneously elegant Merlot. On the nose and palate, wild berries, currants, spices, Mediterranean herbs and *garrigue*, all coming together as a coherent whole. Long and generous. Drink now–2014. Score 92. K

BUSTAN, MERLOT, 2004: Aged in *barriques* for 22 months, dark, almost impenetrable garnet in color, but despite that casting purple and orange reflections. Full-bodied, with big but velvety smooth tannins and showing a tempting array of blackberries, spices, dark chocolate, green olives and a light note of grilled meat. Luscious and long. Drink now. Score 92. K

BUSTAN, MERLOT, 2003: Deep, dark, rich and aromatic. Full-bodied, with soft tannins, this smooth and round wine opens to reveal generous blueberry, cherry and currant fruits on a spicy floral background, all lingering nicely on the generous finish. Drink now. Score 91. K

BUSTAN, SYRAH, 2007: A bold and rich, full-bodied wine, the opening nose catching the attention with notes of blueberries and smoked goose breast, opening in the glass to reveal layer after layer of blueberries, black cherries, raspberries and plums Oak-aged for 18 months, with soft tannins and Asian spices and a finish that seems to go on forever. Supple and generous. Drink now–2016. Score 92. K

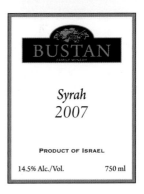

BUSTAN, SYRAH, 2006: Syrah with a distinctly Mediterranean note. Full-bodied, with generous but gently mouth-coating tannins in fine balance with spicy wood and fruits. On first attack wild berries and plums, those yielding comfortably to notes of blackberries and cassis and, in the background, tantalizing

THE WINERIES AND THEIR WINES

hints of leather and game meat. Long, generous and mouth-filling. Drink now–2015. Score 92. K

BUSTAN, SYRAH, 2005: Full-bodied, with a burst of super-soft sweet and savory tannins and parting in the glass to reveal layer after layer of blackberry, plum and citrus peel notes, complemented by notes of black tea, white pepper and, on the long finish, a hint of peppermint. Concentrated, intense, well focused, supple and harmonious with a super-long finish. Drink now–2013. Score 92. K

BUSTAN, SYRAH, 2004: Dark garnet, full-bodied, with firm tannins and gentle smoky wood influences. On the nose and palate black fruits, exotic spices and hints of saddle leather and earthy minerals. Long and generous. Drink now. Score 90. K

BUSTAN, SYRAH, 2003: Aromatic enough to be thought of as perfumed, this full-bodied, chewy and richly tannic wine offers up flavors of blackberries, currants, and boysenberry jam, those with tempting overlays of pepper, wet earth, and just a hint of grilled meat. Deep and intense, with a long, complex finish. Drink now. Score 90. K

Bustan Hameshusheem *

Located on Moshav Had Ness on the Golan Heights, winemaker-owner Benny Josef released his first wines to the market from the 2001 vintage. Production of 8,000 bottles annually is primarily of Cabernet Sauvignon, Merlot, Barbera and Sangiovese, the grapes drawn from the Upper Galilee and nearby vineyards.

BUSTAN HAMESHUSHEEM, CABERNET SAUVIGNON, 2006: Medium- to full-bodied, a country-style wine with generous black fruits and Mediterranean herbs, but sharp tannins and a distinct note of volatile acidity. Drink up. Score 78.

BUSTAN HAMESHUSHEEM, CABERNET SAUVIGNON, 2005: Full-bodied, with chunky, country-style tannins and smoky oak holding back the black fruits and spices. Past its peak. Drink up. Score 78.

BUSTAN HAMESHUSHEEM, CABERNET SAUVIGNON, 2004: Dark in color, with generous firm tannins, those balanced nicely by spicy oak, currant and wild berry aromas and flavors. Showing age. Drink up. Score 76.

BUSTAN HAMESHUSHEEM, SANGIOVESE-CABERNET SAUVIGNON, 2005: Light in body, color and tannins, with a stewed fruit nose and overly sweet on the palate. Drink up. Score 75.

Carmel ✶✶✶✶

Carmel was founded as a cooperative of vintners in 1882 with funding provided by the Baron Edmond de Rothschild. Its first winery was constructed that same year in Rishon Letzion, in the central coastal region of the country, followed in 1890 by a winery in Zichron Ya'akov, in the Mount Carmel area. Carmel receives grapes from about 300 vineyards throughout the country, some owned by the winery, others by individual vintners and by kibbutzim and moshavim. Even though their share of the local wine market has dropped from over 90% in the early 1980s to somewhat under 50% today, Carmel remains the largest wine producer in the country, currently producing over ten million bottles of table wine annually.

For many years, Carmel was in a moribund state, producing wines that, while acceptable, rarely attained excellence and failed to capture the attention of more sophisticated consumers. In the last eight years, Carmel has taken dramatic steps to improve the level of its wines and its better wines place it comfortably as one of the best wineries in the country.

Under the guidance of senior winemaker Lior Lacser and CEO Israel Ivzan, the winery is developing new vineyards in choice areas of the country and gaining fuller control over contract vineyards. In the 1990s Carmel was the first winery to plant major vineyards in the Negev Desert, and a new state-of-the-art winery has been partly completed at Ramat Dalton in the Upper Galilee. Carmel is also the owner of the Yatir boutique winery.

Current releases include the top-of-the-line varietal Limited Edition, the Mediterranean release, the Single Vineyard series, and the Regional series (sometimes referred to as the Appellation Series), the wines in these series earning the winery's stars. Following these are the wines in the Private Collection series, Reches series (labeled as Ridge outside of Israel), Zichron Ya'akov series, Selected series (sometimes known as Vineyards or Vineyards Selected Series outside of

Israel) and the popularly priced Young Selected series. The vineyards mentioned in the tasting notes of the Single Vineyard Wines – Zarit, Ben Zimra and Kayoumi – are located in the Upper Galilee, and Sha'al is on the Golan Heights.

Limited Edition

LIMITED EDITION, 2009: A Bordeaux blend of 61% Cabernet Sauvignon, 30% Petit Verdot and 3% each of Cabernet Franc, Malbec and Merlot. Deep garnet in color, with a generous cigar-box and black-fruit nose, opens with blackberries and blackcurrants, those parting to reveal ripe red plums and, on the long finish, a hint of roasted herbs. Best from mid-2012–2017. Score 92. K

LIMITED EDITION, 2008: From three fine vineyards in the Upper Galilee (Kayoumi, Alma and Ben Zimra), almost impenetrably dark garnet in color, full-bodied, well extracted and muscular with still-firm tannins waiting to integrate with spicy wood and fruits. No fear though, for the balance and structure are definitely here, those boding very well for the future. Aged in *barriques* for 15 months, a blend of Cabernet Sauvignon, Petit Verdot, Malbec, Cabernet Franc and Merlot (this year's blend – 60%, 30%, 4%, 4% and 2% respectively). On the nose and palate blackcurrant, purple plums and raspberries, those on a background of roasted herbs, spicy oak and, on the long, long finish an appealing note of *garrigue*. Drink now–2020. Score 93. K

LIMITED EDITION, 2007: Full-bodied and concentrated but not at all bombastic, developed in Burgundy-sized barrels (45% of which are new), showing fine balance and structure that bode well for the future. A blend of 57% Cabernet Sauvignon, 31% Petit Verdot, 5% each of Merlot and Malbec, and 2% Cabernet Franc, with a generous array of blackcurrant, blackberry and dark plum fruits, those supported by gentle notes of spicy oak and fresh acidity. Needs time for all of the elements to come together. Drink now–2018. Score 93. K

LIMITED EDITION, 2005: A Bordeaux blend of Cabernet Sauvignon, Petit Verdot, Merlot and Cabernet Franc (65%, 17%, 15% and 3% respectively). Dark ruby toward garnet, medium- to full-bodied, with generous soft tannins and reflecting its 15 months in *barriques* with light toasty and spicy oak. Blackberry and black cherry fruits on first attack, yielding to blackcurrants and appealing hints of lead pencil and vanilla and, on

CARMEL WINERY

Limited Edition
2005

No.

the moderately long finish, a near-sweet and elegant tobacco note. Drink now–2013. Score 92. K

LIMITED EDITION, 2004: This blend of 65% Cabernet Sauvignon, 20% Petit Verdot and 15% Merlot shows soft tannins and generous but gentle wood, those in fine balance with currant, blackberry and black cherry fruits, all melding together with light hints of pepper, anise and cigar-box aromas and flavors. Round and caressing, elegant and long. Drink now–2013. Score 93. K

LIMITED EDITION, 2003: A full-bodied blend of 50% Cabernet Sauvignon, 32% Petit Verdot, 17% Merlot and 1% Cabernet Franc. Deeply aromatic, with soft tannins and generous wood in fine balance with fruits and well-tuned acidity. On the nose and palate blackcurrants, blackberries, spices and sweet cedar, all leading to a remarkably long and elegant finish. Drink now–2015. Score 93. K

LIMITED EDITION, 2002: Deep royal purple in color, showing signs of clearing at the rim and taking on a light hint of oxidation. A Bordeaux blend of 60% Cabernet Sauvignon, 30% Merlot and 10% Cabernet Franc, each variety vinified separately and developed for 14 months in French oak. Medium- to full-bodied, with soft tannins and good balance between sweet and smoky wood, aromas and flavors of blackcurrants, berries and dark chocolate, all leading to a long cigar-box finish. Still drinking nicely but throwing sediment freely. Decant or pour carefully. Rapidly sliding past its peak. Drink up. Score 88. K

Mediterranean

MEDITERRANEAN, 2009: A true Mediterranean blend indeed of 27% each of Carignan, Shiraz and Petite Verdot, with 15% Petite Sirah, 3% Malbec and 1% Viognier. A wine that many will label as "feminine" in that it is soft, round and gentle or, in another phrase, anything but a blockbuster. Starts off with the Shiraz plums and a hint of leather, that parting to make way for blackberries and a hint of citrus peel, and on the long finish notes of mocha, all lingering nicely. Best starting in 2013. Tentative Score 90–92. K

MEDITERRANEAN, 2008: A blend this year of 33% Carignan, 24% Shiraz, 23% Petit Verdot, 16% Petite Sirah and 2% each of Malbec and Viognier. Similar to the blend of the 2007 (see the tasting note that follows) and, like that wine, oak-aged for 15 months in largely used oak. Deeper, darker and somewhat more full in body and tannins than the 2007 but maintaining its gentle and elegant personality. On the nose and palate wild berries, black cherries and currants, those parting to make way for notes of raspberries. In the background appealing gentle notes of spicy oak and green peppercorns. A round and long wine. Drink now–2019, perhaps longer. Score 93. K

MEDITERRANEAN, 2007: Youthful dark garnet toward royal purple, casting orange and violet reflections, a full-bodied remarkably gentle blend of 37% Carignan, 26% Shiraz, 20% Petit Verdot, 15% Petite Sirah and 2% Viognier, each fermented separately and developed for seven months in oak before blending and passing eight further months in oak. Deeply aromatic, on first attack so full of ripe red and black fruits and then opening to show an appealing array of blackberry, raspberry and cassis notes, those supported nicely by not at all imposing notes of smoky oak, black pepper and juniper berries. The wine reflects its time in oak with gentle wood influences and abundant but soft and gently caressing tannins. Round, complex and long. Drink now–2018. Score 93. K

Single Vineyard

SINGLE VINEYARD, CABERNET SAUVIGNON, KAYOUMI, 2009: Made entirely from Cabernet Sauvignon, with gentle notes of smoky and spicy oak and chewy but gentle tannins to complement traditional blackcurrant and blackberry fruits. From mid-palate on hints of what seems at one moment to be green olives and at the next, freshly picked Mediterranean herbs. Long and satisfying. Drink now–2016. Score 90. K

SINGLE VINEYARD, CABERNET SAUVIGNON, KAYOUMI, UPPER GALILEE, 2008: Opens with a deep currant nose, goes on to reveal wild berries, blackberries and cassis fruits, those on a background of mocha, baking chocolate and, on the long, long finish hints of coffee beans and black pepper. Full-bodied, well extracted and muscular but remarkably round, gentle and elegant. Drink now–2018, perhaps longer. Score 93. K

SINGLE VINEYARD, CABERNET SAUVIGNON, KAYOUMI, UPPER GALILEE, 2007: Garnet toward royal purple, oak-aged in French *barriques* for 14 months, a distinctive full-bodied Cabernet, showing cherry, raspberry and red currant fruits

on a background of freshly turned earth, tobacco and espresso coffee, all leading to a finish that goes on seemingly without end. Well focused and with excellent integration between fruits, tannins and wood. Drink now–2015. Score 93. K

SINGLE VINEYARD, CABERNET SAUVIGNON, KAYOUMI, UPPER GALILEE, 2006: Super-dark garnet in color, with a traditional Cabernet nose, a long, round and concentrated wine, medium- to full-bodied with generous but gently mouth-coating tannins, opening to show currant, wild berry, chocolate and espresso coffee notes. Deep, round, nearly chewy and with a deep fruit finish. Drink now–2014. Score 91. K

SINGLE VINEYARD, CABERNET SAUVIGNON, KAYOUMI, 2005: Dark garnet with green and orange reflections, full-bodied, open tex-tured and generous showing a spicy, peppery mouthful of blackberry, currant, coffee and black olive notes all leading to a long, round and mouth-filling finish. As this one develops look for an appealing hint of smoked meat rising. Drink now–2013. Score 91. K

SINGLE VINEYARD, CABERNET SAUVIGNON, KAYOUMI, 2004: Aged in oak for 15 months, the wine is dark, almost impenetrable purple in color. Firm tannins and smoky wood come together with currant, blackberry, plum and mineral aromas and flavors, those showing hints of Mediterranean herbs and light Oriental spices. Long and generous. Drink now. Score 91. K

SINGLE VINEYARD, CABERNET SAUVIGNON, KAYOUMI, 2003: Lus-cious and elegant, deep garnet, full-bodied and softly tannic. The nose and palate are still showing the blackcurrant, berry and spicy wood that were here but now these are complemented by hints of smoked meat, together with Oriental spices and tobacco. Long and complex. Drink now. Score 92. K

SINGLE VINEYARD, CABERNET SAUVIGNON, ZARIT, 2004: Deep garnet toward royal purple, reflecting its 15 months in *barriques* with judicious oak integrating nicely with solid tannins. Opens with currants and dusty wood, moving on to spices and blackberries, and from first sip to last, hints of vanilla, freshly hung tobacco leaves and an intimation of mint. Long and generous. Drink now. Score 91. K

SINGLE VINEYARD, CABERNET SAUVIGNON, ZARIT, 2003: Dark garnet, with firm, near-sweet tannins that yield nicely in the glass to reveal an appealing touch of rustic earthiness that adds dimension to rich, ripe black fruits. Complex, concentrated and elegant. Drink up. Score 90. K

SINGLE VINEYARD, CABERNET SAUVIGNON, SCHECH, 2004: From a not-yet-well-known vineyard on the Golan Heights, this red lives up nicely to the stereotypes of what makes a wine "feminine." Soft, round and caressing, elegant without being intense, full-bodied without being muscular, with tempting aromas and flavors of black cherries, currants and anise. Drink now. Score 90. K

SINGLE VINEYARD, MERLOT, SHA'AL, 2009: Aged for ten months in small oak barrels, showing dark garnet toward royal purple in color. Medium- to full-bodied (leaning to the full), opens with a generous hint of mint on a black-fruit nose, going on to reveal purple plums and then to raspberries and red currants. Drink now–2016, perhaps longer. Score 91. K

SINGLE VINEYARD, MERLOT, BEN ZIMRA, 2004: Dark toward inky garnet in color, full-bodied enough to be thought of as dense, with firm tannins integrating now to show fine structure and balance. Opens with a strong gamey aroma, but that fades quickly in the glass to reveal blackcurrants, purple plums and black olives, those highlighted by reined acidity and notes of tar and smoky oak. Long, with meaty flavors and fruits rising on the juicy finish. Drink now. Score 91. K

SINGLE VINEYARD, SHIRAZ, KAYOUMI, 2009: Shiraz blended, as is the wont these days, with 2% of Viognier. Dark garnet, reflecting its 15 months in oak with full-body, gentle notes of spicy cedarwood and dark fruits, those parting to make way for hints of leather and, on the long finish, a tempting note of tar. Generous and mouth-filling. Drink now–2016. Score 91. K

SINGLE VINEYARD, SHIRAZ, KAYOUMI, UPPER GALILEE, 2008: Shiraz blended with 2% Viognier and oak-aged for 15 months. True to the Shiraz varietal, super-dark royal purple in color, with generous but gently mouth-coating tannins. On first attack, raspberries and cherries, those parting to make way for blackberry and cassis. In the background and playing nicely on the palate, notes of saddle leather, fresh forest floor and finally, on the long finish, a hint of sweet cedarwood. Drink now–2018. Score 93. K

SINGLE VINEYARD, SHIRAZ, KAYOUMI, UPPER GALILEE, 2007: Almost impenetrably dark garnet in color, a big, bold and expressive wine, showing generous black cherry, red plum and raspberry fruits, those on a background of Oriental spices. Developed in French oak for

14 months, concentrated and generous, opening in layers on the palate and then lingering long and comfortably. Well crafted. Drink now–2015. Score 92. K

SINGLE VINEYARD, SHIRAZ, KAYOUMI, UPPER GALILEE, 2006: Deep garnet with hints of royal purple and casting orange and green reflections, a concentrated wine, full-bodied and deeply extracted yet showing remarkably soft tannins and spicy wood that almost melts on the palate. On first attack plums and currants, those making way for black cherries, hints of saddle leather and notes of asphalt. On the long and generous finish with tannins rising, a comfortable overlay of freshly roasted herbs and cedarwood. Drink now–2016. Score 93. K

SINGLE VINEYARD, SHIRAZ, KAYOUMI, 2005: Dark, almost impenetrable garnet, full-bodied, with silky tannins and showing fine balance and structure. Opens with a burst of dark plum and currant fruits, those yielding to notes of asphalt, bitter herbs and sweet-and-spicy cedarwood. Comes together as elegant, complex and long. Drink now. Score 91. K

SINGLE VINEYARD, SHIRAZ, KAYOUMI, 2004: Full-bodied, intense and concentrated, with soft tannins integrating nicely and showing layer after layer of spicy oak, smoked meat and tar, those highlighting red berries, black cherries and licorice. Drink now. Score 90. K

SINGLE VINEYARD, SHIRAZ, KAYOUMI, 2003: Firm and well structured, a soft, caressing and elegant wine. Generous soft tannins highlight a tempting array of currant, plum, blackberry and anise flavors and aromas, all of which culminate in a long, mouth-filling finish. Drink now. Score 91. K

SINGLE VINEYARD, CHARDONNAY, KAYOUMI, 2006: With 75% developing in stainless steel and 25% in 300 liter Burgundy oak, this white is showing an aromatic Chablis-like personality, with minerals and light spices backing up hazelnuts, pears, figs and citrus. On the long finish a hint of toasted brioche. Drink now. Score 90. K

SINGLE VINEYARD, GEWURZTRAMINER, LATE HARVEST, SHA'AL, GOLAN, 2010: Made entirely from Gewurztraminer grapes from the Golan Heights, with its moderate sweetness set off by fine balancing acidity. On the nose and palate exotic spices, tropical and dried fruits. Medium-bodied and refreshing, as appealing as an aperitif as with fruit-based desserts. Drink from release–2016. Tentative Score 88–90. K

SINGLE VINEYARD, GEWURZTRAMINER, LATE HARVEST, SHA'AL, GOLAN, 2009: Impacted on by about 15–20% of botrytis, a beautifully funky honeyed and floral nose. As were earlier releases of this wine, generously sweet but with fine balancing acidity, a complex and generous wine showing clear notes of eucalyptus honey, litchis and dried apricots, all on a just-spicy-enough background. A heady wine that lingers and lingers, seemingly forever. Drink now–2020. Score 93. K

SINGLE VINEYARD, GEWURZTRAMINER, LATE HARVEST, SHA'AL, GOLAN, 2008: Generously sweet but with fine balancing acidity, a rich dessert wine, with honey and floral notes to highlight notes of litchi, lemon curd and spices. Complex, long and rich, delicious and complex enough not to accompany dessert but as dessert. Drink now–2016, perhaps longer. Score 93. K

SINGLE VINEYARD, GEWURZTRAMINER, LATE HARVEST, SHA'AL, 2007: Gold, with orange and green tints, medium- to full-bodied, with generous sweetness balanced by lively acidity. Shows litchi, ripe peaches, rose petals, honey, and pineapple aromas and flavors, all coming together in a harmonious whole and, on the long finish, notes of freshly baked pecan pie. Drink now. Score 90. K

SINGLE VINEYARD, GEWURZTRAMINER, LATE HARVEST, SHA'AL, 2006: Made from grapes harvested in the upper Golan Heights, some affected by botrytis. Moderately sweet, with rose petal and orange peel overtones and honeyed pear, apricot and litchi fruits. Succulent, with a long-lingering finish. Drink up. Score 90. K

SINGLE VINEYARD, GEWURZTRAMINER, LATE HARVEST, SHA'AL, 2005: This medium- to full-bodied white shows generous sweetness and fine balancing acidity along with traditional Gewurztraminer litchis and spiciness, those matched by peach and nectarine fruits and, on the long finish, hints of rosewater and honey. Drink up. Score 91. K

Regional (Appellation)

REGIONAL, CABERNET SAUVIGNON, UPPER GALILEE, 2008: 90% Cabernet Sauvignon blended with Malbec and Petit Verdot. Oak-aged for 14 months, dark garnet, full-bodied, with soft, near-sweet tannins and fine balance between those, the wood and the fruits. Forward and ripe but not at all vulgar fruits, those including blackcurrants and blackberries, supported comfortably by notes of spicy wood, Mediterranean herbs and a hint of bittersweet chocolate. Drink now–2015. Score 90. K

REGIONAL, CABERNET SAUVIGNON, UPPER GALILEE, 2007: Full-bodied, with silky tannins and generous but well-balanced spicy and vanilla-rich wood, those parting to reveal traditional blackcurrant and blackberry fruits complemented nicely by notes of grilled Mediterranean herbs. On the long finish, generous fruits with a hint of near-sweet kirsch liqueur. Drink now. Score 90. K

REGIONAL, CABERNET SAUVIGNON, UPPER GALILEE, 2006: Dark garnet with orange reflections, medium- to full-bodied, with firm tannins now settling in nicely. On the nose and palate, spicy wood, currant and blackberry fruits along with hints of Mediterranean herbs and dark chocolate. Drink now. Score 88. K

REGIONAL, CABERNET SAUVIGNON, UPPER GALILEE, 2005: Blended with 7% Cabernet Franc, this firm, concentrated red shows bright, juicy currant and raspberry fruits, those with overlays of near-sweet cedarwood and sage and, on the long finish, a hint of licorice. Drink up. Score 89. K

REGIONAL, MERLOT, UPPER GALILEE, 2007: A dark-garnet blend of 85% Merlot and 15% Petit Verdot, reflecting its 12 months in oak with gentle spicy wood, and still-firm tannins, those starting to settle in comfortably. Filtered roughly, opens in the glass to show an appealing array of blackberry, blueberry and citrus peel, those matched by notes of Oriental spices. Full-bodied, long and generous. Drink now. Score 89. K

REGIONAL, MERLOT, UPPER GALILEE, 2006: Dark garnet toward royal purple, with soft tannins integrating nicely with spicy wood. Medium- to full-bodied, opens with a plum-rich nose shifting on the palate to berry, black cherry and cassis fruits all supported nicely by hints of white pepper and eucalyptus. Drink now. Score 89. K

REGIONAL, CABERNET FRANC, UPPER GALILEE, 2009: About 85% Cabernet Franc, the balance made up of Petit Verdot, Malbec and Cabernet Sauvignon. Oak-aged for ten months in mostly second- and third-year barrels. Dark royal purple, medium- to full-bodied, round and generous with gently caressing tannins, showing crushed blueberries on the nose and then going on to reveal notes of tobacco, anise and mulberries, all lingering nicely. Headed for elegance. Drink from release–2016. Score 90. K

REGIONAL, CABERNET FRANC, UPPER GALILEE, 2008: Made primarily from Cabernet Franc grapes, those fleshed out with a bit each of Petit Verdot, Malbec and Cabernet Sauvignon. Developed in mostly used *barriques* for ten months, dark garnet, with appealing spicy oak on the nose, full-bodied and concentrated, an intense wine opening to reveal its faithfulness to the variety. On the nose and palate raspberries, blackberries and plums, those on background of Mediterranean herbs and what seems one moment to be eucalyptus and the next, mint. Fine balance and structure here. Drink now–2016. Score 91. K

REGIONAL, CABERNET FRANC, UPPER GALILEE, 2007: With grapes from the Netua and Alma vineyards in the Upper Galilee, developed for ten months in oak, some new and some used. Blended with 8% of Petit Verdot and 7% Malbec, a medium- to full-bodied, deep garnet wine showing soft tannins and gentle spicy oak influences integrating nicely and opening to show red fruits and vanilla as well as a clear cigar-box note. Drink now. Score 90. K

REGIONAL, CARIGNAN, OLD VINES, ZICHRON YA'AKOV, 2008: Made from 30–40-year-old vines (indeed entitled to be thought of as *vieilles vignes* by Israeli standards). Dark garnet in color, with generous soft tannins and an appealing influence of spicy wood. On the nose and palate opens with purple plums and currants and then goes to raspberries. Long and generous with the tannins rising on the finish. Drink now–2015. Score 90. K

REGIONAL, CARIGNAN, OLD VINES, ZICHRON YA'AKOV, 2007: Made from thirty-year-old vines, blended with 10% Petit Verdot, oak-aged (minimal new oak) for 14 months. Dark garnet, a fruit-forward blend showing blackcurrant, vanilla and violet notes on a background of fine tannins. Full-bodied, with abundant fruits and fine balance, needs a bit of time for the elements to come together. Drink now–2013. Score 91. K

REGIONAL, CARIGNAN, OLD VINES, ZICHRON YA'AKOV, 2006: A super-dark garnet blend of 85% Carignan and 15% Petit Verdot, the Carignan from 35–40-year-old, very low-yield vines with no irrigation. A blockbuster on first attack, but the firm tannins and generous wood settling down nicely to reveal a rich array of plum, red cherry, raspberry and currant fruits all supported nicely by hints of cocoa and spices. Look as well for a generous mocha-rich finish. Drink now. Score 90. K

REGIONAL, CARIGNAN, OLD VINES, ZICHRON YA'AKOV, 2005: Blended with 10% Petit Verdot and oak-aged for 12 months. Medium- to full-bodied, with soft, caressing tannins and spicy wood in fine balance with blackberry, cherry and peppery chocolate aromas and flavors, those leading to a medium-long espresso-rich finish. Drink up. Score 91. K

REGIONAL, PETITE SIRAH, OLD VINES, JUDEAN HILLS, 2008: Made from unwatered and almost untended vines so close to the ground that one can think of these as bush vines,* a dark garnet and deeply aromatic wine with fine concentration and generous spicy notes, those including nutmeg, allspice and cinnamon, those yielding comfortably to cherry and berry flavors and an appealing hint of mint

---

* "Bush vines" are vines pruned by the gobelet system, that involving no wires or other systems of support, in which the gnarled trunk of the vine is kept quite close to the ground.

on the long finish. Firm and intense, with gripping tannins needing some time to settle in. Drink now–2014, perhaps longer. Score 90. K

REGIONAL, PETITE SIRAH, OLD VINES, JUDEAN HILLS, 2007: Aged for 14 months in oak, partly new, partly used, made from 35+-year-old vines, a concentrated and full-bodied red, showing royal purple in color and with generous tannins in fine balance with spicy and vanilla-rich wood. On the nose and palate a fine array of red and black fruits, those complemented by notes of black pepper, olives and Mediterranean herbs. Drink now. Score 90. K

REGIONAL, PETITE SIRAH, OLD VINES, JUDEAN HILLS, 2006: A big wine, full-bodied, deep garnet toward royal purple, with gripping tannins just starting to settle down but showing fine balance between tannins, wood and fruits. Ripe plum, blackberry and boysenberry notes on a background of minerals, minted chocolate and spicy cedarwood. Drink now. Score 90. K

REGIONAL, PETITE SIRAH, OLD VINES, JUDEAN HILLS, 2005: Developed in French oak for 12 months, made from grapes from 35-year-old vines, this almost impenetrably dark purple, still-firmly tannic wine opens in the glass to reveal a rich array of dark plum, blueberry, peppery, herbal and spicy cedar notes. Dense enough to be thought of as chewable but opens to show harmony and grace. Drink now. Score 91. K

REGIONAL, CABERNET SAUVIGNON-SHIRAZ, UPPER GALILEE, 2009: Dark garnet with violet reflections, showing medium- to full-bodied, with fine concentration and using its muscles in a subdued and elegant manner. On first attack purple plums and leather notes (reflecting, methinks, the Shiraz here), those parting to make way for generous blackberry and blackcurrant fruits. Fruit forward but never vulgar, with a long, mouth-filling finish. Drink now–2016. Score 90. K

REGIONAL, CABERNET SAUVIGNON-SHIRAZ, UPPER GALILEE, 2007: A blend of equal parts of Cabernet Sauvignon and Shiraz, those developed for 12 months in 30% new oak, the balance being older, showing gentle sweet and spicy oak. With the Shiraz clearly dominant, showing full-bodied, with soft tannins and opening to reveal red and black berries, plums and a hint of saddle leather. Finishes long and spicy. Drink now. Score 90. K

REGIONAL, CABERNET SAUVIGNON-SHIRAZ, UPPER GALILEE, 2006: A medium- to full-bodied blend of 50% of each of the varieties, those oak-aged for 12 months in French oak barrels of which about 30%

were new. Dark garnet in color, with soft, gently mouth-coating tannins parting to reveal a tempting array of blackberry and plum fruits, those on a background of spices and, coming in near the finish and lingering nicely, hints of leather and vanilla. Drink now. Score 88. K

REGIONAL, CHARDONNAY, UPPER GALILEE, 2010: With about 75% now in oak and destined to remain there for a total of seven months, the remainder developing in stainless steel, showing gold with green tints. Medium-bodied, opening with melon and tropical fruits, those parting to make way for notes of honeydew melon. Round and generous. Drink now–2014. Score 89. K

REGIONAL, CHARDONNAY, UPPER GALILEE, 2009: Light golden straw in color, with a nose rich with citrus flowers but flavors that are subdued, showing quince, apple and pear compote and herbal notes that may not be appreciated by all. Be prepared for major bottle variation with this release. Drink now. Score 84. K

REGIONAL, CHARDONNAY, UPPER GALILEE, 2008: The color of damp straw, medium-bodied, with apple, citrus and pineapple fruits. Not complex but a good quaffer. Drink now. Score 88. K

REGIONAL, SAUVIGNON BLANC, UPPER GALILEE, 2010: Light glistening gold, unoaked and showing fine aromatics and lively acidity to support aromas and flavors of passion fruit, pink grapefruit and star fruit (carambola), all on a background that hints appealingly of freshly mown grass. Very nice indeed, reflecting the ongoing local improvement with this variety. Drink now–2013. Score 90. K

REGIONAL, SAUVIGNON BLANC, UPPER GALILEE, 2009: Made entirely from Sauvignon grapes, intentionally unoaked. A crisply clean and nicely aromatic wine, light gold in color, with tropical and citrus fruits on a background of stony minerals, citrus peel and a hint of freshly cut grass. Refreshing and with just enough complexity to grab the attention. Drink now. Score 89. K

REGIONAL, SAUVIGNON BLANC, UPPER GALILEE, 2008: Made from 25-year-old vines, unoaked, showing light golden straw in color, freshly aromatic, and on the nose and palate citrus, tropical fruits and citrus peel notes. Not a complex wine but one that is lively and remarkably full of flavor and charm. As good as a cocktail party offering as with food. Drink now. Score 89. K

REGIONAL, VIOGNIER, UPPER GALILEE, 2010: Medium-bodied, lightly oaked, showing fine aromatics but somewhat muted flavors. On the nose and palate dried apricot leather and mixed citrus fruits, those going a bit "flat" in the glass. Drink now. Score 85. K

REGIONAL, VIOGNIER, UPPER GALILEE, 2009: Made entirely from Viognier grapes, this year from the Olive Tree vineyard, some early harvested and others late harvested, and with about 30% developed in oak, the rest in stainless steel. Aromatic, medium-bodied, crisply dry and with lively acidity to highlight aromas and flavors of apricots, white peaches and green apples, all lingering on a long, generous and lightly floral finish. As the wine matures look for notes of crème brûlée sneaking gently in. Drink now. Score 90. K

REGIONAL, VIOGNIER, UPPER GALILEE, 2008: With 25% of the wine developed in oak, the rest in stainless steel, some of the grapes early harvested and other late harvested, a ripe, creamy-near-full-bodied white showing concentrated citrus, pear and green apple notes, those on a background of dried apricots and, even though crisply dry, a tantalizing honeyed note. Fine balance between fruits and acidity lead to a long and delicate finish. Drink up. Score 90. K

REGIONAL, VIOGNIER, UPPER GALILEE, 2007: With 75% cold fermented in stainless steel and the remainder in *barriques*, that aged *sur lie* for four months. Shows a bare, tantalizing hint of spicy oak on the nose as it opens, yielding to an array of spicy pear, grapefruit and tangerine fruits all on a supple and just-spicy-enough frame. Refreshing and rich. Drink up. Score 88. K

REGIONAL, JOHANNISBERG RIESLING, UPPER GALILEE, 2009: A late-harvest wine, showing a gentle hint of sweetness and fine balancing acidity. On the nose and palate baked apples, lemon custard and crème patisserie notes, all lingering nicely. Drink now. Score 89. K

REGIONAL, JOHANNISBERG RIESLING, UPPER GALILEE, 2008: Unoaked, medium-bodied, with fine aromatics. Categorized (the law is strange) as off-dry but with a hint of sweetness so gentle that in Germany the wine would be labeled as *trocken* (i.e., dry), and on the palate generous green apple, grapefruit, lemon curd, minerals and a nice hint of white pepper to add to its charm. Drink now. Score 91. K

REGIONAL, JOHANNISBERG RIESLING, UPPER GALILEE, 2007: Late harvested, having undergone cold fermentation and developed entirely in stainless steel. Opens with a petrol-rich nose, that going on to reveal green apple, lemon custard and mineral flavors and aromas, all leading to a rich pink-grapefruit finish. Off-dry but with good balancing acidity. Drink up. Score 89. K

REGIONAL, GEWURZTRAMINER, UPPER GALILEE, 2010: Fermented and developed in stainless steel tanks, semi-dry, with fine balancing acidity to keep the wine lively. Shows traditional Gewurztraminer aromas and flavors of litchis, tropical fruits and rose petals and, from mid-palate on, notes of date honey and spring flowers. Drink now–2014. Score 89. K

REGIONAL, GEWURZTRAMINER, UPPER GALILEE, 2009: From the Kayoumi and Sha'al vineyards on the northern Golan, cold-fermented to guard the aromas and flavors. Off-dry, with good balancing acidity and showing peaches, litchis and spices on the nose and palate. Rising on the long finish, a bare but tantalizing hint of honey and eucalyptus. Drink now. Score 90. K

REGIONAL, GEWURZTRAMINER, UPPER GALILEE, 2008: An off-dry, unoaked white, made from grapes selected from the Kayoumi and Sha'al vineyards. Light gold with green tints, showing typical Gewurztraminer litchi and spicy notes, those matched nicely by notes of ripe peaches and apricots. Fine balancing acidity and a comfortably long finish. Drink up. Score 90. K

REGIONAL, CARMEL VINTAGE, JUDEAN HILLS, 2007: Fortified with grape alcohol, made entirely from old vine Petite Sirah grapes, a wine that will make you smile as it calls to mind a fine Tawny Port. With moderate sweetness set off nicely by acidity, the first attack on both nose and palate is absolutely laded with chocolate, that giving way comfortably to notes of fresh grapes and raisins, Brazil nuts and almonds, all with a tantalizing note of bitterness to flesh out the sweetness. Drink now. Score 90. K

REGIONAL, CARMEL VINTAGE, FORTIFIED PETITE SIRAH, JUDEAN HILLS, 2004: With Tawny-Port-style chocolate, raisins and spice box aromas, this rich dessert wine opens to reveal coffee and a hint of bitter almonds to balance the sweetness. Drink now. Score 89. K

Private Collection

Note: The Private Collection wines made for the U.S.A. and U.K. prior to 2007 were *mevushal* (flash pasteurized), while those distributed in Israel were kosher but not *mevushal*. Because *mevushal* wines cellared a year or longer tend to show "cooked" flavors and aromas, they should be consumed in their youth. Starting with the 2007 harvest, the Private Collection wines were no longer *mevushal*. The tasting notes that follow are for non-*mevushal* wines.

PRIVATE COLLECTION, CABERNET SAUVIGNON, 2008: Dark garnet, medium- to full-bodied, with somewhat chunky tannins but those settling down nicely in the glass to reveal light hints of spicy wood to complement wild berries, currants and cassis. On the medium-long finish a hint of espresso coffee. Drink up. Score 86. K

PRIVATE COLLECTION, CABERNET SAUVIGNON, 2007: Made entirely from Cabernet Sauvignon grapes, developed partly in stainless steel and partly in French and American oak *barriques* for eight months. Full-bodied, with somewhat gripping tannins, opens with a blueberry nose and then goes on to reveal currant and plum fruits on a lightly spicy background with a hint of espresso coffee that makes itself felt. Drink up. Score 86. K

PRIVATE COLLECTION, MERLOT, 2008: Soft, round and easy to drink, a more-or-less internationalized Merlot for those who enjoy that kind of thing. Medium- perhaps medium- to full-bodied, with a fruit-forward berry-rich nose and currant, plum and cassis notes on the nose and palate. Drink now. Score 85. K

PRIVATE COLLECTION, MERLOT, 2007: Aged partly in stainless steel and partly in *barriques*, medium- to full-bodied, with gently mouth-coating tannins and notes of spicy cedarwood. On the nose and palate wild berry, cherry and currant fruits, those supported nicely by hints of licorice and chocolate. Drink up. Score 87. K

PRIVATE COLLECTION, SHIRAZ, 2008: Having spent eight months in a combination of stainless steel vats and *barriques*, medium- to full-bodied, with a gentle note of smoky wood and silky tannins that grip nicely. On the nose and palate traditional currant and blackberry fruits, those complemented by notes of blueberries and a hint of espresso on the finish. Drink now. Score 86. K

PRIVATE COLLECTION, SHIRAZ, 2007: Developed partly in stainless steel and partly in *barriques* for eight months. Dark garnet, medium- to full-bodied with chunky, somewhat country-style tannins, appealing cedarwood overtones and opening in the glass to reveal blackberry, plum and leathery notes. Not complex but sits comfortably with food. Drink up. Score 86. K

PRIVATE COLLECTION, CABERNET SAUVIGNON-MERLOT, 2008: A blend of 50% each of Cabernet Sauvignon and Merlot, those aged partly in stainless steel, partly in oak for eight months. Medium- to full-bodied, with gently gripping tannins and a hint of vanilla, perhaps from the wood in which it partially aged. Opens to reveal a tempting array of currants, blackberries, and from mid-palate on notes of dark chocolate and licorice. The best Private Collection wine to date. Drink now. Score 89. K

PRIVATE COLLECTION, CABERNET SAUVIGNON-MERLOT, 2007: Medium- to full-bodied, with soft tannins and a gentle spicy wood influence, opening in the glass to show black and red berries and notes of purple plums on a background that hints of vanilla and cinnamon. Drink up. Score 87. K

PRIVATE COLLECTION, CABERNET SAUVIGNON-SHIRAZ, 2007: Deep garnet, medium- to full-bodied with chunky tannins that give the wine a rustic note. Opens to show blackberries and purple plums, those with light hints of roasted herbs. Drink up. Score 85. K

PRIVATE COLLECTION, CHARDONNAY, 2009: Light golden straw in color, medium-bodied with grapefruit and navel oranges on first attack, those followed by notes of Anjou pears and citrus peel. A fine quaffer. Drink now. Score 88. K

PRIVATE COLLECTION, SAUVIGNON BLANC, 2008: Light golden straw in color with green and orange tints, medium-bodied, with citrus and ripe peaches on the nose and palate, those supported nicely by a hint of freshly cut grass. Straightforward and refreshing, a very good quaffer. Drink up. Score 87. K

PRIVATE COLLECTION, EMERALD RIESLING, 2008: Light gold in color, light in body with its sweetness set off by generous acidity. Grape-fruit, tropical and floral aromas here. Drink up. Score 84. K

PRIVATE COLLECTION, BRUT, N.V.: Made by the Charmat method (with the second fermentation accomplished in pressurized stainless steel tanks), a blend of French Colombard, Chardonnay and Viognier (50%, 40% and 10% respectively), with a portion of the Chardonnay oak-aged, shows simple but appealing aromas and flavors of apples, pears and citrus. A short mousse and sharp but not well-focused bubbles here make one think more of Spanish Cava than of French Champagne. Drink now. Score 86. K

PRIVATE COLLECTION, MUSCAT, DESSERT WINE, 2008: Light gold in color, with generously sweet apricots, white peach and citrus notes supported by good acidity. Not overly complex but very pleasant. Drink now. Score 87. K

Reches (Ridge)

CARMEL WINERY
— Since 1882 —

רכס אדום

CARMEL RIDGE RED

ZICHRON YA'ACOV זכרון יעקב

2007

RECHES, RED, ZICHRON YA'AKOV, 2008:
A deep-purple, softly tannic, medium-bodied
ruby blend of Carignan and Shiraz. Round
and gentle with generous red fruits. A simple
but good quaffer. Drink now. Score 85. K

RECHES, ROSÉ, GALILEE, 2007: A blend
of Carignan and Shiraz grapes, light- to
medium-bodied and barely off-dry with
strawberry, raspberry and gooseberry fruits.
Pleasant "as is" but a delight with a few ice
cubes added to the wine when it is already
well chilled. Well past its peak. Drink up.
Score 84. K

RECHES, WHITE, 2008: A golden-straw-col-
ored potpourri of Sauvignon Blanc, French
Colombard and Semillon showing simple summer fruits on a lemon-
and-lime background. An easy quaffer. Drink up. Score 84. K

Selected (Vineyard)

SELECTED, CABERNET SAUVIGNON, 2010: Medium-dark garnet in
color, a soft, round and generously acidic wine showing primarily red
fruits along with a hint of white pepper on a medium-bodied base. A
good entry-level wine. Drink now. Score 85. K

SELECTED, CABERNET SAUVIGNON, 2009: Garnet toward royal
purple, medium-bodied, with gently gripping tannins and a note of
spicy wood parting to reveal wild berry and black cherry fruits, those
on a lightly spicy background. Drink now. Score 85. K

SELECTED, CABERNET SAUVIGNON, 2008: Dark garnet, medium-
bodied, with soft tannins and a hint of what "feels like" spicy oak, opens
to show generous blackberry, black cherry and wild berry fruits. A
crowd pleaser that sits comfortably on the palate. Drink up. Score 84. K

SELECTED, CABERNET SAUVIGNON, 2007: Medium-dark garnet,
medium-bodied, with soft tannins. Shows black fruits along with hints
of spicy wood. An entry-level wine. Drink now. Score 83. K

SELECTED, MERLOT, 2010: Medium-bodied and gently tannic. Medium-dark garnet with orange reflections, opens with a fruity-floral
nose, that settling down nicely in the glass to reveal light oak notes in

fine balance with blackberry, currant and earthy minerals. Drink now–2013. Score 87. K

SELECTED, MERLOT, 2009: Ruby toward garnet, medium-bodied, with soft tannins and appealing red fruits. Nothing complex here but an easy-to-drink quaffer. Drink now. Score 85. K

SELECTED, MERLOT, 2008: Medium-bodied, with somewhat chunky tannins, a pleasant country-style wine with blackberry and black cherry fruits on a lightly spicy background. Not complex, but with its appeal and at its best with grilled, well-spiced meats. Drink up. Score 84. K

SELECTED, CABERNET SAUVIGNON-MERLOT, 2010: Bright garnet, medium-bodied, with soft, gently caressing tannins and showing an appealing array of black and red berries, currants and blueberries on a lightly spicy background. Drink now–2013. Score 87. K

SELECTED, CABERNET SAUVIGNON-MERLOT, 2009: Dark ruby toward garnet, medium- to full-bodied, with soft tannins and notes of spicy cedarwood integrating nicely to show appealing currant, blackberry and blueberry fruits, those coming together in a generous and mouth-filling whole. Drink now. Score 86. K

SELECTED, CABERNET SAUVIGNON-MERLOT, 2008: Garnet toward royal purple in color, medium-bodied, with gently gripping tannins and a hint of spicy wood to highlight aromas and flavors of black fruits and earthy minerals. Drink up. Score 84. K

SELECTED, CABERNET-MERLOT-SHIRAZ, 2010: Cherry red toward garnet, medium-bodied, with light, almost unfelt tannins. On the nose and palate crushed berries, red plums and a note of herbaceousness. A good entry-level wine. Drink now. Score 85. K

SELECTED, CABERNET SAUVIGNON-SHIRAZ, 2009: Medium-deep garnet in color, medium-bodied with gently mouth-coating tannins and a generous array of plum, wild berry and cassis notes, those on a background that hints of black licorice. Drink now. Score 86. K

SELECTED, CABERNET-MERLOT-SHIRAZ, 2008: Dark garnet in color, medium- to full-bodied, with soft, gently caressing tannins. On the nose and palate an interesting mélange of red and black fruits, plums and berries dominating nicely and lingering comfortably. Just enough complexity to grab the attention. Drink up. Score 85. κ

SELECTED, CHARDONNAY, 2008: Plain and simple, a refreshing and lively white wine with pineapple, citrus and topical fruits. Drink up. Score 84. κ

SELECTED, SAUVIGNON BLANC, 2009: Damp straw in color, light-to medium-bodied, falls somehow flat, its fruits muted and without enough acidity to keep it lively. Drink up. Score 80. κ

SELECTED, SAUVIGNON BLANC, 2008: Light and easy, a light straw colored and lively wine with a core of citrus, pineapple and ripe peaches. Nothing complex but a good summer-time quaffer. Drink up. Score 84. κ

SELECTED, SAUVIGNON BLANC, 2007: Light straw colored, with generous acidity to keep it lively and an appealing array of citrus and summer fruits. Drink up. Score 84. κ

SELECTED, EMERALD RIESLING, 2008: Light, flowery and aromatic with green apple and citrus notes, its moderate sweetness balanced nicely by fresh acidity. Drink up. Score 83. κ

SELECTED, MUSCATO, 2009: Off-dry, light and fizzy, with lemon and lime, grapefruit and tropical fruits, a fun wine for breakfast or picnics. The young will adore this one. Drink well chilled. Drink up. Score 84. κ

Young Selected

YOUNG SELECTED, CARIGNANO, 2010: Lightly *frizzante*, cherry red, light in body and with no perceptible tannins, a young wine, quite frivolous on the nose and palate and not meant to be taken the least bit seriously but offering up a good deal of uncomplicated pleasure. Aromas and flavors of cherries and red berries, a low alcohol content (6%) and light sweetness that is carried nicely by lively acidity. A fun wine for breakfast or picnics. Drink up. Score 85. κ

YOUNG SELECTED, CARIGNANO, 2009: Bright purple in color, light in both body and alcohol, with no noticeable tannins at all and an appealing *frizzante* note. Off-dry but clean and crisp with plenty of balancing acidity. A fun party wine, especially for the young and young at heart. Drink up. Score 84. κ

YOUNG SELECTED, CARIGNANO, 2008: So deep royal purple in color is this wine that one almost expects it to glow in the dark (I checked. It does not.) Light in body, off-dry and lightly *frizzante*, with a low alcohol content of 5.5%, this wine is packed with blueberry, blackberry and black cherry flavors. The kind of wine to serve at parties with lots of young people in attendance. To tone down the sweetness, serve as well chilled as you would a white wine. Drink up. Score 82. K

YOUNG SELECTED, MOSCATO, 2010: Think of this as a ginger ale made from grapes and with a 5.5% alcohol content. With about the same level of sweetness as the aforementioned ginger ale, a light and simple wine for those who enjoy their wines on the sweet side. Drink now. Score 84. K

YOUNG SELECTED, MOSCATO, 2009: A near-twin to the wine in the Selected series (see the review above). Fun and frivolous. Drink well chilled and drink now. Score 84. K

YOUNG SELECTED, MOSCATO, 2008: About the same color as ginger ale and just about as *frizzante* but, with its 6% alcohol content, definitely a wine, with its generous sweetness set off by lively acidity. My guess is that the young and those just "getting into wine" will find this one peachy-keen, especially when served after having been placed in the freezer until just before ice-crystals begin to form. (Be sure though not to keep it in the freezer too long as true freezing may cause the bottle to explode.) Drink up. Score 80. K

Carmey Avdat ✶✶

Founded by Eyal Izrael, this small winery is based on a private farm on the heights of the Negev Desert not far from Kibbutz Sde Boker. The winery's vineyards of Cabernet Sauvignon and Merlot grapes are planted in a wadi and rely on water from 1,500-year-old water terraces built by the Nabateans. The winery's first releases were 4,500 bottles from the 2005 vintage and current production is about 6,000 bottles annually.

CARMEY AVDAT, CABERNET SAUVIGNON, 2008: Oak-aged for 12 months in new and older American oak, showing dark garnet, medium- to full-bodied, with soft tannins and, as not infrequently, typifies the wines of the region in its generous acidity. Opens with plums and wild berries, goes on to reveal currants, spices and a hint of anise on the finish. Drink now. Score 86.

CARMEY AVDAT, CABERNET SAUVIGNON, SOMEQ, 2008: Unoaked, showing deep ruby in color, a light- to medium-bodied wine with clean cherry, raspberry and red currant fruits. Nothing complex here but a refreshing quaffer. Drink up. Score 85.

CARMEY AVDAT, CABERNET SAUVIGNON, 2007: Dark garnet, medium- to full-bodied, with soft tannins and notes of spicy wood. On the nose and palate blackcurrant, blackberry and cherry fruits, those on a background of earthy minerals and a hint of mint on the finish. Drink now. Score 85.

CARMEY AVDAT, CABERNET SAUVIGNON, 2006: Deep garnet toward royal purple, medium- to full-bodied, with soft tannins and a gentle wood influence. On the nose and palate berries, black cherries and currants, those with light vanilla and earthy-herbal overlays. Round and generous. Drink up. Score 85.

CARMEY AVDAT, MERLOT, 2008: Deep garnet, medium-bodied, with soft tannins opening in the glass to show generous blackcurrants, purple plums and blackberries, those supported by notes of fresh herbs and brown spices. Easy to drink but complex enough to get our attention. Drink now. Score 87.

CARMEY AVDAT, MERLOT, 2007: Dark garnet with a hint of adobe, medium- to full-bodied with good concentration and extraction, its tannins and spicy wood now integrated, opens to show appealing blackberry, black cherry, purple plums and chocolate, all lingering nicely on the palate. Drink now. Score 87.

CARMEY AVDAT, MERLOT, 2006: Dark ruby toward royal purple, medium- to full-bodied, with still-gripping tannins and generous wood influences but those in good balance with fruits and acidity. On the nose and palate berries, cherries, cassis and appealing chocolate and peppery overlays that linger nicely. Drink up. Score 86.

CARMEY AVDAT, MERLOT, 2005: Holding even better than predicted at earlier tastings. Showing ruby toward garnet with just the first hint of clearing at the rim but fully maintaining its freshness. Soft, gently caressing tannins, a light note of oak in the background and, on the nose and palate, berry and black cherry fruits on a light herbal background. Showing age. Drink up. Score 84.

CARMEY AVDAT, CABERNET SAUVIGNON-MERLOT, TISHREY, 2009: A blend of equal parts of Cabernet Sauvignon and Merlot. Medium- to full-bodied and softly tannic. Aged for 12 months in new oak, opens with a minty and red-fruit nose, going on to reveal aromas and flavors of currants, wild berries and brown spices all lingering nicely. Drink now–2013. Score 88.

CARMEY AVDAT, KEDEM, 2008: A deep-garnet, full-bodied blend of Cabernet Sauvignon and Merlot. On the nose black fruits and pepper. Opens in the glass to show blackcurrant, blackberry and tobacco notes and, on the finish, what seems at one moment to be pepper, at another ginger and at yet another anise. Drink now. Score 88.

CARMEY AVDAT, KEDEM, 2006: A blend of 60% Merlot and 40% Cabernet Sauvignon, oak-aged for 12 months in American oak. Full-bodied, with gently gripping tannins and just the right hand with spicy oak, opens to reveal generous blackberry, blackcurrant and blueberry fruits along with a hint of vanilla, those leading to a long fruity finish. Drink up. Score 87.

CARMEY AVDAT, ROSÉ, 2010: At first glance it seems that with its dark-garnet color, calling this wine a rosé is somewhat of a misnomer. The depth of color comes because the early harvested Cabernet Sauvignon grapes used were allowed 18 hours' skin contact. What surprises pleasantly is that both on nose and palate the wine indeed comes across as a rosé, crisply dry, light- to medium-bodied with blueberry, raspberry and strawberry aromas and flavors and a hint of minerality on the finish. Drink now. Score 86.

Castel ★★★★★

Starting as a micro-winery, the Domaine du Castel grew gradually and now produces approximately 100,000 bottles annually. Since the release of a mere 600 bottles of his first wine in 1992, owner-winemaker Eli Ben Zaken – who now works with his sons Ariel and Eytan – has consistently made some of the very best wines in the country. The fully modern and attractive winery, with its exquisitely designed barrel room holding more than 500 *barriques*, is located on Moshav Ramat Raziel in the Jerusalem Mountains. The winery relies entirely on grapes grown in the area, mostly in its own vineyards, some in vineyards under its full supervision. Grape varieties include Cabernet Sauvignon, Merlot, Petit Verdot, Cabernet Franc, Malbec and Chardonnay.

Until the 2009 vintage the winery produced only three wines annually. The flagship wine, Grand Vin Castel, is a superb Bordeaux-style blend; the fine second label, Petit Castel, an often no-less exciting wine, is one meant for somewhat earlier drinking; and the "C" Blanc du Castel has often been one of the most exciting Chardonnay wines produced in Israel. With the 2009 vintage the winery presented its Rosé du Castel. The Castel wines have all been kosher since 2003.

As rules of thumb, the Castel reds and whites are approachable and thoroughly enjoyable on release; the "C" Blanc du Castel wines will maintain their vivacity, complexity and elegance comfortably for 5–6 years beyond their vintage year; the Petit Castel for 5–7 years; and the Grand Vin for 7–9 years. Beyond that, it is up to each wine lover to determine just how mature he/she best likes their wines.

Grand Vin Castel

GRAND VIN CASTEL, 2009: A tentative blend, with more Cabernet Sauvignon and a bit less Cabernet Franc and Malbec than sometimes found in this flagship wine. Dark ruby toward garnet, full-bodied, with creamy mocha-tinted oak, and still-firm tannins. On first attack notes of curing tobacco and minerals, those yielding comfortably to blackcurrant, blackberry and purple plums. Rich and complex, a long, elegant and well-focused wine. Best starting in 2012 or 2013. Tentative Score 91–93. K

GRAND VIN CASTEL, 2008: A blend of Cabernet Sauvignon, Merlot, Petit Verdot, Cabernet Franc and Malbec (60%, 20%, 10%, 6% and 4% respectively). Deeply aromatic, full-bodied and with fine concentration and opening to show true elegance with layer after layer of complexity and depth. Near-sweet tannins that caress gently come together with lightly spicy cedarwood to highlight aromas and flavors of blackcurrants, blackberries and fresh Mediterranean herbs and, on the super-long finish, a tantalizing note of baking chocolate. Perhaps Castel's best to date. Drink now–2018. Score 93. K

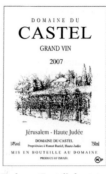

GRAND VIN CASTEL, 2007: The by-now traditional Grand Vin blend of Cabernet Sauvignon, that flushed out with Merlot, Petit Verdot, Cabernet Franc and Malbec. Full-bodied, dark and well extracted, firm on opening but yielding comfortably in the glass to reveal gently caressing tannins, notes of spicy oak and generous blackcurrant, blackberry and blueberry fruits, those supported by notes of mocha, orange peel and black olives. On the super-long finish a tempting note of licorice. Long, generous and coherent. Drink now–2015. Score 93. K

GRAND VIN CASTEL, 2006: A blend focused on Cabernet Sauvignon and Merlot, those fleshed out with Petit Verdot and Malbec. Solid and intense, dark garnet in color, full-bodied and firm on first attack but then opening to show a generous array of blackberries, black cherries, currants and dark chocolate. Dense, rich and complex, with hints of near-sweetness that toy comfortably on the palate, with tannins that grip comfortably and in fine balance with wood and fruits. Long and generous, muscular and intense but with a distinct note of elegance. Drink now–2013. Score 92. K

GRAND VIN CASTEL, 2005: Dark toward inky garnet, with just a bit of clearing at the rim, with firm tannins now integrating nicely with spicy and smoky oak. Deeply aromatic, opens in the glass to show a nose and palate of blackcurrant, blackberry and purple plum fruits on a background of roasted herbs and near-sweet tobacco. On the long finish hints of citrus peel, anise and cherry-flavored dark chocolate. Drink now–2013. Score 92. K

GRAND VIN CASTEL, 2004: Dark garnet with the once-firm tannins now integrating nicely with spicy wood. On the nose and palate currants and blackberries, those supported very nicely indeed by notes of raspberries, licorice and tobacco, all lingering long and comfortably on the palate. An elegant wine. Drink now–2013. Score 93. K

GRAND VIN CASTEL, 2003: Dark garnet and full-bodied, with its once-firm tannins now gently caressing. On the nose appealing notes of fresh sawdust and black fruits, those making way in the glass for currants, wild berries, sweet herbs and a hint of green olives. At its peak now, but as this one continues to develop in the bottle expect the fruits to recede and make room for more earthy-herbal notes. Drink now. Score 90. K

GRAND VIN CASTEL, 2002: Remaining rich and round, continuing to show black fruits, anise and hints of olives and cedarwood, but sliding past its peak and not for further cellaring. Drink up. Score 90.

GRAND VIN CASTEL, 2002 (KOSHER EDITION): Maturing nicely, its once-exuberant currant, cherry and plum fruits now more subdued though still pronounced, and yielding to the minerals and cedar that were once in the background. Full-bodied, with wood, tannins and fruits nicely balanced and taking on a more earthy-herbal note. Past its peak. Drink up. Score 88. K

GRAND VIN CASTEL, 2001: Maturing and now showing earthy currant, black cherry, sage and cedarwood aromas and flavors. Full-bodied and concentrated, the wine possesses great elegance and features long lingering flavors rich in hints of coffee and chocolate. A bit of earthy funk creeping in. Showing signs of age. Drink up. Score 91.

GRAND VIN CASTEL, 2000: With its once-firm tannins now well integrated, this medium- to full-bodied wine continues to show fine balance between spicy blackcurrant, plum and blackberry fruits, those matched nicely by hints of Mediterranean herbs and clean earthy aromas and flavors. Muscular, with firm tannins as well as a long, spicy finish. Sliding past its peak. Drink up. Score 90.

GRAND VIN CASTEL, 1999: In its youth, deep ruby toward dark purple, now garnet going to brick red. Full-bodied, continues to show good balance between generous, well-integrated tannins and currant, plum and blackberry fruits but with notes of Band-aids and oxidation creeping in. Showing a bit flabby on the palate. Past its peak and maturing rapidly. Drink up. Score 87.

GRAND VIN CASTEL, 1998: An elegant wine in its youth, its once-deep garnet color now going somewhat dull and taking on an adobe-brick color, its once gently caressing tannins taking on a somewhat flabby sensation. Continues to show spicy wood, plums and currants on the palate but those with a near-stewed nature. A wine to be appreciated primarily by those who enjoy their wines on the distinctly mature side. Drink up. Score 86.

GRAND VIN CASTEL, 1997: A luxurious wine in its youth, with remarkably intense blackcurrant and black cherry fruits, Mediterranean herbs, abundant but very well-balanced oak and a long finish with pepper and anise. Supple and harmonious as it developed but now well past its peak and fading rapidly. Drink up. Score 85.

GRAND VIN CASTEL, 1996: Fully mature now, this still-complex and full-bodied wine continues to show fine balance between wood, tannins, and an array of aromas and flavors of currants, herbs, tobacco, hints of mint and sweet cedar that unfold nicely on the palate. Fine when first poured but fades quickly in the glass, herbal and earthy notes coming to dominate. Past its peak so drink up. Score 87.

GRAND VIN CASTEL, 1995: In its youth a concentrated, intense and simultaneously elegant wine, showing a rich array of currant, purple plum and black cherry fruits on a background of dark chocolate, and in the background notes of cigar tobacco and spicy cedar. Still harmonious but now showing its age with a hint of adobe brick in the color and clearing at the rim, the once-generous fruits now more subdued and taking on a near-stewed nature, loamy notes of cured leather and tobacco rising as the wine sits in the glass. Well past its peak. Drink up. Score 86.

Petit Castel

PETIT CASTEL, 2009: A blend this year of 60% Merlot and 40% Cabernet Sauvignon. Reflecting its 16 months' development in French oak with notes of spicy wood and soft, gently caressing tannins, opens in the glass to reveal an appealing array of black fruits and crushed wild berries, those on a background that

hints lightly of tobacco and dark chocolate. Drink now–2015. Score 90. K

PETIT CASTEL, 2008: Superb. As almost always, a Bordeaux blend of Cabernet Sauvignon, Merlot and Petit Verdot, the wine aged in French oak for 16 months and in truth a Bordeaux-styled wine that could come only from the Mediterranean sunshine. Deep garnet in color, full-bodied, with soft tannins and bare but tantalizing notes of spicy wood already integrating nicely. A rich blackberry nose followed on the palate by aromas and flavors of blackcurrants, blackberries and black cherries. Pure, round, rich, well focused and with touches of anise and cedarwood on the finish, a complex, deep and long wine. Drink now–2015. Score 93. K

PETIT CASTEL, 2007: A blend of Cabernet Sauvignon, Merlot and Petit Verdot. Deep garnet, a full-bodied wine reflecting its 16 months' development in oak with gently caressing tannins, those integrating nicely with notes of spicy cedarwood. On first attack red plums and a hint of *garrigue*, those yielding comfortably to currants, wild berries and a note of bitter citrus peel. Wood and tannins rise on the finish. Drink now–2013, perhaps longer. Score 90. K

PETIT CASTEL, 2006: Dark garnet, full-bodied, with soft tannins and a gentle spicy wood influence that give the wine a comfortable roundness. Makes me smile as the opening aromas include a distinct note of butterscotch, that yielding to cedary wood and tobacco notes. Showing a generous array of currant, purple plum, bittersweet chocolate and sage, the tannins rising on the long and mouth-filling finish. Drink now–2013. Score 90. K

PETIT CASTEL, 2005: Deep, almost impenetrable garnet in color, medium- to full-bodied, with soft tannins. On the nose an appealing hint of spicy wood, that supported by black fruits and then going on to reveal aromas and flavors of red and black berries, black cherries, licorice and bittersweet chocolate. As in its youth a tantalizing hint of sweetness on the long finish. Drink now. Score 90. K

PETIT CASTEL, 2004: Dark garnet with a hint of clearing at the rim, medium- to full-bodied, with soft tannins, gentle notes of spicy oak and fine balancing acidity. A caressing wine that opens with a chocolate and berry-rich nose, those joined by cassis, black cherries, dark plums, bittersweet chocolate and pepper, all lingering on a long, polished and round finish. Remains elegant and supple but showing first signs of aging. Drink up. Score 91. K

PETIT CASTEL, 2003: Garnet, with a bit of clearing at the rim, opens with a slightly medicinal-iodine note, but that blows in the glass, and then shows medium- to full-bodied, with generous blackcurrant, blackberry and purple plum fruits, those on a softly tannic background. As the wine develops in the glass, look as well for wild berry and a light earthy-herbal note. Drink up. Score 90. K

PETIT CASTEL, 2002: Dark ruby toward garnet, this medium-bodied red shows soft, well-integrated tannins and generous currant and wild berry fruits together with generous touches of sweet cedar, spices and herbs on the moderately long finish. Fully mature and showing signs of age. Drink up. Score 88.

"C", Chardonnay, Blanc du Castel

"C", CHARDONNAY, BLANC DU CASTEL, 2010: Light, bright gold in color, medium-bodied and thus somewhat lighter in body than many earlier releases. Showing fine balance and, even at this very early stage, complexity. On the nose and palate floral notes that highlight nectarine, citrus and pear fruits, those on a light toasty note and finishing with fresh minerality. Drink from release–2015. Tentative Score 91-93. K

"C", CHARDONNAY, BLANC DU CASTEL 2009: Delightful on release but now showing as a wine that has gone seriously wrong in the bottle. The cause of the problem may be the action of mercaptans, those chemical compounds that can make themselves felt as wine develops if the yeasts do not have enough exposure to nitrogen. Whatever the cause, the result is a wine whose aromas and flavors are now buried under an overlay that some will associate with those of burning rubber, cooked cabbage or sewage. In fairness, Eli Ben Zaken of Castel feels that these faults will vanish in time. I shall re-taste the wine periodically but until that time when the wine becomes appealing, I find the wine unscorable and cannot recommend it. K

"C", CHARDONNAY, BLANC DU CASTEL, 2008: Light, bright gold in color, full-bodied but with balance so finely tuned that the wine seems to float on the palate. On first attack, grapefruit and grapefruit pith on a seductive creamy and vanilla nose, the wine then opening in the glass to reveal pear, apricot, fig and melon aromas and flavors, all on a mineral-rich background. Long, deep, complex and elegant. Drink now–2014. Score 93. K

"C", CHARDONNAY, BLANC DU CASTEL, 2007: Delicious in its youth but now with its oak on the ascendant and with a light note of bitter almonds, those happily yielding in the glass to free aromas and flavors of white peaches, ripe pears and honeydew melon, those on a generously acidic and mineral-rich background. Drink now or in the next year or so. Score 89. K

"c", CHARDONNAY, BLANC DU CASTEL, 2006: Tasted from a magnum-format bottle. Rich, shining gold in color, its once somewhat heavy wood influence now receding. On the nose and palate a generous array of Anjou pears, green apples and citrus, those complemented by notes of raisins, roasted Brazil nuts and spices. As at past tastings a concentrated and intense wine, not so much a lively quaffer as a meditation wine. Drink now. Score 90. K

"c", CHARDONNAY, BLANC DU CASTEL, 2005: Developed beautifully, still a peaches-and-cream wine but now in place of the youthful citrus, figs and summer fruits, notes of ripe peaches, pears and toasty oak, all coming together nicely and leading to a long and elegant finish. Not for further cellaring. Drink up. Score 92. K

"c", CHARDONNAY, BLANC DU CASTEL, 2004: Its color now gone from its youthful damp golden straw to a deeper, almost burnished gold. Gentle oak influences and good balancing acidity highlight citrus, melon and pear fruits. As noted at an earlier tasting, a mature Chardonnay, long and generous with an appealing spicy note that rises on the finish. Past its peak. Drink up. Score 87. K

Rosé du Castel

ROSÉ DU CASTEL, 2009: Castel's first rosé and a rousing success. Made by the *saignée* method (i.e., making a wine from red grapes and allowing the free-run juice to run off with minimal skin contact), showing a lively color somewhere between neon orange and mandarin orange. Made entirely from Merlot grapes, medium-bodied and boasting a hefty 14% alcohol content, but don't let that upset you for this is a wine with fine balance between alcohol, acidity and fruits. On the nose and palate strawberries, blueberries, cranberries and light hints of Oriental spices and even a gentle dollop of tannins to add to one's pleasure. Wonderfully fruity and complex. Drink now. Score 90. K

The Cave ✴✴✴✴

Releasing its first red wine from the 2000 vintage, this small winery has its barrel storage facilities in a cave at the foothills of Mount Carmel, not far from the town of Zichron Ya'akov. It should be understood that The Cave is not so much an independent winery as it is an extension of Binyamina, the wines made by the same winemakers, vinified at the main winery and only then transferred to *oak barrels* for aging in an artificial cave, built in the sixteenth century. The cave itself is breathtaking – ninety meters long and nine to ten meters high, with stone-lined walls and roof, maintaining a constant natural temperature and humidity. The winery is currently releasing about 30,000 bottles annually. The Cave also released its first old-vine Cabernet Sauvignon from the 2007 vintage, the grapes coming from a single vineyard in Kerem Ben Zimra in the Upper Galilee.

THE CAVE, 2007: A blend of 65% Cabernet Sauvignon, 33% Merlot and 2% Petit Verdot, each variety vinified separately and oak-aged for 24 months before the blend was selected. Dark garnet in color, with a nose that bursts forth with blackberries and chocolate, opens in the

glass to reveal full-bodied, with gently gripping notes of spicy wood that come together nicely with currant, blackberry and citrus peel notes. On the moderately long finish appealing hints of licorice. Drink now–2014. Score 91. K

THE CAVE, OLD VINE CABERNET SAUVIGNON, 2007: A limited edition, showing dark, almost impenetrable garnet with just a hint of royal purple at the rim. Full-bodied, with generous but remarkably round tannins and gentle notes of spicy wood. On the nose red fruits, vanilla and a hint of cinnamon. Opens in the glass to reveal traditional Cabernet blackcurrant and blackberry fruits, those complemented by notes of bittersweet chocolate and freshly cured tobacco. Concentrated but showing its strength in ways that are discrete and elegant. Fully enjoyable now but best from mid-2012–2020, perhaps longer. Elegance on the grand scale and indeed the best ever from The Cave and from Binyamina. Score 94. K

THE CAVE, CABERNET SAUVIGNON, 2006: Blended with 3% of Petit Verdot, a full-bodied wine, surprisingly soft and round, opening with red fruits that turn in the glass to blackberries and currants. In the background an appealing note of a forest floor after a light rain. Drink now–2013. Score 90. K

THE CAVE, CABERNET SAUVIGNON-MERLOT-PETIT VERDOT, 2007: Dark garnet toward youthful royal purple in color, with generous blackberry, purple plum and peppery notes here, those supported by hints of smoke and saddle leather on the finish. Drink now–2014. Score 88. K

THE CAVE, CABERNET SAUVIGNON-MERLOT, 2006: Full-bodied, with firm tannins and an array of currant, berry and black cherry fruits. Good balance and structure here leading to a moderately long finish. Drink now. Score 88. K

THE CAVE, CABERNET SAUVIGNON-MERLOT, 2005: Full-bodied, with soft tannins integrated nicely and showing a moderate dose of spicy cedarwood, all in fine balance with fruits and acidity. A blend of 65% Cabernet Sauvignon and 35% Merlot, those vinified separately before the final blend was made near bottling time. Dark garnet toward royal purple in color, with currant, blackberry, spices and hints of bitter orange peel all coming together as a long and coherent whole. Drink up. Score 90. K

Chateau Golan *****

Located on Moshav Eliad on the Southern Golan Heights, Chateau Golan released its first wines from the 1999 vintage. From its onset the wines have been made by Oregon- and California-trained winemaker Uri Hetz, who has, in the decade since the winery's founding, demonstrated himself to be one of the best winemakers in the country, his wines comfortably reflecting his style and philosophy of wine.

Set in a fully modern winery which owns its own vineyards, those currently planted in Cabernet Sauvignon, Merlot, Cabernet Franc, Petit Verdot, Syrah, Petite Sirah, Carignan, Mourvedre, Grenache and Touriga Nacional on the red side, and on the white, Sauvignon Blanc, Mourvedre, Roussanne, Grenache Blanc and Viognier. Other experimental plantings have also been made. Production is currently about 75,000 bottles annually. The winery releases wines in three unofficially announced series: Royal Reserve, Eliad and Geshem.

Royal Reserve

ROYAL RESERVE, CABERNET SAUVIGNON, 2010: Traditional Cabernet. In fact, if you mistake this for anything but Cabernet Sauvignon it may be a sign that you need a neurosurgeon. Full-bodied, well extracted but remaining soft and round, with muscles that hold themselves in check to reveal elegance. On the nose and palate blackcurrants, blackberries, black cherries and melted chocolate all coming together in ways that are graceful, polished and long. Best from 2014. Tentative Score 90–92.

ROYAL RESERVE, CABERNET SAUVIGNON, 2009: Dark ruby toward garnet, medium- to full-bodied, with soft, gently caressing tannins and appealing red currants, black cherries and spices, all on a background that hints of sage. Not a concentrated or intense wine but a juicy one that fills the mouth comfortably and then lingers nicely. Drink now–2016, perhaps longer. Score 90.

ROYAL RESERVE, CABERNET SAUVIGNON, 2008: Blended with 10% Merlot and 3% Syrah, oak-aged for about 12 months. Dark garnet, still young and concentrated, with a 14.5% alcohol content and generous gripping tannins, those needing a bit more time to allow the generous fruits here to be felt. On first attack a clear note of black cherries, yielding comfortably to aromas and flavors of black and red currants, plums and a near-sweet cedarwood overlay, finishing with hints of green olives and Mediterranean herbs. Drink now–2018. Score 91.

ROYAL RESERVE, CABERNET SAUVIGNON, 2007: A medium- to full-bodied blend of 85% Cabernet Sauvignon, 7% each Cabernet Franc and Syrah, and a 1% smidgeon (I always wanted to use that word in a tasting note) of Petite Sirah. Vinified separately for 12 months in French and American *barriques* before blending. Dark garnet, with gently mouth-coating tannins and notes of spicy oak and cedar. Opens to show appealing aromas and flavors of blackberries, blackcurrants and violets, and, on the generous finish, a hint of bittersweet chocolate. Drink now–2014. Score 90.

ROYAL RESERVE, CABERNET SAUVIGNON, 2006: Cabernet Sauvignon blended with 9% Cabernet Franc, 3.5% Syrah and 1.5% Petit Verdot. Oak-aged for 12 months, medium-dark garnet, with a hint of sweetness on the nose, turning firm on the palate with mouth-coating tannins and hints of wood. Opens to light oak and mocha, which support currants, blackberries and a hint of vanilla bean that adds a nice touch; tannins, alcohol and a note of sweet chewing tobacco rising on the finish. Drink now–2013. Score 90.

ROYAL RESERVE, CABERNET SAUVIGNON, 2005: Almost impenetrably dark garnet in color, this wine is both concentrated and elegant. A blend of 89% Cabernet Sauvignon and 11% Cabernet Franc, opening with spicy, mocha-tinged blackcurrants, those yielding to blackberries, herbs and light oak. Hints of light sea salt and leather on the super-long finish make the wine intriguing. Perhaps the best yet from the winery. Drink now–2015. Score 94.

ROYAL RESERVE, CABERNET SAUVIGNON, 2004: Blended with 15% Cabernet Franc, and aged in French and American oak for 12 months, this medium- to full-bodied wine's tannins and lightly smoky wood are integrating nicely to highlight blackberry, currant and purple plum fruits, those opening to hints of strawberries and spices. Drink now. Score 91.

ROYAL RESERVE, CABERNET SAUVIGNON, 2003: Dark garnet, full-bodied, with its once-firm tannins now integrated nicely and continuing to show excellent focus and concentration. On the nose, still-youthful aromas and flavors of currants, black cherries and anise, along with attractive earthy-herbal overtones and hints of green olives. Drink now. Score 90.

ROYAL RESERVE, MERLOT, 2010: Surprisingly developed for a wine so young, opening to show medium- to full-body with gently caressing tannins and an appealing array of blackberries, currants, bay leaves and cloves all on a crisp background. Round, supple and long. Drink from release–2016. Tentative Score 89–91.

ROYAL RESERVE, MERLOT, 2009: Ruby toward garnet, well extracted but showing soft and round, with aromas and flavors of wild berries and plums on a background of licorice and earthy minerals. Drink now–2016. Score 90.

ROYAL RESERVE, MERLOT, 2008: When originally tasted from the barrel, the winemaker observed: "If my 2007 Merlot was a dragon, this one is a teddy bear." He was correct. Blended with 10% Cabernet Sauvignon, oak-aged for about 12 months, medium- to full-bodied, with soft, gently caressing tannins. A distinctly Old-World wine, medium-dark garnet in color, with fine concentration and opening to real blackberry, raspberry and cassis along with notes of chocolate-coated citrus peel that rise on the long finish. Drink now–2017. Score 91.

ROYAL RESERVE, MERLOT, 2007: Dark, almost impenetrable garnet in color, a full-bodied blend of 86% Merlot, 9% Petit Verdot and 5% Syrah. Aged for 14 months in French oak, deeply extracted, muscular and intense. A whopping 15% alcohol here but that in fine balance with generous soft tannins and notes of near-sweet cedarwood. On the nose and palate blackberry, raspberry and cassis fruits, those on a background of licorice and bittersweet chocolate. Tannins and a note of toasty oak rise on the long finish. A powerhouse, but one with grace. Drink now–2014. Score 90.

ROYAL RESERVE, MERLOT, 2006: Showing more full-bodied than at earlier tastings, with soft, near-sweet tannins. Opens with a somewhat veggie nature, but shifts quickly to show tempting black fruits, damson plums and crushed berries, those complemented nicely by an exotic near-sweet spicy note that lingers through the finish. Drink now. Score 90.

ROYAL RESERVE, MERLOT, 2005: A thoroughly modern but still-Old-World wine, with good acidity, gentle wood and fruits in fine balance. Showing a bit green now, but opening to currant and blueberry fruits, those complemented nicely by mocha, chocolate and vanilla. Look for a long, lightly spicy finish. Balance, harmony and finesse here. Drink up. Score 90.

ROYAL RESERVE, MERLOT, 2004: A blend of Merlot, Syrah and Cabernet Franc (89%, 6% and 5% respectively) aged in oak for 13 months, this medium-dark garnet wine shows near-sweet tannins and a light, earthy minerality, those supporting generous red currant, berry and cherry aromas and flavors. On the long finish tantalizing hints of sage and anise. Drink up. Score 92.

ROYAL RESERVE, MERLOT, 2003: Aged in oak for 12 months, this deep garnet toward royal purple, medium- to full-bodied blend of Merlot, Syrah and Cabernet Sauvignon (86%, 13% and 1% respectively) shows fine balance between generous tannins, spicy wood and currants, berry fruits and herbaceousness. On the long finish hints of licorice and green olives. Concentrated and well focused. Drink up. Score 90.

ROYAL RESERVE, SYRAH, 2010: Dark garnet, full-bodied, aromatic and well extracted for the vintage and happily avoiding being a block-buster. On the nose and palate blackberries, blueberries and black cherries on a lightly spicy background. Round and generous. Drink from release–2015. Tentative Score 88–90.

ROYAL RESERVE, SYRAH, 2009: Dark, almost impenetrable garnet toward royal purple, full-bodied with silky tannins that grip gently and part to reveal notes of spicy cedarwood. On the nose and palate blackberries, plums and black cherries, those complemented by notes of vanilla and minerals. Drink now–2018. Score 90.

ROYAL RESERVE, SYRAH, 2008: Dark, almost impenetrable garnet toward purple, full-bodied, with a floral nose and then going on to re-veal generous near-sweet tannins and a tantalizing bitter-almond note that runs from first attack to the long finish. A blend of 85% Syrah, 13% Mourvedre and 2% Carignan showing aromas and flavors of red and purple plums, wild berries, tobacco and earthy mineral notes. Intense and concentrated, needing only a bit more time to show its complexity and elegance. Drink now–2018. Score 92.

ROYAL RESERVE, SYRAH, 2007: A Rhone-like wine with a Mediterranean twist. Youthful royal purple in color, a blend of 95% Syrah and 5% Mourvedre, those fermented entirely on natural yeasts and oak-aged in French oak for 12 months. Youthful royal purple in color, full-bodied, with its generous 14.6% alcohol level in fine balance with spicy wood, near-sweet tan-nins, acidity and fruits. On first attack near-sweet plums and crushed berries, those yielding comfortably to blueberries and what seems at one moment notes of saddle leather, the next of espresso coffee. A wine that is simultaneously complex and elegant and, at the same time, surprisingly easy to drink. Drink now–2015. Score 91.

ROYAL RESERVE, SYRAH, 2006: Medium-dark garnet toward royal purple in color, full-bodied, this blend of 89% Syrah, 8% Grenache and 3% Petite Sirah was aged in oak for 12 months. Generous but soft tannins and spicy wood along with a fairly high alcohol content (14.7%), those in fine balance with fruits and acidity. On the nose and palate ripe blackberries, raspberries and red plums, those matched nicely by spices and hints of citrus peel and saddle leather. Drink now. Score 90.

ROYAL RESERVE, SYRAH, 2005: Blended with 3% Cabernet Sauvignon and aged in large French barrels for 11 months. Dark, rich and plush from first attack, opening to show a tempting array of spicy blackberry, raspberry, red currants and pomegranate fruits, those matched nicely by hints of citrus peel. Bold, with distinctly Old-World charm, showing a light greenness, minerality and tantalizing meaty notes. Long and generous. Drink now. Score 92.

ROYAL RESERVE, SYRAH, 2004: Aged in large oak barrels for 14 months, this medium- to full-bodied and firmly tannic wine opens beautifully in the glass to reveal ripe blackberry, currant and raspberry fruits, all with a delicate hint of near-sweetness and spring flowers. On the long and generous finish hints of spices, licorice and smoked meat. Drink now. Score 90.

ROYAL RESERVE, SYRAH, 2003: Blended with 15% Grenache, this is a classic and elegant Syrah with distinct Mediterranean overtones. Fine balance between wood and soft tannins, a generously gamey wine that offers up smoke and black pepper along with deep raspberry and floral aromas and flavors. Drink up. Score 90.

ROYAL RESERVE, SYRAH, 2002: Tasted from the winery's library, my most recent tasting note holds firmly. Big, dense and tannic, continuing to show round and rich. Deep garnet-to-purple color with a bit of clearing now appearing at the rim, show-ing generous plum, herbal and earthy aro-mas and flavors. Drinking well but fully  mature and not for further cellaring. Drink up. Score 90.

ROYAL RESERVE, CABERNET FRANC, 2007: This could be a textbook Loire Valley Cabernet Franc, especially when one considers the area of Chinon. Smooth and velvety, with plenty of tannins, but those soft and gently mouth-coating and opening to show black cherry, currant, blueberry and tobacco notes, those complemented by hints of tobacco. As this one develops look for hints of green olives and briar. Drink from release–2013. Tentative Score 90–92.

ROYAL RESERVE, CABERNET FRANC, 2005: Subtle and seductive, with generous tannins integrating nicely. On the nose and palate fresh currant, dark berry and black cherry fruits matched nicely by bell peppers, cigar-box and lead-pencil notes. Good length, depth and a distinct note of elegance. Drink now. Score 90.

ROYAL RESERVE, CABERNET FRANC, LIMITED EDITION, 2003: Full-bodied, earthy and aromatic with an appealing array of currant, plum and wild berry fruits, those backed up nicely by vanilla and spices from the oak as well as an appealing hint of earthiness on the moderately long finish. Rich and concentrated. Drink now. Score 90.

ROYAL RESERVE, PETIT VERDOT, 2010: Dark garnet, firm and generously tannic, opens in the glass to reveal blackcurrants and blackberry fruits and ends with generous acidity. Possibly destined for a varietal release. Best from 2013. Tentative Score 89–91.

ROYAL RESERVE, GRENACHE, 2005: Ripe, rich and with generous oak-accented blackberry, black cherry, spicy and black pepper flavors. True to its variety, with an attractive hint of greenness. Drink now. Score 90.

ROYAL RESERVE, GRENACHE, 2003: Loyal to its varietal traits, this attractive, pale ruby wine is medium-bodied, with soft tannins and tempting blackberry, black cherry and red currant fruits as well as spicy oak. Drink up. Score 89.

ROYAL RESERVE, TOURIGA NACIONAL, 2010: As in 2008 and 2009, this wine was allowed to go through spontaneous fermentation (that is to say, based on wild yeasts) and then basket-pressed, fortified with French Ferrand Cognac to an alcohol level of about 18% and then oak-aged in 400 liter casks for about 12 months. Inky dark, with a texture best described as creamy, with soft tannins that caress gently and its natural sweetness in fine proportion to acidity and fruits. Look for aromas and flavors of blueberries, blackberries, black cherries and plums, all with an appealing note of licorice that makes itself felt from mid-palate on. Long and generous. Drink from release–2020. Tentative Score 89–91.

ROYAL RESERVE, TOURIGA NACIONAL, 2009: Made entirely from Touriga Nacional, Portugal's best wine grape and an integral part of many of the best vintage Ports as well as in an increasing number of dry red wines. Not a Port, not a Madeira – in fact, not any wine that I know of from the past, but a unique and exciting creation of winemaker Uri Hetz. Aging in 400 liter oak casks for a maximum of 12 months, fortified with French Cognac to a 17.5% alcohol content, a seductive wine with generous sweetness set off comfortably by balancing acidity and an array of black cherry, cassis and dark chocolate flavors. Generous soft tannins here and a powerful sweet and peppery finish. As I wrote in my first tasting note: It's delicious, it's delightful, it's delovely! Drink from release–2019. Score 92.

ROYAL RESERVE, TOURIGA NACIONAL, 2008: The winery's and the country's first venture into a wine based entirely on the Portuguese Touriga Nacional grape. Trodden by foot, allowed to go through spontaneous fermentation (that is to say, based on natural yeasts) and then basket-pressed. The wine is then fortified with French Ferrand Cognac to 17.2% alcoholic strength and oak-aged in 400 liter barrels for about 12 months. As I wrote when I first tasted it, a seductive wine, inky-colored, deep and intense with an abundance of fine-grained tannins and generous sweetness balanced well by natural acidity and fruits. On the nose and palate lanolin, blackberry, cherry and gamey notes, those followed by hints of plums and black cherries, all with generous licorice flavors that come in on the long finish. Delicious and fascinating. Only 400 bottles were produced. Worth fighting for to lay hands on a few bottles. Drink now–2018. Score 93.

ROYAL RESERVE, OG, 2009: If any wine has ever demonstrated a joint sense of adventure and humor, it is winemaker Uri Hetz's Og, the 2009 edition of which continues what started in 2008 and may well become a legend in its time. As in 2008, the winemaker is willing to give no clues whatever to what grape may have been used  here but whatever the grapes, a full-bodied wine, round, generous and aromatic with fine balance and structure. On the nose and palate black fruits, dark chocolate, a hint of leather and, on the long finish, a generous note of black cherries. As Hetz put it at our tasting: "Og will get us all." It has certainly "got" me. Best from 2013–2018. Score 93.

ROYAL RESERVE, OG, 2008: Winemaker Uri Hetz has always made fine and often exciting wines but this is his first venture into a wine that shows a fully post-modern sense of humor. Let's start with the name. Og translates from Hebrew more or less as Ogre. Og was, of course also the Amorite king of Jerusalem. He was also thought by some to be a giant who, although not invited to join Noah on the Ark, managed to hang on to that noble ship and then to survive for quite a few centuries. The giant, who lived 3,000 years, was also said to have been king of the Bashan. As to which Og this one is, Hetz will say not a word. Nor, no matter how his arm may be twisted, will he reveal to anyone (not even others at the winery) what varieties of grapes were used. Whatever, intensely dark, full-bodied, firmly tannic with a black fruit nose and then on nose and palate rich, loamy aromas and flavors of cassis, black cherries and dark chocolate, all coming together as a fascinating and coherent whole. A country-style powerhouse with a distinct sense of charm and elegance. Drink now–2016, perhaps longer. Score 91.

ROYAL RESERVE, ROSÉ, 2009: A shift in style for the winery. Until now the rosé wines have been made entirely from Cabernet Franc. This year the wine contains 80% Cabernet Franc and 20% Grenache, both with very short skin contact and then fermented partly in oak and partly in stainless steel before being blended. The winemaker accurately describes the color as "provocatively not pink," being in fact an attractive faint copper hue. With a generous 14% alcohol content for a rosé, a fascinating wine, medium-bodied, with notes of white peaches on the nose and a palate rich with cherry, currant and orange peel notes along with a hint of spices. And don't be at all surprised to find a tantalizing hint of super-soft tannins here. Drink now. Score 88.

ROYAL RESERVE, ROSÉ, 2008: Almost a twin to the 2007 wine. Pale toward blushing pink in color, made entirely from Cabernet Franc grapes, partly developed in stainless steel and for a short while in used *barriques*. Medium-bodied, with appealing red and black berries, strawberries and red currants, those on a spicy background. Plenty of good acidity here. A more than usually complex rosé. Drink now. Score 89.

ROYAL RESERVE, ROSÉ, 2007: A rosé made entirely from Cabernet Franc grapes, the wine developed partly in stainless steel and part for a short while in old *barriques*. Blushing peach in color, medium-bodied, with appealing wild berries, cassis and notes of strawberries, those on a lightly spicy background. Mouth-filling and generous for a rosé. Drink up. Score 88.

ROYAL RESERVE, SAUVIGNON BLANC, 2010: Light and refined, crisply dry with an appealing note of lively acidity that runs through to highlight aromas and flavors of green apples, lime and grapefruit, those on a background that hints at one moment of freshly mown grass and at another of citrus peel. Refreshing and generous. Drink now. Score 90.

ROYAL RESERVE, SAUVIGNON BLANC, 2009: Golden straw in color, aged partly in *barriques* for four months, the remainder in stainless steel. Medium-bodied, with generous citrus, apple and grassy notes, a fresh, lively and just complex enough wine to grab the attention. Drink now. Score 90. Royal Reserve, Sauvignon Blanc, 2008: Light and lively gold in color, with green and orange tints, developed partly in oak and partly in stainless steel, a wine that is simultaneously lively and refreshing as well as complex and thought provoking. Gently floral, with traditional Sauvignon Blanc aromas and flavors, those including freshly cut grass, gooseberries and tropical fruits, all on a background of well-balanced acidity. Long and generous. Drink up. Score 91.

ROYAL RESERVE, SAUVIGNON BLANC, 2007: 60% of this wine was fermented and developed *sur lie* in old 350 liter barrels, and 40% in stainless steel for about six months. Medium-bodied and aromatic with generous notes of citrus, pineapple and orange peel. Drink up. Score 87.

ROYAL RESERVE, SAUVIGNON BLANC, 2006: Developed partly in oak, partly in stainless steel, now in its fifth year and still going strong. Light gold, with fine aromatics, a bright, lithe wine showing unusual concentration for a Sauvignon Blanc, that reflected in generous citrus, summer fruits and passion fruits, a bare hint of spicy oak making itself nicely felt. Drink up. Score 90.

Eliad

ELIAD, 2009: Cabernet Sauvignon with about 3% Petit Verdot blended in. Showing dark garnet, full-bodied, round and soft, with chewy near-sweet tannins in fine balance with wood and fruits. On the nose and palate blackcurrants, crushed blackberries and ripe plums on a background that hints at one moment of mocha and at another of bittersweet chocolate. Long and generous. Approachable on release but best 2013–2017. Score 91.

ELIAD, 2008: Super-dark garnet with orange and purple reflections, full-bodied and remarkably rich on both nose and palate. A blend of Cabernet Sauvignon and smaller amounts of Petit Verdot and Syrah (93%, 4% and 3% respectively), reflecting its 12 months in oak with still-gripping tannins and toasty oak, those in fine balance with fruits and acidity. On first attack currant and blackberry fruits, followed by hints of baking chocolate and roasted herbs. As this one continues to develop in the bottle it will become softer and rounder and may well develop notes of green olives. Long, generous and mouth-filling. Drink now–2018, perhaps longer. Score 92.

ELIAD, 2007: A blend of 89.5% Cabernet Sauvignon, 7% Petit Verdot and 3.5% Merlot. Almost inky dark in color, a distinctly Old World wine in its elegance, the grapes vinified separately for 13 months in oak before being blended and aged for three months longer. On first attack blackberries and black cherries, those yielding comfortably to notes of toasty oak and bittersweet chocolate, and, on the long finish, as we have come to know with this wine, hints of olives and Mediterranean herbs. Plenty of alcohol here (14%) but not at all a "blockbuster" and given time this one will indeed show elegance. Drink now–2016, perhaps longer. Score 90.

ELIAD, 2006: Dark garnet, full-bodied and with fine balance and structure, a blend of 93% Cabernet Sauvignon and 3.5% each of Merlot and Petit Verdot, oak-aged for 12 months. Opens with red and black berries, those joined by blackcurrant and black cherries supported by a light note of spicy oak, sweet cedarwood and milk chocolate. Ripe, round and generous, will most assuredly call to mind Bordeaux with a Mediterranean hint added by notes of fresh herbs and black olives. Drink now–2013. Score 91.

ELIAD, 2005: Aged in French oak for 13 months, this blend of 94% Cabernet Sauvignon and 6% Syrah opens with rich, almost syrup-like fruits on the nose, and goes on to show depth and grace. Soft, fine-grained tannins, light smoky wood, in good balance with berry, black cherry, currants and licorice. Drink now–2013. Score 93.

ELIAD, 2004: A blend of Cabernet Sauvignon, Merlot, Cabernet Franc and Petit Verdot (70%, 21%, 3% and 6% respectively), this may be the most intense wine released to date by the winery. Dark garnet in color, ripe and complex, showing deep plum, berry, floral, coffee, peppery and earthy aromas and flavors all coming together beautifully in a long and graceful finish. Drink now. Score 92.

ELIAD, 2003: Oak-aged, this deep garnet blend of 66% Cabernet Sauvignon, 20% Merlot and 14% Cabernet Franc is already showing rich, intense and complex. Concentrated plum, berry, currant and spicy oak aromas and flavors matched nicely by spices and a hint of tobacco. Drink now. Score 92.

Geshem

GESHEM, ROUGE, 2010: A blend of Grenache, Mourvedre and Syrah, those coming together in a medium-, perhaps medium- to full-bodied, wine, the color of black cherry juice, showing generous acidity in fine balance with fruits and soft tannins. Soft, juicy and round with generous raspberry and crushed blackberries on the nose and palate, those supported nicely by notes of mint and red licorice. Easy to drink and with just enough complexity to grab the attention. Drink now–2014. Score 90.

GESHEM, ROUGE, 2009: A blend of 68% Grenache and 32% Mourvedre, with a distinct red-fruit nose. Deep ruby toward garnet, medium-,perhaps medium- to full-bodied, with an array of raspberries, cassis and bitter citrus peel. Generously alcoholic (15%) and avoids heat but with a few rough edges, needing a bit of time for the elements to come together. Drink now–2015. Score 90.

GESHEM, ROUGE, 2008: A blend of Grenache, Syrah, Carignan and Mourvedre (54%, 39%, 5% and 2% respectively), the Grenache dominating nicely and giving the young wine a Grand Marnier nose. Full-bodied, with ample but gently gripping tannins, opens with a distinct note of sweetened chewing tobacco, then going on to show generous currants, raspberries and huckleberries, all with light hints of anise and tar that come in and linger on a long and broad finish. Drink now–2018. Score 92.

GESHEM, ROUGE, 2007: At 15%, plenty of alcohol here, but that showing neither heat nor sweetness as it is in fine balance with spicy wood, near-sweet tannins and fruits. Full-bodied, soft, round, rich and deep, showing almost incense-like anise notes and then opening to reveal berry, black cherry and currant fruits. A blend of 70% Grenache with 15% each of

Mourvedre and Syrah, oak-aged for 13 months, with a tempting *liquoreux* finish. Drink now–2014. Score 90.

GESHEM, ROUGE, 2006: A blend of 80% Grenache, 14% Syrah and 6% Mourvedre, each developed separately and having spent a total of 13 months in *barriques*. Medium garnet in color, medium- to full-bodied, opening quietly on the nose but showing very nicely indeed on the palate, revealing raspberry, cherry and red currant fruits, those supported well by vanilla and hints of spices and bittersweet chocolate. Long and generous. Drink now. Score 91.

GESHEM, ROUGE, 2005: Medium-dark garnet, a blend of 70% Grenache and 30% Syrah, reflecting its aging in French oak for 12 months with a light, pleasingly musky overtone. Opens with a near-raspberry liqueur nose, that settling down to reveal oak-accented aromas and flavors of blackberries, cherries and black pepper. Deep and long. Drink now–2013. Score 93.

GESHEM, ROUGE, 2004: The first blend of Syrah and Grenache from the winery (62% and 38% respectively). Dark ruby toward garnet, medium- to full-bodied, with soft, ripe tannins integrating well and showing currant and berry fruits, those matched nicely by spices, freshly crushed herbs and, as the wine sits on the palate, hints of orange peel and black tea. Long, super-fruity finish. Drink now. Score 91.

GESHEM, ROSÉ, 2010: Another shift in style for this wine, this year made from Grenache, Barbera and Syrah (92%, 5% and 3%, the Barbera made by and with a nod of appreciation to the talents of winemaker Gaby Sadan of Shvo winery). Reflecting absolutely minimal skin contact with a pale pink color, but there is nothing whatever pale about this wine. It delights the nose and palate with its array of raspberries, strawberries and savory spices, those including cinnamon and a tantalizing hint of cloves. Bursting with personality, almost guaranteed to bring a smile to the face. Drink now. Score 89.

GESHEM, BLANC, 2010: A blend of Roussanne, Grenache Blanc and Viognier, the three grapes complementing each other nicely (the Grenache supplying the tart and juicy elements, the Roussanne adding a mineral touch; and the Viognier contributing aromatics). Plenty of lively acidity here but that in fine balance with summer and citrus fruits, notes of green almonds and flinty minerals, a wine destined for dishes such as grilled fish or chicken in a spicy tomato sauce. Drink now–2014. Score 90.

GESHEM, BLANC, 2009: A blend of about 40% Roussanne and 30% each Viognier and Grenache Blanc. Medium-bodied, bright, shining gold in color, round and generously but not overly alcoholic (about 14%). Opens with a light vanilla nose, going on to show lightly tart with appealing notes of summer fruits, citrus peel and bitter almonds, all on a background of stony minerals. Drink now. Score 90.

GESHEM, BLANC, 2008: Light golden straw in color, a medium-bodied and nicely aromatic blend of Viognier, Grenache Blanc and Roussanne (58%, 37% and 5% respectively). A distinctly Mediterranean blend, opening with an appealing floral nose and then going on to show apple, nectarine and quince fruits, with a tantalizing hint of spiciness on the long finish. Drink now. Score 91.

Chemla ✶✶✶

CHEMLA, CABERNET SAUVIGNON, RESERVE, 2008: Medium- to full-bodied, reflecting 14 months of aging in French oak with soft, gently gripping tannins and notes of spicy wood. Opens to an appealing array of blackberry, wild berry and cassis fruits, those complemented by hints of roasted herbs. Drink now–2013. Score 88.

CHEMLA, MERLOT, RESERVE, 2008: Dark cherry red toward garnet, reflecting its oak-aging in American oak for 14 months with soft, near-sweet tannins and a note of vanilla. Medium-bodied, opens with a bit of bottle stink but that blows off quickly to reveal an array of red fruits, those set on a lightly spicy background. On the moderately long finish an appealing note of green olives. Drink now. Score 88.

CHEMLA, CABERNET SAUVIGNON-SHIRAZ-PETIT VERDOT, RE-SERVE, 2008: An increasingly popular "Bordeaux-Australia" blend, this one oak-aged for ten months in French oak and showing medium- to full-bodied. Generous but soft tannins and sweet cedarwood part comfortably to make way for aromas and flavors of plums, blueberries and dark chocolate. Drink now. Score 87.

CHEMLA, MERLOT-SHIRAZ-PETIT VERDOT, 2008: Developed for ten months partly in French and partly in American oak, medium-bodied, soft and round. Shows currant and blackberry fruits on a background that hints simultaneously of bell peppers and earthy-minerals. Drink now. Score 85.

Chillag ✦✦✦✦

After studying oenology in Piacenza, Italy, and working at the Antinori wineries in Tuscany, Orna Chillag released her first wines in Israel in 1998. Now located in a new facility in the industrial area of the town of Yahud, on the central plain, the winery relies on Merlot and Cabernet Sauvignon grapes from the Upper Galilee and the Judean Mountains and recently planted its own Syrah, Petit Verdot and Petite Sirah. Production has grown from 4,000 bottles in 2002 to current releases of about 20,000 bottles annually. Until 2005 the winery released wines in two series, Primo Riserva and Giovane. More recently the wines have been appearing in Primo, Solo and Vivo series, the first two meant for cellaring and the third released early and meant for drinking in their youth.

Primo and Primo Riserva

PRIMO, CABERNET SAUVIGNON, UPPER GALILEE, 2009: Even at this early stage showing fine concentration and balance. Medium- to full-bodied (leaning toward the full), opens with red plums and raspberries, those going on to blackcurrant and blackberries, those on a background of cigar tobacco. On the long finish, notes of bittersweet chocolate and licorice. Best from 2013. Tentative Score 89–91.

PRIMO, CABERNET SAUVIGNON, UPPER GALILEE, 2008: Perhaps Chillag's best to date. Full-bodied, with dense ripe fruits and gripping but almost velvety tannins coming together in fine balance and structure. On the nose and palate opens with sweet raspberries and strawberries, those yielding to blackberry and currant notes. Calls to mind fine Brunello di Montalcino. Destined for length, breadth and elegance. Drink now–2016. Tentative Score 92.

PRIMO, CABERNET SAUVIGNON, 2007: Deep garnet in color, full-bodied, with silky-smooth tannins and gentle hint of sweet and spicy cedarwood. On the nose and palate berry and chocolate notes following through to show mineral and floral hints. Round, long and generous. Drink now–2016. Score 90.

PRIMO, CABERNET SAUVIGNON, UPPER GALILEE, 2005: Blended with 10% Merlot, reflecting its 22 months in French oak with generous but judicious spicy wood in fine balance with soft tannins and opening to show a tempting array of blackberries, currants and Oriental spices, all leading to a rich, long and blueberry-laden finish. Drink now. Score 91.

PRIMO, CABERNET SAUVIGNON, 2004: Impenetrably dark garnet, picking up a note of adobe brick in its color as perhaps the first signs of maturity. Opens quietly but then blossoms in the glass to reveal a full-bodied blend of 90% Cabernet Sauvignon and 10% Merlot, those with smoky cedarwood on the nose, soft tannins and an appealing array of currants, blackberries and raspberries. From mid-palate on notes of bittersweet chocolate and on the long finish an appealing note of licorice. Maturing but still drinking very nicely indeed. Drink now. Score 91.

PRIMO RISERVA, MERLOT, 2005: Supple and round with fine structure, Chillag's best to date. Blended with 10% of Cabernet Sauvignon, aged for 22 months in French *barriques*, showing dark garnet in color. Full-bodied with tannins integrating nicely with spicy wood, fresh acidity and generous fruits. On the nose and palate black cherries, plums, toasty oak and roasted coffee, finishing with plum and lead-pencil notes. Drink now. Score 92.

PRIMO RISERVA, MERLOT, 2004: Medium- to full-bodied, with now-soft, round tannins, minerals and generous toasty oak reflecting the 21 months the wine spent in *barriques*. Comes together to show appealing blueberries, blackberries and mineral aromas and flavors that linger comfortably. Drink up. Score 89.

PRIMO, SYRAH, 2009: Super-dark garnet, remarkably concentrated, intense and dense but already showing fine balance and structure that bode well for the future. Full-bodied, with ample but gently gripping tannins, opens to reveal a generous array of plums, blackberries and leathery notes, all with an overlay of Mediterranean herbs. Drink from release. Tentative Score 89–91.

PRIMO, CARIGNAN, 2009: Still in embryonic form but already showing dark royal purple in color and with fine concentration. Made from old-vine grapes (25 years), medium- to full-bodied, with soft tannins parting comfortably to reveal notes of spicy oak, blackberries and citrus peel, all on a tantalizing background of mesquite. Possibly to be released as a varietal wine, possibly to be used as a blending agent. Drink from release. Tentative Score 90–92.

PRIMO, BLEND, 2007: A dark-garnet, full-bodied blend of 50% Cabernet Sauvignon, 30% Syrah and 20% Merlot, reflecting its 26 months in French oak with generous tannins, those gripping when the wine is first poured but becoming soft and caressing in the glass. On first attack red fruits and a note of licorice, those parting to make way for currants, red and black berries and a note of bitter citrus peel. Tannins and fruits rise comfortably on the long and generous finish. Drink now–2016. Score 91.

Solo

SOLO, CABERNET SAUVIGNON, UPPER GALILEE, 2006: Reflecting its 18 months in French *barriques* with notes of oriental spices and sweet cedarwood, opens to reveal generous currant, blackberry and herbal notes. Mouth-filling and generous. Drink now–2013. Score 89.

SOLO, CABERNET SAUVIGNON, UPPER GALILEE, 2005: Medium- to full-bodied (leaning toward the full), a blend of 90% Cabernet Sauvignon and 10% Merlot. Aged in new and one-year-old French *barriques* for 18 months and showing a distinct Tuscan flair. Dark garnet, with soft tannins and an appealing array of wild berries and currants on a spicy background. Lingers nicely on the palate. Drink now. Score 90.

SOLO, MERLOT, JUDEAN MOUNTAINS, 2006: Oak-aged in French *barriques* for 18 months and blended with 10% Cabernet Sauvignon. Medium- to full-bodied, with gently gripping tannins, opens with a floral and licorice nose, goes on to reveal generous black and red fruits, all complemented nicely by notes of spicy wood. Lingers nicely on the palate. Drink now–2013. Score 89.

SOLO, MERLOT, JUDEAN MOUNTAINS, 2005: Deep garnet toward royal purple, a full-bodied blend of 90% Merlot and 10% Cabernet Sauvignon. Developed in French oak for 18 months, showing generously spicy wood, that in fine balance with mouth-coating tannins and fruits. On the nose and palate ripe plums, wild berries, a hint of cherry liqueur, and, on the long finish, a generous touch of bittersweet chocolate. Drink now. Score 90.

Vivo

VIVO, CABERNET SAUVIGNON, KEREM BEN ZIMRA, 2007: Dark garnet, full-bodied reflecting its 18 months in French *barriques* with gently gripping tannins and notes of oriental spices and sweet cedarwood, opens to reveal generous currant, blackberry and herbal notes. Mouth-filling and generous. Drink now–2014. Score 89.

VIVO, MERLOT, 2007: Dark cherry red toward garnet, a full-bodied blend of 85% Merlot, 10% Cabernet Sauvignon and 5% Syrah. Reflecting its 14 months in *barriques* with soft tannins and tantalizing hints of spicy cedarwood, opens in the glass to reveal red currant and raspberry fruits on a background of Mediterranean herbs and Madagascar green peppercorns. Long and generous. Drink now–2015. Score 89.

VIVO, MERLOT, JUDEAN MOUNTAINS, 2006: Super-dark garnet in color, reflecting its 12 months in new and one-year-old French *barriques*, with gently spicy cedar notes and opening to reveal purple plums, wild berries and notes of spices on the moderately long finish. Mouth-filling and generous. Drink now. Score 89.

VIVO, SYRAH, 2007: Blended with 10% Cabernet Sauvignon and 5% Merlot, reflecting its 19 months in oak with soft tannins and tantalizing hints of spicy cedarwood and licorice. On the nose and palate a generous array of plums, currants and blackberries, those on a background of freshly tanned leather and, on the long finish, an appealing note of bitter herbs. Drink now–2015. Score 90.

VIVO, BLEND, 2007: Cabernet Sauvignon, Merlot and Syrah come together in a distinctly Mediterranean wine. Oak-aged for 14 months, showing dark garnet, medium- to full-bodied with gently caressing tannins, opens in the glass to reveal blackcurrants, plums and huckleberries, those supported nicely by notes of exotic spices. A bit poetic for a tasting note, I know, but you will feel sunshine in this wine. Drink now–2015. Score 80.

VIVO, BLEND, JUDEAN MOUNTAINS, 2006: A garnet toward royal purple, medium- to full-bodied blend of 55% Cabernet Sauvignon and 22.5% each of Merlot and Syrah. Oak-aged for 12 months, opens to reveal purple plums, raspberries and notes of milk chocolate and espresso coffee. Drink now. Score 89.

Giovane

GIOVANE, CABERNET SAUVIGNON, 2007: Dark garnet toward royal purple, medium- to full-bodied, with soft tannins and a note of spicy oak integrating nicely with currant, wild berry, cigar tobacco and chocolate notes. Drink now–2014. Score 88.

GIOVANE, MERLOT, 2006: A blend of 86% Merlot, 12% Cabernet Sauvignon and 2% Petite Sirah. Developed for ten months in French *barriques*, showing medium- to full-bodied with soft, gently mouth-coating tannins and opening to reveal plum and blackberry fruits, those highlighted by notes of sweet toast, vanilla and minerals. Drink now. Score 89.

GIOVANE, CABERNET SAUVIGNON-PETITE SIRAH, 2005: A blend of equal parts Cabernet Sauvignon and Petite Sirah. Oak-aged for 20 months, showing medium- to full-bodied and with still-firm, near-sweet tannins, those just starting to settle down and opening to reveal generous black fruits, on a light background that hints nicely of licorice and bitter almonds. Easy to drink but with just enough complexity to grab and hold our interest. Drink up. Score 90.

Chillag

CHILLAG, CABERNET SAUVIGNON, LATE HARVEST, 2009: Fascinating! Made by blending together Cabernet Sauvignon harvested in the usual manner with 25% of late-harvest Cabernet and 25% of grapes that were allowed to dry before being vinified. Relying in part on winemaking practices in Valpolicella and in Tuscany, but a distinctly Mediterranean wine. Richly aromatic, showing raisins, earth, black olives and dried herbs on the nose, deeply tannic and with flavors of chocolate running through, opens to reveal spicy red and black fruits. Long, round, mouth-filling and irresistible even now. Drink from release. Tentative Score 90–92.

CHILLAG, PETITE SIRAH, 2006: From a vineyard in the Jerusalem Mountains at 750 meters above sea level, Petite Sirah as Petite Sirah should be. Oak-aged for 24 months, almost impenetrably dark garnet in color, dense and concentrated, opening with lavender and peppery notes, those yielding to chocolate and licorice and only then black cherry, blackberry, cassis and plum flavors. In the background look for tobacco and toasty oak and, on the long, chewy finish, a note of espresso coffee. Unfiltered, so do not be surprised if you find a bit of sediment here, that doing no harm whatever to this muscular but oh-so-enchanting wine. Drink now–2016. Score 92.

SEA HORSE-CHILLAG, 60–60, 2008: A cooperative venture, between two wineries, Sea Horse and Chillag. When asked to suggest a name for this cooperative effort, Orna Chillag suggested "60–60," saying that "after all it was an effort half of one winery, half of the other." Chillag may not be very good on calculating percentages but between her efforts and those of Dunie, a quite successful collaboration. Based on 50% Cabernet Sauvignon supplied by Chillag, 45% Mourvedre and 5% of Syrah from Dunie, a super-dark garnet, full-bodied, generously tannic and spicy, wood-rich wine. Showing generous black fruits, purple plums and blueberries on a background of olives and notes of licorice. Long and mouth-filling. Drink now–2014. Score 90.

Chotem HaCarmel ✶✶

Founded in 2005 by Eli Sidi and set in the Moshava of Bin-yamina. Current production is about 3,000 bottles annually, the winery drawing on Merlot, Cabernet Sauvignon, Shiraz and Petite Sirah grapes from their own vineyards.

CHOTEM HACARMEL, CABERNET SAUVIGNON, 2006: Light ruby toward garnet, medium-bodied, with near-sweet tannins integrating nicely and showing a primarily blackberry-black cherry personality. Light enough on the palate that one might take it for wine made from Gamay grapes. Easy to drink. Drink now. Score 84.

CHOTEM HACARMEL, CABERNET SAUVIGNON, 2005: Light garnet, medium- to full-bodied, with gently gripping tannins and notes of sweet and spicy oak parting to reveal currant and blackberry fruits on a lightly spicy background. Drink up. Score 85.

CHOTEM HACARMEL, MERLOT, 2006: Light garnet in color, medium-bodied, with softly caressing tannins, and forward raspberry, cherry and plum fruits. Nothing complex here but a pleasant quaffing wine. Drink now. Score 84.

CHOTEM HACARMEL, SHIRAZ, 2006: Medium-bodied, with soft tannins and crisp acidity to highlight strawberry and dried berry aromas and flavors, those with a few hints of Mediterranean herbs. A good entry-level quaffer. Drink now. Score 84

CHOTEM HACARMEL, PETITE SIRAH, 2005: Dark garnet, medium- to full-bodied, with light tannins and spicy wood. Opens with a somewhat musky aroma but that blows off quickly enough to show an interesting array of red and black fruits. Marred a bit by a somewhat muddy note that comes in on the finish. Drink up. Score 82.

Clos de Gat ★★★★★

Located on Kibbutz Har'el in the Jerusalem Mountains, this joint project of the kibbutz and Australian-trained wine-maker Eyal Rotem released its first wines from the 2001 vintage. The name "Clos de Gat" is a play on words – the French *clos* is an enclosed vineyard surrounded by stone walls or windbreaks, while the Hebrew *gat* is an antique wine press. Grapes come from the winery's own vineyards, which now include Cabernet, Merlot, Petit Verdot, Syrah and Chardonnay. Production is currently about 50,000 bottles annually.

The winery releases wines in three series, Sycra (Aramaic for "bright red"), the Bordeaux-blend Clos de Gat, and Har'el. From the 2003 vintage, the wines have been made with wild yeasts.

Sycra

SYCRA, MERLOT, 2006: Full-bodied, reflecting its 20 months in new oak with generous spicy wood and equally generous but softly mouth-coating tannins, those in fine balance with fruits and acidity. Opens with currant, purple plum and mocha notes, those yielding to blackberry, citrus peel and light herbal and tobacco overtones. Drink now–2014. Score 93.

SYCRA, MERLOT, 2003: With 24 months in wood and a generous 15% alcohol content, this super-dark garnet-colored wine is full-bodied enough to be chewy and shows tannins that, although gripping, seem soft and comforting. On the nose and palate touches of spice and freshly turned earth supporting currant, blackberry and floral notes, all leading to a finish that goes on and on. Drink now–2013. Score 93.

SYCRA, SYRAH, 2007: Super-dark garnet toward royal purple, full-bodied and reflecting its 14 months in French oak *barriques* with abundant but gently mouth-coating tannins and notes of cinnamon and vanilla on the palate. Deeply aromatic, opens to reveal generous raspberries and red currants on the first attack, those yielding comfortably to plums, notes of saddle leather and a hint of green tobacco on the remarkably long finish. Caressing and elegant. Drink now–2018. Score 94.

SYCRA, SYRAH, 2006: An opulent wine, almost impenetrably deep garnet in color, full-bodied, with silky-smooth tannins that caress gently and opening in the glass to reveal aromas and flavors of wild berries, grilled meat and spices, those leading to a fruit-rich finish on which you will find tempting chocolate and vanilla undertones. Long, round and generous. If this one does not make you fall in love you're a hard-hearted wine lover indeed. One of the best wines ever from Israel. Approachable and enjoyable now but best from 2013–2019, perhaps longer. Score 95.

SYCRA, SYRAH, 2004: Oak-aged for 20 months. Full-bodied, with oak that at one moment seems spicy and at the next smoky but never dominating; with firm tannins integrating nicely now. A dense, almost muscular wine, but one that sits gently and opens to show a tempting array of cherry, berry and currant fruits, those on a just-spicy-enough background to highlight hints of freshly roasted coffee. Well focused, intense and long. Drink now–2014. Score 93.

Clos de Gat

CLOS DE GAT, AYALON VALLEY, 2007: As always, a Bordeaux blend of Cabernet Sauvignon, Merlot and Petit Verdot (60%, 30% and 10% respectively), showing full-bodied and reflecting its 18 months in new oak with gentle influences of spicy oak and abundant but soft, gently caressing tannins. Impenetrably dark garnet in color, showing black fruits on the nose, opening in the glass to reveal currant and blackberry fruits and, from mid-palate on, hints of blueberries. Long and generous with tannins rising together with the fruits on the finish. Approachable now but best 2013–2019. Score 94.

CLOS DE GAT, AYALON VALLEY, 2006: A Bordeaux blend of Cabernet Sauvignon, Merlot and Petit Verdot, and showing a clear kinship to the releases of 2004 and 2005. Full-bodied, with generous but soft and gently gripping tannins, notes of spices and a hint of smoke from the wood in which it aged. On first attack blackcurrants and blackberries, those yielding to blueberries and clear notes of espresso coffee. On the long finish, tannins rise together with notes of red licorice. Intense, complex and worthy of cellaring. Drink now–2018. Score 94.

CLOS DE GAT, AYALON VALLEY, 2005: A Bordeaux blend of Cabernet Sauvignon, Merlot and Petit Verdot (63%, 30% and 7%), given a distinct Mediterranean note by touches of black olives and mint. Dark garnet, opens with a sweet red nose, that overlaid with notes of spicy cedarwood. Showing soft, mouth-coating tannins that go on to reveal currant, blackberries and notes of slate. On the long and generous finish, look for notes of raspberries and mocha. Drink now–2014. Score 93.

CLOS DE GAT, AYALON VALLEY, 2004: Dark, full-bodied, firmly tannic, with generous spicy wood, this blend of 65% Cabernet Sauvignon, 30% Merlot and 5% Petit Verdot shows fine harmony but still needs time to integrate. The wine opens to reveal currant, blackberry, spicy oak and hints of licorice and light earthiness. Drink now. Score 93.

CLOS DE GAT, 2003: Predominantly Cabernet Sauvignon, fleshed out with Merlot and Petit Verdot. Dark garnet, medium- to full-bodied, with firm tannins integrating nicely, this elegant wine shows blackcurrant, black cherry and berry fruits, those supported well by hints of vanilla and licorice, all leading to a long spicy finish. Drink now. Score 92.

CLOS DE GAT, 2002: With generous but soft tannins, this dark red toward black, medium- to full-bodied blend of 70% Cabernet Sauvignon and 30% Merlot reflects its 18 months in oak with spicy but not exaggerated wood. On the nose and palate ripe currants and plums matched nicely by hints of coffee, sweet cedar, vanilla and Mediterranean herbs. Drink up. Score 90.

CLOS DE GAT, CABERNET SAUVIGNON-MERLOT, AYALON VALLEY, 2001: A deep ruby-garnet, full-bodied unfiltered blend of 70% Cabernet Sauvignon and 30% Merlot, with generous, soft tannins that integrate beautifully, a wine that can honestly be said to reflect its *terroir*. Overlaying traditional Cabernet blackcurrants are generous hints of green olives, basil, tarragon and other Mediterranean herbs. The wine shows good balance and structure, with chocolate and leather coming in on the long finish. Maturing nicely. Drink up. Score 90.

CLOS DE GAT, CHANSON ROUGE, 2010: The winery's first release of a red Chanson and quite a happy success. A blend about 63% Merlot, 30% Syrah and 7% Mourvedre, oak-aged for three months in well-used barrels to give the wine just a kiss of sweet and spicy oak. On the nose berries and cherries, opening in the glass to reveal medium-bodied, with soft tannins and fresh raspberry, cherry and cassis flavors, those complemented nicely by a light note of milk chocolate. An ideal match to the Chanson Blanc and like that, with an easy-going complexity. Drink now–2013. Score 90.

CLOS DE GAT, CHARDONNAY, 2009: As is the wont of the wine-maker, fermented entirely on wild yeasts, developed in French oak for 12 months, deep gold with a distinct green tint. Deeply aromatic, the opening nose replete with lime and tangerines, showing fabulous depth of aromas and flavors that blossom in the glass as the wine opens. Round and almost thick, full-bodied but with plenty of fine acidity. On first attack, navel oranges and summer fruits, those parting to make way for notes of fresh figs, spices and gently subdued oak, all in fine balance and all lingering on a super-long and near creamy finish. If this one does not call to mind a fine Burgundian Montrachet, nothing will. Drink now–2016. Score 94.

CLOS DE GAT, CHARDONNAY, 2008: Made entirely from Chardonnay grapes, fermented on wild yeasts and with no battonage in French oak *barriques* in which the wine developed for 12 months. Full-bodied, rich, complex and opulent, with fig, citrus and melon fruits, those on a background of minerals and butterscotch. Deep gold in color, and on the long finish rising notes of kumquats and minerals. Drink now–2014. Score 93.

CLOS DE GAT, CHARDONNAY, 2007: Deep bright gold in color, full-bodied, reflecting its 12 months *sur lie* in oak with no *battonage*, with a near-creamy texture, opening with delicate honeyed green apple and pear notes, those concentrated and well focused and showing fine balance with just enough acidity to keep the wine fresh. Closes with an earthy-mineral overlay that lingers nicely. Generous, mouth-filling and almost extravagant. Drink now–2015. Score 93.

CLOS DE GAT, CHARDONNAY, 2006: Developed *sur lie* for 12 months in French oak, wisely using only 25% of new oak before the final blend was made, and thus showing a light, almost tantalizing hint of the wood. Medium- to full-bodied, with fine balance between wood, acidity and fruits. Opens with citrus, citrus flowers and citrus rind, those yielding to hints of melon and spiced apples all lingering long and comfortably on the finish. Hedonistic, elegant and complex. Drink now. Score 92.

CLOS DE GAT, CHARDONNAY, 2005: Dark gold, full-bodied, but so well balanced that it floats on the palate. Reflects its year in oak with generous spicy wood that turns creamy on the palate and with citrus and green apple notes that develop into peaches, apricots, ginger and lightly chalky-mineral notes that linger comfortably through the long finish. Drink up. Score 92.

CLOS DE GAT, CHARDONNAY, 2004: Deep but lively gold, full-bodied, simultaneously floral and creamy, with fine balancing acidity to show off citrus, pear, green apples and, on the long finish, hints of figs and ginger. Long, generous and mouth-filling. Sliding past its peak. Drink up. Score 92.

CLOS DE GAT, CHANSON BLANC, 2010: Bright, shining gold in color, an unoaked bend of 65% Chardonnay, 20% Semillon and the remainder of Viognier and Chenin Blanc. Medium-bodied, with notes of citrus and white peaches, opening in the glass to show tantalizing hints of tropical fruits and minerals. As in the past, a mouth-filling wine that is simultaneously easy to drink and possessed of just enough complexity to grab the attention. Drink now–2013. Score 90.

CLOS DE GAT, CHANSON, 2009: The usual well-tempered blend for this wine of Chardonnay, Semillon, Viognier and Chenin Blanc (this year in proportions of 65%, 25%, 7% and 3% respectively). Unoaked and not subjected to malolactic fermentation, deep gold in color, with medium- to full-body, finely tuned balancing acidity. On first attack fresh apricots, those yielding nicely to notes of citrus and minerals and, on the long finish, a hint of guava. Simultaneously easy to drink and complex. Drink now–2013. Score 91.

CLOS DE GAT, CHANSON BLANC, 2008: Showing light gold in color, medium-bodied, with crisp acidity to highlight citrus, pear and melon fruits. A blend of Chardonnay, Semillon, Viognier and Chenin Blanc, with generous mineral overtones. Refreshing and with just enough complexities. Drink now. Score 90.

CLOS DE GAT, CHANSON, 2007: A well-crafted unoaked blend of Chardonnay, Semillon, Viognier and Chenin Blanc (about 75%, 15%, 7% and 3% respectively). Pale gold in color with orange reflections, medium-bodied, opening with minerals and citrus fruits, those opening in the glass to reveal passion fruits and ripe melon. Long, lively and thought-provoking. Drink up. Score 91.

CLOS DE GAT, WHITE DESSERT WINE, 2006: A deep, youthful gold toward orange blend of 75% Muscat Alexandroni and 25% Viognier, those aged in well-tempered barrels (those previously used for Chardonnay) and reinforced with grape alcohol to a 16% alcohol content. Generously sweet, but with fine balancing acidity, opens with notes of citrus peel, goes on to reveal honeyed peach and apricot notes and then, surprisingly, to tropical fruits, all coming together as a well-structured and coherent whole. Long and generous. One of the very best dessert wines made in Israel and certainly the one destined for the longest cellaring ability. Drink now–2040, perhaps longer. Score 95.

Har'el

HAR'EL, CABERNET SAUVIGNON, 2009: Blended with small amounts of Merlot and Petit Verdot, showing medium- to full-bodied, reflecting its 12 months in oak with a tempting note of fresh hardwood sawdust on the nose, that matched nicely by notes of crushed berries. On the palate blackcurrant, blackberry and black cherry fruits, those going on to reveal a clear flavor of raspberries, all matched by notes of what at one moment seems to be mocha and the next espresso coffee. Round and long with soft, gently caressing tannins that rise on the finish. Drink now–2017. Score 92.

HAR'EL, CABERNET SAUVIGNON, 2008: Deep, dark and intensely tannic, a rich, full-bodied red showing fine balance and structure, reflecting its 12 months in *barriques* with spicy and vanilla-tinged oak and still-firm tannins yielding to highlight well-focused blackberry, blackcurrant and black cherry fruits. On the long finish, with chewy tannins rising, tempting notes of licorice, mint and bitter almonds. Drink now–2017. Score 94.

HAR'EL, CABERNET SAUVIGNON, 2007: A blend of 87% Cabernet Sauvignon, 9% Merlot and 4% Petit Verdot. Deep garnet in color, medium- to full-bodied (leaning toward the full) and firmly tannic, opens with an unusual but very appealing light musky note and then goes on to well-focused red currants and cherries, those supported nicely by notes of freshly turned earth and Mediterranean herbs. Supple, rich and deep, with a finish that goes on seemingly without end. Drink now–2016. Score 92.

HAR'EL, CABERNET SAUVIGNON, 2006: Dark, almost inky-garnet in color, full-bodied, with tannins that are firm on first attack but yield nicely in the glass to reveal fine balance with a genteel hand, with spicy oak, good balancing acidity and fruits. Blended, Bordeaux style, with 9% Merlot and 4% Petit Verdot. On the nose and palate opens with raspberries, those then going to purple plums, blackberries and currants, all intertwined with a pleasing overlay of Mediterranean herbaceousness. Well crafted. Drink now. Score 91.

HAR'EL, CABERNET SAUVIGNON, 2005: Blended with 8% of Merlot and 3% of Petit Verdot and aged in oak for 12 months, this deep garnet toward royal purple, full-bodied red shows generous, fine-grained tannins that highlight lightly spicy wood and generous red currant and black cherry fruits. On the moderately long finish, an appealing mineral streak. Drink now. Score 90.

HAR'EL, CABERNET SAUVIGNON, 2004: Full-bodied and firmly tannic, reflecting its 12 months in oak with spicy wood which yields in the glass to reveal currants, black cherries and purple plums, those supported nicely by hints of chocolate and cigar tobacco. Fine balance and structure. Drink now. Score 90.

HAR'EL, MERLOT, 2009: Dark garnet toward royal purple, a concentrated and intense wine that shows layer after layer of complexity. On first attack, black fruits and wild berries, those parting to make way for red currants and cherries all on a background of freshly picked herbs. On the long finish notes of mocha and Oriental spices. Drink now–2016. Score 92.

HAR'EL, MERLOT, 2008: An intense wine, as far as you can get from the "internationalized Merlot" that has become so ubiquitous. Deep, almost impenetrable garnet, full-bodied, with still-firm tannins and spicy wood reflecting its youth, those in fine balance with fruits and natural acidity and showing fine qualities for cellaring. On first attack blackberries and black cherries, those yielding to clear notes of white chocolate, mint and spices, all lingering through to a long and generous finish. Remarkably rich. Drink now–2018. Score 94.

HAR'EL, MERLOT, 2007: Royal purple toward black, muscular, with bold tannins and spicy oak integrating nicely. Made entirely from Merlot grapes, aged in *barriques* for 14 months. On first attack near-sweet plum and cocoa aromas and flavors, those yielding to notes of currant jam and licorice. A solid finish on which arise notes of citrus peel. Drink now–2015. Score 92.

HAR'EL, MERLOT, 2005: Deep and dark, full-bodied, with still-gripping tannins integrating well and with generous spicy wood all coming together to show round and generous. Deeply aromatic, opens to reveal aromas and flavors of red currants, raspberries and chocolate, those yielding later to generous hints of chocolate and toasted rye bread. On the long, intense finish look for hints of minerals and licorice. Drink now. Score 92.

HAR'EL, MERLOT, 2004: Deep and dark, opening with a chocolate-rich nose and firm tannins, those opening to show near-sweet oak and generous currants, plums and berries. A long, mouth-filling and deeply aromatic finish that picks up notes of smoke. Drink up. Score 90.

HAR'EL, MERLOT, 2003: A dense, muscular wine showing deep, dark and absolutely beautiful. Complex oak-accented blackberry, currant and black cherry aromas and flavors on a background of chewy tannins, sweet cedar and hints of pepper and vanilla, all of which linger beautifully. Drink now. Score 92.

HAR'EL, SYRAH, 2009: Dark royal purple, reflecting its 14 months in *barriques* with still-gripping tannins and notes of spicy cedarwood on the nose, opening slowly in the glass to show black and red currants, dried berries, those matched by notes of sage and graphite. Firm and mineral-rich, needing time for its elements to come fully together and show its well-focused complexity. Dense and chewy at this stage but destined to be an alluring and elegant wine. Drink now–2019. Score 93.

HAR'EL, SYRAH, 2008: Blended with 15% Cabernet Sauvignon and developed for 15 months in *barriques*, showing super-dark garnet toward royal purple. Full-bodied, with generous but softly caressing tannins making the wine more than approachable despite its youth. Opens to show blackcurrant and blueberry fruits, those parting to make way for blackberries and black cherries with gentle hints of black pepper and grilled meat rising on the remarkably long finish. Drink now–2017. Score 93.

HAR'EL, SYRAH, 2007: Dark, almost impenetrable royal purple, full-bodied, with generous soft tannins integrating nicely. Blended with 15% of Cabernet Sauvignon and oak-aged for 16 months, a generously spicy wine opening to show wild berry, plum and black cherry fruits, those going on to reveal notes of sage, minerals and dark chocolate. Deep and complex, with a long finish on which tannins, red cherries and floral notes make themselves comfortably felt. Drink now–2016. Score 93.

HAR'EL, SYRAH, 2006: Dark garnet toward royal purple, blended with 15% of Cabernet Sauvignon and oak-aged for 15 months (about ⅓ new oak). Full-bodied, with soft, gently mouth-coating tannins and fine balance and structure. Opens slowly in the glass at this stage but when it does, it does so with gusto, showing plum, red berry and cassis fruits, those on a generous but well-proportioned spicy background. Long, round and elegant. Drink now–2013, perhaps longer. Score 93.

HAR'EL, SYRAH, 2005: Oak-aged for 16 months and blended with 7% Cabernet Sauvignon, this dark royal purple, deeply aromatic, mouth-filling and lush red shows medium- to full-bodied, and boasts tannins that are soft but comfortably gripping. A generous array of plum, cherry and berry fruits, those backed up by juniper and white pepper. On the nose near-sweet black fruits and on the long finish hints of leather and citrus peel. Drink now–2014. Score 93.

HAR'EL, SYRAH, 2004: Dark, almost impenetrable garnet, this medium- to full-bodied blend of 85% Syrah and 15% Cabernet Sauvignon shows soft, round tannins and, on the nose and palate, a generous array of plum, blueberry and blackberry, those complemented by spices and appealing hints of fresh herbs and toffee. Drink now. Score 92.

HAR'EL, SYRAH, 2003: Medium-dark garnet, this blend of 85% Syrah and 15% Cabernet Sauvignon shows generous peppery overtones. Medium- to full-bodied, with firm but nicely integrating tannins and complex plum, red berry and earthy aromas and flavors, all with a hint of leather on the finish. Drink now–2013. Score 92.

Dadah ✶✶

Founded by Jackie Hazan and Nechemia Katabi after the harvest of 2007, this boutique winery is located on the Makura Ranch on the western slopes of Mount Carmel. The winery currently produces about 12,000 bottles annually, those primarily from Cabernet Sauvignon, Merlot, Shiraz, Malbec and Barbera grapes.

DADAH, CABERNET SAUVIGNON, 2008: Dark garnet, medium- to full-bodied, showing almost stinging tannins and a medicinal aroma from first to last sip, that hiding the black fruits that never quite make themselves felt. A somewhat coarse country-style wine. Drink up. Score 78.

DADAH, CABERNET SAUVIGNON-SHIRAZ, 2007: Garnet toward royal purple, medium- to full-bodied, with soft tannins, a blend of 60% Cabernet Sauvignon and 40% Merlot, those oak-aged in French *barriques* for 14 months. Round and gentle, with red currants and wild berries on the nose and palate, the tannins rising on a spicy finish. Drink now. Score 88.

DADAH, MERLOT-SHIRAZ, 2007: Dark garnet, medium-bodied, reflecting its 14 months in French oak with lightly chunky but caressing tannins and notes of vanilla and showing primarily red fruits with an appealing herbal overlay. Not a complex wine but a pleasant one. Drink now. Score 85.

DADAH, MALBEC-BARBERA, 2008: Dark ruby toward garnet, with soft, almost unfelt tannins, spicy oak and a hint of volatile acidity hiding the black fruits that try to make themselves felt here. Drink up. Score 82.

DADAH, MALBEC-BARBERA, 2007: Medium-dark garnet in color, a gently tannic and richly acidic blend of 50% each of Malbec and Barbera. Oak-aged for 14 months, showing red and black cherries and wild berries on the nose and palate, those complemented nicely by earthy minerals and spices. Appealing. Drink now. Score 84.

Dalton ✦✦✦✦

Founded by the Haruni family in 1993, this fully modern winery located in the industrial park of Dalton in the Upper Galilee has vineyards in Kerem Ben Zimra and several high-altitude sites along the Lebanese border. New vineyards are also being developed. Australian- and Californian-trained winemaker Na'ama Sorkin is currently producing wines in seven series, the age-worthy Single Vineyard, Reserve, Dalton Estate and Safsufa Vineyards wines, as well as the Alma, Dalton and Canaan series, those of similar varieties but which are intended for early drinking. With the 2006 vintage, a wine under the Matatia label was released, that destined to become the winery's flagship wine and to be released only in vintage years determined appropriate by the winemaker.

Grapes under cultivation include Cabernet Sauvignon, Merlot, Shiraz, Barbera, Zinfandel, Chardonnay, Sauvignon Blanc, Viognier and Muscat. First production was 50,000 bottles, and current production is about 850,000 bottles annually. Dalton has earned a consistently good name for high-quality wines, providing excellent value for money. Among major developments in recent years has been the expansion of the Alma series, now containing a white blend, a Bordeaux blend and a Rhone blend.

Matatia

MATATIA, 2008: A full-bodied blend of 71% Cabernet Sauvignon, 28% Merlot and 1% Cabernet Franc. Generously mouth-filling and concentrated, keeps its muscles nicely in check in order to show its elegance. On the nose and palate blackberries, espresso and licorice notes and, from mid-palate on, notes of tobacco and graphite, all of the elements coming together as a coherent and generous whole. "Classy." Drink now–2016, perhaps longer. Score 92. K

MATATIA, 2006: A Bordeaux blend of 80% Cabernet Sauvignon, 15% Merlot and 5% Cabernet Franc. Developed in new French oak, showing deep and dark but not at all mysterious. On first attack aromas of mint, tar and a hint of iodine, those remarkably and perhaps surprisingly pleasing. Yields in the glass to reveal generous blackberry, blackcurrant and bitter-orange-peel notes, and finally, on the long finish, hints of espresso coffee. With fine balance between wood, acidity, tannins and fruits, a thought-provoking and delicious wine. Produced in a limited edition of 6,000 bottles. If I had to find a single word to describe the wine, that word would be "scrumptious." Drink now–2014. Score 93. K

Single Vineyard

/6500

DALTON

CABERNET SAUVIGNON

MERON VINEYARD

FOR MANY YEARS NOW, THE MERON VINEYARD HAS CONSISTENTLY PRODUCED WINE OF SINGULAR
AND OUTSTANDING CHARACTER. THE WINE IS SO RICH WITH EUCALYPTUS, CASSIS AND MINT CHARACTERS
THAT, THIS YEAR, IT HAS MERITED ITS OWN BOTTLING. *Alex Haruni*

קברנה סוביניון כרם מירון
2004

SINGLE VINEYARD, CABERNET SAUVIGNON, MERON, 2008: Medium- to full-bodied, rich and intense but not heavy, showing ripe currants and blackberries, those on a background that hints of sandalwood and cedar and ends with a note of anise. Drink now–2015, perhaps longer. Score 91. K

SINGLE VINEYARD, CABERNET SAUVIGNON, MERON, 2004: Developing beautifully. Dark ruby toward garnet, medium- to full-bodied, this well-balanced wine was aged in French oak for eight months and then bottled without filtration. Generous soft tannins and ample wood, those integrated nicely and revealing an appealing array of red currant, raspberry and citrus peel on a peppery, lightly herbal, minty background. Round, long and mouth-filling with a hint of earthy minerals on the long finish. Drink now. Score 92. K

SINGLE VINEYARD, MERLOT, MERON, 2005: Supple, rich and generous. Aged in oak for 16 months, with soft, near-sweet, mouth-coating tannins and fine balancing acidity to add liveliness to the blueberry and currant fruits. Hints of spices and mint run through to the long finish. Ripe, round and polished. Drink now. Score 91. K

Reserve

RESERVE, CABERNET SAUVIGNON, 2009: Dark garnet with red fruits and cigar box on the nose. Opens in the glass to reveal appealing black and red berries, those matched nicely by notes of minted dark chocolate. Medium- to full-bodied, soft and round, a good effort for the vintage. Drink now–2014. Score 89 K

RESERVE, CABERNET SAUVIGNON, 2008: Super-dark garnet in color, with a floral and plum-rich nose. Full-bodied, with silky near-sweet tannins and gentle notes of spicy sweet cedarwood part to reveal traditional currant, blackberry, herbal and spicy notes. Drink now–2015. Score 91. K

RESERVE, CABERNET SAUVIGNON, 2007: Deep garnet toward royal purple, its once-firm tannins and generous wood now settling in to show the wine's fine balance and structure. On the nose and palate traditional Cabernet blackcurrant and blackberry fruits, those supported by hints of freshly cured tobacco and bittersweet chocolate. Long and generous and on the finish an appealing hint of green olives. Drink now–2016. Score 92. K

RESERVE, CABERNET SAUVIGNON, 2006: Super-dark in color, firmly tannic, showing good structure and fine balance between wood, tannins and fruit that bodes well for the future. A full-bodied, rich and concentrated wine, with dense blackberry and blackcurrant fruits, notes of freshly roasted coffee and gentle layers of currants, spices, green olives and cedarwood. Drink now–2013. Score 92. K

RESERVE, CABERNET SAUVIGNON, 2005: Dark garnet with orange and green reflections, medium- to full-bodied, with still-firm tannins integrating nicely and showing light spicy oak. Opens with currants and plums, goes on to wild berries and hints of black licorice and chocolate. Long, round and generous. Drink now. Score 91. K

RESERVE, CABERNET SAUVIGNON, 2004: Medium- to full-bodied, with a layer of spicy and toasty wood to show for its 18 months in oak, this dark garnet toward royal purple wine shows moderately soft tannins and acidity coming together nicely. On the nose and palate blackberries, currants and an intimation of purple plums, those complemented by hints of spices and minty chocolate on the long finish. Drink now. Score 91. K

RESERVE, MERLOT, 2007: Developed for 18 months in French *barriques*, half of which were new, showing soft, gently caressing tannins, spicy cedarwood and generous wild berry and cassis, those supported by herbal, tobacco notes and on the long finish a flavor of red plums rising. Drink now–2013. Score 90. K

RESERVE, MERLOT, 2006: Oak-aged for 18 months, dark, youthful royal purple in color, full-bodied, with soft, gently mouth-coating tannins integrating nicely with light spices and vanilla from the oak in which it is aging. Opens to reveal ripe and generous red plum, raspberry and coffee aromas and flavors, those supported nicely by a tantalizing hint of cigar tobacco. Long, ripe and generous. Drink now–2013. Score 90. K

RESERVE, MERLOT, 2005: Soft and round but well focused, opening in the glass to reveal silky tannins and a gentle touch with the wood, those supporting currant, berry, cocoa and light hints of mint, all of which linger very nicely on the palate. Drink up. Score 89. K

RESERVE, SHIRAZ, 2009: Blended with 2% Viognier, deep garnet in color, medium- to full-bodied with gently gripping tannins. On the nose black fruits and cigar tobacco and on the palate crushed blackberries and notes of roasted herbs. Medium- to full-bodied, an easy-to-drink but not overly complex wine. Drink from release–2014. Tentative Score 87–89. K

RESERVE, SHIRAZ, 2008: Blended and fermented together with 7% Viognier, the blend developed for 14 months in 60% of new French oak, showing forward blackberry, currant and purple plums, those matched by a generous note of black licorice. Long, concentrated and, given time, will show elegance. Drink now–2014, perhaps longer. Score 91. K

RESERVE, SHIRAZ, 2007: Dark garnet in color, medium- to full-bodied, blended with 5% of Viognier and developed in new French oak. Opens with an appealing floral and bitter-nutty nose, that going on to show spicy wood and gently mouth-coating tannins. On the palate a generous array of black and purple fruits, those complemented nicely by notes of Mediterranean herbs and cigar tobacco. Drink now–2014. Score 91. K

RESERVE, SYRAH, 2005: Blended with 10% of Viognier, nearly black in color, but a wine of remarkable elegance. Aromatic, with spicy and floral scents on first attack, those yielding to aromas and flavors of berries and plums, all backed up by hints of white pepper, and on the long finish, surprising notes of peaches and apricots. Drink now. Score 91. K

RESERVE, CABERNET SAUVIGNON-MERLOT, 10th ANNIVERSARY EDITION, 2003: Dark cherry toward garnet, medium-bodied, this gently oaked wine shows an appealing array of aromas and flavors. On first attack blackberries and a hint of mint, those yielding to strawberries, cherries, licorice and earthy minerals. Nicely balanced and moderately long but starting to show signs of age. Drink up. Score 89. K

RESERVE, SAUVIGNON BLANC, 2010: Light, refined and polished, with a nose rich in hints of freshly cut hay and warm grass. Opens to show a tempting array of citrus, ripe pear and apple blossoms all lingering nicely on a generous and refreshing finish. Drink now. Score 89. K

RESERVE, SAUVIGNON BLANC, 2009: Damp golden straw in color, light- to medium-bodied with appealing citrus and tropical fruits and gooseberries on a background of flinty minerals. Drink now. Score 88. K

RESERVE, SAUVIGNON BLANC, 2008: An unoaked white, developed on its lees in stainless-steel tanks. The color of damp straw, light- to medium-bodied, showing crisp and refreshing with its grapefruit, pineapple and gooseberry fruits complemented nicely by notes of stony minerals and freshly cut grass. Drink up. Score 88. K

RESERVE, VIOGNIER, 2009: Bright gold with an orange tint, medium-bodied, opens with a floral and peach nose, goes on to show pears, white peaches, litchis and notes of white pepper. Oak-aged for just four months, crisply dry with lively acidity and despite its dryness a tantalizing hint of sweetness (perhaps from the wood). Give this one a bit of time and it will show a hint of sweet cream as well. Drink now. Score 90. K

RESERVE, VIOGNIER, RESERVE, 2008: Light gold in color, fermented with wild yeasts and with a deeply aromatic nose. A rich array of aromas and flavors including honeyed nectarine and pineapple fruits, those with a hint of white pepper. Rich, lively and harmonious despite its high 15% alcohol content. Drink now. Score 91.

RESERVE, VIOGNIER, 2007: Perhaps the Israeli Viognier most loyal to the grape to date. Fermented partly with wild yeasts, developing in *barriques* on its lees, showing intense, vibrant and complex with spice, floral, fig and melon aromas and flavors. Deep and rich with a long, broad finish. Showing signs of age. Drink up. Score 89. K

Dalton Estate ("D" Label)

DALTON ESTATE, CABERNET SAUVI-GNON, 2009: Dark ruby toward garnet, medium- to full-bodied, with gently gripping tannins. On the nose and palate traditional Cabernet blackberries and blackcurrants, those complemented by notes of currant jam and pepper. A generous and mouthwatering finish. Drink now–2014. Score 89. K

DALTON ESTATE, CABERNET SAUVI-GNON, 2008: Deep garnet in color, opens with a fruit-rich nose, goes on to show generous wild berries, blackcurrants and spices, those on a medium- to full-bodied frame with gently gripping tannins and light cedar notes, all lingering nicely. Drink now–2013. Score 89. K

DALTON ESTATE, CABERNET SAUVIGNON, 2007: Just complex enough to grab attention, showing ripe and distinctive for cherry, blackberry, blueberry and herbal aromas and flavors framed by gentle notes of sweet-and-spicy oak. Medium-bodied with soft tannins, and lingering nicely on the palate. Drink up. Score 90. K

DALTON ESTATE, MERLOT, 2009: Developed for ten months in older *barriques*, showing medium-bodied, with just a kiss of the wood and soft tannins. Ruby toward garnet, with a blueberry and currant nose, opens in the glass to show aromas and flavors of blackberries, black cherries and bittersweet chocolate. Lingers nicely. Drink now–2014. Score 89. K

DALTON ESTATE, MERLOT, 2008: Reflecting its ten months in French oak with gentle notes of spicy wood to highlight blackberry, black cherry and notes of bittersweet chocolate and tobacco. Medium- to full-bodied, with gently gripping tannins and lingering nicely, the fruits and aromas rising on the long finish. Drink now–2013. Score 89. K

DALTON ESTATE, MERLOT, 2007: Lightly gripping tannins on a medium- to full-bodied frame, showing fine balance and reflecting its ten months in oak with generous but gentle sweet cedar. Opens to show generous wild berry, cassis and spices, all lingering nicely. Drink now. Score 88. K

DALTON ESTATE, MERLOT, 2006: Garnet toward royal purple, medium-bodied and generously aromatic, showing soft, well-integrated tannins and lightly spicy oak. On the nose and palate wild berries, currants and a hint of white chocolate on the long, round finish. Drink up. Score 88. K

DALTON ESTATE, SHIRAZ, 2009: Dark garnet, medium-bodied, with gentle oak influences and silky tannins, opens to reveal generous blackberries, purple plums and notes of bitter citrus peel, all on a lightly spicy background. As this one develops somewhat look as well for notes of vanilla, tobacco and saddle leather. Drink now–2014. Score 90. K

DALTON ESTATE, SHIRAZ, 2008: Aged in new American oak for ten months, dark garnet, full-bodied, with gently gripping tannins and notes of spicy wood. Opens to show spicy red and black fruits complemented by hints of saddle leather and black tea. Drink now–2013, perhaps longer. Score 90. K

DALTON ESTATE, SHIRAZ, 2007: Made entirely from Shiraz grapes, a distinctly New-World wine, fruit forward, medium- to full-bodied, with generous but not at all overpowering oak and soft, near-sweet tannins in fine balance with fruits. At first sip a virtual attack of berry and plum fruits, those yielding on the palate to blackberries and peaches (yes, peaches!) and an array of spices. Long and generous. Drink now. Score 90. K

DALTON ESTATE, SHIRAZ, 2006: Dark, almost impenetrable garnet, medium- to full-bodied, and with soft and gently mouth-coating tannins in good balance with fresh acidity and fruits. On the nose and palate blackberries, purple plums, licorice, black pepper and hints of saddle leather and vanilla that come in on the generous finish Drink now. Score 87. K

DALTON ESTATE, BARBERA, 2008: Royal purple in color, medium-, perhaps medium- to full-bodied, with notes of spices and vanilla to complement berry, cherry and citrus peel notes. Oak-aged for ten months, showing a gentle note of spicy oak with a note of red licorice rising on a medium-long finish. Drink now. Score 87. K

DALTON ESTATE, BARBERA, 2007: Dark ruby toward garnet, medium-bodied, with soft tannins and a bright and lively set of cherry, berry and citrus peel aromas and a background of light spicy oak. Aged in used French oak for ten months, showing generous fresh fruit on a medium finish. Drink up. Score 87. K

DALTON ESTATE, PETITE SIRAH, 2009: The winery's first varietal release of Petite Sirah and by heaven, Petite Sirah as Petite Sirah should be. Dark garnet with a purple robe, generously fragrant, medium- to full-bodied with notes of black pepper, licorice and blackberries on the nose, those yielding on the palate to ripe, near-jammy huckleberry and blackberry fruits on a background of vanilla-tinged spicy notes and, on the long finish a hint of black olives. Generous and well focused. Drink now–2016, perhaps longer. Score 90. K

DALTON ESTATE, FUMÉ BLANC, OAK-AGED, 2010: With ⅔ of the wine developed in *barriques* and ⅓ in stainless steel, and with fermentation taking place in 500 liter barrels by spontaneous fermentation. Light gold in color, medium-bodied, offering notes of pears and citrus on the nose, those complemented by a light note of smoke. On the palate an almost oily texture that coats the tongue comfortably and showing aromas and flavors of white peaches, ripe yellow apples and citrus, those backed up by light herbal notes. Lively, with just enough complexity to grab the attention. Drink now. Score 89. K

DALTON ESTATE, FUMÉ BLANC, 2009: Allowed to ferment spontaneously and then developed *sur lie* for three to four months in new 500 liter oak barrels, that just to pass on a hint of smoky and spicy wood. Fragrant, and on the nose and palate an appealing smoky quality that comes together nicely with citrus, grapefruit, peach and spicy notes. Fine acidity makes this an easy-to-drink wine but one with just enough complexity to grab our attention. Drink now. Score 89. K

DALTON ESTATE, FUMÉ BLANC, 2008: With the addition of 9% Viognier to add body, medium-bodied and reflecting its four months in oak with light hints of spices and a tantalizing smoky note. On the nose and palate citrus fruits, nectarines and what at one moment seems like papaya and another like mango. Round and generous. Drink up. Score 88. K

Safsufa Vineyards

SAFSUFA VINEYARDS, CABERNET SAUVIGNON, 2009: Reflecting its eight months in barriques with silky tannins and light notes of cedarwood, opening to show round, soft and medium-bodied. On the nose and palate wild berries, black cherries and a hint of mint and, on the moderately long finish a note of spicy oak. Drink now–2013. Score 88. K

SAFSUFA VINEYARDS, CABERNET SAUVIGNON, 2006: Dark garnet with purple reflections, medium- to full-bodied, reflecting its 12 months in used French oak *barriques* with gentle notes of spices. On the nose and palate, traditional Cabernet blackcurrant and blackberry fruits, those on a light background of near-sweet cedar and minted chocolate. Drink up. Score 88. K

SAFSUFA VINEYARDS, MERLOT, 2009: Dark ruby toward garnet, medium-bodied, a soft, round wine showing appealing notes of almost jammy cherries, wild berries and Oriental spices. Generous acidity rises on the finish. Drink now. Score 85. K

SAFSUFA VINEYARDS, MERLOT, 2006: Deep royal purple, medium- to full-bodied, showing appealing hints of vanilla and spices from its 12 months in used French oak. Soft tannins highlight aromas and flavors of red berries, cherries and cassis, all coming to a near-jammy fruit finish. Drink up. Score 87. K

SAFSUFA VINEYARDS, SAUVIGNON BLANC-VIOGNIER, 2009: The color of damp straw, medium-bodied, opens with a clean note of grape-fruit, yielding as the wine develops in the glass to tangerines and orange peel, those supported by lively acidity. Not complex but quite pleasant. Drink now. Score 86. K

Alma

ALMA, BORDEAUX BLEND, 2009: Garnet toward royal purple, a full-bodied blend of 64% Cabernet Sauvignon, 27% Merlot and 9% Cabernet Franc. A deep black fruit and chocolate nose parts to reveal a soft, round wine with a generous array of blackberries, plums, coffee and Mediter-ranean herbs. Rich tannins here, but those caressing gently. A round and tempting wine. Best from 2013–2017. Tentative Score 89–91. K

ALMA, RHONE BLEND, 2009: A blend of Shiraz, Mourvedre and Viog-nier (79%, 15% and 6% respectively). Deep garnet in color, full-bodied and round, with notes of tobacco and black fruits on the nose. On the palate an array of cassis, black cherries, minerals and tobacco and, from mid-palate on, tastes of white pepper and juniper berries. Drink from release–2015. Tentative Score 88–90. K

ALMA, 2008: A full-bodied blend of 47% each Cabernet Sauvignon and Merlot with 6% Cabernet Franc. Deep and dark, with gently caressing tannins and moderate notes of spicy cedarwood, opens to reveal an array of wild berries, currants and citrus peel, those hinting of roasted herbs and espresso coffee. Drink now–2015. Score 91. K

ALMA, 2007: Almost impenetrably dark garnet in color, a full-bodied blend of 65% Cabernet Sauvignon, 22% Merlot and 13% Cabernet Franc. Developed in French *barriques* for 14 months, showing gently mouth-coating tannins and light notes of sweet cedarwood, opens with ripe black and purple fruits, those on a background of chocolate and sweet chewing tobacco. Drink now–2014. Score 90. K

ALMA, 2006: Dark, almost impenetrable garnet, a full-bodied blend of Cabernet Sauvignon, Merlot and Cabernet Franc (56%, 25% and 19% respectively), showing soft tannins and a black fruit nose. Opens to reveal wild berries, purple plums and notes of chocolate and vanilla along with a hint of jammy sweetness on the medium-long finish. Drink now. Score 89. K

ALMA, 2005: Garnet toward purple, medium- to full-bodied, this blend of 53% Cabernet Sauvignon and 47% Merlot spent 16 months in French oak. Firm tannins integrating nicely with light notes of spicy oak. On the nose and palate blackberries, purple plums and a teasing hint of bitter oranges, the fruits backed up nicely by Oriental spices. Hints of bitterness, spicy oak and acidity all in fine balance. Drinking well but showing first signs of sliding past its peak and thus not for further cellaring. Drink up. Score 89. K

ALMA, WHITE, 2010: A blend of 66% Viognier and 34% Chardonnay, half developed in *barriques* and half in stainless steel. Fresh and generous, smooth and round, with fine acidity set off by a light creamy note. On the nose and palate spicy pears, pineapple and a hint of cloves and, from mid-palate on to the generous finish, a hint of litchi. At its best with fish and seafood dishes in lightly spicy cream sauces. Drink now. Score 88. K

Dalton

DALTON, ZINFANDEL, 2009: Oak-aged in American *barriques* for 12 months, blended with 13% Petite Sirah, medium- to full-bodied (leaning to the full), a deeply aromatic wine showing a nose rich with mahogany and smoke and a note of smoked goose breast. Fine tannins here parting to reveal generous black fruits, sweet tobacco and notes of spicy oak all lingering nicely. Drink now–2015. Score 90. K

DALTON, ZINFANDEL, 2008: Showing bigger than at early tastings but no less tempting despite its 15% alcohol content. A big wine, dark garnet toward royal purple, blended with 12% of Petite Sirah, oak-aged in new American oak for 12 months, showing fine balance between wood, soft tannins and fruits. On the nose and palate ripe wild berry, blackberry and boysenberry fruits. Elegant and polished, generously mouth-filling without ever feeling heavy. Drink now–2014. Score 91. K

DALTON, ZINFANDEL, 2007: Deep, almost impenetrable garnet in color, developed in new American oak and blended with about 7% Merlot. Generously aromatic, with gently gripping tannins and not at all imposing oak notes, those in fine balance with black and red fruit, including red currants, blackberries, blueberries and huckleberries, all on a generously spicy background. Although the wine boasts a 15.5% alcohol content it manages to keep nicely in balance and shows elegance. Drink now. Score 90. K

DALTON, ZINFANDEL, 2006: As has become traditional at the winery, a single vineyard wine. Blended with about 7% of Merlot but fully faithful to the variety, with full body, wild berries, plums, vanilla and notes of white chocolate and cinnamon, all with a bare and tantalizing hint of sweetness. Aged in new American *barriques* for 12 months, showing fine balance between sweet and spicy oak, notes of black pepper, soft tannins and fruits. 15% alcohol here but not a hot spot to be found. Drink up. Score 90. K

DALTON, ROSÉ, 2010: A departure from earlier Dalton rosé wines, those having been made entirely from Cabernet Sauvignon grapes. This cuvée, a blend of 38% Barbera, 32% Cabernet Sauvignon and 30% Zinfandel shows bubble-gum pink in color, but don't let that put you off for bubble gum flavors are as far as you will get from this delightful wine. Light- to medium-bodied, barely off-dry, with fine acidity to keep the wine lively, shows notes of raspberries, strawberries, cassis and citrus peel. A fine summertime quaffer and a good choice with Mediterranean mezes or Spanish tapas. Drink now. Score 88. K

DALTON, ROSÉ, 2008: As has become traditional at Dalton, made entirely from Cabernet Sauvignon grapes with a very short skin contact. Peach-blossom pink, with wild berry and cassis fruits matched by an appealing hint of grapefruit peel. Off-dry and lively, fine on its own or a good match to fish, seafood and chicken salads. Drink up. Score 87. K

DALTON, CHARDONNAY, 2009: Unoaked, light gold in color, with lively acidity and appealing apple, citrus and tropical fruits on a light mineral background. A wine that consistently calls to mind Petit Chablis. Drink up. Score 88. K

DALTON, LIQUEUR MUSCAT, N.V.: Deep gold toward bronze in color, a late-harvest wine fermented for a short time, the fermentation stopped by the addition of neutral spirits and then developed in old barrels. At this stage showing generous sweetness, that balanced by natural acidity, and on the nose and palate, honeyed summer fruits, citrus and even notes of guava. A contemplation wine to sip quite slowly, not with dessert but in the late hours of the evening. Eventually to become part of a solera system. Drink from release. Score 91. K

DALTON, MOSCATO, 2010: A virtual twin in its aroma and flavor profile to the 2009 release. See the tasting note that follows.

DALTON, MOSCATO, 2009: Lightly *frizzante*, with generous sweetness set off nicely by acidity to keep it lively. On the nose and palate citrus, citrus peel and tropical fruits. Serve as well chilled as you would a Champagne. *Mevushal* (pasteurized) but that seems to highlight the freshness of the fruits. A fun wine that will make you smile. Drink up. Score 87. K

Canaan

CANAAN, CABERNET SAUVIGNON, 2010: Developed entirely in stainless steel, showing ruby toward garnet, medium-bodied and softly tannic. Fresh aromas and flavors of blackberries and black cherries, those complemented by a hint of sage, make for a pleasant, easy-to-drink wine that will match nicely with pasta dishes or small cuts of meat. Drink now. Score 87. K

CANAAN, CABERNET SAUVIGNON, 2008: Dark royal purple in color, medium-bodied, with gently caressing tannins and a bare hint of spicy wood, showing cassis, raspberries and red plums, those opening to show notes of green olives and mint. An appealing Mediterranean wine. Drink up. Score 85. K

CANAAN, MERLOT, 2010: Shining garnet in color, medium-bodied and with lightly chewy tannins. On the nose and palate blackberries, cassis and appealing notes of spices and earthy minerals. Drink now. Score 86. K

CANAAN, MERLOT, 2008: Deep ruby toward garnet, medium-bodied, reflecting its four months in used oak with light notes of spicy wood, soft tannins and generous plums and blackberries, all on an appealingly spicy background. Drink up. Score 86. K

CANAAN, RED, 2010: An unoaked blend of Cabernet Sauvignon, Merlot, Shiraz, Petite Sirah and Mourvedre that might have come together as a "kitchen sink" but turns out to be quite pleasant indeed. Dark ruby toward garnet, with soft tannins, a round wine showing aromas and flavors of wild black and red berries, cherries and notes of white pepper and cinnamon that come in from mid-palate on. Drink now. Score 86. K

CANAAN, RED, 2008: Dark royal purple, medium-bodied, softly tannic, a blend of 64% Cabernet Sauvignon and 24% Merlot, the rest of Petite Sirah and Shiraz. Light tannins and good acidity in fine balance with spicy purple plum and blackberry fruits. Drink up. Score 85. K

CANAAN, WHITE, 2010: A blend of Sauvignon Blanc, Chardonnay, Viognier and a bit of Muscat. Categorized as off-dry but with fine balancing acidity to keep the wine lively. On the nose and palate apple, melon and Anjou pears, those with an attractive hint of minerals. Not a complex wine but a very appealing one. Drink now. Score 86. K

CANAAN, WHITE, 2009: A simple white, off-dry with just enough acidity to keep it going. Continues to show summer and tropical fruits but not for further cellaring. Drink up. Score 82. K

Derekh Eretz ✶✶✶

Settled in on an individual ranch on the Negev Heights at which his stone sculptures can be seen everywhere, Daniel Kish planted his first vines in 2006, those of Cabernet Sauvignon, Merlot, Zinfandel, Petite Sirah, Petit Verdot and Shiraz grapes. A rugged individual living in and thriving on rugged circumstances, with no power yet connected to the national grid but relying entirely on generators, as of now wines are made in large plastic vats with the addition of oak chips. First releases, of 3,000, bottles are all from the 2010 vintage.

DEREKH ERETZ, MERLOT, 2010: Dark garnet, full-bodied, with soft tannins and notes of smoky wood in fine balance with fruits and acidity. With an appealing herbal nose, opens to reveal raspberries, red currants and sweet spices. Round and generous. Drink from release. Tentative Score 86–88.

DEREKH ERETZ, SHIRAZ, 2010: Full-bodied, round, ripe and generous with aromas and flavors of red berries and cherries supported by notes of earthy minerals and sweet spices, all lingering nicely. Drink from release. Tentative Score 86–88.

DEREKH ERETZ, ZINFANDEL, 2010: Blended with 20% Cabernet Sauvignon, impenetrably dark garnet with a royal purple robe. Full-bodied and muscular, with still-gripping tannins needing time to integrate, opens in the glass to revel a generous array of raspberries, blackberries and crushed wild berries, those with an overlay of earthy minerals and, on the finish, hints of brown spices. Drink from release. Tentative Score 86–88.

DEREKH ERETZ, PETIT VERDOT, 2010: With an abundance of chocolate on the nose, a full-bodied, softly tannic and generously acidic wine, showing red currants, sage and briar, all on a generously spicy background. Drink from release. Tentative Score 87–89.

DEREKH ERETZ, PETITE SIRAH, 2010: Super-dark garnet in color, full-bodied with moderate notes of spicy oak. Opens to show true Petite Sirah characteristics. On the nose, licorice, black pepper and huckleberries, those parting to make way for generous blackberry fruits, all on a firmly tannic background. Generous and long. Drink from release. Tentative Score 86–88.

Domaine Herzberg ✳✳✳

Founded by Max Herzberg on Moshav Sitria (the winery uses the French spelling of Sitrya), not far from the city of Rehovot and in the foothills of the Judean Mountains, the winery released its first wines from the 2007 vintage. Now cultivating their own vineyards with Cabernet Sauvignon, Merlot, Malbec and Petite Sirah, the winery relies largely on organic techniques and uses a minimum of pesticides. Plans are to release a varietal Malbec from the 2009 vintage. Production for 2007 was 2,000 bottles, for 2008, 3,500 and projected production for 2009 is for 6,000 bottles.

DOMAINE HERZBERG, MERLOT, CÔTEAUX DE SITRYA, SPECIAL RESERVE, 2008: Dark garnet, medium- to full-bodied, with soft tannins and forward red fruits supported by notes of pepper and Mediterranean herbs. Drink now–2013. Score 88. K

DOMAINE HERZBERG, MERLOT, CÔTEAUX DE SITRYA, 2008: Showing spices and vanilla from the oak in which it was briefly aged, and opening to reveal black cherry, cassis and cedar aromas, those on a background of purple plums and spices. Young and still showing some rough edges so give this one a bit of time. Drink now–2013. Score 87. K

DOMAINE HERZBERG, MERLOT, CÔTEAUX DE SITRYA, 2007: Dark ruby toward garnet, lightly oak-aged, a supple, fruit-forward wine with attractive black cherry and wild berry fruits supported by notes of spices. Medium- to full-bodied, with soft tannins and an appealing hint of licorice that lingers on the finish. Drink now. Score 87. K

DOMAINE HERZBERG, RESERVE, CÔTEAUX DE SITRYA, 2007: Deep garnet in color, a medium- to full-bodied blend of 50% each Cabernet Sauvignon and Merlot. Reflecting its nine months in French and American *barriques* with firm tannins and spicy wood in fine balance with blackcurrant, wild berry and licorice notes. Drink now–2013, perhaps longer. Score 88. K

DOMAINE HERZBERG, RED BLEND, RESERVE, 2008: A medium- to full-bodied blend of 40% Cabernet, 40% Merlot and 20% Malbec, softly tannic, showing gentle spicy wood influences and opening to show an appealing array of blackcurrant, wild berry and blueberry fruits, those on a background of bitter citrus peel and white pepper. A charmer. Drink now–2013. Score 89. K

Domaine Netofa ✶✶✶

Located on Mitzpe Netofa in the Lower Galilee, the Netofa winery was founded by winemaker Pierre Miodownick, for many years the winemaker in charge of producing many of the French wines made for, imported and distributed by Royal Wines. Miodownick relies entirely on his own vineyards, those containing Syrah, Mourvedre, Tempranillo, Touriga Nacional, Chardonnay and Chenin Blanc grapes. The first wines were released from the 2009 vintage. Until a winery is constructed, Netofa relies on separate facilities at the Or HaGanuz winery. Production for 2009 was about 25,000 bottles and from the 2010 vintage about 80,000.

DOMAINE NETOFA, LATOUR NETOFA, GALILEE 2009: Developed in French oak, showing garnet toward royal purple, a medium- to full-bodied red with gently caressing tannins. On first attack plums and black cherries, those parting to make way for blackberries and rising on the moderately long finish notes of black pepper and bittersweet chocolate. Mouth-filling and generous. Drink now–2014, perhaps longer. Score 90. K

DOMAINE NETOFA, GALILEE, 2009: A Rhone blend of Syrah and Mourvedre, dark ruby toward garnet, medium- to full-bodied with its once-chunky tannins now settling down to reveal an array of blackberry, cassis and dark chocolate, those on a lightly spicy background. Finely tuned balance here that calls to mind similar blends from the Coteaux d'Aix-en-Provence and Bandol. Drink now–2013. Score 88. K

DOMAINE NETOFA, ROSÉ, NAHAL TABOR, GALILEE, 2010: Light- to medium-bodied, a blend of Syrah and Mourvedre showing salmon pink and opening with appealing raspberry, cranberry and blueberry fruits on a crisply dry background. Drink up. Score 86. K

DOMAINE NETOFA, ROSÉ, GALILEE, 2010: A crisply dry rose, blending Syrah and Mourvedre. Salmon pink in color, medium-bodied with aromas and flavors of black berries, cherries and raspberries on a crisp mineral background. Not complex but lively and refreshing. Drink now. Score 87. K

DOMAINE NETOFA, ROSÉ, NAHAL TABOR, GALILEE, 2009: A dry rose made from a blend of Syrah and Mourvedre grapes. Rose petal toward salmon pink, medium-bodied and showing aromas and flavors of red and black berries, those on a background of stony minerals.

Lacking that extra hint of what might have made the wine more lively, and showing a bit austere but a fine match to cold chicken and seafood dishes (think chicken salad and cold fish cocktails). Drink up. Score 86. K

DOMAINE NETOFA, CHARDONNAY, GALILEE, 2010: A clean, round wine, opening to show red apples, grapefruit pith and grassy notes, those followed by a taste of honeysuckle. Neither an opulent or an austere wine but one that reminds of the fruity whites of Macon or Macon-Villages. Give this one time to open in the glass. Drink now. Score 87. K

Domaine Ventura ✳✳✳

Domaine Ventura was founded in 2005 by David Ventura and is located in the community of Ofra, north of Ramallah. Annual production is about 50,000 bottles, those based on Cabernet Sauvignon, Merlot, Cabernet Franc, Petite Sirah and Petit Verdot grapes, with Mourvedre soon coming on line. The Ventura wines, consistently reflecting the winemaker's French background, have shown increasing complexity and quality on a regular basis. Because 2008 was a *shmita* year in which many observant winemakers choose to leave their fields lying fallow, no wines were produced in that year.

DOMAINE VENTURA, CABERNET SAUVIGNON, GRAND VIN, HAUTE JUDÉE-SAMARIE, 2009: Developed for 15 months in French oak, opens with a nose rich in black fruits and licorice. Full-bodied with ample tannins that grip gently, opens slowly in the glass to reveal aromas and flavors of blackcurrants, black cherries and violets, those followed on the long and generous finish with appealing notes of anise and black pepper, the tannins and fruits rising together. Approachable and fully enjoyable now but best mid-2012–2015 perhaps longer. Score 90. K

DOMAINE VENTURA, CABERNET SAUVIGNON, GRAND VIN, HAUTE JUDÉE-SAMARIE, 2007: Made entirely from Cabernet Sauvignon grapes, showing deep garnet, medium- to full-bodied, and reflecting its 18 months in French *barriques* with notes of dusty cedarwood. Opens with a light medicinal aroma that never quite blows off but does allow the blackcurrant, blackberry and plum fruits to come through nicely, the fruits on a background of freshly turned earth and cigar tobacco. Showing better than at an earlier tasting. Drink now. Score 86. K

DOMAINE VENTURA, CABERNET SAUVIGNON, GRAND VIN, HAUTE JUDÉE-SAMARIE, 2006: Dark garnet toward adobe-brick red, already showing clearing at the rim. On the nose and palate some black fruits, those dominated by notes of tobacco, smoke and earthy minerals. Drink up. Score 80. K

DOMAINE VENTURA, MERLOT, GRAND VIN, HAUTE JUDÉE-SAMARIE, 2009: As is the wont of the winemaker with his red wines, aged for 15 months in French oak. Medium- to full-bodied (leaning to the full) with gently caressing tannins and again as reflected in many of the 2009 wines with acidity that creeps up slowly to highlight cassis, blackberries and raspberries, those on a background of earthy minerals. Drink now–2015. Score 89. K

DOMAINE VENTURA, MERLOT, GRAND VIN, LIMITED EDITION, HAUTE JUDÉE-SAMARIE, 2006: Garnet toward royal purple in color, medium-bodied, with soft, near-sweet tannins, and developed in French *barriques* for 12 months. Opens to show aromas and flavors of raspberries and red currants, those on a light earthy-herbal background. Put aside its somewhat grandiose labeling information and you will find a pleasant-enough quaffer. Drink now. Score 86. K

DOMAINE VENTURA, CABERNET FRANC, HAUTE JUDÉE-SAMARIE, 2009: A fresh and supple wine, full-bodied and round, with fresh acidity to highlight aromas and flavors of blackberries and plums, those on a background of tobacco leaf and earthy minerals. Long, smooth and harmonious. Drink now–2014. Score 91. K

DOMAINE VENTURA, RUBENS, GRAND VIN, HAUTE JUDÉE-SAMARIE, 2009: The winery's only red blend, in this case of 55% Cabernet Sauvignon, 35% Merlot, 6% Petit Verdot and 4% Cabernet Franc. A true Bordeaux blend but happily showing a distinct Mediterranean palate, its blackberry and blackcurrant fruits complemented very nicely indeed by notes of anise and freshly picked sweet herbs. Full-bodied, with tannins that caress gently, blossoming on the nose and palate and then lingering on the palate as the fruits and tannins rise together. Approachable and enjoyable now but best from mid-2012–2016, perhaps longer. Score 91. K

DOMAINE VENTURA, RUBENS, GRAND VIN, HAUTE JUDÉE-SAMARIE, 2007: Dark ruby toward garnet, a medium-bodied Bordeaux blend of 55% Cabernet Sauvignon, 35% Merlot, and 6% Petit Verdot and 4% Cabernet Franc. Oak-aged for 18 months, with its once-firm tannins and spicy wood integrating nicely. Opens to reveal red currant and raspberries on a background that hints of raisins and milk chocolate, with tannins and fruits rising on the moderately long finish. Drink now. Score 86. K

DOMAINE VENTURA, RUBENS, GRAND VIN, HAUTE JUDÉE-SAMARIE, 2006: A Bordeaux blend, medium- to full-bodied with gripping tannins and spicy wood that seem not to want to integrate. On the nose and palate muted black fruits and herbal notes. Drink up. Score 84. K

DOMAINE VENTURA, AARONS, GRAND VIN, HAUTE JUDÉE-SAMARIE, 2007: A blend of equal parts of Cabernet Sauvignon and Shiraz. Oak-aged for 18 months, showing dark garnet in color, with somewhat chunky tannins parting to reveal currant, raspberry and plum fruits on a lightly spicy background. Drink now. Score 85. K

DOMAINE VENTURA, AARONS, GRAND VIN, RUBENS, HAUTE JUDÉE-SAMARIE, 2005: Dark ruby toward garnet, medium- to full-bodied, with searing tannins and generous wood that seem not to want to settle in and hide the black fruits that struggle to make themselves felt. Drink up. Score 83. K

DOMAINE VENTURA, SHIRAZ, GRAND VIN, 2007: Oak-aged for 24 months in two- and three-year-old oak, dark ruby toward garnet, medium-, perhaps medium- to full-bodied, opening with a dark chocolate and sweet, almost oxidized Port-like nose. Given a few minutes in the glass the wine reveals notes of blackberries, plums and currants. Alas, the fruits play second-fiddle to the oak and too-generous acidity. Drink now. Score 85. K

DOMAINE VENTURA, CABERNET FRANC, GRAND VIN, HAUTE JUDÉE-SAMARIE 2006: Dark, almost impenetrable ruby toward garnet in color, medium-bodied, reflecting its 20 months in French oak barriques with generously spicy wood and firm tannins just now starting to integrate On the nose and palate plums, blackberries and bittersweet chocolate, those on an appealing herbal background, with fruits and tannins rising on the long finish. Drink now. Score 89. K

DOMAINE VENTURA, ISAAC'S, GRAND VIN, HAUTE JUDÉE-SAMARIE, 2007: Showing dramatically better than at an earlier tasting. Dark, almost impenetrable garnet, medium- to full-bodied, a blend of 74% Pinot Noir and 26% Cabernet Sauvignon. A light medicinal aroma on opening but that blows off in the glass to reveal gently gripping tannins and generous spicy oak from its 24 months in oak. On the nose and palate plums, blackberries and currants, those lingering on a generous finish. Drink now–2013. Score 87. K

DOMAINE VENTURA, MARGOT, 2006: An unabashedly sweet red wine made from an unstated potpourri of grapes. Sweet enough that you almost feel grains of sugar grinding on the teeth, showing aromas and flavors of raspberry and currant jam, those on a generously earthy background. Somewhat cloying because it lacks the acidity that might have made it more lively. Drink now. Score 75. K

DOMAINE VENTURA, CUVÉE ROSÉ, HAUTE JUDÉE-SAMARIE, 2009, 2010: Medium-bodied, bright cherry red, a blend of 75% Merlot and 25% Cabernet Franc. Crisply dry, with acidity that "creeps in on little cat's paws" to surprise pleasantly and complement aromas and flavors of raspberries, strawberries and both red and black cherries. Fresh and refreshing and just complex enough to give pause for thought. Drink now. Score 89. K

DOMAINE VENTURA, CHARDONNAY, GRAND VIN BLANC, HAUTE JUDÉE-SAMARIE, 2009: Reflecting its 12 months in new French *barriques* with a creamy texture and the barest hint of smoky oak. Shining gold in color and opening with a nose on which generous white peach and nectarine fruits. Medium- to full-bodied, with the acidity rising slowly in the glass to comfortably set off aromas and flavors of pears, melon and citrus peel. Drink now–2013. Score 89. K

Dror **

Located on Moshav Kfar Shamai not far from the city of Safed in the Upper Galilee, this young winery is currently producing about 3,500 bottles annually.

DROR, CABERNET SAUVIGNON, 2008: Dark garnet, medium- to full-bodied, with soft tannins integrating nicely and showing appealing blackberry and blackcurrant fruits on a background that hints at one moment of Oriental spices and at the next of cigar tobacco. Drink now. Score 86.

DROR, MERLOT, 2008: Developed in *barriques* for eight months, ruby toward garnet in color, medium-bodied with silky tannins and a hint of spicy cedar. Soft, fresh and round, with plenty of black fruits that make themselves felt nicely. A good quaffing wine. Drink now. Score 84.

DROR, NEBBIOLO, 2008: Blended with 10% Cabernet Sauvignon and oak-aged for six months. Light- to medium bodied, light ruby in color, with fresh raspberry, cranberry and blueberry notes, a simple, easy-to-drink quaffer. Drink now. Score 84.

Ein Nashut **

Situated near Moshav Kidmat Tzvi and named after a Talmudic-period Jewish community on the Golan Heights, this small winery released its first wines from the 2007 vintage. The winery relies on Cabernet Sauvignon, Merlot and Shiraz grapes from its own vineyards.

EIN NASHUT, CABERNET SAUVIGNON, ALIKA, 2008: Developed together with oak chips for two months after fermentation, showing soft, near-sweet tannins and generous raspberry, cherry and currant fruits, those with a light overlay of bitter herbs that rises on the finish. An acceptable entry-level wine. Drink now. Score 84.

EIN NASHUT, CABERNET SAUVIGNON, 2007: A blend of Cabernet Sauvignon, Merlot and Shiraz (85%, 10% and 5% respectively), cold fermented and then exposed to oak chips for 14 months. Medium-bodied, showing raspberry, cherry and wild strawberry fruits. Somewhat-chunky tannins and a hint of raisined fruits make this a simple but pleasant enough little country-style wine. Drink now. Score 84.

EIN NASHUT, SYRAH, ALIKA, 2008: An unoaked wine, dark garnet, medium- to full-bodied, with gently gripping tannins. On the nose and palate an appealing array of plums, raspberries and cassis, those complemented by notes of spices and bitter herbs. Drink now. Score 84.

EIN NASHUT, FRENCH SHIRAZ, 2007: Precisely how the winery chose to name this particular wine is not known. A medium- to full-bodied blend of 85% Shiraz with 15% of Cabernet Sauvignon, oak-aged for 14 months, showing red plums and white pepper but those struggling to make themselves felt through a simultaneously too-astringent and too-bitter background. Drink up. Score 79.

Ein Teina ✳✳✳

Founded by Yotam Ben-Tzvi on Moshav Givat Yoav on the southern Golan Heights, this small winery released its first wines in 2004. First year's releases were of 900 bottles, and current production is about 4,000 bottles annually. The winery relies on Cabernet Sauvignon, Merlot and Syrah grapes from the southern Golan.

EIN TEINA, CABERNET SAUVIGNON, 2008: After undergoing cold fermentation in open vats using a combination of wild and cultured yeasts, the wine was transferred to French and American oak *barriques* in which it aged for 13 months. Full-bodied, with somewhat chunky country-style tannins and a hint of sawdust on the nose, opens in the glass to reveal traditional Cabernet Sauvignon blackcurrants and blackberries. Tannins, fruits and notes of licorice and citrus peel rise on the long finish. Drink now–2015. Score 90.

EIN TEINA, CABERNET SAUVIGNON, RESERVE, 2007: Aged in *barriques* for 14 months, showing dark garnet toward royal purple. Full-bodied, with still-firm tannins needing time to settle down but showing balance and structure that bode well for the future. On the nose and palate traditional Cabernet blackcurrant and blackberry fruits, those complemented by notes of citrus peel and, rising on the finish, notes of dark chocolate and cigar tobacco. Best to date from the winery. Drink now–2015. Score 91.

EIN TEINA, CABERNET SAUVIGNON, 2007: Developed in French oak for 12 months, dark garnet in color, showing black fruits and wild berries on a background of tobacco and fresh herbs. Medium- to full-bodied, with good balance and structure, with a sweet nose and a surprising but quite pleasant note of cloves coming in on the long finish. Drink now. Score 88.

EIN TEINA, MERLOT, 2007: Dark garnet toward royal purple, medium- to full-bodied, with gently gripping tannins and notes of spicy and vanilla-rich cedarwood. An appealing array of black fruits, bitter citrus peel and Oriental spices, all lingering nicely on the palate. Drink now–2013. Score 88.

EIN TEINA, SYRAH, 2008: Fermented entirely on wild yeasts and developed for 16 months in French oak *barriques*, a deeply extracted wine showing fine balance and structure. On opening attack spicy oak, that making way comfortably for generous notes of cassis, red plums, citrus peel and licorice. On the long finish tannins rise along with a hint of saddle leather. Drink now–2015. Score 90.

EIN TEINA, CABERNET SAUVIGNON-SYRAH, 2008: Cabernet Sauvignon and Syrah with small amounts of Merlot and Viognier, each of the varieties fermented separately before blending and aging in French oak for 15 months. Medium- to full-bodied, with notes of spicy wood, wild berries, red plums and baking chocolate, all coming together in a long and coherent whole. Drink now–2014. Score 89.

EIN TEINA, CABERNET SAUVIGNON-SYRAH, 2006: A blend of 75% Cabernet Sauvignon and 25% Syrah. Oak-aged for 14 months, showing soft tannins and hints of spicy wood, and opening in the glass to reveal red and black berries, cassis and notes of freshly roasted herbs. Round and generous. Drink now. Score 88.

EIN TEINA, CABERNET SAUVIGNON-MERLOT, 2007: Medium- to full-bodied, with still-firm tannins, generous wood and acidity needing time to integrate but already showing a fine array of currant, blackberry and purple plums, those supported comfortably by a peppery note that comes in on the long finish. Drink now–2013. Score 88.

EIN TEINA, TALIA'S BLEND, 2008: Garnet toward royal purple, a medium- to full-bodied, gently tannic blend of Cabernet Sauvignon, Merlot and Syrah, those developed in French oak for 14 months. On the nose blueberries and chocolate, those making way for an appealing array of currants, purple plums and licorice, all with a hint of earthy minerals on the generous finish. Drink now–2015. Score 90.

EIN TEINA, VIOGNIER, 2009: Full-bodied, with a deeply burnished gold color and what on a blind tasting I assumed to be severe oxidation but, when reading the label later, had to do a complete turnabout, for the wine was cold-fermented together with chunks of toasted olive wood. A noble experiment perhaps but one that seems to have failed, as this treatment imparts to the wine a coarse texture and far-too-generous notes of charred wood and bitter almonds that dominate the apple and melon flavors lurking here. Drink now. Score 78.

Ella Valley Vineyards ✳✳✳✳

Located on Kibbutz Netiv Halamed Hey in the Jerusalem Mountains, the winery has vineyards that might well serve as a model of efficiency and beauty anywhere in the world. Cultivation started in 1997 in the Ella and Adulam Valleys in the Judean Hills, and now includes Cabernet Sauvignon, Cabernet Franc, Merlot, Shiraz, Pinot Noir, Petite Sirah, Chardonnay, Sauvignon Blanc, Viognier, Semillon and Muscat grapes. Under the supervision of French-trained winemaker Doron Rav Hon, the winery released its first wines, 90,000 bottles, from the 2002 harvest. Current production is about 160,000 bottles annually.

In addition to a flagship wine, "E", wines are released in three series: Vineyard's Choice, Ella Valley Vineyards and Ever Red, the first two destined for moderately long cellaring and the third for early drinking. The winery occasionally releases wines under the label of Manne, those entirely for export.

"E"

"E", 2006: A limited edition of 2,200 bottles, a full-bodied and generously tannic blend of 35% Syrah, 15% Cabernet Franc and the balance of Cabernet Sauvignon and Merlot, each variety fermented separately and developed in primarily new French oak for 12 months before blending. After the blending, the wine was given an additional eight months in oak for its elements to marry comfortably. Firm, near-sweet tannins and spicy wood come together on first attack with aromas and flavors of cassis and licorice, those followed by notes of blackcurrants and tobacco and, on the super-long finish, a hint of dried figs. A concentrated and intense wine that needs a bit more time in bottle to show its elegance. Drink now–2017, perhaps longer. Score 92. K

Vineyard's Choice

VINEYARD'S CHOICE, CABERNET SAUVIGNON, 2007: Developing beautifully in the bottle. Full-bodied, dark garnet with a royal purple robe, and its once gripping tannins and generous oak now integrating nicely. A nose rich with dark red fruits and plums yields in the glass to aromas and flavors of blackcurrants, blackberries, exotic spices and a clear not of licorice. On the long and generous finish an appealing note of sweet Mediterranean herbs. Showing polished, silky and elegant. Drink now–2017. Score 93 K

VINEYARD'S CHOICE, CABERNET SAUVIGNON, 2005: Full-bodied, with moderately firm tannins, a gentle wood influence, and fine balance. Blended with 10% of Merlot, this soft, round wine opens with near-sweet berries and spices, those yielding to reveal lush currant and blackberry aromas and flavors. Drink now–2013. Score 91. K

VINEYARD'S CHOICE, CABERNET SAUVIGNON, 2003: Blended with 3% of Cabernet Franc and aged in oak for 17 months, this is a deep and brooding wine. Dark royal purple, full-bodied, with ripe, rich fruits showing harmony and finesse. Layers of currants, juicy cherries and tempting oak shadings. Drink now. Score 91. K

VINEYARD'S CHOICE, MERLOT, 2005: Deep and dark, with blockbuster tannins that promise to soften with time to show the wine's complexity and balance. A tempting array of black cherry, blackberry and currant flavors all coming together in a long finish. Drink now. Score 91. K

VINEYARD'S CHOICE, MERLOT, 2004: Dark garnet, with firm tannins integrating nicely now and showing sweet-and-spicy cedar notes, opening to reveal red and black berries, currants and light tobacco with herbal notes that come in on the long finish. Drink now. Score 90. K

VINEYARD'S CHOICE, MERLOT, 2003: Its youthful royal purple color and generous black cherry, berry and spices show this to be an exuberant wine, but as those come together in the glass showing full body and firm structure, one begins to feel the elegance. Softening nicely now and showing long and round with an appealing spicy oak note that rises on the finish. Sliding past its peak. Drink up. Score 90. K

VINEYARD'S CHOICE, SYRAH, 2007: Notably dark garnet in color, full-bodied, with fine balance between still-gripping tannins and wood, and just waiting patiently for all of its elements to come together. On first attack currants, wild berries and an appealing loamy note, those opening to reveal hints of bay leaves, juniper berries and mint, all leading to a long and intense finish. Drink now–2016. Score 92. K

VINEYARD'S CHOICE, CABERNET SAUVIGNON-MERLOT, 2005: Dark garnet toward purple, deeply aromatic, a full-bodied blend of 60% Cabernet Sauvignon and 40% Merlot. Muscular and tannic at this time but with balance and structure that bode well for the future. Currant, cherry and berry fruits with generous hints of toasty oak on an appealing base of exotic spices. Overtones of cedar come in on the long finish. Drink now. Score 90. K

VINEYARD'S CHOICE, RR, 2004: A blend of 60% Merlot and 40% Cabernet Sauvignon, oak-aged for 16 months. Showing generous oak, firm but well-integrating tannins, plums and black cherries on a spicy and harmonious background and with hints of vanilla that rise on the moderately long finish. Drink up. Score 88. K

VINEYARD'S CHOICE, MERLOT-CABERNET FRANC, 2006: A full-bodied blend of 80% Merlot and 20% Cabernet Franc, dark ruby toward garnet in color, and reflecting its time in oak with Oriental spices and firm tannins. Opens nicely in the glass to reveal blackberry, raspberry and dried currant fruits. Generously spicy, with a tantalizing hint of red chili rising on the super-long finish. Drink now–2013. Score 92. K

Ella Valley Vineyards

ELLA VALLEY VINEYARDS, CABERNET SAUVIGNON, 2010: Deep garnet with a robe of royal purple, full-bodied, with generous gripping tannins in fine proportion with wood and fruits. Tight but lively and well focused with its blackberry, blackcurrant and licorice aromas and flavors showing a tantalizing light hint of caramel. Long and seductive. Drink from release–2017. Tentative Score 90–92. K

ELLA VALLEY VINEYARDS, CABERNET SAUVIGNON, 2008: Medium- to full-bodied, with soft tannins integrating nicely. Opens with a bare and tantalizing hint of freshly cut Mediterranean herbs, and then goes on to generous cherry and currant fruits. Supple and generous. Drink now–2014. Score 90. K

ELLA VALLEY VINEYARDS, CABERNET SAUVIGNON, 2007: Developed in French oak for 16 months, blended with 15% of Merlot, ripe and rich, with near-sweet tannins, a soft, round wine showing a light touch of spicy oak. On first attack purple plums and notes of freshly turned earth, those parting to make way for currant and blueberry fruits and finally, leading to a long finish, red cherries, roasted Mediterranean herbs and a tantalizing hint of dark chocolate. Generous and elegant. Drink now–2014. Score 91. K

ELLA VALLEY VINEYARDS, CABERNET SAUVIGNON, 2006: Developed in *barriques* for 16 months, blended with 15% Merlot, medium- to full-bodied with fine concentration and showing soft, gently mouth-coating tannins. On the opening nose, black fruits and mocha, those going on to reveal blackcurrants, blackberries and hints of pepper. On the long finish hints of chocolate and earthy minerals. Drink now–2014. Score 91. K

ELLA VALLEY VINEYARDS, CABERNET SAUVIGNON, 2005: Dark royal purple, medium- to full-bodied, with tannins and wood in fine balance with fruits. On first attack blackcurrants, blackberries and a light earthy overlay, those opening to reveal spicy oak and hints of dark cocoa. Long, generous and elegant. Drink now. Score 89. K

ELLA VALLEY VINEYARDS, CABERNET SAUVIGNON, 2004: Full-bodied, ripe and complex, with soft tannins integrating nicely and showing currant and red plums along with intimations of anise, black pepper and spicy oak. On the finish hints of earthiness and freshly tanned leather. Round and long. Well crafted. Drink up. Score 91. K

ELLA VALLEY VINEYARDS, CABERNET SAUVIGNON, 60TH ANNIVERSARY EDITION, 2004: Vinified separately from the regular release, but a near-twin to that wine (see above). Full-bodied, dark garnet, with soft tannins integrating nicely with spicy wood and fruits. On the nose and palate blackcurrants, plums and blackberries, those supported nicely by notes of Oriental spices and black pepper along with a hint of earthy minerality that comes in on the long finish. Drink up. Score 91. K

ELLA VALLEY VINEYARDS, MERLOT, 2010: Deep royal purple, full-bodied, with soft tannins that caress gently and just the right notes of sweet cedarwood. On first attack raspberries and red currants, those yielding to blackberries, espresso coffee and notes of spices, all going on to a long and supple finish. As this one continues to develop it promises to develop a near-creamy texture. Drink from release–2016. Tentative Score 89–91. K

ELLA VALLEY VINEYARDS, MERLOT, 2009: Dark, deep and concentrated, opening slowly at this stage to reveal generous plum and blackberry fruits, those enhanced nicely by notes of mocha and licorice, all leading to a long, mouth-filling finish. Drink from release–2015. Tentative Score 89–91. K

ELLA VALLEY VINEYARDS, MERLOT, 2008: Deep garnet in color, full-bodied with still-gripping tannins but already showing fine balance and structure that bode well for the future. Rich and round, a fruity red with an abundance of blackberry, raspberry and currant notes, those showing an appealing floral note. From mid-palate on to the long finish, hints of citrus peel and milk chocolate. Drink now–2014. Score 90. κ

ELLA VALLEY VINEYARDS, MERLOT, 2007: Blended with 15% Cabernet Sauvignon, opens with a hint of dusty wood and near-sweet tannins. A full-bodied and firm Merlot showing round and well balanced, the tannins complemented nicely by light spicy oak. On the nose and palate generous blackberry, currant, wild berry and exotic spices highlighted nicely by notes of minerals and light toasty oak. Drink now–2013. Score 90. κ

ELLA VALLEY VINEYARDS, MERLOT, 2006: Blended with 6% Cabernet Sauvignon and developed in French oak for 16 months, full-bodied, a solid, almost muscular wine, but with gently gripping tannins and turning round and smooth in the glass. Dark ruby toward garnet, showing a tempting array of plums, cherries and spices on a tempting earthy-mineral overlay. Long and generous with an appealing note of *garrigue* on the finish. Drink now–2013. Score 90. κ

ELLA VALLEY VINEYARDS, MERLOT, 2005: Dark and brooding, with once-gripping tannins now setting in nicely, this dense wine offers up generous currant and black cherry aromas and flavors. Showing muscular elegance. Drink now. Score 92. κ

ELLA VALLEY VINEYARDS, MERLOT, 2004: Blended with 5% of Cabernet Sauvignon, deep royal purple toward garnet in color, a firm but round and well-balanced wine showing black cherry, blackcurrant and spicy cedarwood, all coming to a long finish on which the fruits rise nicely. Drink now. Score 90. κ

ELLA VALLEY VINEYARDS, SYRAH, 2010: Fresh, lively and aromatic, with a complex aroma and flavor profile that goes from floral and wild berry flavors on to blackberries, black cherries and loamy earthy notes. Full-bodied and concentrated with a long and spicy finish. Best from 2013–2018, perhaps longer. Tentative Score 91–93. κ

ELLA VALLEY VINEYARDS, SYRAH, 2009: Made from very low-yield Syrah vines (150 kilos per dunam) and now blended with 10% Merlot. Inky-dark garnet toward royal purple in color. Full-bodied and with generous gripping tannins, an intense wine opening with mineral and leathery notes and then going on to reveal blackberry and purple plums, those with hints of tar and earthy minerals. Powerful but well focused and not at all weighty, and destined for muscular elegance. Best 2013–2018, perhaps longer. Tentative Score 91–93. K

ELLA VALLEY VINEYARDS, SYRAH, 2008: Showing every bit as well as at barrel tastings. Super-dark garnet in color, full-bodied, with gripping tannins and spicy wood that part slowly in the glass to reveal a fine array of blackberries, black cherries, plums and black and white pepper. On the long and mouth-filling finish, notes of sweet cedarwood. A wine that opens with boldness and then turns toward finesse and elegance. Best from 2013–2018 Score 93. K

ELLA VALLEY VINEYARDS, SYRAH, 2007: Developed in French oak for 16 months, made entirely from Syrah grapes, a super-dark and concentrated wine that opens with a tantalizing note of bitter almonds that lingers nicely through and complements aromas and flavors of plums, wild berries, citrus peel and, from mid-palate on, notes of dark chocolate and saddle leather. Drink now–2017. Score 91. K

ELLA VALLEY VINEYARDS, SYRAH, 2006: Deep royal purple, full-bodied, with its tannins and wood now integrating nicely with the fruits. Blended with 5% each Cabernet Sauvignon and Merlot, aged in French oak for 16 months, opening to show a generous array of currants, plums and wild berries, those on an appealing loamy note. From mid-palate on, tantalizing hints of bay leaves and mint. Rounds off nicely to a long and generous finish. Drink now–2016. Score 92. K

ELLA VALLEY VINEYARDS, PINOT NOIR, 2010: The most true to its variety Pinot Noir of the winery to date. Rich and complex, full-bodied and dense but seems to float on the palate. On the nose raspberries, wild berries and earthy minerals, those carrying through to the palate, which also shows cherries, raspberries, orange peel and notes of exotic spices. Rich, complex and long, a wine that comfortably reflects its Mediterranean roots. Best from 2013–2017, perhaps longer. Tentative Score 91–93. K

ELLA VALLEY VINEYARDS, PINOT NOIR, 2009: Deeply aromatic, deep royal purple in color, full-bodied for a Pinot but not overly tannic and with a still-gentle wood influence. Ripe and spicy and, on the nose and palate, plums, black cherries, cola and mineral notes. On the long fresh finish a note of cedarwood rising. Drink now–2016. Score 90. K

ELLA VALLEY VINEYARDS, PINOT NOIR, 2008: Dark cherry-red toward garnet, medium- to full-bodied with fine tannins and spices. A well-focused wine, elegant and stylish showing wild berry, black cherry and cassis fruits, with a tantalizing bitter-herbal finish that rises on the long, generously fruity finish. Drink now–2014. Score 91. K

ELLA VALLEY VINEYARDS, PINOT NOIR, 2005: Ruby toward garnet in color, medium-bodied, with soft, caressing tannins and generous cherry, cassis, strawberry and cranberry aromas and flavors, those backed up nicely by minerals, hints of white pepper and vibrant acidity. Drink now. Score 92. K

ELLA VALLEY VINEYARDS, CABERNET FRANC, 2010: Dark garnet with a robe of royal purple, medium- to full-bodied (leaning to the full), with soft, gently caressing tannins, a wine that is simultaneously concentrated and gentle. Abundant rose-petal, pomegranate and raspberry aromas and flavors that part to make way for notes of spicy cedarwood, tobacco and red licorice. Lithe and supple, a well-balanced and long wine. Best from 2013–2017, perhaps longer. Tentative Score 90–92. K

ELLA VALLEY VINEYARDS, CABERNET FRANC, 2009: Super-dark garnet in color, on first attack seeming medium- to full-bodied but gaining depth and breadth as it opens in the glass. Opens to reveal sleek tannins and notes of spicy wood in support of plum and black cherry fruits, those with hints of freshly hung tobacco and minerals. Give this one time to show its supple and refined nature. Drink now–2017, perhaps longer. Score 92. K

ELLA VALLEY VINEYARDS, CABERNET FRANC, 2008: Developed in French *barriques* for 16 months, a full-bodied blend of 85% Cabernet Franc, 10% Merlot and 5% Cabernet Sauvignon, with softly gripping tannins and gentle notes of spicy wood offset by fresh acidity and fine fruits. Opens to reveal black cherry, blackberry, tobacco and mineral notes, the fruits and a light nutty flavor rising on the long finish. Drink now–2015. Score 91. K

ELLA VALLEY VINEYARDS, CABERNET FRANC, 2007: Oak-aged in French *barriques* for 16 months, Cabernet Franc blended with 5% each of Cabernet Sauvignon and Merlot. Dark royal purple, medium- to full-bodied with softly caressing tannins. Opens with a distinct veggie Cabernet Franc note, that yielding comfortably to cherry, blackberry, licorice and citrus peel and, on the long and generous finish, a clear hint of bittersweet chocolate. Drink now–2014. Score 90. K

ELLA VALLEY VINEYARDS, CABERNET FRANC, 2006: Blended with 3% each of Merlot and Cabernet Sauvignon, dark garnet in color, medium- to full-bodied, deeply aromatic and showing a generous array of blackberry, black cherry and currant notes. Long, round, rich and mouth-filling. Drink now. Score 92. K

ELLA VALLEY VINEYARDS, CABERNET FRANC, 2005: Blended with 12% of Merlot, oak-aged for 15 months, this dark garnet, medium- to full-bodied wine shows appealing vegetal aromas on first attack, those parting to reveal gently spicy cedarwood, raspberries, blackberries, red currants and generous hints of herbaceousness and white chocolate that come in on the long, well-balanced finish. Drink now. Score 91. K

ELLA VALLEY VINEYARDS, CABERNET FRANC, 2004: Intensely dark royal purple, opens with a somewhat funky and loamy nose, but that passes quickly and reveals a medium- to full-bodied wine, showing appealing red fruits, those supported nicely by notes of vanilla and cinnamon. From mid-palate on, notes of cigar box and traditional Cabernet Franc veggie notes. Long and generous. Drink up. Score 91. K

ELLA VALLEY VINEYARDS, PETITE SIRAH, 2010: From 12-year-old vines, dark and dense, with chunky tannins that give the wine a rustic note, those parting to reveal notes of spices and cedarwood and finally making way for a generous array of blackberries, huckleberries, spices and tobacco. On the long and mouth-filling finish an appealing note of sandalwood. Best from 2013–2019, perhaps longer. Tentative Score 91–93. K

ELLA VALLEY VINEYARDS, PETITE SIRAH, 2009: Full-bodied and concentrated, with still firmly gripping tannins waiting to settle down but already showing fine balance and structure. Opens to reveal ripe blackberry, purple plum and huckleberry fruits, those highlighted nicely by notes of white pepper, all with the tannins rising on the long flavorful finish. Drink from release–2017, perhaps longer. Tentative Score 90–92. K

ELLA VALLEY VINEYARDS, PETITE SIRAH, 2008: Petite Sirah at its muscular best, showing fine balance between thick, near-sweet tannins, dusty cedarwood, acidity and fruits. Full-bodied, with ripe blackberry, boysenberry and huckleberry fruits, those on a peppery background. Well focused and with fine structure that bodes well for future cellaring ability. Drink now–2018. Score 91. K

ELLA VALLEY VINEYARDS, PETITE SIRAH, 2007: Made from grapes from ten-year-old vines, intensely dark royal purple in color, full-bodied, showing gripping tannins, spicy oak and fine fruit concentration. On the nose and palate blackberries, raspberries and loganberry fruits, those matched nicely by notes of mint and tobacco. Firm and chewy with a long, near-muscular finish. Drink now–2014. Score 90. K

ELLA VALLEY VINEYARDS, CABERNET SAUVIGNON-SYRAH, 2005: Dark purple toward brick red, full-bodied, with soft tannins, this blend of 65% Cabernet Sauvignon and 35% Syrah is young, generous and remarkably lively, with cherry, raspberry and plum aromas and flavors, those with overlays of cedarwood, freshly turned earth and spices. Drink now. Score 89. K

ELLA VALLEY VINEYARDS, MERLOT-PETITE SIRAH, 2006: Deep purple, medium- to full-bodied, with somewhat chunky tannins that give the wine a few sharp edges but showing generous plum and black-currant fruits. An appealing country-style quaffer. Drink now. Score 87. K

ELLA VALLEY VINEYARDS, ROSÉ, 2010: A medium-bodied rosé blend of Syrah and Merlot. Categorized as half-dry, opens with a red wine nose and a light sweetness, the sweetness seeming to rise as the wine develops in the glass and at least somewhat hiding the raspberry and strawberry fruits that struggle  to make themselves felt. Lacks liveliness as is but perhaps an ice cube or two might help. Drink now. Score 85. K

ELLA VALLEY VINEYARDS, CHARDONNAY, 2010: A blend from two vineyards (Aderet and Nes Harim), aging in 25% new oak, promising to be simultaneously buttery and crisp. An appealing array of aromas and flavors shifting on the palate from tropical to citrus fruits, those focused most intensely on kiwi, pineapple, red grapefruit and lime, the fruits complemented very nicely indeed by a tantalizing hint of green almonds on the long finish. Drink now–2015. Score 90. K

ELLA VALLEY VINEYARDS, CHARDONNAY, 2009: With 30% developed in new oak for 11–12 months, showing medium-bodied, with a lively gold color. Moderate acidity gives an almost creamy texture on which roasted nuts, citrus, pear and apricot fruits sit nicely with a hint of lime on the long finish. Bound for elegance. Drink now–2014. Score 90. K

ELLA VALLEY VINEYARDS, CHARDONNAY, 2008: Developed partly in new oak, partly in stainless steel, not so much lively as it is well focused and complex. On the nose and palate greengage plums, pears and yellow apples, all with a crème vanilla note. Firm and tight with a mouth-filling and elegant finish. Drink now–2014. Score 92. K

ELLA VALLEY VINEYARDS, UNOAKED CHARDONNAY, 2008: Light and glistening golden straw in color, developed on its fine lees in stainless steel tanks and with no racking, a medium-bodied white. Generous lemon curd, lime and green apple notes. Crisp and tangy enough to make you smile with pleasure. Drink up. Score 87. K

ELLA VALLEY VINEYARDS, CHARDONNAY, 2007: Developed partly in barriques, partly in stainless steel for 11 months, a medium-bodied, crisply freshly and aromatic wine. Freshly dampened golden straw in color, showing a gentle hand with the wood, the nose and palate opening with hints of honey, flaky pastry and minerals, and then showing yellow plum and citrus blossoms. Well structured, long and elegant. Look as well for a creamy hint that is creeping in nicely. Drink now. Score 90. K

ELLA VALLEY VINEYARDS, UNOAKED CHARDONNAY, 2007: Light gold in color, medium-bodied, with crisp acidity to support appealing tropical and citrus fruits, those on a background of light, near-flinty minerals and finishing with a hint of white pepper. Sliding past its peak. Drink up. Score 88. K

ELLA VALLEY VINEYARDS, SAUVIGNON BLANC, 2010: As is the winemaker's wont, blended with about 10% Semillon. Reflecting early harvest, initial fermentation in stainless steel and only then being partly transferred to oak with clean, fresh aromatics and fine acidity to keep the wine lively along with just the right level of complexity. On the nose and palate pear, pink grapefruit and passion fruit, those complemented nicely by a note of a well-trimmed lawn after a light rain. Drink now–2014. Score 90. K

ELLA VALLEY VINEYARDS, SAUVIGNON BLANC, 2009: Blended with 10% of Semillon, showing light gold in color, deeply aromatic with grapefruit and pear, those fruits supported comfortably by lively notes of tropical fruits that toy on the palate. Long and harmonious, easy to drink and simultaneously complex. If ever a wine deserved to be called "jazzy," this is it. Drink now–2013. Tentative Score 90. K

ELLA VALLEY VINEYARDS, SAUVIGNON BLANC, 2008: Blended with 10% of Semillon, the wine oak-aged in small part, showing light gold in color with lively and crisp acidity. Opens with notes of kiwis, guava and grapefruit, those supported nicely by light hints of freshly cut grass, all with just enough complexity to grab our attention. Drink up. Score 88. K

ELLA VALLEY VINEYARDS, SEMILLON-VIOGNIER, 2010: A blend of about 60% Semillon and 40% Viognier, fermented partly in stainless steel and partly in oak, showing more blonde than gold in color, medium-bodied, with fine acidity and aromatics. A rich floral nose parts to make way for aromas and flavors of ripe summer fruits and grapefruit peel, those with a light spicy overtone. Long and generous. Drink now–2014. Score 88. K

ELLA VALLEY VINEYARDS, MUSCAT DESSERT WINE, 2006: Full-bodied with lots of glycerin, avoiding the sometimes too-too flowery nature of the Muscat grape, and with fine balancing acidity to set off the generous sweetness. Dark gold in color, sitting almost thickly but comfortably on the palate and showing both fresh and dried honeyed apricots, those yielding to pear and raisin compote. Generous and long. Perhaps best not with dessert but as dessert. Drink now. Score 90. K

ELLA VALLEY VINEYARDS, MUSCAT DESSERT, 2003: Medium-bodied, unabashedly sweet but with fine balance between sugar, acidity and alcohol. On the nose and palate aromas and flavors of honeyed summer fruits, stewed pears, sesame seeds and spring flowers. Generous, mouth-filling and long. Drink now. Score 90. K

Ever Red

EVER RED, 2007: A medium-bodied blend, gently tannic red, this year of 60% Merlot and 40% Cabernet Sauvignon. Developed for 14 months in *barriques*, shows appealing near-sweet blackberry, currant and black cherry fruits, those on a background of light and just-spicy-enough oak. Not complex but comfortable drinking. Drink up. Score 87. K

EVER RED, 2006: A medium-bodied blend of Cabernet Sauvignon, Merlot and Petite Sirah (45%, 45% and 10% respectively) that was developed for 14 months in *barriques*. Soft, near-sweet tannins integrating nicely with red berries, red currants and light oak, all showing a gentle spicy note. Drink up. Score 88. K

Manne

MANNE, MERLOT, 2008: Medium-bodied, developed in stainless-steel tanks together with oak staves, showing soft tannins and near sweet blackberry and black cherry fruits on a lightly spicy background. Not complex but a good quaffer. Drink up. Score 85. K

MANNE, ANDROMEDA, 2008: A blend of 50% each of Cabernet Sauvignon and Merlot, developed in stainless steel with oak staves. Dark ruby toward garnet, with soft tannins and gentle wood influences and showing currant and wild berry fruits. A good entry-level quaffer. Drink up. Score 85. K

Erle ★★★

Ari Erle comes from a family of vintners, their Aroyo Vineyard located on Moshav Givat Nili (not far from Zichron Ya'akov). Releasing its first wines from the 2006 vintage, this is an artisanal winery producing about 3,000 bottles annually, those from Merlot, Carignan, Argaman and Sauvignon Blanc grapes.

ERLE, MERLOT, AROYO VINEYARD, ISRAEL, 2007: Blended with a bit of Argaman, deep royal purple in color, medium- to full-bodied with gently gripping tannins and hints of sweet cedarwood parting to reveal a generous mouthful of wild berry, currant and purple plums. From mid-palate on peppery notes that linger nicely on the finish. Long and generous. Drink now. Score 89.

ERLE, CARIGNAN, AROYO VINEYARD, ISRAEL, 2007: Medium-dark garnet toward royal purple in color, medium-bodied, developed primarily in used oak, showing soft, round and smooth. On the nose and palate berries and black fruits along with notes of toasty oak and pepper and, on the finish, tannins rise along with an appealing hint of dark cocoa. Drink now. Score 90.

ERLE, ARGAMAN, AROYO VINEYARD, ISRAEL, 2007: Like all wines made from Israel's own cultivar, the Argaman grape, this one has excellent color, excellent color and excellent color. Although it lacks any discernible nose, the wine is medium-bodied, has soft tannins (those perhaps more from the wood in which it was aged than the grape itself) and some appealing wild berry and black cherry notes. Neither long nor complex but a good quaffing wine. Drink now. Score 85.

ERLE, SAUVIGNON BLANC, AROYO VINEYARD, ISRAEL, 2007: Light golden straw in color, medium-bodied, showing fine balancing acidity and a light frizzante note, opens to reveal aromas and flavors of citrus, pineapple and tropical fruits, those with a vague but tantalizing grassy note, all lingering long and comfortably on the palate. Don't be put off by the white crystals you see in the bottom of the bottle as those are nothing but tartrate crystals that have formed because the wine was not cold stabilized." Whatever, the crystals are absolutely harmless. Simultaneously refreshing and complex, this would be judged a well-made Sauvignon Blanc no matter from where it came. Drink now. Score 90.

Essence **

Located in the community of Ma'aleh Tsvia in the Western Galilee, the winery was founded by Yaniv Kimchi, Eitan Rosenberg and Itzhak Avramov, and released its first wines in 2001. Grapes, including Cabernet Sauvignon and Merlot, are raised in the winery's organic vineyards at the foothills of Mount Kamon, and the wines are made in accordance with international organic standards. The winery's output is currently about 10,000 bottles annually.

ESSENCE, CABERNET SAUVIGNON, 2006: Garnet toward royal purple, medium-bodied, with firm but nicely integrating tannins and revealing currant, wild berry and blackberry fruits. Drink now. Score 84.

ESSENCE, CABERNET SAUVIGNON, RESERVE, 2005: Dark ruby toward garnet, medium- to full-bodied, with chunky country-style tannins and generous spicy wood. Opens to reveal berry, black cherry and cassis fruits. Drink up. Score 85.

ESSENCE, MERLOT, 2006: Showing generous spicy and smoky wood, with chunky, country-style tannins, those settling down slowly to reveal blackberry, raspberry and citrus peel. Drink up. Score 83.

ESSENCE, MERLOT, 2005: Oak-aged for 14 months, with now–soft tannins and once-generous wood now integrating, this medium-bodied red opens in the glass to show berry and cherry fruits. Drink up. Score 84.

ESSENCE, ELECTRUM, 2005: Aged in *barriques* for 24 months, this medium-bodied blend of equal parts of Cabernet Sauvignon and Merlot shows drying tannins and a distinctly bitter note that overlays black cherry and currant notes. Drink up. Score 84.

Eyal Winery ∗∗∗

Located on Moshav Givat Nili, not far from Zichron Ya'akov and Wadi Ara, this family-owned winery was established by Eyal Ochayaon and first releases are from the 2008 vintage. Grapes, including Cabernet Sauvignon, Merlot, Shiraz and Carignan, are from family-owned vineyards. Current releases are about 4,000 bottles annually. The wines will be kosher from the 2009 vintage.

EYAL, CABERNET SAUVIGNON, 2009: Destined as are all of the wines of this boutique winery for 14 months in *barriques*, and even now showing near-sweet tannins and spicy oak. Opens in the glass to show traditional blackcurrant and blackberry fruits, those complemented nicely by a note of green olives on the long finish. Drink now–2016. Score 88. K

EYAL, CABERNET SAUVIGNON, 2008: Oak-aged in French *barriques* for 14 months and blended with 15% Merlot. Showing light garnet in color, medium-bodied and with silky soft, almost unfelt tannins. Aromas and flavors of black cherries, wild berries and spices. A pleasant quaffer. Drink now. Score 86.

EYAL, MERLOT, 2009: Dark garnet, medium- to full-bodied with still-gripping tannins and spicy oak needing time to integrate but already opening to show black cherries and black and red berries on a background that hints nicely of roasted herbs and baking chocolate. Drink from release–2015. Tentative Score 87–89. K

EYAL, MERLOT, 2008: Merlot blended with 15% Cabernet Sauvignon and oak-aged for 14 months. Ruby toward garnet, medium-bodied, with soft tannins and generous cherry, berry and cassis fruits that sit comfortably on the palate. A simple quaffer. Drink now. Score 85.

EYAL, SHIRAZ, 2009: Dark royal purple, medium- to full-bodied, with soft tannins and notes of smoky oak. Opens to an appealing array of blackcurrants, plums, Oriental spices and, on the long finish, notes of licorice. Drink now–2015. Score 88. K

EYAL, CARIGNAN, 2009: Medium-bodied, with soft tannins and notes of spicy cedarwood, a round and well-balanced wine showing generous black fruits on a stony-mineral background. Appealing. Drink now. Score 87. K

Flam ★★★★★

Located in a thoroughly modern facility not far from the town of Beit Shemesh at the foothills of the Jerusalem Mountains, the Flam winery has produced consistently excellent and exciting wines since its first releases from the 1998 vintage. Established by brothers Golan and Gilad Flam; Golan, having trained and worked in Australia and Tuscany, is the winemaker; Gilad is in charge of the business aspects. Also working with the two brothers is their father, Israel Flam, who was for many years the senior winemaker at Carmel.

The winery is currently producing age-worthy varietal Cabernet Sauvignon and Merlot wines in their Reserve and Superiore series; a second wine, Classico, which is a blend of Cabernet Sauvignon and Merlot that is meant for relatively early drinking; and a label for white wine, Flam.

Starting with the 2008 vintage the winery is also scheduled to release a new flagship wine, a special reserve that has yet to receive an official name. Current production is about 130,000 bottles annually. Of those about 15,000 are white wines.

Grapes come primarily from vineyards over which the winery has full control, in the Judean Mountains and the Galilee. In addition to current reliance on Cabernet Sauvignon, Merlot, Syrah, Chardonnay and Sauvignon Blanc, other varieties including Cabernet Franc, Petit Verdot and Mourvedre are soon to come on line. Starting with the 2010 vintage the Flam wines will be kosher.

Special Reserve

SPECIAL RESERVE, CABERNET SAUVIGNON (NOT OFFICIAL NAME), 2009: Destined for oak-aging in tight-grained new oak for 20 months, already showing dark garnet and boasting a generously spicy nose. A ripe, full-bodied wine, rich and layered, opening in the glass to reveal a complex array of aromas and flavors, those including plums, blackberries, wild berries and blackcurrants, all unfolding in ways that are graceful and complex. On the super-long finish notes of spices rise together with black licorice and mocha. Scheduled for release in 2012, but give this one the time it needs to show its true elegance. Best from 2013–2020. Tentative Score 92–94.

Reserve

RESERVE, CABERNET SAUVIGNON, 2010: Made from grapes from Kerem Ben Zimra, waiting to be blended with small amounts of Merlot and/or Petit Verdot. Impenetrable inky garnet in color, full-bodied and with still-gripping tannins but already showing fine potential. Opens with jammy red currants and raspberries, the jammy sensation passing quickly and going on to black fruits on a spice- and licorice-rich background. Best from 2014. Tentative Score 91–94. K

RESERVE, CABERNET SAUVIGNON, 2009: Made from Cabernet Sauvignon grapes from the Ben Zimra and Dishon vineyards in the Upper Galilee, developing in French oak *barriques*, and blended with a bit of Petit Verdot, showing fine potential. Full-bodied, with soft, gently mouth-coating tannins, opening in the glass to reveal red and black currants, blackberries and wild berry fruits. On the long, fresh finish notes of freshly turned earth. Best from 2013. Tentative Score 90–92.

RESERVE, CABERNET SAUVIGNON, 2008: Developed in new French oak for 18 months, a blend of 92% Cabernet Sauvignon and 4% each of Merlot and Petit Verdot. Deep, almost impenetrable garnet in color, with spicy oak on the nose, that oak having the grace of showing only gently in the glass. On the nose and palate wild berries, blackcurrants and spiced plums, all on a background that hints at one moment of garrigue and another of roasted herbs. Drink now–2020. Score 94.

RESERVE, CABERNET SAUVIGNON, 2007: A blend of 87% Cabernet Sauvignon, 9% Merlot and 4% Petit Verdot, oak-aged for 16 months and showing gently caressing tannins and a not at all imposing note of spicy cedarwood. Dark, almost impenetrable garnet, full-bodied, opening to reveal ripe berry, currant and citrus peel notes on first attack, those yielding to Mediterranean herbs and notes of licorice. Long and generous. Drink now–2016. Score 91.

RESERVE, CABERNET SAUVIGNON, 2006: Oak-aged for about 16 months, a full-bodied, gently tannic and concentrated blend of 87% Cabernet Sauvignon, 10% Merlot and 3% Petit Verdot. Firm on first attack but unfolding beautifully in the glass, showing dark cherry red toward garnet with soft, near-sweet tannins and notes of spicy wood, opens with a mélange of black cherry, blackberry and currant notes, and reveals hints of red berries, brown spices and chocolate. Long, broad and elegant. Drinking beautifully now but don't hesitate to cellar until 2016. Score 92.

RESERVE, CABERNET SAUVIGNON, 2005: The first thing to hit you (albeit a rather nice blow) is the bittersweet chocolate on the nose and only then spicy oak, now settled down comfortably from earlier tastings. A blend of 88% Cabernet Sauvignon with 6% each of Merlot and Petit Verdot, opening firm and gripping but yielding nicely in the glass to show a complex array of blackcurrant, black cherry, anise and Mediterranean herbs and, on the long finish, hints of red licorice. Drink now–2016. Score 93.

RESERVE, CABERNET SAUVIGNON, 2004: Deep garnet toward black, full-bodied, with once-searing tannins now integrating nicely. This blend of 88% Cabernet Sauvignon and 12% of Merlot reflects its 18 months in *barriques* with spicy wood and tannins in fine balance with natural acidity and currant, plum and blackberry fruits. On the long finish hints of mint and spices. Drink now–2014. Score 91.

RESERVE, CABERNET SAUVIGNON, 2003: This full-bodied, dark garnet toward inky-purple wine, blended with 7% of Merlot, was oak-aged for about 14 months. Generous blackcurrant and cherry fruits come together elegantly with mineral, herbal and light earthy aromas and flavors, all with a hint of smoky-toasty oak. Super-smooth tannins and a long finish. Drink now–2014. Score 93.

RESERVE, CABERNET SAUVIGNON, 2002: Made from Cabernet Sauvignon grapes from the Upper Galilee and blended with a small amount of Merlot from Karmei Yosef, this elegant, deep garnet toward black wine shows good integration between wood, soft tannins, sweet cedar and generous currant and ripe red fruits. A long fruity and lightly herbal finish. Holding its own nicely. Drink now or in the next year or so. Score 90.

RESERVE, CABERNET SAUVIGNON, 2001: Dark garnet, a deeply extracted wine still holding its own and showing remarkable softness. A full-bodied, now softly tannic and distinctly Mediterranean red continuing to show fine balance between wood, tannins and fruit. Traditional Cabernet blackcurrants are well set off by cherries, berries, spices and hints of black olives and leather. Drink now. Score 93.

RESERVE, CABERNET SAUVIGNON, 2000: Dark garnet, medium- to full-bodied blend of 90% Cabernet Sauvignon and 10% Merlot reflecting its 15 months in oak with now-soft tannins and a bare "kiss" of the wood. On the nose and palate still-fresh black and red currants, those matched now by appealing notes of earthy minerals and brown spices. Showing first signs of fading in the glass so drink up. Score 90.

RESERVE, CABERNET SAUVIGNON, 1999: Fully mature but remaining as dark garnet in color today as during its youth, albeit with a hint of browning, this deep and profound oak-aged blend of 85% Cabernet Sauvignon and 15% Merlot has intense berry, mint and cassis aromas and flavors, along with still-ample hints of spicy oak. On the outer cusp of its peak but still elegant and refined, with silky tannins and a succulent finish. Drink up. Score 90.

RESERVE, MERLOT, 2010: Made from Merlot grapes from the Dishon vineyard in the Upper Galilee, destined to be blended with small percentages of Petit Verdot and/or Cabernet Sauvignon. Deep, youthful royal purple, full-bodied with soft, gently caressing tannins opening with red berry and cassis fruits, those parting to reveal black cherries and plums, all complemented by notes of spicy cedarwood and a hint of cinnamon that tantalizes. Drink from release–2017. Tentative Score 90–93. K

RESERVE, MERLOT, 2009: Made from grapes from the Dishon vineyard in the Upper Galilee and now developing in French oak. My second barrel tasting, its once-gripping tannins now settling in nicely. On the nose and palate spicy oak, wild berry, red currant and black cherry fruits complemented nicely by notes of roasted herbs and earthy minerals. Long and generous, a touch of red licorice on the finish. Drink from release–2016, perhaps longer. Tentative Score 89–91.

RESERVE, MERLOT, 2008: Oak-aged in French barriques for 15 months, a blend of 90% Merlot and 5% each of Petit Verdot and Cabernet Sauvignon. Dark garnet toward royal purple, with ample soft tannins and a gentle hand with the oak, showing aromas and flavors of currants and black cherries, those supported nicely by notes of peppermint, spring flowers and spices, a tempting light, earthy note rising on the long finish. Drink now–2018. Score 92.

RESERVE, MERLOT, 2007: Oak-aged for 15 months, a full-bodied blend of 92% Merlot and 4% each Cabernet Sauvignon and Petit Verdot with the firm tannins and spicy wood of youth now integrating nicely. Opens with a generous array of blackberries, blueberries and cigar-box aromas and flavors, those leading to a long finish on which bittersweet chocolate and cherry liqueur. Drink now–2016. Score 91.

RESERVE, MERLOT, 2006: Dark garnet, full-bodied, with firm tannins and generous oak in fine balance with fruits and acidity but still needing a bit of time for its elements to fully integrate. A blend of 90% Merlot and 10% Petit Verdot. Opens in the glass to show a fine array of raspberry, blueberry and cassis fruits, those on a background of espresso coffee and sweet cedar. Drink now–2015. Score 92.

RESERVE, MERLOT, 2005: Dark garnet toward royal purple, medium- to full-bodied, reflecting its oak-aging with soft, gently mouth-coating tannins and notes of spicy wood. Look for a tempting light earthiness that supports blackberries, currants, and a touch of spiciness that weaves its way through the wine and then lingers nicely on a long, elegant finish. Drink now–2013. Score 92.

RESERVE, MERLOT, 2004: Dark garnet with orange and green reflections. Made entirely from Merlot grapes, full-bodied and tannic. On first attack peppery wood reflecting 16 months in oak, that opening slowly to reveal firm, mouth-coating tannins, then showing a tempting array of currant, berry and black cherry fruits, those backed up nicely by spices and, on the long finish, a hint of crème Anglaise. Continuing to develop nicely. Drink now. Score 92.

RESERVE, MERLOT, 2003: Blended with 7% Cabernet Sauvignon, dark, deep and intense, with soft, almost sweet tannins and layer after layer of berry, black cherry, anise and spice aromas and flavors that linger nicely on the palate. The once-marked wood influence is now receding and the wine is showing soft, round and long. Drink now. Score 90.

RESERVE, SYRAH, 2010: Deep royal purple, full-bodied and concentrated with blackberries, black cherries, red plums and wild berries, those supported by notes of spring flowers. As the wine continues to develop look as well for notes of cherry pie. Well structured, tight, deep and long. Best from 2013. Tentative Score 90–93. K

RESERVE, SYRAH, 2009: More an elegant Rhone than a blockbuster Australian or Californian, showing medium-dark garnet, full-bodied, with soft tannins and a gentle wood influence. Opens to reveal plum, blackberry and nutty aromas and flavors. Potentially a round and elegant wine. Drink from release–2016. Tentative Score 88–90.

RESERVE, SYRAH, 2008: Developed in 80% first- and second-year French oak and 20% new American oak, shows full-bodied, well concentrated and round, with soft, gently mouth-coating tannins and spicy and vanilla notes integrating nicely. Aromatic, and on the nose and palate red fruits, leather, roasted herbs and tempting notes of mocha and baking chocolate. Drink now–2016, perhaps longer. Score 92.

RESERVE, SYRAH, 2007: Dark garnet with purple reflections, medium- to full-bodied with round, gently caressing tannins and a generously fruity personality. Look for raspberries and red currants on a lightly meaty and spicy background, all lingering nicely on the palate. Drink now–2013. Score 90.

RESERVE, SYRAH, 2005: Dark garnet in color, with hints of dusty wood on first attack, those yielding to appealing plum, wild berry and mint. Full-bodied and chewy but soft and elegant. Drink now. Score 90.

RESERVE, SYRAH, 2004: Garnet to royal purple, aged in French and American *barriques*, this aromatic, medium- to full-bodied wine shows firm but yielding tannins, gentle wood and a tempting array of berry and plum fruits, those backed up by hints of Oriental spices, chocolate and light earthiness. Drink now. Score 90.

Superiore

SUPERIORE, SYRAH, 2009: Deep, almost impenetrable royal purple in color, oak-aged for 12 months in French and American oak, a full-bodied and rich wine. Almost chewy but nicely rounded, a distinctly European style wine with aromas and flavors of blueberries, currants and raspberries, those supported by notes of espresso and licorice. Long and generous. Drink now–2016. Score 91.

SUPERIORE, SYRAH, 2008: A graceful wine, filled with rich, fresh flavors. Medium- to full-bodied, with silky-smooth tannins and with well-focused blueberry, blackberry and huckleberry fruit. Remarkably easy to drink, but look beyond that ease and find a very appealing complexity here. Drink now–2015. Score 91.

SUPERIORE, 2007: Youthful ruby toward royal purple, medium- to full-bodied, with gently mouth-coating tannins and notes of spicy and toasty oak, a blend of 72% Syrah and 28% Cabernet Sauvignon. Aromatic, with black fruits and a note of leather first attack, opens to reveal blackberry, cassis and vanilla notes. From mid-palate on a tantalizing note of resin and on the long finish a hint of cigar smoke. Soft, round and comfortably elegant. Drink now. Score 90.

SUPERIORE, 2006: A blend of 86% Syrah and 14% Cabernet, oak-aged for 12 months in French and American oak. Medium- to full-bodied, with soft tannins integrating nicely and a nice "bite" of spicy wood. Concentrated on the palate, showing purple plum, blackberry and raspberry fruits, those supported by tantalizing hints of leather and smoked meat. Drink now. Score 91.

SUPERIORE, 2005: A blend of 81% Syrah and 19% Cabernet Sauvignon. After 12 months in oak, this dark ruby-red is medium- to full-bodied, with fine-grained tannins and lively cherry, raspberry and cassis fruits, those supported nicely by hints of herbs, cedar and spring flowers. About to pass its peak. Drink up. Score 90.

SUPERIORE, 2004: A blend of 80% Syrah and 20% Cabernet Sauvignon showing toasty oak, smoke and generous but soft tannins, those matched nicely by spicy plum, berry and black cherry fruits. A long, round and elegantly near-sweet finish. Drink up. Score 90.

Classico

CLASSICO, 2009: The by now traditional blend of equal parts of Cabernet Sauvignon and Merlot, 30% of which aged in new oak, the remainder in second- and third-year oak for six months. Generous black fruits on the nose, medium- to full-bodied, with gently caressing tannins and an appealing array of blackberry, currant and wild berry fruits, those showing hints of dark chocolate and licorice. Drink now–2014. Score 89.

CLASSICO, 2008: A blend of equal parts of Cabernet Sauvignon and Merlot, oak-aged in American oak for six months. Dark royal purple in color, opens to show light notes of toasty wood that complement appealing cherry, berry and currant fruits. Soft, round and generous with just enough complexity to catch our attention. Drink now. Score 89.

CLASSICO, 2007: A gently oak-aged blend of Cabernet Sauvignon and Merlot, showing light hints of tobacco, chocolate and spicy cedarwood to highlight currant, blackberry and black cherry fruits. Medium- to full-bodied, with soft tannins throughout and, on the long finish, a hint of Mediterranean herbs. Drink up. Score 89.

Flam

FLAM, ROSÉ, 2010: Made this year entirely from Cabernet Franc grapes, those allowed three to four hours on the skins after crushing. Rose-petal pink, light- to medium-bodied, with fine balancing acidity, a lively and just complex enough rosé wine showing aromas and flavors of strawberries, cherries and cassis and, if you let the wine sit on the tongue for a few minutes, a bare and tantalizing hint of tannins. Delicious and refreshing. Drink now. Score 90. K

FLAM, ROSÉ, 2009: Oh what a lovely rosé! A blend of 70% Cabernet Franc and 30% Merlot, those allowed only short skin contact, showing cherry-red in color and on the nose and palate red cherries, raspberries and cassis fruits. Fresh, lively and crisp, with an appealing flinty mineral note that lingers nicely. Drink now. Score 89.

FLAM, SAUVIGNON BLANC-CHARDONNAY, 2010: An intentionally unoaked blend of 67% Sauvignon Blanc and 33% Chardonnay. Not subjected to malolactic fermentation in order to safeguard the natural flavors of the grapes, light golden straw in color, medium-bodied, with finely tuned acidity keeping the wine crisp and refreshing while not losing its complexity. Look for aromas and flavors of spicy citrus and tropical fruits, those hanging on through a long, lively finish on which fine notes of stony minerals. Drink now. Score 90. K

FLAM, SAUVIGNON BLANC-CHARDONNAY, 2009: As always an unoaked, crisply clean wine, this year a blend of 60% Sauvignon Blanc and 40% Chardonnay. Golden straw in color, medium-bodied, showing citrus fruits and flowers, stony minerals and from mid-palate on notes of guava. Refreshing enough to drink in large gulps but complex enough to savor comfortably. Drink up. Score 89.

FLAM, SAUVIGNON BLANC-CHARDONNAY, 2008: A blend this year of 80% Sauvignon Blanc and 20% Chardonnay, those wisely unoaked to maintain the wine as crisply fresh and aromatic. Shows tropical and citrus fruits along with citrus flowers and flinty minerals. Fine balance here between fruits and acidity to make the wine both lively and fascinating. Drink up. Score 90.

Flegmann ✶✶

To the best of my knowledge, this is not so much an independent winery as it is a set of private label wines made especially for the Flegmann family at the Psagot Winery.

FLEGMANN, CABERNET SAUVIGNON, JUDEAN HILLS, 2007: Garnet to royal purple, medium- to full-bodied with gripping tannins and generous spicy wood that seem not to want to settle in. When the wine does open it shows muted black fruits and Mediterranean herbs on a background of freshly turned earth. Drink now. Score 86. K

FLEGMANN, CABERNET SAUVIGNON, JUDEAN HILLS, 2006: Dark garnet, medium- to full-bodied, with somewhat chunky country-style tannins. On the nose and palate traditional Cabernet currant and blackberry fruits and, on the moderately long finish, hints of licorice and green olives. Drink up. Score 87. K

FLEGMANN, MERLOT, JUDEAN HILLS, 2007: Garnet toward royal purple, medium- to full-bodied with gripping tannins that part slowly to show blackberry, raspberry and purple plum fruits, Not typical of the variety but an appealing quaffer. Drink now. Score 85. K

FLEGMANN, MERLOT, JUDEAN HILLS, 2006: Ruby toward garnet, medium-bodied, with soft tannins and well-balanced, a pleasant albeit somewhat internationalized Merlot, opening to show blackberry and black cherry fruits, those on a lightly spicy and minty background. Drink up. Score 86. K

Gad *

Located on Moshav Sdot Micha in the Ella Valley, this boutique winery was founded by Amir Baruch in 2000. Production, primarily from Cabernet Sauvignon, Merlot, Syrah and Petite Sirah grapes from vineyards in Karmei Yosef, is currently about 10,000 bottles annually.

GAD, CABERNET SAUVIGNON, RESERVE, 2006: Dark but not clear garnet in color, with gripping tannins and searing alcohol, already oxidizing and showing Port-like aromas and flavors. Lacks balance or charm. Score 65. K

GAD, CABERNET SAUVIGNON, 2006: Dark ruby, with too-generous dusty and smoky oak reflecting the simultaneous use of oak barrels and oak chips for five months. Muddy flavors hold back whatever fruits may be lurking here. Score 70. K

GAD, CABERNET SAUVIGNON, RESERVE, 2005: An oak-aged blend of 90% Cabernet Sauvignon and 10% Merlot. Medium-bodied, with coarse tannins and a far-too-generous dose of wood on the palate and nose. Lacks balance. Score 72. K

GAD, CABERNET SAUVIGNON, 2005: Garnet-red, with chunky, country-style tannins and spicy berry-black cherry fruits. Lacks depth, breadth or length. Drink up. Score 78. K

GAD, MERLOT, 2005: Dark ruby-red, light- to medium-bodied, with chunky tannins, a few berry, cherry fruits and a too-herbal finish. One-dimensional. Drink up. Score 76. K

GAD, BLEND, 2005: A potpourri of Cabernet Sauvignon, Merlot, Syrah, Petite Sirah and Argaman grapes. Medium-bodied, with flabby tannins, far too acidic and not fruity enough. Score 70. K

Galai ✷✷

Sigalit and Asaf Galai established this small winery at Moshav Nir Akiva in the northern part of the Negev Desert in 2002 and use the facilities of the Asif service winery to make their wines. The winery has vineyards containing Cabernet Sauvignon and Merlot as well as experimental sections of Cabernet Franc, Shiraz and Zinfandel. Current production is about 7,000 bottles annually.

GALAI
ESTATE WINE

2002
Cabernet Sauvignon

12.5% vol.　　Unfiltered　　℮750 ml.

GALAI, CABERNET SAUVIGNON, 2007: Medium- to full-bodied, with somewhat chunky country-style tannins and generous wood. On the nose and palate blackberries, cherries and currants supported by notes of freshly roasted herbs. A not-complex but appealing country-style wine. Drink now. Score 85.

GALAI, CABERNET SAUVIGNON, 2006: Garnet toward royal purple, medium-bodied, with firm tannins and generous wood needing time to settle in. Opens in the glass to reveal black cherry, blackberry and peppery notes that linger nicely. Drink up. Score 85.

GALAI, CABERNET SAUVIGNON, 2005: Dark garnet and medium-bodied, with firm but yielding tannins and light smoky oak. On the nose and palate generous blackcurrant, red and black berries and a hint of white pepper that comes in on the finish. Drink up. Score 85.

GALAI, MERLOT, 2007: Dark royal purple in color, with soft, gently caressing tannins, and opening to show wild berry, cassis and smoky herbal notes. Drink now. Score 86.

GALAI, MERLOT, 2006: Medium- to full-bodied, dark garnet, with silky tannins and showing appealing black fruits on a lightly smoky and spicy background. Drink up. Score 85.

Galil Mountain ✳✳✳✳

Having celebrated its tenth anniversary in 2010, with its physically beautiful, ecologically friendly, state-of-the-art winery located on Kibbutz Yiron in the Upper Galilee, this joint venture between the Golan Heights Winery and the kibbutz has vineyards located in some of the best wine-growing areas of the Upper Galilee, including Yiron, Meron, Misgav Am, Yiftach and Malkiya. Senior winemaker Micha Vaadia and winemaker Boaz Mizrachi Adam produce distinctly terroir-based wines in two series. The first labels are Yiron, a blend of Cabernet Sauvignon and Merlot, and Meron, a unique blend of Syrah, Cabernet Sauvignon and Petit Verdot. The regular labels, Galil Mountain and Avivim, contain varietal releases of Cabernet Sauvignon, Merlot, Pinot Noir, Syrah, Sangiovese, Chardonnay and Sauvignon Blanc. Production from the 2000 vintage was about 300,000 bottles. Since then the winery has grown to an output of approximately one million bottles annually and further vineyards are being developed.

Yiron

YIRON, 2009: A blend at this stage largely of Cabernet Sauvignon, that fleshed out with Merlot and Petite Sirah. Dark garnet with a youthful royal purple robe, showing vanilla-scented red fruits on the nose, those yielding comfortably to currants, wild berries and vanilla, all on a pleasingly spicy background. Still-gripping tannins and spicy wood here but those in fine balance with fruits and acidity and boding well for the future. A lovely and promising baby. Best from 2013. Tentative Score 89–91. K

YIRON, 2008: Dark garnet, full-bodied, with still-gripping tannins waiting to settle down, showing a moderate hand with spicy oak. A blend primarily of Cabernet Sauvignon and Merlot, those fleshed out with Cabernet Franc and Petit Verdot. On first attack ripe red berries and spices, those parting to make way for blackberries, currants and hints of vanilla and mocha, all lingering long and nicely. Needs a bit of time for its elements to come fully together but they will, indeed they will! Best from 2013–2018. Score 92. K

YIRON, 2007: A well-balanced and firmly structured full-bodied blend of 62% Cabernet Sauvignon, 31% Merlot and 7% Syrah, living up nicely to its earlier promise. On the nose and palate blueberries, blackberries and stony minerals, those yielding to blackcurrants and purple plums all sitting comfortably on a background that hints of saddle leather and dark chocolate. Long and elegant. Drink now–2017. Score 92. K

YIRON, 2006: Dark garnet in color, full-bodied, with soft tannins and gentle spicy and vanilla notes from the oak in which it aged, a blend of Cabernet Sauvignon, Merlot and Syrah (58%, 37% and 5% respectively). Showing fine balance and structure. On first attack raspberries on a lightly spicy background, those yielding to currants, blackberries and purple plums. Round, long and elegant. Drink now–2016. Score 91. K

YIRON, 2005: Dark, almost impenetrable garnet in color, a blend of 50% Cabernet Sauvignon, 44%, 4% Syrah and 2% Petite Sirah (depending on which of the winemaker's notes you read that might be 2% of Petit Verdot). Whatever, full-bodied, with its once-firm tannins now integrated nicely and reflecting its 16 months in barriques with a gentle overlay of spicy cedarwood. Opens to reveal aromas and flavors of blackberries, cassis, purple plums and vanilla, those leading to a long dark chocolate and licorice-tinged finish. Drink now–2015. Score 93. K

YIRON, 2004: A blend of 72% Cabernet Sauvignon, 25% Merlot and 3% Syrah. Intense garnet toward royal purple, full-bodied, with firm, near-sweet tannins integrating nicely with smoky and vanilla-tinged wood. Opens with wild berries on the nose and palate, those yielding to black cherry, cassis and spices, and finally, on the long finish, a tantalizing hint of bitterness. Drink now–2013. Score 91. K

YIRON, 2003: A blend of Cabernet Sauvignon, Merlot and Syrah (61%, 32% and 7% respectively), showing dark, almost impenetrably garnet in color. Full-bodied, with now-soft tannins and hints of spicy wood in fine proportion with fruits and acidity. On the nose and palate blackberries, blackcurrants and black cherries, those with an appealing overlay of earth minerals. Long, generous and mouth-filling. Drink now. Score 90. K

YIRON, 2002: Medium- to full-bodied, a dark-garnet blend of 54% Cabernet Sauvignon and 46% Merlot, its once-firm tannins and generous wood now fully integrated. A mature wine, continuing to show abundant currant, purple plum and berry fruits on a background of sweet cedarwood with the once-light, herbal-earthy overtone now on the ascendant. Sliding past its peak. Drink up. Score 89. K

YIRON, 2001: Dark, impenetrable garnet but with a hint of browning at the rim showing its maturity, the still-fresh nose starting to hint at a light balsamic overlay. Generous fruits still here, those including blackberries and currants on a cherry-liqueur background. Throwing sediment now, with earlier hints of tobacco and dark chocolate starting to take on a somewhat medicinal note. Past its peak and not for further cellaring. Drink up. Score 88. K

YIRON, SYRAH, 2005: Dark, almost inky-garnet in color, medium- to full-bodied, with fine balance between soft tannins, spicy wood and fruits. On first attack raspberries and chocolate, those yielding to blackberries, currants and a rich floral note. On the long finish the tannins rise along with fruits and an appealing hint of red licorice. Drink now–2013. Score 91. K

YIRON, SYRAH, 2004: Dark royal purple with orange and green reflections, opening with a rich fruity and floral nose. Full-bodied, with bold but soft tannins integrating nicely with spicy wood and showing black fruits, dusty wood and light meaty and earthy overlays. Long and deep. Drink now. Score 91. K

YIRON, SYRAH, 2003: Full-bodied, showing soft tannins with just enough grip to catch the attention, those yielding nicely to light spicy wood. Dark garnet in color, aromatic, with blackberries, purple plums and hints of white pepper and chocolate as well as a light meaty-earthy sensation that comes in on the round and comfortably medium-long finish. Drink now. Score 91. K

Meron

MERON, 2008: A blend of 69% Syrah, 21% Petit Verdot and 10% Cabernet Sauvignon. Full-bodied, with generous soft tannins that caress

rather than grip, opens with a red-fruit nose, making way in the glass for blackberries and purple plums, all on a background of bittersweet chocolate, freshly picked herbs, green olives and earthy minerals. Approachable now but best 2013–2018. Score 92. K

MERON, 2007: Oak-aged for 16 months, a dark-garnet blend of Syrah, Cabernet Sauvignon and Petit Verdot (81%, 10% and 9% respectively). Full-bodied and concentrated, with a generous 15% alcohol content but simultaneously soft and round, with gentle notes of spicy cedarwood, opens to show an appealing array of cassis, blackberries and red plums, those supported nicely by notes of grilled herbs and earthy minerals. Drink now–2016. Score 91. K

MERON, 2006: An unusual but highly successful blend of Syrah, Cabernet Sauvignon and Petit Verdot. A full-bodied, softly tannic blend of 78% Syrah and 11% each of Cabernet Sauvignon and Petit Verdot, most assuredly representing the terroir of the Upper Galilee. Aromatic, with a distinctly blueberry-scented nose, opens nicely in the glass to reveal a rich array of blackberries, cassis, cranberries and freshly snipped rosemary and thyme, those yielding on the generous finish to hints of what at one moment seems to be spearmint, at another, eucalyptus. Long and generous, reflecting its 16 months in French oak with a tantalizing note of white pepper. Drink now–2016. Score 92. K

Galil Mountain

GALIL MOUNTAIN, CABERNET SAUVIGNON, 2010: Tasted from components, showing garnet toward royal purple, medium- to full-bodied, with soft tannins and hints of sweet-and-spicy oak already integrating nicely. On the nose and palate traditional Cabernet blackcurrant and blackberry fruits, those supported comfortably by notes of figs, boysenberry and cocoa. On the long finish a hint of lead pencil. Drink from release–2016. Tentative Score 88–90. K

GALIL MOUNTAIN, CABERNET SAUVIGNON, 2009: Unoaked, showing medium dark garnet with purple and orange reflections, medium-bodied and with soft, gently caressing tannins. On the nose and palate blackcurrants, blackberries and blueberries and, lurking comfortably in the background, notes of green olives and freshly hung tobacco. Drink now–2013. Score 88. K

GALIL MOUNTAIN, CABERNET SAUVIGNON, 2008: Medium- to full-bodied, deep garnet, with ample and gently mouth-coating tannins to highlight aromas and flavors of cassis and black cherries, those supported comfortably by notes of minted chocolate. Drink now. Score 88. K

GALIL MOUNTAIN, CABERNET SAUVIGNON, 2007: Dark ruby toward garnet, medium-bodied, with soft, gently caressing tannins, and showing an appealing array of blackberries, blackcurrants and fruits on a background that hints nicely of minted chocolate. Drink now. Score 87. K

GALIL MOUNTAIN, CABERNET SAUVIGNON, 2006: Super-dark garnet, showing moderate spicy and vanilla notes and soft, near-sweet tannins. On the nose and palate blackberries and blueberries, currants and, coming in from mid-palate, hints of earthiness and freshly turned mushrooms. Drink up. Score 90. K

GALIL MOUNTAIN, MERLOT, 2010: Moderately deep garnet in color, medium- to full-bodied, with a nose that hints nicely of eucalyptus and freshly picked herbs. On the nose and palate forward dark berries and peppery notes, those complemented by notes of raspberries and sweet spices. Drink from release–2014, perhaps longer. Tentative Score 87–89. K

GALIL MOUNTAIN, MERLOT, 2009: Garnet toward royal purple, an unoaked red, medium- to full-bodied, with soft, gently caressing tannins, showing currant, wild berry and purple plums on a lightly spicy background. Not complex but making for very pleasant drinking and at its best with small cuts of beef or veal. Drink now–2013. Score 86. K

GALIL MOUNTAIN, MERLOT, 2008: Garnet toward royal purple, medium- to full-bodied, an unoaked, softly tannic red with an array of wild berries, purple plums and *garrigue* on the nose and palate. Easy to drink with just enough complexity to catch our attention. Drink now. Score 87. K

GALIL MOUNTAIN, MERLOT, 2007: Unoaked, with soft, near-sweet tannins and showing inky-garnet in color. On the nose and palate red and black berries, cassis and hints of Oriental spices and dark chocolate. Drink up. Score 88. K

GALIL MOUNTAIN, MERLOT, 2006: Dark ruby toward garnet, medium- to full-bodied, with firm tannins settling in nicely now. On the nose and palate an array of red and black berries, purple plums and orange peel notes, those on a light background of Mediterranean herbs. Drink up. Score 90. K

GALIL MOUNTAIN, SHIRAZ, 2009: Dark ruby toward garnet, medium-perhaps medium- to full-bodied, with just firm enough tannins gripping gently. On the nose and palate purple plums, blackberries and black cherries, those on a background that hints at one moment of saddle leather and the next of licorice and roasted herbs. Drink now–2014. Score 89. K

GALIL MOUNTAIN, SHIRAZ, 2008: Unoaked, deep royal purple in color, medium- to full-bodied and generously fruity, showing appealing blackberry, cassis and black cherry fruits on a background of freshly turned earth. Gently tannic, round and moderately long, showing a bit of muscle on the finish. Drink now. Score 90. K

GALIL MOUNTAIN, SHIRAZ, 2007: Medium- to full-bodied, oak-aged for 13 months, with gently mouth-coating tannins and showing an appealing array of cherry, wild berry and peppery notes, with a hint of bitter almonds on the long finish. Drink now. Score 89. K

GALIL MOUNTAIN, SHIRAZ, 2006: Dark garnet, medium- to full-bodied, and aromatic with soft tannins integrating nicely and showing a generous array of red and black berries, cherries and plums, those on a lightly spicy background. Easy to drink but with enough complexity to command our attention. Sliding past its peak. Drink up. Score 86. K

GALIL MOUNTAIN, PINOT NOIR, 2010: Moderately deep ruby toward garnet, medium-, perhaps medium-to full-bodied, with a nose rich in currants and plums, those making way in the glass for an array of dried berries, currants, white pepper and spices, all unfolding, playing nicely and then lingering comfortably on the palate. As the wine continues to develop look for notes of licorice and dark chocolate. Well focused and long, rich and generous. Drink from release–2018. Tentative Score 90–92. K

GALIL MOUNTAIN, PINOT NOIR, 2009: Living up nicely to barrel-tasting promise. Developing in French *barriques*, dark ruby in color, medium-bodied, gently tannic, showing a lovely fruit-rich nose and equally tempting flavors. On the nose and palate red and black berries, black cherries and cassis, those reflecting a gentle hand with spicy wood. From mid-palate on hints of stony minerals and cedarwood. Pinot Noir true to its variety and happily reflecting its Galilean roots. A fine effort for the vintage. Drink now–2016. Score 90. K

GALIL MOUNTAIN, PINOT NOIR, 2008: Developed in one-year-old French *barriques*, showing deep ruby toward garnet in color, medium- to full-bodied, with soft tannins integrated nicely. On the opening attack black cherries, those going on to reveal notes of red and black berries, cassis and spices, all on a gentle background of spicy wood and stony minerals. Complex, generous and long. Drink now–2014. Score 90. K

GALIL MOUNTAIN, PINOT NOIR, 2007: Developed in one-to-three-year-old French barrels, those imparting gentle spicy and vanilla notes. Dark cherry red toward garnet, medium-bodied, with soft tannins integrating nicely and opening to reveal red and black berries, cherries and earthy minerals. Soft and round, with just enough complexity to keep our attention. Drink now. Score 88. K

GALIL MOUNTAIN, PINOT NOIR, 2006: Medium-bodied, oak-aged in French *barriques* for ten months, its once dark cherry red color now picking up a note of browning. On the nose and palate red berries, cherries and spices, those now taking on a marked earthy-mineral note. Sliding rapidly past its peak. Drink up. Score 85. K

GALIL MOUNTAIN, BARBERA, 2010: Deep garnet, with a traditional Barbera nose of cherries and spring flowers, medium-bodied, with soft, gently caressing notes of spicy oak. On the nose and palate plums, black cherries and cassis, those highlighted by notes of violets. Destined to have a velvety texture and a moderately long finish. Drink from release–2014, perhaps longer. Tentative Score 89–91. K

GALIL MOUNTAIN, BARBERA, 2008: Neither Barbera d'Asti nor Barbera d'Alba, but a distinct Barbera de Galilee wine. Tasted from components still in tanks before being transferred to its nine months' anticipated stay in *barriques*, but already showing great charm. Dark garnet toward royal purple, with almost muscular concentration and firm, near-sweet tannins, opening to show a dark chocolate nose, and, on the palate, black and blue berries, purple plums and floral notes. Destined to be a concentrated wine, but as it continues to develop it will soften comfortably. Drink now. Score 90. K

GALIL MOUNTAIN, BARBERA, 2007: Reflecting its nine months in French oak with notes of smoky oak, medium-dark garnet in color, opening with a quiet nose but going on to reveal a generous array of berries, black cherries, purple plums and spring flowers. Tannins and oak rise along with a hint of bitter almonds on the finish, so give this one a bit of time for its elements to come together. Drink now. Score 89. K

GALIL MOUNTAIN, BARBERA, 2006: Developed for nine months in French oak, dark, almost inky ruby toward garnet in color, with its impressive 15% alcohol content in fine balance with wood, tannins and fruit. On the nose and palate blackberries, blueberries, plums and violets supported nicely by notes of vanilla, milk chocolate and, rising on the long finish, notes of black pepper. Gently mouth-coating tannins and fine concentration. Drink up. Score 91. K

GALIL MOUNTAIN, PETIT VERDOT, 2010: Perhaps to be released as a varietal, perhaps to be used as a blending agent. Dark garnet, with earthy minerals, plums and black pepper on the nose, opens in the glass to show a rich core of currants and plums. Medium- to full-bodied, with still-firm tannins just settling in and a welcome modicum of oak. Finishes with hints of licorice and iron. If released as a varietal, best from 2013–2018. Tentative Score 89–91. K

GALIL MOUNTAIN, SHIRAZ-CABERNET SAUVIGNON, 2008: Garnet red in color, a medium- to full-bodied, softly tannic blend of 50% each Shiraz and Cabernet Sauvignon. On the nose and palate cherries, raspberries, a gentle hint of dusty oak and an appealing hint of white pepper that rises on the finish. Drink now–2013. Score 88. K

GALIL MOUNTAIN, SHIRAZ-CABERNET SAUVIGNON, 2007: A blend of 58% Shiraz and 42% Cabernet Sauvignon, aged in American oak for ten months. Deep garnet toward royal purple, with abundant but soft and gently mouth-coating tannins and fine concentration. A generous 15% alcohol content but that matched nicely by wood and fruits and showing fine structure. Opens to reveal a medium- to full-bodied wine with plum, berry and cassis notes on a lightly spicy smoked-meat background. Drink now. Score 90. K

GALIL MOUNTAIN, SHIRAZ-CABERNET SAUVIGNON, 2006: Smooth, round and aromatic, reflecting its ten months in American oak with gently spicy wood and hints of vanilla. Opens in the glass to show a generous mouthful of currant, blackberry, cherry and licorice notes. On the finish look for a hint of pomegranates. Drink now. Score 89. K

GALIL MOUNTAIN, ROSÉ, 2010: A rose-petal pink blend of Sangiovese, Pinot Noir, Cabernet Sauvignon and Barbera (64%, 14%, 12% and 10% respectively). Crisply dry, with raspberries, strawberries and cherries.

Medium-bodied, not so much a lively wine as one to sip slowly with grilled seafood or fish tartar. Drink now. Score 89. K

GALIL MOUNTAIN, ROSÉ, 2009: Light- to medium-bodied, rose petal to light strawberry pink in color, with strawberry, raspberry and even a note of blueberries, all with fine balancing acidity. Crisp and refreshing, a fun wine to drink. Drink up. Score 88. K

GALIL MOUNTAIN, ROSÉ, 2008: Light- to medium-bodied, with refreshing acidity, a crisply dry, rose-petal-pink-colored wine showing an appealing tutti-frutti array of red fruits. Drink up. Score 87. K

GALIL MOUNTAIN, CHARDONNAY, 2010: Light gold, medium-bodied with a note of sweet-and-spicy cedar. On the nose and palate white peaches, grapefruit and a hint of tropical fruits, all on a light mineral background. Drink now–2013. Score 89. K

GALIL MOUNTAIN, CHARDONNAY, 2009: Light, lively gold in color, medium-bodied, with just a bare and tantalizing hint of spicy oak, opens in the glass to show summer fruits, citrus and citrus peel on a background of flinty minerals. Drink now. Score 88. K

GALIL MOUNTAIN, CHARDONNAY, 2008: Lightly oaked, with a lively golden color, opens with a distinct peachy nose and goes on to show appealing citrus, apple and white peach fruits, all with a fine overlay of minerality. Look as well for a note of peach and cherry pits that comes in on the finish. Drink up. Score 89. K

GALIL MOUNTAIN, CHARDONNAY, 2007: Developed partly in oak, partly in stainless steel vats. Golden straw in color, medium-bodied, with a gentle hint of spicy oak and showing citrus, apple and pear fruits, those with a tempting hint of bitterness that creeps in on the finish. Drink up. Score 88. K

GALIL MOUNTAIN, SAUVIGNON BLANC, 2010: Light gold with green and orange tints. Unoaked, pure, crisp and well focused, with peach, citrus, tangerine and mango aromas and flavors. From mid-palate on delightful notes of key lime pie and stony minerals. Refreshing, with appealing complexity. Drink now. Score 90. K

GALIL MOUNTAIN, SAUVIGNON BLANC, 2009: Unoaked, as is the rule for this wine, light golden straw in color, a fresh and aromatic wine with aromas and flavors of citrus, melon and a hint of a fresh lawn after a light spring shower. Lively and refreshing and with just enough complexity to grab the attention. Drink up. Score 89. K

GALIL MOUNTAIN, SAUVIGNON BLANC, 2008: An unoaked white, light straw in color, with a generously aromatic nose and crisply refreshing acidity, showing a tempting array of melon, citrus and kiwi fruits, those on a background that hints nicely of freshly mown grass. Drink up. Score 88. K

GALIL MOUNTAIN, VIOGNIER, 2010: Medium-bodied, light bright gold showing a hint of smoky oak to complement a generous mouthful of green gage plums, litchis, Anjou pears and, from mid-palate on, a note of honeydew melon. Tangy, lively and long. Drink now. Score 90. K

GALIL MOUNTAIN, VIOGNIER, 2009: The color of damp golden straw, medium-bodied, with bare hints of spicy and toasty oak. On the nose and palate citrus, white peaches and mineral notes, those yielding from mid-palate on to flavors of ripe cantaloupe melon. Fragrant and moderately long. Drink now. Score 88. K

GALIL MOUNTAIN, VIOGNIER, 2008: Developed in new French oak barrels, with a light toasted white bread overlay. Light golden straw in color, with fine balancing acidity to highlight citrus and summer fruits, those hinting of a buttery overlay and peach pits. Medium-bodied but seems to float comfortably on the palate and finishing generous and long. Drink now. Score 90. K

GALIL MOUNTAIN, VIOGNIER, 2007: Medium-bodied, dark golden straw with orange and green reflections, showing good balance between wood, acidity and fruit. On the nose and palate floral, light mineral, summer fruits and melon come together nicely. Drink up. Score 89. K

Avivim

AVIVIM, 2009: A blend of 71% Viognier and 29% Chardonnay. Oak-aged for 9 months *sur lie*, medium-bodied with a hint of cinnamon on the nose and opening in the glass to show green gage plums, ripe pears, citrus and melon notes, all on a lightly floral background. Simultaneously refreshing and complex. Drink now. Score 90. K

AVIVIM, 2008: Oak-aged on its lees for nine months, a blend of 75% Viognier and 25% Chardonnay, deep fruit and light herbs on the deeply aromatic nose, medium- to full-bodied with fine concentration and acidity to keep it lively. Aromas and flavors of pears, honeydew melon and citrus, all coming together as a long, coherent and charming whole. Drink now. Score 90. K

AVIVIM, 2007: Medium-bodied, light golden straw in color, a blend of 69% Viognier and 31% Chardonnay, those aged on their lees in new French oak *barriques* for nine months. Youthful and zesty, with lightly spicy cedarwood notes highlighting an array of tropical fruits, pears and honeydew melon. Lurking comfortably in the background a hint of red grapefruit. Drink up. Score 90. K

Gat Shomron *

Founded by Avigdor Sharon and Lior Nachum on Karnei Shomron, not far from Kfar Saba, in 2003, this small winery released its first wines from that harvest in 2005, and is currently producing about 7,000 bottles annually of oak-aged Cabernet Sauvignon, Merlot and Chardonnay. Grapes are sourced from the areas of Shomron and the Upper Galilee.

GAT SHOMRON, CABERNET SAUVIGNON, GALILEE, 2006: Aged for one year in 300 liter oak casks, medium-bodied, with somewhat chunky, country-style tannins and opening to reveal berry, currant and black cherry fruits on a lightly spicy background. Drink up. Score 84. K

GAT SHOMRON, CABERNET SAUVIGNON, SHOMRON, 2006: Deep garnet in color, full-bodied, with still-firm tannins needing time to integrate. Opens in the glass to show plum, blackberry and blueberry notes, those complemented by hints of cedarwood and tobacco, all leading to a medium-long finish. Drink up. Score 85. K

GAT SHOMRON, MERLOT, GALILEE, 2006: Super-dark garnet in color, full-bodied, with firm tannins, generous spicy wood and a whopping 15.8% alcohol content. Opens with a marked alcoholic nose but that yields to berry, black cherry and plum fruits, those on a light spicy background. With tannins and alcohol rising, finishes hot. Drink up. Score 83. K

GAT SHOMRON, RED BLEND, 2007: A potpourri of Cabernet Sauvignon, Cabernet Franc, Syrah, Merlot and Petit Verdot, oak-aged for six months. Medium-bodied, with chunky tannins that give the wine a somewhat country style, but that pleasant enough with berry, cherry and currant notes making themselves felt nicely along with hints of Mediterranean herbs. Drink up. Score 85. K

Gesher Damia *

Founded in 1999 by Moshe Kaplan in the town of Pardes Hannah on the northern Coastal Plain, this small winery receives Cabernet Sauvignon, Merlot, Argaman, Petite Shiraz, Gewurztraminer and Chardonnay grapes from Gush Etzion, the Jerusalem Hills and the center of the country. Production is currently about 6,000 bottles annually.

GESHER DAMIA, CABERNET SAUVIGNON, 2006: Garnet-red, medium-bodied, with soft tannins, hints of peppery wood and a basic berry-black cherry personality. Drink up. Score 79.

GESHER DAMIA, CABERNET SAUVIGNON, 2005: Ruby toward garnet, light- to medium-bodied, with almost unfelt tannins, spicy oak and a few blackberry fruits. Drink up. Score 78.

GESHER DAMIA, CABERNET SAUVIGNON, 2004: Dark ruby, medium-bodied, with chunky tannins, smoky oak and skimpy black fruits. Drink up. Score 79.

GESHER DAMIA, MERLOT, 2006: A simple country-style wine with chunky tannins, and near-sweet sur-ripe berry, cherry and cassis notes. Drink up. Score 79.

GESHER DAMIA, MERLOT, 2005: Medium-bodied, with almost unfelt tannins and stewed plum and berry fruits. Drink up. Score 78.

GESHER DAMIA, MERLOT, 2004: Medium-bodied, with soft, near-sweet tannins and blackberry, cherry and cassis fruits, those on a lightly spicy background. Drink up. Score 80.

Ginaton **

Founded in 1999 by Doron Cohen and Benju Duke on Moshav Ginaton on the Central Plain not far from the city of Lod, the winery draws Cabernet Sauvignon, Muscat and Chardonnay grapes from Karmei Yosef and Kerem Ben Zimra. The first commercial releases were 3,000 bottles from the 2000 vintage. Current annual production is about 5,500 bottles.

GINATON, CABERNET SAUVIGNON, 2007: Garnet in color, medium-bodied with soft tannins and opening to show currant and wild berry fruits. An entry-level wine. Score 83.

GINATON, CABERNET SAUVIGNON, 2006: Dark ruby toward garnet, medium- to full-bodied, with soft tannins and a hint of sawdust on the nose. Opens to show currant and berry fruits. An entry-level wine. Drink up. Score 84.

GINATON, CABERNET SAUVIGNON, 2005: Youthful royal purple, medium-bodied, with once-firm tannins integrating nicely and showing lightly spicy black fruits. Drink now. Score 84.

GINATON, CABERNET SAUVIGNON, 2004: Garnet toward royal purple, medium-bodied, with soft tannins integrating nicely to show blackberry and currant fruits on a light spicy background. Drink up. Score 84.

GINATON, MERLOT, CARMEI YOSEF, 2006: Garnet in color, medium- to full-bodied, with somewhat chunky tannins giving the wine a rustic note. On the nose and palate black fruits and notes of candied citrus peel. Drink up. Score 84.

GINATON, MERLOT, BEN ZIMRA, 2005: This medium-bodied wine shows generous, spicy and vanilla-rich oak with soft tannins rising on the finish. Opens slowly to reveal plum, blackberries and black cherry fruits that linger nicely. Not complex but easy to drink. Drink now. Score 85.

GINATON, SHIRAZ, 2007: Ruby toward garnet, medium-bodied, with soft, barely felt tannins, showing straightforward plum and berry fruits on a lightly spicy background. An acceptable quaffer. Drink now. Score 84.

Givon ✱✱

Established by Nir Ernesti and Shuki Segal in the village of Givon Hachadasha, north of Jerusalem in the Judean Mountains, and relying on Cabernet Sauvignon and Merlot grapes from nearby vineyards, this winery released its first wines from the 2002 vintage. Current production is about 5,000 bottles annually.

GIVON, CABERNET SAUVIGNON, 2005: Somewhat cloudy dark garnet, medium- to full-bodied, with chunky tannins, generous smoky oak and currant, berry and black cherry fruits. A simple country-style wine. Drink up. Score 85.

GIVON, MERLOT, 2006: Oak-aged for 24 months, full-bodied, with gripping tannins and spicy wood on opening, those parting with time in the glass to reveal currant, red plum and black cherry fruits on a background of cigar tobacco and licorice. Drink up. Score 86.

GIVON, CABERNET SAUVIGNON-MERLOT, 2005: Dark garnet, full-bodied, with once-firm tannins now integrating nicely. Reflecting generous spicy oak from its 16 months in oak, opening in the glass to reveal appealing currant, blackberry and chocolate notes, those lingering nicely. Showing age. Drink up. Score 83.

Gizo ★★★

Producing under 2,000 bottles annually, this is the smallest of the wineries to enter this guide, that largely because even though production is very low, the wines are of definite interest. Established about five years ago by Yoav Alon in the village of Gizo which is on the Yoav-Yehuda wine route not far from Beit Shemesh, the winery makes primarily red wines, those based on Cabernet Sauvignon, Merlot and Petit Verdot.

GIZO, CABERNET SAUVIGNON, NACHAL HAREL, 2009: Garnet toward royal purple, medium- to full-bodied, and blended with 5% of Petit Verdot, reflecting its 13 months in oak with gently gripping tannins and notes of spicy wood. On the nose and palate aromas and flavors of currants, wild berries, green olives and citrus peel, all on a background of earthy minerals. Drink now–2014. Score 87.

GIZO, CABERNET SAUVIGNON, SPE-
CIAL RESERVE, 2008: Dark garnet, medium- to full-bodied, reflecting its 13 months in *barriques* with soft, gently mouth-coating tannins and light notes of spicy wood. A blend of 85% Cabernet Sauvignon, 12% Merlot and 3% Petit Verdot, opens in the glass to reveal generous back fruits, those supported comfortably by notes of roasted herbs and earthy minerals. Drink now–2013. Score 86.

GIZO, MERLOT, BORDEAUX, 2009: Dark cherry red, medium- to full-bodied, blended with 3% of Petit Verdot, reflecting its development in *barriques* for 13 months with soft, gently gripping tannins and notes of vanilla. Opens in the glass to reveal an appealing array of blackberry, cassis and black cherry fruits, those on a background that hints of earthy minerals and freshly cut herbs. Drink now–2014. Score 87.

GIZO, MERLOT, TU BEYAV, 2009: A medium- to full-bodied blend of 85% Merlot and 15% Petit Verdot. Oak-aged for 13 months, showing garnet toward royal purple. A whopping 14.9% alcohol here but that in fine balance with spicy wood, soft tannins and fruits. On the nose and palate opens with blueberries, those going to blackberries and blackcurrants, all on a background of bitter citrus peel and a hint of eucalyptus. Drink now–2015. Score 88.

GIZO, MERLOT, TU BEYAV, 2008: Blended with 3% Petit Verdot and

with a generous 15% alcohol content, the alcohol noticeable but in good balance with wood and still-firm tannins. On the nose and palate blackberry, blueberry and cassis fruits, those on a background of earthy minerals and, on the finish, a note of baking chocolate. Not the "usual" Merlot and worth trying to see if it is to your taste. Drink now. Score 88.

GIZO, MERLOT, SOREQ, 2008: Garnet toward royal purple, oak-aged for 13 months, blended with 3% Petit Verdot. On first attack black fruits and mocha, those yielding to notes of cassis and black olives. With tannins rising, the 14.7% alcohol content makes itself felt with a light touch of heat on the finish. Drink now–2013, perhaps longer. Score 86.

GIZO, CHARDONNAY, NACHAL AYALON, 2010: The winemaker says that he decided to make a Chardonnay that would be "somewhat out of the box." By blending the Chardonnay with 8% Riesling and 2% Muscat of Alexandria, he succeeded. As does the wine. Reflecting its nine months sur lie in American oak with medium to full body and notes of vanilla and peach pits on the nose, opens in the glass to reveal an array of passion fruit, mango and citrus. On the long finish an appealing hint of bitter peach pits. Best from the winery to date. Drink now–2014. Score 90.

Golan Heights Winery ★★★★★

From the moment they released their first wines in 1984, there has been no doubt that the Golan Heights Winery was and is still today largely responsible for placing Israel on the world wine map. Be there no question but that after nearly 30 years the Golan Heights Winery remains the quality leader in Israeli wines. A good deal of state-of-the-art attention to technical and scientific details concerning the various soil and climatic conditions in the vineyards does not indicate any diminishing whatever in that most important of all skills of the winemaker – intuition. Indeed, although scientific methodology plays an increasingly crucial part in the development and maintenance of vineyards, there is nothing that can replace a winemaker's "gut feeling" of what will do well in specific locations and in the ability to make blends. The winery, with its state-of-the-art facilities located in Katzrin on the Golan Heights, and fine vineyards on the Golan and in the Upper Galilee, is owned by eight of the kibbutzim and moshavim that supply them with grapes. Maintaining rigorous control over the vineyards and relying on a combination of New and Old World knowledge and technology, senior winemaker Victor Schoenfeld and his team of winemakers, all of whom trained in California, France or Australia, produce wines that often attain true excellence.

The winery has three regular series, Yarden, Gamla and Golan, the wines in the first two series often being age-worthy while those in the Golan series are meant for early drinking. Within the Yarden series the winery also releases single vineyard wines, and those often prove to be among the best wines in the country. There is also the top-of-the-line Katzrin series that includes an often-superb red Bordeaux-style blend that is released only in years considered exceptional, and a Chardonnay that has been released annually since 1995. The winery recently released its first wine under the label of Rom, intended to parallel the Katzrin in quality.

The winery is currently producing more than six million bottles annually and of this production nearly thirty percent is destined for export. Among the regularly released varietal wines are Cabernet Sauvignon, Merlot, Pinot Noir, Gamay, Sangiovese, Sauvignon Blanc, Chardonnay, Johannisberg Riesling, Muscat Canelli and Gewurztraminer, and the winery is currently cultivating experimental plantings of Nebbiolo and Malbec. The winery also produces sparkling Blanc de Blanc and Brut, both made in the traditional *Champenoise* method; Heightswine (a play on the words Ice Wine); and several dessert wines.

In as simple terms as I can find, this Israeli winery consistently earns reviews and scores that rival the best of California and many of the best of France and Italy. Victor Schoenfeld and his team must be doing something very right indeed.

Katzrin

KATZRIN, 2007: A blend of 91% Cabernet Sauvignon and 9% Merlot, showing dark garnet to royal purple in color, reflecting its 18 months in oak with spicy and smoky oak and gently mouth-coating tannins, all in fine balance with fruits. On first attack blackcurrants, blackberries and black cherries, those making way for notes of honey-sweetened chewing tobacco, roasted herbs and, on the super-long finish with fruits and tannins rising comfortably, a generous hint of baking chocolate. Drink now–2025. Score 93. K

KATZRIN, 2004: Aged in new French *barriques* for 18 months, a blend of 94% Cabernet Sauvignon and 6% Merlot. Dark garnet toward royal purple, with orange and violet reflections. Shows still-generous oak and firm tannins, those in fine proportion and well balanced by blackberry, blackcurrant and cherry fruits, on a background of white pepper, Mediterranean herbs and tobacco, and, on the long and generous finish, hints of vanilla and peppermint. Drink now–2018, perhaps longer. Score 93. K

KATZRIN, 2003: Dark garnet, a full-bodied blend of 83% Cabernet Sauvignon, 14% Merlot and 3% Cabernet Franc, with gently mouth-coating tannins and smoky oak integrating nicely. Shows layers of blackcurrant, black cherry and berry fruits, those yielding and coming together with peppery and herbal aromas and flavors culminating in a long blueberry and white chocolate finish. Drink now–2018. Score 93. K

KATZRIN, 2000: A blend of 89% Cabernet Sauvignon, 9% Merlot and 2% Cabernet Franc. Showing beautifully now, its blackberry, cherry and currant fruits supported by spicy oak, notes of cigar tobacco and hints of freshly turned earth. Dense, deep and intense, with finely tuned balance and structure, a simultaneously bold and elegant wine. Drink now–2015. Score 92. K

KATZRIN, 1996: Vibrant and complex, with an array of aromas and flavors that include currants, cherries and plums overlaid by smoky oak, chocolate, spices and tobacco, this full-bodied, young tannic red is only now beginning to reveal its charms. Excellent integration between fruit, tannins and oak indicates that the wine will continue to develop beautifully. Drink now–2015. Score 93. K

KATZRIN, 1993: Deep, broad, long and complex, this full-bodied Cabernet-Merlot blend continues to live up to its promise. Abundant tannins are well balanced by wood and fruits that include cassis, black cherries and orange peel, along with generous overlays of milk chocolate and toasty oak. Elegant and graceful. Drink now. Score 94. K

KATZRIN, 1990: Still holding its own as it approaches its twentieth year. A blend of 90% Cabernet Sauvignon and 10% Merlot, this deep, elegant, full-bodied wine maintains its dark garnet color and excellent balance between fruits, wood, acidity and tannins. Still showing blackcurrants, black cherries, vanilla, cloves and chocolate, now with a light herbal note creeping in. Long and generous but not for further cellaring. Drink up. Score 93. K

KATZRIN, CHARDONNAY, 2008: Lighter gold and, although full-bodied, neither as dense or as oaky as with past releases. All of which is just fine, for after distinct notes of butterscotch and poached pears the wine opens to reveal citrus, melon and light toasty notes that prove both subtle, complex, elegant and long. Drink now–2018. Score 92. K

KATZRIN, CHARDONNAY, 2007: Dark, almost bronzed in color, full-bodied, with a generous dose of creamy wood that runs through. Sounds like a wine dominated by wood, but the balance is there, the wood matched at first by notes of butterscotch and then by pear, pineapple, spices and hazelnuts, all of which come together as a concentrated and well-focused whole. Drink now–2016, perhaps longer. Score 92. K

KATZRIN, CHARDONNAY, 2006: Rich and supple, deep gold in color, full-bodied but not quite as dense as earlier releases, with abundant toasty oak and vanilla integrating nicely and in fine balance with fruits. Opens in the glass to reveal peach, greengage plums and mineral aromas and flavors, those hinting at one moment of figs, at another of pears. Hints of butterscotch on first attack and, on the long finish, notes of spices, all coming together as a thoroughly coherent and contemplative whole. Drink now–2016. Score 92. K

KATZRIN, CHARDONNAY, 2005: A creamy and buttery Chardonnay, deep, almost bronzed gold in color and marked from first attack to its long finish with super-generous toasty oak and hazelnuts. Opens slowly on the palate to reveal fig, melon and pear fruits, but those always under the oaky notes. A good wine, but not up to the Katzrin standards and mostly for those who can take the intense oak. Drink now. Score 88. K

KATZRIN, CHARDONNAY, 2004: Dark golden-yellow, full-bodied and concentrated. Developed in new oak for ten months, notably yeasty on first attack but that yielding beautifully to a buttery, oak-rich texture and opening to reveal nutty, fig, pear, tropical fruits and butterscotch, all on a spicy background. Rich, long and complex. Drink now. Score 92. K

KATZRIN, CHARDONNAY, 2003: Rich, ripe, concentrated and complex with generous layers of figs, tangerines, summer fruits and hazelnuts. Generous but not imposing oak on the finish makes it especially elegant, as does a hint of butterscotch that comes in on the long finish. Drink up. Score 92. K

KATZRIN, CHARDONNAY, 2002: Fully mature, almost bronzed gold in color, remaining as full-bodied and complex as in its youth but now, with its oak nicely subdued, showing only the barest hint of smoky wood, that serving as a backdrop for summer fruits, pears and citrus. Earlier roasted nuts, minerals and a hint of cream continue to play nicely on the palate but look as well for notes of herbs and spices that are creeping in. Drink up. Score 91. K

Yarden – Rom

YARDEN, ROM, 2008: Victor Shoenfeld and his team of winemakers keep turning out wines that earn between 95–96 points. That, of course, is no cause for complaint. A blend this year of 41% Syrah, 33% Merlot and 26% Cabernet Sauvignon. Super-dark garnet in color, full-bodied, ripe and expressive, showing still-firm tannins and generous smoky/spicy oak that needs only time to settle down. On first attack black cherries, blackberries and peppery overtones, those yielding to purple plums and sweet spices, all leading to a remarkably long and polished finish that goes on and on, seemingly without end. Approachable on release but best 2015–2025, perhaps longer. Score 95. K

YARDEN, ROM, 2007: Impenetrably dark garnet in color, with fine aromatics, a blend of 53% Cabernet Sauvignon and 24% Syrah and 23% Merlot. Full-bodied, with still-firm tannins and generous wood but showing finely tuned balance that bodes well for the future. On first attack blueberries and spices, those followed by notes of near-jammy black and red currants, red plums, citrus peel and dark chocolate. On the super-long finish, tannins and fruits rise along with hints of raspberries and red licorice. As to the somewhat jammy note, that will integrate within the next year to 18 months. Although the wine is approachable now it will come to its best only between 2013–2022. Score 95. K

YARDEN, ROM, 2006: A blend of Syrah, Cabernet Sauvignon and Merlot (37%, 34% and 29% respectively), a selection of grapes from eight different vineyards, seven on the Golan and one in the Upper Galilee, the wines blended nine months after harvest. Oak-aged in French *barriques* for a total of 21 months and bottled without filtration. A wine to follow in stages, for at this point in its development it opens so fruit-forward, with ripe blueberries, cherries and red currants, that some may actually mistakenly think it sweet. Even now, however, that sensation passes quickly to reveal a full-bodied, well-extracted and remarkably intense wine with aromas and flavors that literally flood the palate. As the wine continue to develop and as its elements come fully together look for notes of fresh herbs, espresso coffee and hints of both anise and cinnamon. Israel's best wine ever. Superb now but best from 2014–2022, perhaps longer. Score 96. K

Yarden – Single Vineyard Wines

YARDEN, CABERNET SAUVIGNON, ODEM VINEYARD, 2009: Still in its infancy but already showing beautifully. Somewhat lighter than usual Odem releases but don't let that hold you back, for the concentration and intensity are both here along with the promise of elegance. On the nose and palate red and black currants, wild berries, abundant but gentle tannins and light notes of Mediterranean herbs, spicy cedarwood and a hint of chocolate that creeps in on the finish. Destined for both elegance and complexity. Best 2014–2024, perhaps longer. Tentative Score 92–94. K

YARDEN, CABERNET SAUVIGNON, ELROM VINEYARD, 2008: Intensely dark garnet in color, deep and powerful, with ripe blackberry, blackcurrant and black cherry fruits. Still in its infancy with the tannins, wood and fruits starting to come together and with the kind of balance and structure that bode well for a well-focused and cellar-worthy wine. Destined for elegance so give this one the time it deserves. Approachable by 2012 but best only from 2014 or 2015 and then cellaring well until 2024, perhaps longer. Tentative Score 94–96. K

YARDEN, CABERNET SAUVIGNON, ELROM VINEYARD, 2007: Full-bodied, dark enough in color to be thought of as garnet toward black, with still-firm tannins and notes of sweet cedarwood integrating nicely. Opens with a near-chocolate nose, that parting to make way for raspberries and then to aromas and flavors of blackcurrants, wild berries and bitter oranges. Fine balance and structure, with tannins and fruits rising simultaneously on the long finish. Approachable on release but best 2013–2020, perhaps longer. Score 93. K

YARDEN, CABERNET SAUVIGNON, ELROM VINEYARD, 2004: Showing almost inky-dark garnet, full-bodied, with still-firm tannins and spicy wood well on the way to integrating and already showing elegance and finesse. Look for layer after layer of currant, blackberry and wild berry fruits, those supported beautifully by notes of sweet herbs and tar, all leading to a near-sweet fruity finish that lingers on and on. Drink now–2020. Score 94. K

YARDEN, CABERNET SAUVIGNON, ELROM VINEYARD, 2003: Intensely dark ruby toward royal purple, full-bodied, with caressing tannins and a moderate oak influence. Opens with blackcurrants, blackberries and minerals, goes to meaty, earthy and herbal aromas and flavors, and then to spices and a long and elegant fruity finish. Firmly structured with excellent grip and complexity. Drink now–2020. Score 95. K

YARDEN, CABERNET SAUVIGNON, ELROM VINEYARD, 2001: Dark, almost impenetrable garnet-purple, full-bodied, with finely tuned balance between generous well-integrated tannins and judicious oak, this exquisite wine shows complex tiers of aromas and flavors of red currants, berries and spices on the first attack, those opening to include light earthy and herbal overlays. Plush and opulent, with a long, complex finish. Certainly one of the best wines ever made in Israel. Drink now–2017. Score 95. K

YARDEN, CABERNET SAUVIGNON, YONATAN VINEYARD, 2010: Dark, almost impenetrable garnet in color, full-bodied, with chewy, still-gripping tannins needing only time to integrate and already showing fine balance and structure. On the nose generous black fruits and on the palate traditional Cabernet Sauvignon blackcurrant and blackberry fruits, those supported well by notes of spicy wood, freshly cut herbs and a note of anise. Destined to be round and elegant. Best from 2014–2020. Tentative Score 91–93. K

YARDEN, CABERNET SAUVIGNON, YONATAN VINEYARD, 2007: Deep and intense garnet in color, full-bodied, showing fine balance and structure, with still-generous spicy oak on the nose and firm tannins needing time to integrate. On first attack, wild berries and currants, those parting to make way for notes of roasted herbs and black olives and then, on the long finish, mocha and berry fruits rising together. Approachable now but best 2013–2020, perhaps longer. Score 92. K

YARDEN, MERLOT, KELA (SHA'AL) VINEYARD, 2008: Full-bodied, concentrated and well-focused, showing layer after layer of blackberries, plums, espresso coffee and fresh sage and roasted herbs. Give this one time and it will show hints of leather. An intense wine but with the potential for elegance. Drink now–2018, perhaps longer. Score 93. K

YARDEN, MERLOT, ODEM VINEYARD, 2010: Not a deep or concentrated wine but one that is full-bodied, rich, round and seductive, showing a generous array of wild berries, pomegranate and cassis aromas and flavors, those coming together in a lightly oaky but well-balanced finish. Drink from release–2017. Tentative Score 89–91. K

YARDEN, MERLOT, ODEM VINEYARD, 2009: Deep, almost inky garnet in color, full-bodied, with chewy but gentle tannins and hints of new wood. Opens with blackberries on the nose and palate, goes on to reveal blackcurrants, notes of citrus peel and a hint of rose petals, all coming to a long and mouth-filling finish on which a tinge of black pepper. Drink from release–2018. Tentative Score 90–92. K

YARDEN, MERLOT, ODEM ORGANIC VINEYARD, 2007: Super-dark ruby toward garnet, full-bodied, with silky tannins and gentle spicy wood influences. Opens to reveal a generous array of ripe red currants, black cherries, mocha and spices, with the tannins rising on the finish. Opulent and bold. Drink now–2018. Score 91. K

YARDEN, MERLOT, ODEM ORGANIC VINEYARD, 2006: Dark, almost inky purple, with sweet and smoky oak notes matched nicely by generous but gently mouth-coating tannins. On first attack near-sweet black cherries, those yielding to blackcurrants, blackberries, notes of Mediterranean herbs and, on the super-long finish, hints of bitter orange peel. Lovely. Drink now–2018. Score 92. K

YARDEN, MERLOT, KELA VINEYARD, 2008: Deep, almost impenetrable garnet in color, full-bodied, concentrated and well focused, reflecting its 14 months in French *barriques* with chewy tannins and notes of spicy cedar, those parting to make way for aromas and flavors of blackberries, plums, espresso and sage. On the long finish notes of roasted herbs. Give this one some time and it will show appealing earthy minerals and hints of citrus peel. Drink now–2018, perhaps longer. Score 93. K

YARDEN, MERLOT, KELA VINEYARD, 2006: Now fully out of a dumb period through which the wine passed, showing a nose rich with plums and leathery notes. Impenetrably dark garnet in color, full-bodied, with its once-generous wood and gripping tannins now integrating nicely, opens to reveal blackberry, black cherry and currant fruits, those on a background of earthy minerals. Drink now–2016. Score 91. K

YARDEN, MERLOT, KELA VINEYARD, 2005: Rich, intense and concentrated, with chewy tannins and generous but well-moderated wood. Aged for 14 months in French oak, ⅔ of which was new, showing bold aromas and flavors of plum, red currant, blackberry, red licorice and spices, all rising to a long tannic and mineral, herbal and tobacco-rich finish. Drink now–2017. Score 92. K

YARDEN, MERLOT, TEL PHARES VINEYARD, 2005: Almost impenetrably dark garnet in color, full-bodied, with gently caressing tannins and notes of toasty oak, opens in the glass to show chocolate ganache, jammy blackberry and red plum fruits, those with tantalizing hints of truffles and Christmas pudding. On the long and juicy finish appealing notes of roasted herbs. Drink now–2016. Score 92. K

YARDEN, MERLOT, ORTAL VINEYARD, 2004: Showing as splendidly as ever! Dark garnet toward inky black, full-bodied, with once-firm tannins and generous spicy wood integrating nicely now. Opens to reveal a tempting array of blackberry, raspberry, plum and cassis fruits, those supported nicely by hints of smoky cedarwood and chocolate, all leading to a gently spicy and notably long finish. Simultaneously complex, concentrated and elegant. Drink now–2018. Score 93. K

YARDEN, MERLOT, ORTAL VINEYARD, 2001: Deeply aromatic, reflecting its 14 months in mostly new French barrels with generous spicy oak, that in harmony with ample but seamless tannins, all coming together in a dense but plush and luxurious wine. Full-bodied, showing appealing aromas and flavors that open in layer after layer, those including blackberries, near-jammy plums, chocolate, fresh herbs, and on the long finish, a rising hint of Oriental spices, all with a light herbal bitterness, that offset comfortably by a hint of orange peel. Drink now–2014. Score 94. K

YARDEN, SYRAH, AVITAL SLOPES (FORMERLY PART OF THE ORTAL VINEYARD), 2007: Deep, dark and concentrated, with soft, lightly dusty tannins and notes of cedarwood. Full-bodied and aromatic, opening in the glass to show generous purple plums, blackberries and black cherries, those yielding to a comfortable hint of crème de cassis. On the long finish notes of earthy minerals and a light and tempting hint of bitterness. Drinking well now but best from 2014–2022. Score 93. K

YARDEN, SYRAH, YONATAN VINEYARD, 2007: A candidate for Israel's best Syrah to date. Almost impenetrably deep garnet in color, a deep and concentrated wine, showing still-firm tannins and generous spicy wood but those integrating nicely and showing fine balance and structure. On first attack red plums, cherries and a note of cassis liqueur, those yielding to currant and berry fruits all on a background of earthy minerals. From mid-palate on look for hints of small game birds and a note of leather that lingers nicely on to the long, long finish. Drinking well now but best from 2013–2024. Score 94. K

YARDEN, SYRAH, ORTAL VINEYARD, 2004: One of the two very best Syrah wines ever in Israel, both by the Golan Heights Winery. Extraordinarily deep ruby, full-bodied, with near-sweet tannins integrating nicely with spicy wood. Opens with a burst of almost jammy raspberries and kirsch liqueur, those yielding to blackberry, cherry and plum fruits. In the background generous hints of anise and Oriental spices and a hint of freshly tanned leather. Drink now–2018. Score 94. K

YARDEN, SYRAH, TEL PHARES VINEYARD, 2010: Ripe and rich, medium- to full-bodied, even at this early stage of its development showing blackberry, plum and raspberry fruits, those with hints of spicy cedarwood and earthy minerals. Tannins and fruits rise nicely on the finish. Drink from release–2018. Tentative Score 89–91. K

YARDEN, SYRAH, TEL PHARES VINEYARD, 2008: Deep and concentrated enough to be thought of as muscular but even at this stage gentle and polished. With firm tannins starting to settle in, opens slowly in the glass at this stage to reveal richness, intensity and depth of flavor, opening with blackberry and currant fruits, moving on to plums and wild berries and then opening to reveal minerals, spices, *garrigue* and sage, all coming to a long and firmly tannic finish. As the wine continues to develop look for a note of bittersweet chocolate. Approachable and enjoyable now but best 2013–2024. Score 93. K

YARDEN, SYRAH, TEL PHARES VINEYARD, 2007: Still in its infancy but already showing fine balance and structure. Still-tight, gripping and intense tannins but those settling in nicely with creamy and spicy oak. With fine balance, opens even now to reveal blackberry, blueberry and red currant fruits, those on a background of generously peppered smoked meat and roasted herbs. Give this one time and it will show notes of saddle leather and mocha. Drink now–2018. Score 93. K

YARDEN, SYRAH, TEL PHARES VINEYARD, 2006: Dark garnet toward royal purple, full-bodied, its once-firm tannins now soft and gently mouth-coating, and integrating nicely with notes of spicy wood. Opens to reveal a complex array of plum, currant and berry fruits, those supported nicely by notes of earthy minerals, and generously peppered game meat with tannins and fruits rising comfortably on the long, round finish. Drink now–2017. Score 92. K

YARDEN, PINOT NOIR, MAROM GALIL VINEYARD, 2008: Deeply aromatic, a lighter-than-usual-style Pinot from Yarden, showing red berries, cherries, sage and minerals. Medium-bodied, with light tannins that linger nicely through and lead to a long, persistent finish. Drink now–2016. Score 91. K

YARDEN, PINOT NOIR, EIN ZIVAN VINEYARD, 2008: Full-bodied, showing ripe black cherries, plums and spices, and picking up a mineral edge on a long finish. Ripe, pure and fleshy. Drink now–2016. Score 91. K

YARDEN, CHARDONNAY, ODEM ORGANIC VINEYARD, 2009: Deep gold with green tints, on first attack pears and apricots, those yielding to clear notes of tropical fruits, minerals and, on the long finish, a tempting hint of bitter almonds. At this stage unfolds slowly in the glass. Drink now–2016. Score 91. K

YARDEN, CHARDONNAY, ODEM ORGANIC VINEYARD, 2008: Bright burnished gold in color, full-bodied, opening with a note of butterscotch on the nose. On first attack summer fruits and pears, those yielding to notes of citrus and crème brûlée. Gentle wood and a near-buttery texture balanced finely with acidity. Not a lively wine but indeed destined to be complex, mouth-filling and, for lack of a better term, delicious. Drink now–2018. Score 94. K

YARDEN, CHARDONNAY, ODEM ORGANIC VINEYARD, 2007: Full-bodied, deep golden with a distinct tint of orange that plays in the glass, a wine reflecting generous wood but that in fine proportion to acidity and fruits. Opens with pears, grilled nuts and pie crust notes, those going on to show ripe fig, pineapple and baked apple aromas and flavors. Long and creamy with the oak rising on the finish. Elegance on a grand scale. Drink now–2016. Score 92. K

YARDEN, CHARDONNAY, ODEM ORGANIC VINEYARD, 2006: Full-bodied, opening with subtle aromas of figs, pears and apples, going on to show a generous dash of smoky, toasty oak and then blossoming forth with pineapple, citrus peel and minerals leading to a long finish that is simultaneously creamy and bright. Drink now–2013. Score 92. K

YARDEN, CHARDONNAY, ODEM ORGANIC VINEYARD, 2005: Full-bodied, opening with floral and citrus, those going on to tropical fruits and figs, all set off by hints of smoky oak, ginger and, on the long finish, ripe pears. Drink now. Score 91. K

YARDEN, CHARDONNAY, ODEM ORGANIC VINEYARD, 2004: With its once-generous oak now subdued, rich and complex, full-bodied and creamy, with pears, ripe apricots, citrus and mango fruits backed up by light spicy and mineral overtones. Drink now. Score 91. K

Yarden

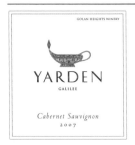

YARDEN, CABERNET SAUVIGNON, 2008: A component tasting from the Elrom vineyard. Super-dark garnet toward royal purple, full-bodied with still-gripping tannins, those in fine balance with wood and fruits. On first attack a generous array of currants and blueberries, those yielding to spicy plum and near-sweet cedarwood, and, on the long finish, a broad array of spices. Drink from release–2022. Tentative Score 91–93. K

YARDEN, CABERNET SAUVIGNON, 2007: Medium- to full-bodied (leaning to the full), with soft tannins and sweet-and-spicy wood integrating nicely. An aromatic black fruit and chocolate nose, going on to show a fine array of blackberry, blackcurrant, black cherry and wild berry fruits, all leading to a long and generous earthy-mineral finish. Drink now–2024. Score 92. K

YARDEN, CABERNET SAUVIGNON, 2006: Full-bodied, with gently mouth-coating tannins, sweet cedarwood and notes of tobacco integrating nicely. On the nose and palate wild berries, purple plums and currants on a background of spicy oak, all touched with hints of spices, coffee and light mineral-earthy overtones. On the long finish a hint of red cherries that brings a comfortable smile to the eyes. Drink now–2018. Score 92. K

YARDEN, CABERNET SAUVIGNON, 2005: Brooding, almost impenetrably dark ruby-red, full-bodied, with near-sweet tannins and spicy oak wrapped around blackcurrants, berries, spices and a hint of dark chocolate. Look as well for enchanting hints of citrus peel on the long finish. Fine balance and structure bode well for the future. Drink now–2018. Score 92. K

YARDEN, CABERNET SAUVIGNON, 2004: Dark, almost impenetrable garnet, with generous wood in fine balance with acidity and fruits. Opens to show currants and crushed berries, those yielding to cranberries, ripe purple plums and dark chocolate, all on a background of spices, asphalt and earthiness. Drink now–2016. Score 92. K

YARDEN, CABERNET SAUVIGNON, 2003: Aged in French oak for 18 months and showing generous but gentle wood influence. Soft mouth-coating tannins support generous blackberry, black cherry and plum fruits, and on the long finish, hints of Oriental spices and a light herbal-tobacco sensation. Drink now–2014. Score 93. K

YARDEN, CABERNET SAUVIGNON, 2002: Dark garnet, full-bodied, with once-firm tannins and spicy oak now settled in nicely and opening to show aromas of red currants, black cherries and berries on first attack, those giving way to layers of sweet cedar, vanilla, leather, and on the long finish, hints of Mediterranean herbs. Rich, generous and elegant. Drink now. Score 92. K

YARDEN, CABERNET SAUVIGNON, 2001: Full-bodied with finely tuned balance between wood, tannins and fruits. Showing plum, wild berry and spicy currant fruits, and reflecting its 18 months in oak with appealing overlays of vanilla, cedar, tobacco and cocoa. Drink now–2013. Score 91. K

YARDEN, CABERNET SAUVIGNON, 2000: Full-bodied, still youthful, with firm tannins and generous oak well balanced by currants, blackberries and spicy cedarwood, those opening to plums and black cherries, all matched nicely with vanilla and an appealing herbal overlay followed by a long finish. Drink up. Score 92. K

YARDEN, MERLOT, 2008: Dark garnet in color, a powerful Merlot but one that holds its muscles in check nicely to show off its silky smoothness. On the nose and palate blackcurrants, purple plums and espresso coffee, those on a background of toasty oak and mocha, the tannins and fruits rising nicely on the long finish. Drink from release–2017, perhaps longer. Score 91. K

YARDEN, MERLOT, 2007: Impenetrably dark garnet in color, the most full-bodied Yarden Merlot in recent years, with gripping but velvety-smooth tannins and toasty oak. On first attack ripe raspberries and blackcurrants, those making way for light herbal and earthy notes and finally plums and Oriental spices, all culminating in a long, mineral-rich finish. Drink now–2016, perhaps longer. Score 91. K

YARDEN, MERLOT, 2006: Almost impenetrably dark garnet, medium- to full-bodied, with soft, gently mouth-coating tannins and opening to show blackberry and raspberry fruits, those supported nicely by notes of minerals and licorice. As this continues to develop look as well for notes of cigar tobacco. Drink now–2014. Score 90. K

YARDEN, MERLOT, 2005: Super-dark garnet in color, medium- to full-bodied, with spicy wood and firm, mouth-coating tannins in fine balance with fruits. On the nose and palate ripe purple plums and blackcurrants with overlays of smoke and roasted Mediterranean herbs. Long and elegant. Drink now–2015. Score 91. K

YARDEN, MERLOT, 2004: Dark garnet toward purple, medium- to full-bodied, with tannins and spicy wood now integrated nicely and showing a generous array of berry, cassis and plum fruits, those supported by minerals, sweet cedarwood and, rising on the medium-long finish, an overlay of spices and tobacco. Drink now. Score 90. K

YARDEN, MERLOT, 2003: Dark garnet, full-bodied and with generous tannins, a well-polished wine showing a generous array of cherry, currant and berry fruits, those supported nicely by layers of Mediterranean herbs, vanilla and a gentle hand with smoky oak. On the long finish a tantalizing hint of green olives tiptoes in nicely. Drink now–2014. Score 91. K

YARDEN, SYRAH, 2007: Inky and impenetrably dark garnet in color, full-bodied, with tremendous intensity and concentration. Opens slowly in the glass to reveal blackcurrants, black cherries, plums and raspberries, those supported very comfortably by Oriental spices, all leading to notes of red licorice on the extra-long finish. Approachable now but best 2013–2022. Score 92. K

YARDEN, SYRAH, 2006: Super-dark garnet in color, full-bodied, opens slowly, going on to reveal still-chewy tannins and spicy wood, those in good balance with fruits and acidity. Dense and powerful. On the nose and palate showing black cherry, blackberry and plum fruits on a background of licorice and black olives, all going to a long meaty finish. Drink now–2020. Score 92. K

YARDEN, SYRAH, 2005: Garnet toward inky-black, full-bodied, with spicy oak and generous soft tannins in fine balance with fruits. Opens with raspberry, purple plum and currant notes, those going on to show generous hints of black pepper, anise and wild berries, all coming to a long and generous chocolate and smoky finish. Drink now–2015. Score 91. K

YARDEN, SYRAH, 2004: Having taken on a far deeper garnet color than its youth but holding all of its charms intact, the once-firm tannins and spicy wood now well integrated and parting to make way for aromas and flavors of near-jammy blackberry, raspberry and black cherry fruits, those on a background of spices and saddle leather. Drink now–2014. Score 91. K

YARDEN, SYRAH, 2003: Super-dark garnet in color, with soft, gently mouth-coating tannins and an appealing array of spicy cedarwood. Oak-aged for 18 months, opens with a clear note of bittersweet chocolate on the nose, goes on to show blackberries, purple plums and earthy-herbal aromas and flavors. Long and generous, the chocolate rising on the finish together with a note of blackberry jam. Drink now. Score 92. K

YARDEN, PINOT NOIR, 2010: Medium-dark ruby toward garnet, medium- to full-bodied, opening with a nose of crushed berries and chocolate, going on to reveal blackberries and raspberries, those on a background of licorice and graphite with a hint of anise rising on the long finish. Drink from release–2016. Score 90. K

YARDEN, PINOT NOIR, 2009: Dark ruby toward garnet, medium- to full-bodied, a generously aromatic wine, opening to reveal black cherry, blackberry and crushed berry fruits, those on a mineral-rich and lightly peppery background. Full-bodied and intense but subtle and complex. Drink from release–2018, perhaps longer. Score 91. K

YARDEN, PINOT NOIR, 2008: Round and well balanced, dark cherry-red toward garnet in color and medium- to full-bodied. On the opening nose spices and chocolate, and on the palate blackberries, black cherries and roasted herbs. Fresh, aromatic and concentrated with a tantalizing hint of licorice on the long finish. Drink now–2017, perhaps longer. Score 92. K

YARDEN, PINOT NOIR, 2007: Dark, almost rusty garnet in color, medium- to full-bodied, with soft tannins that caress gently. On the opening nose freshly picked Mediterranean herbs and blackberry fruits, those going on to reveal aromas and flavors of blackberries, blackcurrants and red cherries, all on a lightly spicy background. On the moderately long finish notes of sandalwood and red plums. Drink now–2014. Score 90. K

YARDEN, PINOT NOIR, 2006: Intense ruby toward garnet, medium- to full-bodied, with well-focused cherry fruits at the core, those opening to reveal plums, dark chocolate and espresso coffee, all leading to a blackberry-rich finish. Generous, balanced and long, with wood and firm tannins, those nicely integrated. Drink now–2014. Score 90. K

YARDEN, PINOT NOIR, 2005: Dark ruby with a hint of clearing at the rim, full-bodied enough to be thought of as fleshy, and with spicy wood and gentle tannins in fine balance with acidity and fruits. Opens with near-sweet, liqueur-like berry aromas and flavors, those yielding in the glass to reveal a crisply dry wine on which you will feel hints of kirsch and dark chocolate, all coming together in a long and generous blackberry-rich finish. Drink now–2013. Score 93. K

YARDEN, PINOT NOIR, 2004: Super-dark garnet, medium- to full-bodied, with firm but well-integrated tannins and showing a generous array of blackberry, plum and black cherry fruits, those supported very nicely by hints of pine nuts. On the fruity finish tantalizing hints of earthiness and anise. Drink now. Score 90. K

YARDEN, PINOT NOIR, 2003: Garnet-red, medium- to full-bodied, with soft, mouth-coating tannins and a moderate hand with spicy oak. On the nose and palate, forward but elegant black cherry, blackberry and cassis fruits supported nicely by hints of lightly spicy floral and earthy notes. Drink now. Score 90. K

YARDEN, MOUNT HERMON RED, 2010: Dark ruby in color, a soft, round Bordeaux blend of Merlot, Cabernet Sauvignon, Cabernet Franc and Petit Verdot. Medium-bodied, with soft tannins, showing forward aromas and flavors of crushed red berries, cherries and currants. Nothing complex here but a fine entry-level wine. Drink now. Score 84. K

YARDEN, MOUNT HERMON RED, 2009: Ruby toward garnet, medium-bodied with soft tannins, a gently tannic Bordeaux blend made for drinking in its youth. A rather basic cherry-berry personality this year along with a hint of sweetness that may not be appreciated by all. Drink now. Score 84. K

YARDEN, MOUNT HERMON RED, 2008: Dark ruby toward garnet, medium-bodied with soft tannins, this blend of Merlot, Cabernet Sauvignon, Cabernet Franc, Malbec and Petit Verdot shows forward cherry, berry and cassis fruits. A very pleasant, easy-to-drink wine, well suited to Italian and Mediterranean dishes. Drink up. Score 87. K

YARDEN, CHARDONNAY, 2009: If there is a problem at all with the Golan Heights Chardonnays in the Yarden and Katzrin series, it is only that most people too often open and drink them too early – that is to say, before the wines reach their peak. At this stage, this particular release opens with nose of toasty wood and only then aromas of pears. Give this one the time it deserves and that oak will show far more subdued, the pear fruits will blossom and make way for the creamy yellow apple, honeysuckle and buttery notes that are waiting patiently to make themselves felt. Promising to be long and elegant. Drink now–2016. Score 90. K

YARDEN, CHARDONNAY, 2008: Think of this as a "super-Chardonnay" if you will. Rich, full-bodied and well-focused, with generous but not at all imposing oak in fine balance with fruits, spices and acidity. On first attack melon, pears and toasty oak, those yielding to notes of nutmeg and butterscotch, all on a full-bodied but never heavy background and all becoming more subtle on the super-long finish. Drink now–2016. Score 92. K

YARDEN, CHARDONNAY, 2007: Concentrated and full-bodied, with aromas and flavors of pears, figs, apricots and lemon peel, all with an overlay of spicy, toasty oak. Rich, elegant and persistent, with notes of tangerines and nectarines that come in on the long finish. Drink now–2014. Score 91. K

YARDEN, CHARDONNAY, 2006: Rich and supple, deep gold in color, full-bodied, with abundant toasty oak and vanilla but those well integrated. Opens in the glass to reveal peach, yellow plum and mineral aromas and flavors, those hinting at one moment of figs, at another of pears. Hints of cream and spice come in but in the end the fruits carry through beautifully to an effusive finish that will remind many of Grand Cru Chablis. Drink now–2014. Score 92. K

YARDEN, CHARDONNAY, 2005: Oak-aged for seven months, full-bodied, bright gold in color, with nutty, floral and woody notes highlighting ripe tropical fruits, pears and citrus. On the background a nice hint of white pepper, all leading to a long finish. Drink up. Score 89. K

YARDEN, SAUVIGNON BLANC, 2010: Light shining gold in color, medium-bodied, opens with a hint of butterscotch and then goes on to show subdued but elegant aromas and flavors of pears, white peaches and honeydew melon and, from mid-palate on, a note of lemon custard. Ripe and smooth with just enough acidity to keep it going through a long finish. Drink now–2013. Score 89. K

YARDEN, SAUVIGNON BLANC, 2009: Light gold in color, with a nose replete with tropical fruits, starts off a bit flat on the palate but within moments opens to reveal generous citrus and apple notes all on a light herbal background. Drink now–2014. Score 89. K

YARDEN, SAUVIGNON BLANC, 2008: Light golden straw in color, light- to medium-bodied, a crisply refreshing wine with just enough complexity to catch our attention. On the nose and palate generous green apple, lime and grapefruit, those complemented nicely by hints of pine needles and freshly cut grass, all lingering nicely on the finish. Drink now. Score 89. K

YARDEN, VIOGNIER, 2009: On the opening nose light notes of oak and flowers, those parting to make way for aromas and flavors of white peaches, pears and spices and, from mid-palate to a generous finish, notes of green gage plums. Drink now–2013. Score 90. K

YARDEN, VIOGNIER, 2008: Almost burnished gold in color, with buttery, floral and caramel notes on the nose, opens to reveal spicy wood, pineapple, guava and peach fruits, a rich, ripe and lush wine. Long and simultaneously refreshing and complex. Drink now–2013. Score 92. K

YARDEN, VIOGNIER, 2007: Medium-bodied, deep gold, with a near-buttery texture and showing a tantalizing hint of spicy oak. Opens with citrus and herbal notes, goes on to reveal pears, papaya and peach blossoms. Shows an appealingly creamy note on the long finish. Drink now. Score 89. K

YARDEN, VIOGNIER, 2006: Shows a thoroughly traditional Viognier personality. Following an aromatic and floral nose, flavors and aromas of ripe Anjou pears, peaches, spring flowers and minerals along with hints of citrus. Lively, clean, fresh and long. Drink up. Score 91. K

YARDEN, GEWURZTRAMINER, 2010: Dark golden straw in color, medium-bodied, lightly off-dry and showing appealing litchi, orange and orange-peel notes on a background that is just floral and spicy enough to grab the attention. Drink now–2013. Score 89. K

YARDEN, GEWURZTRAMINER, 2009: Rich gold, off-dry, deeply aromatic and lithe, with fine balance between mouthwatering acidity and fruits. On the nose and palate grapefruit, litchi and floral notes all lingering nicely. Drink now. Score 89. K

YARDEN, GEWURZTRAMINER, 2008: The color of freshly dampened straw, showing medium-bodied with traditional Gewurztraminer spices, litchis and floral notes. In the background, ripe peaches and a note of citrus peel, and finishing with notes of rose petals and minerals. Even though categorized as off-dry, there is but a bare hint of sweetness here, that tantalizing and refreshing. Drink now. Score 90. K

YARDEN, GEWURZTRAMINER, 2007: Golden straw in color, off-dry, medium-bodied, with appealing spicy and floral notes running through, those including white pepper, anise and cinnamon. A lovely wine with tempting summer and litchi fruits. On the long finish, hints of rose petals and grapefruit peel. Drink now. Score 89. K

YARDEN, MOUNT HERMON WHITE, 2010: Light- to medium-bodied, with aromas and flavors of pineapple, citrus and summer fruits. Not a hint of complexity but fruit-forward enough to make some think it has the hint of sweetness for which they search. A good entry-level wine. Drink now. Score 84. K

YARDEN, MOUNT HERMON WHITE, 2008: A pleasant enough entry-level wine, with peach, citrus and pineapple fruits. Drink up. Score 84. K

YARDEN, MOUNT HERMON WHITE, 2007: Nothing complex here, but appealing summer fruits and pineapple to make a good entry-level wine. Drink up. Score 84. K

YARDEN, NOBLE SEMILLON, BOTRYTIS, 2005: Deep golden with orange and green reflections, medium-bodied, impacted upon by botrytis in the winery, showing an appealing array of ripe apricots, white peaches and citrus peel. In the background notes of white pepper, and spring flowers, all with just the right level of acidity to balance the generous sweetness. Delicious and complex. Drink now–2018. Score 91. K

YARDEN, NOBLE SEMILLON, BOTRYTIS, 2004: Golden in color, with fine concentration and balance, and developing deep honeyed botrytis-impacted spices and funkiness. On the nose and palate dried apricots, orange peel, toasty oak, and tropical fruits that come in toward the long, caressing finish. Drink now–2018. Score 92. K

YARDEN, NOBLE SEMILLON, BOTRYTIS, 2003: Deep and rich, with a concentrated personality of citrus peel, honeyed peaches and botrytis spice. Generously sweet, with fine balancing acidity and a long, sweet and caressing finish on which tropical fruits and butterscotch arise. Drink now–2015. Score 91. K

YARDEN, NOBLE SEMILLON, BOTRYTIS, 2002: Golden toward subdued orange in color, medium- to full-bodied and showing generous botrytis influence. Honeyed sweetness complemented nicely by aromas and flavors of orange peel and apricots. Soft, round and creamy on the palate, with good balancing acidity and hints of heather and white pepper on the moderately long finish. Drink now–2015. Score 90. K

YARDEN, NOBLE SEMILLON, BOTRYTIS, 2001: This lively, golden, medium-bodied dessert white offers up unabashed honeyed sweetness along with aromas and flavors of orange marmalade, pineapple and ripe apricots that

meld comfortably into a soft, almost creamy texture. Plenty of balancing natural acidity and a medium-long finish boasting hints of spring flowers and spices. Promises to darken and attain greater complexity and depth in the future. Drink up. Score 90. K

YARDEN, HEIGHTSWINE, 2009: Deep gold, medium- to full-bodied with generous sweetness set off by fine balancing acidity. On the nose and palate eucalyptus honey, dried summer fruits and notes of ginger and apples. Rich and long. Drink now–2016, perhaps longer. Score 90. K

YARDEN, HEIGHTSWINE, 2008: Bright, shining gold in color, medium-bodied, with honeyed sweetness and showing appealing peach, apricot and tropical fruits, those on a background of ginger-flavored baked apples. Rich and long, with fine acidity to keep it lively. Best with cheesecake or fruit-based pies. Drink now–2018. Score 92. K

YARDEN, HEIGHTSWINE, 2007: Richly honeyed, with generous aromas and flavors of ripe white peaches, apricots, litchis and passion fruit, all with overlays of sweet ginger and, on the long, long finish, notes of baked apples that have been treated to hints of cinnamon and sweet cream. Medium- to full-bodied, rich and with good balancing acidity, a fine wine indeed. Drink now–2018. Score 92. K

YARDEN, HEIGHTSWINE, 2006: Showing varietal typicity with litchis, apricots and tropical fruits, all on a spicy background. Now starting to develop the floral and honeyed characteristics of an ice wine. Drink now–2014. Score 90. K

YARDEN, HEIGHTSWINE, 2005: Made entirely from Gewurztraminer grapes frozen at the winery. Pale gold in color, with a complex nose and palate that offers up pineapple, citrus, litchi, orange peel and floral aromas and flavors, those with a light hint of seawater that adds to the wine's charm and complexity. Drink now. Score 91. K

YARDEN, HEIGHTSWINE, 2004: Generous sweetness set off by lively acidity. Elegant and rich, deep gold with a bronze overlay, with apricots, peaches and spices on the nose and palate set to a honeyed and floral background. Drink up. Score 90. K

YARDEN, HEIGHTSWINE, 2003: A tantalizing dessert wine, light- to medium-bodied with delicate honeyed apricot and peach aromas and flavors, good balancing acidity and an elegant, lingering finish. Drink up. Score 90. K

YARDEN, HEIGHTSWINE, 2002: Light gold in color, medium-bodied, with excellent balance. Plenty of natural acidity to back up the sweetness and keep it lively while allowing the peach, apricot and quince fruits to make themselves nicely felt. Honeyed and floral, generous and round. Showing first signs of age. Drink up. Score 90. K

YARDEN, HEIGHTSWINE, 2001: Well balanced, generous and elegant, this honeyed dessert wine has a lively golden color and offers up a generous array of yellow peaches, apricots, melon, orange marmalade and quince, all on a floral and just-spicy-enough background. Drink up. Score 91. K

YARDEN, MUSCAT DESSERT WINE, 2008: Light gold with orange tints, a reinforced dessert wine showing ripe apricots, peaches and pineapple notes. Generously sweet but lacking the balancing acidity that might have made it more lively. Drink now. Score 85. K

YARDEN, MUSCAT DESSERT WINE, 2006: With a light brandy reinforcement, a light- to medium-bodied, generously sweet wine with good balancing acidity and showing dried summer fruits with a gentle honeyed touch. Somewhat one-dimensional. Drink now. Score 86. K

Yarden – Sparkling Wines (*Methode Champenoise*)

YARDEN, BLANC DE BLANCS, 2000, LATE DISGORGED: The policy at the winery is to disgorge* sparkling wines only five years after the wine has gone through its fermentation in the bottle. Although the 2000 Blanc de Blancs was originally released in 2005, the winery held back a limited number of bottles for late disgorgement. The bottle from which I sampled was hand-disgorged for this tasting. Opening with a nose that is rich in toasty aromas and then showing a tempting range of oranges, apples and figs, those on a background of toasted hazelnuts and vanilla.

---

* The process of disgorgement involves chilling or freezing the neck of the bottle and then opening it to let the block of yeast that has fallen to the neck pop out. In anything but the most absolutely dry of Champagnes a small amount of sugar is then added and the bottle is immediately recorked in order to keep the carbon dioxide that has developed as a result of the fermentation process and given the wine its bubbles. Some Champagne producers leave a small percentage of their wine to remain on its yeasts for ten or more years, allowing the wine to mature and take on a tantalizing set of secondary aromas and flavors.

Displaying a rewarding note of age but with remarkably youthful zest, a wine that shows richness, finesse, with fine, near-miniscule bubbles that go on and on, all leading to a mineral-rich finish. A wine that demands luxurious dishes such as blinis with crème fraiche or foie gras. Drink from release–2020, perhaps longer. Score 93. K

YARDEN, BLANC DE BLANCS, 2005: When I first reviewed this wine, I borrowed a line from Cole Porter and wrote, "It's delicious, it's delightful, it's delovely." And so it still is. With a long mousse, sharp, well-focused and long-lasting bubbles, as brut-dry as one could hope for, opens to notes of yeasty white bread, going on to show tropical and citrus fruits all on a lightly floral background. Long, generous and elegant. Drink now–2018. Score 91. K

YARDEN, BLANC DE BLANCS, 2001: A truly fine sparkling wine by any standard. Made, as all of the winery's Blanc de Blancs, entirely from Chardonnay grapes and by the traditional *methode Champenoise*, continuing to show all of the charm of its youth. Finely tuned balance between aromas and flavors of yeasty sourdough bread, white peaches, citrus, citrus peel and minerals, showing a long mousse and sharp, well-focused bubbles that go on and on. Crisp, sophisticated and with a mouth-filling finish. Drink now–2013. Score 92. K

YARDEN, SPARKLING ROSÉ, 2010: Still in near-embryonic form but already showing as delicious and complex. On the nose and palate rose petals, citrus and wild berries, those with light overlays of candied citrus peel, vanilla. Destined to be creamy, full-bodied and elegant. Due to be released in 2014. Drink from release–2020, perhaps longer. Tentative Score 90–92. K

YARDEN, SPARKLING ROSÉ, 2009: Still in its toddlerhood, light baby-blanket pink in color, a crisply dry sparkling wine of great finesse with subtle aromas and flavors of wild berries, citrus and minerals, those in fine harmony with a floral note that floats through. Sharp, concentrated bubbles and fine grip, all leading to a finish of dried berries and minerals. Drink from release–2020, perhaps longer. Tentative Score 90–92. K

YARDEN, SPARKLING ROSÉ, 2008: Still undergoing its aging process but already showing fine precision and balance. Light salmon pink in color, with an appealing array of aromas and flavors that include pomegranates, black cherries and cassis, those on a background that hints at one moment of almonds, at another of candied citrus peel and at yet another of violets. Fresh, complex and lively with a long, mineral-rich finish. Scheduled for release about 2014. Drink from release–2022. Score 92. K

Gamla

GAMLA, CABERNET SAUVIGNON, 2008: Dark garnet, medium- to full-bodied, with gently gripping tannins and notes of spicy wood. On the nose and palate traditional Cabernet Sauvignon blackcurrants and blackberries, those complemented nicely by notes of crushed berries, pepper and chocolate all leading to a medium-long finish. Drink now–2014. Score 89. K

GAMLA, CABERNET SAUVIGNON, 2007: Medium- to full-bodied, a solid wine, opening with notes of spicy cedar, briar and cassis, those followed by currants, plums and blackberries, all on a background of sweet spices. Soft, round, spicy and generous. Drink now. Score 88. K

GAMLA, CABERNET SAUVIGNON, 2006: Oak-aged for 12 months, medium-bodied, with soft tannins and light notes of spicy wood integrated nicely to show black cherry and blackberry fruits on a background that hints of freshly roasted coffee. Drink now. Score 88. K

GAMLA, CABERNET SAUVIGNON, 2005: Medium- to full-bodied, dark garnet, a traditional Bordeaux blend showing soft, gently mouth-coating tannins and opening to reveal blackcurrant, wild berry and light Mediterranean herbal notes. Fine balance between oak, tannins, acidity and fruit and a generous, just-spicy-enough finish. Drink up. Score 88. K

GAMLA, MERLOT, 2008: Oak-aged in French barriques for nine months. Dark garnet, medium- to full-bodied, with a generous 14.5% alcohol content and firm but gently gripping tannins. On the nose, black fruits and hints of vanilla. Opens in the glass to reveal wild berries, blackcurrants and notes of roasted herbs, all leading to a mouth-filling and lightly peppery finish. Drink now–2013. Score 88. K

GAMLA, MERLOT, 2007: Medium-dark garnet, medium- to full-bodied with soft tannins and a note of spicy oak. On the nose and palate currant, black cherry and notes of citrus peel. Drink now. Score 87. K

GAMLA, MERLOT, 2005: Garnet-red, medium- to full-bodied, with silky tannins and showing an appealing array of berry, black cherry and cassis fruits on a lightly spicy background, and reflecting its development in *barriques* with light overlays of spices and white chocolate. Drink up. Score 88. K

GAMLA, PINOT NOIR, 2008: Dark ruby in color, medium-bodied, with soft tannins integrating nicely. On the nose and palate red currants and black and red cherries, those complemented nicely by notes of spices and minerals. Complex enough to grab our attention and simultaneously easy to drink. Drink now–2013. Score 88. K

GAMLA, PINOT NOIR, 2007: Medium-, perhaps medium- to full-bodied, medium-dark garnet in color, with near-sweet tannins, opens to reveal generous berry, cherry and cassis fruits. Lacks complexity but a fine quaffing wine. Drink now. Score 86. K

GAMLA, PINOT NOIR, 2006: Medium-bodied but intense and well-focused, with generous raspberry and black cherry fruits supported nicely by notes of minerals and anise that rise from mid-palate on. Drink now. Score 89. K

GAMLA, PINOT NOIR, 2005: Ruby toward garnet, medium-bodied, with soft tannins integrating nicely and showing appealing hints of spicy and vanilla-rich wood. Opens to show blackberry, blueberry and black cherry fruits with a hint of lemon-cola on the finish. Round and easy to enjoy. Drink up. Score 88. K

GAMLA, SANGIOVESE, 2008: Developed in *barriques* for 12 months, showing medium-bodied, with soft, gently caressing tannins. On the nose and palate currants, blackberries and black cherries, those complemented by hints of Mediterranean herbs. Drink now–2014. Score 88. K

GAMLA, SANGIOVESE, 2007: Dark ruby toward garnet, medium-bodied, with caressing tannins, a smooth, round wine with raspberry and blackberry aromas and flavors on a chocolate and mocha-scented background, all lasting through the long and easy-going finish. Drink now–2013. Score 88. K

GAMLA, SANGIOVESE, 2006: Showing more developed but fully consistent with an earlier tasting. Aromas and flavors of raspberries, strawberries and cassis, those on a medium-bodied frame with soft tannins, and showing appealing hints of spicy oak and sawdust, all leading to a fresh finish. Drink up. Score 87. K

GAMLA, SANGIOVESE, 2005: Medium- to full-bodied, with chewy but gentle tannins coming together to show an appealing array of berry, minted chocolate and spiced tea. Long and caressing. Drink now. Score 90. K

GAMLA, NEBBIOLO, 2009: With a lavender-scented nose, full-bodied, with soft tannins and generous blackberry and strawberry flavors, reminds of a very young Barolo still in development. Drink from release. Tentative Score 89–91. K

GAMLA, NEBBIOLO, 2008: Super-dark, medium- to full-bodied with gently gripping tannins, showing fine balance and structure. On the nose and palate plums and raspberries, those opening to reveal blackberries and earthy minerals. A wine that plays on the palate, at one moment showing hints of licorice, at another, black pepper and at yet another, dark chocolate. Does not taste like Nebbiolo, but a generous and intriguing wine. Drink now–2014. Score 89. K

GAMLA, NEBBIOLO, 2006: The winery's first Nebbiolo varietal release. Reflecting its 12 months in French oak, dark ruby toward garnet, medium- to full-bodied, with generous but softly caressing tannins. Opens to reveal a tempting array of blackberries, cherries and, in the background from first attack to the long finish, notes of licorice and tar. Drink now–2013. Score 89. K

GAMLA, CHARDONNAY, 2009: Medium-bodied and gently oaked, showing an appealing combination of citrus, pineapple and tropical fruits, all on a gently spicy background. Lively and crisply refreshing. Drink now. Score 88. K

GAMLA, CHARDONNAY, 2008: Light- to medium-bodied, with appealing melon and apple notes. Needs a bit more acidity, but a pleasant little wine. Drink up. Score 85. K

GAMLA, CHARDONNAY, 2007: Light gold, light- to medium-bodied, with citrus, peach and melon fruits on a pleasing gentle mineral background. Crisp, clean and delightful. Drink up. Score 88. K

GAMLA, SAUVIGNON BLANC, 2010: Straw colored with green tints, light and refreshing with generous citrus and tropical fruits set off by a hint of freshly mown grass. Drink now. Score 86. K

GAMLA, SAUVIGNON BLANC, 2009: Light gold in color, light- to medium-bodied with a generous array of citrus, apple and melon fruits. Lively and refreshing. Drink now. Score 87. K

GAMLA, SAUVIGNON BLANC, 2008: The color of damp straw, medium-bodied, with fine acidity, a lively wine showing appealing citrus, green apples and passion fruits on a lightly spicy background. Drink now. Score 87. K

GAMLA, SAUVIGNON BLANC, 2007: Light straw colored, light- to medium-bodied, showing traditional green apple, citrus and passion fruits. Plenty of spices and acidity to keep the wine lively. Drink up. Score 87. K

GAMLA, WHITE RIESLING, 2009: Light gold, medium-bodied, with generous ripe peach and apricot fruits supported nicely by notes of white pepper. Fruit forward enough that some will think it near-sweet. Best as an aperitif. Drink now. Score 87. K

GAMLA, WHITE RIESLING, 2008: Light golden straw in color, showing appealing floral, ginger and white peach aromas and flavors, those on a near creamy and lightly oily background. Lingers nicely on the palate. Drink now. Score 87. K

GAMLA, WHITE RIESLING, 2007: Light gold in color, medium-bodied, with citrus fruits overlaid with ripe pear and peach flavors. A somewhat short finish but that with a very appealing mineral overlay. Drink up. Score 86. K

GAMLA, BRUT, 2007: Light gold in color, drier and more tempting than the earlier N.V. release of this wine, with a gently yeasty hint on the nose and palate and opening to show fine citrus and apple fruits. A good mousse, long-lingering and sharp bubbles with a note of toasted brioche on the finish. Drink now–2014. Score 89. K

GAMLA, BRUT, N.V.: As is its wont, a blend of near-equal parts of Pinot Noir and Chardonnay and made by the *Methode Champenoise*. The best cuvée of this wine ever. Medium-bodied, light golden straw in color, showing sharp, well-focused bubbles and generous aromas and flavors of black cherries, citrus, citrus peel and apples. Crisply dry with a light mineral overlay. Score 89. K

Golan

GOLAN, CABERNET SAUVIGNON, 2009: Made entirely from Cabernet Sauvignon grapes, ruby toward garnet, medium-bodied, with soft tannins and friendly blackcurrant and black cherry fruits on a background that hints of black pepper. A good quaffer. Drink now. Score 85. K

GOLAN, CABERNET SAUVIGNON, 2008: Dark ruby toward garnet, medium-bodied, soft and round, gently tannic and with appealing blackberry, wild berry and black cherry fruits supported nicely by notes of black pepper and licorice. Drink now. Score 85. K

GOLAN, CABERNET SAUVIGNON, 2007: With soft tannins and just a bare hint of vanilla from the American oak in which the wine developed for six months, showing wild berry and black cherry fruits on a lightly spicy background. Drink up. Score 86. K

GOLAN, CABERNET SAUVIGNON, 2006: Medium-bodied, with caressing tannins, a gentle hint of vanilla from the oak in which it developed for six months and appealing berry, currant and black cherry fruits. Round and generous, a good entry-level wine. Drink up. Score 86. K

GOLAN, MERLOT, 2008: Medium-bodied, garnet toward royal purple in color, with soft tannins and bare hints of spicy wood integrating nicely to show a basic berry-cherry personality, the fruits overlaid lightly with hints of dried herbs and earthy minerals. A good quaffer. Drink now. Score 86. K

GOLAN, MERLOT, 2007: Lightly oak-aged, dark garnet toward royal purple, a medium-bodied, gently tannic wine with generous currant, berry and spicy notes. An easy-to-drink wine. Drink up. Score 87. K

GOLAN, SION CREEK, RED, 2009: A light and frivolous blend of Pinot Noir, Sangiovese, Syrah and Nebbiolo. Ruby toward garnet, with almost unfelt tannins and generous raspberry, cherry and wild berry fruits. A pleasant enough entry-level wine. Drink up. Score 84. K

GOLAN, CHARDONNAY, 2008: Very lightly oaked, with crisp citrus, pineapple and tropical fruits, a lively and pleasant little wine. Drink now. Score 85. K

GOLAN, CHARDONNAY, 2007: Light gold in color, light, bright and refreshing, showing crisply dry with citrus and tropical fruits with an appealing flinty-mineral overlay. Drink up. Score 86. K

GOLAN, MOSCATO, 2010: Nicely frizzante, with a nose that is fresh and just floral enough to tantalize, opens to show fruity and delicate, with hints of melon, pear and white peach flavors. Generous sweetness here but one will not suffer at all from that because the sweetness, fruits and acidity are in fine balance. Reminds of a fine Moscato d'Asti. Drink now. Score 87. K

GOLAN, MOSCATO, 2009: With just the lightest hint of fizz and its generous sweetness set off nicely by natural acidity. Light- to medium-bodied, with generous lemon and lime grapefruit, green apple and white peach fruits, a distinctly fun wine that serves as well as an aperitif as a dessert wine. Hard to believe, but also a good match to hummus, eggplant salad and yoghurt, especially when served very, very well chilled. Drink up. Score 86. K

GOLAN, MOSCATO, 2008: Made in the style of Moscato d'Asti entirely from Muscat Canelli grapes, with generous sweetness set off nicely by lively acidity and a light fizzy nature. Nothing complex here, but delightful aromas and flavors of wild flowers, green apples, peaches and passion fruit and minerals. Light- to medium-bodied, low in alcohol (6%) and remarkably refreshing, as good as an aperitif as a dessert wine with fruit-based pies, tarts and mousses. An ebullient wine to drink as well chilled as you would a Champagne. Drink up. Score 87. K

GOLAN, SION CREEK, WHITE, 2009: A half-dry blend of Sauvignon Blanc, Gewurztraminer and Riesling. A fair amount of sweetness here, that set off nicely by balancing acidity and showing ripe peach and tropical fruits. A good entry-level wine. Drink up. Score 84. K

Greenberg ✶✶✶

Located in Herzliya, not far from Tel Aviv, this micro-winery owned by Motti Greenberg is now producing about 2,000 bottles annually. First wines were released from the 2003 vintage, using Cabernet Sauvignon, Merlot and Shiraz grapes from the Karmei Yosef vineyards at the foothills of the Jerusalem Mountains.

GREENBERG, CABERNET SAUVIGNON, 2006: Dark garnet toward royal purple, lithe and open-textured. Soft tannins and spicy wood integrating nicely to show currant and blackberry fruits, those with hints of espresso coffee and eucalyptus on the long finish. Drink now. Score 88.

GREENBERG, CABERNET SAUVIGNON, 2005: Aged in oak for 12 months and racked four times before blending 85% Cabernet Sauvignon with 10% of Merlot and 5% Shiraz. Dark ruby toward garnet, medium- to full-bodied, with generous, soft tannins and light spicy wood opening to show blackcurrant, blackberry and spicy notes. On the finish a hint of eucalyptus. Drink up. Score 88.

GREENBERG, MERLOT, 2006: Dark, almost impenetrable garnet, a plush wine showing layers of raspberry, blackberry and fig aromas and flavors, those complemented by spices, minerals and a hint of lead pencil. Bodes for elegance. Drink now. Score 89.

GREENBERG, MERLOT, 2005: Garnet toward royal purple, this medium- to full-bodied blend of 85% Merlot, 10% Cabernet Sauvignon and 5% Shiraz opens with generous, near-sweet tannins and spicy wood, those coming together nicely to show blackberry, black cherry and spicy aromas and flavors. Drink up. Score 87.

GREENBERG, SHIRAZ, 2006: Complex and supple, with layers of spices, wild berries, anise and leather, all coming together beautifully. A firm tannic grip here that carries through to the long finish. Drink now. Score 91.

GREENBERG, SHIRAZ, 2005: Deep purple, with soft tannins and light spicy wood influences, this is a medium- to full-bodied blend of 85% Shiraz, 10% Merlot and 5% Cabernet Sauvignon. On the nose and palate black fruits matched nicely by hints of saddle leather and earthiness. Generous and moderately long. Drink now. Score 89.

Gush Etzion ✶✶✶

Located at the Gush Etzion Junction near Jerusalem, the winery is owned largely by vintner Shraga Rozenberg and partly by the Tishbi family, and has its own vineyards in the Jerusalem Mountains providing Cabernet Sauvignon, Merlot, Pinot Noir, Shiraz, Cabernet Franc and Petit Verdot as well as Chardonnay, Viognier and Johannisberg Riesling grapes. First releases were of about 2,000 bottles in 1998 and the winery currently produces about 40,000 bottles annually. Now in a recently constructed facility, the winery is capable of producing up to 50,000 bottles annually.

Most recently released wines are in four series. The top-of-the-line wines in the Emek Bracha series are blended reds aged for 20–22 months; the two mid-range series of varietal wines are Alon HaBoded (The Lone Oak) and Gush Etzion; and the basic line is Nachal HaPirim.

Emek Bracha

EMEK BRACHA, MERLOT, 2008: Oak-aged for 22 months, a garnet toward royal purple blend of 81% Merlot and 19% Cabernet Sauvignon. Medium- to full-bodied, with soft tannins and a fine array of currant, wild berry and red plums, those complemented nicely by hints of black pepper and dark chocolate. Long and generous. Drink now–2013. Score 90. K

EMEK BRACHA, MERLOT, 2007: A blend of 87% Merlot and 13% Cabernet Franc, showing dark garnet with a note of adobe brick. Oak-aged for 20 months, showing full-bodied with firm tannins and generous spicy wood and in need of decanting at this stage of its development. Opens to reveal black and red berries, cassis and notes of freshly picked Mediterranean herbs, all on a light earth background. Drink now–2014. Score 90. K

EMEK BRACHA, MERLOT, 2006: Aged in French oak *barriques* for 22 months, a dark-garnet blend of 82% Merlot and 18% Cabernet Sauvignon. Opens with a blow of spicy wood and firm tannins, those happily receding in the glass to reveal blackberry, raspberry and licorice notes with tannins and wood rising on the finish. Drink up. Score 87. K

Alon HaBoded

ALON HABODED, CABERNET SAUVIGNON, 2008: Medium- to full-bodied, garnet toward royal purple in color, reflecting its time in oak with soft tannins and spicy cedarwood. On the nose and palate black and red berries, cassis and notes of earthy minerals. Not complex but a fine match to food. Drink now. Score 86. K

ALON HABODED, CABERNET FRANC, 2009: Dark garnet, medium- to full-bodied and aromatic, showing a comfortable note of spicy oak and soft tannins. On first attack distinct notes of green herbs, those parting to make way for black fruits and a note of mocha. Drink now–2015. Score 89. K

ALON HABODED, CHARDONNAY, 2009: Damp golden straw in color, medium-bodied, reflecting very light exposure to oak with a hint of sweet cedar. Opens in the glass to reveal citrus, melon and tropical fruits on a background that hints of stony minerals. Drink now. Score 86. K

ALON HABODED, SAUVIGNON BLANC, 2010: Light straw colored, light- to medium-bodied. On the nose and palate summer fruits, melon and citrus flowers on a background that hints of freshly cut grass. Drink now. Score 89. K

ALON HABODED, SAUVIGNON BLANC, 2009: Golden straw in color, light and fragrant with generous melon, peach, nectarine and lemon fruits highlighted by notes of freshly picked herbs. Juicy and refreshing. Drink up. Score 88. K

ALON HABODED, WHITE RIESLING, 2009: Fresh and bright, this dry Riesling opens with notes of peaches and peach pits, those going on to reveal quince and green apples. Fine lime-flavored acidity and a hint of pea blossoms rise on the finish. Drink now. Score 89. K

ALON HABODED, GEWURZTRAMINER, 2009: Light gold in color, opening with a nose of browned butter, freshly cut flowers and slate-like minerals. On the nose and palate a potpourri of summer fruits, lemons and tangerines, those matched nicely by a note of eucalyptus honey. Ripe and refined. Drink now. Score 89. K

Nachal HaPirim

NACHAL HAPIRIM, 2008: As always, a Bordeaux blend of Cabernet Sauvignon, Merlot, Petit Verdot and Cabernet Sauvignon. Medium- to full-bodied, with firm tannins and spicy oak that part nicely in the glass to reveal aromas and flavors of blackcurrants, wild berries and citrus peel, those on a background that hints one moment of roasted herbs and at another of earthy minerals. Drink now–2013. Score 89. K

NACHAL HAPIRIM, 2007: A full-bodied Bordelaise blend of Cabernet Sauvignon, Merlot, Petit Verdot and Cabernet Franc (60%, 26%, 9% and 5% respectively). Aged in French *barriques*, showing gently mouth-coating tannins and a subtle note of spicy cedarwood, those parting to reveal currant, blackberry and earthy notes. Drink now. Score 89. K

NACHAL HAPIRIM, 2005: A medium-to full-bodied blend of Cabernet Sauvignon, Merlot, Cabernet Franc and Petit Verdot (60%, 25%, 10% and 5% respectively). Reflecting oak-aging in new French oak for 12 months with lightly smoky cedar hints, showing soft tannins and opening to reveal currant and blackberry fruits, those on a light background of a fresh forest floor. Drink now. Score 87. K

NACHAL HAPIRIM, WHITE WINE, 2009: A half-dry blend of 75% Sauvignon Blanc, 14% White Riesling and 11% Gewurztraminer. Light gold in color, deeply floral, opening with generous tropical and citrus fruits, those going on to quince and green apples. Lacking that extra bit of acidity that would have made the wine more refreshing. Drink up. Score 85. K

Gush Etzion

GUSH ETZION, CABERNET SAUVIGNON, 2008: Medium- to full-bodied, with gently gripping tannins and a light hand with spicy oak. Opens to reveal traditional blackcurrant, blackberry and smoky cedar notes, all on a background of a fresh forest floor. Drink now–2013. Score 88. K

GUSH ETZION, MERLOT, ORGANIC VINEYARD, 2006: Dark garnet, medium- to full-bodied, reflecting its 17 months in oak with gently caressing tannins and notes of sweet cedarwood. On the nose and palate an appealing array of red and black berries, cassis and notes of toasted rye bread. Generous and mouth-filling. Drink now. Score 88. K

GUSH ETZION, SHIRAZ, 2007: Dark garnet toward royal purple, medium- to full-bodied, a ripe and intense wine with wild berry, black cherry and notes of green peppers and freshly turned earth all leading to a long and generous finish. Drink now. Score 88. K

GUSH ETZION, SHIRAZ, 2006: Vibrant and lively, dark garnet in color, medium- to full-bodied, with tight tannins and spicy wood that part in the glass to reveal ripe berries, black cherries and citrus peel notes. In the background appealing hints of roasted herbs and earthy minerals. Drink now. Score 88. K

GUSH ETZION, CABERNET FRANC, 2008: Garnet toward royal purple, full-bodied with soft tannins and spicy wood integrating nicely. Opens to show generous black fruits, roasted herbs and hints of cigar tobacco. Drink now. Score 89. K

GUSH ETZION, CABERNET FRANC, 2007: Dark garnet in color, medium- to full-bodied, with generous soft tannins and notes of spices and vanilla from the oak in which it aged for 18 months. On the nose and palate an appealing array of blackberries, black cherries, cassis and, from mid-palate on, notes of Mediterranean herbs and saddle leather. Drink now. Score 89. K

GUSH ETZION, CABERNET FRANC, 2005: Medium- to full-bodied, reflecting its 14 months in oak with generous soft tannins and notes of spicy oak. On first attack plums, tar and minerals, those yielding comfortably to notes of dried cherries, blackcurrants, minerals and a hint of mint. Drink up. Score 90. K

GUSH ETZION, CABERNET SAUVIGNON-MERLOT, 2006: Aged in oak for 14 months. Full-bodied and with soft tannins that make the wine simultaneously sleek, complex and bold. Opens with dried berries, currants and earthy minerals, goes on to reveal notes of spices and tobacco that linger long and comfortably. Drink now. Score 90. K

GUSH ETZION, CHARDONNAY, 2008: The color of damp golden straw, light- to medium-bodied, with citrus, melon and tropical fruits. Lively, rich and easy to drink. Drink up. Score 87. K

GUSH ETZION, WHITE RIESLING, 2008: Blended with 10% Gewurztraminer, opens with a floral and citrus nose, goes on to reveal white peaches and tropical fruits all with a tempting, lightly oily texture. Drink now. Score 87. K

GUSH ETZION, GEWURZTRAMINER, 2009: Gold with a hint of bronze, medium-bodied, with traditional Gewurztraminer litchi and rosewater aromas and flavors, those complemented by an appealing note of mint. Not complex but very pleasant. Drink now. Score 86. K

GUSH ETZION, GEWURZTRAMINER, 2008: Light golden in color, opens with a light petrol note that calls to mind Riesling more than Gewurztraminer. On the nose and palate apricots, pears and spices.

Lacks the acidity that might have given it more liveliness and with a not-fully-wanted hint of sweetness that rises on the finish. Drink now. Score 84. K

GUSH ETZION, HAR ETZION (MOUNT ETZION), WHITE, 2008: An unoaked potpourri of Gewurztraminer, Riesling, Sauvignon Blanc and Chardonnay showing apples, mangos, pineapple and citrus peel on the nose and palate. Not complex but a pleasant little dry white. Drink up. Score 85. K

GUSH ETZION, CHARDONNAY, DESSERT WINE, 2006: The color of damp straw, reflecting its five months in oak with hints of spices that come together with not at all cloying sweetness. On the nose and palate appealing ripe peach and apricot fruits and vanilla. Drink now. Score 88. K

GUSH ETZION, CHARDONNAY, DESSERT WINE, ORGANIC VINE-YARD, 2006: Oak-aged for five months, golden toward apricot in color, medium- to full-bodied with moderate sweetness balanced by fresh acidity, and showing an appealing array of lightly honeyed tropical and summer fruits. Drink now. Score 87. K

Gustavo & Jo ✶✶✶✶

Located in the village of Kfar Vradim in the Western Galilee, and drawing on grapes from the Golan Heights and the Upper Galilee, this small winery was founded in 1995 by Gideon Boinjeau and produced only Cabernet Sauvignon wines until the release of a first white in 2005. Production of two series, Premium and Gustavo & Jo, averages 3,000 bottles annually.

Premium

PREMIUM, CABERNET SAUVIGNON, 2006: Dark garnet, full-bodied with gripping tannins and toasty oak needing time to settle down. On the nose and palate black fruits and wild berries, those with a note of mocha. Lingers nicely. Drink now–2014. Score 90.

PREMIUM, CABERNET SAUVIGNON, 2005: Full-bodied and aromatic with its once-gripping tannins and generous spicy wood now integrating nicely. Opens to reveal currant, blackberry, blueberry and chocolate-covered citrus peel, those yielding to notes of freshly hung tobacco. Long and generous. Drink now–2014. Score 91.

PREMIUM, CABERNET SAUVIGNON, 2004: Deep ruby toward garnet, medium- to full-bodied, with firm tannins that need time to integrate but already showing fine balance and structure. Aromas and flavors of blackberries, currants, near-sweet cedarwood and white pepper lead to a long tobacco and chocolate-rich finish. Drink now. Score 91.

PREMIUM, CABERNET SAUVIGNON, 2003: Dark garnet toward black, full-bodied, with firm tannins integrating nicely, those well balanced by spicy wood and blackcurrant, blackberry and cassis fruits all on a background of minty chocolate. Long and complex. Drink now. Score 90.

Gustavo & Jo

GUSTAVO & JO, CABERNET SAUVIGNON, 2009: Dark, almost impenetrable garnet, full-bodied, with silky smooth tannins and gentle notes of spicy oak. A few rough edges but give this one some time and it will show a soft, round wine opening in the glass to reveal blackcurrants, blackberries, citrus peel and notes of bittersweet chocolate. Drink now–2016. Score 88.

GUSTAVO & JO, CABERNET SAUVIGNON, 2006: Deep garnet in color, full-bodied, with gently gripping tannins and near-sweet cedar in fine balance with black and red currants. Spicy and long with the tannins rising on the finish. Drink now–2013. Score 89.

GUSTAVO & JO, CABERNET SAUVIGNON, 2005: Garnet toward royal purple, full-bodied with soft tannins and spicy oak. Showing a rich array of blackcurrant, blackberry and raspberry fruits on a background of spices and licorice. Drink now. Score 90.

GUSTAVO & JO, CABERNET SAUVIGNON, UNFILTERED, INBAR, 2005: Inky-dark garnet in color, full-bodied, with fine balance between gently gripping tannins and spicy oak. On the nose and palate generous black fruits, those supported nicely by notes of bitter orange peel and spices. Long and generous. Drink now. Score 91.

GUSTAVO & JO, CABERNET SAUVIGNON, 2004: Medium-dark garnet in color, with grapes primarily from the Upper Galilee, this spicy, generously oaked and tannic wine shows fine balance and structure and appealing black fruits. Hints of licorice and green olives come together nicely on a long and mouth-filling finish. Drink now. Score 90.

GUSTAVO & JO, CABERNET SAUVIGNON, 2003: Dark garnet toward black, full-bodied, with still-firm tannins well balanced by spicy wood and blackcurrant, blackberry and cassis fruits all on a background of minty chocolate. Long and complex but starting to show age. Drink up. Score 89.

GUSTAVO & JO, FUMÉ BLANC, SHANI, 2009: An oak-aged Sauvignon Blanc, deep gold in color, showing aromas of pineapple and over-ripe peaches all with a somewhat bitter overlay that tends to dominate. Drink up. Score 84.

Gvaot ✴✴✴✴

Founded by Shivi Drori and Amnon Weiss on Shiloh in the Shomron region, with vineyards at an altitude of 700–900 meters above sea level, this boutique winery released its first wines from the 2005 vintage. Current production is about 20,000 bottles annually, those drawing on Cabernet Sauvignon, Merlot, Pinot Noir, Petit Verdot, Cabernet Franc, Chardonnay and Gewurztraminer grapes. The winery is currently releasing wines in three series, Gofna Reserve, Masada and Herodion.

Gofna Reserve

GOFNA RESERVE, CABERNET SAUVIGNON, 2009: Oak-aged for 16 months, showing full-bodied with still-gripping, near-sweet tannins and spicy wood in fine balance with fruits but needing a bit of time to settle down. Opens in the glass to reveal generous blackcurrants, blackberries and bitter citrus peel on a background that hints at one moment of baking chocolate and at another of espresso. Long and firm but not at all aggressive. Best from mid-2012–2016. Score 91. K

GOFNA RESERVE, CABERNET SAUVIGNON, SINGLE VINEYARD, HAR'EL, 2007: New World Cabernet, full-bodied, with caressing tannins and forward blackberry and blackcurrant fruits, those supported by generous hints of spices and sweet Mediterranean herbs, all leading to a dark chocolate and tobacco finish. Drink now–2013. Score 89. K

GOFNA RESERVE, CABERNET SAUVIGNON, 2005: Generous spicy wood here after 24 months' development in French oak, but showing smooth and round. Almost inky-dark garnet in color, full-bodied, with concentrated black cherry and blackberry fruits. The tannins rise from mid-palate on and lead to a long and intense finish. Drink up. Score 87. K

GOFNA RESERVE, MERLOT, 2006: Dark garnet toward royal purple, medium- to full-bodied with gently mouth-coating tannins. Blended with 10% Cabernet Sauvignon and oak-aged for 14 months, opens to reveal blueberry and black cherry fruits on a background of roasted chestnuts and licorice. Long and generous. Drink now. Score 89. K

GOFNA RESERVE, PINOT NOIR, 2009: Made from still-young vines and showing light garnet, a rich, medium-bodied and elegant wine. Oak-aged for 12 months, opens with a cherry-berry nose, going on to show soft, gently caressing tannins and abundant wild berry, plum and cherry fruits, those on a just-spicy-enough background to tantalize. Well focused and long with fruits and tannins rising nicely on the finish. Drink now–2016. Score 91. K

GOFNA RESERVE, CABERNET FRANC, 2007: As predicted at an early tasting, the best yet from this winery. Medium- to full-bodied, opening with notes of freshly turned earth and loam, those parting to reveal black and blue berries along with spicy and toasty oak notes. Firm tannins but with fine balance and structure, a simultaneously muscular and elegant wine. Drink now. Score 90. K

GOFNA RESERVE, GEWURZTRAMINER, 2009: Blended with 5% of Chardonnay, light gold in color, showing appealing litchi, tropical and citrus fruits on a lightly peppery background and with a hint of rosewater that rises on the nose. Drink now. Score 87. K

GOFNA RESERVE, CHARDONNAY-CABERNET SAUVIGNON, 2009: An odd marriage between 80% Chardonnay and 20% Cabernet Sauvignon, the red grapes having undergone very cold pressing to keep coloration to an absolute minimum. Light gold in color, reflecting four months in new French *barriques* with gentle hints of spicy cedar. Full-bodied, a white that hints comfortably of tannins and opens on the palate to reveal a rich array of tropical and citrus fruits, those complemented nicely by notes of wild berries. Well made and fascinating. Drink now–2013. Score 89. K

Masada

MASADA, 2009: A blend of Cabernet Sauvignon, Merlot and Petit Verdot (50%, 35% and 15% respectively), destined for oak-aging of 21 months. Super-dark garnet, one feels the spicy oak and the still-firm tannins, those needing only a bit more time to meld together with the fruits and acidity. Opens in the glass to reveal a richly textured wine, with well-focused currant, plum and blueberry fruits, those complemented nicely by notes of wild berries and Mediterranean herbs. Give this one the time it needs. Drink now–2016, perhaps longer. Score 90. K

MASADA, 2008: A full-bodied, dark-garnet blend of 60% Cabernet Sauvignon and 40% Merlot. Developed for 20 months primarily in new French *barriques* with hints of dusty oak and firm tannins that yield in the glass to fruits and spices. Concentrated and rich, showing generous blackberry, blackcurrant and wild berry fruits, those supported by notes of earthy minerals and Mediterranean herbs. Showing the kind of balance and structure that bode well for the future. Drink now–2016, perhaps longer. Score 91. K

MASADA, 2007: Showing all the best Cabernet Sauvignon traits. Deep, concentrated and full-bodied, with still-gripping tannins waiting to settle down but already showing fine balance and structure. Generous black fruits supported comfortably by notes of licorice and dark chocolate. A tantalizing bitter note complemented by the illusion of sweetness makes one think somewhat of a fine Amarone. Long and generous. Drink now–2014. Score 91. K

MASADA, 2006: Made from Cabernet Sauvignon and Merlot grapes that had partly dried on the vines, cold-fermented before being transferred to oak barrels. Medium-, perhaps medium- to full-bodied, with a vague hint of sweetness set off nicely by aromas and flavors of ripe berries and black cherries and, on the moderately long finish, a touch of eucalyptus. Drink up. Score 88. K

MASADA, MERLOT, 2006: Dark, almost impenetrable garnet in color, full-bodied, firm and concentrated, opening with peppery cedarwood, that yielding comfortably to blackberry and spicy and earthy aromas and flavors. A distinct personality and a long-lingering finish. Drink now. Score 89. K

MASADA, MERLOT, 2005: Dark royal purple with orange reflections, this wine reflects its 18 months in *barriques* with spicy oak and mouth-coating near-sweet tannins in fine balance with herb-scented cherry and berry flavors, those with overlays of milk chocolate and mint. Full-bodied, with fine tannins and a caressing finish. Drink now. Score 89. K

Herodion

HERODION, CABERNET SAUVIGNON, 2009: Blended with 10% Merlot, dark garnet toward royal purple, opens with a bit of funk on the nose but that blows off quickly to reveal appealing aromas of crushed berries and spring flowers. Medium- to full-bodied (leaning to the full), with light notes of spicy oak and silky tannins that grip gently, those making way for blackberries, purple plums, espresso and earthy minerals. On the  long finish with the tannins rising, freshly picked herbs. Drink from release–2018. Score 90. K

HERODION, CABERNET SAUVIGNON, 2008: Blended with 10% Merlot, oak-aged for 12 months in French and American casks. Soft, well-integrating tannins and notes of spices and vanilla highlight generous blackcurrant and blackberry fruits, those complemented by notes of roasted herbs and black olives. Drink now. Score 89. K

HERODION, CABERNET SAUVIGNON, 2007: Reflecting its 12 months in *barriques* with gentle spicy oak, this medium- to full-bodied red has soft tannins and a round, fruity personality. On the nose and palate appealing black fruits, spices and hint of Oriental spices, all lingering nicely, the fruits and tannins rising on a long and mouth-filling finish Drink now. Score 88. K

HERODION, CABERNET SAUVIGNON, 2006: Opens with a lightly funky aroma, that passing quickly. Reflecting its development in *barriques* with full body, firm tannins and generous spicy wood, those integrating nicely and showing appealing currant, blackberry, green olives and Mediterranean herbs. Drink up. Score 88. K

HERODION, CABERNET SAUVIGNON, 2005: A blend of 85% Cabernet Sauvignon and 15% Merlot, reflecting sweet and spicy cedarwood from its 14 months' development in French oak, the wood in good balance with soft, gently mouth-coating tannins and fruits. Medium- to full-bodied, aromatic, and showing deep currant, black cherry and dark red fruits. Finishes with a touch of heat but that will integrate nicely in time. Drink now. Score 88. K

HERODION, MERLOT, 2009: Dark garnet toward royal purple, full-bodied with ample tannins caressing nicely and notes of spicy and smoky wood. Developing half in French and half in American *barriques*, opens with an unmistakable blueberry nose and then opens in the glass to show purple plums, blackberries and currants on a lightly spicy background. Showing fresh and long and destined for complexity and elegance. Drink now–2015. Score 90. K

HERODION, MERLOT, 2008: Dark garnet, full-bodied, with silky tannins and light notes of spicy wood parting to reveal a fine array of wild berry, blackberry and minted chocolate, all leading to a long, mouth-filling finish. Drink now. Score 89. K

HERODION, MERLOT, 2007: Blended with 10% Cabernet Sauvignon, oak-aged for 12 months, medium- to full-bodied, with soft, caressing tannins and appealing blackcurrant and black cherry fruits, a generous and near-elegant wine with a long, licorice-hinted finish. Drink now. Score 88. K

HERODION, VINEYARDS DANCE, 2009: A blend of 60% Cabernet Sauvignon, 30% Merlot and 10% Petit Verdot, each variety fermented separately until the final blend was made. Oak-aged for 12 months in French and American oak barriques, about 40% of which were new, showing dark garnet, medium- to full-bodied with soft tannins that almost dance in the mouth. Ripe and generous, offering up a generous array of blackberry, plum and floral aromas and flavors that take one to a long, firm-textured finish. Combines intensity with style and grace. Drink now–2016, perhaps longer. Score 91. K

HERODION, VINEYARDS DANCE, 2008: A blend of 60% Cabernet Sauvignon, 25% Merlot and 15% Cabernet Franc. Showing dark ruby toward garnet, medium- to full-bodied, with silky tannins that caress gently, a round and elegant wine opening with red plum and red currant fruits, those yielding to black cherries and blackberries, the fruits supported nicely by notes of bittersweet chocolate and, on the long finish, a hint of Oriental spices. Drink now–2014. Score 90. K

HERODION, VINEYARDS DANCE, 2007: A full-bodied Bordeaux blend of Cabernet Sauvignon, Merlot and Cabernet Franc (60%, 30% and 10%). Showing spicy and toasty notes from its oak-aging, and on the nose and palate appealing blackberry, purple plum and currant fruits. Long and mouth-filling. Drink now–2013. Score 89. K

HERODION, CABERNET SAUVIGNON-MERLOT, 2006: Dark ruby toward garnet, aged for 14 months primarily in used French *barriques*, this blend of 60% Cabernet Sauvignon and 40% Merlot shows medium-bodied, with gently mouth-coating tannins. Round, soft and rich with appealing red berry and cassis notes, those on a lightly spicy background. Long and generous. Drink up. Score 88. K

HERODION, CHARDONNAY-GEWURZTRAMINER, 2010: A barely off-dry and deeply aromatic blend of 83% Chardonnay and 17% Gewurztraminer. Medium-bodied, with fine balancing acidity. On first attack guava and pineapple, those followed by hints of litchi, and nectarines. As this one develops in the bottle look as well for notes of dried apricots and dried apples. Best as an aperitif or with desserts such as kadaif or peach pie. Drink now–2015. Score 91. K

Hakerem *

Founded in 2001 by Isaac Herskovitz and located in Beit-El, north of Jerusalem, this winery produces Cabernet Sauvignon and Merlot wines, drawing on grapes from various vineyards. The winery sometimes releases more than one wine under the same label. Annual production is currently about 6,000 bottles.

HAKEREM, CABERNET SAUVIGNON, KEDUSHAT SHVI'IT, 2008: The best wine to date from this small winery. Dark ruby toward garnet, medium- to full-bodied, with generous, softly caressing tannins and notes of spicy wood. On the nose and palate traditional Cabernet Sauvignon blackberry and blackcurrant fruits, those matched by generous hints of tobacco and earthy minerals. Drink up. Score 88. K

HAKEREM, CABERNET SAUVIGNON, 2005: Ruby toward cloudy garnet, aged in oak for 24 months, showing far-too-generous acidity and some barnyard aromas that tend to hide the black fruits here. Showing age. Drink up. Score 76. K

HAKEREM, MERLOT, 2005: Medium-bodied, with somewhat coarse tannins and an overriding earthy note that tends to hide whatever fruits may be hidden. Showing age. Drink up. Score 75. K

HAKEREM, MUSCAT, 2007: Dark bronzed-gold in color, thick, and even though categorized as half-dry, so sweet that it is cloying. Comes in a bottle closed with a plastic screw-cap, one more appropriate for fruit juice than wine. Score 60. K

Hamasrek ★★

Established by brothers Nachum and Hanoch Greengrass in 1999 on Moshav Beit Meir in the Jerusalem Mountains, this kosher boutique winery draws on grapes from their own area as well as from Zichron Ya'akov and the Upper Galilee. In 2000 the winery released 5,000 bottles of Merlot and Chardonnay, and since then the winery has added Cabernet Sauvignon and Gewurztraminer to their line. Current production is about 20,000 bottles and wines are released in two series – The King's Blend and Hamasrek.

The King's Blend

HAMASREK, THE KING'S BLEND, JUDEAN HILLS, N.V.: A blend of Cabernet Sauvignon, Merlot and Zinfandel grapes (80%, 15% and 5% respectively) from the 2004 and 2005 vintages. Dark garnet, medium- to full-bodied, with soft tannins integrating nicely and showing generous berry, black cherry and herbal aromas and flavors. Lingers nicely. Showing age. Drink up. Score 83. K

HAMASREK, THE KING'S BLEND, JUDEAN HILLS, N.V.: A blend of Cabernet Sauvignon, Merlot and Zinfandel grapes from the 2003 and 2004 vintages. Medium- to full-bodied, with chunky tannins, a strong influence of the wood and only bare hints of black fruits. Flat, one-dimensional and showing age. Drink up. Score 80. K

Hamasrek

HAMASREK, CABERNET SAUVIGNON, 2006: Oak-aged for ten months, garnet-red, showing chunky, country-style tannins and a moderate spicy-oak influence. Appealing red fruits here when first poured but turns somewhat flat and flabby on the finish. Drink up. Score 82. K

HAMASREK, CABERNET SAUVIGNON, LIMITED EDITION, SINGLE VINEYARD, JUDEAN HILLS, 2005: Dark royal purple toward garnet in color, full-bodied and reflecting its time in *barriques* with near-sweet tannins and toasty oak. On the nose and palate, red and blackcurrants, raspberries and light pepper-cedarwood notes, those leading to a long, espresso-coffee-rich finish. Drink up. Score 88. K

Hans Sternbach ✶✶

Founded by Gadi and Shula Sternbach on Moshav Givat Yeshayahu in the Judean Hills, the Domaine Hans Sternbach's
first release was of 1,800 bottles from the 2000 harvest. With
the winery located on the moshav and relying primarily on
Cabernet Sauvignon, Syrah, Petit Verdot, Sauvignon Blanc,
Viognier and Marsanne grapes from its own and nearby
vineyards, production from the 2003 vintage was about 3,000
bottles and from 2004–2007 about 10,000 bottles annually.
With Bordeaux-trained partner Emmanuel Madar now serving as winemaker, the winery is currently releasing about
18,000 bottles annually.

Janaba Reserve

JANABA RESERVE, 2010: Made entirely
from Cabernet Sauvignon grapes, full-
bodied, with gripping, somewhat chunky
tannins that give the wine a rustic note.
On the nose and palate blackberries, black
cherries and cassis, the fruits supported by
notes of spicy oak, all leading to a moderately long finish. Best 2013–2016. Tentative
Score 85–87.

Hills of Judea - Ella Valley

HS
W

HANS STERNBACH
Giv'at Yesha'ayahu

Reserve 2003
Hakhlil Valley
JANABA - ג'נבא

Grown, Produced & Bottled on the Property
14.5% by Volume / *Produce of Israel* / 750 ml

JANABA RESERVE, 2009: Medium- to full-
bodied, with still-gripping and drying tannins waiting to settle in, opens slowly in the
glass to reveal cassis, blackberry and wild berry fruits, those supported
nicely by notes of grilled herbs. Made entirely from Cabernet Sauvignon
grapes, with a light note of spicy wood running through, and with fruits
and tannins rising on the finish. Drink now–2014. Score 86.

JANABA RESERVE, 2008: Dark garnet toward royal purple, full-bodied,
reflecting its two years in oak with generous spicy wood but that in fine
balance with tannins and fruits. A deep wine, with tannins destined
always to be on the gripping side but parting to reveal blackcurrant,
raspberry and blackberry fruits, those supported by a comfortable note
of vanilla. Drink now. Score 87–89.

JANABA RESERVE, CABERNET SAUVIGNON, HAKHLIL VALLEY,
2006: Showing better than an earlier tasting. Made entirely from

Cabernet Sauvignon grapes, oak-aged for 12 months in new oak and 12 in used oak, dark garnet toward royal purple, full-bodied with once-firm tannins settling in nicely now and showing an appealing array of currant and blackberry fruits on a spicy and lightly herbal background and leading to a round and caressing finish. Drink now. Score 86.

Nachal Hakhlil

Hills of Judea - Ella Valley

HS
W

HANS STERNBACH
Giv'at Yesha'ayahu

| 2008 |

Hakhlil Valley

נחל חכליל

Produced & Bottled on the Property / Produce of Israel / 14% by Volume 750 ml

NACHAL HAKHLIL, 2010: Reflecting oak-aging with notes of spices and vanilla. Medium- to full-bodied with chunky country-style tannins that part in the glass to make way for black fruits and notes of earthy minerals. Drink from release. Tentative Score 85–87.

NACHAL HAKHLIL, 2009: Oak-aged for 12 months, a blend of two-thirds Cabernet Sauvignon and one-third Syrah. Dark cherry red in color, with an aromatic nose and soft tannins on a medium-bodied framework. On the nose and palate cherries, wild berries and light spicy and stony minerals. Just enough complexity to grab our attention. Drink from release–2014. Tentative Score 85–87.

NACHAL HAKHLIL, 2008: Cabernet Sauvignon, showing medium- to full-bodied, with soft tannins, notes of spicy wood and a distinct acidic note that may not be fully wanted. On the nose and palate wild berries along with hints of eucalyptus and Mediterranean herbs. Drink up. Score 84.

NACHAL HAKHLIL, GIVAT YESHA'AYHU, 2007: Made entirely from Cabernet Sauvignon grapes, oak-aged for 12 months, medium-bodied, with soft tannins, gentle influences of spicy wood and a hint of sweetness, showing a basic black-fruit personality. Without complexities but a good quaffer. Drink up. Score 85.

NACHAL HAKHLIL, 2006: Dark royal purple in color, this oak-aged blend of 70% Cabernet Sauvignon and 30% Merlot is showing medium- to full-bodied, with firm tannins opening to reveal generous currant, blackberry and Mediterranean herbs. Drink up. Score 84.

Emek Ha'Ella

EMEK HA'ELLA, 2010: Deep royal purple, a medium-bodied blend of ⅔ Syrah and ⅓ Cabernet Sauvignon. Light tannins caress gently and part to reveal aromas and flavors of ripe red plums and crushed berries. Not complex but fun to drink. Drink from release. Tentative Score 83–85.

Nouveau

HANS STERNBACH, NOUVEAU, 2010: Youthful royal purple in color, a medium-bodied, softly tannic blend of ⅔ Syrah and ⅓ Cabernet Sauvignon. Showing forward blackberry and cassis notes on a lightly spicy background. Meant for youthful consumption. Drink up. Score 85.

Har Bracha ✶

HAR BRACHA, CABERNET SAUVIGNON, HEART LANDER, 2007: My first exposure to this new small winery (now producing about 5,000 bottles annually). Cabernet Sauvignon blended with 5% each of Shiraz and Merlot. Somewhat cloudy garnet in color, medium- to full-bodied, with chunky tannins giving the wine a distinctly rustic note. On the nose and palate blackberry and black cherry fruits, those together with not distinct and not completely wanted notes of bitter herbs. Drink up. Score 77. K

Hatabor ✶

Located in the village of Kfar Tabor in the Lower Galilee, this winery was founded by Shimi Efrat in 1999 and released its first wines from the 2002 harvest. Grapes come primarily from nearby vineyards, and production is currently about 7,000 bottles annually.

HATABOR, CABERNET SAUVIGNON, 2006: Medium- to full-bodied, dark garnet in color, with firm tannins and generous spicy wood but opening slowly to reveal currant and blackberry fruits. One-dimensional. Drink up. Score 79.

HATABOR, CABERNET SAUVIGNON, 2005: Full-bodied, with almost searing tannins and far-too-generous wood hiding the fruits that struggle to make themselves felt. Drink up. Score 78.

HATABOR, MERLOT, 2005: Deep royal purple, medium- to full-bodied, with firm tannins yielding somewhat in the glass to reveal raspberry, cassis and herbal aromas and flavors. Drink up. Score 84.

HATABOR, MERLOT-CABERNET SAUVIGNON, 2005: Medium-bodied, with soft tannins and a gentle wood influence. Showing appealing black and red berry as well as black cherry fruits. A good quaffer. Drink up. Score 85.

HATABOR, CHARDONNAY, 2006: Medium-bodied, with lively acidity and appealing citrus and tropical fruits. Simple but easy to drink. Drink up. Score 84.

Hevron Heights **

Located in Kiryat Arba, not far from the heart of the city of Hebron, this winery was founded in 2001 by a group of French investors and initially produced about 150,000 bottles per year, the target audience largely being observant Jews abroad. At my last contact with them the winery reported production of about 600,000 bottles annually, consisting of varietal and blended wines of Cabernet Sauvignon, Merlot, French Colombard, Sauvignon Blanc and Malbec grapes, drawing largely on grapes from the Judean Hills as well as vineyards near Hebron. The winery has a broad and somewhat confusing labeling system with a large number of series and brands including Hevron Heights, Noah, Hevron, Tevel, Shemesh, Pardess, Judea and Jerusalem Heights, some labels released locally, others for export, and several of which are also released as private labels.

Hevron Heights

HEVRON HEIGHTS, CABERNET SAUVIGNON, ELONE MAMRE, RESERVE, 2006: My third tasting of this wine and, like many of the wines from the winery, shows dramatically different at each tasting. Dark, almost impenetrable garnet in color, full-bodied, with generous but soft and gently mouth-coating tannins and a temperate hand with the oak in which the wine aged for 20 months. On first attack distinctly sweet plums and crushed berries, those followed by notes of blackcurrants and spices. Drink now–2013. Score 87.

HEVRON HEIGHTS, CABERNET SAUVIGNON, GEDEON, 2009: Garnet with a royal purple robe, medium- to full-bodied, with somewhat chunky tannins giving the wine a rustic note. On the nose and palate blackcurrants, purple plums and toasty oak, all on a background of cigar tobacco and roasted herbs. Drink now–2013. Score 85. K

HEVRON HEIGHTS, CABERNET SAUVIGNON, GEDEON, 2006: Garnet in color, medium-bodied, with soft tannins and hints of smoky wood. Opens to show raspberry, cherry and berry fruits. Not complex but a pleasant enough quaffer. Drink up. Score 84. K

HEVRON HEIGHTS, CABERNET SAUVIGNON, ISAAC'S RAM, 2005: Oak-aged for 18 months, medium- to full-bodied, with chunky tannins and aromas of not-quite-fresh earth that linger and tend to mask the black fruits that are hidden here. Past its peak. Drink up. Score 76. K

HEVRON HEIGHTS, CABERNET SAUVIGNON, JUDEAN HEIGHTS, 2005: Dark garnet with a bit of clearing at the rim, medium- to full-bodied with chunky, country-style tannins. Oak-aged for 12 months, opens to reveal a basic blackberry, black cherry personality, all on a somewhat barnyard-like background. Past its peak. Drink up. Score 78. K

HEVRON HEIGHTS, CABERNET SAUVIGNON, KIDRON, 2004: Dark garnet, this medium- to full-bodied wine reflects its 12 months' exposure to oak with spices and soft tannins. On the nose and palate black fruits and hints of pepper and star anise. An acceptable entry-level wine in its youth but now showing age. Drink up. Score 82. K

HEVRON HEIGHTS, ISAAC'S RAM, 2006: Medium- to full-bodied, perhaps leaning to the full, with smoky wood, that yielding slowly to unfolding black fruits on the nose and then opening to show blackcurrants, raspberries and dark chocolate, the wine marred somewhat by a bitter-herbal sensation that comes in from mid-palate and then lingers on to the moderately short finish. Drink now. Score 87. K

JUDEAN VINEYARDS
5761
Cabernet Sauvignon
2001
ISAAC'S RAM
HEVRON HEIGHTS WINERY
13% Vol.   750 ml

HEVRON HEIGHTS, SYRAH, RESERVE, 2004: Dark royal purple, medium- to full-bodied, with firm tannins integrating nicely. On the nose and palate plums, blackberries and spices with a moderately long earthy-mineral finish. Past its peak. Drink up. Score 80. K

HEVRON HEIGHTS, PETITE SIRAH, GEDEON, 2009: Dark garnet, generously tannic and reflecting its development in French oak with gently gripping tannins. On the nose and palate blackberries, plums and notes of white chocolate. On the moderately long finish a note of cigar tobacco. Drink now–2014. Score 85. K

HEVRON HEIGHTS, ARMAGEDDON (MEGIDDO IN NORTH AMERICA), 2002: An unfiltered blend of 80% Cabernet Sauvignon, 15% Merlot and 5% Syrah, aged in new French oak for 24 months. To my palate, this wine has been so vastly different from tasting to tasting that it defies a firm description or consistent scoring. Overall, it continues to reflect generous sweet and smoky wood and gripping tannins. At this most recent tasting, the tannins and wood seem to finally be integrating, allowing the blackcurrant, red and black berries, and ripe red plum aromas and flavors to show. Drink up. Scores range from 79–84. K

HEVRON HEIGHTS, MAKHPELAH, 2005: To the best of my knowledge, a blend of Cabernet Sauvignon and Merlot reflecting its development in barriques with generously gripping tannins and a rather heavy dose of spicy oak. Full-bodied, the too-generous wood hiding the black fruits that struggle to make themselves felt. Showing first signs of oxidation. Drink up. Score 78. K

HEVRON HEIGHTS, MAKHPELAH, 2002: A blend of 70% Cabernet Sauvignon, 26% Merlot and 4% Marsanne, oak-aged for more than 20 months. This dark garnet-going-to-adobe-brown wine is full-bodied, almost thick in texture, with chunky tannins and generous wood tending to hide the plum and blackberry fruits that never fully make their way to the surface. Well past its peak. Drink up. Score 76. K

HEVRON HEIGHTS, SPECIAL RESERVE, 2002: Developed in French and American oak for 20 months, this blend of Cabernet Sauvignon, Merlot and Shiraz (65%, 25% and 10% respectively) shows full-bodied, with gripping tannins and generous spicy and smoky wood. Opens to reveal plum, wild berry and cassis fruits, those leading to a moderately long and generously peppery finish. Well past its peak. Drink up. Score 74. K

HEVRON HEIGHTS, MOUNT HEVRON RED, JERUSALEM HILLS, 2009: So impenetrably dark garnet in color it makes me think of the mega-purple that some wineries use. Full-bodied and with intensely gripping tannins, opens slowly in the glass to reveal black fruits, toasty oak and baking chocolate. Try decanting, even double or triple decanting this one to help it open. Drink now. Score 84. K

HEVRON HEIGHTS, JERUSALEM HILLS, 2005: A medium-bodied blend of Petite Sirah, Merlot and Cabernet Sauvignon (60%, 30% and 10% respectively). Ruby toward garnet in color, with chunky tannins and black fruits. A country-style wine that ends on a somewhat bitter note. Drink up. Score 80. K

HEVRON HEIGHTS, CABERNET SAUVIGNON-MERLOT, 2005: A blend of equal parts of the two varieties, oak-aged for 18 months in new French and American *barriques*. Dark garnet with distinct hints of browning and oxidation now making themselves felt, those pushing the black fruits too far into the background. Past its peak. Drink up. Score 74. K Hevron Heights, Cabernet-Merlot, Jerusalem Heights, 2002: Perhaps the best from the winery. A full-bodied, softly tannic blend of

50% each of Cabernet Sauvignon and Merlot, opening to reveal juicy blackberry, raspberry and cassis fruits on a background of spices and leather. Showing age. Drink up. Score 80. K

HEVRON HEIGHTS, CABERNET SAUVIGNON-SHIRAZ, JERUSALEM HILLS, 2009: Medium- to full bodied, with near-sweet tannins and a not-entirely-vegetal undertone that runs through the jammy plum, blackberry and cherry fruits. Drink now. Score 83. K

Noah

NOAH, CABERNET SAUVIGNON, 2006: Dark garnet, medium-bodied, with firm, chunky tannins. A hint of barnyard aromas that linger, and on the palate a note of mold that hides the skimpy berry fruits. Score 69. K

NOAH, CABERNET SAUVIGNON, TEVEL, 2005: Oak-aged for 18 months, dark ruby toward garnet, medium-bodied, with soft tannins and showing berry, cassis and cedarwood notes. A pleasant entry-level wine in its youth but now well past its peak. Drink up. Score 80. K

NOAH, MERLOT, 2006: Garnet toward purple, medium- to full-bodied, with too-flabby tannins and somewhat muddy berry and cherry flavors. Drink up. Score 70. K

NOAH, MERLOT, TEVEL, 2005: Dark ruby toward garnet, oak-aged for 12 months, showing soft and round, with berry, black cherry and purple plums, a simple country-style wine. Drink up. Score 84. K

NOAH, PETITE SIRAH, GEDEON, 2006: Loaded with volatile acidity that gives the wine a distinct taste of sour, unripe plums. Medium-bodied, with neither complexity nor charm. Score 68. K

NOAH, PETITE SIRAH, GEDEON, 2005: Dark purple, medium-bodied, with chunky and somewhat coarse tannins, this distinct country-style wine shows skimpy berry and black cherry fruits, all with a not-entirely-wanted sweet aftertaste. Past its peak. Drink up. Score 78. K

NOAH, CABERNET SAUVIGNON-MERLOT, 2006: Oak-aged for 12 months but showing a rather generous hand with spicy wood, that tending to hide the black fruits and bittersweet chocolate that lie underneath. Drink up. Score 83. K

NOAH, SHIRAZ-CABERNET SAUVIGNON, TEVEL, 2005: Aged in *barriques* for 12 months, a dark garnet blend of 60% Syrah and 40%

Cabernet Sauvignon. Medium- to full-bodied, with blackberry, plum and black cherry fruits. Past its peak. Drink up. Score 78. K

NOAH, MUSCAT DESSERT, 2005: Golden-yellow in color, not so much full-bodied as it is thick. Unabashedly sweet and flowery, with apricot, peach and nutty aromas and flavors, but lacking balancing acidity. Drink up. Score 79. K

Jascala ✦✦✦

Founded by the Kharich family and set in the village of Gush Halav (Jish) in the Upper Galilee, this family-owned winery released its first wines from the 2004 vintage. The extraordinarily attractive boutique winery currently relies on grapes from various sources in the Galilee, but its own vineyards, those containing Cabernet Sauvignon, Cabernet Franc, Shiraz, Merlot, Petit Verdot and Dabukki grapes, will be coming on line in the next year or two. Current production is about 6,500 bottles annually and plans are to grow to an annual output of 20,000 bottles.

JASCALA, CABERNET SAUVIGNON, 2009: Deep youthful royal purple in color, medium- to full-bodied with generous near-sweet tannins and spicy wood notes. On the nose and palate traditional blackcurrant and blackberry fruits, those matched nicely by notes of cigar tobacco and sweet herbs. Drink from release. Tentative Score 86–88.

JASCALA, CABERNET SAUVIGNON, 2008: Dark garnet, medium- to full-bodied, with spicy oak and soft, near-sweet tannins making way for blackcurrant, wild berry and citrus peel notes. On the moderately long finish hints of bittersweet chocolate and green olives. Drink now. Score 85.

JASCALA, CABERNET SAUVIGNON, 2007: Dark garnet, oak-aged for 16 months, a blend of 85% Cabernet Sauvignon, 10% Shiraz and 5% Cabernet Franc. On the nose and palate appealing black fruits and hints of licorice, those complemented by notes of earthy minerals. Drink up. Score 85

JASCALA, CABERNET SAUVIGNON, RESERVE, 2006: Oak-aged for 18 months, dark garnet, medium- to full-bodied, with soft tannins integrating well with not at all imposing but well-felt notes of spicy and vanilla rich wood. On the nose and palate blackberries, a hint of cassis liqueur and Far Eastern spices all coming together comfortably. Drink up. Score 89.

JASCALA, CABERNET SAUVIGNON, 2006: Glistening clear deep garnet in color, medium-, perhaps medium- to full-bodied, reflecting its 14 months in barriques with notes of vanilla and spices and gently gripping tannins. Appealing currants and crushed berries along with hints of bittersweet chocolate. Drink up. Score 86.

JASCALA, MERLOT, 2009: Impenetrably dark garnet in color, opening with spicy and smoky wood and firm tannins, those residing in the glass and making way for a rich, round wine. On the nose and palate black and red berries, cassis and dark chocolate and on the long finish a hint of red licorice. Potentially the best from the winery. Drink now–2013. Score 88.

JASCALA, MERLOT, 2007: Blended with about 10% of Cabernet Sauvignon and reflecting its 16 months of development in oak with a pronounced smoky-wood note. Dark brick-red and clearing at the rim, the wine is too flabby and its black fruits carry a rather heavy overlay of earthy minerals. Sliding past its peak. Drink up. Score 79.

JASCALA, MERLOT, 2006: Garnet with a hint of brick red, medium-bodied, with chunky country-style tannins. Reflecting its 14 months in oak with an appealing spicy overlay and opening to show crushed wild berries and cassis, those complemented by notes of earthy minerals. Past its peak. Drink up. Score 86.

JASCALA, SHIRAZ, 2009: Deep garnet toward royal purple, medium- to full-bodied, with generous gripping tannins and spicy wood needing time to integrate. Opens to reveal plum, wild berry and citrus peel notes, those supported nicely by notes of cigar tobacco and mocha. Drink now–2013. Score 86.

JASCALA, SHIRAZ, 2008: Dark, almost impenetrable garnet in color, full-bodied, with still-gripping tannins needing time to settle in but already showing good balance between the tannins, smoky oak and fruits. On the nose and palate red and purple plums, those complemented by notes of saddle leather and earthy minerals. Drink now. Score 86.

JASCALA, SHIRAZ, 2007: Dark garnet, reflecting its aging in French barriques for 17 months, and showing medium- to full-bodied. Plenty of red fruits and earthy minerals here but the wine is marred by an excess of volatile acidity that gives the wine too close a resemblance to vinegar. Drink up. Score 70.

JASCALA, CABERNET FRANC, 2009: Medium- to full-bodied, with soft, near-sweet tannins and a gentle note of spicy oak, those parting to reveal black fruits, earthy minerals and green olives, all lingering nicely, the tannins rising on the finish. Drink now. Score 86.

JASCALA, CABERNET FRANC, 2008: Dark royal purple, with still-firm tannins and generous wood just starting to integrate. Opens nicely to reveal cassis, raspberry and black cherry fruits on a background of freshly roasted herbs, green olives and baking chocolate. Drink now. Score 87.

JASCALA, CABERNET FRANC, 2007: Deep garnet toward royal purple, with a nose that shows nicely of jammy plums and chocolate. Medium- to full-bodied, with gripping tannins and spicy wood in good balance with fruits, opens to show generous wild berries, blackcurrants and a light leathery note. Notes of green herbs rise on the finish. Drink now. Score 86.

JASCALA, BLENDED RED, 2008: Oak-aged for 18 months, a dark garnet, full-bodied blend of Cabernet Sauvignon, Merlot and Petit Verdot (about 80%, 12% and 8% respectively). With soft tannins and a gentle wood influence parting to make way for blackcurrants, wild berries, licorice and roasted herbs. Best to date from the winery. Drink now. Score 87.

JASCALA, BLENDED RED, 2006: An oak-aged blend of Cabernet Sauvignon, Merlot and Shiraz, showing medium- to full bodied, with somewhat generous oak and tannins that seem to not want to settle down. Opens slowly to reveal basic black fruits and notes of fresh herbs. Drink up. Score 84.

Kadesh Barnea ✶✶

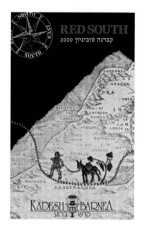

Established in 1999 by Alon Tzadok on Moshav Kadesh Barnea on the Negev Heights, the winery owns its own vineyards, near the ruins of the Byzantine city of Nitzana, just north of the Egyptian border. Among the grapes utilized in varietal releases and blends are Cabernet Sauvignon, Merlot, Petit Verdot, Shiraz, Cabernet Franc, Mourvedre, Sauvignon Blanc and Chardonnay.

Initial production was about 5,000 bottles, and current annual production is currently about 75,000 bottles annually. Target production is 150,000 bottles annually. New equipment has been introduced to the winery and Tzadok's son Yogev who studied winemaking in Florence, Italy and returned to Israel in 2009 is now fully in charge of the winemaking process. The wines have been kosher since the 2002 vintage.

Alon

ALON, CABERNET SAUVIGNON, 2009: Destined for oak-aging for a total of 14–18 months, already showing dark garnet with a nose of dark fruits and chocolate. Medium- to full-bodied, with soft tannins integrating nicely, showing appealing currant and raspberry fruits on a lightly spicy background. Round and long. Drink from release. Tentative Score 87–89. K

ALON, MERLOT, 2009: Blended with 10% Cabernet Sauvignon and reflecting its ten months in American oak with a gentle influence of the wood and soft tannins. Garnet toward royal purple, with a red-fruit nose, opens to reveal blackcurrant and black and red berries on a background of roasted herbs, brown spices and earthy minerals. Drink now–2013, perhaps longer. Score 87. K

ALON, MERLOT, 2007: Garnet toward royal purple, medium- to full-bodied, with somewhat chunky tannins parting in the glass to reveal cassis and wild berries, those on a background of green olives and roasted herbs. Drink up. Score 84. K

ALON, MERLOT, 2006: Dark royal purple, this medium- to full-bodied wine shows gripping, near-sweet tannins that yield slowly to reveal generous wild berry, currant and spices on first attack, those in turn opening to Mediterranean herbs and an appealing hint of black olives. Sliding rapidly past its peak. Drink up. Score 83. K

ALON, BLENDED RED, RESERVE, 2009: A blend of 45% each Cabernet Sauvignon and Merlot, those fleshed out by 5% each of Petit Verdot and Shiraz. Medium-to full-bodied (leaning to the full), reflecting its 18 months in half-French, half-American oak, with sweet and spicy oak and generous but soft tannins. With a distinct note of chocolate on the opening nose, that yielding in the glass to aromas and flavors of black and red berries, cassis and stony minerals, tannins and a hint of brown spices rising on the finish. Easy to drink but too generous acidity holds the wine back from true excellence. Drink now–2013. Score 86. K

ALON, BLENDED RED, 2008: A blend of Cabernet Sauvignon, Merlot and Petit Verdot (50%, 45% and 5% respectively). Oak-aged for 12 months, showing chocolate and brown spices on the nose. Dark garnet, medium- to full-bodied with soft tannins and generous blackcurrant, blackberry and citrus peel aromas and flavors, those supported by notes of stony minerals. Drink now or in the next year or so. Score 86.

Silver Label

SILVER LABEL, CABERNET SAUVIGNON, 2009: Oak-aged for six months in American *barriques*, showing near-sweet tannins and sweet cedar notes that complement a basic berry-cherry personality. A medium-bodied quaffer. Drink now. Score 86. K

SILVER LABEL, CABERNET SAUVIGNON HAMESHUBACH, SILVER LABEL, 2007: Dark garnet, medium- to full-bodied, with generous spicy wood influences that tend to hide the black fruits that are here. One-dimensional. Drink up. Score 84. K

SILVER LABEL, MERLOT, HAMESHUBACH, 2007: Reflecting its 16 months in French oak with rather heavy-handed spicy cedarwood notes, those tending to overpower the currant and berry fruits that struggle to make themselves felt. Drink up. Score 82. K

SILVER LABEL, MIDBAR, HAMESHUBACH, SILVER LABEL, 2009: A blend of Cabernet Sauvignon, Merlot and Petit Verdot (60%, 30% and

10% respectively). Oak-aged for six months in American oak, showing garnet toward royal purple, medium-bodied, with somewhat chunky tannins giving the wine a rustic note. Opens to reveal wild berry, currant and black cherry fruits, all with a hint of licorice that lingers nicely. Drink now. Score 87. K

SILVER LABEL, MIDBAR, HAMESHUBACH, 2007: Garnet toward royal purple, a blend of 60% Cabernet Sauvignon, 35% Merlot and 5% Petit Verdot. Reflecting its 16 months in French oak barriques with a generous dose of spicy wood, that parting in the glass to reveal currant and blackberry fruits. Not complex but good with food. Drink now. Score 85. K

Kadesh Barnea

KADESH BARNEA, CABERNET SAUVIGNON, 2009: A blend of 90% Cabernet Sauvignon and 10% Shiraz. Oak-aged for ten months, showing medium-dark garnet in color, medium-bodied with soft tannins. A somewhat quiet nose but opening in the glass to reveal aromas and flavors of blackberries and purple plums, those on a background that hints of bitter herbs. Somewhat short but a good quaffer. Drink–2013 Score 84. K

KADESH BARNEA, CABERNET SAUVIGNON, GILAD, 2008: Blended with 15% of Merlot, oak-aged for ten months, medium-bodied with soft tannins and generous acidity showing mostly red fruits. A simple entry-level wine. Drink now. Score 82. K

KADESH BARNEA, CABERNET SAUVIGNON, GILAD, 2005: A blend of Petit Verdot, Merlot and Shiraz. Medium-bodied, showing generous spicy wood and firm tannins that need time to integrate, this red opening slowly in the glass to reveal berry, black cherry and earthy-tobacco notes. Sliding past its peak. Drink up. Score 85. K

KADESH BARNEA, MERLOT, GILAD, 2008: Dark garnet, medium-bodied, a soft, round wine with forward red fruits and notes of Oriental spices. An easy-to-drink quaffer. Drink now. Score 84. K

Kadita ✶✶✶✶

Jonathan Goldman made wines at his home in Bikta Bekadita in the Upper Galilee for several years before he released his first commercial output of 600 bottles in 2001, a blend of Cabernet Sauvignon and Merlot. Grapes are currently drawn from the winery's own nearby vineyards and from Kerem Ben Zimra. Annual production is currently about 4,000 bottles.

KADITA, CABERNET SAUVIGNON, 2007: Dark garnet, showing medium- to full-bodied with fine concentration, soft tannins and generous berry, black cherry and currant notes on a background of white pepper, green olives and eucalyptus. Fruits and tannins rise on the finish. Drink now. Score 89.

KADITA, CABERNET SAUVIGNON, 2006: Full-bodied, intense and concentrated, showing deep, almost inky purple, with still-firm tannins and spicy wood in fine balance with natural acidity and fruits. Opens with aromas and flavors of raspberries and minty chocolate, those yielding to blackcurrants and red plums and finally to a long fruity finish with hints of white chocolate. Drink now–2013. Score 90.

KADITA, CABERNET SAUVIGNON, 2005: Deep royal purple, full-bodied, with firm tannins and spicy oak integrating nicely. On the nose and palate an array of blackberry, currant and black cherry fruits matched handsomely by hints of roasted herbs, green olives and, on the long finish, a hint of black licorice. Drink now. Score 89.

KADITA, CABERNET SAUVIGNON, 2004: Youthful, deep royal purple, full-bodied, with generous soft tannins integrating nicely with concentrated black fruits, Mediterranean herbs, eucalyptus and hints of spicy cedarwood from the oak barrels. Long, concentrated and mouth-filling. Drink now. Score 90.

KADITA, CABERNET SAUVIGNON, 2003: A blend of grapes from two vineyards, one with volcanic soil, one with red soil, this still-youthful, deep royal purple wine shows full body, firm tannins promising to integrate nicely and a tempting array of blackcurrant and wild berry fruits, those on a long, spicy tobacco and chocolate finish. Sliding past its peak. Drink up. Score 89.

KADITA, MERLOT, 2006: Dark cherry-red toward garnet, medium- to full-bodied, with soft, mouth-coating tannins and a gentle wood influence. Showing red and black berries, cassis and just the right hint of herbaceousness. Long and generous. Drink now. Score 89.

KADITA, MERLOT, 2005: Full-bodied, deep and aromatic, with black pepper highlighting cherry, currant, chocolate and light licorice aromas and flavors, all lingering on the generous finish. Drink now. Score 91.

KADITA, MERLOT, 2004: Full-bodied and aromatic, with firm but already well-integrating tannins, and showing a tempting array of blueberry, raspberry and purple plum fruits, those on a background of chocolate and Mediterranean herbs. Drink up. Score 89.

KADITA, SHIRAZ, 2004: Rich, ripe and generous, full-bodied, with liberal but refined tannins. On the nose and palate plum, blueberry, black cherry and gentle spices, all coming together with lively acidity. Powerful and graceful with flavors that linger on and on. Drink up. Score 91.

KADITA, CABERNET SAUVIGNON-MERLOT, 2008: Tasted from a tentative blend. Aging in French oak, already showing full-bodied, with silky tannins and a generous array of currant, wild berry and citrus peel, those on a background of Mediterranean herbs and white pepper, the tannins and fruits rising in harmony on the long finish. Drink now–2016. Score 90.

KADITA, CABERNET SAUVIGNON-MERLOT, 2007: Deeply extracted dark garnet, showing medium- to full-bodied with fine concentration, soft tannins and generous berry, black cherry and currant notes on a background of white pepper, green olives and eucalyptus. Fruits and tannins rise on the finish. Drink now–2015. Score 91.

KADITA, CABERNET SAUVIGNON-MERLOT, 2006: Oak-aged for 25 months, full-bodied, intense and concentrated, showing deep, almost inky purple, with still-firm tannins and spicy wood in fine balance with natural acidity and fruits. Opens with aromas and flavors of raspberries and minty chocolate, those yielding to blackcurrants and red plums and finally to a long fruity finish with hints of white chocolate. Drink now–2015. Score 90.

KADITA, CABERNET SAUVIGNON-MERLOT, 2005: Dark, almost intense royal purple, full-bodied, with once-firm tannins and spicy oak now integrating nicely. On the nose and palate an array of blackberry, currant and black cherry fruits matched handsomely by hints of roasted herbs, green olives and, on the long finish, a hint of black licorice. Drink now. Score 90.

KADITA, CABERNET SAUVIGNON-MERLOT, 2004: Kadita's traditional blend of 60% Cabernet Sauvignon and 40% Merlot, oak-aged for 21 months, continuing to show youthful, deep royal purple, full-bodied, with its generous soft tannins integrated nicely to show ripe but not at all overripe black and red fruits, Mediterranean herbs, eucalyptus and hints of spicy cedarwood from the oak barrels. Long, concentrated and mouth-filling. Starting to slide past its peak. Drink up. Score 90.

Kahanov *

Located in Gadera on the Central Plains, winemaker Avi Kahanov is producing about 4,500 bottles annually, those based largely on Cabernet Sauvignon, Merlot and Petit Verdot grapes sourced from the winery's own vineyards.

KAHANOV, CABERNET SAUVIGNON, 2007: Oak-aged for 18 months, dark garnet, full-bodied, with firm tannins and notes of smoky oak and earthy minerals. Opens in the glass to reveal currant, berry and licorice aromas and flavors. Drink now. Score 83.

KAHANOV, CABERNET SAUVIGNON, 2006: Medium- to full-bodied, a country-style wine reflecting its 16 months in oak with chunky tannins and generous earthy minerals and herbs hiding the black fruits that try to make themselves felt. On the coarse side. Drink up. Score 76.

KAHANOV, CABERNET SAUVIGNON, 2005: Dark garnet, with chunky tannins giving the wine a distinct country style. Good blackberry fruits here but with earthy, weedy and dusty cedary oak more prominent than fruit. Somewhat coarse. Drink up. Score 78.

KAHANOV, MERLOT, 2008: Medium- to full-bodied, with a generous 15.5% alcohol content, soft tannins and aromas and flavors primarily of prunes and raisins, reminds of a not-successful Amarone. Drink up. Score 78.

KAHANOV, MERLOT, 2007: Oak-aged for 20 months, blended with 5% Petit Verdot, showing dark garnet with a hint of browning creeping in. Lots of chunky, coarse tannins and Brett here that tends to overpower the black fruits that are lurking beneath. Drink up. Score 76.

KAHANOV, MERLOT, 2006: Medium-bodied, with chunky tannins and notes of sawdust and spices, showing a basic cherry-berry personality. Well past its peak. Drink up. Score 75.

KAHANOV, BILUIM, PETIT VERDOT, 2008: Oak-aged for four months, showing soft tannins and gentle notes of wood, opening to reveal appealing black fruits, citrus peel and chocolate. Best to date from the winery. Drink now. Score 85.

KAHANOV, PETIT VERDOT, 2005: Full-bodied, with generous spicy wood and firm tannins and alcohol hanging on as if they do not want to yield. Some good black cherry fruits here, but that overpowered by gamey and tobacco notes. Drink up. Score 77.

Karmei Yosef ★★★★

Founded in 2001 by Ben-Ami Bravdo and Oded Shosheyov, both professors of oenology at the Hebrew University of Jerusalem, the winery sits in the heart of the vineyards at Karmei Yosef on the western slopes of the Judean Mountains. The winery released 2,800 bottles of its first wine in 2001. Current production is about 45,000 bottles annually. The winery relies largely on grapes grown in their own vineyards, among those Cabernet Sauvignon, Merlot, Shiraz and Chardonnay. The wines have been kosher since the 2007 vintage.

KARMEI YOSEF, CABERNET SAUVIGNON, BRAVDO, 2010: Full-bodied, intensely dark garnet and deeply extracted with still-abundant tannins and notes of spicy wood, those in fine balance with fruits and needing only time for its elements to come together. On the nose and palate nuanced black and red currants, blackberries and licorice and, on the long finish, notes of red plums, kirsch and spices. Best from 2013–2018. Tentative Score 91–93. K

KARMEI YOSEF, CABERNET SAUVIGNON, BRAVDO, 2009: Almost impenetrably dark garnet in color, a true Cabernet nose of black fruits and cigar-box aromas, those parting to reveal a rich, full-bodied and gently tannic wine with currant, blackberry and blueberry fruits on a background of Oriental spices. Tannins and an appealing note of crushed berries rise together on the long finish. Best from 2013–2017. Score 91. K

KARMEI YOSEF, CABERNET SAUVIGNON, BRAVDO, 2008: Full-bodied, with once-super-firm tannins and generous spicy oak now settling in nicely. Dark garnet, with gently gripping tannins that part to reveal traditional blackcurrant and blackberry fruits, those on a background of bay leaves and dark chocolate. On the long finish an appealing note of roasted herbs. Deep, long and complex. Best 2011–2016, perhaps longer. Score 92. K

KARMEI YOSEF, CABERNET SAUVIGNON, BRAVDO, 2007: My most recent tasting note holds firmly. Deep garnet in color, full-bodied, with deep tannins and spicy wood, those opening to reveal a rich core of currant, wild berry, toasty oak and minted chocolate, all lingering nicely. Drink now. Score 89. K

KARMEI YOSEF, CABERNET SAUVIGNON, BRAVDO, 2006: Dark garnet toward royal purple in color, showing more full-bodied than in the past and maintaining fine balance between once-firm tannins and spicy wood that are integrating well to allow the fruits to show. On the nose and palate currants, wild berries and mint notes, those lingering nicely. Drink now–2013. Score 90.

KARMEI YOSEF, CABERNET SAUVIGNON, BRAVDO, 2005: At its peak now, deep garnet in color, medium- to full-bodied with tannins and wood receding nicely. On the nose gentle notes of cedar sawdust and black fruits, those parting to reveal aromas and flavors of blackberries, currants and raspberries, complemented by notes of lead pencil and roasted herbs. As intense now as it was during its youth and showing the potential for further cellaring. Drink now. Score 90.

KARMEI YOSEF, CABERNET SAUVIGNON, BRAVDO, 2004: Holding its own very nicely, thank you. Medium to full-bodied with soft, near-sweet tannins and spicy wood well balanced by blackcurrant, wild berry and black cherry fruits. Round, generous and long. Drink now. Score 91.

KARMEI YOSEF, CABERNET SAUVIGNON, BRAVDO, 2003: Dark garnet with a bit of clearing at the rim, continuing to show its inherently fine balance and structure. A blend of 80% Cabernet Sauvignon and 20% Merlot, with generous aromas and flavors of blackcurrants, purple plums, black cherries and minted chocolate. Medium- to full-bodied, showing somewhat lighter than in the past. Still drinking elegantly. Not for much further cellaring. Drink now. Score 90.

KARMEI YOSEF, CABERNET SAUVIGNON, BRAVDO, 2002: A blend of 90% Cabernet Sauvignon and 10% Merlot, continuing to show full-bodied, its once-gentle leathery base now rising as is a first hint of oxidation. Still drinking well and showing aromas and flavors of ripe blackberries, currants and black cherries, those on a background of Oriental spices. Leathery and earthy notes rising. Drink now. Score 90.

KARMEI YOSEF, CABERNET SAUVIGNON, BRAVDO, 2001: Still-deep garnet but with a distinct note of clearing at the rim and showing a hint of adobe brick, a blend of 85% Cabernet Sauvignon and 15% Merlot. Still drinking well and showing good black and red fruits, those on a background of roasted Brazil nuts, licorice and roasted herbs but clearly past its peak. Drink up. Score 89.

KARMEI YOSEF, MERLOT, BRAVDO, 2010: Destined as are all of the winery's red wines for 12 months oak-aging, showing dark royal purple, opening with a distinct red-fruit nose and showing even now full-bodied, with soft, gently caressing tannins. Deeply aromatic, with ripe plums and blueberries on the nose, those parting in the glass to make way for aromas and flavors of black cherries, blackberries and Mediterranean herbs. Lithe and supple and, on the long finish, an appealing note of freshly turned earth. Best from 2013–2017. Tentative Score 90–92. K

KARMEI YOSEF, MERLOT, BRAVDO, 2009: Deep garnet toward royal purple, medium- to full-bodied (leaning to the full) with gently caressing tannins and not at all exaggerated notes of spicy wood, those complementing a generous array of blackcurrant, wild berry and raspberry fruits. Deep and round, with notes of cigar tobacco and a tantalizing hint of sweetness on the long finish. Finely tuned balance and structure bode well for an elegant wine as this one continues to develop. Drink now–2016, perhaps longer. Score 92. K

KARMEI YOSEF, MERLOT, BRAVDO, 2008: Dark garnet, with green and orange reflections, showing more full-bodied than at barrel tastings. Soft tannins and gentle wood influences give the wine round, well-balanced notes, those coming together nicely on first attack with cherries and red currants, in turn yielding to black fruits, exotic spices and a note of minted chocolate. A hedonistic wine, rich and opulent, finishing long and with fruits rising nicely. Drink now–2016. Score 91. K

KARMEI YOSEF, MERLOT, BRAVDO, 2007: Dark garnet toward royal purple, medium- to full-bodied, with soft, near-sweet tannins and showing a generous array of blackberry, blueberry, spicy and earthy aromas and flavors. Drink now. Score 89. K

KARMEI YOSEF, MERLOT, BRAVDO, 2006: Blended with 15% of Cabernet Sauvignon, aged in *barriques* for 12 months, deep garnet toward royal purple in color, with once-gripping tannins now integrating nicely with spicy wood. Full-bodied, opens to reveal a core of plums, blackberries and blueberries, those on a background of exotic spices and hints of chocolate and mocha that linger nicely on the palate. Drink now. Score 90.

KARMEI YOSEF, MERLOT, BRAVDO, 2005: After developing for 12 months in French and American oak, this dark ruby toward garnet wine is showing medium- to full-bodied, with near-sweet tannins and dusty wood highlighting intense currant, blackberry, black cherry and mocha aromas and flavors. A hint of unwanted sweetness creeping in on the finish. Drink now. Score 88.

KARMEI YOSEF, MERLOT, BRAVDO, 2004: Oak-aged for 12 months, with 10% of Cabernet Sauvignon blended in, this medium-bodied red shows appealing smoky oak and moderately firm tannins well balanced with cassis, blueberry and black cherry fruits. On the long finish, hints of anise, sweet cedar, sage and tobacco. Drink up. Score 90.

KARMEI YOSEF, SHIRAZ, BRAVDO, 2010: Dark and dense, well extracted with a nose that boasts cherries and spices, opening in the glass to reveal aromas and flavors of raspberries, wild berries and plums all on a background that hints at one moment of saddle leather and at another of exotic spices. Round and generous, with a hint of bitter almonds that comes in on the long finish. Drink from release–2016. Tentative Score 90–92. K

KARMEI YOSEF, SHIRAZ, BRAVDO, 2009: Full-bodied and well extracted, showing super-dark garnet toward black in color. On the nose spicy cedarwood and purple plums, those parting in the glass to reveal aromas and flavors of blackberries, black olives and roasted herbs. Still-firm tannins here but those in fine balance with wood and fruits and needing only time for the elements to come together. A powerful wine at this stage but one whose muscles will become more discrete over time and show the wine's elegance. Approachable now but best 2013–2017. Score 91. K

KARMEI YOSEF, SHIRAZ, BRAVDO, 2008: Deep royal purple in color, a rich and aromatic wine made intentionally from late-harvested grapes. On the nose and palate ripe red berries, plums and blueberries, those supported comfortably by notes of cedar sawdust, spicy oak and an appealing overlay of white pepper and, on the long finish, a note of saddle leather. Drink now–2016. Score 92. K

KARMEI YOSEF, SHIRAZ, BRAVDO, 2007: Almost impenetrably dark garnet in color, an intense and spicy wine, offering wild berry and black-berry fruits, those with leathery overtones. Muscular but fine-grained tannins and a relatively high alcohol content (almost 16%) make this a near-blockbuster. Drink now–2013. Score 90. K

KARMEI YOSEF, COUPAGE, BRAVDO, 2009: The winery's first blended wine, in this case of Cabernet Franc, Shiraz and Cabernet Sauvignon (40%, 33% and 27% respectively), the grapes vinified separately and oak-aged for 12 months before blending. A chewy wine, showing the traits of each of the varieties, black fruits and spicy berries from the Cabernet Sauvignon, an appealing note of earthy greenness from the Cabernet Franc and notes of plums and leather from the Shiraz. Full-bodied and concentrated, needs time to show its elegance. Best from 2013–2017, perhaps longer. Score 92. K

KARMEI YOSEF, CHARDONNAY, BRAVDO, 2010: With half of the wine developed *sur lie* in French oak for three months, the rest in stainless steel tanks, showing bright shining gold. Full-bodied, a generously aromatic wine with fine balancing acidity and a bare hint of the wood, opens in the glass to reveal citrus, ripe summer fruits and a hint of mango. On the long near-creamy finish an appealing note of honeydew melon. Drink now–2014. Score 90. K

KARMEI YOSEF, CHARDONNAY, BRAVDO, 2009: Oak-aged in new French *barriques* for just three months, that passing on appealing hints of spicy wood to complement generous citrus, green apple, melon and tangerine fruits. A lively yet complex wine, well balanced by acidity and, on the long finish, an appealing note of crème fraiche. Drink now. Score 91. K

KARMEI YOSEF, CHARDONNAY, BRAVDO, 2008: Wisely developed in new oak *barriques* for just three months, showing tantalizing notes of spicy wood and toasted white bread, those parting comfortably to reveal generous nectarine, citrus and green apple notes, all leading to a finish hinting of sweet cream. Lively and easy to drink with just enough complexity to grab our attention. Drink now. Score 89. K

KARMEI YOSEF, CHARDONNAY, BRAVDO, 2007: Made from 100% Chardonnay grapes, developed in oak for only three months to guard the aromas and freshness of the variety, this medium-bodied white shows forward pineapple, citrus and pear fruits, those with good acidity and a light mineral note keeping the wine lively. Lacks complexity but refreshing and easy to drink. Drink up. Score 87. K

KARMEI YOSEF, CHARDONNAY, BRAVDO, 2006: Fermented partly on its lees in new French and American oak and partly in stainless steel, this deeply golden white shows a green tint, and is bursting with layers of figs, apples, apricots, melon and light cedary oak. Rich, with mineral flavors that linger nicely on the finish. Drink up. Score 89.

Karmei Ziv ★

Founded in 2006 by Benji Shavit, currently planting their own vineyards but until now relying on purchased grapes and producing some 3,000 bottles annually.

KARMEI ZIV, CABERNET SAUVIGNON, 2008: Garnet toward royal purple, medium- to full-bodied, with vanilla and spicy notes from the oak chips with which it was developed. Gently tannic with appealing blackberry and cassis fruits. Drink up. Score 84.

KARMEI ZIV, MERLOT, 2008: Soft and round with not much in the way of tannins but lots of spicy oak from the oak chips with which the wine was developed. A basic berry-black cherry wine without complexities. Perhaps acceptable as an entry-level quaffer. Drink up. Score 80.

KARMEI ZIV, SHIRAZ, 2008: Light ruby in color, light- to medium-bodied, with chunky country-style tannins and a few berry, cherry fruits. Drink now. Score 78.

Katamon ✴✴

Founded by Avital Goldner, who released his first wines in 2004, this boutique winery currently produces some 4,000 bottles annually, those based on Cabernet Sauvignon, Merlot, Cabernet Franc, Chardonnay, Riesling and Semillon grapes.

KATAMON, CABERNET SAUVIGNON, 2004: Garnet toward purple in color, a medium- to full-bodied blend of 80% Cabernet Sauvignon and 20% Merlot, that aged in new French oak for 12 months and then in stainless steel for another year. Showing clean, fresh black- and blueberry notes along with hints of licorice and dark chocolate, and faulted only by a hint of unwanted volatile acidity. Drink up. Score 85. K

KATAMON, MERLOT, 2007: Ruby toward garnet, medium-bodied, reflects its 24 months in French oak with generous but not overpowering notes of spicy cedar. On the nose and palate blackberries, cassis and notes of earthy minerals. Drink now. Score 86. K

KATAMON, MERLOT, 2005: Dark garnet, medium- to full-bodied, a blend of 90% Merlot and 10% Cabernet Franc that spent 26 months partly in new American and one-year-old French *barriques*. Soft and round, with gently mouth-coating tannins and appealing blackberry and purple plum fruits on a lightly spicy background. Past its peak. Drink up. Score 85. K

KATAMON, RED BLEND, 2006: A blend of Merlot, Cabernet Sauvignon and Cabernet Franc (50%, 40% and 10% respectively), now developing in French oak *barriques*. Medium- to full-bodied, with soft, near-sweet tannins integrating nicely with smoky cedarwood. Generous berry, black cherry and currant fruits backed up by an appealing hint of bitter herbs on the moderately long finish. Drink up. Score 86. K

KATAMON, CHARDONNAY, 2009: Developed in French and American *barriques* for 12 months, light gold with orange reflections, medium-bodied with spicy oak and hints of vanilla on the nose. Opens in the glass to show basic citrus, citrus peel and melon fruits. Drink up. Score 85. K

KATAMON, CHARDONNAY, 2007: Light golden in color, medium-bodied, with refreshing acidity to support pear, melon and citrus fruits. Not a complex wine but a very pleasant one and at its best with food. Showing age. Drink up. Score 85. K

KATAMON, RIESLING, 2006: A dry white based on 60% Emerald Riesling and 40% Johannisberg Riesling. Developed for one year in one-year-old French and American *barriques*, an open-knit dry wine, its lime, apple, citrus and slate notes calling to mind the Rieslings of New York's Finger Lake Region. Lacks intensity but has an appealing bouncy note that lingers through to the finish. Drink up. Score 85. K

KATAMON, SEMILLON, 2005: A light golden, medium-bodied blend of 80% Semillon and 20% Chardonnay showing relatively high alcohol (14.5%), low acidity, generous herbal overlays on the palate and only skimpy aromas and flavors of tropical fruits. Past its peak. Drink up. Score 76. K

Katlav ✶✶✶

Cabernet Sauvignon
2003

יין 750 ml. 14.5 Alc.
Katlav Winery, Nes Harim 99885, Israel

Owner-winemaker Yossi Yittach founded this small winery on Moshav Nes Harim in the Jerusalem Mountains in 1996 and released his first wines from the 2000 vintage. The winery draws on Cabernet Sauvignon, Merlot, Petit Verdot and Syrah grapes from local vineyards. Production for the 2009 vintage was about 20,000 bottles. Because of the *shnat shmita* (Sabbatical year for the vineyards), no wines were produced from the 2008 vintage.

KATLAV, CABERNET SAUVIGNON, 2009: Medium-dark garnet with purple and orange reflections, medium- to full-bodied, a polished and well-focused wine with earthy, licorice and fruitcake notes to highlight aromas and flavors of blackcurrants, blackberries and figs, all leading to a velvety finish. Drink from release–2015. Tentative Score 88–90. K

KATLAV, CABERNET SAUVIGNON, LIMITED EDITION, 2007: Developed for 14 months in new light- to medium-toasted French *barriques*. Opens with a light medicinal note on the nose but that blows off quickly to reveal aromas of black fruits and licorice. On first attack plums and cranberries, those parting to reveal currants, figs and black cherries, all supported comfortably by notes of spices and tobacco leaf. Full-bodied and complex, with fruits and tannins rising on the long finish. The best to date from Katlav, probably not to be released until mid-2012. Best 2013–2017. Score 91. K

KATLAV, CABERNET SAUVIGNON, 2007: Deep ruby toward garnet, full-bodied, showing rich and round with near-sweet tannins and light notes of cedar and spices. On the nose and palate a tempting array of blackcurrant, blackberry and purple plum fruits, those complemented by hints of mocha and Mediterranean herbs, all lingering nicely. Drink now. Score 89. K

KATLAV, CABERNET SAUVIGNON, 2006: Oak-aged for 24 months, dark ruby toward garnet, medium- to full-bodied, with soft tannins and light spicy oak coming together nicely with notes of red plums, cherries and raspberries. Faulted only by a light medicinal note that rises on the medium-long finish. Drink up. Score 85. K

KATLAV, CABERNET SAUVIGNON, RESERVE, 2005: Dark garnet, medium- to full-bodied, with soft tannins integrating nicely and showing generous hints of spicy oak. Blackcurrant and blackberry fruits, those well supported by hints of black pepper and Mediterranean herbs. Flawed by a hint of volatile acidity. Past its peak. Drink up. Score 84. K

KATLAV, CABERNET SAUVIGNON, 2005: Oak-aged for 18 months, garnet toward royal purple in color, with soft tannins and toasty wood. Medium-bodied, with a basic berry, cherry and light spicy personality. Drink up. Score 85. K

KATLAV, MERLOT, 2009: Medium-dark garnet, medium- to full-bodied, showing generous soft tannins and just the right note of spicy oak. On the nose and palate blackberries, blueberries and herbal notes, those lingering nicely on the well-balanced finish, on which a note of roasted herbs. Drink from release–2014. Tentative Score 88–90. K

KATLAV, MERLOT, 2007: Made entirely from Merlot grapes, dark ruby toward garnet in color, medium- to full-bodied, with soft tannins integrating nicely and showing black cherry, cola and nutmeg on toasty oak, those yielding on the finish to hints of mocha and sage. Spoiled somewhat by a medicinal note that seems on the ascendant. Drink now. Score 85. K

KATLAV, MERLOT, 2006: Garnet toward royal purple, medium- to full-bodied, with soft tannins promising to integrate nicely with light oak. Showing dried currants and berries, those overlaid with spices and mint and a tantalizing hint of earthy bitterness. Drink up. Score 86. K

KATLAV, SHIRAZ 2005: Oak-aged for 22 months, medium- to full-bodied, with traditional Syrah leathery, meaty and spicy notes highlighting red plum, cherry and cassis fruits. Hints of licorice and chocolate on the long finish. Drink up. Score 87. K

KATLAV, PINOT NOIR, 2007: Oak-aged for 24 months, medium-dark ruby in color, a soft, round and easygoing Pinot opening to show black cherry, red berry and spicy aromas and flavors. Light tannins and a gentle note of the wood make this an easy-to-drink and just-complex-enough Pinot. Drink up. Score 86. K

KATLAV, PETIT VERDOT, 2009: Super-dark garnet toward royal purple, medium- to full-bodied (leaning to the full), with gently gripping tannins and an easy hand with spicy oak. Already well focused, opens with red berry, raspberry and cherry fruits on the nose and palate, those followed by notes of cassis and cigar tobacco. Long and round. Drink from release–2013. Tentative Score 87–89. K

KATLAV, PETIT VERDOT, 2007: Dark garnet in color, full-bodied, with tannins as intense as the acidity and fruits. Opens slowly to reveal blackcurrants, blackberries and black cherries, those complemented nicely by mocha and spicy oak notes. Potentially the best yet from the winery. Drink up. Score 88. K

KATLAV, WADI KATLAV, 2007: An oak-aged blend of 50% Cabernet Sauvignon, 35% Merlot and 15% Petit Verdot. Deeply aromatic, dark ruby toward garnet, medium-bodied, opens with a medicinal aroma but that blows off rapidly to reveal straightforward black fruits on a lightly spicy background. Not complex but pleasant. Drink up. Score 86. K

KATLAV, WADI KATLAV, 2006: Medium- to full-bodied, dark garnet toward royal purple and oak-aged for 24 months, this blend of Cabernet Sauvignon, Merlot and Shiraz (60%, 30% and 10%, respectively), with its once-firm tannins now integrating nicely with spicy wood and opening to reveal blackberry, black cherry and red currant fruits, those on a background of spices and earthy minerals. Tannins and wood rise on the long finish. Drink now. Score 87. K

KATLAV, PINOT NOIR-CABERNET SAUVIGNON, 2007: A strange animal in its way but not one that frightens at all, the Cabernet adding body and tannins, those perhaps better suited to what many perceive as the popular Israeli taste than varietal Pinot Noir. Medium- to full-bodied, with cherry, berry and currant notes supported by lightly gripping tannins and hints of spicy wood. Drink up. Score 86. K

KATLAV, CABERNET SAUVIGNON, DESSERT WINE, 2009: Made from selected grapes dried on mats in the sun before gentle rushing. As was the case with Katlav's first dessert wine release, deep garnet in color, showing the kind of browning typical to wines made from dried grapes in their youth, that brown certain to vanish as the wine continues to age in oak. Full-bodied, with still-gripping tannins waiting to integrate, with generous sweetness set off nicely and kept lively by natural acidity. Give this one time and it will show its elegance. Best from 2013. Tentative Score 90–92. K

KATLAV, CABERNET SAUVIGNON, DESSERT WINE, 2005–2006: Not Port-style, not Madeira- or Sherry-style, a rather unique dessert wine, super-dark garnet in color, full-bodied, with soft tannins yielding in the glass to generous sweetness, that balanced by natural acidity. On the nose and palate abundant ripe plums, berries and cassis, those with overlays of white pepper and chocolate, all leading to a fresh and long finish. Drink now–2014. Score 91. K

Katz *

Founded by Jossi Katz in 2001 and located on Moshav Mesilat Tzion in the foothills of the Judean Mountains, this small winery, producing what are admittedly "idiosyncratic wines," is currently producing about 7,000 bottles annually and plans to grow to an output of about 20,000.

KATZ, DRY RED RESERVE, RENOIR, 2007: An oak-aged blend of Cabernet Sauvignon, Merlot and Petite Sirah. Medium-bodied, opens with a rather severe bottle stink that never quite dissipates and showing a good deal of volatile acidity, the two of those hiding whatever fruits may be lurking here. Score 65.

KATZ, MATISSE, 2007: Cloudy garnet in color, a late-harvest blend of Cabernet Sauvignon, Merlot and Petite Sirah. Categorized as off-dry but with cloying sweetness and showing distinct notes of caramelization. If there are aromas and flavors of fruits here they are of dried sour cherries and dried apricots that have gone moldy. Score 60.

Kella David ⋆

Founded in 1995 by Amos Barzilai on Moshav Givat Yeshayahu in the Jerusalem Mountains, this small winery produces about 10,000 bottles of white wines annually, taking a break in production for 2005.

KELLA DAVID, MERLOT, 2007:
Dark garnet, with generous spicy oak and chunky tannins that give the wine a rustic note. On the nose and palate berries, black cherries and a perhaps too generous dose of earthy minerals. Drink up. Score 83.

KELLA DAVID, PETITE SIRAH, 2007: Impenetrably dark garnet in color, reflecting its two years in oak with firm tannins and generous notes of spicy oak. Full-bodied, opens slowly in the glass to reveal purple plum, licorice and herbal notes. Drink up. Score 84.

KELLA DAVID, DRY WHITE, 2007: An unoaked dry blend of 60% French Colombard and 40% Emerald Riesling, in its youth showing a floral and spicy nose and flavors of citrus and tropical fruits but those now clearly oxidizing. Score 65.

KELLA DAVID, SEMI-DRY WHITE, 2007: Semi-dry as its label states, but with the distinct kind of bitterness that one associates with overly roasted coffee or nuts. Shows only minimal fruits. A blend of 60% French Colombard and 40% Emerald Riesling. Score 65.

Kfir **

Founded in 2003 by Meir Kfir in the village of Gan Yavne on the southern Coastal Plain, this small winery was originally known as Gefen Adderet and changed its name to Kfir in 2006. Although producing only about 8,000 bottles annually, it releases a large variety of labels, those from Cabernet Sauvignon, Merlot, Cabernet Franc, Sangiovese, Nebbiolo, Syrah, Petite Sirah, Zinfandel, Malbec, Viognier, Riesling, Gewurztraminer and Chardonnay grapes from the vineyards of Karmei Yosef, the Jerusalem Mountains and the Galilee.

KFIR, SHIRAZ, BAR, 2005: Ruby toward garnet, medium-bodied, with chunky, near-sweet tannins. Showing basic plum and black cherry fruits, those with a hint of Oriental spices. Past its peak. Drink up. Score 80.

KFIR, CABERNET FRANC, 2005: Made entirely from Cabernet Franc grapes and aged in *barriques* for 12 months, this medium-bodied and softly tannic wine is showing signs of premature aging. Opens with medicinal and barnyard aromas, the once-youthful sweet cherry and currant fruits now taking on a stewed and oxidized note. Drink up. Score 76.

KFIR, BARBERA, 2008: Light in color and in body, reflecting its 20 months in barriques with more than generous notes of spicy cedar and chunky tannins and a high level of acidity inappropriate for either the variety or the body of the wine. Straightforward cherry-berry fruits. Drink now. Score 82.

KFIR, BARBERA, 2005: Opens with an iodine-medicinal aroma, but that blows off quickly. 86% Barbera with 14% Cabernet Sauvignon blended in to add backbone, this medium-bodied, oak-aged, dark ruby toward purple wine shows soft tannins integrating nicely with acidity, spicy wood and appealing berry and currant fruits. On the long and generous finish a hint of smoky tobacco. Drink up. Score 86.

KFIR, CABERNET SAUVIGNON-MERLOT-SYRAH, 2007: Garnet toward royal purple, medium-bodied, with gently gripping tannins and notes of smoky wood. On the nose and palate blackberries, cassis and raspberries on a lightly spicy background. Drink now. Score 84.

KFIR, AVICHAI, 2006: Medium-garnet toward purple, an oak-aged blend of Merlot, Cabernet Sauvignon and Syrah, showing spicy and vanilla-rich wood, chunky, country-style tannins and black fruits. An appealing entry-level wine. Drink up. Score 84.

KFIR, GILAD, 2005: Dark garnet toward royal purple, this oak-aged blend of Sangiovese, Zinfandel, Nebbiolo, and Barbera grapes (64%, 26%, 8% and 2% respectively) has a distinctly Italian character. Medium- to full-bodied, with soft tannins integrating nicely, it shows appealing raspberry, cherry and red currant fruits overlaid with hints of black olives and anise, all with a light spicy oak overlay. Showing age. Drink up. Score 80.

KFIR, SYRAH-PETITE SIRAH, 2008: A medium- to full-bodied blend of 60% Syrah and 40% Petite Sirah, showing a heavy hand with oak and somewhat chunky tannins that give the wine a distinct countrified note. Aromas and flavors of plums, blackberries and dark chocolate. Drink now. Score 84.

KFIR, SYRAH-PETITE SIRAH, 2007: Dark garnet, with generous spicy and smoky wood and still-youthful and gripping tannins that need time to integrate but already opening nicely in the glass to reveal blackberry, plum and black cherry fruits on a spicy background. Long and generous. Drink up. Score 86.

KFIR, SYRAH-PETITE SIRAH, 2006: Dark garnet toward royal purple in color, its once-youthful spicy wood and gripping tannins now integrated nicely and showing blackberry, purple plum and black cherry fruits. Spicy and long. Drink up. Score 84.

KFIR, SYRAH-PETITE SIRAH, 2005: Deep royal purple in color, this oak-aged blend of 58% Syrah and 42% Petite Sirah shows generous but not dominating spicy wood and tannins. Medium- to full-bodied, a round wine with plum, wild berry and black cherry fruits on a spicy background. Drink up. Score 85.

KFIR, LEOPON, 2006: A medium-to full-bodied, garnet-colored blend of Cabernet Sauvignon and Merlot. Gentle notes of wood, soft tannins and appealing berry and cherry fruits make this a pleasant little quaffer. Drink up. Score 84.

KFIR, ZOHARA, 2007: A blend of 34% each Cabernet Sauvignon and Merlot and 16% each Shiraz and Petite Sirah. Dark garnet, medium-bodied, with soft tannins, a round and fruity wine showing appealing red and black berries and cassis on a lightly spicy and herbal background. Drink now. Score 86.

KFIR, ZOHARA, 2006: A light- to medium-bodied blend of Syrah, Petite Sirah and Cabernet Franc. Medium-dark garnet, with soft tannins and forward blackberry and blueberry fruits. A pleasant and easy-to-drink entry-level wine. Drink up. Score 84.

KFIR, GEWURZTRAMINER, 2008: Light straw colored, medium-bodied, with fine balancing acidity, showing not so much traditional Gewurztraminer litchi and spices but with appealing peach, pear and citrus that make for a not at all traditional but quite pleasant wine. Drink now. Score 85.

KFIR, GEWURZTRAMINER, WHITE NIGHTS, 2007: Light golden straw in color, light- to medium-bodied, and with a bare hint of honeyed sweetness to an overall dry persona. Spicy apples and pears supported by lively acidity. Drink up. Score 85.

KFIR, CABERNET FRANC, DESSERT WINE, 2004: Generously sweet, with good balancing acidity. Medium-full on the palate, maintaining the blackberry fruits and greenness typical to the variety. Appealing as an aperitif. Drink up. Score 86.

Kitron **

Founded by Maeir Bitoen and set on Kibbutz Ma'abarot, not far from the city of Hadera, and drawing on Cabernet Sauvignon, Shiraz and Merlot grapes from the Upper Galilee and the Judean Hills, this boutique winery released its first wines from the 2006 vintage, when production was about 14,000 bottles. Current production is about 26,000 bottles annually. Wines are released only in a reserve series.

KITRON, CABERNET SAUVIGNON, RESERVE, 2008: Showing fine extraction, deep garnet color and generous tannins. Shows traditional black fruits and spices. Promising. Drink now. Score 86. K

KITRON, CABERNET SAUVIGNON, RESERVE, 2007: Dark garnet in color, full-bodied, with somewhat generous spicy and smoky wood and chunky, country-style tannins. Opens in the glass to show black fruits, those on a somewhat muddled background of cloves, cinnamon and chocolate. Drink now. Score 84. K

KITRON, CABERNET SAUVIGNON, RESERVE, 2006: Full-bodied, with gently gripping tannins and notes of spicy oak in fine balance with currants, blackberries and spicy aromas yielding to black cherry, roasted herbs and espresso flavors. Tannins and fruits rise on the finish. Drink now. Score 88. K

KITRON, MERLOT, RESERVE, 2007: Deep and dark, medium- to full-bodied, with firm tannins and spicy wood integrating nicely with purple plum, blueberry and cassis fruits. Not complex but a good quaffer. Drink now. Score 85. K

KITRON, MERLOT, RESERVE, 2006: Blended with 5% Cabernet Sauvignon and oak-aged for 14 months. Dark ruby toward garnet, medium- to full-bodied, smooth and spicy with ripe berry, cherry and chocolate flavors, with tannins and hints of sweet cedarwood rising on the finish. Drink up. Score 85. K

KITRON, SHIRAZ, RESERVE, 2007: Garnet toward royal purple, with its generous wood and tannins now settling in comfortably and opening to show blackberry and black cherry fruits, those on a background of Mediterranean herbs and green olives. A bit of coarseness but that does not stop this from being a rewarding country-style wine. Drink now. Score 85. K

KITRON, CABERNET SAUVIGNON-SHIRAZ, LIKA, RESERVE, 2007: A blend of 47% Cabernet Sauvignon, 31% Merlot and 22% Shiraz, showing dark garnet in color, medium- to full-bodied, with somewhat chunky tannins that give the wine a countrified quality. Opens to reveal generous currant, plum and blackberry fruits, those on a lightly spicy background, spicy oak and tannins rising on the finish. Drink now. Score 86. K

Kleins ✶

Founded in 2004 by Yom-Tov Klein, this winery is set in the old city of Hebron, and is producing wines from Merlot, Cabernet Sauvignon, Chardonnay, Sauvignon Blanc and other grapes, though none of them indicate either the grape variety or the vintage year on their labels. Production is reported at about 110,000 bottles annually.

KLEINS, DRY RED, N.V.: Dark garnet, with hints of browning, and distinctly barnyard aromas that hide whatever fruits may be trying to make themselves felt. Score 60. K

KLEINS, SEMI-DRY WHITE, N.V.: Crisply floral on the nose, but on the palate overly sweet, without balancing acidity and only the skimpiest of lemon and lime aromas and flavors. Score 68. K

KLEINS, YASMIN DESSERT, RED, N.V.: Super-sweet, coarse, alcoholic, oxidized and caramelized. Score 55. K

KLEINS, YASMIN DESSERT, WHITE, N.V.: Golden straw in color, heavy on the palate and cloyingly sweet with overripe peach fruits. Score 60. K

KLEINS, PORT WINE, ANATOT, N.V.: Pale ruby in color, medium-bodied and with burned rubber and muddy aromas and flavors. Score 55. K

Lachish ✶✶

Established on Moshav Lachish on the Central Plain by Oded Yakobson, Oscar Meisels and Gai Rosenfeld, this small winery relies entirely on Cabernet Sauvignon, Merlot and Shiraz grapes from their own vineyards. Current production is about 3,000 bottles annually.

LACHISH, CABERNET SAUVIGNON, 2006: Medium-bodied, with chunky tannins and ripe berry, black cherry and spices on the nose and palate. A simple but appealing country-style wine. Drink up. Score 83.

LACHISH, CABERNET SAUVIGNON, 2005: Garnet toward royal purple, medium- to full-bodied, a somewhat coarse but pleasing country-style wine with generous black fruits, spices and hints of Mediterranean herbs. Drink up. Score 84.

LACHISH, CABERNET SAUVIGNON, 2004: Medium- to full-bodied, with chunky, firm tannins that yield slowly in the glass to show ripe blackberry and currant fruits. Drink up. Score 84.

LACHISH, SHIRAZ, 2004: Medium- to full-bodied, with soft, mouth-coating tannins and spicy wood yielding in the glass to reveal plum, berry and citrus peel aromas and flavors. Drink up. Score 84.

Lagziel *

Founded on Moshav Even Menachem on the Lebanese border in the Western Galilee by Moshe and Yariv Lagziel, the winery released its first wines in 2005. Current production is about 3,000 bottles annually.

LAGZIEL, CABERNET SAUVIGNON, 2006: Reflecting 20 months of oak-aging in a combination of new and older *barriques*, a medium- to full-bodied red with generous but not overpowering toasted oak notes and chunky tannins. Opens to show blackberry and black cherry fruits, those on spicy background. Not complex but a pleasant little country-style wine. Passing its peak. Drink up. Score 84.

LAGZIEL, MERLOT, 2005: The winemaker admits that he might have "gone a bit overboard" by letting this wine develop in oak for 30 months. He is correct, for indeed this medium- to full-bodied is dominated by its wood, that largely hiding the black fruits that try hard but do not quite succeed in making themselves fully felt. Past its peak. Drink up. Score 78.

La Terra Promessa **

Parma-born Sandro Pelligrini comes from a family of winemakers, and he and his wife Irit founded this small winery in 1998 at their home on Moshav Shachar on the fringes of the northern Negev Desert. The winery relies on Cabernet Sauvignon and Merlot grapes from the Upper Galilee and Ramat Arad, as well as from a vineyard near the winery with Shiraz, Zinfandel, Sangiovese and Petite Sirah. The winery is currently producing about 4,500 bottles annually, in four series: the

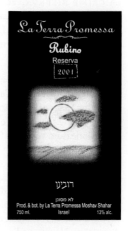

premium Rubino and La Crime Riserva and the regular La Crime and La Terra Promessa.

The winery recently moved to a new facility and took on a partner. Sadly, there was a falling out of partners and no wines were produced from the 2009 and 2010 vintage years. The future of the winery is open to question.

Rubino Riserva

RUBINO RISERVA, 2005: Full-bodied, with generous wood and firm tannins opening slowly to reveal black fruits on a licorice and earthy background. Drink up. Score 85.

RUBINO RISERVA, 2004: Dark garnet toward royal purple, full-bodied, with generous caressing tannins in fine balance with wood, natural acidity and fruits. On the nose and palate blackcurrants, blackberries and ripe plums, all with a hint of black truffles that makes itself felt on the finish. Past its peak. Drink up. Score 87.

RUBINO RISERVA, 2003: Reflecting its 24 months in *barriques* with generous spicy oak. Full-bodied, softly tannic and well balanced, this blend of 60% Cabernet Sauvignon and 40% Merlot offers up aromas and flavors of blackcurrants, plums and black cherries matched nicely by hints of cocoa and mint on the moderately long finish. Showing signs of aging. Drink up. Score 85.

La Crime Riserva

LA CRIME RISERVA, 2005: Medium- to full-bodied, dark garnet toward royal purple, a blend of 45% Sangiovese, 45% Shiraz and 10% Cabernet Franc. Oak-aged for 24 months, opens with dusty cedarwood aromas that hang on and interfere with the black fruit flavors. Drink up. Score 85.

LA CRIME RISERVA, 2004: A dark garnet, medium- to full-bodied of 45% each Sangiovese and Cabernet Sauvignon and 10% Cabernet Franc. Reflecting 24 months in *barriques* with generous dusty oak and tannins, those yielding slowly in the glass to reveal an appealing array of plums, blackberries and a light leathery note. Past its peak. Drink up. Score 83.

La Crime

LA CRIME, 2006: A blend of Syrah, Sangiovese and Cabernet Franc. Garnet toward royal purple, medium-bodied, with soft tannins and forward ripe berry, black cherry and currant fruits. Somewhat one-dimensional but a good quaffer. Drink up. Score 84.

LA CRIME, 2005: Showing medium-bodied, with generous black fruit, tobacco and chocolate. Long, round and well-balanced in its youth but now well past its peak. Drink up. Score 83.

La Terra Promessa

LA TERRA PROMESSA, CABERNET SAUVIGNON, 2006: Medium-bodied, with somewhat chunky tannins opening slowly to show black fruits on a light earthy-herbal background. A pleasant country-style wine. Drink up. Score 84.

LA TERRA PROMESSA, CABERNET SAUVIGNON, 2005: Garnet-red, medium-bodied, with soft tannins and an appealing hint of sweet herbs backing up plum and currant fruits. Lacking complexity and past its peak. Drink up. Score 83.

LA TERRA PROMESSA, MERLOT, 2006: Dark garnet, medium-bodied, with soft tannins and hints of spicy wood, showing straightforward black fruits and hints of Mediterranean herbs. Drink up. Score 84.

LA TERRA PROMESSA, SYRAH, 2005: Medium-dark garnet, medium-bodied, showing a tempting array of red and black berries along with notes of cassis, smoky oak and earthy minerals. Round and soft, generous and long. Drink up. Score 88.

LA TERRA PROMESSA, PRIMITIVO, 2005: Made entirely from Primitivo grapes and aged for 12 months in 400 liter oak casks, this bright garnet wine shows soft, near-sweet tannins, spicy oak and ripe raspberry, cassis and cherry aromas and flavors. Drink up. Score 86.

LA TERRA PROMESSA, DESERT ROSE, NEGEV, 2005: Dark ruby toward garnet, medium-bodied, a blend of Sangiovese, Cabernet Sauvignon and Syrah (70%, 20% and 10% respectively). Developed in *barriques* for 14 months, showing appealing spicy cedar notes that complement red currants, plum and red berry notes. Just enough complexity to get attention. Drink up. Score 86.

LA TERRA PROMESSA, DRY EMERALD RIESLING, 2008: Unlike most local Emerald Rieslings, this one is dry and shows only the least hint of sweetness. Damp straw in color, light- to medium-bodied, with aromas and flavors of citrus, pineapple and spring flowers. Finishes with a generously acidic dose of citrus. Drink up. Score 81.

Latroun ✶

Located in an idyllic setting at the foothills of the Judean Mountains midway between Jerusalem and the coast, the Trappist monks at this monastery have been producing wine since their arrival from France in the 1890s. For many years before the onset of the local wine revolution, weekend outings to the monastery to purchase wines were an important part of the social life of many. With over 400 dunams of land adjoining the monastery planted in grapes, the winery was the first to introduce Gewurztraminer, Riesling, Pinot Noir and Pinot Blanc grapes to the country and is currently producing about 300,000 bottles annually from twenty varieties of grapes. The winemaker is Father René.

LATROUN, CABERNET SAUVIGNON, 2009: Garnet with a hint of adobe brick, a simple rustic wine with chunky tannins and a few basic berry fruits, those overlaid with a too-strong note of Brett. Drink up. Score 72.

LATROUN, CABERNET SAUVIGNON, 2008: Royal purple, medium-bodied, with chunky, country-style tannins and berry-cherry fruits. Alas, enough Brett here to give the wine a musty, barnyard personality. Drink up. Score 70.

LATROUN, CABERNET SAUVIGNON, 2007: Light- to medium-bodied, with soft, almost flabby tannins and a basic berry-cherry personality. A simple country-style wine. Drink up. Score 79.

LATROUN, MERLOT, 2009: A simple country-style wine, medium-bodied, light in tannins and with a few basic black fruits. Drink up. Score 78.

LATROUN, MERLOT, 2008: A somewhat coarse medium-bodied wine, its black fruits almost hidden by aromas of wet fur. Score 70.

LATROUN, MERLOT, 2007: As many of the wines of Latroun, a simple, somewhat coarse country-style wine. Generous blackberry and plum notes make this an easy-to-drink quaffer. Drink now. Score 80.

LATROUN, PINOT NOIR, 2009: Dark ruby, medium-bodied, with soft tannins, a pleasant little wine with black cherry, berry and citrus peel notes. Drink now. Score 84.

LATROUN, PINOT NOIR, 2007: Ruby toward garnet in color, medium-bodied, a pleasant but simple little wine showing berry, cherry and light spicy notes. Drink up. Score 82.

LATROUN, PINOT NOIR, 2006: Light garnet in color, light- to medium-bodied, with soft, almost unfelt tannins, and with its berry and cherry aromas spoiled by a too-heavy Brett influence. Drink up. Score 76.

LATROUN, CHARDONNAY, 2008: Dark, almost bronzed gold, showing a bit of caramelization despite its youth, that hiding its citrus and tropical fruits. Drink up. Score 75.

LATROUN, SAUVIGNON BLANC, 2010: A simple but pleasant wine, medium-bodied with grapefruit and tropical fruits on a background that hints of tobacco and roasted herbs. Drink now. Score 84.

LATROUN, SAUVIGNON BLANC, 2009: A simple little white, light- to medium-bodied with tropical fruits and a somewhat strong earthy note. Drink up. Score 74.

Lavie **

Located in the community of Ephrata not far from Jerusalem, the first wine of Asher Bentolila and Yoav Guez was from the 2002 vintage. Drawing largely on grapes from the Jerusalem Mountains, the winery is currently producing about 3,000 bottles annually.

LAVIE, CABERNET SAUVIGNON, 2007: Garnet toward royal purple, medium-bodied, with chunky tannins and a heavy hint of spicy wood that somewhat hides the currant and blackberry fruits. Drink up. Score 80.

LAVIE, CABERNET SAUVIGNON, 2006: Medium-dark garnet, medium-bodied, with soft tannins and hints of spicy wood. Opens to show blackberry and purple plum fruits. A good quaffer. Drink up. Score 82. K

Levron **

Established by Segal and Yehuda Levron, with the winery located in their Haifa home, first releases are from the 2004 vintage. Drawing on Merlot and Cabernet Sauvignon grapes from Kerem Ben Zimra and the Gush Chalav area in the Galilee, the winery is currently producing 4,000 bottles annually and plans to expand to 6,000.

LEVRON, CABERNET SAUVIGNON, 2007: Garnet-red, medium-bodied, with soft tannins and showing aromas and flavors of currants, blackberries and black cherries. On the finish notes of spices and bitter orange peel. Drink now. Score 84.

LEVRON, CABERNET SAUVIGNON, 2006: Ruby toward garnet, medium-bodied, with softly mouth-coating tannins and opening to show wild berry, black cherry and currant notes, all on a light background of earthy minerals. Finishes with an appealing spicy note. Drink up. Score 85.

LEVRON, MERLOT, 2007: Medium-bodied, dark garnet in color, with good balance between near-sweet tannins, spicy wood and black fruits. Not complex but a good quaffer. Drink now. Score 85.

LEVRON, MERLOT, 2006: Medium-bodied, with hints of spicy oak and vanilla accompanied by soft tannins. Opens in the glass to reveal berry, purple plum and light herbaceous notes. Drink up. Score 84.

Lewinsohn ✶✶✶✶

After formal winemaking studies and the garnering of experience in Italy, France, Israel and Australia, and currently as one of the winemaking team of Israel's Recanati Winery, Ido Lewinsohn, together with his father, Amnon, opened their own artisanal winery. With the winery located literally in a residential garage in the Tel Aviv suburb of Hod HaSharon, Lewinsohn relies on purchased contract grapes, those at this stage including Cabernet Sauvignon, Merlot, Petite Sirah, Syrah and Chardonnay from various vineyards in selected spots throughout the country. First releases, from the 2007 vintage, were of about 2,000 bottles and current releases are of about 6,000 bottles annually.

This small winery relies on a combination of modern and traditional winemaking methods and produces only two wines annually. The playful naming of those as "Garage de Papa" Blanc and Rouge is in itself a fine calling card but far more important is that the Lewinsohn wines are demonstrating a unique personality that is indeed attracting a cult-like audience.

LEWINSOHN, ROUGE, GARAGE DE PAPA, 2010: Based on about 75% Merlot, that fleshed out with Petite Syrah, Syrah and about 1% of Viognier, showing dark cherry red toward garnet, full-bodied, with abundant but gently caressing tannins and fine balancing acidity. Lush and rich, polished and round, opening to show an appealing array of red and black currants, plums and notes of loamy earth and spices. An expressive wine, on the long finish tannins rising together with a note of mocha. Approachable on release but best 2013–2020. Tentative Score 92–94.

LEWINSOHN, ROUGE, GARAGE DE PAPA, 2009: About 65% Merlot, that blended with Petite Sirah, Carignan, Cabernet Sauvignon and 23%

of Viognier. Dark royal purple, full-bodied, with soft tannins that caress gently and a bare hint of vanilla from the oak in which it aged. Ripe but not at all overripe, a round, soft wine showing generous blackberries, blackcurrants and a note of licorice, those complemented nicely by notes of tobacco and mocha. Long and elegant. Approachable and enjoyable now but best 2013–2020. Score 93.

LEWINSOHN, ROUGE, GARAGE DE PAPA, 2008: A blend of about 40% Merlot and equal parts of Petite Sirah, Cabernet Sauvignon and Carignan, those complemented by about 3% of Viognier, each of the grapes vinified separately in Burgundy-sized barrels before blending together. Reflecting its 12 months in oak with a gentle hand, the wine opens with distinct cherry-berry aromas, those carrying over to the first attack and then yielding to red and blackcurrants and purple plums, on a background of mocha and green olives. Finally, tannins and fruits rise together and on the long finish a note of eucalyptus. Because the wine was intentionally submitted to only the coarsest of filtration, do not be surprised to see some sediment developing even in the next year or two. Do not hold that against the wine in any way, however, for it shows itself as simultaneously muscular and gentle, complex and delicious. Drink now–2018. Score 93.

LEWINSOHN, CABERNET SAUVIGNON, 2007: Dark ruby toward royal purple, an unfiltered blend of 85% Cabernet Sauvignon and 15% Petite Sirah. Medium- to full-bodied, with firm and chewy but polished tannins, those parting in the glass to reveal raspberries and spices on first attack and then on to blackberry and licorice notes, all supported nicely by a note of espresso, the raspberries rising again on the long finish. Drink now–2017, perhaps longer. Score 92.

LEWINSOHN, MERLOT, 2007: Deeply aromatic, kingly royal purple in color, full-bodied, with gripping tannins that take their time parting in the glass to reveal the wine's fine balance and structure. Notes of toasty oak here to complement black cherry, currant and vanilla aromas, those on a background of a roasted bouquet garni of Mediterranean herbs. Long and generous, the tannins rise on the finish. Drink now–2017. Score 91.

LEWINSOHN, BLANC, GARAGE DE PAPA, 2010: Showing bright, shining golden in color, with the crisp mineral-rich notes of a fine Chablis and the well-focused and stylish notes of a fine Meursault, most assuredly a Burgundy-style white. Full-bodied, opening to reveal lime, green apple, citrus and rich flinty minerals along with a hint of vanilla, a thoroughly well-balanced white that is mouthwatering and long. Not a "big" wine but one that fills the mouth beautifully. Approachable and enjoyable on release but best 2013–2019. Tentative Score 92–94.

LEWINSOHN, BLANC, GARAGE DE PAPA, 2009: Made entirely from Chardonnay grapes developed in new and older barriques, rich, not at all buttery but crisply refreshing with fine balance between generous but wisely utilized acidity, low alcohol (about 12.5%) and fruits. Opens with elegantly subdued aromas and flavors that hint of pears, apples and citrus, those on a background of lightly toasted oak and crisp minerality. Goes on to reveal candied limes, peaches and vague but tantalizing notes of exotic spices and blanched almonds. Lush and mouth-watering, the vibrant acidity leading to a long, long finish on which a hint of baked pie pastry. Chardonnay in its purest form and calls to mind a fine Puligny-Montrachet. Firmly structured, the wine is thoroughly enjoyable now but will develop a more fleshy texture as it develops. Drink now–2018. Score 93.

LEWINSOHN, BLANC, GARAGE DE PAPA, 2008: Chardonnay at its best. Light, shining gold with tantalizing hints of green and orange reflections, showing fine balance between acidity, minerals and fruit. On first attack a distinct note of grapefruit, that yielding to notes of lemon, melon, green apples and a tantalizing combination of chalky and flinty minerals, all with an appealing floral overlay. Full-bodied but not at all fat, with gentle notes of spicy wood, calls to mind a fine 1er cru Chablis, and like those wines will age nicely. Mouth-filling yet graceful and elegant. Drink now–2018. Score 93.

LEWINSOHN, CHARDONNAY, 2007: Lightly burnished gold with an orange tint, gently oaked and opening with a burst of lime flowers, spicy oak and citrus peel, those yielding in the glass to hints of white peaches, all on a near-buttery background and finishing with a note of pastry dough. Fine acidity and good balance keep this one deep, complex and elegant. Drink now–2015. Score 92.

Livni ✴✴✴

In vineyards not far from Kiryat Arba, on the line where the Judean Hills meld into the Judean Desert, Menachem Livni has been raising Cabernet Sauvignon, Pinot Noir and Shiraz grapes since 1994. In 2003 he opened his own winery and the first releases from the Livni winery were of 3,000 bottles. Today, with the winery located on Moshav Carmel in the Hebron Hills and working with French-born winemaker Bruno Darmon, the winery is producing about 10,000 bottles annually.

LIVNI, CABERNET SAUVIGNON, SDEH CALEV, 2009: Full-bodied, and dark garnet in color with orange and purple reflections, reflecting its 13 months in oak with just chewy enough tannins and notes of spicy cedar. Opens with a distinctly black-fruit nose, goes on to reveal traditional Cabernet Sauvignon aromas and flavors of blackcurrants, blackberries and freshly turned earth and, from mid-palate on notes of red licorice and cherries, all lingering nicely. Rich, with tannins and fruits rising nicely on the long finish. Drink now–2015. Score 90. K

LIVNI, CABERNET SAUVIGNON, SDEH CALEV, 2007: Medium- to full-bodied (leaning toward the full), reflecting its 22 months in second- and third-year barriques with soft tannins, showing round and generous. On first attack wild berries and cherries, those followed by notes of currants and roasted herbs. Drink now–2014. Score 90. K

LIVNI, PINOT NOIR, 2009: Made entirely from Pinot Noir grapes grown and aged for 12 months in French and American barriques, a full-bodied, impenetrably dark-garnet wine with almost chewy tannins. Opens with a black-fruit nose, goes on to show crushed wild berries, ripe cherries and raspberry fruits, those with overlays of licorice and earthy minerals. Rich, deep and layered, perhaps not fully typical of the variety but certainly a very tempting Pinot Noir. Approachable and enjoyable now but best from 2013–2017. Score 90. K

Lueria **

Drawing on vineyards planted on the slopes of Mt. Meron in the Upper Galilee, this winery is a cooperation between vintner Yossef Sayida and winemaker Yariv Lavie. With vineyards containing a large number of grape varieties, first releases were from the 2006 vintage and current production is about 25,000 bottles annually.

LUERIA, GRAND VIN, VITAL, 2008: Dark garnet, medium-, perhaps medium- to full-bodied, with chunky, country-style tannins and sweet-and-spicy oak. On the nose and palate black currants, blueberries and citrus peel, those on a background of grilled meat and roasted herbs. Drink now. Score 84.

LUERIA, GRAND VIN, HAUT GALILEE, 2007: Dark garnet, a medium- to full-bodied blend of Cabernet Sauvignon and Cabernet Franc. Gently gripping tannins and notes of spicy oak part to make way for aromas and flavors of currants and wild berries, those on a background of roasted herbs and earthy minerals. Drink now–2013. Score 87.

LUERIA, GRAND VIN, HAUT GALILEE, 2006: A wine that seems to have "crashed" since my first tasting, its elements seeming now at odds with each other. Dark garnet, medium- to full-bodied, with once-chunky tannins and spicy oak now far too pronounced and searing, those hiding the fruits that struggle to make themselves felt. Developing an odd medicinal aroma. Drink up. Score 80.

LUERIA, GRAND VIN, HAUT GALILEE, 2005: Oak-aged for two years in barriques, a blend of Cabernet Sauvignon and Cabernet Franc. Showing generous spicy wood and firm, somewhat chunky tannins. Opens in the glass to reveal aromas and flavors of blackcurrants and citrus peel. Somewhat one-dimensional and past its peak. Drink up. Score 80. K

LUERIA, ROUGE, HAUT GALILEE, 2007: A medium-bodied blend of Sangiovese, Barbera and Cabernet Sauvignon (60%, 30% and 10% respectively). With a fresh, fruity nose, soft tannins and generous wild berry, currant and black cherry fruits, a not-complex wine and somewhat acidic, but an acceptable entry-level quaffer. Drink now. Score 84. K

Maccabim ✶✶

Founded in 2002 by Eitan Rosenthal, Gari Hochwald, Yoav Heller and Ami Dotan in the community of Maccabim, at the foothills of the Jerusalem Mountains, and drawing grapes from that area as well as from the Galilee and the Ella Valley, this start-up winery's first release was of 1,200 bottles in 2002. Now producing Cabernet Sauvignon and Merlot wines, the winery releases about 5,000 bottles annually.

MACCABIM, CABERNET SAUVIGNON, 2006: Dark garnet toward royal purple, medium- to full-bodied, with notes of sweet cedar. Straightforward currant and berry fruits make for a good quaffer. Drink now. Score 84. K

MACCABIM, CABERNET SAUVIGNON, 2005: Medium- to full-bodied, with soft, near-sweet tannins and spicy wood integrating nicely. On the nose and palate currant, red berry and spices all leading to a medium-long finish. Drink up. Score 85. K

MACCABIM, CABERNET SAUVIGNON, 2004: Deep garnet, medium- to full-bodied, with spicy oak and soft tannins highlighting currant, black cherry and plum fruits. Drink now. Score 85. K

MACCABIM, MERLOT, 2006: Medium-bodied, a simple but pleasant little country-style wine with chunky tannins. Spicy oak and a berry-cherry personality. Drink now. Score 84. K

MACCABIM, MERLOT, 2005: Dark royal purple, medium- to full-bodied, with firm tannins and spicy wood along with blackberry, currant and plum fruits. Drink up. Score 85. K

Maor ✦✦✦

Established by Danny and Tal Maor on Moshav Ramot on the Golan Heights, the winery's first release was of 3,200 bottles from the 2003 vintage. Current production is about 20,000 bottles annually, drawing on grapes from the Golan Heights and the Upper Galilee, those including Cabernet Sauvignon, Merlot, Syrah and Cabernet Franc.

MAOR, CABERNET SAUVIGNON, 2006: Dark garnet toward royal purple, with a nose rich with chocolate and licorice, opening to reveal medium- to full-bodied, with soft tannins integrating nicely. On the nose and palate blackcurrants, wild berries, and hints of freshly roasted herbs and espresso. Drink now. Score 88.

MAOR, CABERNET SAUVIGNON, 2005: Blended with 15% Merlot and 3% Cabernet Franc, this generously oaked, dark garnet wine shows aromatic and tempting. Soft tannins give the wine a round, well-balanced personality, that flushed out by traditional currant, berry, black cherry and light herbal aromas and flavors. On the long finish a hint of freshly roasted coffee. Drink now. Score 89.

MAOR, CABERNET SAUVIGNON, CLASSIC, 2004: Blended with 20% of Merlot, this deep ruby toward garnet wine is medium-bodied, with soft tannins integrating nicely with spicy wood. Look for aromas and flavors of raspberries, red plums and cranberries, those supported nicely by hints of freshly turned earth and green olives. Drink up. Score 88.

MAOR, CABERNET SAUVIGNON, 2004: Dark garnet, medium- to full-bodied, with generous but not dominating wood and firm tannins well balanced by fruits and acidity. On the nose and palate currants, wild berries and vanilla, all lingering nicely. Drink up. Score 87.

MAOR, SYRAH, 2007: Made entirely from Syrah grapes, dark royal purple in color, full-bodied, with gently gripping tannins and just the right hint of sweet-and-spicy cedar. On the nose and palate plums, red currants and wild berries, those on a background of lightly roasted herbs and, on the long finish, a hint of mocha. Drink now–2014. Score 88.

MAOR, SYRAH, 2006: Dark garnet toward royal purple in color, with generous but soft tannins and hints of spicy wood. Well balanced and showing appealing red plum, cassis, herbal and chocolate aromas and flavors, all leading to a generous and mouth-coating finish. Drink now. Score 88.

MAOR, SYRAH, 2005: Dark garnet in color, with solid but yielding tannins and spicy oak, those in fine balance with fruits and acidity. Opens to show plum, currant, tar, tobacco and mineral notes, leading to a long and chocolate-tinted finish. Best yet from the winery. Drink now. Score 89.

MAOR, CLASSIC, 2007: A medium- to full-bodied Bordeaux blend of mostly Cabernet Sauvignon and Merlot. Gently gripping tannins part to reveal aromas and flavors of currants, crème de cassis and freshly cut herbs, all lingering nicely. Drink now–2013. Score 88.

MAOR, CABERNET SAUVIGNON-MERLOT, 2007: As we have come to expect with this wine, medium- to full-bodied with gently gripping tannins and truly Mediterranean in its personality. On the nose and palate blackcurrants and blackberries are complemented by notes of licorice and black olives, all on a background of freshly picked herbs. On the long finish an appealing hint of porcini mushrooms. Drink now–2014. Score 89.

MAOR, CABERNET SAUVIGNON-MERLOT, 2006: Dark ruby toward garnet, medium- to full-bodied, with soft tannins, fine concentration and a complex array of black and red fruits, those complemented by generous hints of Mediterranean herbs and, on the long finish, an appealing hint of freshly unearthed mushrooms. Drink now. Score 88.

MAOR, SYRAH-MERLOT, 2006: Deep purple toward inky black in color, firm and well focused and capturing the traditional herbaceousness of Merlot and the minty, berry and meaty flavors of Syrah. Concentrated but soft and round. Drink now. Score 88.

MAOR, ROSÉ, 2010: Salmon pink in color, light- to medium-bodied, with tutti-frutti aromas. Opens in the glass to reveal black and red berries, strawberries and, perhaps despite itself, a tempting note of tannins. Round, clean and refreshing. Drink now. Score 86.

Margalit ✶✶✶✶✶

There are very few who know the wines of Israel who are not familiar with the wines of the Margalit winery. All of which is fair enough, for this was among the first boutique wineries in the country, and most certainly the first to capture the imagination of sophisticated wine lovers. Founded by Ya'ir Margalit in 1989, the winery was first located on Moshav Kfar Bilu near the town of Rehovot, and since 1994 has been set in the heart of a citrus orchard not far from the town of Hadera, at the foothills of Mount Carmel.

Father-and-son team Ya'ir and Assaf Margalit are most renowned for their Bordeaux-style reds that are released in both a regular and a reserve series. In his role as a physical chemist, Ya'ir Margalit has published several well-known textbooks. Assaf, now the winemaker, studied in the agriculture faculty of Hebrew University at Rehovot and also trained in California and is now firmly placing his own mark on the wines. Happily, the passing of the baton from one generation to the next shows itself as fully successful.

As to changes in the wines since Assaf became the winemaker, I would be hard pressed to say that the wines of either the father or the son are "better," the overall signature on the wine maintaining its consistency, but under Assaf the wines showing somewhat less massive, more approachable during their youth and taking a clear turn toward elegance. The wines under both father and son are generously cellar-worth and have the reputation for being among the most long-lived in the country.

Margalit's earliest release, in 1989, was of 900 bottles of Cabernet Sauvignon. More recent releases, including Cabernet, Merlot, Petite Sirah, Cabernet Franc and Syrah, are made primarily of grapes from their own vineyards in Kadita in the Upper Galilee, while the Cabernet Franc is grown in their Binyamina vineyard. The winery offers three series: the top-of-the-line Special Reserve, Margalit, and, starting with the 2003 harvest, Enigma, a Bordeaux-style blend. All of Margalit's wines are meant for cellaring. Production varies at between 17,000–21,000 bottles annually.

Special Reserve

SPECIAL RESERVE, CABERNET SAUVI-
GNON, 2009: Cabernet Sauvignon blended
with 17% of Margalit's remarkably intense
Petite Sirah. Super-dark garnet, full-bodied
and concentrated, a broad and rich, multi-
layered wine opening with blackcurrants and
blackberries, those parting to make way for
notes of spices, cedarwood and green olives
and, finally, on the remarkably long finish
notes of dusty oak and sage. At an estimate,
in a few years this one will start to show notes

of black licorice and dill. If you must, try it now and you'll find it surprisingly approachable. If you have the patience, give this one the time it demands to show its depth, elegance and finesse. Best 2013–2023. Score 95.

SPECIAL RESERVE, CABERNET SAUVIGNON, 2008: Cabernet Sauvignon, as always blended with Margalit's "special" and remarkably
concentrated Petite Sirah, this year 88% and 12% respectively. Intensely
dark garnet, throwing purple, orange and green reflections, full-bodied
and with spicy wood and still-firm tannins just starting on the road
to integration but showing fine balance and structure. On first attack
traditional blackcurrant and blackberry fruits on a spicy background,
the wine opening in the glass to reveal black cherries and then raspberries and espresso coffee. Nor is this the end, for on the long, long finish
tempting hints of black olives and saddle leather. Perhaps the best to
date from Margalit and certainly one of the best wines ever produced
in Israel. Approachable now but best only from 2013–2025. Score 95.

SPECIAL RESERVE, CABERNET SAUVIGNON, 2007: Intense and
concentrated, with still-firm tannins, those receding as the wine opens
in the glass and in fine balance with wood and fruit, and showing an
enviable structure. Destined to always be muscular, those muscles with
an elegant and not at all showy note. On the nose and palate currant,
black cherry and blackberry fruits, those with hints of black pepper,
nutmeg and licorice, all leading to a long, generous finish. Approachable
and enjoyable now but best 2013–2020. Score 94.

SPECIAL RESERVE, CABERNET SAUVIGNON, 2006: Cabernet Sauvignon blended with about 13% of Margalit's Petite Sirah. Full-bodied,
dense and intense, but at the same time round and yielding, offering up
chocolate-covered cherries, cassis, wild berry and kirsch, those balanced
nicely by spicy-cedary oak. Long, complex and destined for elegance.
Drink now–2017. Score 93.

SPECIAL RESERVE, CABERNET SAUVIGNON, 2005: A blend of 85% Cabernet Sauvignon and 15% of Margalit's special Petite Sirah. Deep garnet toward inky black, remarkably concentrated and intense; still-firmly tannic at this stage but with fine balance and structure. Now starting to show a glorious array of currant, blackberry and plums on the first attack, those melding into hints of coffee, dusky spices and smoky notes. On the super-long finish, the tannins recede to let the fruits and a hint of espresso coffee rise to the surface. Potentially Margalit's longest-lived wine. Drink now–2022. Score 94.

SPECIAL RESERVE, CABERNET SAUVIGNON, 2004: A limited edition of 600 bottles, this full-bodied blend of 86% Cabernet Sauvignon and 14% Petite Sirah shows fine balance between tannins that are now integrating nicely, hints of sweet oak and generous but subdued blackcurrant, plum and chocolate aromas and flavors. Drink now–2014. Score 93.

SPECIAL RESERVE, CABERNET SAUVIGNON, 2003: Rich, ripe and concentrated, with layer after layer of dark plum, currant, anise, mocha, black cherries and sage. An oak-aged blend of Cabernet Sauvignon and Petite Sirah (87% and 13% respectively), this distinctly Old World wine has excellent balance between wood, lively acidity and well-integrated tannins. Complex and long. Drink now–2014. Score 93.

SPECIAL RESERVE, CABERNET SAUVIGNON, 2002: Coming into its own now, the once almost unbearable intensity now residing and letting the wine show its elegance. This almost impenetrable garnet toward inky-black blend of 80% Cabernet Sauvignon, 12% Petite Sirah and 8% Cabernet Franc remains remarkably concentrated and heavy enough to chew, but through its muscles shows great finesse. Ripe currants, purple plums, wild berries, spices and cedar flavors on a complex licorice and tobacco core and a long, intense finish. Drink now–2014. Score 93.

SPECIAL RESERVE, CABERNET SAUVIGNON, 2001: Dense and concentrated, with its once-gripping tannins now settled in nicely. A full-bodied and rich blend of 85% Cabernet Sauvignon and 15% of Margalit's very special Petite Sirah now showing layer after layer of currants, wild berries, plums and black cherries along with toasty oak, minerals and just the right hints of earthiness and sage on the very long finish. Drink now. Score 91.

SPECIAL RESERVE, CABERNET SAUVIGNON, 2000: Showing every bit as elegant and luxurious as during its youth. A blend of 80% Cabernet Sauvignon, 15% Petite Sirah and 5% Merlot, opens with an earthy-mineral nose, that going to spring flowers and then on to aromas and flavors of blackcurrants, wild berries, black cherries and cigar box notes. On the long finish hints of dark chocolate and cigar tobacco. Drink up. Score 92.

SPECIAL RESERVE, CABERNET SAUVIGNON, 1999: Harmonious, dense and tannic, this full-bodied and elegant blend of 87% Cabernet Sauvignon and 13% Carignan offers tempting spices and ripe fruit aromas and flavors of currants, plums, chocolate and coffee. Mature but showing great elegance. Drink up. Score 93.

Margalit

MARGALIT, CABERNET SAUVIGNON, 2009: Dark garnet, big and broad, a stylish wine with fine concentration and structure, opening slowly in the glass to reveal an array of currant, blackberry and black licorice on a background of near-sweet tannins. Generous and elegant, and on the long finish a surprising but most pleasant hint of raspberries. Drink now–2021, perhaps longer. Score 94.

MARGALIT, CABERNET SAUVIGNON, 2008: Blended with 10% Merlot, deep ruby toward garnet, full-bodied, showing its muscles but those in a gentlemanly manner, that is to say, powerful but full of grace. On the nose and palate black and red currants, blackberries and cigar-box notes, those complemented nicely by notes of white pepper and freshly picked herbs. On the long finish a tantalizing hint of porcini mushrooms. Drink now only if you must. Drink now–2018, perhaps longer. Score 93.

MARGALIT, CABERNET SAUVIGNON, 2007: Made from intentionally early-harvested grapes, full-bodied, green and tannic, with brambly undertones and black licorice on first attack, those yielding to blackcurrant, tobacco and espresso coffee aromas and flavors. As the wine develops, look as well for notes of olives and truffles. Still quite solid but showing fine balance and structure and already starting to open to reveal an underlying finesse. Drink now–2017. Score 92.

MARGALIT, CABERNET SAUVIGNON, 2006: Almost inky-black in color, offering a generous mouthful of currant, cherry, blackberry and blueberry fruits, those matched by layers of sweet spices. Big, broad and intense but yielding on the palate to show grace and elegance, and closing with a long, fruity finish. Drink now–2016. Score 92.

MARGALIT, CABERNET SAUVIGNON, 2005: Deep garnet toward royal purple, medium- to full-bodied, with soft but gripping tannins and fine balance and structure. Opens with red currant, raspberry and red plum fruits, those yielding to blueberries and appealing earthy-herbal overtones with gentle spicy wood on the long finish. Drink now–2015. Score 93.

MARGALIT, CABERNET SAUVIGNON, 2004: Dark garnet toward royal purple with orange reflections, this well-balanced, medium- to full-bodied wine is showing generous currant and berry fruits, those matched nicely by spicy wood, dark chocolate and espresso coffee. Long and luxurious. Drink now–2013. Score 92.

MARGALIT, CABERNET SAUVIGNON, 2003: Drinking beautifully, this blend of 88% Cabernet Sauvignon and 12% Cabernet Franc, both from the Kadita vineyard in the Upper Galilee, is showing full-bodied, remarkably rich and with fine balance and structure. Opens as it did in its youth with earthy currants and black cherry fruits, and then goes on to reveal notes of raspberries, mocha and chocolate. Generous tannins here but those now gently caressing, giving the wine both roundness and elegance, all leading to a super-long finish on which one finds at one moment a note of anise and another a hint of saddle leather. At its best now, but this one will hold its peak comfortably until 2015. Score 94.

MARGALIT, CABERNET SAUVIGNON, 2002: This full-bodied blend of 85% Cabernet Sauvignon, 8% Merlot and 7% Cabernet Franc, its once-firm tannins softening now, is showing aromas and flavors of blackcurrants, berries and game meat, together with a long finish. Complex and sophisticated, but not for much longer cellaring. Drink up. Score 92.

MARGALIT, CABERNET SAUVIGNON, 2001: This dark, dense and richly flavored oak-aged blend of 90% Cabernet Sauvignon and 10% Merlot offers generous currant, blackberry, sage and mineral aromas and flavors. Still-firm tannins, those integrating nicely now, and a long finish with tempting coffee, dark chocolate and hints of licorice and mint. Drink now. Score 91.

MARGALIT, CABERNET SAUVIGNON, LOT 37, 2001: Vastly different in style from every other Margalit wine released, this wine was aged in *barriques* for two years, in contrast to all of Margalit's other wines, aged for only one. The blackcurrants that typify so many of this winery's wines have been replaced here by plums, and the oft-searing tannins that sometimes take years to integrate are already soft and now showing a sweet and dusty nature. Drink now. Score 92.

MARGALIT, CABERNET SAUVIGNON, 2000: This full-bodied, still-tannic blend of 88% Cabernet Sauvignon and 12% Merlot had some rough edges in its youth but has now come fully into its own. Look for an abundance of raspberry, black cherry, sage, and spicy aromas and flavors, all with delicious leathery, cedarwood overtones. Drink now. Score 91.

MARGALIT, MERLOT, 2007: Anything but one of those rather boring internationalized Merlots that we have come to dread! Medium- to full-bodied, earthy, with big but velvety tannins and ripe purple plum, currant and blackberry fruits. Long and soft on the palate, with a finish that goes on and on. Drink now–2017. Score 93.

MARGALIT, MERLOT, 2005: Inky purple in color, offers up generous near-sweet oak, black cherries, blackberries and currants on first attack, those yielding to red plums and jammy raspberries. Dark and brooding at this time, with the tannins rising on the long finish. Drink now–2014. Score 93.

MARGALIT, MERLOT, 2004: Fresh, ripe and generous, with appealing blackberry, plum, cassis, mocha and vanilla aromas and flavors finishing with a hint of grilled herbs. Medium- to full-bodied, with soft tannins, a gently spicy wine that lingers nicely. Drink now. Score 90.

MARGALIT, MERLOT, 2002: Full-bodied, deep purple toward inky black in color and blended with 10% Cabernet Sauvignon to add backbone, this ripe, bold and delicious wine shows well-integrated tannins that give it a welcome softness, those matched nicely by aromas and flavors of plums, currants and black cherries, and a long spicy and cedar-flavored finish. Drink up. Score 92.

MARGALIT, MERLOT, 2001: This complex, intense and well-balanced 85% Merlot and 15% Cabernet Sauvignon blend has abundant soft tannins and plenty of earthy and mineral notes overlaying spicy currant, wild berry and coffee aromas and flavors. Look for a long, lingering finish with an array of hazelnuts, coffee and anise. Drink up. Score 91.

MARGALIT, CARIGNAN, 1999: A surprise when it was released, the one and only varietal Carignan released by Margalit. Blended with 5% Cabernet Sauvignon grapes, the wine was remarkably tight and closed during its youth but even then showing fine balance and structure. Full-bodied, with a still-young, garnet toward royal purple color, but with tannins that have subsided and now fully complement red berry, chocolate and notes of licorice all leading to a round and mouth-filling finish. Drink up. Score 90.

MARGALIT, CABERNET FRANC, 2009: Dark cherry red toward garnet, a supple, round and thoroughly graceful wine, full-bodied but seeming to float on the palate with soft tannins that caress rather than grip and gentle wood influences giving the wine a plush mouth-feel. On the nose distinct notes of red fruits, those yielding comfortably in the glass to aromas and flavors of ripe cherries, currants, spices and, from mid-palate on, a tantalizing hint of mint. A fascinating marriage between power and elegance. Approachable and thoroughly enjoyable now but best from 2013–2021. Score 93.

MARGALIT, CABERNET FRANC, 2008: Oak-aged, as are nearly all of the Margalit wines for 12 months, at this stage showing dark but bright ruby in color. Full-bodied, richly aromatic, rich and velvety, packed with plum, blueberry, cherry and exotic spices all on a softly tannic background and showing a tantalizing hint of *garrigue*. Blended with 7% Cabernet Sauvignon, a seductive wine that will be approachable early but will cellar very nicely. Drink now–2018, perhaps longer. Score 94.

MARGALIT, CABERNET FRANC, 2007: Still a baby and because of that not yet showing its full charms, but already revealing remarkable promise. Full-bodied, with gently mouth-coating tannins, opens to reveal traditional Cabernet Franc "greenness," yielding comfortably to blackberry, blueberry and cassis fruits, those complemented by notes of sweet peppers, green olives and an appealing note of *garrigue*. Give this one time to show its elegance. Drink now–2018. Score 93.

MARGALIT, CABERNET FRANC, 2006: Dark garnet toward royal purple, medium- to full-bodied. Blended with 5% of Cabernet Sauvignon and showing rich blackcurrant, cherry and blackberry fruits matched nicely by floral and light earthy aromas and flavors, all coming to a long, round and caressing finish. Drink now–2015. Score 92.

MARGALIT, CABERNET FRANC, 2005: Dark cherry toward garnet and full-bodied, this round and polished wine shows abundant blackberry, currant and black cherry fruits, those matched nicely by hints of spices and cedarwood, all leading to a long, generously tannic finish. Elegant and faithful to the variety. Drink now–2013. Score 92.

MARGALIT, CABERNET FRANC, 2004: Deeply fragrant, this full-bodied wine was blended with 12% Cabernet Sauvignon. Silky-smooth tannins, black and red fruits, hints of tobacco and chocolate come together on a long, mouth-filling finish with an appealing hint of freshly turned earth. Drink now. Score 90.

MARGALIT, CABERNET FRANC, 2003: Almost impenetrable deep purple, full-bodied, with excellent balance between soft, luxurious tannins and a tempting array of dark plum, wild berry and herbal aromas and flavors. Oak-aged, with the addition of 10% Cabernet Sauvignon, the wine is mouth-filling and long, showing a tantalizing hint of mint on the finish. Drink now. Score 90.

MARGALIT, CABERNET FRANC, 2002: This deep royal purple, full-bodied, concentrated Cabernet Franc with 12% Cabernet Sauvignon blended in, opens with a subdued nose hinting that the wine may be just a wee bit too mature. That is put to the lie rather nicely by the palate, the first impression being not so much of fruits but of bittersweet chocolate and roasted herbs. After five or six minutes in the glass one sits back with an "oh wow" look on the face as both nose and palate blossom, the wine unfolding to reveal fresh and dried black and red currants, cigar tobacco, sage and hickory, and finally, on the long finish, an appealing note of minerality. As full-bodied as ever it was, with the tannins and wood now comfortably in the background. Drink now. Score 93.

Enigma

ENIGMA, 2009: A Bordeaux blend, this year of 60% Cabernet Sauvignon, 22% Merlot and 18% Cabernet Franc. Dark cherry red in color, full-bodied and concentrated but showing its muscles with discretion and grace. On the nose chocolate and smoked goose breast, and on first attack aromas and flavors of red cherries and raspberries, those yielding comfortably in the glass to notes of currants, blueberries and hints of cedarwood and herbs, all on a softly tannic background. On the long finish notes of tobacco and minerals along with an appealing hint of loam. Approachable now but best 2013–2021. Score 93.

ENIGMA, 2008: A full-bodied blend of 58% Cabernet Sauvignon, 24% Merlot and 18% Cabernet Franc reflecting its aging in *barriques* for 12 months with firm but not at all searing and almost caressing tannins and notes of spices and vanilla from the wood. On first attack raspberries and red plums, those yielding to blackcurrants, and notes of bittersweet chocolate. Rich and concentrated but not at all bombastic. Destined for elegance. Drink now–2020. Score 92.

ENIGMA, SPECIAL RESERVE, 2007: The winery's first release of a special reserve in the Enigma line. Unlike the regular Enigma release (see the following tasting note, tasted on return from my visit to the winery), this one was aged for two years in oak, not so much adding a feeling of wood to the wine as allowing its elements to come together while still in the *barriques*, that affording a certain desirable level of micro-oxidation. A blend of Cabernet Sauvignon, Merlot and Cabernet

Margalit

2007

ENIGMA
SPECIAL RESERVE

Kadita & Binyamina

C. Sauvignon 51% / Merlot 26% / C. Franc 23%

Product of Israel

Alc 13.9% by volume   750 ML

Franc (51%, 26% and 23% respectively), full-bodied with gently gripping tannins and notes of lead pencils and earthy herbaceousness and on the super-long finish a note of licorice. Give this one time to round out and it will develop a most welcome overlay of smoked meat. Best from 2013–2025. Score 94.

ENIGMA, 2007: Developing very nicely. Full-bodied, with gently mouth-coating tannins and tantalizing hints of sweet cedarwood. On first attack black cherries, wild berries and blackcurrants, those on a background of roasted herbs and notes of both *garrigue* and fresh forest floor. Drink now–2017. Score 92.

ENIGMA, 2006: Full-bodied, subtle and round, a softly tannic blend of 60% Cabernet Sauvignon, 23% Cabernet Franc and 17% Merlot. Opens with red currants and red plums, goes to black cherries and a pleasing light spiciness, and closing with a long, fruity and persistent finish. Drink now–2016. Score 93.

ENIGMA, 2005: This medium- to full-bodied blend of Cabernet Sauvignon, Cabernet Franc and Merlot (60%, 22% and 18% respectively) shows generous cassis, raspberry and cherry fruits, those matched nicely by caressingly soft tannins, lightly spicy oak and chocolate, all coming together elegantly on a long and mouth-filling finish. Drink now–2015. Score 93.

ENIGMA, 2004: A blend of 60% Cabernet Sauvignon, 21% Cabernet Franc and 19% Merlot. A Bordeaux blend with the clear Margalit signature, showing generous but near-sweet soft tannins and a moderate hand with the wood. On the nose and palate dark purple plum and currant fruits, those matched nicely by spices and a hint of red licorice that creeps in on the long finish. Drink now. Score 93.

ENIGMA, 2003: Fully living up to its earlier promise, this Bordeaux blend of 70% Cabernet Sauvignon, 18% Merlot and 12% Cabernet Franc is showing remarkably rich, ripe and polished. Dark garnet, round and approachable, with a complex array of currant, plum and wild berry aromas and flavors, those well focused and long, and matched by a gentle spiciness and a hint of freshly roasted coffee that run through to the long finish. Drink now–2013. Score 92.

Meishar ✳✳✳✳

Founded in 1991 by Ze'ev and Chaya Smilansky on Moshav Meishar on the southern coastal plains, this small winery relies entirely on its own vineyards of Cabernet Sauvignon, Merlot, Shiraz and Muscat grapes, and currently produces about 10,000 bottles annually of red wines in a Reserve and a Meishar series.

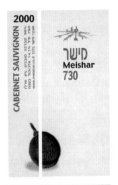

Reserve

RESERVE, 730, CABERNET SAUVIGNON, 2007: Developed in barriques for about 16 months, showing dark garnet, medium- to full-bodied. A round wine, with silky tannins and appealing notes of sweet and spicy cedarwood, opens in the glass to reveal traditional Cabernet Sauvignon aromas and flavors of blackcurrants and black berries. Lively acidity and overlays of dark chocolate and Mediterranean herbs add to the complexity of the wine. Drink now–2015. Score 90.

RESERVE, 730, CABERNET SAUVIGNON, 2005: Dark royal purple in color, full-bodied, with softly caressing tannins and notes of sweet and spicy cedarwood, opening to reveal blackcurrants, blackberries and cherry fruits, those supported nicely by notes of bittersweet chocolate, and, on the moderately long finish, a hint of smoke. Drink now. Score 87.

RESERVE, 730, CABERNET SAUVIGNON, 2004: Dark garnet, with just a hint of clearing at the rim. Full-bodied, this red reflects its 18 months in oak with its once near-searing tannins and sweet cedar notes now integrated nicely with black cherries, currants and light chocolate mousse flavors that sneak in quietly on the finish. Drink up. Score 89.

RESERVE, 731, MERLOT, 2008: Medium- to full-bodied, medium-dark garnet with a violet robe and showing silky soft tannins and a bare kiss of spicy wood that caress gently. Opens in the glass to reveal raspberries, red currants and light notes of roasted herbs. On the long finish tannins rise together with fruits and a hint of red licorice. Drink now–2016. Score 90.

RESERVE, 730, MERLOT, 2005: Showing dark and spicy, with an enchanting earthy character that highlights cherry, blackberry and spice aromas and flavors. Long and mouth-filling. Drink up. Score 89.

RESERVE, 730, MERLOT, 2004: Made entirely from Merlot grapes, showing medium- to full-bodied along with a gentle hand with the oak and generous earthy-herbal overtones, those in fine balance with ripe currant and blackberry fruits. On the long finish, hints of Oriental spices and grilled meat. Sliding past its peak. Drink up. Score 89.

Meishar

MEISHAR, CABERNET SAUVIGNON, 2005: Dark garnet toward royal purple, medium- to full-bodied, with fine balance between still-firm but already integrating tannins, spicy wood and well-focused currant, dark plum and black cherry fruits. Hints of ground pepper and anise that linger nicely. Drink up. Score 90.

MEISHAR, CABERNET SAUVIGNON, 2004: Dark garnet, medium- to full-bodied, with generous but soft tannins and smoky oak opening nicely to reveal aromas and flavors of blackcurrants, purple plums, white chocolate and spices. Long and mouth-filling. Drink now. Score 89.

MEISHAR, MERLOT, 2009: Dark cherry red toward garnet, reflecting its ten months in oak with gently caressing tannins and a light note of vanilla. On first attack cassis and raspberries, those making way in the glass for notes of crushed wild berries, all on a background of earthy minerals and mocha. Drink from release–2016. Tentative Score 88–90.

MEISHAR, MERLOT, 2006: Deep ruby, medium- to full-bodied, oak-aged for 18 months and showing soft tannins that grip gently and stand up nicely to notes of spicy wood. Opens with raspberries and black cherries, those making way for blueberry, cassis and citrus peel notes, all on a background of freshly picked Mediterranean herbs. Simultaneously complex and easy to drink. Drink now–2013. Score 90.

MEISHAR, MERLOT, 2005: Medium-dark garnet, medium-bodied and with silky tannins allowing raspberry, blackberry and cassis fruits to show through nicely, those complemented by generous hints of cocoa and a light earthy-graphite sensation that lingers nicely. Drink up. Score 88.

MEISHAR, SHIRAZ, 2007: Dark ruby, medium- to full-bodied, with soft tannins and a gentle touch of the oak in which the wine aged for about ten months. Not an intense or concentrated Shiraz but a gentle and elegant one, showing rich and round, with aromas and flavors of wild berries and ripe plums complemented by notes of what at one moment seems like bittersweet chocolate and at the next espresso. Drink now–2015. Score 90.

MEISHAR, BLENDED RED, #41, 2006: Oak-aged for 11 months, a blend of 60% Shiraz and 20% each of Merlot and Cabernet Sauvignon. Moderately dark garnet, medium- to full-bodied with a red-fruit nose, opens to reveal aromas and flavors of red plums, black cherries and bitter citrus peel all on a background that hints of cigar tobacco and saddle leather. Very nice indeed. Drink now–2013. Score 89.

MEISHAR, SHIRAZ-MERLOT-CABERNET SAUVIGNON, #41, 2004: Dark garnet, medium-bodied, with gentle sweet cedar and spicy oak overtones highlighting blackberries, black cherries and an array of herbs and spices. Look for hints of minerals and anise on the crisp finish. Drink up. Score 89.

MEISHAR, TACSUM, 2003: Perhaps the winemakers were in a playful mood when they named this wine by spelling "Muscat" backward. Made from Muscat Canelli grapes that were sun-dried and then frozen before pressing, this is a wine as much in the Italian *appasimento* style as it is an ice wine. Not so much full-bodied as it is "thick," the wine shows unabashed sweetness and a dark, burnished bronze color. Good balancing acidity and flavors of apricots, ripe peaches and honeydew melon keep it lively. Drink up. Score 88.

Meister *

Founded by Ya'akov Meister in Rosh Pina in the upper Galilee and drawing on Cabernet Sauvignon, Merlot, Shiraz and Carignan grapes from his own and other Galilee vineyards, this small winery released its first wines to the market with 2,000 bottles in 2003. Current production is about 6,000 bottles annually.

MEISTER, CABERNET SAUVIGNON, 2008: Medium- to full-bodied, with chunky, country-style tannins, opens to show a basic berry–black cherry personality, the fruits a somewhat barnyardy background. Drink up. Score 70.

MEISTER, CABERNET SAUVIGNON, 2007: Dark garnet, full-bodied and spoiled by far too many medicinal, moldy and sour notes that hide whatever fruits may be lurking here. Score 60.

MEISTER, CABERNET SAUVIGNON, 2006: A funky, muddy wine, with charred herbs, tar and searing tannins that end with a chalky aftertaste. Score 65.

MEISTER, MERLOT, 2008: Garnet toward adobe brick in color, medium- to full-bodied, with compost-like aromas that make the wine difficult to approach. Score 60.

MEISTER, MERLOT, 2007: Dark but not perfectly clear garnet and medium- to full-bodied. Dominated by unclean barnyard aromas that make the wine unappealing. Score 60.

MEISTER, MERLOT, 2006: Dry and bitter, with green earthy and tobacco ash aromas and flavors. Score 60.

MEISTER, SHIRAZ, 2006: Medium-bodied, with barnyard aromas and flavors of slightly sour stewed plums and cherries that lead to an earthy and balsamico finish. Score 55.

MEISTER, CARIGNAN, 2006: Medium-bodied, with spicy oak, weedy and vegetable aromas and flavors that hide the black fruits struggling without much success to make themselves felt. Score 65.

Miles ✯✯✯

Founded by vintner Eyal Miles in
2001 on Moshav Kerem Ben Zimra
in the Upper Galilee, with its own
vineyards containing Cabernet Sauvignon, Merlot, Shiraz, Sauvignon
Blanc and Gewurztraminer, this
winery is currently producing about
7,000 bottles annually. Wines are
released in a regular and a reserve
series.

Reserve

MILES, CABERNET SAUVIGNON, RESERVE, 2008: Oak-aged in
French and American *barriques* for 20 months. Dark garnet, medium- to
full-bodied with tannins and spicy oak in fine balance with plums, red
and black berries and a note of earthy minerals. Long and generous.
Drink now–2014. Score 89.

MILES, CABERNET SAUVIGNON, RESERVE, 2007: Developed in
French oak *barriques* for 20 months, showing almost inky garnet in
color, with firm tannins that coat the mouth nicely but yield to reveal
spicy wood and an appealing array of black and red berries, cassis and
Mediterranean herbs, all lingering nicely. Drink now–2013. Score 89.

MILES, CABERNET SAUVIGNON, RESERVE, 2006: Dark garnet,
full-bodied, reflecting its 20 months in partly new, partly used French
and American oak with generous spicy wood and somewhat chunky
country-style tannins. Firm and closed when first poured but opens
in the glass to show traditional blackcurrant and blackberry fruits,
those supported by hints of spices and Mediterranean herbs. Drink
up. Score 86.

MILES, CABERNET SAUVIGNON, RESERVE, 2005: Reflecting 18
months of oak-aging with generous smoky wood and gripping tannins
only now starting to integrate. Opens to reveal currant, blueberry and
plum fruits, those on a light background of earthy minerals. Drink
up. Score 85.

MILES, SHIRAZ, RESERVE 2007: Best to date from the winery. Oak-
aged for 18 months, full-bodied, concentrated and chewy, opens with
freshly crushed raspberries, goes on to reveal red plums, those on a

background of white pepper, saddle leather and tobacco. Well balanced and needs a bit of time for its elements to come together. Drink now–2014. Score 89.

Miles

MILES, MERLOT, 2006: Made entirely from Merlot grapes, oak-aged in new and older French and American oak for 26 months, showing chunky, country-style tannins and a generous hand with the oak that tends to hide the black fruits that are here. Sliding past its peak. Drink up. Score 84.

MILES, CABERNET SAUVIGNON-MERLOT, 2007: A blend of 60% Cabernet Sauvignon and 40% Merlot, oak-aged for 11 months, showing soft tannins, gentle notes of spicy wood and opening to show blackberry, currant, and Mediterranean herbs, all lingering nicely. Drink up. Score 86.

MILES, CABERNET SAUVIGNON-MERLOT, 2006: Oak-aged for 18 months, a blend of 60% Cabernet Sauvignon and 40% Merlot. Opens with a tarry-medicinal aroma but that blows off in the glass to reveal medium-to-full body and somewhat chunky tannins, those yielding to blackberry, blueberry and citrus peel notes, all on a lightly spicy background. Drink up. Score 85.

Miller *

Established in 2003 by Dan Ashkenazi in the community of Sha'arei Tikva on the western slopes of the Samarian Mountains, this small winery is currently producing 7,000 bottles annually, relying primarily on Cabernet Sauvignon and Merlot grapes from local vineyards and vineyards in the Galilee.

MILLER, CABERNET SAUVIGNON, 2007: Dark garnet, medium- to full-bodied, with soft tannins integrating nicely and showing black and red berries, cassis and notes of mint. Simple but pleasant. Drink now. Score 84. K

MILLER, CABERNET SAUVIGNON, 2006: Garnet toward purple, medium-bodied, soft and round, with straightforward red berry, cherry and cassis fruits. Drink up. Score 80. K

MILLER, CABERNET SAUVIGNON, 2005: This dark cherry-red wine is unoaked and medium-bodied, with soft tannins and simple but pleasant raspberry and cherry aromas and flavors. Already showing signs of age. Past its peak. Drink up. Score 75. K

MILLER, MERLOT, 2007: Medium-bodied, garnet toward royal purple with cassis and wild berry fruits. Clean and refreshing, an entry-level wine. Drink now. Score 84. K

MILLER, MERLOT, 2006: Unoaked, light- toward medium-bodied, with soft tannins and forward berry and cherry fruits on a lightly spicy background. A simple quaffer. Drink up. Score 84. K

MILLER, MERLOT, 2005: Ruby toward garnet, this medium-bodied, unoaked country-style wine has appealing berry, black cherry and cassis aromas and flavors. Drink up. Score 80. K

Mond ✳✳

Located in a pastoral setting on Moshav Mishmeret, not far from Kfar Saba, this boutique winery was founded by Moshe Keren, and the first wines were released from the 2004 vintage. The winery relies on Cabernet Sauvignon and Merlot grapes from the Ella Valley and from the Upper Galilee. Current production is about 25,000 bottles annually.

MOND, CABERNET SAUVIGNON, RESERVE, 2007: Oak-aged for 24 months, which is considerably longer than earlier releases and reflecting that with somewhat coarse and chunky tannins and a generous overlay of spicy wood, those holding back the black fruits that fight to make themselves felt. Medium- to full-bodied, showing a rather heavy dose of dark chocolate. Lacks balance. Drink now. Score 80. K

MOND, CABERNET SAUVIGNON, RESERVE, 2006: Oak-aged in barriques for 16 months, showing dark garnet, full-bodied and with generous wood and firm, somewhat chunky tannins starting to integrate with blackcurrant and wild berry fruits, those on a background of licorice and lightly bitter herbs. Drink up. Score 84. K

MOND, CABERNET SAUVIGNON, RESERVE, 2005: Garnet toward royal purple, medium- to full-bodied, reflecting its 18 months in oak with firm tannins and a generous spicy overlay. Opens to reveal currant, berry and red-plum fruits along with notes of bittersweet chocolate and tobacco. Sliding past its peak. Drink up. Score 86. K

MOND, MERLOT, RESERVE, 2007: Dark ruby toward garnet, medium-bodied, reflecting its 22 months in oak with hints of spices and smoke. On the nose and palate blackberries, blueberries and cassis. Not complex but soft, round and easy to drink. Drink up. Score 86. K

MOND, MERLOT, RESERVE, 2006: Showing somewhat better than at a pre-release tasting. Garnet in color, full-bodied, with firm, chunky tannins that are just starting to integrate. Opens with time in the glass to reveal blackberry, dark chocolate and licorice notes. An appealing country-style wine. Drink up. Score 85. K

MOND, MERLOT, RESERVE, 2005: Dark garnet, medium- to full-bodied, with gripping tannins and spicy wood just now starting to settle in. Opens to show wild berries, cassis and black cherries, those on a background of earthy minerals. Drink up. Score 87. K

MOND, MERLOT, RESERVE, 2004: Dark garnet with a hint of browning at the rim, but holding its own very nicely. Full-bodied, with soft tannins and spicy wood now well integrated and showing a generous array of blackberry, cassis and citrus peel, those supported by a hint of green olives. Sliding past its peak. Drink up. Score 85. K

MOND, SHIRAZ-CABERNET SAUVIGNON, RESERVE, 2007: Dull garnet in color, a blend of 70% Shiraz and 30% Cabernet Sauvignon. Oak-aged for 18 months, showing medium- to full-bodied, with somewhat chunky tannins and straightforward aromas and flavors of currants, wild berries and spices. Easy to drink and with just enough complexity to grab the attention. Drink now. Score 86. K

MOND, BLENDED RED, 2007: Medium-dark garnet in color, a blend of 40% Merlot and 20% each of Cabernet Sauvignon, Syrah and Cabernet Franc. Developed for 16 months in second-year oak, showing medium-bodied, soft and round, with caressing tannins and light notes of smoky oak. On the nose and palate blackberries, cassis and hints of spices, saddle leather and green olives. Drink now. Score 87. K

Mony ✳✳✳

Located in the foothills of the Jerusalem Mountains on the grounds of the Dir Rafat Monastery, the Mony winery was operated for many years by the resident monks. About ten years ago, control of the vineyards and winery passed to the Ertul family, long-time vintners for the monastery. Grapes in the vineyards include Cabernet Sauvignon, Cabernet Franc, Merlot, Zinfandel, Shiraz, Carignan, Argaman, Petite Sirah, Chardonnay, Semillon and Emerald Riesling. Annual production is close to 185,000 bottles. The winery is currently producing wines in three series: the upper-level Reserve, Sunny Farms and the regular Mony. From the 2005 vintage, the wines have been kosher. In 2009 winemaker Sam Soroka came aboard and the wines are now showing vast improvement over earlier releases.

Reserve

RESERVE, CABERNET SAUVIGNON, 2009: Medium-dark garnet toward royal purple, with generous fruits and vanilla on the nose, aging in 60% new and 40% older French barrels. Medium- to full-bodied, with soft tannins showing aromas and flavors of strawberries, raspberries and cassis, those supported by a tantalizing note of black olives. Soft, round and generous Drink from release. Tentative Score 87–89. K

RESERVE, CABERNET SAUVIGNON, 2006: Dark but not perfectly clear garnet, with sharp and chunky tannins and perhaps too-generous spicy wood. Opens slowly to reveal stingy currant and berry fruits. Past its peak. Drink up. Score 80. K

RESERVE, MERLOT, 2009: Blended with 10% Petit Verdot and developing in primarily French oak, light- to medium-garnet in color, with a fresh nose packed with raspberries. Medium- to full-bodied, with gently caressing tannins, opens to show a fine array of currants, wild berries and light spicy notes, all with a hint of earthy minerals. Drink from release. Tentative Score 87–89. K

RESERVE, SHIRAZ, 2009: Dark garnet, full-bodied with still-gripping tannins waiting to settle down, but already showing good balance and structure. On the nose and palate red berries and red currants, those complemented nicely by notes of leather, game meat and spices and, on the long finish, a note of white chocolate. Drink now–2015. Score 88. K

RESERVE, BORDEAUX BLEND (TENTATIVE NAME), 2009: A blend of equal parts of Petite Verdot and Cabernet Sauvignon. Medium- to full-bodied (leaning to the full), well extracted and showing dark garnet toward royal purple. On the nose and palate currant and wild berry fruits, those complemented nicely by notes of spices, saddle leather and a hint of earthy-minerals. Drink from release. Tentative Score 87–89. ĸ

RESERVE, CHARDONNAY, 2010: With 95% of the wine developed in new and one-year French barriques for about six months and the remainder in stainless steel vats, a light gold, medium-bodied white with notes of spicy oak and vanilla, showing fresh acidity and an appealing array of pineapple and tropical fruits along with notes of citrus peel and minerals. Lively and refreshing with just enough complexity to catch our attention. Drink now. Score 86. ĸ

RESERVE, CHARDONNAY, 2009: Showing fine on release but something seems to have gone wrong in the bottle. Dark golden straw in color, medium-bodied, with its once-crisp acidity now taking too sharp a turn and the flinty minerals that were there having become rather earthy and thus hiding the peach, pear and tropical fruits that fail to make themselves adequately felt. Drink up. Score 80. ĸ

Mony

MONY, CABERNET SAUVIGNON, SUNNY HILLS, 2010: Dark ruby toward garnet, medium-bodied, an unoaked red with soft tannins. Round and generous, showing wild berries, black cherries and a hint of earthy minerals. Drink now. Score 85. ĸ

MONY, CABERNET SAUVIGNON, SUNNY HILLS, 2009: An unoaked Cabernet Sauvignon showing dark cherry red toward garnet, with clean, fresh fruits on the nose. Medium-bodied, with tannins so gentle they almost "kiss" instead of grip, and with forward red and black berries and a light hint of freshly picked herbs. Nothing complex here but a very pleasant quaffer. Drink up. Score 85. ĸ

MONY, MERLOT, SUNNY HILLS, 2010: Ruby toward garnet, medium-bodied, a soft and round red showing black and red berries on a background of roasted herbs. Not complex but a good entry-level quaffer. Drink now. Score 84. ĸ

MONY, MERLOT, SUNNY HILLS, 2009: Ruby toward garnet, with chunky, country-style tannins and a basic berry-cherry personality. A not at all complex but easy-to-drink rustic wine. Drink up. Score 84. K

MONY, SHIRAZ, 2009: Medium- to full-bodied, dark garnet with a fruity nose and showing gently gripping, near-sweet tannins. On the nose and palate currant, wild berry and herbal notes on a background of light spices. Drink now. Score 87. K

MONY, CABERNET SAUVIGNON-PETITE SYRAH, 2009: Garnet toward royal purple, medium-bodied, with somewhat chunky tannins that grip nicely. On the nose and palate crushed blackberries and notes of mocha and Mediterranean herbs. An appealing country-style wine that needs a hearty beef or lamb stew. Drink now. Score 86. K

MONY, CLARET, 2009: Dark garnet, a blend of Cabernet Sauvignon, Petit Verdot and Merlot (46%, 34% and 20%), developed in stainless steel together with oak staves. Medium-bodied, with soft tannins, opens to show appealing cassis and red berries, those on a background of gently spicy oak and, on the moderately long finish, a note of red licorice. Easy to drink yet with just enough complexity to grab the attention. Drink now. Score 86. K

MONY, RHONE BLEND (TENTATIVE NAME), 2009: Made from equal parts of Shiraz and Syrah clones, calls to mind the Southern Rhone. Developed in stainless steel with oak staves, medium- to full-bodied, opens with black fruits, those going to raspberries and cherries. Dark garnet in color, medium- to full-bodied with gently caressing tannins. Drink from release. Tentative Score 86–88. K

MONY, EIN GEDI, 2009: A blend of 60% Cabernet Sauvignon and 20% each of Cabernet Franc and Argaman. A simple, almost coarse rustic red with near-sweet berry and currant fruits and a too-generous herbal nature. Drink up. Score 75. K

MONY, ELAT, 2009: Garnet in color, a blend of 65% Cabernet Sauvignon and 35% Merlot showing somewhat chunky tannins and relatively high acidity that do not allow the black fruits here to make themselves fully felt. Drink up. Score 74. K

MONY, ROSH HANIKRAH, 2009: A medium-bodied blend of 50% Merlot, 30% Cabernet Sauvignon and 20% Petite Sirah showing blackberry, blueberry and cassis aromas and flavors. Alas, a bit flabby on the palate. Drink up. Score 76. K

MONY, KIKAR HASHABBOS, 2009: Medium-dark ruby, medium-bodied, with chunky tannins, a simple rustic wine with not quite enough in the way of fruits to carry it. Drink up. Score 74. K

MONY, ROSÉ, 2009: With skin contact of about 12 hours, made entirely from first-run must from Cabernet Sauvignon grapes, showing dark pink toward ruby in color, and with enticing strawberry, raspberry and blueberry notes. Dry, crisp and appealing. Drink up Score 86. K

MONY, COLOMBARD, 2010: A dry white, not at all complex but a pleasant quaffer, light golden straw in color, medium-bodied, with plenty of lively acidity. On the nose and palate grapefruit, tropical fruits and a hint of citrus peel. A good summertime refresher. Drink up. Score 85. K

MONY, FRENCH COLOMBARD, GFANIM, 2009: One may not expect much from French Colombard (a cross between Gouais Blanc and Chenin Blanc) but this one is most pleasant indeed. Wisely unoaked, a crisply fresh dry white wine with good acidity, showing a floral nose and opening on the palate to show red grapefruit, kiwi and lime notes. An easy-to-drink and thoroughly refreshing little wine. Drink up. Score 86. K

MONY, MASSADA, 2009: Made entirely from French Colombard grapes, an off-dry white wine with good balancing acidity and generous grapefruit and tropical fruits on the nose and palate. Nothing complex but an acceptable entry-level wine. Drink up. Score 80. K

MONY, GEWURZTRAMINER, 2010: Light golden straw in color, medium-bodied, a half-dry white with traditional Gewurztraminer rosewater, litchis and citrus on the nose and palate. Fine balancing acidity keeps the wine lively. Drink now. Score 86. K

MONY, SEMILLON-CHARDONNAY, SUNNY HILLS, 2009: Categorized as off-dry but lacking the balancing acidity that might have added liveliness. Opens in the glass to reveal straightforward citrus and tropical fruits. Drink up. Score 80. K

MONY, MUSCAT DESSERT WINE, SUNNY HILLS, 2009: Floral on the nose, light gold with green and orange reflections, a generously sweet wine with good balancing acidity. On the nose and palate mango, kiwi and citrus, those balanced nicely by a light hint of bitter citrus peel on the finish. Medium-bodied, with a moderate 10.5% alcohol content, an easy-to-drink dessert wine. Drink now. Score 89. K

Na'aman ✳✳✳

Founded by Rami and Bettina Na'aman on Moshav Ramot Naftaly in the Upper Galilee, this boutique winery released their first wines from the 2004 vintage. With their own vineyards containing Cabernet Sauvignon, Merlot, Cabernet Franc, and Petit Verdot grapes, releases from 2004 were just under 1,000 bottles. Current production is about 10,000 bottles annually. As at past tastings, the Na'aman wines reflect a sophisticated country-style nature. More than that, they show what in stereotypical terms might be thought of as "masculine" wines – that is to say, concentrated, intense and muscular, happily the muscles showing themselves in a gentle and mannerly fashion. It is interesting to note that the winemaker takes special pleasure in naming his blended wines after musical groups, e.g., Pink Floyd, and songs, such as Black Velvet.

NA'AMAN, CABERNET SAUVIGNON, 2009: Medium- to full-bodied, with gently gripping tannins and appealing notes of spicy oak. On the nose black fruits and licorice, opening in the glass to show a generous array of currants and blackberries, those on a background that hints of garrigue and, on the long finish, an appealing note of bitter herbs. Drink from release–2016. Score 90.

NA'AMAN, CABERNET SAUVIGNON, 2008: Well extracted, showing deep garnet, blended with 6% Malbec. Full-bodied, with generous soft tannins and notes of vanilla and cinnamon from the oak in which it aged. On the nose and palate currants, blackberries, purple plums and dark chocolate and, on the long finish, hints of raspberries and red licorice. Drink now–2015. Score 90.

NA'AMAN, CABERNET SAUVIGNON, 2007: Dark garnet, medium- to full-bodied, with once-chunky tannins and generous spicy oak now settling in nicely. On the nose and palate traditional blackcurrants, berries, black cherries and Mediterranean herbs. An appealing country-style wine. Drink now. Score 88.

NA'AMAN, CABERNET SAUVIGNON, 2006: Dark garnet in color, full-bodied, with firm tannins and a gentle hand with spicy oak. Opens with red plum and berry notes, those yielding to currant and orange peel, and goes on to a tannic finish with appealing herbal overtones. Drink up. Score 88.

NA'AMAN, MERLOT, 2010: Unoaked, made entirely from free-run juice, showing light garnet in color. Medium-bodied with soft tannins and notes of black and red berries, those highlighted by notes of tutti-frutti bubble gum. As many young people would say these days, an "achla" wine – one that makes you smile. Meant for easy quaffing. Drink now. Score 87.

NA'AMAN, MERLOT, 2008: Medium-dark garnet, medium- to full-bodied, with black fruits on the nose but then opening on a bitter note that lingers too prominently and tends to hide the black fruits that fail to make themselves fully felt. Not a bad wine but one that fails to come together as a coherent whole. Perhaps better with time. Drink now. Score 84.

NA'AMAN, MERLOT, 2007: Richly aromatic, with berries and wildflowers on the nose, a full-bodied and generously tannic oak-aged Merlot showing good balance and structure. On the nose and palate wild berries, cassis and hints of baking chocolate, those on a background that hints of a fresh forest floor. Deep and long. Drink now. Score 90.

NA'AMAN, CABERNET FRANC, 2009: Blended with 4% Merlot and 2% Cabernet Sauvignon, developed in second-year-oak for 14 months, showing dark ruby toward garnet. Medium- to full-bodied, with crushed berries on the nose and opening in the glass to reveal generous black fruits on a background of garrigue and earthy minerals. Long and mouth-filling. Drink now–2015. Score 89.

NA'AMAN, CABERNET FRANC, 2008: Blended with 10% Cabernet Sauvignon, dark garnet, medium- to full-bodied, a solid wine, with firm tannins and spicy wood notes starting to settle in now. A bit sharp on first attack but given time in the glass, opens to reveal generous plum, cherry, blackberry and tobacco notes. Sleek and ripe with notes of espresso coffee and earthy minerals on the finish. Long and mouth-filling. Drink now–2015. Score 90.

NA'AMAN, CABERNET FRANC, 2007: Made entirely from Cabernet Franc grapes, gently oak-aged, medium- to full-bodied, with softly mouth-coating tannins and spicy wood integrating nicely. Opens to show generous berry and currant fruits, those well supported by notes of roasted herbs. Medium-long with a hint of cigar tobacco on the finish. Drink now. Score 88.

NA'AMAN, PETIT VERDOT, 2009: Almost impenetrably dark garnet, full-bodied, with fine concentration and muscles that hold back in a genteel fashion. On first attack mocha, chocolate and spices, those parting to make way for blackberries, black currants and, on the long finish, a note of boysenberries. Generous and mouth-filling. Drink now–2016. Score 90.

NA'AMAN, PETIT VERDOT, 2008: Blended with 6% Merlot, dark, almost dense purple, medium- to full-bodied, with an appealing note of peppermint on the nose and opening to show fresh cassis, blackberry and toasty oak, all lingering nicely with good acidity to keep the wine lush and fresh. Very appealing. Drink now–2014. Score 90.

NA'AMAN, PETIT VERDOT, 2007: Dark garnet, with a light herbal nose and still-gripping tannins and generous spicy wood. Opens in the glass to reveal red and black berries, cassis and notes of bittersweet chocolate on a light earthy background. A country-style wine in a most pleasant fashion Drink now. Score 88.

NA'AMAN, DEEP PURPLE, 2009: Reflecting its development in French *barriques* with notes of spicy wood and vanilla, full-bodied, with abundant tannins that grip comfortably yet make room for aromas and flavors of black fruits, Mediterranean herbs and freshly picked mushrooms. Plenty of muscles here but those have the good grace to linger quietly in the background. Drink now–2016. Score 90.

NA'AMAN, DEEP PURPLE, 2008: A dark-garnet, medium- to full-bodied blend of Cabernet Sauvignon, Cabernet Franc, Merlot and Petit Verdot (40%, 30%, 20% and 10% respectively). Reflecting its 13 months in *barriques* with softly caressing tannins and spicy cedarwood, opens to reveal appealing blackcurrants, black cherries, chocolate and licorice notes, all leading to a long and generous finish. Drink now–2014. Score 90.

NA'AMAN, DEEP PURPLE, 2006: Oak-aged for 13 months, a blend of Cabernet Sauvignon, Cabernet Franc, Merlot and Petit Verdot (40%, 30%, 20% and 10% respectively). Dark royal purple in color, medium- to full-bodied with still-firm tannins needing time to integrate. Opens to reveal blackberry, purple plum and cassis fruits along with generous hints of saddle leather and earthy minerals. Drink up. Score 86.

NA'AMAN, KING CRIMSON, 2009: Cabernet Sauvignon and Merlot (75% and 25% respectively), showing medium- to full-bodied with gentle notes of spicy wood and abundant but soft tannins that caress comfortably. On the nose and palate blackberries, currants, Oriental spices and notes of freshly turned earth, all coming together in a moderately long finish. Drink from release–2014. Score 89.

NA'AMAN, KING CRIMSON, 2008: Garnet toward royal purple, a medium- to full-bodied blend of 75% Cabernet Sauvignon and 25% Merlot, softly tannic with appealing spicy cedarwood notes and opening to reveal currant, wild berry and purple plum fruits, those on a lightly spicy background. On the finish appealing touches of mocha and tobacco. Drink now–2015. Score 90.

NA'AMAN, KING CRIMSON, 2007: Deep royal purple in color, with roasted herbs on the nose, gently gripping tannins on a medium- to full-bodied frame. A blend of 75% Cabernet Sauvignon and 25% Merlot showing a gentle spicy wood influence and opening to reveal currant, wild berry and a note of bittersweet chocolate. A good mouth-feel here. Drink now–2013. Score 88.

NA'AMAN, KING CRIMSON, 2006: A blend of Cabernet Sauvignon and Merlot. Dark garnet, full-bodied, with still-firm tannins starting to integrate with spicy wood. Showing an appealing array of currant, berry and black cherry fruits, those with hints of earthy minerals and spices. Lingers nicely. Drink up. Score 86.

NA'AMAN, BLACK VELVET, 2009: A blend of 60% Merlot, 30% Cabernet Franc and 10% Petit Verdot, the wine developed in barriques for 14 months. Super-dark garnet, a deep and intense wine with gripping tannins and appealing earthy notes, those parting to make way for blackcurrant, black cherry and blueberry notes, the tannins and earthy notes rising comfortably on the long and generous finish. Drink now–2015, perhaps longer. Score 89.

NA'AMAN, BLACK VELVET, 2008: Merlot, Cabernet Franc and Petit Verdot (60%, 30% and 10% respectively) come together in a medium- to full-bodied, firmly tannic wine that blossoms slowly in the glass to reveal generous blackberry, currant and herbal notes, those showing fine balance and structure that bode well for the future. The best to date from the winery. Drink now–2016. Score 91.

NA'AMAN, PINK FLOYD, ROSÉ, 2010: Deep rose-petal pink, with a red-fruit nose, showing medium-bodied with a generous but not overpowering 13% alcohol level and even a bare and tantalizing hint of tannins. Look for aromas and flavors of red currants, cranberries and a hint of bitter earth on the finish. Not your usual run-of-the-mill rosé, but one that will go as nicely with lamb chops as it will with grilled salmon. Drink now. Score 88.

Nachshon **

Founded in 1996 on Kibbutz Nachshon in the Ayalon Valley at the foot of the Jerusalem Hills, the winery raises its own Cabernet Sauvignon, Merlot, Shiraz, Cabernet Franc and Argaman grapes and, until 2007, produced about 20,000 bottles annually under the careful eye of winemaker Shlomi Zadok. No wines were produced in 2008 and the 2009 vintage will be quite limited. With new partners now aboard, renovations to the winery under way and Nathan Lifshitz as the new winemaker, several blends will soon be released from wines still in the barrels from older vintages. Anticipated releases from the 2010 vintage will be about 10,000 bottles.

Ayalon

AYALON, SYRAH, 2005–2006–2007: A "salvage job," the new winemaker blending barrels from three vintages. Garnet, with a hint of clearing at the rim showing its maturity. Somewhat chunky tannins give the wine a countrified personality, but that's fine as the wine shows appealing black cherry, blackberry and raspberry fruits, those on a background of tobacco leaf and licorice. Drink now. Score 86.

AYALON, SYRAH, 2006: Garnet toward royal purple in color, this round and generous blend of 90% Syrah and 10% Cabernet Sauvignon is medium-bodied, with soft tannins, and shows raspberry, leathery and meaty aromas and flavors. Sliding rapidly past its peak. Drink up. Score 85.

AYALON, CABERNET FRANC, 2006: Dark garnet, this medium- to full-bodied softly tannic blend of 90% Cabernet Franc and 10% Cabernet Sauvignon shows complex currant, plum, cedarwood and tobacco aromas and flavors. Well balanced and round, with an appealing finish highlighted by spicy oak and orange peel. Drink up. Score 86.

Sela

SELA, CABERNET FRANC, 2007: Dark garnet, developed in older oak barriques for two years, showing full-bodied and round, with gentle notes of spicy cedarwood. On the nose and palate earthy currant, plum and mineral notes, those supported by hints of licorice. Black fruits and chewy tannins rise on the finish. Drink now. Score 87.

SELA, FRENCH BLEND, 2006–2007: Made by blending wines in barrels from the 2006 and 2007 vintage, one might think of this as a "salvage job." Fortunately, the salvage was successful A blend of Syrah, Merlot and Cabernet Franc from both vintages, showing medium- to full-bodied, with soft, gently gripping tannins and appealing blackberry, black cherry and cassis fruits on a background that hints of smoked meat. Drink now. Score 87.

SELA, FRENCH BLEND, 2005: Medium-dark garnet with silky tannins, this blend of Syrah, Cabernet Sauvignon, Cabernet Franc and Petit Verdot (41%, 33%, 16% and 10% respectively) shows an appealing array of wild berries, currants and plums, those on a gently spicy background. Rich, round and moderately long. Past its peak. Drink up. Score 82.

Nahal Amud ✳

Established by Avi Abu in 1998 and located on Moshav Kfar Shamai near Safed in the Upper Galilee, the winery draws on grapes from its own vineyards, those including Cabernet Sauvignon, Cabernet Franc, Merlot and Petite Sirah. Current production is about 8,000 bottles annually.

NAHAL AMUD, CABERNET SAUVIGNON, 2006: Dark garnet, full-bodied, with sharp-edged tannins and too-generous acidity that make the black fruits seem almost sour. Drink up. Score 70. K

NAHAL AMUD, CABERNET SAUVIGNON, 2005: Garnet toward purple, medium-bodied, with chunky, somewhat coarse tannins, minimal fruits and an excessive earthy overlay. Drink up. Score 72. K

NAHAL AMUD, CABERNET SAUVIGNON, 2004: Medium-bodied, with coarse tannins and far-too-generous and not entirely clean earthy overlays and only the skimpiest of black fruits. Showing first signs of aging. Drink up. Score 75. K

NAHAL AMUD, MERLOT, 2006: Dark royal purple in color with chunky, country-style tannins. On the nose a strong herbaceousness and a near-sweetness hide whatever fruits may be here. Drink up. Score 70. K

NAHAL AMUD, MERLOT, 2005: Dark garnet with a hint of browning, medium-bodied, with firm tannins and an underlying sweetness of stewed red fruits. Drink up. Score 70. K

NAHAL AMUD, MERLOT, 2003: Dark but not fully clear royal purple, medium-bodied, with searing tannins and aromas and flavors that call to mind cherry liqueur. Score 68. K

NACHAL AMUD, BLENDED RED, 2008: A blend of Cabernet Sauvignon, Merlot and Sangiovese. Medium- to full-bodied, with chunky country-style tannins, opens with a medicinal and tarry nose that lingers throughout. Far too acidic and earthy. Score 65.

NAHAL AMUD, BLENDED RED, 2007: A blend of 60% Sangiovese and 20% each Cabernet Sauvignon and Merlot. Oak-aged for 12 months, a clean, fresh, distinctly Mediterranean country-style wine, medium-bodied, with generous red fruits and soft tannins. A good quaffer, especially when served lightly chilled. Drink up. Score 85.

Nahar Dalton *

A family-owned artisanal winery located in the Upper Galilee, producing about 3,500 bottles annually based on Merlot and Cabernet Sauvignon grapes.

NAHAR DALTON, CABERNET SAUVIGNON, 2007: Developed with oak chips for one year, dark garnet, with a distinct note of iodine on the nose and earthy-herbal rather than fruity aromas and flavors. Score 69. K

NAHAR DALTON, MERLOT, 2006: Opens with a medicinal aroma that lingers throughout and interferes with the red fruits that never quite make themselves felt. Soft enough to be thought of as flabby. Score 68. K

Nashashibi ✶

Founded in 2001 by brothers Munir and Nashashibi Nashashibi, the winery is located in the village of Eehbelin in the southwestern reaches of the Lower Galilee, and set on a site where wine has been made since Roman times. Current production is about 15,000 bottles annually, that of Cabernet Sauvignon, Merlot and Chardonnay in two series, Special Reserve and Nashashibi. Grapes come from the Upper Galilee as well as from the winery's own vineyards at the foothills of the Carmel Mountains.

Special Reserve

SPECIAL RESERVE, CABERNET SAUVIGNON, 2006: Garnet toward adobe brick in color, with firm, chunky tannins giving the wine a countrified style. Look for aromas and flavors of wild berries and currants, those with just a bit too much Brett to make drinking comfortable. Drink up. Score 73.

SPECIAL RESERVE, CABERNET SAUVIGNON, 2005: Dark garnet and medium-bodied, with firm tannins starting to integrate. Showing generous smoke and spices from the wood casks in which it aged. On the nose and palate currants and berries. Starting to develop a barnyard aroma. Drink up. Score 80.

SPECIAL RESERVE, MERLOT, 2004: Medium-bodied, with almost unfelt tannins, this dark cherry-red toward purple wine reflects its fourteen months of aging with generous smoky oak. Not much in the way of fruits here. Drink up. Score 75.

Nashashibi

NASHASHIBI, CABERNET SAUVIGNON, 2006: Dark garnet with a bit of browning at the rim, a country-style wine that has aged well before its time. Score 70.

Natuf **

Founded in 1997 by Meir Akel and Ze'ev Cinnamon on Moshav Kfar Truman in the Central Plains, not far from Ben Gurion Airport, this winery draws on grapes from the Ayalon Valley, and its releases have been primarily of Cabernet Sauvignon. Current production is about 4,500 bottles annually.

NATUF, CABERNET SAUVIGNON, 2007: Dark garnet, full-bodied, with still-tight tannins needing time to settle down but showing good balance and structure. A blend of 85% Cabernet Sauvignon, 10% Merlot and 5% Shiraz, developed in American oak for 15 months. Opens slowly, at first revealing primarily blackcurrants and blackberries and then blossoming to show notes of blueberries, chocolate and freshly ground coffee. Drink now–2013. Score 88.

Shiraz
2006

משק יין כפר טרומן
Natuf Winery
750 Ml. 13.6% Alc.

Cabernet
Sauvignon
2007

משק יין כפר טרומן
Natuf Winery
750 Ml. 14.3% Alc.

NATUF, CABERNET SAUVIGNON, 2006: Dark ruby toward garnet, full-bodied and reflecting its 14 months in *barriques* with firm tannins and spicy wood, those integrating to show ripe berry and black cherry fruits. Drink up. Score 84.

NATUF, MERLOT, 2006: Blended with 10% of Cabernet Sauvignon and 5% Shiraz, with the soft Merlot dominating. Deep garnet toward royal purple, medium- to full-bodied with once-chunky tannins now showing far softer. On the nose and palate wild berries, cherries, raspberries and a hint of black licorice. A good dose of acidity makes this a refreshing quaffer. Drink up. Score 85.

NATUF, SHIRAZ, 2007: Shiraz blended with 15% Cabernet Sauvignon and 5% Merlot and oak-aged for 14 months in French and American oak. Full-bodied, with firmly gripping tannins and a generous wood influence but those starting to settle in now. Opens in the glass to reveal plum and black cherry fruits, those supported by hints of spices and saddle leather. Drink up. Score 86.

NATUF, SHIRAZ, 2006: A blend of 85% Shiraz, 9% Cabernet Sauvignon and 6% Merlot. Medium- to full-bodied, with once-firm tannins and generous spicy wood now integrated nicely and parting to reveal plum, blackberry, licorice and meaty aromas and flavors. On the moderately long finish a hint of bittersweet chocolate. Drink now. Score 85.

NATUF, MERLOT-CABERNET SAUVIGNON, 2007: A blend of 55% Merlot, 37% Cabernet Sauvignon and 8% Shiraz. Oak-aged for 14 months, showing full-bodied, with its once-gripping tannins and wood now well integrated. On the nose and palate an appealing array of red and black berries, red plums and spices. Tannins and wood rise on the finish. Drink now–2013. Score 87.

NATUF, MERLOT-SHIRAZ, CABERNET SAUVIGNON, 2007: Dark garnet, medium- to full-bodied with soft tannins and gentle notes of spicy wood. Round and smooth, opening to reveal red berries, cassis and notes of white pepper and red licorice. Drink now–2013. Score 88.

Neot Smadar ✶

This small winery, the southernmost in the country, is located on an oasis on Kibbutz Neot Smadar in the Jordan Valley, 60 kilometers north of Eilat. The winery released its first wines from the 2001 vintage and since its inception has relied entirely on organically raised grapes of Cabernet Sauvignon, Merlot, Chardonnay, Sauvignon Blanc and Muscat Canelli, all grown in vineyards on the kibbutz. Due to the unique climate conditions, theirs is invariably the earliest harvest in the country. The winery is currently producing about 4,000 bottles annually.

NEOT SMADAR, CABERNET SAUVIGNON, 2007: Ruby toward garnet, with soft, almost unfelt tannins and hints of spicy wood. Opens to show berry, currant and black cherry aromas. A simple but pleasant quaffer. Drink now. Score 84.

NEOT SMADAR, CABERNET SAUVIGNON, 2006: Medium-bodied, with soft tannins, hints of spicy wood and appealing currant and berry fruits. A simple quaffer. Drink up. Score 80.

NEOT SMADAR, MERLOT, 2007: Light garnet, medium-bodied, with chunky tannins and with a basic berry-cherry personality. A simple country-style wine. Drink up. Score 79.

NEOT SMADAR, MERLOT, 2006: Ruby toward garnet, medium-bodied, with soft tannins and gentle spicy wood notes. On the nose and palate appealing berry, currant and black cherry fruits. Drink up. Score 84.

NEOT SMADAR, CHARDONNAY, 2007: The color of damp straw, medium-bodied, with good balancing acidity to highlight citrus, apple and tropical fruits. Drink up. Score 82.

NEOT SMADAR, SAUVIGNON BLANC, 2008: Light straw in color, light-to medium-bodied, with aromas and flavors of green apples, citrus and freshly mown grass. Drink up. Score 85.

NEOT SMADAR, MUSCAT DESSERT WINE, 2004: Light- to medium-bodied, generously sweet, with good balancing acidity and appealing dried-apricot, apple and peach fruits. Drink up. Score 85.

Nevo ✳

Founded in 2002 by Nevo Chazan and located on Moshav Mata, not far from Jerusalem, the winery produced 2,000 bottles from the 2007 vintage and about twice that from the 2008 vintage. The wines will be kosher from the 2010 vintage.

NEVO, CABERNET SAUVIGNON, 2007: Not showing as well as when first tasted, the once-appealing garnet color now turning to adobe brick. A pleasant enough country-style wine, medium-bodied, with chunky tannins and notes of cinnamon from the wood. Opens to reveal blackberry and blueberry fruits, those taking on notes of sour-ball candies from mid-palate on. Drink up. Score 81.

NEVO, MERLOT, SAPIR, 2007: Garnet colored, medium-bodied, with soft tannins and notes of spicy wood that run throughout, opens to show a basic berry–black cherry personality. A light medicinal aroma from first attack to the finish. Nothing complex here. Drink up. Score 74.

NEVO, CHOSHEN, 2007: A medium-bodied blend of Cabernet Sauvignon and Merlot (60% and 40% respectively). Aged in second- and third-year *barriques*, with chunky, country-style tannins and a good deal of Brett that adds a stinky note, that hiding the black fruits that fail to make themselves felt. Score 70.

Noga ∗

Owned by the Harari family and located between Gedera and Moshav Kidron on the Southern Plains, the winery's first release was of 2,000 bottles from the 2004 vintage. Current production is about 5,000 bottles annually and those under two labels, Noga and Tom, both blends of Cabernet Sauvignon and Merlot.

NOGA, 2007: Ruby toward garnet, a medium-bodied, softly tannic blend of Merlot and Cabernet Sauvignon. Opens to show berry, black cherry and licorice notes. A pleasant quaffer. Drink up. Score 84.

NOGA, 2006: An oak-aged blend of 80% Merlot and 20% Cabernet Sauvignon. Medium-bodied, with soft tannins, a round and easy-to-drink wine with currant, berry and black cherry fruits on a lightly spicy background. Drink up. Score 83.

TOM, 2007: Light spicy and toasted white bread notes from its oak-aging, medium-bodied, with black fruits and an overlay of vanilla. A simple country-style wine. Drink up. Score 83.

TOM, 2006: A dark garnet, medium-bodied blend of 80% Cabernet Sauvignon and 20% Merlot, reflecting its oak-aging with spices and vanilla and showing appealing currant and black cherry fruits. Past its peak. Drink up. Score 80.

Odem Mountain ✳✳✳✳

Founded by the Alfasi family in 2003, the winery is situated in a modern facility on Moshav Odem in the northern Golan Heights. It relies primarily on grapes grown in its own vineyards – one of which is organic – those supplemented by grapes from other vineyards on the Golan, in the Upper Galilee and in the Judean Hills. Currently producing wines based on Cabernet Sauvignon, Merlot, Shiraz and Cabernet Franc, production for the 2008 vintage was about 75,000 bottles and from the 2009 vintage about 85,000.

The top-of-the-line series are Alfasi and Reserve, and mid-range series are Odem Mountain and Volcanic. The wines have been kosher since the 2007 vintage.

Alfasi

ALFASI, 2007: Oak-aged for 24 months in a combination of new and older *barriques*, ruby toward garnet in color, a full-bodied blend of Cabernet Sauvignon and Merlot. With spices and vanilla from the oak in which it aged, those parting to reveal blackberries, purple plums and cassis, the fruits supported nicely by peppery notes along with a hint of a Mediterranean bouquet garni. Round and rich. Drink now–2014, perhaps longer. Score 90. K

ALFASI, 2006: Dark, almost inky garnet in color, full-bodied, with still-firm tannins just starting to settle in but already showing fine balance and structure. The usual Alfasi blend of 60% Cabernet Sauvignon and 40% Merlot, oak-aged for 24 months in partly used *barriques* and opening in the glass to reveal fine blackcurrant and wild berry fruits, those backed up by notes of freshly cut herbs and bittersweet chocolate. Long and generous. Drink now–2014, perhaps longer. Score 90.

ALFASI, 2005: An oak-aged blend of 60% Cabernet Sauvignon and 40% Merlot. Dark garnet, medium- to full-bodied, with soft tannins integrating nicely and unfolding on the palate to show a generous array of ripe currant and berry fruits, those supported by hints of sweet herbs and green olives. Drink now. Score 88.

ALFASI, CABERNET-MERLOT, 2004: This oak-aged blend of 60% Cabernet Sauvignon and 40% Merlot shows fine balance between still-firm tannins and spicy wood, those yielding in the glass to reveal black fruits, sweet herbs and, on the long finish, hints of green olives and anise. Sliding past its peak. Drink up. Score 88.

Reserve

RESERVE, CABERNET SAUVIGNON, 2007: Full-bodied, with soft tannins integrating nicely and reflecting its 15 months in oak with notes of smoky vanilla. On the nose and palate traditional blackcurrant and blackberry fruits, those complemented by notes of roasted herbs and tobacco. Drink now. Score 88. K

RESERVE, CABERNET SAUVIGNON, 2006: Dark garnet toward royal purple in color, made entirely from Cabernet Sauvignon grapes, medium- to full-bodied, and oak-aged for 15 months. Opens with a low but appealing fruity and floral nose. Goes on to show blackcurrants and purple plums, those matched nicely by hints of spicy and vanilla-rich wood. Tannins and alcohol rise together on the finish, but given a bit more bottle time this may well vanish and give way to hints of raspberries and cranberries. Drink now. Score 88.

RESERVE, CABERNET SAUVIGNON, 2005: Deep garnet toward royal purple, medium- to full-bodied, with generous, soft tannins and spicy wood in good balance with blackberry, currant and cassis fruits. On the moderately long finish, hints of cedar and freshly cut herbs. Drink up. Score 90.

RESERVE, MERLOT, 2008: Dark garnet, medium- to full-bodied with soft, gently caressing tannins and a moderate hand with the oak. On the nose and palate currants, wild berries, black cherries and a gentle hint of licorice on the long finish. Drink now–2015. Score 90. K

RESERVE, MERLOT, 2007: Aged in new oak, mostly French for one year and then wisely transferred to used oak (two years old) for an additional six months, showing a well-tempered hand with the wood. Medium- to full-bodied, soft and round, with just a hint of earthy minerals to support blackberry, black cherry and currant notes. On the finish appealing hints of black olives and bitter herbs. Drink now–2015, perhaps longer. Score 90. K

RESERVE, MERLOT, 2006: Aged in new French *barriques* for 15 months, dark ruby toward garnet, showing blueberries and black cherries on first attack, those yielding comfortably to notes of licorice and near-sweet tobacco. Long and generous. Drink now. Score 89.

RESERVE, MERLOT, 2005: Garnet toward purple, reflecting ten months in oak with spicy and vanilla overlays and showing appealing berry and cassis fruits. Medium-bodied, with soft tannins integrating nicely and with a moderately long finish. Past its peak. Drink up. Score 85.

RESERVE, CABERNET SAUVIGNON-MERLOT, 2006: Oak-aged for 15 months, this blend of 60% Cabernet Sauvignon and 40% Merlot shows generous but gentle spicy wood in fine balance with soft tannins and acidity. Opens to reveal currant, berry and black cherry fruits on a background of chocolate, sweet spices and tarry notes. Long and generous. Drink now. Score 89.

RESERVE, CABERNET SAUVIGNON-MERLOT, 2005: Deep ruby toward garnet, medium-bodied, with soft tannins integrating nicely with spicy and vanilla-rich wood. On the nose and palate, berry, black cherry and cassis, those backed up by sweet herbs and a hint of anise. Moderately long and complex. Drink up. Score 89.

Odem Mountain

ODEM MOUNTAIN, CABERNET SAUVIGNON, 2008: Dark garnet with orange reflections, full-bodied, a soft, caressing and mouth-filling wine, its elements coming together very nicely and already showing generous blackberry, blackcurrant and plum fruits, those on a lightly spicy background. Long and generous. Drink now–2015. Score 89. K

ODEM MOUNTAIN, CABERNET SAUVIGNON, 2006: Dark garnet, medium- to full-bodied, gently tannic but nicely concentrated, showing generous blackcurrant and purple plum fruits, those well matched by hints of mocha and espresso coffee. Ripe, round and moderately long. Drink now. Score 86.

ODEM MOUNTAIN, CABERNET SAUVIGNON, 2005: Dark ruby toward garnet, medium-bodied, with soft tannins integrating nicely and well balanced by spicy oak. On the tangy nose and palate, traditional Cabernet blackcurrant and wild berry fruits. Drink up. Score 86.

ODEM MOUNTAIN, MERLOT, 2008: Medium- to full-bodied, with soft, gently gripping tannins and notes of cedar and spicy oak integrating nicely with blackberry, blueberry and cassis fruits. Round and generous and, in the background, gentle hints of licorice and star anise. Drink now–2014. Score 88. K

ODEM MOUNTAIN, MERLOT, 2007: Oak-aged for 18 months, a dark, well-extracted wine. Medium- to full-bodied and with fine concentration, opens to reveal blueberry, blackberry and cassis notes, those supported by an appealing hint of Oriental spices. Long, mouth-filling and luxuriant. Drink now. Score 90. K

ODEM MOUNTAIN, MERLOT, 2006: Medium-dark garnet, medium- to full-bodied, with soft, near-sweet tannins. Showing generous berry and black cherry fruits matched nicely by hints of cigar tobacco, tar and bittersweet chocolate. Drink now. Score 85.

ODEM MOUNTAIN, SYRAH, 2008: Super-dark, almost inky garnet in color, full-bodied with fine balance between wood, acidity, fruits and an overall peppery note that runs comfortably through the wine. On first attack blueberries and spicy wood, those yielding comfortably to blackberries and appealing hints of roasted herbs on the long finish. Drink now–2015. Score 90. K

ODEM MOUNTAIN, CABERNET SAUVIGNON-SYRAH, 2006: This blend of 70% Cabernet and 30% Syrah is showing spicy, floral and earthy aromas and flavors on first attack, those opening to reveal currant, berry and black cherry fruits. Finishing with appealing leathery and cigar-box hints. Drink now. Score 85.

Volcanic

VOLCANIC, CABERNET SAUVIGNON, 2008: Deep ruby toward garnet, oak-aged for 12 months, showing gently gripping tannins and a "just-right" note of sweet cedar. Opens in the glass to reveal a well-tuned mélange of black and red fruits, those with an appealing overlay of red licorice. Generous and mouth-filling. Drink now–2014. Score 90. K

VOLCANIC, CABERNET SAUVIGNON, 2007: Opens with a lovely fruit and chocolate-rich nose, and in the glass reveals ripe, near-jammy black fruits, those well balanced by spicy oak and notes of roasted herbs. Oak-aged for ten months. Not overly complex but very comfortable to drink. Drink now. Score 87. K

VOLCANIC, CABERNET SAUVIGNON, 2005: Garnet-red, medium-bodied, softly tannic and generously fruity, this unoaked blend of 87% Cabernet Sauvignon and 13% Merlot was made from organically grown grapes. On the nose and palate blackberry and currant fruits, a hint of wood and abundant acidity that makes the wine refreshing but somewhat one-dimensional. Drink up. Score 85.

VOLCANIC, MERLOT, 2008: Deep royal purple in color, medium- to full-bodied, reflecting its 12 months in half-new, half-two-year-old *barriques* with gentle notes of spicy wood. On the nose and palate a generous array of blackberries, raspberries, cassis and licorice. On the generous finish an appealing hint of bitter almonds. Drink now. Score 89. K

VOLCANIC, MERLOT, 2007: Oak-aged for ten months, showing garnet with a hint of burnt Sienna, opening on a bitter note that lingers too heavily despite appealing black fruits. Somewhat firm chunky tannins give the wine a country-style personality. Drink now. Score 85. K

VOLCANIC, SHIRAZ, 2008: Dark garnet toward royal purple, a concentrated and full-bodied wine with its once-firm tannins now integrating nicely with notes of vanilla and cinnamon from the *barriques* in which it aged. On the nose and palate plums, wild berries, cassis and, on the long finish with tannins rising, appealing notes of anise and leather. Deep, long and complex. Drink now–2015. Score 91. K

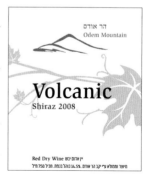

VOLCANIC, CABERNET SAUVIGNON-MERLOT, 2007: Medium- to full-bodied, dark garnet, with generous wood and rustic, chunky tannins, opens in the glass to show blackberry, plum and spicy notes. An appealing country-style wine. Drink up. Score 87. K

VOLCANIC, CHARDONNAY, 2010: Developed *sur lie* in oak for about five months, showing light golden straw in color and nicely aromatic. Opens in the glass to reveal aromas and flavors of grapefruit, melon and citrus peel, those leading to a long, gently spicy finish. Drink now–2013. Score 88. K

VOLCANIC, CHARDONNAY, 2008: Oak-aged for about six months, light gold in color, with citrus, tropical fruits and notes of bitter citrus peel complemented nicely by a note of flinty minerals. Drink up. Score 87. K

Or HaGanuz ✴✴

Founded in 2005 in the Upper Galilee village of Or HaGanuz, the winery lies about six kilometers north west of Safed and at the foothills of Mt. Meron. An interesting story behind the founding of the winery, as the community is one of highly orthodox Jews, the name of the winery and village taken from the kabbalah – *Or HaGanuz*, meaning "Hidden Light," referring to what many consider the first act of creation. The winery is currently producing 140,000 bottles annually, many of which are intended to bring the American Orthodox crowd into the world of wine. The winery is also a "service winery," allowing other winemakers to use their facilities to make wine under their own labels.

OR HAGANUZ, CABERNET SAUVIGNON, MERON, 2009: A medium- to full-bodied blend of 80% Cabernet Sauvignon and 20% Merlot. Labeled as semi-dry but with far-too-generous sweetness, that overshadowing the red fruits, prunes and raisins that are here. Said to be "in the style of Port" but I could not help but smile in thinking that this might be the modernists' answer to Manischewitz. Drink up. Score 74. K

OR HAGANUZ, CABERNET SAUVIGNON, SAHAR, PREMIUM, 2007: Blended with about 12% Merlot, oak-aged for 12 months, showing garnet toward royal purple in color. Medium- to full-bodied, with soft tannins and generous red fruits, an easy-to-drink quaffer but somewhat one dimensional. An entry-level wine. Drink now. Score 83. K

OR HAGANUZ, CABERNET SAUVIGNON, NAMURA, 2009: Medium- to full-bodied, garnet in color, reflecting its development for 14 months in French oak and showing soft tannins and hints of spicy cedar. On the nose and palate crushed red and black berries, cassis and notes of freshly cut herbs. Easy to drink. Drink now. Score 85. K

OR HAGANUZ, CABERNET SAUVIGNON, NAMURA, 2007: Made entirely from Cabernet Sauvignon grapes, oak-aged for 24 months, showing dark garnet, full-bodied and firmly tannic with perhaps too-generous spicy wood tending to hide the black fruits that lie underneath and never make themselves fully felt. Drink up. Score 84. K

OR HAGANUZ, CABERNET SAUVIGNON, 2007: Blended with 15% of Merlot, an oak-aged wine showing full-bodied, with soft tannins and opening to reveal wild berry, black cherry and cassis, those supported by notes of white pepper and licorice. Drink up. Score 84. K

OR HAGANUZ, MERLOT, NAMURA, 2009: Oak-aged for 14 months, deep garnet toward royal purple in color, with somewhat chunky tannins giving the wine a rustic note. Medium- to full-bodied, opens in the glass to reveal stewed fruits, crushed berries and notes of earthy herbaceousness. Drink now. Score 84. K

OR HAGANUZ, CABERNET FRANC, 2009: Oak-aged for 14 months, showing medium-dark garnet with a robe of royal purple. On the nose and palate purple plums and blackberries, all with perhaps too-generous overlays of cigar tobacco and roasted herbs. Drink now. Score 84. K

OR HAGANUZ, BARBERA, AMUKA, 2009: Medium-bodied, softly tannic, showing generous sweet cherries, plums and blackberry fruits, those on a background of light tannins and hints of exotic spices. Soft, round and fresh, a pleasant quaffer. Drink now. Score 86. K

OR HAGANUZ, ELIMA, 2009: A blend of 75% Cabernet Sauvignon and 25% Cabernet Franc, said to "contain no sulfites." Dark garnet, with a hint of adobe brick, opens with a somewhat medicinal aroma but that blows off quickly enough to reveal a medium- to full-bodied wine with chunky tannins that provide a rustic note. On the nose and palate some black fruits those showing a somewhat stewed nature and sitting on a background of earthy herbaceousness. Drink now. Score 80. K

OR HAGANUZ, SELECT, NAMURA, 2009: A medium-bodied blend of Cabernet Sauvignon, Merlot and Shiraz (48%, 32% and 20% respectively). Showing dark garnet, reflecting its 18 months in French oak with soft tannins and generous notes of sweet-and-spicy cedarwood. Turns somewhat earthy on the finish. Drink now. Score 84. K

OR HAGANUZ, CABERNET SAUVIGNON-MERLOT, HAR SINAI, 2009: Said on the label to be "in the style of Cahors" but I cannot help but wonder who thought that up, as the wines of Cahors are made largely from Malbec and Tannat grapes and can be very tannic and nearly black in color on release. Made from different grapes, medium-, perhaps medium- to full-bodied, with soft tannins and lacking concentration or intensity, the personality of this release reminds more of a young cru Beaujolais wine. On the nose and palate black cherries, wild berries and a hint of Mediterranean herbs. A simple but pleasant entry-level wine. Drink now. Score 84. K

OR HAGANUZ, CABERNET SAUVIGNON-MERLOT-SHIRAZ, SAFSUFA, 2007: A light-garnet, medium-bodied blend of Cabernet Sauvignon, Merlot and Shiraz (48%, 32% and 20% respectively). Oak-aged for 18 months but surprisingly showing super-soft tannins that go barely noticed, opens to show forward berry, cherry and cassis fruits.

Perhaps a good entry-level wine but somewhat one-dimensional and fails to excite. Drink up. Score 84. K

OR HAGANUZ, MERLOT-CARIGNAN-PETIT VERDOT, AMUKA, 2009: Based on 60% Merlot, 30% Carignan and 10% Petite Verdot, a young, fruity red with soft tannins and an appealing array of blackberry, blueberry and citrus peel, those complemented nicely by notes of milk chocolate and white pepper. Drink now–2013. Score 86. K

Pelter ✶✶✶✶✶

The Pelter winery was established in 2002 on Moshav Zofit in Central Israel and since 2005 has been located on Kibbutz Ein Zivan on the Golan Heights. Winemaker Tal Pelter, who studied oenology and worked at several wineries in Australia draws on Cabernet Sauvignon, Merlot, Cabernet Franc, Shiraz, Petit Verdot, Grenache, Tempranillo, Semillon, Sauvignon Blanc, Gewurztraminer and Chardonnay grapes, mostly from the Golan and the Upper Galilee with some coming from the Jerusalem Mountains. The winery, one of only four in the country to produce a sparkling wine, releases wines in two series: T-Selection and Pelter. The winery has introduced a new flagship wine, "I", from the 2008 vintage. Production from the 2002 vintage was about 4,000 bottles. Growth has been well planned, and current production is about 85,000 bottles annually.

This is the kind of winery that critics most enjoy, the wines rising in both quality and interest on a regular basis. More than that, since its inception the winery has clearly reflected the philosophy of its winemaker. In my 2005 and 2006 books, the Pelter winery earned three stars; in the 2007 and 2008 books it moved up to four stars, and since the 2009 edition has earned the top rating of five stars, that indicating a world-class winery, regularly producing excellent wines. The winery comfortably holds on to its five stars and continues to demonstrate itself as one of the best and most exciting in the country.

Pelter "I"

PELTER, "I", 2008: The new flagship wine of the winery, a Bordeaux blend of Cabernet Sauvignon, Merlot, Cabernet Franc and Petit Verdot in approximately equal parts, those aged in French oak, deeply extracted, opening with raspberries and chocolate on the nose, going on to a complex array of aromas and flavors, among which currants, plums, black olives and citrus peel. Despite the blend, not so much a Bordeaux wine as a deeply elegant wine with a distinctly Mediterranean note. Full-bodied and concentrated, needs time for its elements to come together. Approachable now but best from 2013–2018, perhaps longer. Score 94.

T-Selection

T-SELECTION, CABERNET SAUVIGNON, 2009: Deep, youthful royal purple in color, destined for 20 months of oak-aging, full-bodied, with soft but pleasingly chewy tannins. On first attack blackberries and currants, those parting to make way for aromas and flavors of blackberries, plums and wild berries, those on a lightly spicy background. A graceful, multi-layered and complex wine that lingers on and on. Approachable on release but best from 2013–2020. Tentative Score 92–94.

T-SELECTION, CABERNET SAUVIGNON, 2008: Full-bodied, dark garnet in color, with soft, gently caressing tannins and notes of spicy wood in fine balance with fruits. On first attack black and red berries and chocolate, those yielding comfortably to blackcurrants and notes of mint and freshly clipped Mediterranean herbs. Long and generous. Drink now–2018. Score 94.

T-SELECTION, CABERNET SAUVIGNON, 2007: Garnet toward royal purple, full-bodied, with silky smooth tannins integrating beautifully. Powerful and concentrated but not at all a "blockbuster." Opens with blackcurrant and berry fruits, those yielding to notes of ripe plums and, from first sip to the long finish, notes of raisins, earthy minerals and anise. Ripe and supple. Drink now–2017. Score 92.

T-SELECTION, CABERNET SAUVIGNON, 2006: Showing much as at earlier tasting and drinking beautifully now. With 20 months in new French *barriques*, a generously oaked wine, near-sweet because of its 15% alcohol content. Dark garnet in color, with generous velvety tannins that match the oak. Opens in the glass to reveal blackcurrants and black cherries, those along with tarry and spicy notes, and, rising on the very long finish, notes of sweet chewing tobacco. A California-style blockbuster but yielding in the glass to show its own kind of muscular elegance. Drink now–2015. Score 93.

T-SELECTION, CABERNET SAUVIGNON, 2004: Dark, dense and concentrated, this spicy and complex red shows muscular and earthy currants and blackberries, backed up by herbal and spicy oak, all with a generous dose of firm tannins. Turns smooth and polished as it opens to reveal tempting mineral, sage and cedar flavors. Long and generous, with a promise for true elegance. Drink now. Score 92.

T-SELECTION, MERLOT, MIA, 2008: A special cuvée made for Chloé-lys restaurant in Ramat Gan. Dark royal purple in color, with generous near-sweet tannins and reflecting its 14 months in French oak with gentle spicy overlays. Full-bodied, with soft tannins, concentrated but round and smooth, with generous wild berries, blackberries and cassis notes. On the long finish notes of tobacco and grilled herbs. Drink now–2017. Score 91.

T-SELECTION, MERLOT, 2004: Big and bold, full-bodied, with firm tannins that take time to recede in the glass and then open to reveal blackberry, cassis and smoky oak on a generously spicy background that takes on depth and richness toward the long finish, on which a burst of fruit makes itself felt. Drink now. Score 90.

T-SELECTION, SHIRAZ, 2006: Oak-aged for 18 months, dark ruby, full-bodied but with such fine balance between tannins, oak, acidity and fruits that it seems to almost float on the palate. On first attack generous near-jammy blackberry and currant fruits, those yielding comfortably to plum, licorice and spices, all of which carry on to a long and generous finish. Drink now–2013. Score 91.

T-SELECTION, SHIRAZ, 2005: Dark crimson in color, opening with lightly sweet vanilla notes on the nose, this full-bodied, round and elegant wine shows a generous array of plum and currant fruits, freshly tanned leather and an appealing, light earthy-herbaceousness. The soft but gripping tannins linger well into the long finish. Look as well for a tempting hint of bittersweet chocolate developing. Drink now. Score 91.

T-SELECTION, SHIRAZ, 2004: Developed for 18 months in French oak, and showing fine balance and structure. Full-bodied, deeply tannic and concentrated enough to be thought of as chewy, but under that, red currants, plums and red berries along with black pepper, rosemary, thyme and a very appealing hint of peppermint. Fruits rise nicely on the long finish. Might easily be taken for a fine Australian Shiraz. Drink now. Score 91.

T-SELECTION, PINOT NOIR, 2009: Dark cherry red toward garnet, medium- to full-bodied, with silky tannins. Soft and round, with wild berry and blueberry fruits coming together nicely with hints of toasty oak. Supple, well balanced and concentrated with a long and generous finish, that with an appealing note of bitter almonds. Drink now–2016. Score 92.

T-SELECTION, PINOT NOIR, 2008: Showing every bit as well as at barrel tastings. A robust and concentrated wine, medium- to full-bodied, deep garnet in color, with generous soft and gently caressing tannins. On first attack wild berries and black cherry fruits, those yielding to notes of blueberries, white pepper and a note of *garrigue*. From mid-palate on appealing notes of cinnamon and freshly cut herbs. A captivating and distinctly Mediterranean wine, perhaps more interesting than "great." Drink from release–2015. Score 92.

T-SELECTION, PINOT NOIR, 2006: Dark cherry-red toward garnet, medium- to full-bodied, with a generous 14.5% alcohol content, but don't let that throw you off because all is here in fine balance and enviable structure. Ripe and distinctive in flavor, with blackberry, currant, raspberry and floral aromas and flavors supported by minerals and a hint of raw beef all coming together beautifully with delicate spices. A multi-layered and complex wine. Drink now–2013. Score 92.

T-SELECTION, CABERNET FRANC, 2009: Dark ruby toward garnet, full-bodied with still-firm tannins that need time to integrate. On the nose black fruits and freshly tanned leather, and on the palate currants, freshly picked Mediterranean herbs and earthy minerals. Even now showing fine depth and length. This one will be approachable on release but best only from 2013–2019, perhaps longer. Tentative Score 92–94.

T-SELECTION, CABERNET FRANC, 2008: Having lost the first flush of youth and with its elements now coming together beautifully. Dark cherry red toward garnet, full bodied, and with gently gripping tannins, opens in the glass to reveal aromas and flavors of blackberries, blueberries and red currants, those on a background of cigar tobacco and roasted herbs. Finishes with an appealing earthy-mineral overlay. Approachable and enjoyable now but best from mid-2012–2018. Score 92.

T-SELECTION, CABERNET FRANC, 2007: Dark ruby toward garnet, medium- to full-bodied (leaning to the full), reflecting its 14 months in French oak with now well-integrated, gently chewy tannins and a note of spicy oak. On the nose and palate blueberries, blackberries, raspberries and freshly picked herbs. On the long finish tannins rise along with a tempting note of milk chocolate. Drink now–2014. Score 92.

T-SELECTION, CABERNET FRANC, 2006: Ruby toward royal purple in color, full-bodied, with silky tannins and a gentle hand with the oak. Showing gorgeous plum, blackberry and floral aromas and flavors on a background of sweet spices and, coming in on the finish, a tempting hint of semi-sweet chocolate. Long and generous. Drink now. Score 92.

T-SELECTION, CABERNET FRANC, 2005: This full-bodied wine reflects its 14 months in new French oak with spicy wood and mouth-coating tannins, both integrating nicely. A generous array of black fruits on first attack, those opening to reveal overlays of fresh Mediterranean herbs, and finally, on the long finish, espresso coffee, dark chocolate and the barest but tantalizing hint of crushed raspberries. Drink now–2013. Score 92.

T-SELECTION, CABERNET FRANC, 2004: Deep, almost impenetrable in color, lush and elegant with a rich array of ripe raspberry, cassis and berry fruits, those matched nicely by herbal and bittersweet chocolate aromas and flavors. Firm tannins, especially on the finish, but with just the right levels of French oak influence and both balance and structure that bode well for the future. Drink now. Score 91.

T-SELECTION, CABERNET FRANC, 2003: Oak-aged for 14 months in new French *barriques*. Smooth, rich and supple, with ripe plum, currant and berry fruits together with an array of mocha, tobacco and espresso coffee, all complemented well by a hint of vanilla-scented oak. Tannins and fruits rise on the finish. Showing its elegance nicely. Drink now. Score 90.

T-SELECTION, PETIT VERDOT, 2009: Super-dark garnet, a rich, concentrated wine opening with currants, blackberries and mocha, going on to show notes of bittersweet chocolate and, on the long, long finish, hints of anise and candied ginger. Approachable on release but far better to give this one the time it needs to show its smooth and polished elegance. Best 2013–2019. Score 93.

T-SELECTION, PETIT VERDOT, 2008: Oak-aged for 14 months, full-bodied, with fine concentration and gently mouth-coating tannins and notes of spicy cedar. On first attack blackcurrants and blackberries, those yielding comfortably to notes of purple plums and citrus peel and, to add to its charms, underlying hints of ripe Kalamata olives and a potpourri of Oriental spices. Fruit forward, firm and concentrated at this stage and even now with a super-long finish. Give this one some time in the bottle and it will show earthy minerals and (as an educated guess) a tantalizing note of licorice. Drink now–2019. Score 93.

T-SELECTION, PETIT VERDOT, 2006: A luxurious wine, deeply concentrated, thick, tannic and complex, showing wild berries, cassis, blackberry and pomegranate fruits, those complemented nicely by notes of cola and ginger, all with a light and tantalizing bitter citrus peel note that runs through to the super-long finish. Unique, expressive and cellar-worthy. Drink now–2017. Score 93.

T-SELECTION, SHIRAZ-GRENACHE, 2009: As always, a blend of 60% Shiraz and 40% Grenache, developed in French oak for 14 months. Dark garnet, medium- to full-bodied (leaning to the full) and gently tannic, opens with a red-fruit nose. On the nose and palate a generous array of cherry and rhubarb fruits, those complemented nicely by notes of green Madagascar peppercorns. Finely tuned balance between wood, acidity and fruits leads to a long and harmonious finish. Drink from release–2016, perhaps longer. Score 90.

T-SELECTION, SHIRAZ-GRENACHE, 2008: A blend of 60% Shiraz and 40% Grenache, oak-aged in primarily French *barriques*. Showing dark ruby toward garnet in color, with soft tannins and gentle spicy oak notes in fine balance with red currant and wild berry fruits. Smooth, round and, on the long finish, hints of cigar tobacco and Mediterranean herbs. Drink now–2015. Score 90.

T-SELECTION, SHIRAZ-GRENACHE, 2006: Opens with a hint of iodine but that blows off quickly to reveal a black-fruit nose. Deep garnet with a hint of clearing at the rim, medium- to full-bodied, with silky tannins and reflecting its 14 months in oak with a gentle spicy touch. Supple and graceful, showing cherry, blueberry and pomegranate fruits all on a background of white pepper, and on the finish hints of leather and star anise. Drink now–2014. Score 93.

T-SELECTION, SHIRAZ-GRENACHE, 2005: Deep, almost inky-garnet in color, full-bodied, with firm tannins integrating nicely. Reflecting its 14 months in French *barriques* with spicy cedar, this blend of 60% Shiraz and 40% Grenache shows concentrated purple plum, blackberry and citrus peel notes on a background of sweet herbs and red licorice. Drink now–2014. Score 92.

T-SELECTION, SHIRAZ-GRENACHE, 2004: Medium-dark garnet toward purple, full-bodied, with generous tannins well balanced by the influence of aging in French oak casks for 14 months. Distinctive, ripe and luxurious, with near-sweet plum, blueberry and citrus peel intertwined beautifully with spicy, herbal and pomegranate aromas and flavors. Drink now. Score 91.

T-SELECTION, SHIRAZ-GRENACHE, 2003: Dense purple in color, this rich, big and juicy wine is absolutely loaded with blackberry and plum fruits, those set off nicely by hints of cloves, coffee, citrus peel and black pepper, all on super-soft tannins. Harmonious, generous, long and mouth-coating. Drink now. Score 91.

T-SELECTION, SEMILLON, 2009: Developed in French oak for three months, at this stage showing gentle spicy wood to highlight fig, tangerine and mineral notes. Still a baby and a few years away from release, which is a wise move because as this one continues to develop the oak will recede and secondary aromas and flavors will arise – those including pine nuts, white asparagus and pears, all with a gentle overlay of sage and, if my estimate is accurate, a creamy finish. Drink now–2018, perhaps longer. Score 92.

Pelter

PELTER, CABERNET SAUVIGNON-SHIRAZ, 2009: Full-bodied, with soft, gently caressing tannins and showing dark, youthful royal purple in color. Opens with a red-fruit nose, going on to reveal currant, blackberry and licorice aromas and flavors and on the long, velvety finish a hint of smoky oak. Drink now–2016, perhaps longer. Score 91.

PELTER, CABERNET SAUVIGNON-SHIRAZ, 2008: Dark garnet toward royal purple, a big full-bodied wine, one that is ripe, soft, round and well focused. On first attack blackberries and plums, those followed by notes of licorice, smoke and spices. Fine soft tannins and gentle wood integrating beautifully. Drink now–2017. Score 91.

PELTER, CABERNET SAUVIGNON-SHIRAZ, 2007: Dark garnet in color, with generous spicy wood in fine balance with soft tannins and fruits. Full-bodied, opening with notes of spicy wood and black fruits, those yielding in the glass to wild berries, red currants and earthy minerals, all on a background that hints gently of cigar tobacco and licorice. Long and mouth-filling. Drink now–2015. Score 92.

PELTER, CABERNET SAUVIGNON-SHIRAZ, 2006: Oak-aged for 18 months in 30% new oak, dark garnet in color, with generous spicy oak opening on the nose, but that residing nicely to show an appealing array of cherry, raspberry, currant and peppery notes, the soft tannins caressing as the full-bodied wine fills the mouth. With fine balance and structure, showing elegance and length. Drink now–2013. Score 92.

PELTER, CABERNET SAUVIGNON-SHIRAZ, 2005: Deep ruby toward garnet, full-bodied, with a generous backbone of wood and tannins, those integrating nicely and in fine balance with fruits. On the nose and palate blackcurrants, blackberries, raspberries and black cherries, all supported by appealing earthy and herbal undercurrents. Deep, long and smooth. Drink now. Score 91.

PELTER, CABERNET SAUVIGNON-SHIRAZ, 2004: Aged in American oak for 18 months, this blend of 50% each of Cabernet Sauvignon and Shiraz shows a medium-dark garnet color, a strong acidic backbone and appealing spices and vanilla from the wood, none of which hold back layers of blackberry, cherry, herbal and earthy aromas and flavors. Good concentration, ripeness and smoothness lead to a long and generous finish, on which one will find appealing hints of minted bittersweet chocolate. Drink now. Score 91.

PELTER, CABERNET SAUVIGNON-SHIRAZ, 2003: Deep ruby toward garnet, full-bodied, with gently caressing tannins, and on the nose and palate blackberry and blackcurrant fruits, those supported well by hints of espresso coffee and dark chocolate. Tannins and wood rise on the finish. Still drinking very nicely but showing signs of full maturity. Drink now. Score 89.

PELTER, SHIRAZ-CARIGNAN, 2006: A blend of 60% Shiraz and 40% Carignan, reflecting gentle oak influences from its 14 months in older barrels. Dark garnet, with soft tannins and generous acidity integrating nicely, opening to show plum, wild berry and dark chocolate. Drink now. Score 89.

PELTER, QUARTO, LIMITED EDITION, 2005: A rich Bordeaux blend of Cabernet Sauvignon, Merlot, Cabernet Franc and Petit Verdot. Deep royal purple, full-bodied, with still-firm tannins just starting to settle down. Opens to show berry and cassis fruits on a lightly spicy background, with a long red fruit finish. Drink now. Score 90.

PELTER, TRIO, 2009: A blend of 70% Cabernet Sauvignon and 15% each of Merlot and Cabernet Franc. Garnet toward royal purple, gently tannic, reflecting its 14 months in French oak with hints of lead pencils and vanilla. On the nose and palate blackberries, blueberries and cassis, those complemented by notes of roasted herbs and earthy minerals. Tannins and fruits rise nicely on the long finish. Drink now–2014, perhaps longer. Score 90.

PELTER, TRIO, 2008: Dark cherry red toward garnet, a medium- to full-bodied blend of Cabernet Sauvignon, Merlot and Cabernet Franc. Reflects its oak-aging with notes of sweet and spicy wood, showing soft tannins and lively acidity. Opens to show aromas and flavors of currants, red and black berries and, on the long finish, a bouquet garni of dried herbs. Drink now–2013. Score 90.

PELTER, TRIO, 2007: Dark cherry toward garnet in color, a blend of 70% Cabernet Sauvignon and 15% each of Merlot and Cabernet Franc. Reflecting its 14 months in used *barriques*, shows a gentle influence of spicy wood and soft, gently mouth-coating tannins that highlight red currant, raspberry and red cherry notes. Soft, round and generous, a medium-bodied wine with a hint of eucalyptus on the moderately long finish. As good with grilled fish or seafood as with small cuts of beef, pork or lamb. Drink now. Score 90.

PELTER, TRIO, 2006: A blend of 70% Cabernet Sauvignon and 15% each of Merlot and Cabernet Franc. Dark ruby toward garnet, medium- to full-bodied, showing gentle spicy oak and soft tannins that yield to show currant, red and black berries and cherries on a light earthy-mineral background. Long and mouth-filling. Drink now. Score 91.

PELTER, ROSÉ, 2010: Baby-blanket pink in color, made entirely from Tempranillo grapes that were allowed 12 hours of skin contact. Medium-bodied, with a bare and tantalizing hint of sweetness that plays on the palate, that set off nicely by crisply balancing acidity. Opens with aromas and flavors of raspberries, goes on to reveal notes of dried citrus, glazed pears and a light spicy note. Well balanced and elegant. Drink now–2013. Score 90.

PELTER, ROSÉ, 2009: Made entirely from Tempranillo grapes, those allowed 12 hours of skin contact, showing salmon pink toward orange in color. Light- to medium-bodied, with fresh aromas of blueberries, raspberries and strawberries, the wine off-dry but crisp and refreshing. Not a frivolous little rosé but one with enough complexity to grab the attention. Drink now. Score 88.

PELTER, CHARDONNAY, 2010: As it is every year an unoaked white, damp golden straw in color, medium-bodied and opening to show an appealing array of citrus, tropical fruits and white peaches, all coming together as a refreshing and elegant whole. Drink now. Score 90.

PELTER, CHARDONNAY, 2009: Unoaked, light golden straw in color, medium-bodied, with fine balancing acidity. Muted when first poured, opens in the glass to delight first with notes of minerals and tropical fruits, then with pears and guava fruits and finally with notes of ripe white peaches. Surprisingly complex for an unoaked white, not so much a lively wine as an elegant one. Drink now. Score 90.

PELTER, CHARDONNAY, 2008: Unoaked to show off the wine's rich mineral, summer fruits, kiwis and peach pits. Medium-bodied, with good balancing acidity. Perhaps not as lively as one expects of an unoaked Chardonnay, but showing a generous share of elegance. Drink now. Score 90.

PELTER, CHARDONNAY, 2007: Golden straw in color, light- to medium-bodied and unoaked, opens with grapefruit and pineapple notes, those going on to citrus, green apples and pears. Stylish, juicy and long, finishing on a light flinty-mineral note. Drink up. Score 90.

PELTER, SAUVIGNON BLANC, 2010: Light golden straw with green and orange tints, an unoaked, medium-bodied white with fine balancing acidity. On first attack navel oranges and red grapefruit, those making way for guava and mineral notes that linger nicely. Drink now. Score 90.

PELTER, SAUVIGNON BLANC, 2009: Unoaked to maintain the natural aromas, flavors and liveliness of the wine. The color of damp straw, an "oh wow" white, opening with and maintaining a burst of aromas and flavors, those including tangerine, grapefruit, key lime and papaya, all of which play beautifully on the palate together with notes of fresh acidity and minerals. Fresh and refreshing while simultaneously long and complex. Drink now. Score 91.

PELTER, SAUVIGNON BLANC, 2008: Medium-bodied, light, bright straw in color, unoaked and with generous lively acidity to show off tropical fruits, red grapefruit and notes of grapefruit peel, all on a mineral-rich background. Drink now. Score 89.

PELTER, SAUVIGNON BLANC, 2007: Light, bright and lively, with pears and passion fruit at its core, those opening to show grapefruit, floral and light mineral notes in the background. Unoaked, a fresh and thoroughly appealing wine finishing with an elegant note. Drink up. Score 89.

PELTER, GEWURZTRAMINER, 2010: Off-dry but with fine acidity keeping the wine lively and refreshing. Opens to show traditional Gewurztraminer aromas and flavors of rosewater and litchis, those complemented nicely by notes of green apples, ripe pears and green almonds. Lingers long and comfortably on the palate. Drink now–2014. Score 90.

PELTER, GEWURZTRAMINER, 2009: Traditional Gewurztraminer aromas and flavors on a tantalizingly off-dry background. Spicy and ripe, with apple, pineapple, litchi and citrus peel along with notes of candied almonds, and with fine balancing acidity. On the long finish notes of white peaches and peach pits. Lovely. Drink now–2013. Score 90.

PELTER, GEWURZTRAMINER, 2008: The first wine in the country to use a glass stopper instead of a cork. Full-bodied, with fine balancing acidity and generous yeasty white bread notes, opens on the palate to reveal a charming array of pineapple, litchi and grapefruit, those supported nicely by Oriental spices that come in from mid-palate and then linger long and comfortably. Lovely as an aperitif, with goose liver dishes or as an accompaniment to fruit-based desserts. Drink now. Score 90.

PELTER, GEWURZTRAMINER, 2007: Medium-bodied, showing traditional Gewurztraminer aromas and flavors of rose petals, ginger, litchi and peppermint on first attack, those opening to show generous pineapple fruits, and going to dried apricots. Spicy, just barely off-dry and long, a generous and delightful mouthful. Drink now. Score 90.

PELTER, SEMILLON, 2007: Light, tasty and tangy, with green pineapple, grapefruit and white peach fruits supported nicely by spring flowers and a tantalizing light hint of honey. Long and elegant. Capable of some age. Drink now. Score 91.

PELTER, SEMILLON, 2006: Fermented partly in stainless steel and partly in *barriques* for three months, this straw-colored wine opens with citrus peel and pear aromas and flavors, those going to melon and green apples, all with an appealing spicy overlay. Drink up. Score 90.

PELTER, CHENIN BLANC, 2010: Light, shining gold with a green tint, showing a subtle and tantalizing hint of wood (is that oak, cedar or mahogany that one senses?). Medium- to full-bodied, with a buttery texture opening to reveal aromas and flavors of figs, melon and pears and, from mid-palate on, a tempting hint of honeysuckle. Fine acidity that leads to a long finish on which a note of bitter almonds. Drink from release–2014. Tentative Score 90–92.

PELTER, SPARKLING WINE, 2009: As much a guess as an estimate, for this was tasted not only from components but from the base wines, that is to say the Chardonnay and the Pinot that will eventually be blended to make this traditional Champagne-style sparkling wine. With the Pinot showing just the right hint of micro-oxidation (natural and not man-made) and notes of peppermint along with blackberry and blueberry, and the Chardonnay lively and showing generous acidity, a most promising combination indeed. Destined for release in 2012 or 2013. Drink from release–2018. Tentative Score 90–92.

PELTER, BRUT NATUREL, BLANC DE BLANCS, 2007: In place of the traditional *dosage*, the second fermentation here was started by adding some of the sparkling wine of the last release. Tempting aromas and flavors of lime and grapefruit on a lively and racy background showing notes of vanilla, candied fruits and minerals, those complemented by gentle hints of lightly toasted sourdough bread. Fine and concentrated bubbles that go on and on to a super-long finish. Drink now–2014. Score 92.

PELTER, BLANC DE BLANCS, BRUT, N.V.: Even though this sparkling wine is categorized as non-vintage, it was made entirely from Chardonnay grapes from the 2005 vintage. With sharp bubbles that go on and on, a fresh and aromatic wine, showing gentle notes of yeasty white bread that highlight notes of lime and grapefruit, those complemented by hints of Oriental spices. On the long finish look as well for hints of roasted nuts. Drink now. Score 91.

Special Edition

SPECIAL EDITION, SYRAH, 2009: Dark ruby toward garnet, medium- to full-bodied with silky tannins and a generously aromatic nose. Opens to reveal aromas and flavors of currants, purple plums and notes of fresh herbs and saddle leather. Drink now–2014. Score 89.

Poizner ✦✦✦

Located in Zichron Ya'akov and founded by Yoav Poizner in 2002, the winery released about 2,500 bottles from each of the 2005, 2006 and 2007 vintages. Releases from 2008 are anticipated at about 3,500 bottles. The winery relies on Cabernet Sauvignon, Merlot, Syrah, Carignan and Malbec from their own vineyards. Mourvedre and Petit Verdot will be coming on line shortly, and all of the wines are aged for at least 12 months in French oak.

POIZNER, CABERNET SAUVIGNON, KFAR YUVAL, 2007: An oak-aged blend of 90% Cabernet Sauvignon, 7% Syrah and 3% Merlot. Dark garnet with orange and purple reflections, full-bodied, with gently gripping tannins and spicy wood in fine balance with blackcurrants, cassis and black cherry fruits and, on the generous finish, notes of chocolate with the tannins and fruits rising. Drink now–2013, perhaps longer. Score 89.

POIZNER, CABERNET SAUVIGNON, KFAR YU-VAL, 2006: Dark garnet in color, medium- to full-bodied, with soft tannins integrating nicely and reflecting its 14 months in French oak with gentle spicy and vanilla overlays. Opens to reveal traditional Cabernet aromas and blackcurrant and blackberry fruits, those with an appealing hint of minted chocolate, black licorice and a note of red cherries on the long finish. Drink now. Score 90.

POIZNER, CABERNET SAUVIGNON, 2005: Oak-aged in French *barriques* for 14 months, this blend of 85% Cabernet Sauvignon and 15% Merlot shows fine balance between soft, gently mouth-coating tannins, a light hand with spicy wood and an array of traditional Cabernet, blackcurrant and blackberry fruits. In the background generous hints of lead pencil and green olives. Drink up. Score 88.

POIZNER, MERLOT, 2007: Deep garnet in color, medium-bodied with soft tannins integrating nicely to show a lightly spicy berry-cherry personality. Not complex but very appealing. Drink now. Score 86.

POIZNER, MERLOT, ZICHRON YA'AKOV, 2006: Blended with 4% of Carignan, oak-aged in French *barriques* for 15 months and showing medium- to full-bodied. Dark garnet in color with nicely integrating

431

soft tannins and spicy wood supporting aromas and flavors of black-berries, cassis and bitter orange peel. Long, round and generous. Drink now. Score 88.

POIZNER, MERLOT, 2005: Full-bodied, dark ruby toward garnet, opening with firm tannins and generous wood influence from its 12 months in French oak, but those integrating well with raspberry and plum fruits, backed up nicely by spicy and toasty hints on the finish. Drink up. Score 87.

POIZNER, SYRAH, KFAR YUVAL, 2007: A dark-garnet blend of Syrah grapes from two different vineyards. Reflecting its 21 months in oak with still-firm tannins and notes of smoky wood, opening in the glass to reveal red plum, black cherry and cassis notes, those supported nicely by hints of earthy minerals. A generous wine. Drink now–2015. Score 88.

POIZNER, CARIGNAN, OLD VINES, 2006: Showing much as at barrel tastings. Dark garnet with purple and orange reflections, full-bodied and firm. Made from grapes from 35-year-old vines, reflects its 16 months in French oak with light spicy and dusty wood, that highlighting aromas and flavors of red cherries, red currants, raspberries and spice. On the lingering finish generous hints of cocoa and vanilla. Drink up. Score 88.

POIZNER, SYRAH-SHIRAZ-CARIGNAN, 2006: Dark ruby toward garnet, oak-aged for 16 months, this blend of French and Australian clones of Syrah and Shiraz and Carignan (50% Syrah and 25% of Shiraz and Carignan) shows full-bodied, with soft tannins integrating nicely. Reflecting the oak with vanilla and white pepper, those parting to reveal raspberry, red plum and cassis notes along with a generous note of Mediterranean herbs. Drink up. Score 87.

Psagot ✶✶✶✶

Located in the community of Psagot in the northern Jerusalem Mountains, overlooking Wadi Kelt (Nachal Prat), the winery was founded by Na'ama and Ya'akov Berg, who planted their first vineyards in 1998. The oak *barriques* used by the winery are stored in a cave dating to the Second Temple, containing both ancient pressing facilities and fully modern winemaking tools. The cave maintains 90% humidity throughout the year, with winter temperatures of about 12 degrees Celsius and summer temperatures that do not exceed 18 degrees Celsius.

With Ya'akov Berg and Josh Hexter as co-winemakers, the winery relies on Cabernet Sauvignon, Merlot, Cabernet Franc, Viognier and Chardonnay grapes, with the top-of-the-line wine being a Bordeaux blend named Edom. Regular varietal wines are produced in the Psagot series and there is also a Port-style wine. The winery also releases a single vineyard Cabernet Sauvignon in years deemed appropriate. Production has been growing annually, with the winery expecting to release 100,000 bottles from the 2010 vintage. From the aspect of both quality and wines that command our attention, clearly a winery on its continuing way up.

Edom

EDOM, 2009: An ever-shifting blend, this year of Cabernet Sauvignon, Cabernet Franc, Merlot and Petite Verdot (61%, 17%, 15% and 7% respectively), each variety fermented separately until blending. Super-dark garnet in color, full-bodied, with gently caressing near-sweet tannins and just the right amount of spicy oak in the background. On the nose and palate blackcurrants, blueberry and purple plum fruits, those complemented by hints of Mediterranean herbs and, on the long finish, an appealing hint of bitter-citrus peel. Drink now–2016, perhaps longer. Score 90. K

EDOM, 2008: A blend of 81% Cabernet Sauvignon, 11% Petit Verdot and about 4% each of Cabernet Franc and Merlot. Super-dark garnet, with its once firmly gripping tannins now settling in nicely and with cigar-box notes in fine balance with fruits, minerality and acidity. Big and ripe with intense currant, wild berry, spices, cedar and sage aromas and flavors, the berry notes rising on a long, mouth-coating finish. Drink now–2016. Score 90. K

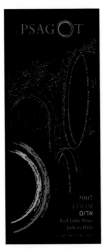

EDOM, 2007: A Bordeaux blend of 59% Cabernet Sauvignon, 19% Merlot, 12% Cabernet Franc and 10% Petit Verdot. Showing medium- to full-bodied (leaning toward the full), with its once-firm tannins and generous spicy wood and acidity now integrating nicely, opens in the glass to show generous spicy black fruits, those yielding to notes of cassis and Mediterranean herbs. Long and generous. Drink now–2013. Score 89. K

EDOM, 2006: A blend of 57% Cabernet Sauvignon and 33% Merlot, with the remainder made up of Petit Verdot and Cabernet Franc. Medium- to full-bodied, generously but not aggressively oaked, with firm tannins just now starting to settle in. Opens with red currants and raspberries, those parting to make way for plums and black fruits on an earthy-herbal background, all with a light bitter streak that some will find appealing and others not. Drink now. Score 86. K

EDOM, 2005: Deep garnet in color, a blend of 75% Cabernet Sauvignon and 25% Merlot. Opens with a rich vanilla and white chocolate nose, then settles down in the glass to reveal aromas and flavors of black cherries, plums and currants. Medium- to full-bodied, with soft but mouth-coating tannins, a good touch of spicy cedarwood, and, on the finish, an appealing earthy minerality. Sliding past its peak. Drink up. Score 88. K

Psagot Single Vineyard

PSAGOT, CABERNET SAUVIGNON, SINGLE VINEYARD, 2009: Full-bodied enough to be thought of as brawny, with deep black-fruit aromatics and still-generous notes of spicy oak, all showing fine balance and structure, and needing only time for its elements to come more fully together. On the nose and palate blackcurrants, crushed berries and figs, those supported by notes of espresso and roasted Brazil nuts. As the wine develops in the bottle it will show its long and expressive finish. Drink now–2016, perhaps longer. Score 90. K

PSAGOT, CABERNET SAUVIGNON, SINGLE VINEYARD, 2007: Almost impenetrable inky-dark garnet in color, full-bodied, and reflecting its 13 months of oak-aging, with youthful, gripping tannins now integrating nicely and reflecting the wine's inherent good balance. On the nose and palate ripe currant, blackberry and citrus peel, complemented by notes of sweetened chewing tobacco, green olives and mocha. Drink now–2014. Score 90. K

Psagot

PSAGOT, CABERNET SAUVIGNON, 2009: Dark garnet, medium- to full-bodied, with silky smooth tannins. On the opening nose dusty oak, with that parting in the glass to show aromas and flavors of red and black currants and bitter-citrus peel, those in turn followed by notes of vanilla and smoke, all leading to a long and mouth-filling finish. Drink now–2016. Score 89. K

PSAGOT, CABERNET SAUVIGNON, 2008: Perhaps the best to date from the winery. Medium- to full-bodied, leaning to the full, dark garnet in color, with still-firm tannins and spicy cedarwood waiting to integrate but already showing fine balance and structure. Opens in the glass to reveal generous aromas and flavors of black cherry, blackcurrant and plum fruits, and, on the finish, appealing hints of green olives and fresh herbs. Drink now–2016. Score 92. K

PSAGOT, CABERNET SAUVIGNON, 2007: Developing beautifully. Deep garnet toward royal purple, oak-aged for 13 months, full-bodied, with firm tannins and smoky wood settling in nicely now and showing rich, generous and complex with well-focused red and blackcurrant fruits overlaid with hints of cocoa and cedarwood. Drink now. Score 90. K

PSAGOT, CABERNET SAUVIGNON, 2006: Garnet toward royal purple in color, with firm but yielding tannins, and at this stage showing medium- to full-bodied. On the nose and palate traditional Cabernet blackberry and blackcurrant fruits, those complemented by spices and hints of Mediterranean herbs. Drink up. Score 86. K

PSAGOT, MERLOT, 2009: Made entirely from Merlot grapes, moderately-dark garnet in color and medium- to full bodied, reflecting its 13 months in oak with notes of spicy cedarwood. A distinctly red-fruit wine, showing red-berry and raspberry fruits, those supported nicely by notes of earthy minerals and lightly peppery spices, all leading to a generous finish on which a hint of dark chocolate. Drink now–2014. Score 89. K

PSAGOT, MERLOT, 2008: Part of the signature line of the Psagot wines is a clear, clean minerality and that shows nicely on this 100% Merlot. Dark garnet in color, medium- to full-bodied, reflecting its 14 months in oak with soft, gently gripping tannins and spicy cedarwood notes integrating well and parting to reveal raspberries, red currants and an appealing note of dark chocolate on the finish. Round, long and generous. Drink now–2013. Score 89. K

PSAGOT, MERLOT, 2007: Medium- to full-bodied, with ample but gentle tannins and reflecting its 13 months in oak with spicy and vanilla notes. On the nose and palate purple plums, raspberries, cassis and a note of red licorice. Round and long. Drink now. Score 89. K

PSAGOT, MERLOT, 2006: Dark garnet in color, with generous oak and gripping tannins receding nicely and showing good balance and structure. Fine spices and vanilla here to highlight plum, currant and orange-peel notes that go on to a medium-long finish. Drink up. Score 88. K

PSAGOT, SHIRAZ, 2009: Medium- to full-bodied, with a red-fruit nose and gently chewy tannins. On the palate blueberries, cassis and plums, those on a background of brown spices, dried tomatoes and, on the finish, with tannins rising, a hint of pomegranates. Best now–2016, perhaps longer. Score 89. K

PSAGOT, SHIRAZ, 2008: From four-year-old vines that have just come on line, the winery's first varietal Shiraz release. Oak-aged, as are nearly all of the Psagot wines, for about 13 months, showing deep garnet, full-bodied with soft tannins and gentle spicy wood notes integrating nicely. On the nose and palate an appealing array of ripe cherry, boysenberry and pomegranate fruits, those on a spicy, medium- to full-bodied background with tannins and notes of minerals rising on the finish. Drink now–2013. Score 88. K

PSAGOT, CABERNET FRANC, 2009: So distinctly Cabernet Franc in its personality that anyone tasting this who mistakes it for Cabernet Sauvignon or Merlot is almost certainly sure to be at least half brain-dead. Medium- to full-bodied (leaning to the full), with just chewy enough tannins, a round, supple and complex wine. On the nose and palate pomegranate, raspberry fruits and floral notes, those supported by generous hints of cigar tobacco and licorice, all going on to a long and generous finish. Drink now–2016. Score 90. K

PSAGOT, CABERNET FRANC, 2008: Dark ruby in color and fully faithful to the variety, offering up an array of complex and elegant black cherries and purple plums, those matched nicely by notes of cedar, minerals and asphalt and, from mid-palate on, hints of tobacco and sage. A supple and long wine. Drink now–2015. Score 91. K

PSAGOT, CABERNET FRANC, 2007: Aromatic, opening with a nose of eucalyptus, tar and spicy wood. Medium- to full-bodied, showing a hint of muscle going on to reveal dark plum, currant, tobacco and mocha notes, those on an appealing background of freshly cut herbs. A solid effort. Drink now. Score 90. K

PSAGOT, CABERNET FRANC, 2006: Medium-dark ruby toward garnet in color, medium-bodied, with soft, gently caressing tannins and appealing spicy oak. Showing pleasant red currant and raspberry fruits on a background of earthy minerals and herbs and saddle leather. Drink now. Score 88. K

PSAGOT, CHARDONNAY, 2010: Reflecting its six months in new oak with hints of both spices and vanilla, deep gold in color and deeply aromatic. On the nose and palate pineapple and citrus fruits, those yielding in the glass to notes of yellow peaches and melon and, on the moderately long finish, a tempting flavor of almonds. Drink now. Score 88. K

PSAGOT, VIOGNIER, 2010: Developed in new French oak for six months, light, bright gold in color, medium-bodied, with generous acidity that calls to mind green apples, the acidity in fine balance with notes of spicy oak. Opens in the glass to reveal appealing spiced pears, litchis and almonds. Generous 14% alcohol here but not a sign of heat. Drink now or in the next year or so. Score 88. K

PSAGOT, VIOGNIER, 2009: Golden straw in color, lightly oaked, with appealing aromas and flavors of pears and blood oranges supported by light pepper notes and coming to a lively near-creamy finish. Drink now. Score 88. K

Ra'anan ✶✶

Established by Ra'anan Margalit in 1994 on Moshav Ganei Yochanan in the Southern Plains, the winery utilizes Cabernet Sauvignon, Merlot and Chardonnay grapes from its own vineyards, located nearby at Karmei Yosef. Current production is about 8,000 bottles annually.

RA'ANAN, CABERNET SAUVIGNON, RESERVE, 2006: Garnet toward royal purple, medium- to full-bodied, with gently mouth-coating tannins and spicy, toasty oak. Opens to show appealing blackcurrant and berry fruits. Drink up. Score 84.

RA'ANAN, MERLOT, 2006: Medium-bodied, with soft tannins, spicy oak and black fruits. Not complex but a good quaffer. Drink up. Score 84.

RA'ANAN, MERLOT, 2005: Garnet to purple, medium-bodied, with soft, near-sweet tannins and hints of spices, licorice and earthy minerals supporting berry and cassis aromas and flavors. Drink up. Score 84.

Rajum **

Located on the Tzel HaMidbar Ranch at Mitzpe Ramon,
which by any standards is one of the most exquisitely beautiful places on the planet, this small winery was founded in
2008 by Ziv Spector and Ilan Tifti. The winery is now producing 3,000–3,500 bottles annually from Malbec, Cabernet
Sauvignon, Merlot, Shiraz and Pinot Noir grapes sourced
from various Negev vineyards. The winery has no kashrut
certificate but labels its wines as "kosher on trust," this im-
plying that all of the rules of kashrut are enforced in both
the vineyards and the winery.

RAJUM, CABERNET SAUVIGNON, YETER, 2009: Made entirely from
Cabernet Sauvignon grapes, developed in French oak for 12 months and
showing medium- to full-bodied, round and generous. On the nose and
palate currants, raspberries, and an appealing hint of the wood. On the
finish sweet spices and a note of licorice. Drink now–2014. Score 87.

RAJUM, CABERNET SAUVIGNON, AROD, 2008: Oak-aged for 12
months, opens with a somewhat medicinal aroma but that blows off
quickly enough in the glass to reveal a medium- to full-bodied wine,
garnet in color with blackcurrant and blackberry fruits on a background
that hints of sea salt and earthy minerals. Drink now. Score 84.

RAJUM, MERLOT, ARDON, 2008: Dark garnet, medium-bodied, with
chunky tannins that give the wine a rustic note. Developed in oak for
eight months, shows a somewhat bitter note that tends to hide the
black fruits that struggle to make themselves felt. Drink up. Score 80.

RAJUM, SHIRAZ, KEMER, 2009: Cherry red toward garnet, reflecting its 12 months in oak with somewhat chunky tannins. Medium- to
full-bodied, opening in the glass to reveal an array of red and black
berries, those on a background of grilled herbs. On the finish a note of
bittersweet chocolate. Drink now. Score 86.

RAJUM, CABERNET SAUVIGNON-MERLOT, RAMON, 2009: Developed for 12 months in 100 liter demijohns with oak chips, an unusual blend (to say the least) but comes together nicely as medium- to full-bodied, with gently gripping tannins to highlight aromas and flavors of red and black berries, milk chocolate and earthy minerals, the tannins and fruits rising on the finish. Drink now–2013, perhaps longer. Score 86.

RAJUM, CABERNET SAUVIGNON-MALBEC, KARKOM, 2009: Aged, as all of the winery's releases, for 12 months in barriques, a medium- to full-bodied, gently tannic blend of equal parts of Cabernet Sauvignon and Malbec. On the nose and palate ripe raspberry and black and red currants coming together with notes of toasty oak and a hint of cocoa. Drink now–2013, perhaps longer. Score 86.

Ramim *

Founded in 1999 on Moshav Shachar in the Southern Plains by Nitzan Eliyahu and producing its first wines from the 2000 harvest, the winery draws grapes from three self-owned vineyards, in Kfar Yuval and Safsufa, both on the Lebanese border, and on Moshav Shachar. Red varieties include Cabernet Sauvignon, Merlot, Sangiovese, Cabernet Franc, Syrah from France and Shiraz from Australia, as well as early plantings of Barbera, and Nebbiolo. White varieties include Zinfandel, Chardonnay, Gewurztraminer, Riesling, Semillon and Muscat.

The winery, which relies on Hungarian, French and American oak barrels, releases wines in a variety of series and under a large number of labels, some released only periodically. Among the series are Special Reserve, Art Reserve, Reserve and Ramim. The winery also produces several private-label wines for both local sale and export. Production in 2002 was 22,000 bottles, in 2003 it was 55,000 bottles, and in 2005 and 2006 it jumped to about 70,000 bottles. Current production is not known. The wines have been kosher since the 2003 vintage.

Special Reserve

SPECIAL RESERVE, CABERNET SAUVIGNON, 2003: Dark garnet, medium- to full-bodied, with firm tannins and generous spicy wood influences, those somewhat holding back the currant and blueberry fruits that are here. One-dimensional, short and past its peak. Drink up. Score 79. K

Art Reserve

ART RESERVE, CABERNET SAUVIGNON, 2006: Dark garnet in color, medium-to full-bodied, with tight tannins that seem not to want to integrate. On the nose and palate skimpy black fruits and a too-generous green note that lingers on the finish. Drink up. Score 82. K

ART RESERVE, CABERNET SAUVIGNON, 2005: Medium-bodied, with chunky, country-style tannins and showing generous herbal, green olive and cherry aromas and flavors. Lacks complexity but an easy-to-drink quaffer. Drink up. Score 84. K

ART RESERVE, MERLOT, 2005: Oak-aged for 18 months, dark ruby toward garnet, medium-bodied, showing black cherry, toasty oak and nutmeg notes, and, on the tannic finish, hints of mocha and sage. Showing age. Drink up. Score 80. K

Ramim

RAMIM, CABERNET SAUVIGNON, SHACHAR, 2007: Medium- to full-bodied, with chunky and tight tannins and spicy cedar notes that tend to hide the blackberry and currant flavors that are barely felt. Drink now. Score 84. K

RAMIM, CABERNET SAUVIGNON, SHACHAR, 2005: A medium-bodied, modest wine with spicy wood and ripe and earthy plum, herb and sage notes, those fading somewhat on the finish. Showing age. Drink up. Score 85. K

RAMIM, MERLOT, 2006: An easygoing wine with spicy cherry, cola and plum fruits. Medium-bodied with soft tannins. A good entry-level wine. Drink up. Score 83. K

RAMIM, MERLOT, SHACHAR, 2005: Deep garnet, medium- to full-bodied, with firm tannins, perhaps too-generous smoky oak, and only skimpy berry-cherry aromas and flavors. Past its peak. Drink up. Score 82. K

RAMIM, MOSAIC, 2005: A somewhat odd blend of Cabernet Sauvignon, Merlot, Pinot Noir and Shiraz (54%, 31%, 8% and 7% respectively) aged in Hungarian and American oak for six months. Light- to medium-bodied, with almost unfelt tannins and a berry-cherry personality. A simple quaffing wine. Well past its peak. Drink up. Score 78.

RAMIM, CABERNET SAUVIGNON-MERLOT, 2005: Medium-bodied, with mineral and cedar notes complementing berry and cherry flavors. A simple quaffer. Drink up. Score 82. K

RAMIM, GEWURZTRAMINER, 2007: Pleasant enough, although not at all typical of the varietal, showing soft peach, tangerine and nutmeg aromas and flavors. Drink up. Score 82. K

RAMIM, CHARDONNAY, DESERT ICE, 2003: Showing dramatically better than at an earlier tasting, almost as if my palate were discerning two different wines. Medium-bodied, dark golden in color, with generously sweet kiwi, pineapple and citrus fruits backed up by gentle acidity. At its best served icy-cold. Drink up. Score 84. K

Ramot Naftaly ✱✱✱

Founded on Moshav Ramot Naftaly in the Upper Galilee in 2003 by vintner Yitzhak Cohen (working at first with winemaker Tal Pelter as a regular consultant but now acting only as a colleague sharing advice), this small winery owns vineyards planted with Cabernet Sauvignon, Merlot, Shiraz, Petit Verdot, Barbera and Malbec. With a new visitors' center now opened, current production is about 10,000 bottles annually, those in regular and reserve series. The wines have been kosher from the 2009 vintage.

RAMOT NAFTALY, CABERNET SAUVIGNON, 2010: Dark cherry red toward garnet, medium- to full-bodied, with soft gently caressing tannins. On first attack red berries and spices, those yielding in the glass to currants and crushed wild berries, all leading to a long, gently spicy finish. Drink from release–2014. Tentative Score 88–90. K

RAMOT NAFTALY, CABERNET SAUVIGNON, KADESH VALLEY, SPECIAL EDITION, 2009: A blend primarily of Cabernet Sauvignon, that fleshed out with Malbec, Merlot and Petit Verdot. Oak-aged for 12 months, showing garnet in color, medium- to full-bodied with soft tannins and a generous hint of spicy wood. On the nose and palate, blackcurrants, blueberries and a note of earthy minerality. Drink now–2013. Score 87. K

RAMOT NAFTALY, CABERNET SAUVIGNON, 2008: Deep garnet, full-bodied, with generous tannins needing time to integrate but showing fine structure and balance. Oak-aged for 24 months but happily reflecting that with gentle notes of spices and smoke, opens to reveal an array of blackcurrant, blackberry and wild berry fruits, those supported nicely by hints of roasted herbs. Long and generous. Drink now–2014. Score 90.

RAMOT NAFTALY, CABERNET SAUVIGNON, 2007: Dark garnet toward royal purple, medium- to full-bodied, with soft tannins and notes of spicy wood reflecting its 24 months in oak. Opens to reveal traditional currant and berry fruits, those supported nicely by hints of Oriental spices. A distinctly Mediterranean wine. Drink now. Score 88.

RAMOT NAFTALY, CABERNET SAUVIGNON, RESERVE, 2007: Medium-dark garnet in color, full-bodied, with gently mouth-coating tannins and vanilla-rich wood settling in well. On the nose and palate traditional Cabernet fruits of blackcurrants and blackberries, those supported nicely by notes of freshly picked Mediterranean herbs and, on the long finish, hints of vanilla and bitter-orange peel. Drink now–2014. Score 90.

RAMOT NAFTALY, CABERNET SAUVIGNON, 2007: Dark garnet toward royal purple, medium- to full-bodied, with soft tannins and notes of spicy wood reflecting its 12 months in oak. Opens to reveal traditional currant and berry fruits, those supported nicely by hints of Oriental spices. Not overly complex but a distinctly Mediterranean wine. Drink now. Score 88.

RAMOT NAFTALY, SHIRAZ, 2010: Garnet toward royal purple, medium- to full-bodied (perhaps leaning to the full), with soft, well-integrating tannins and light notes of sweet cedar. On the nose and palate Santa Rosa plums, red currants and spices with a comfortable note of saddle leather coming in on the finish. Drink from release–2015, perhaps longer. Tentative Score 87–89. K

RAMOT NAFTALY, SYRAH, 2008: Medium- to full-bodied, opening with light, leathery, earthy notes on the nose. Medium- to full-bodied, with soft, already well-integrating tannins and appealing blueberry, blackberry and wild strawberry fruits, all on a just-spicy-enough background and, on the mouth-filling finish, a hint of minted chocolate. Drink now–2014. Score 91.

RAMOT NAFTALY, SYRAH, 2007: Medium- to full-bodied, with still-gripping tannins and generous acidity that need some time to settle in. On the nose and palate ripe red berry, plum and licorice notes. Drink now–2013. Score 88.

RAMOT NAFTALY, BARBERA, 2010: Ruby toward garnet, medium-bodied, showing silky tannins, a light wood influence and generous acidity. Opens in the glass to show raspberry, black cherry and cranberry fruits, those highlighted by notes of violets, all leading to a moderately long finish. Drink from release–2013. Tentative Score 86–88. K

RAMOT NAFTALY, BARBERA, 2009: Dark garnet, surprisingly full-bodied for the vintage with light notes of spicy oak and what might be thought of as "laid-back tannins." Deeply aromatic, opening in the glass to reveal boysenberries, raspberries and notes of white pepper, the tannins rising on the finish to give off an appealing black tea flavor that lingers nicely. Drink now–2014. Score 89. K

RAMOT NAFTALY, BARBERA, 2008: A rich nose of crushed blackberries and licorice, opens to reveal a medium- to full-bodied, gently tannic red on which blackberries, blueberries, flowers and earthy minerals make themselves felt nicely. On the generous finish a hint of citrus to add liveliness. Drink now. Score 87.

RAMOT NAFTALY, BARBERA, 2007: An appealing Barbera, medium-bodied, with soft tannins, good acidity and a wild berry and chocolate personality. Opens with a bit of bottle stink but that blows off quickly revealing generous fruits on a light earthy background. Drink up. Score 87.

RAMOT NAFTALY, PETIT VERDOT, 2010: Deep, youthful royal purple in color, medium- to full-bodied with soft tannins that make way for aromas and flavors of raspberries, boysenberries and notes of crème patisserie, and from mid-palate on notes of tobacco and white pepper. Ripe and well focused. Drink from release–2014. Tentative Score 88–90. K

RAMOT NAFTALY, PETIT VERDOT, 2009: Surprisingly dense for the vintage, with a red-fruit nose, a light touch of oak and good, gently gripping tannins. On the nose and palate ripe plums, black cherries and notes of bittersweet chocolate. On the long finish a hint of minted chocolate mousse that cannot help but make you smile. Drink from release–2014. Tentative Score 89–91. K

RAMOT NAFTALY, PETIT VERDOT, 2008: Deep purple in color, medium-bodied, with softly caressing tannins, showing both red and black berries, those on a background of toasty oak. Lively but not exaggerated acidity and notes of spices with fruits and tannins rising on the long finish. Drink now–2013. Score 90.

RAMOT NAFTALY, MALBEC, 2010: Medium-bodied, deep cherry red, with silky tannins, fine balancing acidity and notes of violets and vanilla on the nose. Opens in the glass to show aromas and flavors of raspberries, plum sauce and a note of graphite and, on the moderately long finish, notes of figs and anise. As the wine develops look as well for hints of cigar humidor aromas. Drink from release–2014. Tentative Score 87–89. K

RAMOT NAFTALY, MALBEC, 2009: Lots of invigorating acidity on a medium-bodied frame, opening in the glass to show notes of raspberries, boysenberries and red licorice and, on the finish, an appealing hint of graphite. Not overly complex but easy to drink and a very nice quaffer. Drink from release–2014. Tentative Score 86–88. K

RAMOT NAFTALY, MALBEC, 2008: Oak-aged for 18 months, garnet toward purple, opening with light earthy and tobacco notes on the nose. Medium- to full-bodied with notes of spicy wood and gently gripping tannins. Opens to reveal generous blackberry and purple plum fruits. A round, gentle Malbec with distinct Mediterranean overtones. Drink now. Score 88.

RAMOT NAFTALY, DUET, 2010: A medium- to full-bodied blend of 60% Cabernet Sauvignon and 40% Merlot, showing a generous red-fruit nose. Soft and round, with what might be thought of as "red fruits all the way" – those including raspberries, cranberries, red currants and even a hint of wild strawberries, all lingering nicely on the palate. Not what one would think of as a complex wine but a very nice one indeed. Drink from release–2014 perhaps longer. Tentative Score 87–89. K

RAMOT NAFTALY, DUET, 2009: A blend of Cabernet Sauvignon and Merlot, oak-aged for 12 months, showing bright garnet in color. Soft tannins and a gentle wood influence highlight aromas and flavors of red plums, red and black berries, licorice and, on the long finish, an appealing note of black olives. Drink from release–2013, perhaps longer. Score 89. K

RAMOT NAFTALY, DUET, 2008: A blend of 65% Merlot and 35% Cabernet Sauvignon, aged for 12 months in a combination of new, first-year and second-year oak. Garnet toward purple, with crushed berries on the nose, showing aromas and flavors of currants, wild berries and spices. A gently tannic, medium-bodied and charming wine. Drink now. Score 88.

RAMOT NAFTALY, DUET, 2007: An oak-aged medium- to full-bodied blend of Cabernet Sauvignon and Merlot showing gently gripping tannins and lively acidity. Opens to reveal raspberries, cranberries and red plums, those on a background of lightly peppery citrus peel. A tempting quaffer. Drink up. Score 87.

RAMOT NAFTALY, SHIRAZ-CABERNET SAUVIGNON, 2008: Medium- to full-bodied, with gently caressing tannins, a round and smooth blend of 60% Shiraz and 40% Cabernet Sauvignon. On the nose roasted herbs and red fruits, and in the glass currants, raspberries and tempting notes of espresso. Drink now–2014. Score 90.

Recanati ✶✶✶✶

Established in 2000, this modern winery, located in the Hefer Valley in the north part of the Sharon region, relies on grapes from their own as well as contract vineyards, primarily in the Upper Galilee. Senior winemaker Gil Shatzberg and winemaker Ido Lewinsohn make an experienced, talented and versatile team, the two working with a kind of synergy that demonstrates that the sum can be greater than its parts.

The winery produces wines in several series: the top-of-the-line, age-worthy Special Reserve wines and two varietal series, Reserve and Recanati, which now include Cabernet Sauvignon, Merlot, Syrah, Petite Sirah-Zinfandel, Chardonnay and Sauvignon Blanc. The winery also has a popular-priced series named Yasmine and a Special Edition series produced entirely for one of the Derek HaYain chain of wine shops in Israel. Production is currently about 950,000 bottles annually.

The winery continues to move in the direction of wines that, while no less complex or sophisticated, are less alcoholic, rounder and more distinctly food friendly. Part of this goal is being attained by earlier harvest and the increasing use of fine-grain Burgundy barrels that will impart a more gentle wood influence to the wines. No less important, the wines are showing increasingly cellar worthy.

Special Reserve

SPECIAL RESERVE, 2009: Made from very low-yield vines, dark, almost impenetrable garnet, developed in primarily new French oak, a blend largely of Merlot, that fleshed out with Petite Sirah and Cabernet Sauvignon. Clear notes of crushed berries and spicy oak on the nose, opens to show generous but not overly forward red and black currants, dried spices, bittersweet chocolate and fresh, earthy minerals. Rich, powerfully structured and well focused, this one needs time. Approachable now but showing its

elegance best from 2013 or 2014 and then cellaring nicely until 2019, perhaps longer. Tentative Score 92–94. ĸ

SPECIAL RESERVE, 2008: Recanati's flagship wine, this year a blend of 70% Cabernet Sauvignon and Merlot, the rest made up by Petite Sirah, Syrah and Cabernet Franc, the various components blended only as the wine was ready to be bottled. Developed in Burgundy oak *barriques*, a supple and elegant wine showing fine balance and structure that bode well for its future. On the nose and palate well-focused currant, blueberry and blackberry fruits, those on a background of bittersweet chocolate, freshly hung cigar tobacco and sweet spices, with its tannins now integrating nicely. A seamless, deftly balanced and elegant wine. Drink now–2018. Score 94. ĸ

SPECIAL RESERVE, 2007: With its once-firm tannins now settling in nicely and showing fine balance with spicy wood and fruits, showing very well indeed. Dark garnet in color, full-bodied but with a remarkable sense of "lightness" as it sits on the palate, opens with a berry-cherry nose and then goes on to show aromas and flavors of currants, red cherries and wild berries, those on a background of sweet cedar and dark chocolate. Remarkably approachable despite its youth but still cellar-worthy. Drink now–2015. Score 32. ĸ

SPECIAL RESERVE, 2006: A blend of 82% Cabernet Sauvignon and 18% Merlot. Aged for 19 months in *barriques*, of which 80% were new, showing full-bodied with still-firm tannins along with generous wood and acidity. No fear, however, for those are settling in nicely and show fine balance with fruits yielding a structure that bodes very well for the future. On the nose and palate hints of chocolate, espresso coffee and tobacco to support rich berry, currant and licorice notes, all coming to a powerful but long and graceful finish. Drink now–2018. Score 93. ĸ

SPECIAL RESERVE, 2005: Living up nicely to its earlier promise. Deep royal purple, full-bodied, with firm, still rough-edged tannins, those integrating nicely with light spicy wood and fruits to show fine balance and structure. A blend of 84% Cabernet Sauvignon and 16% Merlot, this is a big, rich and bold wine, with concentrated layers of currant, blackberry, anise and cedary oak flavors. Drink now–2013. Score 93. ĸ

SPECIAL RESERVE, 2004: A blend of 92% Cabernet Sauvignon and 8% Merlot, with generous but not-exaggerated toasty oak and soft tannins, those integrating nicely and opening to reveal a rich array of currant, blackberry and black cherry fruits, with gentle overlays of mint and chocolate. As the wine develops look for a hint of cigar tobacco on the long finish. Drink now. Score 93. ĸ

SPECIAL RESERVE, 2003: This deep, broad, gently tannic blend of 72% Cabernet Sauvignon and 28% Merlot combines Cabernet currants, cassis and spicy-herbal overtones with typical Merlot softness. Good balance between wood, tannins and fruits, and a long finish. Drink now. Score 92. K

SPECIAL RESERVE, 2001: As in its youth, deep garnet toward royal purple, full-bodied, with fine balance between well-integrated soft tannins, spicy and mocha-rich oak, and currant, blackberry and ripe red plum fruits. Some variation between bottles but that primarily in fruit intensity. Drink up. Score 90. K

SPECIAL RESERVE, WHITE, 2009: A blend of Viognier, Chardonnay and Sauvignon Blanc, the wine developed *sur lie* for eight months in Burgundy oak barrels. A full-bodied wine which, by wisely avoiding malolactic fermentation, maintains the integrity of flavors and crispness of the varieties. Mineral-rich, with only the barest trace of wood, a rich and generous wine with abundant peach, nectarine and apricot aromas and flavors, those coming together in a wine best described as "lush." Plenty of juicy acidity here to keep the wine lively through its long finish. Drink now–2014. Score 93. K

SPECIAL RESERVE, WHITE, 2008: The winery's first white release in their Special Reserve series. A blend of about one-third each Viognier, Chardonnay and Sauvignon Blanc (the Sauvignon Blanc from *vieilles vignes*). Oak-aged for eight months in Burgundy oak barrels, an aromatic blend, full-bodied and powerful but with finesse and elegance. Fine balance between light cedar notes, acidity and fruits, opening with peaches and tropical fruit, going on to melon and pears, all lingering nicely on the palate. A wine that will develop a more mineral background as it opens. Drink now–2014. Score 92. K

Reserve

RESERVE, CABERNET SAUVIGNON, KEREM BEN ZIMRA, 2009: Full-bodied, reflecting its 14 months in oak with soft tannins and tantalizing hints of dusty cedarwood. Round and smooth, a polished wine offering up generous blackcurrant, blackberry and black cherry fruits on a background that hints at one moment of mint and at another of Mediterranean herbs. On the long finish a tantalizing note of blueberries. Drink now–2016. Score 92. K

RESERVE, CABERNET SAUVIGNON, 2009: Garnet toward royal purple with orange and green reflections with a richly fruity nose. Full-bodied, with gently caressing tannins and an appealing light overlay of cedarwood, opens to show traditional Cabernet blackcurrants, blackberries and then not-so-traditional blueberries. Tannins and a spicy note rise on the finish. Drink now–2017. Score 92. K

RESERVE, CABERNET SAUVIGNON, 2008: Dark garnet, with black fruits and chocolate on the nose. Reflecting its development in 20% new and 80% in one- and two-year-old *barriques* with gentle notes of spicy oak, opens with aromas and flavors of raspberries, those parting to make way for currants, blackberries and licorice, all on a note of dried, crushed spices. Concentrated and long, showing muscles that are held in reserve to allow the elegance of the wine to make itself comfortably felt. Drink now–2016. Score 91. K

RESERVE, CABERNET SAUVIGNON, 2007: Dark, full-bodied, loaded with chocolate, spices and licorice, opening to reveal a generous array of currants, black cherries and blueberries, all of which linger through a long and supple finish. Drink now–2015. Score 90. K

RESERVE, CABERNET SAUVIGNON, 2006: Dark garnet toward royal purple, medium- to full-bodied (leaning more toward the full), with generous near-sweet tannins, and on the nose and palate a generous array of blackcurrant, blackberry, spice and mocha notes. Juicy and long. Drink now. Score 90. K

RESERVE, CABERNET SAUVIGNON, 2005: Dark garnet, medium- to full-bodied, with softly caressing tannins and showing a generous array of blackcurrant, wild berry and purple plum fruits, those supported nicely by hints of sweet herbs and reflecting its 18 months in *barriques* with lightly toasty oak. Rich, round and generous. Drink now. Score 90. K

RESERVE, CABERNET SAUVIGNON, 2004: Dark garnet with orange and purple reflections, this medium- to full-bodied wine shows soft, gently yielding tannins. Shows generous but well-balanced and a measured hand with spicy wood. Opens to reveal currant, plum and blackberry fruits, those well supported by light hints of herbs and cedarwood. Sliding past its peak. Drink up. Score 91. K

RESERVE, CABERNET SAUVIGNON, 2003: Super-dark garnet in color, ripe and rich, now showing full-bodied with soft tannins integrating nicely. On the nose and palate an appealing array of currant and berry fruits, those complemented by hints of Oriental spices and toasty oak. Generous. Drink up. Score 90. K

RESERVE, MERLOT, MANARA VINEYARD, 2009: Developed in French oak, 50% of which was new for 14 months. Deep royal purple in color, full-bodied, with tannins that grip nicely and a nose of black fruits and spices. True to its variety, opens with blackberries and blueberries, those going on to reveal currant, black cherry, espresso and spicy flavors. In the background light notes of toasty cedarwood along with hints of garrigue and earthy minerals. Long, generous and mouth filling with a note of licorice on the finish. Approachable from release but best from 2013–2018, perhaps longer. Tentative Score 90–92. K

RESERVE, MERLOT, 2008: Made from low-yield, non-irrigated grapes from the Manara vineyard in the Upper Galilee, full-bodied, with soft, gently gripping tannins integrating nicely. Dark garnet and showing a tempting array of wild berries, black cherries and currants, those matched gently by notes of spicy cedarwood. Deep, generous and long, with near-sweet tannins rising on the long finish. Drink now–2016. Score 91. K

RESERVE, MERLOT, 2007: Garnet toward royal purple, medium- to full-bodied with soft tannins and gentle hints of smoky wood and spices. Opens to show currants, wild berries and notes of green olives on a lightly earthy-mineral background. Drink now–2013. Score 89. K

RESERVE, MERLOT, 2006: Full-bodied, firm in texture, with its tannins integrating nicely and showing appealing blackberry, blueberry and currant fruits, those supported by a hint of mocha. Chewy, round and long. Drink now. Score 90. K

RESERVE, MERLOT, 2005: A single-vineyard wine, made entirely with grapes from the Manara Vineyard. Smooth, round and generous, rich and spicy, with a core of raspberry, cherry and creamy oak backed up by hints of minted chocolate that linger nicely. Good balance between fresh acidity, wood and fruits, and a long finish. Drink up. Score 90. K

RESERVE, SYRAH, 2007: Blended, as is the winemakers' wont, with 3% of Viognier (precisely how that white grape adds depth and color to a red wine escapes me, but by heaven, it does). Intensely dark royal purple in color, with a complex fruit and herb-rich nose, opening to reveal aromas and flavors of purple plums, blackcurrants and wild berries, those on a background that hints comfortably of saddle leather and earthy minerals. Drink now–2016. Score 90. K

RESERVE, SYRAH, 2006: Dark garnet in color, with still-firm tannins needing time to settle in but showing fine balance and structure. On the nose and palate black cherry and blackcurrant fruits, those matched by hints of grilled beef, herbal and green olive notes. Drink now. Score 89. K

RESERVE, SHIRAZ, 2008: Dark garnet and full-bodied, a well-focused wine with softly caressing tannins. On the nose and palate purple plums, wild berries and tobacco, those complemented by hints of nutmeg and cloves. Long and generous. Drink now–2015. Score 90. K

RESERVE, SHIRAZ, 2004: Dark cherry-red toward garnet, full-bodied, supple and round, with blackberry, black cherry, herbal and beefy aromas and flavors, those coming together with firm tannins and sweet cedarwood. On the long tannic finish, toasted bread and mocha. Drink up. Score 89. K

RESERVE, CABERNET FRANC, 2008: Oak-aged for 18 months in 40% new oak. Smooth and velvety, with tannins that grip gently and stand up nicely to light toasty wood. Notes of rose petals, black cherries and raspberries on first attack, those yielding comfortably to currants, tar and toasted rye bread. Full-bodied, with tannins and wood in fine balance with the fruits, all leading to a long and persistent finish on which the oak takes on an appealing, sweetish note. Drink now–2015. Score 90. K

RESERVE, CABERNET FRANC, 2006: With its once-firm tannins now integrating nicely, showing medium-dark garnet, full-bodied, and reflecting its 14 months in oak with generous but not-imposing sweet cedar. Dark berry, black cherry and plum fruits highlighted by notes of tobacco, bell peppers and bittersweet chocolate, all lingering nicely on the finish. Drink now. Score 91. K

RECANATI, CARIGNAN, RESERVE, KEREM BA'AL, 2009: Listed on the label as coming from *Kerem Ba'al* (an unwatered vineyard) and as a "wild" wine, that referring to the grapes being raised as bush vines, showing even better than at an earlier barrel tasting. The first varietal Carignan release from the winery, made from old vines with naturally low yield, showing full-bodied and distinctly royal purple, its once-chunky tannins now softened nicely. On the nose unmistakable aromas of raspberries and spices, and in the glass opening to reveal a generous array of blackcurrant and blackberry fruits, those supported by notes of spicy oak, licorice, pepper and tobacco. Powerful but oh so gentle on the palate, with hints of mesquite and a note of fresh acidity livening up the generous finish. Perhaps at its very best with entrecote, T-bone or porterhouse steaks. Drink now–2016. If I were to rate the wine entirely on a hedonistic basis, it would earn a Score of 96–97 for the sheer pleasure it gives. Rating it in a more standard manner – Score 93. K

RESERVE, SYRAH-VIOGNIER, MANARA VINEYARD, 2010: Blended with a small amount of Viognier, developing in Burgundy barrels, deep, almost shining garnet with a royal purple robe. At this youthful stage showing full-bodied with firmly gripping tannins but with fine balance and structure. As the elements marry and integrate look for a wine that will show plum, wild berry and currant fruits, and, unfolding on the palate, notes of roasted meat and earthy minerals. In its youth this one will be concentrated and intense. As the wine continues to develop it will show supple elegance. Drink now–2019. Score 91. K

RESERVE, SYRAH-VIOGNIER, MANARA VINEYARD, 2009: Syrah with a smidgeon of Viognier blended in. Dark royal purple, deeply aromatic, opens in the glass to reveal a generous array of wild berries, cassis and red plums, those on a background of stony minerals. Drink now–2016. Score 90. K

RESERVE, PETITE SIRAH-ZINFANDEL, 2010: Dark royal purple in color, showing more full-bodied than earlier releases, with generous, almost chewy tannins and tempting hints of peppery vanilla from the wood in which it is developing. Destined always to be a concentrated and muscular wine but showing those muscles with grace. On the nose and palate ripe blackberry, huckleberry and purple plums, those complemented by notes of cedarwood and candied violets. Fruits and tannins rise nicely on the long finish. Drink now–2018. Score 91. K

RESERVE, PETITE SIRAH-ZINFANDEL, 2009: With about 90% Petite Sirah blended with Zinfandel, showing dark garnet toward royal purple. Medium- to full-bodied, with soft tannins and notes of spicy wood parting in the glass to show red and black berries, purple plums, exotic spices and hints of eucalyptus. Fruits and tannins rise nicely on the finish. Drink now–2015. Score 90. K

RESERVE, PETITE SIRAH-ZINFANDEL, 2008: Garnet toward royal purple, medium-bodied with silky tannins, opens to show appealing blackberry, black cherry and cassis notes, those complemented nicely by notes of licorice, black olives and sweet cedar. Drink now. Score 89. K

RESERVE, PETITE SIRAH-ZINFANDEL, 2007: Medium- to full-bodied, dark, almost impenetrable garnet, opens with black fruits and a gentle note of spicy wood. Goes on in the glass to reveal red berry and light leathery and peppermint notes. Drink now. Score 90. K

RESERVE, PETITE SIRAH-ZINFANDEL, 2006: Reflecting its eight months in oak with gently smoky and spicy wood and softly caressing tannins, a blend of 80% Petite Sirah and 20% Zinfandel. Youthful royal purple, opens to reveal blackberry, pomegranate, mocha and sage notes. Drink now. Score 90. K

RESERVE, PETITE SIRAH-ZINFANDEL, 2005: Dark and concentrated, its firm, crisp tannins integrating nicely with vanilla-rich spicy oak. On the nose and palate blackberry, raspberry and black cherry fruits, those coming together nicely with hints of minerals and an appealing light earthy note. Long and generous. Drink up. Score 90. K

RESERVE, CHARDONNAY, MANARA VINEYARD, 2009: Very nice indeed. Developed partly in stainless steel, partly in *barriques*, showing generous acidity to keep the wine lively, that in fine balance with fruits. On the nose and palate hints of sweet-and-spicy cedar, complemented nicely by citrus fruits, ripe peaches and a tantalizing hint of white pepper. Drink now–2013. Score 90. K

RESERVE, CHARDONNAY, 2008: Developed partly in mostly one-year-old *barriques* and partly in stainless steel, all on its lees for six months, light gold in color, medium-bodied, with an appealing note of spicy oak to highlight the citrus and summer fruits, those with light hints of pepper and juniper berries. On the long and generous finish a tantalizing note of bitter citrus peel. Drink now. Score 90. K

RESERVE, SAUVIGNON BLANC, 2009: Made from old vines at Kerem Ben Zimra, developed partly *sur lie* and partly in stainless steel, showing notes of sweet and spicy cedarwood, opens to reveal generous tropical and citrus fruits on a background of ginger and Oriental spices and freshly grass. Fresh, lively and with enough complexity to grab the attention. Drink now. Score 88. K

RESERVE, SAUVIGNON BLANC, 2008: Light straw colored, with lively lemon, grapefruit and gooseberry fruits along with chalky minerals. Light, lively and refreshing. Drink up. Score 87. K

Special Edition

SPECIAL EDITION, CABERNET SAUVIGNON-MERLOT-SHIRAZ, 2009: With each variety developed in oak for about nine months before blending, showing tantalizing hints of oak and soft tannins that are integrating nicely. On the nose and palate a fine array of currants, raspberries and wild berries, those complemented by notes of white pepper and earthy minerals. Medium-bodied and round, a just complex enough but easy-to-drink red. Drink now. Score 88. K

SPECIAL EDITION, 2008: A new blend for this wine – in this case of 40% Shiraz and 30% each of Cabernet Sauvignon and Merlot. Ruby toward garnet, medium-bodied, with soft tannins and a gentle note of spicy wood and vanilla reflecting its six months primarily in American oak. A seductive wine, smooth and polished, opening nicely to reveal blueberry, black cherry and plum fruits, those with appealing hints of toasted coconut and bitter orange peel on the finish. Easy to drink and at the same time showing complexity and elegance. Drink now. Score 90. K

SPECIAL EDITION, PETITE SIRAH-SHIRAZ, 2007: A blend this year of 60% Petite Sirah and 40% Shiraz, dark royal purple in color, medium-bodied, showing soft, well-integrated tannins and just the right note of dusty oak. On the nose and palate blackberries, blueberries and cassis, those matched nicely by notes of chocolate and mocha. Simultaneously "fun" and elegant. Drink now. Score 90. K

SPECIAL EDITION, PETITE SIRAH-SHIRAZ, 2006: Dark garnet enough to be thought of as brooding, with a nearly explosive nose packed with raspberries and chocolate. Medium-bodied, with soft, caressing tannins that part comfortably to reveal a generous array of blackberries and blueberries, cassis, tobacco and dark chocolate, all of which linger long and comfortably. Drink up. Score 92. K

SPECIAL EDITION, CHARDONNAY, 2009: Unoaked, blended with a bit of Sauvignon Blanc, both from the Upper Galilee, a most pleasant wine. Light gold in color, medium-bodied, with crisp and fresh aromas and flavors of citrus (leaning to red grapefruit), citrus peel and a hint of tropical fruits all on a light, flinty, mineral background. Crisp and refreshing. Drink now. Score 88. K

457

Recanati

RECANATI, CABERNET SAUVIGNON, 2010: Glistening dark garnet in color, full-bodied, with just a kiss of the oak and showing silky tannins. Unmistakably Cabernet Sauvignon, opening with crushed blackberries on the nose, going on to reveal aromas and flavors of blackcurrants, black cherries and bay leaf, those on a background that hints at one moment of earthy minerals and at another of minted chocolate. Soft, round and long. Drink now–2016. Tentative Score 90. K

RECANATI, CABERNET SAUVIGNON, 2009: Medium-, perhaps medium- to full-bodied, with gently mouth-coating tannins and peppery and vanilla overtones. Opens to reveal traditional Cabernet currant, blackberry and dark chocolate notes. A long, mouth-filling finish on which tannins and fruits rise nicely together. Drink now–2013. Score 90. K

RECANATI, CABERNET SAUVIGNON, 2008: Developed in older barrels and showing a gentle spicy wood influence along with soft, gently mouth-coating tannins. Opens to reveal red currant, berry and orange-peel, those supported nicely by notes of freshly cut Mediterranean herbs and earthy minerals. Drink now. Score 90. K

RECANATI, CABERNET SAUVIGNON, 2007: Garnet with purple and orange reflections, opens with a rich, fruity nose. Medium- to full-bodied, with soft tannins and a gentle spicy overlay from the wood, and an overall currant and black cherry personality. Smooth, rich and concentrated for the vintage, with tannins rising on the finish. Drink up. Score 89. K

RECANATI, MERLOT, 2010: Merlot with clearly recognized traits of the variety. Dark garnet toward royal purple, medium- to full-bodied with gently caressing tannins and just a hint of vanilla from the oak in which it was developed for a short while. On the opening nose violets and blackberries, those making way for aromas and flavors of blackberries, currants and blueberries on a background of bay leaves and stony minerals, all lingering nicely. A soft, supple and well-focused wine. Drink from release–2014, perhaps longer. Score 90. K

RECANATI, MERLOT, 2009: Blended with about 10% Cabernet Sauvignon, allowed to ferment partly by carbonic maceration, opens with a fruity nose and then goes on to show purple plum, blackberry and blueberry fruits. Developed partly in American and partly in French oak, medium-bodied, not overly complex but sits very comfortably on the palate. Drink now–2013. Score 88. K

RECANATI, MERLOT, 2007: Ripe and rich, garnet-colored, reflecting its four months in oak with gentle spices and a tantalizing hint of cedar, those matched by soft tannins and showing black cherry, plum and currant fruits along with light hints of minerals and mocha. Drink up. Score 88. K

RECANATI, SHIRAZ, 2010: Blended with about 3% of Viognier, show-ing deep, youthful royal purple in color, with appealing floral and red-plum notes on the nose. Opens nicely in the glass to show itself as a round, well-balanced and distinctly Mediterranean Shiraz. On first attack wild red and black berries, those yielding comfortably to blackberry and raspberry fruits, those complemented by hints of spices, citrus peel and, on the long finish, a note of saddle leather. As this one develops in the bottle look as well for hints of lightly peppery cream sauce. If one were to seek a single word to describe this wine, it would be "finesse." Drink from release–2016. Score 91. K

RECANATI, SHIRAZ, 2009: Blended with a small amount of Cabernet Sauvignon and developed in French and American oak. Super-dark garnet in color, with lively acidity and gentle wood influences settling, opens to a floral, vanilla and mineral-rich nose and then goes on to reveal peppery plum and berry fruits, all lingering nicely on the palate. Drink now–2014. Score 89. K

RECANATI, SHIRAZ, 2008: Developed partly in stainless-steel vats, partly in *barriques*, showing good color and fruit extraction. Medium-bodied, opening with a floral nose and going on to show purple plum, blackberry and leathery notes, those on a background of violets and spring flowers. Appealing but not meant for aging. Drink now–2014. Score 89. K

RECANATI, BARBERA, 2006: Light garnet toward purple in color, medium-bodied, with soft tannins and generous acidity. Reflects its eight and a half months in *barriques* with light spicy notes and appeal-ing crushed blackberry and cherry and chocolate notes, all leading to a light peppery finish. Drink up. Score 88. K

RECANATI, ROSÉ, 2010: As it has been since 2008, a blend primarily of Barbera, that fleshed out with Merlot, the grapes from the intention-ally unirrigated Manara Vineyard in the Upper Galilee. Cherry red in color, light- to medium-bodied, opens with aromas of freshly crushed strawberries, going on to reveal raspberries and red cherries. Consistent in style from year to year with fine balancing acidity and an appealing hint of super-light tannins. Sits easily on the palate but manages to fill the mouth nicely. Crisply refreshing, as good a choice for breakfast or brunch as with grilled fish and seafood dishes. Drink now–2013. Score 89. K

RECANATI, ROSÉ, 2009: A blend of 70% Barbera and 30% Merlot, the Merlot component made by the saignée method. Almost bright cherry-red, showing light- to medium-bodied, with fine balancing acidity to keep it lively and refreshing. On the nose and palate raspberry, cherry and watermelon notes with a tantalizing hint of super-light tannins to add complexity. Very nice indeed. Drink up. Score 89. K

RECANATI, CHARDONNAY, 2010: Developed *sur lie* with ⅓ developing in oak and ⅔ in stainless steel tanks. Showing gentle notes of yeast but that will pass with time to show a fresh, generously fruity and crisply refreshing wine with concentrated aromas and flavors of Anjou pears, apples and citrus fruits, those supported nicely by a light mineral note. Polished and well focused. Drink now–2013. Score 90. K

RECANATI, CHARDONNAY, 2009: Developed on its lees, 50% in second- and third-year barrels, 50% in stainless steel, showing light yeast notes that part to reveal appealing pear, apple and citrus notes on a light flinty mineral background. Lively and generous. Drink now. Score 89. K

RECANATI, CHARDONNAY, 2008: Developed partly in mostly one-year-old *barriques* and partly in stainless steel, all on its lees for six months, light gold in color, medium-bodied, with an appealing note of spicy oak to highlight the citrus, pear and summer fruits, those with light hints of pepper and juniper berries. On the long and generous finish a tantalizing note of bitter citrus peel. Drink now. Score 90. K

RECANATI, SAUVIGNON BLANC, 2010: Glistening light gold in color, with a rather quiet nose but opening nicely on the palate to show pineapple, grapefruit and green apple flavors, those complemented by hints of citrus peel and thyme. Good acidity adds an appealing juicy note. Drink now. Score 88. K

RECANATI, SAUVIGNON BLANC, 2009: Unoaked, with a moderate 12% alcohol, a crisp and refreshing wine with fine acidity to highlight citrus and apple fruits, all with a hint of white pepper on the finish. Drink up. Score 88. K

Yasmin

YASMIN, RED, 2009: A blend of Cabernet Sauvignon, Merlot, Syrah and Petite Sirah, made partly by carbonic maceration. Ruby toward garnet, light- to medium-bodied and soft, an easy-to-drink entry-level wine showing wild berry and blackberry fruits. Drink up. Score 86. K

YASMIN, RED, 2008: A medium-bodied, softly tannic blend primarily of Cabernet Sauvignon and Merlot, with a bit each of Carignan and Petite Sirah. Made partly by carbonic maceration, deep purple in color, showing appealing wild berry, black cherry and currant fruits with notes of orange peel and a hint of white pepper. Round and soft, a comfortable quaffer. Drink up. Score 86. K

YASMIN, WHITE, 2010: Light straw in color, an unoaked blend of French Colombard, Sauvignon Blanc, Emerald Riesling and Chardonnay, a small part of which was made by carbonic maceration. Opens with notes of pineapple and mango, those going to citrus and citrus peel. Not a complex wine but one that is crisply dry with fine balancing acidity, a lively and easy-to-drink white. Drink now. Score 87. K

YASMIN, WHITE, 2009: An unoaked blend of Sauvignon Blanc, Emerald Riesling, French Colombard and Semillon. With a moderate 12% alcohol, not having undergone malolactic fermentation, showing floral notes to support citrus and tropical fruits. A pleasant-enough quaffer. Drink up. Score 85. K

Red Boat ✶✶✶✶

Not "Red Sails in the Sunset," not "Red Poetry" and not "The Lady in Red," but simply Red Boat. A well-known wine lover, Doron Omer entered into his winemaking venture in 2007, sourcing grapes from Karmei Yosef , the Jerusalem Hills in general and from vineyards on Mount Meron in the Galilee. The winery is currently producing about 2,500 bottles annually.

RED BOAT, CABERNET SAUVIGNON, KARMEI YOSEF, 2007: A dark-garnet blend of 85% Cabernet Sauvignon, 10% Shiraz and 5% Petit Syrah. Medium- to full-bodied, gently tannic, a ripe and velvety wine with well focused blackcurrant and blackberry fruits highlighted by notes of smoky oak and licorice, all coming to a solid and long-lingering finish. Drink now–2014. Score 89.

RED BOAT, KARMEI YOSEF, 2009: A blend of 50% Cabernet Sauvignon, 30% Merlot and 20% Shiraz, reflecting its oak-aging with notes of sweet-and-spicy cedarwood and tannins on their way to being velvety. Opens in the glass to reveal blackcurrant, blackberry and licorice notes, those supported on the long, solid finish by notes of mocha and bittersweet chocolate. Look as well on the finish for a tantalizing hint of raspberries. Best from mid-2012–2015, perhaps longer. Score 91.

RED BOAT, KARMEI YOSEF, 2008: Medium- to full-bodied, deep garnet toward royal purple with gently gripping tannins, a juicy and tangy red showing red plums, cassis and crushed raspberry fruits, those supported nicely by aromas and flavors of blueberries, red currants and hints of cedarwood. Fruits and tannins rise nicely on the finish. A blend of 86% Cabernet Sauvignon and 7% each of Cabernet Franc and Merlot. Drink now–2014. Score 89.

RED BOAT, MOUNT MERON, 2009: Dark garnet toward royal purple, an oak-aging blend of 42% Cabernet Sauvignon, 30% Merlot and 28% Shiraz. Full-bodied, with still-gripping tannins and generous sweet-and-spicy oak, those in fine balance with fruits and needing only time to integrate. On the nose and palate red and black currants, purple plums and a note of minted chocolate (think After Eights). On the long finish an appealing note of bitter citrus peel. Best from mid-2012–2015. Score 90.

RED BOAT, MOUNT MERON, 2008: A dark-garnet oak-aged blend of 40% Cabernet Sauvignon, 30% Merlot and 30% Shiraz. Medium- to full-bodied, with fine density and gripping tannins only now starting to settle in. On the nose and palate purple plums, blackberries and chocolate along with notes of Mediterranean herbs and a hint of green olives. Drink now–2014, perhaps longer. Score 90.

RED BOAT, JERUSALEM FOOTHILLS, 2009: Dark garnet toward royal purple, well-focused and tangy, oak-aged blend of 60% Cabernet Sauvignon, 25% Merlot and 15% Shiraz. On first attack blueberries and minerals, those parting to make way for aromas and flavors of blackcurrants and blackberries, all with an appealing hint of tobacco. Long and generous. Approachable and enjoyable now but best from mid-2012–2015, perhaps longer. Score 90.

RED BOAT, CABERNET SAUVIGNON-MERLOT, JERUSALEM FOOT-HILLS, 2007: An oak-aged Bordeaux-style blend of 41% each of Cabernet Sauvignon and Merlot with 9% each of Cabernet Franc and Petit Verdot. Medium- to full-bodied, leaning to the full, with chunky tannins giving the wine a somewhat rustic note, but don't hold that against the wine, as it opens to reveal a generous array of black and red fruits, among those black and red currants, blackberries and black cherries, on a background of sweet cedarwood and stony minerals. Lingers nicely, tannins smoothing out and fruits rising on the finish. Drink now–2013. Score 89.

RED BOAT, CHARDONNAY, 2010: Destined for 12 months *sur lie* aging in oak, full-bodied, with a distinct grapefruit nose, opening in the glass to reveal lively acidity supporting mouthwatering aromas and flavors of citrus, citrus peel, green apples and floral notes. On the long finish a hint of earthy minerals, the flavors playing nicely on the palate and leading to a long finish. Drink from release–2014. Tentative Score 90–92.

RED BOAT, CHARDONNAY, 2009: Light gold in color, full-bodied, showing generous oak on the nose and palate but that in good balance with fruits and acidity. On the nose and palate white peaches, ripe apricots and citrus, those leading to a moderately long finish. Not so much a lively wine as a contemplative one. Drink now–2013. Score 88.

RED BOAT, CHARDONNAY, 2008: Full-bodied, lightly burnished gold in color, with notes of vanilla and spices from the oak in which it developed. A generous 15.5% alcohol content, but that blending in well with fruits and wood. Opens to reveal citrus and summer fruits, those supported by aromas and flavors of gooseberries and peach pits all on an appealing background of green almonds. Drink now–2013. Score 89.

Red Poetry ✶✶✶

Established in 2001 by Dovi Tal on Havat Tal, the winery has its own vineyards with Cabernet Sauvignon, Merlot, Tempranillo, Carignan, Cabernet Franc, Mourvedre, Petit Verdot, Shiraz, Petite Sirah, Sangiovese, Riesling and Gewurztraminer grapes. The winery releases wines in two series, Reserve and Red Poetry. Current production is about 10,000 bottles annually.

Reserve

RESERVE, CABERNET SAUVIGNON, 2007: Dark, deep and intense, opening at this stage with a hint of freshly cut sawdust on the nose, that yielding to wild berries, currants and tobacco notes, all on a background of spices and finally, on the long finish, a generous hint of white chocolate. Drink now–2013. Score 88,

RESERVE, CABERNET SAUVIGNON, 2006: Blended with 2–3% Petit Verdot and Merlot, dark garnet toward royal purple, medium- to full-bodied, with firm tannins and generous spicy wood but already showing the balance and structure needed. As this one develops look for blackberries, cassis, vanilla and, on the long finish, a generous hint of licorice. Generous and mouth-filling. Drink now. Score 88.

RESERVE, CABERNET SAUVIGNON, 2005: Medium- to full-bodied, showing good concentration and balance between soft tannins, cedarwood and fruits, playing on the nose and palate a combination of red and black fruits. A soft, round wine with a medium-long finish. Drink now. Score 85.

RESERVE, CABERNET SAUVIGNON, 2004: Dark garnet, medium-bodied, with soft tannins. Opens with barnyard aromas but those blow off quickly to reveal appealing blackberry and black cherry fruits. Somewhat short and one-dimensional. Showing age. Drink up. Score 84.

Red Poetry

RED POETRY, CABERNET SAUVIGNON, 2006: Dark garnet, medium- to full-bodied and developed in *barriques* for 14 months, a blend of 85% Cabernet Sauvignon and the balance of Cabernet Franc and Merlot. Showing soft, near-sweet tannins and spicy and vanilla-rich wood that open to show blackcurrant, blackberry and blueberry fruits. On the finish hints of dark chocolate and spices. Drink now. Score 86.

RED POETRY, CABERNET SAUVIGNON, 2005: Ruby toward garnet, medium- to full-bodied, with soft tannins and spicy wood integrating nicely and showing generous plum, currant and wild berry fruits. Oak-aged for 14 months, a blend of 85% Cabernet Sauvignon, 8% Cabernet Franc and 7% Merlot. Moderately long. Drink now. Score 85.

RED POETRY, MERLOT, 2006: Blended with 10% of Cabernet Sauvignon and oak-aged for 18 months. Dark garnet, medium- to full-bodied, with somewhat chunky, near-sweet tannins and notes of spicy wood, opening to show red currant, raspberry and plum fruits on a earthy-herbal background. Drink now. Score 85.

RED POETRY, MERLOT, 2005: Dark ruby in color, medium-bodied, with soft, near-sweet tannins and spices from the oak in which it aged. On the nose and palate appealing red berry and red currant fruits leading to a lightly herbal and green olive finish. Drink up. Score 85.

RED POETRY, CARIGNANE, RED STAINS, 2008: It's spelled Carignan in most of France and Cariñena in Spain, so precisely why the winery chose to use the "e" at the end of the name of the grape as is done only in parts of California eludes me. Spelling doesn't count, however, for the wine shows all of the traits of the variety. Dark garnet with orange reflections, medium- to full-bodied, with notes of sweet cedar on the nose and still-firm tannins waiting to integrate. Opens slowly in the glass to reveal red cherries, wild berries, white pepper and licorice notes and, from mid-palate on, a note of bitter almonds that lingers nicely. Drink now–2013. Score 88.

RED POETRY, CARIGNANE, RED STAINS, 2007: Medium- to full-bodied, with toasty vanilla and licorice notes to highlight red and black cherry and boysenberry fruits and, on the medium-long finish, a touch of earthy minerality. Drink now. Score 88.

RED POETRY, CABERNET SAUVIGNON-MERLOT, 2007: Almost inky garnet in color, full-bodied, with still-gripping tannins but those starting to settle in nicely. On the nose mint and black fruits, and on the palate black fruits and notes of bitter citrus peel, the fruits rising on the long finish. Drink now. Score 88.

RED POETRY, SHIRAZ-CABERNET SAUVIGNON, 2005: Deep royal purple in color, medium- to full-bodied, with soft, near-sweet tannins and hints of smoky oak. A blend of 80% Shiraz and 20% Cabernet Sauvignon, developed in new French oak for 12 months and showing forward plum, wild berry and currant fruits on a background of earthy-herbaceousness. Drink up. Score 86.

RED POETRY, SHARONA, 2007: A blend this year of 70% Cabernet Franc and 30% Merlot. Dark garnet toward royal purple, with gently caressing tannins and a moderate note of spicy cedarwood, opening on the palate to show blackberry, ripe plum and chocolate notes. On the long finish a hint of licorice. Drink now. Score 87.

RED POETRY, SHARONA, 2006: Deep royal purple in color, a blend of 60% Cabernet Franc and 40% Merlot. Full-bodied, concentrated and aromatic, round and tempting, opening to show aromas and flavors of wild berries and cassis, those with light earthy-herbal notes. Soft, generous and long. Drink now. Score 87.

RED POETRY, EHRLICH, 2007: Dark garnet, medium- to full-bodied, a blend primarily of Shiraz and Merlot, showing soft tannins and opening slowly on the nose and palate to show black and purple fruits, those with appealing hints of licorice and cigar tobacco. Drink up. Score 87.

RED POETRY, EHRLICH, 2006: Dark garnet, a medium- to full-bodied blend of 40% each of Merlot and Shiraz, the balance made up of Petite Sirah, Petit Verdot and Cabernet Sauvignon. Soft, caressing tannins in good balance between spicy oak and black fruits, all of which linger nicely. Sliding past its peak. Drink up. Score 86.

RED POETRY, EHRLICH, 2005: Dark garnet toward royal purple, a medium- to full-bodied blend of 40% Merlot, 40% Shiraz and 20% Cabernet Sauvignon. Reflects its 12 months in oak with soft, lightly spicy tannins and a note of vanilla, those parting to reveal wild berries, plums and blackcurrants. In the background an appealing hint of freshly tanned leather. Past its peak. Drink up. Score 84.

RED POETRY, CAPRIOTTI, 2007: A tempting blend of Sangiovese and Merlot, medium-bodied, with generous red berry, plum and citrus peel notes along with hints of milk chocolate that come in on the finish. Pleasant and easy to drink. Drink up. Score 87.

RED POETRY, CAPRIOTTI, 2006: Ruby toward garnet, medium-bodied, with soft, well-integrated tannins and a bare hint of vanilla and spices from its short-term oak-aging. A blend of 80% Sangiovese and 20% Merlot, the Sangiovese clearly dominating and showing blackcurrants and damson plums along with hints of citrus peel and licorice. A just-complex-enough quaffer. Drink up. Score 87.

RED POETRY, VIN FOU, 2008: A dark-garnet, medium- to full-bodied and gently tannic blend of Carignan and Merlot. On the nose and palate blackberries, purple plums and spices, the tannins and a note of cigar tobacco rising on the finish. Drink now–2013. Score 88.

RED POETRY, VIN FOU, 2006: 85% Carignan and 15% Merlot, entitled a "crazy wine," this also claims to be a "traditional Israeli blend," I am not quite sure what a traditional Israeli blend might be but this one shows itself quite nicely, on first attack with black fruits and tobacco, those yielding to ripe red plums and spices all leading to a generous and long finish. Drink up. Score 89.

RED POETRY, AARONSOHN, 2007: A blend of 75% Mourvedre and 25% Syrah, oak-aged for 18 months, showing deep garnet in color with firm tannins and smoky oak starting to settle in nicely now. Opens to show a generously spicy medium- to full-bodied red with ripe blackberry, blueberry and black cherry fruits, those complemented nicely by notes of vanilla and on the medium-long finish what seems at one moment a chocolaty note and at another one of cola. Drink now. Score 89.

Rosh Pina *

Set near the village of Rosh Pina in the
Galilee, this small winery was founded by
Ya'akov Blum in 2001 and released its first
wines in 2002. Grapes are drawn from the
Galilee, those including Cabernet Sauvignon,
Shiraz and Carignan. No wines were released
from the 2005 vintage due to damages done
to the winery during the 2006 war between
Israel and the Hezbollah forces of Lebanon.
The winery is currently releasing about 4,000
bottles annually.

ROSH PINA, CABERNET SAUVIGNON, 2004: Medium-bodied, dark
brick-red in color, with chunky tannins, this is a simple country-style
wine with a few raspberry and plum flavors. Drink up. Score 78.

ROSH PINA, MERLOT, 2004: Garnet-red, medium-bodied, with a few
cherry and wild berry fruits but those overpowered by earthy, musty
aromas and flavors. Drink up. Score 74.

ROSH PINA, MERLOT, 2003: Coarse enough to be thought of as vulgar,
with chunky tannins, far too much acidity, and earthy and only bare
hints of wild berry fruits. Drink up. Score 70.

ROSH PINA, SHIRAZ, 2003: Dark, but not fully clear garnet in color,
with chunky country-style tannins and a bit of coarseness. On the nose
and palate black cherry and cassis fruits, those with a somewhat exaggerated earthy character. Showing age. Drink up. Score 74.

ROSH PINA, CARIGNAN, TEVA, 2004: A few raspberry fruits, but
those struggling to be felt against too-dominant horsy, leathery and
herbal aromas and flavors. Score 70.

ROSH PINA, CABERNET SAUVIGNON-MERLOT, 2004: Opens with
powerful aromas of tobacco, stingy black fruits and an oddly sour
cedarwood note and finishes with a distinct barnyard stink. Score 65.

ROSH PINA, CABERNET SAUVIGNON-SHIRAZ, 2003: This blend of
60% Cabernet and 40% Shiraz is light ruby toward brick-red, light- to
medium-bodied, far too acidic and with chunky country-style tannins.
A few berry and black cherry fruits. Showing age. Drink up. Score 75.

Rota ✱✱✱

Founded by Erez Rota on the Negev Heights, this artisanal winery released its first wines in 2002. The winery and its beautifully planted and tended vineyards are set on an isolated farm, surrounded by magnificent desert mountains. Grapes under cultivation are Cabernet Sauvignon, Merlot, Shiraz and Muscat of Alexandria. In addition, the winery also receives grapes from the Ella Valley. First releases in 2002 were of 1,000 bottles. Current production is about 10,000 bottles annually. The wines will be kosher from the 2010 vintage.

ROTA, CABERNET SAUVIGNON, 2009: Medium-dark garnet in color, medium- to full-bodied, with fine balance between spicy wood, alcohol, soft tannins and fruit. On the nose and palate clean black and red berries, currants and spices. Gentle but with good concentration. Drink now. Score 86.

ROTA, CABERNET SAUVIGNON, YA'EL, 2008: Royal purple toward garnet, medium-bodied, reflecting its aging in barriques for eight months with soft, gently caressing tannins and hints of sweet-and-spicy cedarwood. On the nose and palate currants, crushed berries, earthy minerals and notes of brown spices. Mouth-filling and generous. Drink now. Score 87.

ROTA, CABERNET SAUVIGNON, ADDI, 2008: Oak-aged for 13 months, showing medium- to full-bodied, with gentle notes of spicy oak and chunky, country-style tannins, those tannins supporting aromas and flavors of blackcurrants, blackberries, plums, spices and green olives. Round and easy with just enough complexity to grab the attention. Drink now. Score 86.

ROTA, CABERNET SAUVIGNON, 2007: Dark garnet, medium- to full-bodied, with gripping tannins and spicy wood yielding to black fruits, spices and notes of candied citrus peel. Drink up. Score 85.

ROTA, CABERNET SAUVIGNON, 2006: Garnet toward royal purple, medium-bodied, with somewhat chunky tannins and generous wood, those parting slowly to make way for berry and blackcurrant fruits. Drink up. Score 85.

ROTA, MERLOT, 2009: Ruby toward garnet, with cherries and red berries on the nose, those making way for notes of cranberries and blueberries. Soft tannins, medium-bodied and notably easy to drink. Drink from release. Tentative Score 86–87.

ROTA, MERLOT, 2006: Deep garnet, medium- to full-bodied, with firm tannins and spicy French oak integrating nicely. Opens on the palate to show abundant red currant and raspberry fruits, those matched by hints of white pepper and green olives. Generous and long. Drink now. Score 87.

ROTA, SHIRAZ, 2009: Dark ruby toward royal purple in color, medium- to full-bodied, a generously aromatic wine opening to show fine plum, wild berry and cassis notes, those on a background that hints of saddle leather and roasted herbs. Soft tannins rise comfortably on the finish. Drink from release. Tentative Score 85–87.

ROTA, CABERNET SAUVIGNON-MERLOT, 2010: A medium-bodied, ruby toward garnet, gently tannic blend of 50% each Cabernet Sauvignon and Merlot, those developed with oak chips. Fresh and refreshing, with red berries and cassis fruits matched nicely by notes of stony minerals and an appealing hint of spicy oak. Intended for early drinking. Drink now. Score 87. K

ROTA, CABERNET SAUVIGNON-MERLOT, YA'EL, 2008: A blend of equal parts of Cabernet Sauvignon and Merlot. Dark garnet with a hint of adobe brick in color, with soft, gently gripping tannins and hints of vanilla from the oak in which it aged for eight months, opens

to show cassis and blackberries, those on a lightly spicy background. Drink now. Score 86.

ROTA, CABERNET SAUVIGNON-MERLOT, 2006: Deeply aromatic, this dark garnet, medium- to full-bodied wine is showing soft, mouth-coating tannins and a moderate hand with spicy oak. On the nose and palate berry, black cherry and cassis fruits, those complemented by hints of pepper, anise and light earthiness. Drink up. Score 87.

Rozenbaum *

Founded by Avi Rozenbaum in 1998, this small winery is located on Kibbutz Malkiya in the Upper Galilee near the Lebanese border. Grapes, including Cabernet Sauvignon, Merlot, Sangiovese, Chardonnay and Muscat of Alexandria, come from the Kadesh Valley. Production in 2003 was of 7,000 bottles, no wines were produced in 2004 and, with a new partner, 5,000 bottles were produced from the 2005, 2006 and 2007 harvests.

ROZENBAUM, CABERNET SAUVIGNON, 2006: Ruby toward garnet, medium-bodied with chunky country-style tannins and a far too distinct note of Brett that makes the wine unapproachable. Score 60.

ROZENBAUM, CABERNET SAUVIGNON, 2005: Dark garnet, with coarse tannins and a medicinal overlay that hides whatever fruits may be hiding here. Score 68.

ROZENBAUM, BLEND, 2006: Somewhat muddied garnet-red, with flabby tannins and a simple berry-cherry personality, the fruits hidden by a bit of bottle stink that fails to fade away. Score 60.

ROZENBAUM, BLEND, 2005: A coarse, alcoholic and hot blend of Cabernet Sauvignon and Merlot. Lacks charm. Score 70.

Ruth ★★★

Founded by Tal Maor and located in Kfar Ruth, adjoining the city of Modi'in, this family-owned winery produced several hundred bottles of wine from the 2002 vintage and current production is 20,000 bottles annually. Grapes, including Cabernet Sauvignon, Merlot and Shiraz, are harvested from vineyards on the central plain and in the hills of Jerusalem.

Reserve

RESERVE, CABERNET SAUVIGNON, 2004: Reflecting its prolonged development (30 months) in *barriques* with generous spicy wood along with hints of sawdust, a full-bodied wine showing poached red plums and cherry-pudding notes, those on a background of licorice and Mediterranean herbs, all with a rather sweet overlay. Drink now. Score 80. K

RESERVE, CABERNET SAUVIGNON, 2003: Oak-aged for 30 months, medium-bodied, with generous spicy wood and mouth-coating tannins. Shows red cherry and red berry fruits, those on a background of red licorice and roasted herbs. Drink now. Score 85. K

Ruth

RUTH, CABERNET SAUVIGNON, 2009: Medium-, perhaps medium- to full-bodied, with chunky tannins giving the wine a rustic note. On the nose and palate blackberries, purple plums and freshly hung tobacco. Drink now. Score 85. K

RUTH, CABERNET SAUVIGNON, 2005: Medium-bodied, with soft tannins integrating nicely. Showing appealing blackberry and grape flavors supported nicely by bramble, spice and tobacco notes. Drink up. Score 86. K

RUTH, MERLOT, 2005: Its youthful rough edges now smoothing out nicely, blended with 5% Cabernet Sauvignon and aged for 24 months in *barriques*, this medium- to full-bodied red shows spicy wood and firm tannins, those in fine balance with blackcurrant, plum and berry fruits all on a light licorice background. Drink up. Score 87. K

RUTH, CABERNET SAUVIGNON-MERLOT, 2006: A blend of 60% Cabernet Sauvignon and 40% Merlot, developed in oak for 12 months, showing medium- to full-bodied, soft and round with blackberry, currant and black cherry fruits highlighted by notes of bittersweet chocolate and tobacco. Drink now. Score 88. K

RUTH, CABERNET SAUVIGNON-MERLOT, 2005: A blend of 60% Cabernet Sauvignon and 40% Merlot, aged in *barriques* for 14 months. Dark garnet, medium- to full-bodied, with spicy wood and soft tannins integrating nicely and showing appealing currant and berry fruits on a light licorice background. Drink up. Score 85. K

RUTH, SHIRAZ-MERLOT, 2009: Dark garnet toward royal purple, reflecting its development in oak with soft tannins and notes of spicy wood and vanilla. Medium- to full-bodied, showing plum, cassis and wild berry fruits, those supported by hints of minted chocolate. Drink now. Score 86. K

RUTH, SHIRAZ-MERLOT, 2006: Medium- to full-bodied, a dark garnet blend of equal parts of Shiraz and Merlot, aged in new oak for 15 months. A country-style wine showing generous oak and chunky tannins, but do not take that as negative for the wine opens beautifully on the palate to show red plums and raspberries on a peppery background. Drink now. Score 88. K

Safed (Tsfat HaAttika) ✳

Founded by Moshe Alon in 2002 and located in the heart of the old city of Safed, this winery relies largely on grapes from the Upper Galilee. Production is about 12,000 bottles annually, the wines from Cabernet Sauvignon, Merlot, Cabernet Franc and Gewurztraminer grapes.

SAFED, CABERNET SAUVIGNON, 2007: Medium-bodied, somewhat cloudy garnet in color but opens with a fresh fruity nose and goes on to show appealing black fruits. A simple but acceptable quaffer. Drink up. Score 78. K

SAFED, CABERNET SAUVIGNON, RESERVE, 2006: Blended with Merlot and Cabernet Franc grapes, aged in new *barriques* for 16 months, showing dusty, not-clear garnet in color, opening with a strong barnyard whiff and going on to show a few red fruits, those alas overlaid with soggy cardboard and, rising on the finish, a most unwanted note of vegetal and animal decay. Score 55. K

SAFED, CABERNET SAUVIGNON, 2006: Developed in oak for nine months. Dark garnet, medium-bodied, dominated by earthy, compost pile and barnyard aromas that make it impossible to find whatever fruits may be hiding. Score 55. K

SAFED, CABERNET SAUVIGNON, RESERVE, 2005: Marked by searing tannins, burning alcohol and aromas that call to mind the sewers of Paris. Score 50. K

SAFED, MERLOT, RESERVE, 2006: Developed in *barriques* for 15 months, showing dark garnet in color, medium- to full-bodied with generous raspberry, cherry and cassis fruits. Lacks complexity but a good quaffer. Drink now. Past its peak. Score 82. K

SAFED, MERLOT, 2006: Dark ruby with a hint of off-brown, medium-bodied, with chunky tannins. Aged in used French and Bulgarian oak for 15 months, showing somewhat muddled red fruits and a too-deep earthy-herbal overlay. Past its peak. Drink up. Score 72. K

SAFED, CABERNET FRANC, 2006: Oak-aged for about eight months, a blend of 90% Cabernet Franc and 10% Cabernet Sauvignon. Dark garnet, medium- to full-bodied, opens with a medicinal aroma that, although it fades somewhat, never vanishes and hides the somewhat muddy black fruits that lie underneath. Score 65. K

SAFED, CHARDONNAY, 2006: Despite its youth this bronze-colored wine has gone toward vinegar, that with a distinct aroma of sewage. Score 50. K

SAFED, SAUVIGNON BLANC, 2007: Acidic enough to be thought of as puckering and sour, with a strong petrol-like aroma that one cannot shake. Score 50. K

SAFED, GEWURZTRAMINER, 2007: Damp straw colored, light- to medium-bodied, with stewed apricot and peach fruits but those hidden under a far too acidic and tart note. Noted on the bottle as having an 11.5% alcohol content but alcoholic on the nose and hot on the finish. Score 65. K

Salomon ✶✶

Located on Moshav Amikam in the Ramot Menashe forest not far from Zichron Ya'akov, this winery was founded in 1997 by Itamar Salomon. For several years the winery made only small quantities of wine for home consumption, and the first commercial release was from the 2002 vintage. Grapes are currently drawn from the Golan Heights, but the winery is planting its own vineyards with Cabernet Sauvignon, Merlot, Cabernet Franc and Shiraz grapes in the Upper Galilee. Production in 2004 was about 2,500 bottles and current production is about 10,000 bottles annually.

SALOMON, CABERNET SAUVIGNON, 2006: Medium- to full-bodied, with chunky, country-style tannins and notes of spicy wood that open to show currant and wild berry fruits. A pleasant little country-style wine. Drink up. Score 84.

SALOMON, CABERNET SAUVIGNON, 2005: Despite its youth, showing signs of premature aging. Medium-bodied, with tannins more gripping than at an earlier tasting, with its once-clean cherry, plum and sandalwood aromas and flavors now taking on a hint of barnyard. Past its peak. Drink up. Score 78.

SALOMON, MERLOT, 2006: Deep royal purple in color, medium-bodied, with soft tannins integrating nicely and showing black fruits, espresso coffee and a hint of Mediterranean herbs. Not complex but a good quaffer. Passing its peak. Drink up. Score 84.

SALOMON, SHIRAZ, 2005: Dark garnet toward royal purple, medium- to full-bodied, with silky tannins and showing generous plum, berry and licorice notes all leading to a moderately long finish. Drink up. Score 85.

SALOMON, STAV (AUTUMN), 2005: An oak-aged blend of Cabernet Franc, Cabernet Sauvignon and Shiraz (60%, 30% and 10% respectively), showing garnet toward royal purple in color, medium-bodied, soft and round. On the nose and palate, black and red berries matched by notes of Mediterranean herbs, cigar tobacco and licorice. Appealing but somewhat short on the finish. Drink up. Score 85.

Sarig **

Established in 2005 on Moshav Merchavia by Pini and Amir Sarig, with Amir serving as winemaker. Relying on Syrah, Mourvedre and Grenache Noir grapes, current production is about 4,000 bottles annually.

SARIG, SHIRAZ, 2006: Oak-aged for 12 months, with spicy but soft tannins and hints of vanilla from the wood. Medium- to full-bodied, a smooth, round wine opening to show plum and wild berry fruits, those supported nicely by notes of saddle leather and tobacco. Long and mouth-filling. Drink now. A fine first release. Score 88.

Saslove ✶✶✶✶

Established by Barry Saslove in 1998 on Kibbutz Eyal in the Sharon region, this boutique winery has well-established vineyards in the Upper Galilee planted with Cabernet Sauvignon, Merlot, Syrah and Sauvignon Blanc grapes. More recently planted vineyards with Cabernet Franc, Petit Verdot and Gewurztraminer grapes are now coming on line. The winery also has a facility in the Upper Galilee, not far from its vineyards, primarily for receiving and fermenting grapes. The barrel room and visitors' center remain on Kibbutz Eyal.

Current production of red wines made by the father-and-daughter team of Barry and Roni Saslove is in three series: Reserved, Adom and Aviv. The winery occasionally produces white wines as well. A recent addition to the winery's repertoire are the red, reinforced dessert wines in the Kadita series. Production has grown steadily, from 35,000 bottles in 2002 to about 80,000 bottles in 2009 and 2010. Starting with releases from the 2010 vintage, the Saslove wines will be kosher.

Reserved

RESERVED, CABERNET SAUVIGNON, 2008: Perhaps the best to date from Saslove. Full-bodied, deep garnet in color, with generous but not at all imposing oak in fine harmony with soft tannins and fruits. On first attack aromas and flavors of crushed blackberries, those parting to make way for notes of currants, black cherries and an appealing hint of bitter herbs. Long and mouth-filling, muscular but elegant. Drink now–2018. Score 93.

RESERVED, CABERNET SAUVIGNON, 2007: Youthful, with still-firm tannins and a moderate hand with spicy oak settling in nicely and showing fine balance and structure. Full-bodied, showing finesse and elegance. Traditional blackcurrant and blackberry fruits, those supported by notes of tobacco and roasted herbs. Long, generous and mouth-filling with an appealing note of bitter herbs on the finish. Drink now–2016. Score 90.

RESERVED, CABERNET SAUVIGNON, 2006: Made entirely from Cabernet Sauvignon grapes, oak-aged for 20 months, a deep, full-bodied wine with generous oak and still-firm tannins integrating nicely and showing fine balance and structure. Softening nicely as it develops and showing a concentrated and intense wine that is simultaneously rich and elegant. On the nose and palate blackcurrants, blackberries, raspberries and dried citrus peel notes, those supported by notes of spices Mediterranean herbs and, on the long finish, appealing hints of licorice and baking chocolate. Drink now–2015. Score 91.

RESERVED, CABERNET SAUVIGNON, 2005: Made from organically raised Cabernet Sauvignon grapes from the Kadita vineyard, oak-aged for 24 months in French and American oak, full-bodied with firm but gently mouth-coating tannins parting to reveal traditional Cabernet aromas and flavors of blackcurrants and blackberries. The fruits supported by complex notes of mocha, bittersweet chocolate, Oriental spices and Mediterranean herbs, all of which play nicely on the palate and lead to a long and generous finish. Drink now. Score 91

RESERVED, CABERNET SAUVIGNON, 2004: Developed in French oak for 27 months, still showing generous sweet-and-spicy oak but that in fine balance with soft, mouth-coating tannins, acidity and fruits. On opening attack blackcurrants and wild berries, those followed by notes of earthy minerals and tobacco and, on the long finish, a tantalizing hint of minted chocolate. Round, soft, generous and elegant. Drink now. Score 92.

RESERVED, CABERNET SAUVIGNON, 2003: This oak-aged blend of 88% Cabernet Sauvignon and 12% Merlot is dark garnet and medium- to full-bodied. Showing generous sweet-and-spicy wood and tannins in fine balance with currant, black cherry and blackberry fruits and a complex array of herbs and spices. On the long finish a hint of raspberry liqueur. An elegant wine. Drink up. Score 91.

Adom

ADOM, CABERNET SAUVIGNON, 2009: A wine that some would describe as "masculine" – that is to say, muscular, solid and even somewhat brash, with still-firm tannins waiting to settle down but showing balance and structure that bode well for the future. On the nose and palate red currants, plums and figs, those with notes of sweet cedarwood and espresso. Destined not for elegance but for power. Best starting in 2013. Tentative Score 88–90.

ADOM, CABERNET SAUVIGNON, 2008: Almost impenetrably dark garnet, showing full-bodied and round, with silky tannins and notes of spicy oak that caress gently. On the nose and palate traditional Cabernet Sauvignon blackcurrants and blackberries, those highlighted by hints of licorice and espresso coffee. Ripe, generous and long. Best from 2013–2017. Tentative Score 90–92.

ADOM, CABERNET SAUVIGNON, 2007: Deep garnet in color, full-bodied, reflecting its 20 months in barriques (40% of which were new) with near-sweet tannins and notes of spicy and vanilla-rich wood, those in fine balance with fruits. On the nose and palate blackcurrants, blackberries and black cherries, complemented by notes of mocha and unsweetened cocoa. Drink now–2016. Score 90.

ADOM, CABERNET SAUVIGNON, 2006: Full-bodied, rich, smooth and complex, with firm tannins integrating nicely with spicy wood and opening to reveal currant and berry fruits, those complemented by notes of sage and minerals, and, on the long finish, light sweet cedar and blackberries. Long, and simultaneously concentrated and elegant. Drink now–2015. Score 91.

ADOM, CABERNET SAUVIGNON, 2005: Well-crafted. Full-bodied, reflecting its 20 months in oak with firm tannins integrating nicely with spicy and vanilla-rich cedar. Opens with blackcurrants and wild berry fruits, those yielding to notes of plums, black cherries, orange peel, and, on the long, generous finish, an appealing hint of bittersweet chocolate. As the wine develops, look as well for notes of sweet spices and herbs coming in nicely. Drink now. Score 91.

ADOM, CABERNET SAUVIGNON, 2004: Medium- to full-bodied, with soft, mouth-coating tannins in fine balance with spicy and smoky wood and acidity. On the nose and palate traditional Cabernet blackcurrant and blackberry fruits, those matched nicely by light tobacco and chocolate-coated orange peel on the long finish. Drink up. Score 89.

ADOM, MERLOT, 2007: Dark garnet toward royal purple, medium- to full-bodied, with caressing tannins, a rich, soft and round wine, showing blackberry, espresso coffee and black olive notes all on a lightly spicy background. On the long finish a surprising but appealing note of citrus peel. Tasted from components. Drink now–2013. Score 88.

ADOM, MERLOT, 2006: Soft and round, medium- to full-bodied, this blend of 85% Merlot and 15% Cabernet Sauvignon offers up a generous and well-balanced array of cassis and berry fruits, those on a background of Mediterranean herbs and, on the long finish, a hint of bittersweet chocolate. Drink now–2013. Score 90.

ADOM, MERLOT, 2005: Medium- to full-bodied with fine concentration, yet soft and supple with generous but not-imposing wood after 20 months in French and American oak. Opens with bold aromas and flavors of toasty oak and freshly roasted coffee, yielding nicely to a generous array of cassis, purple plum and black cherry fruits, and those complemented nicely by hints of bittersweet chocolate and spices. Drink up. Score 90.

ADOM, SHIRAZ, 2009: A deeply extracted wine, deep garnet in color with a royal purple robe. Full-bodied, with generous wood and soft tannins in fine balance with fruits and acidity On the nose and palate currants, wild berries, red licorice and, on the long finish, a note of crushed berries. Best 2013–2017, perhaps longer. Tentative Score 88–90.

ADOM, SHIRAZ, 2008: Still early days for this wine but already showing full-bodied, with gently caressing tannins. On first attack notes of minerality underlying raspberries and cherries, those parting to make way for spicy blackberries. On the long finish notes of saddle leather and green tea. Ripe and generous. Drink from release–2016, perhaps longer. Tentative Score 89–91.

ADOM, SHIRAZ-CABERNET SAUVIGNON, 2008: Tasted from components. Already showing medium- to full-, perhaps full-bodied, deeply aromatic, with ripe red and black berries, red currants and orange-peel notes, those complemented by hints of vanilla and, on the finish, hints of licorice and fresh herbs. Drink now–2015. Score 90.

ADOM, SHIRAZ-CABERNET SAUVIGNON, 2007: A super-dark garnet, full-bodied, deep royal-purple blend of 60% Shiraz and 40% Cabernet Sauvignon, in which both varieties make themselves felt. Developed in *barriques* for 20 months, its elements coming together nicely and showing opulence, the generous 14.5% alcohol never imposing. On the nose and palate a tempting array of currants, plum, blueberries and black pepper, those on a background that hints at one moment of earthy minerals, at another of saddle leather and at yet another of freshly hung tobacco. Drink now–2016. Score 91.

ADOM, SHIRAZ-CABERNET SAUVIGNON, 2006: Dark royal purple, full-bodied, with gently gripping tannins and spicy wood integrated nicely. Opens in the glass to reveal spicy currants and berries, the light tarry sensation felt during its youth now black licorice and dried herbs. Drink now–2015. Score 91.

ADOM, SHIRAZ-CABERNET SAUVIGNON, 2005: Developed in oak for 20 months, this blend of 60% Shiraz and 40% Cabernet Sauvignon will remind many of the Mollydooker wines of Australia. Dark garnet, full-bodied, with firm tannins and peppery wood notes, those given a racy feeling by generous currant, cherry and raspberry fruits. On the background, tantalizing hints of pepper and tar, all culminating in a long, mouth-filling finish. Drink now. Score 91.

ADOM, MARRIAGE, 2004: Dark, almost impenetrable garnet, this medium-bodied, smooth and round blend of Cabernet Sauvignon, Merlot and Shiraz opens with generous spicy-dusty oak on the nose but that yielding nicely to black and red currants, crushed berries and appealing hints of licorice. Sliding past its peak. Drink up. Score 88.

ADOM, MARRIAGE, 2003: Aged in a variety of oak barrels, fermented with different yeasts, this full-bodied blend of Cabernet Sauvignon, Merlot and Syrah is one of Saslove's best efforts to date. Full-bodied and tannic but simultaneously soft, round and elegant, on the nose and palate a basic blackcurrant personality but that matched by a generous array of berry, black cherry and spices, all lingering nicely on the finish. Showing age. Drink up. Score 87.

Aviv

AVIV, CABERNET SAUVIGNON, 2008: Deep, almost impenetrable garnet in color, medium- to full-bodied, reflecting its exposure to oak with gently gripping tannins and notes of spicy oak. On first attack raspberries, those parting to make way for red and black currants and blackberries with notes of brown spices and white pepper. Simultaneously easy to drink and complex. Drink now–2014. Score 90.

AVIV, CABERNET SAUVIGNON, 2007: A near-twin to the 2006 edition. Blue-black in color, medium- to full-bodied with firm tannins and smoky wood integrating nicely now and showing fine balance to highlight blackberry, purple plum and currant fruits, those complemented by hints of spices, cloves and espresso coffee. Drink now. Score 88.

AVIV, CABERNET SAUVIGNON, 2006: Almost blue-black in color, medium- to full-bodied with firm tannins and smoky wood integrating nicely now and showing fine balance to highlight blackberry, purple plum and currant fruits, those complemented by hints of spices, cloves and espresso coffee. Drink up. Score 89.

AVIV, MERLOT, 2008: Dark ruby toward garnet, reflecting its six months in *barriques* with soft, gently gripping tannins and hints of near-sweet cedarwood. Medium- to full-bodied, with aromas and flavors of red and black cherries, cassis and generous hints of cloves and cinnamon. On the long finish, tannins and hints of milk chocolate rise nicely. Drink now–2013. Score 89.

AVIV, MERLOT, 2007: Made in stainless-steel vats with oak chips, as are all of the wines in the Aviv series. Medium-bodied, with soft tannins and appealing notes of spicy and vanilla-rich oak, opening to show wild berry, currant and purple plums, those highlighted by light notes of sage and chocolate. Finishes round and smooth and moderately long with fruits rising. Drink now. Score 88.

AVIV, MERLOT, 2006: Soft and round, medium- to full-bodied, this blend of 85% Merlot and 15% Cabernet Sauvignon offers up a generous and well-balanced array of cassis and berry fruits, those on a background of Mediterranean herbs. Long and satisfying. Drink now. Score 89.

AVIV, MERLOT, 2005: Medium-bodied, with caressing, near-sweet tannins and a generous array of black fruits backed up nicely by earthy, herbal and chocolate aromas and flavors that linger nicely on the palate. Drink up. Score 90.

AVIV, MARRIAGE, 2008: Based on 90% Cabernet Sauvignon, Merlot and Shiraz, those fleshed out with 10% of Cabernet Franc, Petit Verdot and Nebbiolo, reflecting its six months' exposure to oak with soft, gently caressing tannins. Medium- to full-bodied, with an array of spicy red and black berries, bittersweet chocolate and from mid-palate on an appealing note of eucalyptus. Drink now–2014. Score 90.

AVIV, MARRIAGE, 2007: A medium-bodied, soft and round blend of 25% Merlot, 65% Cabernet Sauvignon and 10% Shiraz opening to show appealing red currant, raspberry and blueberry notes, those supported by notes of spices and, as traditional to this wine, red licorice. Drink now. Score 88.

AVIV, MARRIAGE, 2006: Deep garnet toward royal purple, medium- to full-bodied, with silky tannins. A blend of 60% Merlot, 33% Cabernet Sauvignon and 7% Petite Sirah, showing black fruits, spices and hints of red licorice on the finish. Drink up. Score 89.

Kadita

KADITA, 2007: Named after the organic vineyard in which the Cabernet Sauvignon grapes were grown, reinforced with fruit alcohol to a 17% alcohol content. Showing the color of mahogany pearl (some refer to that as black garnet), a full-bodied wine, generously sweet but not at all unctuous and opening in the glass to reveal violets, berries, cherries and prune aromas and flavors, those on a background that hints of both citrus peel and pepper. At its best with Stilton, Gouda or sweet Gorgonzola cheeses, or with a plate of walnuts and pears. A fine effort, lingering long and comfortably on the palate. Drink now–2015. Score 90.

KADITA, 2005-2007: A blend from two vintage years, showing dark garnet with a purple robe. Full-bodied, with generous apricots, cherries and spices and, from mid-palate on, hints of dried fruits. As this one develops in the bottle look as well for a hint of maple syrup. Generously sweet but with fine balancing acidity. Drink now–2014. Score 88.

KADITA, 2005: Deep amber toward garnet in color, medium- to full-bodied with polished tannins that make themselves felt nicely. On the nose and palate abundant spring flowers, peppery red cherries, vanilla and citrus peel, all lingering long and comfortably on the palate. At its best with a fine Gouda cheese. Drink now–2013. Score 90.

Saslove

SASLOVE, APRIL, 2010: Developed in French and American oak for four months, a rather hodge-podge blend of 40% Cabernet Franc, Petit Verdot and Nebbiolo, 40% Merlot and 20% Cabernet Sauvignon. Medium-bodied, with chunky tannins, a simple rustic wine with notes of red and black fruits, an overlay of spices and cinnamon aromas on the finish. Drink up. Score 84. K

SASLOVE, LAVAN, 2010: A half-dry blend of 45% each of Gewurztraminer and Viognier with 10% of Sauvignon Blanc. Cold fermented over a prolonged period and developed entirely in stainless steel, showing aromas and flavors of grapefruit, litchis and apricot leather. With its moderate sweetness complemented by fine balancing acidity, a wine that coats the palate comfortably, the flavors lingering very nicely indeed. As good as an aperitif as with beef carpaccio, tuna tartar, and grilled or fried fillets of small fish. Most pleasant. Drink now–2013. Score 90. K

Sassy *

Sasson Bar-Gig established this small winery in 2000 in the town of Bat Yam on the outskirts of Tel Aviv. The winery draws on grapes from Gush Etzion and the Golan Heights, and is currently producing about 8,000 bottles annually, the reds aged in oak for about 12 months.

SASSY, CABERNET SAUVIGNON, 2006: Medium-bodied, with firm tannins, dusty wood and barnyard aromas that tend to hide the black fruits that struggle to make themselves felt. Drink up. Score 72.

SASSY, CABERNET SAUVIGNON, 2005: Ruby toward garnet, medium-bodied, with firm tannins that open slowly to show currant and berry fruits. A simple country-style wine. Drink up. Score 80.

SASSY, CABERNET SAUVIGNON, 2004: A country-style wine, medium-bodied, with an herbal edge to currant and cherry fruits. Well past its peak. Score 70.

SASSY, MERLOT, 2006: Medium- to full-bodied, with chunky tannins and generous Brett giving the wine a distinctly rustic note. Opens to show muted plum and berry fruits. Drink up. Score 75.

SASSY, MERLOT, 2005: Dark garnet but, despite its youth, showing clearing at the edges. Somewhat coarse tannins hold back the black fruits that fail to make themselves fully felt. Drink up. Score 77.

SASSY, MERLOT, 2004: Garnet-red but already showing its maturity with hints of browning. Medium-bodied, still showing some red fruits but now starting to caramelize. Past its peak. Score 75.

Savion ✶✶✶✶

Founded by Ashi Salmon and Eli Pardess and set on Moshav Mesilat Tzion in the Jerusalem Mountains, this micro-winery released its first wine from the 2000 vintage and is currently producing about 2,500 bottles annually. Grapes come primarily from Ramat Dalton and other vineyards in the Upper Galilee, but the winery has new vineyards in which it is raising its own Cabernet Sauvignon, Merlot and Syrah grapes. For primarily logistic reasons, no wines were released from the 2007 vintage.

SAVION, CABERNET SAUVIGNON, 2009: Dark garnet, full-bodied, with still-firm, near-sweet tannins just starting to integrate. Showing an appealing spiciness from the French and American *barriques* in which the wine is developing, that parting to make way for an appealing array of blackcurrants, purple plums and bittersweet chocolate. A blend of 92% Cabernet Sauvignon and 8% Merlot, showing a hint of licorice on the long finish. Best from 2013. Tentative Score 88–90.

SAVION, CABERNET SAUVIGNON, 2008: A concentrated and deep blend of 88% Cabernet Sauvignon, about 8-10% Merlot with the balance of Syrah. Super-dark garnet toward royal purple, with a traditional Bordeaux nose of black fruits and lead-pencil notes, opens in the glass to show generous black fruits, spicy oak and a note of roasted herbs that rises on the finish. Firm and tannic at this stage but showing fine balance and structure that bode well for the future. Drink from release–2015, perhaps longer. Score 90.

SAVION, CABERNET SAUVIGNON, 2006: Made entirely from Cabernet Sauvignon grapes, showing medium- to full-bodied with soft, gently caressing tannins, those integrating nicely with notes of spicy cedarwood and fruits. On first attack ripe plums, those going to blackberries and currants. Tannins, fruits and a note of minted chocolate rise nicely on the finish. Drink now–2014. Score 90.

SAVION, CABERNET SAUVIGNON, 2006: Deep royal purple, firm, concentrated and intense, this medium- to full-bodied wine shows generous soft tannins and complex blackberry, currant, tobacco and anise aromas and flavors. Already revealing sharp focus and tannins that firm up on the long, fruity finish. Drink now. Score 89.

SAVION, CABERNET SAUVIGNON, 2005: Blended with 15% of Merlot and developed partly in American and partly in French oak, medium- to full-bodied, with now–softened tannins and vanilla-rich wood. Opens to reveal currant, blackberry, black cherry, spicy cedar and hints of sage. On the long finish, cherry and berry fruits rise. Drink now. Score 90.

SAVION, CABERNET SAUVIGNON, 2004: Blended with 10% of Merlot and aged for 12 months in primarily French oak. Garnet toward royal purple, medium- to full-bodied, with firm tannins and spicy wood integrating nicely with fruits and acidity. On the nose and palate blackcurrants and berries complemented by herbal and tobacco notes and, on the long finish, a hint of white chocolate. Drink up. Score 89.

SAVION, SOMEQ, 2008: A full-bodied blend of 60% Syrah, 24% Petit Verdot, 10% Merlot and 6% Cabernet Sauvignon. Oak-aged in American *barriques* for 12 months, showing dark ruby toward royal purple. Round and supple, with tannins that grip gently and part to make room on first attack for raspberries and crushed berries, those yielding to notes of blackcurrants and roasted herbs. Drink from release–2015. Score 90.

Sde Boker ✳✳✳

Located on Kibbutz Sde Boker in the heart of the Negev Desert, this small winery was founded in 1998 by former Californian Zvi Remick who studied winemaking at California's Napa Valley College. Relying on Cabernet Sauvignon, Merlot, Malbec, Carignan and Zinfandel grapes grown in the desert, production varies between 3,000–6,000 bottles annually. The winery has recently opened an attractive visitors' center.

SDE BOKER, CABERNET SAUVIGNON, 2008: Medium- to full-bodied, dark garnet in color with soft tannins and generous (perhaps too-generous) acidity. Opens in the glass to reveal black and red currants, wild berries and notes of spices and earthy minerals. Drink now. Score 85.

SDE BOKER, CABERNET SAUVIGNON, 2005: Dark garnet toward inky purple, medium- to full-bodied, with soft tannins integrating nicely and showing generous but not-imposing spicy cedarwood. Look for aromas and flavors of black fruits, Oriental spices and green olives, all lingering comfortably. Drink up. Score 87.

SDE BOKER, MERLOT, 2008: Garnet in color, medium- to full-bodied, with soft tannins and light notes of spicy oak giving the wine a round, easily approachable nature. On the nose and palate red currants and raspberries, those parting to make way for crushed wild berries. Tannins and fruits rise nicely on a moderately long finish. Drink now. Score 86.

SDE BOKER, MERLOT, 2005: Made entirely from Merlot grapes, oak-aged for 24 months in 30% new oak, showing ruby toward garnet, with soft, gently mouth-coating tannins and a spicy wood influence. On the nose and palate blackberries, black cherries and plums, those supported by hints of roasted herbs and earthy minerals. Drink up. Score 86.

SDE BOKER, ZINFANDEL, 2008: Showing true Zinfandel traits but neither a California Zinfandel nor an Italian Primitivo, this is a wine that reflects its desert heritage nicely. Notes of briar and tumbleweed (call that *garrigue* if you like, but tumbleweed is as close as I can get in words), opening to show wild berries, crushed black pepper, dried cherries and licorice notes. Medium- to full-bodied with

somewhat chunky tannins that in this case succeed in giving the wine an appealing rustic character. Well done. Drink now–2013. Score 88.

SDE BOKER, MALBEC, 2009: Made entirely from desert-grown Malbec grapes and developed for 18 months in barriques, 10% of which were new. Garnet with a royal purple robe, a ripe and friendly medium- to full-bodied wine with blackberries, red plums and a note of figs all coming together nicely on a background of licorice and graphite and, on the moderately long finish, an appealing hint of anise. Drink now–2013. Score 87.

SDE BOKER, MALBEC, 2008: Developed in barriques for 12 months, medium-bodied, with now nicely integrating tannins and appealing Malbec spices and smokiness to highlight raspberry and blackberry fruits. A light medicinal note on opening but that passes as the wine opens in the glass. The wine's generous acidity calls for food. Drink now. Score 85.

SDE BOKER, CABERNET SAUVIGNON-MERLOT, 2007: An oak-aged blend of equal parts of Cabernet Sauvignon and Merlot. Dark garnet toward royal purple, full-bodied, with soft tannins that grip gently and showing fine balance between wood, acidity and fruits. On first attack red plums and spices, those parting to make way for clean notes of cassis and blackberries and, on the long finish, the tannins rising together with the fruits a note of roasted herbs. The best to date from the winery. Drink now. Score 90.

SDE BOKER, CABERNET SAUVIGNON-MERLOT, 2006: Deep garnet-red, medium- to full-bodied, with spicy aromas and flavors of blackcurrants, black and red cherries, Mediterranean herbs and pepper. Well balanced, with softly caressing tannins and good focus, with tangy red fruits and smoky oak on the finish. Drink up. Score 88.

SDE BOKER, ZIN ZIN, 2007: Made, as is the winemaker's wont, from late-harvested Zinfandel grapes, a sweet dessert wine with its whopping 15.9% alcohol content and generous sweetness completely natural. Oak-aged and with fine prunes and raisins on the nose, opens in the glass to show super-ripe cherry, berry and plum fruits, those on a background of sweet brown spices and toasty oak. On the long finish cherries, milk chocolate and a tantalizing hint of cinnamon. Drink now–2014. Score 88.

Sea Horse *****

This boutique winery was established in 2000 on Moshav Bar Giora in the Jerusalem Mountains. Ze'ev Dunie has his own vineyards planted in Syrah, Zinfandel and Grenache and draws on Cabernet Sauvignon and other red grapes from the Upper Galilee. Mourvedre, Grenache and Petite Sirah are planted as well, coming on line with the 2010 vintage. The winery's initial production, from the 2001 vintage, was of 1,800 bottles. Growth has been gradual and well measured, and production now stands at 20–24,000 bottles annually. As can be seen in the names he gives, winemaker Dunie has a passion for naming his wines after people he admires. Current releases include two Cabernet Sauvignon-based wines, Elul and Fellini; a Zinfandel-based wine, Lennon; a Syrah-based wine, Antoine; and in selected years, Munch, which is made entirely from Petite Sirah grapes. There are also two blends, Gaudi and Romain. James, the winery's first white wine, a Chenin Blanc, was released from the 2007 vintage. In 2008 the winery unveiled what will now be its flagship wine, Underground, the blend of which will vary, even dramatically, from year to year in the years that it will be produced, all depending on what Dunie considers a blend special enough.

Underground

UNDERGROUND, 2008: A limited edition blend of 66% Petite Sirah and about 17% each of Syrah and Cabernet Sauvignon. Reflecting its development in *barriques* for 18 months, showing full-bodied, with gently gripping tannins and an appealing note of spicy wood. A big but friendly and juicy wine, opening with blueberry and plum fruits, those going on to reveal notes of blackberries, black pepper and licorice. Long and generous Drink now–2016. Score 91.

Elul

ELUL, 2009: A tentative blend of Cabernet Sauvignon, Syrah and Petite Sirah (70%, 20% and 10% respectively), developing in French oak. Deep purple toward black, a full-bodied, concentrated and muscular wine at this stage of its development but already showing good balance and structure. On first attack blackcurrants and baking chocolate, those parting to make way for generous notes of purple plums and blackberries. Needs time but promises to show soft and round as its elements integrate. Best from 2013–2018. Tentative Score 90–92.

ELUL, 2008: A blend of 72% Cabernet Sauvignon and 14% each of Syrah and Petite Sirah, showing a black-fruit and floral nose, opening in the glass to show generous blackberries and cassis, those supported nicely by notes of dark chocolate and licorice and, on the long finish, hints of green olives and Mediterranean herbs. Drink now–2018. Score 92.

ELUL, 2007: Dark, almost impenetrable garnet in color, deeply aromatic with its once-firm tannins now integrating nicely and showing fine balance and structure. A blend of 75% Cabernet Sauvignon, 20% Syrah and 5% Petite Sirah, showing a tempting array of blackcurrant and black and red berries, those on a generously spicy background and coming to a long, caressing finish on which a tempting note of bitter herbs. Drink now–2016. Score 90.

ELUL, 2006: Developed in French and American oak for 20 months, full-bodied, with generous firm tannins and cigar-box notes in fine balance with fruits. A blend of Cabernet Sauvignon, Syrah and Petite Sirah (75%, 20% and 5%, respectively). On first attack blackberry and blackcurrant fruits, those opening to reveal notes of Oriental spices, mocha and cigar tobacco. Look for a long, tantalizing near-sweet finish on which tannins, fruits and notes of roasted herbs rise nicely. Drink now–2014. Score 91.

ELUL, 2005: A blend of 73% Cabernet Sauvignon and about 13.5% each of Syrah and Petite Sirah, developed for 22 months in French and American oak, now showing dark garnet, generously aromatic and full-bodied with firm, near-sweet tannins and spicy oak integrated nicely and gently mouth-coating. Opens with currant, kirsch and black cherry fruits, those yielding to hints of licorice, spices and berries, all leading to a long and complex finish. Drink now–2015. Score 91.

ELUL, 2004: A blend of 75% Cabernet Sauvignon, 20% Syrah and 5% Petite Sirah. Deep, almost impenetrable garnet, medium- to full-bodied (leaning to the full), with firm tannins complemented by spicy oak. On first attack red currants and plums, those yielding to red and black berries, a hint of iron, and finally to bittersweet chocolate and Mediterranean herbs, all lingering comfortably. Ripe, round and mouth-filling but not for further cellaring. Drink up. Score 92.

ELUL, 2003: Holding its peak better than originally predicted, a well-balanced blend of Cabernet Sauvignon, Syrah and Petite Sirah (85%, 10% and 5% respectively), reflecting its development for 20 months in barriques with near-sweet tannins and a gentle overlay of spicy oak. On the nose and palate black cherries, currants and berries along with hints of anise and a light earthiness. Long and generous, an elegant wine. Drink now. Score 92.

ELUL, 2002: Deep garnet toward royal purple, a full-bodied blend of 85% Cabernet Sauvignon, 9% Merlot and 6% Syrah. Generous but soft and well-integrating tannins with jammy currant and berry aromas and flavors set off by spices and toast, all showing appealing overtones of Mediterranean herbs. Continuing to show elegance but sliding rapidly past its peak. Drink up. Score 90.

Fellini

FELLINI, 2009: Dark garnet, a full-bodied blend of 60% Syrah and 40% Cabernet Sauvignon showing notes of spices and vanilla from the oak in which it is developing. On the nose and palate raspberries and cherries, those yielding to purple plums and currants, all supported by notes of roasted herbs. Finishes long with a note of licorice. Best from release–2016. Tentative Score 88–90.

FELLINI, 2008: A blend of 58% Syrah and 42% Cabernet Sauvignon, oak-aged for 18 months. Dark garnet with a youthful royal purple robe, showing full-bodied, with gently gripping tannins. On first attack purple plums and blackcurrants, those parting to reveal generous notes of huckleberries, dark chocolate and tobacco. As has been the case with earlier editions of this wine, a hint of red licorice on the long and mouth-filling finish. Approachable and enjoyable now but best 2013–2018. Score 92.

FELLINI, 2007: Developed in French and American oak for 14 months, dark garnet with green and orange reflections, a full-bodied blend of 55% Syrah and 45% Cabernet Sauvignon, showing heady, near-sweet tannins and sweet-and-spicy cedarwood, those in fine balance with fruit and natural acidity. On the nose and palate generous black fruits complemented by notes of bittersweet chocolate, freshly cured cigar tobacco and, on the long finish, a hint of red licorice. Drink now–2016. Score 91.

FELLINI, 2006: A medium-bodied, soft and round blend of 55% Syrah and 45% Cabernet Sauvignon, those oak-aged for 18 months. Showing soft and round, with silky tannins and a gentle hand with the oak. Opens to show plums, raspberries and cassis, those with notes of vanilla and licorice that linger nicely. Drink now. Score 90.

FELLINI, 2005: A blend of 46% each Cabernet Sauvignon and Syrah, those complemented by 8% of Petit Verdot. Developed in French and American oak for 16 months, this medium- to full-bodied wine shows silky tannins along with cherry, raspberry and licorice aromas and flavors, those opening to reveal tempting hints of Mediterranean herbs and bittersweet chocolate on the finish. Drink now. Score 90.

FELLINI, 2004: Super-dark amber toward inky-black in color, this blend of equal parts Cabernet Sauvignon and Syrah developed in oak for 16 months and shows gentle cedar and cigar-box hints that run throughout. On the nose and palate wild berries, currants and a generous hint of citrus peel, those complemented nicely by light earthy and leathery overtones. Mouth-filling, long and generous. Sliding past its peak. Drink up. Score 90.

Lennon

LENNON, 2009: Deep, almost impenetrable garnet in color, with sweet fruits on the nose, that possibly because of a generous 15% alcohol content. Developing in American oak, a blend of 85% Zinfandel, 10% Petite Sirah and 5% Mourvedre, opening with red berries and going on to purple plums, cassis, black olives and a hint of mocha.

Finishes with a bit of alcoholic heat. Perhaps better as the elements integrate. Drink from release–2014. Tentative Score 86–88.

LENNON, 2008: This year a blend of 80% Zinfandel and 10% each of Petite Sirah and Mourvedre. A simultaneously supple and intense wine, well focused and even at this early stage showing fine balance and structure. On first attack black cherries, anise and pepper, those followed by wild berry, sage and oregano notes and, on the long finish, blueberries and cherries. Plenty of tannins here so no need to rush. Drink now–2016. Score 91.

LENNON, 2007: Primarily Zinfandel, that flushed out with Petite Sirah. Showing more round, gentle and elegant than at barrel tastings. A sophisticated country-style wine, with soft but somewhat chunky tannins and the once-dominant wood now receding nicely. On the nose and palate generous plum, berry and licorice aromas. On the long finish the tannins part to reveal notes of red berries, black pepper and sage. Drink now–2014. Score 91.

LENNON, 2006: Medium- to full-bodied, this blend of 92% Zinfandel and 8% Petite Sirah shows soft and round with gently mouth-coating tannins and a moderate hand with spicy oak. On the nose and palate red plums, blackberries and hints of both Oriental spices and Mediterranean herbs, all lingering nicely. Look for a tantalizing note of bitter chocolate on the finish. Drink now. Score 90.

LENNON, 2005: A blend this year of 90% Zinfandel and 5% each Petite Sirah and Carignan. Aged for about 16 months in used American oak barrels, this full-bodied, deep, dark-garnet wine is richly aromatic, with soft tannins integrating beautifully and highlighting generous plum, wild berry, black berry and notes of roasted herbs. A long and generous spicy finish. Drink up. Score 90.

LENNON, 2004: Deep garnet, medium- to full-bodied, reflecting its 14 months oak-aging with now-soft, well-integrated tannins and spicy wood. A blend of 95% low-yield Zinfandel vines and 5% Petite Sirah, the wine continuing to show good balance between wood, tannins and fruits. Opens to reveal generous raspberry, plum and cassis fruits, those matched nicely by light peppery, vanilla and minty overtones. Firm and concentrated, lingering nicely on the palate but not for further cellaring. Drink up. Score 90.

Take Two

TAKE TWO, 2006: This oak-aged blend of Primitivo, Zinfandel and Petite Sirah shows deep and dark, with fine intensity and generous firm tannins backing up plum, cherry and chocolate aromas and flavors, those on a medium- to full-bodied frame, all leading to a long fruity finish. Drink now. Score 88.

TAKE TWO, 2005: A medium-bodied, softly tannic blend of 85% Zinfandel, 10% Petite Sirah and 5% Carignan that was aged for eight months in primarily American oak. With light peppery and chocolate overtones highlighting plum, raspberry and wild berry fruits, those with hints of anise and minerals. Ripe, round and generous. Drink up. Score 89.

TAKE TWO, 2004: Dark garnet, aged in oak for eight months, this blend of 88% Zinfandel, 10% Petite Sirah and 2% Cabernet Sauvignon shows light meaty and leathery notes. Smooth and round, with wild berry and cassis fruits that make themselves felt nicely. Sliding past its peak. Drink up. Score 90.

Camus

CAMUS, 2008: A dark garnet blend of Syrah and Petite Sirah, distinctly tannic and concentrated but with fine balance and structure that bode well for the future. On first attack blackberries and bitter herbs, those yielding to wild berries and roasted coffee and then to a long finish on which you will find notes of ripe plums. Delicious and with the stuffing for cellaring. Drink now–2018. Score 91.

CAMUS, 2007: The now-traditional blend of Syrah and Petite Sirah, this year for the first time sub-labeled as "New Camus" because the grapes now come entirely from the winery's own vineyards. Dark garnet in color, full-bodied and intense but offering soft tannins that give a round and gentle touch to the wine. Opens with clear notes of raspberries, those parting to make room for juicy plum, wild berry and floral notes. Gripping tannins and wood well in control here giving the wine fine balance and structure. Drink now–2014. Score 90.

CAMUS, 2006: Firm and gripping tannins opening to reveal dense blackcurrant and blackberry fruits, those backed up by aromas and flavors of minerals, black pepper and cigar box. At this stage massive, but with balance and structure that bode well for future elegance. Drink now. Score 90.

CAMUS, 2005: This almost inky-garnet, full-bodied blend of 92% Syrah and 8% Petite Sirah reflects its 12 months in French oak with a gentle layer of spicy wood, that well balanced by generous but yielding tannins and on the nose and palate smoky blackberries and currants, Oriental spices and hints of game meat. Soft, round and well focused with the tannins rising on the long, supple finish along with appealing hints of leather and black pepper. Drink up. Score 90.

CAMUS, 2004: Dark garnet, medium-bodied, and with soft, caressing tannins, this blend of 94% Syrah and 6% Petite Sirah reflects its 12 months in oak with refreshing acidity, and spicy-toasty oak. On the nose and palate blackcurrant, blackberry, tobacco, and a hint of freshly tanned leather, with white pepper and cigar tobacco rising on the long finish. Drink up. Score 90.

Antoine

ANTOINE, 2009: A deeply aromatic Rhone blend of 66% Syrah and 17% each of Grenache and Mourvedre. Dark garnet, medium- to full-bodied, with soft, gently mouth-coating tannins. Showing generous black fruits, and spices along with hints of saddle leather and black olives. Drink now–2017. Score 90.

ANTOINE, 2008: Dark garnet, an oak-aged blend of Syrah, Grenache and Mourvedre (65%, 18% and 17% respectively). The deepest, softest and most elegant Antoine to date, showing silky-smooth tannins and hints of sweet cedarwood. On opening attack blackberries and eucalyptus, the wine opening in the glass to show blueberries and currants, those supported nicely by notes of dark chocolate and freshly tanned leather. Long and mouth filling. Drink now–2016. Score 91.

ANTOINE, 2007: Full-bodied now, showing deeper garnet, greater concentration and more elegant than at previous tastings. A blend of 76% Syrah, 17% Grenache and 7% Mourvedre, with its youthfully firm tannins and generous wood now receding to show the wine's inherent balance. On first attack black fruits, those yielding to raspberries and mint. Dense, almost chewy and muscular, but on the palate soft, round and elegant. Drink now–2015. Score 91.

ANTOINE, 2006: Dark garnet, reflecting its 18 months in oak with generous but soft tannins and tempting notes of spicy cedarwood.

On first attack black fruits and bittersweet chocolate, those parting to make way for red berries and currants and, on the long finish, notes of freshly tanned leather and cigar tobacco. Long and generous. Drink now–2014. Score 91.

ANTOINE, 2005: Made entirely from Syrah grapes, this full-bodied wine spent 16 months in second- and third-year French barriques. Showing dark garnet in color, with once-gripping tannins now integrated nicely and in fine balance with spicy oak. Not an aromatic wine but one rich in flavors, those including purple plums, blackberries, spices and red licorice. Drinking nicely with an appealing hint of bitterness on the finish but showing first, albeit very light, signs of oxidation. Drink now. Score 90.

Munch

MUNCH, 2008: 100% Petite Sirah made from 35-year-old vines. Almost inky black in color, firm and intense, a wine with muscles but that seems to know how to behave like a gentleman. Rich and deeply concentrated, opens with wild berry and chocolate notes, goes on to reveal minerals, anise and sage, all on a gently peppery background. Finishes with the tannins rising together with persistent notes of espresso coffee. Drink from release–2017. Tentative Score 90–92.

MUNCH, 2007: Dark, almost impenetrable royal purple in color, full-bodied and with firmly gripping tannins and spicy wood, those parting in the glass to reveal blackberries and notes of purple plums on a background of garrigue and roasted herbs. Don't expect this one to ever be dainty, rather look for a wine that is simultaneously muscular and elegant. Drink now–2014. Score 90.

MUNCH, 2006: Petite Sirah at its best. Dark, almost impenetrably inky garnet in color, full-bodied, concentrated and intense, showing generous wood and mouth-coating tannins, those in fine balance with red plum, blueberry and currant fruits. Give this one time and it will prove supple, ripe and rich. Drink now. Score 91.

MUNCH, 2005: Made entirely from Petite Sirah grapes from a dry-farmed vineyard. Dark, almost inky teeth-staining purple, with firm, brooding tannins waiting to settle down, and full-bodied enough to be thought of as chewy, but with all of that in fine balance with blackberries, currants, ripe plums and hints of citrus peel and tobacco all on a spicy and near-leathery background. Intense rather than elegant, recalls some of the most interesting wines of this variety from California. Drink now–2013. Score 91.

Gaudi

GAUDI, 2008: As always, a blend of Carignan, Cabernet Sauvignon and Syrah, oak-aged for 12 months, showing notes of spicy cedarwood and soft tannins. Round and approachable, revealing raspberries and blueberries on first attack, those yielding to blackberries and black cherries. Round and generous, meant for early drinking. Drink now. Score 89.

GAUDI, 2007: A blend of 60% Carignan and 20% each of Cabernet Sauvignon and Syrah. Medium- to full-bodied, with gentle spicy oak and comfortably gripping tannins. Developed in *barriques* for six months, opens to reveal red and blackcurrants, those going on to generous wild berry and peppery notes. Soft, round, generous and moderately long. Drink now. Score 89.

GAUDI, 2006: Dark royal purple, medium-bodied, with soft but mouth-coating tannins, this is a "wild" wine in that it seems to almost burst forth on the nose and palate, at first with raspberry and cassis notes and then, with a second burst, tobacco and spices. Happily, all of these integrate nicely and lead to a long, simultaneously tannic and fruity finish. A blend of 50% Carignan, 33% Syrah and 17% Cabernet Sauvignon. Drink up. Score 88.

Romain

ROMAIN, 2009: A Rhone blend of Grenache, Syrah and Mourvedre (55%, 34% and 11% respectively), showing garnet to royal purple, medium- to full-bodied with soft tannins and gentle notes of spicy oak. Generous black fruits on the nose and opening on the palate to reveal plums, black and red berries and a tempting note of red licorice that comes on the long, round finish. Best from release–2017. Tentative Score 89–91.

ROMAIN, 2008: Dedicated, as the winemaker enjoys doing to his intellectual heroes, in this case to author Romain Gary. A blend of 40% Grenache and 30% each Syrah and Mourvedre. Medium- to full-bodied (leaning to the full), dark cherry to brick-red in color, reflecting its 15 months in second- and third-year *barriques* with gently gripping tannins and an overtone of spicy cedarwood. On first attack red berries and freshly cut Mediterranean herbs, those parting to make way for blackberries, black cherries, Oriental spices and a clear hint of mocha. Long, round and generous. Drink now–2014. Score 91.

ROMAIN, 2007: Dark garnet in color, medium- to full-bodied, showing an appealing bittersweet streak that parts to reveal blackberry, red cherry, pomegranate and sweet red pepper flavors, those supported nicely by notes of rose petals and tobacco. A blend of 60% Grenache and 40% Syrah, needing time for its elements to come together but already showing fine balance and structure. Drink now–2013. Score 90.

James

JAMES, 2010: Made entirely from Chenin Blanc grapes and destined for about eight months in oak, already showing more full-bodied than earlier releases, with a texture that reminds one of olive oil. On the nose a light and pleasing musky note, and on the palate summer and tropical fruits, those supported by fine balancing acidity. From mid-palate on a hint of honey-dipped herbs. Drink from release–2016. Tentative Score 90–92.

JAMES, 2009: Light golden straw in color and medium-bodied, developed sur lie in second- and third-year barriques. Showing fine balance between lively acidity and fruits, an enticingly rich and stylish wine with peach, mango and apricot fruits, those supported nicely by notes of cloves and green tea and, on the long finish, hints of candied ginger. Drink now–2014, perhaps longer. Score 90.

JAMES, 2008: Glistening light gold in color, medium- to full-bodied, and now coming of age very nicely. On the nose and palate white peaches, roasted almonds and hints of cardamom, those on a background of heather and stony minerals. Continues now as in the past to call to mind a well-made Vouvray. Drink now–2014. Score 91.

JAMES, CHENIN BLANC, WILD YEASTS, 2008: Fermented entirely with wild yeasts, only about 200 bottles of this wine were made. With light funky-yeasty notes that persist, those adding charm to a mineral-rich white showing bitter almonds, peaches and peach pits along with clear notes of earthy minerals. If the regular release of this wine (see the tasting note above) calls to mind Vouvray, this one seems more something from Where the Wild Things Are. Enchanting. Drink up. Score 90.

Sea Horse

SEA HORSE-CHILLAG, 60–60, 2008: A cooperative venture, just for "fun" between two wineries, Sea Horse and Chillag. When asked to suggest a name for this cooperative effort, Orna Chillag suggested "60–60," saying that "after all it was an effort half of one winery, half of the other." Chillag may not be very good on calculating percentages but between her efforts and those of Dunie, a quite successful collaboration. Based on 50% Cabernet Sauvignon supplied by Chillag and 45% Mourvedre and 5% of Syrah from Dunie, a super-dark garnet, full-bodied, generously tannic and spicy wood-rich wine with its elements waiting to come together. Already showing generous black fruits, purple plums and blueberries on a background of spiced green olives and notes of licorice. Long and mouth-filling with tannins rising on the finish. Drink now–2014. Score 90.

SEA HORSE, MUSCAT, 2009: Made from old vines, oak-aged in French oak for six months, shows a quietly floral nose and opens in the glass to reveal a potpourri of grapefruit, grape, green melon and citrus peel notes, those on a not quite acidic enough background. A simple country-style wine. Drink up. Score 84.

Special Edition

SPECIAL EDITION, SYRAH-GRENACHE, 2009: A blend of 66% Syrah and 34% Grenache. Dark ruby toward garnet, reflecting its 12 months in French oak *barriques* with hints of sweet-and-spicy cedar and generous but soft and gently caressing tannins. A friendly wine, with abundant plum and blackberry fruits, those complemented by notes of anise and, on the long finish, a hint of toasted rye bread. Drink now. Score 89.

SPECIAL EDITION, CARIGNAN, 2008: Made entirely from Carignan grapes and reflecting its 24 months in *barriques* with notes of smoky oak and chewy tannins. Opens to reveal plum and tobacco notes, those intertwined with an intriguing note of white pepper. Muscular but round and elegant. Drink now. Score 88.

Segal ★★★★

Established in the 1950s as Ashkelon Wines and later taking on the name of the Segal family that owned it, in 2001 the company was bought out by Barkan Wineries, but kept its name. Under winemaker Avi Feldstein, with quality vineyards in several regions of the Upper Galilee, and operating now in Barkan's state-of-the-art facilities at Kibbutz Hulda, the winery is now producing several excellent wines, including Single Vineyard and Unfiltered wines, both from Cabernet Sauvignon grapes. Other series are Ben Ami, Marom Galil (including those wines labeled *Single* and *Fusion*), Rechasim, the single-vineyard Dovev varietal wines, Batzir and the popular-priced, entry-level Shel Segal series. The winery relies on Cabernet Sauvignon, Merlot, Argaman, Chardonnay, Sauvignon Blanc, Emerald Riesling and French Colombard grapes, and current production is about 1.5 million bottles annually, of which nearly one million are in the Shel Segal series.

Single Vineyard

SINGLE VINEYARD, CABERNET SAUVIGNON, DISHON, 2006: Garnet toward purple, medium- to full-bodied, already showing a rather generous hand with smoky wood that tends to hold back the fruits and herbal notes here. Drink now–2013. Score 87. K

SINGLE VINEYARD, CABERNET SAUVIGNON, DISHON, 2005: Dark, almost inky-garnet in color, concentrated and intense. Full-bodied and tannic enough to be thought of as chewy, the tannins integrating nicely and showing fine balance with the wood in which the wine was aged. Generous black fruits here, but not so much a fruity wine as a spicy one, led by aromas and flavors of smoked bacon, licorice and espresso coffee. Drink now. Score 90. K

SINGLE VINEYARD, MERLOT, DOVEV, 2004: Dark garnet toward royal purple, this medium- to full-bodied wine was super-generous with its tannins in its youth, so waiting to release this one was a wise move on the part of the winery. With those tannins now integrating nicely, spicy and showing well-tuned balance and structure. Aromas and flavors of black cherries, blackberries and purple plums, those matched well by spicy oak accents and, on the long finish, hints of espresso and dark chocolate. Drink up. Score 87. K

SINGLE VINEYARD, MERLOT, DOVEV, 2003: Developed in French and American *barriques* for 19 months, this wine is showing full-bodied, with firm tannins and spicy wood integrating well and opulent blueberry, currant and plum flavors, those with spicy and floral notes with hints of licorice in the background. Long, smooth, round and polished. Drink up. Score 91. K

Unfiltered

2005

קברנה סוביניון
ללא סינון

התווים עשויים להפתח ענבים ומעץ חות-תנייר הגדל בכרם | סדרה בת 8300 בקבוקים

UNFILTERED, CABERNET SAUVIGNON, 2008: Dark, almost impenetrable garnet, full-bodied, with its still-firm tannins now starting to settle in nicely. On the nose notes of spicy oak and crushed berries. Opens in the glass to reveal a generous array of blackcurrants, black cherries and bitter-citrus peel. Long and mouth-filling destined to always be a muscular wine, one that will do very well indeed with large cuts of beef. Drink from release–2014. Tentative Score 90–92. K

UNFILTERED, CABERNET SAUVIGNON, 2007: My earlier tasting note holds firm. Perhaps the best of Segal's unfiltered Cabernet Sauvignon releases to date. Dark garnet, full-bodied, with a black-fruit and spicy nose, showing firm tannins that yield comfortably in the glass to reveal on first attack blackberries and bittersweet chocolate, those followed by notes of red and black currants, matched nicely by notes of cloves, dill and black olives all lingering on a long and generous finish. Drink now–2017. Score 92. K

UNFILTERED, CABERNET SAUVIGNON, 2006: Full-bodied, concentrated, deeply tannic and with generous wood even at this early stage, the tannins and wood holding back the black fruits and Oriental spices that are trying to make themselves felt. Drink now–2014. Score 88. K

UNFILTERED, CABERNET SAUVIGNON, 2005: Blended with 10% Merlot, aged partially in partly new, partly used French and American oak for 30 months, showing full-bodied with generous but gently mouth-coating tannins, the wood and the tannins in fine balance with the fruits. With almost liqueur-like flavors of kirsch and cassis, those yielding comfortably to notes of purple plums and pepper. Long and generous. Drink now. Score 90. K

UNFILTERED, CABERNET SAUVIGNON, 2004: Blended with 10% of Merlot and oak-aged in French and American *barriques* for 22 months, showing dark, firm and intense. Full-bodied, with still-gripping tannins and generous but not-dominating oak with good balance between those and the red and blackcurrants, black cherries, sage and spicy cedarwood on the nose and palate. On the finish, an overlay of minerals and an appealing hint of bitterness. Sliding past its peak. Drink up. Score 90. K

Rechasim

RECHASIM, CABERNET SAUVIGNON, DISHON, 2008: Deep royal purple, a concentrated and intense wine at this stage, with still firmly gripping tannins and generous spicy oak, the wine already showing fine balance and structure that bode well for the future. On the nose and palate traditional Cabernet aromas and flavors of blackcurrants and blackberries, those on a background of bittersweet chocolate and, from mid-palate to the long finish, appealing hints of red berries and cigar tobacco. Drink now–2016. Score 90. K

RECHASIM, CABERNET SAUVIGNON, DISHON, 2007: Oak-aged for 18 months in American, French and Central European oak for 18 months, a dark-garnet, full-bodied red with soft, gently caressing tannins and notes of spicy cedarwood. Generously aromatic, opens to reveal blackcurrants and black cherries, those supported nicely by notes of tobacco and earthy minerals, with fruits and tannins rising on the finish. Drink now–2013. Score 90. K

RECHASIM, CABERNET SAUVIGNON, DISHON, 2005: Garnet toward royal purple, medium- to full-bodied with fine concentration. Generous spicy wood and soft tannins part to reveal blackberry, purple plum and currant fruits, those with appealing spicy and herbal notes lingering comfortably on the finish. Drink up. Score 89. K

RECHASIM, MERLOT, DOVEV, 2007: Super-dark garnet toward royal purple, full-bodied, with its once-firm tannins and generous acidity now integrating nicely with spicy wood and fruits, showing fine concentration and balance. On opening attack red fruits, those going on to blackberries and blackcurrants overlaid with aromas and flavors of freshly cut Mediterranean herbs. Drink now–2014. Score 89. K

RECHASIM, MERLOT, DOVEV, 2006: Dark garnet toward royal purple, full-bodied, with firm tannins just now starting to settle down. With generous spicy wood and crisp acidity, opens to reveal an array of near-sweet black fruits and, on the finish, a note of green gage plums. Drink now. Score 87. K

RECHASIM, MERLOT, DOVEV, 2005: Deeply aromatic, full-bodied with chewy tannins needing time to settle in but showing good balance and structure. Opens to reveal spicy oak along with black cherry and raspberry fruits, goes on to reveal a tempting herbaceousness and, on the finish, a hint of eucalyptus. Drink up. Score 89. K

RECHASIM, MERLOT, DOVEV, 2004: With its once-firm tannins now well integrated, showing dark garnet, medium- to full-bodied, with aromas and flavors of purple plums, black cherries and blackberries, those complemented by notes of spicy oak and, on the long finish, hints of espresso and bittersweet chocolate. Generous and mouth-filling. Drink up. Score 91. K

RECHASIM, ARGAMAN, DOVEV, 2008: Soft and round, almost impenetrably dark garnet toward royal purple, with super-soft tannins and notes of smoke coming not from the grape but from the oak in which it aged. On the nose and palate somewhat amorphous blueberry, blackberry and cassis flavors (not much in the way of aromatics here). Not at all a "bad" wine but one that fails to inspire. Drink now. Score 86. K

RECHASIM, ARGAMAN, DOVEV, 2007: Oak-aged for 18 months in new American, French and other European barriques, the wine shows deep royal purple in color. Although the nose is somewhat quiet, the flavors are pronounced, on first attack showing raspberries, those yielding comfortably to black fruits and a hint of mint, all of which are complemented by soft, gently gripping tannins. Drink now. Score 90. K

Marom Galil

MAROM GALIL, CABERNET SAUVIGNON, SINGLE, 2008: Oak-aged for 18 months, showing dark garnet, medium- to full-bodied and with gently gripping tannins that highlight currant, blackberry and black cherry fruits, those on a background that hints at one moment of mint and at another of green olives and Mediterranean herbs. Drink now–2013. Score 88. K

MAROM GALIL, CABERNET SAUVIGNON, SINGLE, 2007: Reflecting its 18 months in oak with gently gripping tannins, vanilla and a hint of Oriental spices. Super-dark garnet, medium- to full-bodied, showing traditional Cabernet blackcurrant, blackberry and black cherry notes. Moderately long. Drink now. Score 88. K

MAROM GALIL, CABERNET SAU-VIGNON, SINGLE, 2005: Dark garnet toward royal purple, medium- to full-bodied, with soft tannins and its youthful generous oak now integrated nicely. Opens to show ripe blackcurrant, blackberry and black cherry fruits, those complemented by notes of spices and minted chocolate. Long, mouth-filling and generous. Drink up. Score 90. K

MAROM GALIL, MERLOT, SINGLE, 2008: Dark garnet toward royal purple, medium- to full-bodied with tannins that start off as rather chunky and then turn smooth and soft as the wine opens in the glass. On the nose and palate blackberries and blueberries, those supported nicely by notes of spicy oak and, toward the finish, a note of bittersweet chocolate. Drink now–2013. Score 88. K

MAROM GALIL, MERLOT, SINGLE, 2007: Dark garnet, medium-bodied, a blend of 85% Merlot and 15% Cabernet Sauvignon. Oak-aged for 14 months, showing soft tannins and spicy wood, both integrating nicely to highlight blackberry and blueberry fruits on a lightly spicy background. Drink now. Score 87. K

MAROM GALIL, RED FUSION, SINGLE, 2009: A medium-bodied, softly tannic, unoaked blend of Merlot, Cabernet Franc and Cabernet Sauvignon (60%, 25% and 15% respectively). Dark and well extracted, with ample berry, black cherry and cassis aromas, a young, easy-to-drink wine. Drink now. Score 86. K

MAROM GALIL, CHARDONNAY, SINGLE, 2008: Lightly oaked, deep gold in color, medium- to full-bodied, showing fine balancing acidity and a hint of mint on the nose with tropical and summer fruits on a lively background. Not complex but a good quaffer. Drink up. Score 86. K

MAROM GALIL, WHITE FUSION, 2009: A blend of 60% Chardonnay and 40% French Colombard, those exposed to minimum wood. Light gold in color, aromatic with citrus, green apple and hints of bitter almonds. A fine quaffer. Drink up. Score 87. K

MAROM GALIL, MUSCAT DESSERT, 2006: Unabashedly sweet and lacking balancing acidity, not so much a fruity wine as one of honeyed herbs. Drink up. Score 84. K

Ben Ami

BEN AMI, CABERNET SAUVIGNON, 2009: Ruby toward garnet, medium-, perhaps medium- to full-bodied, with sharp tannins and showing flavors and aromas of blackberries, currants, blueberries and earthy minerals. Drink now. Score 84. K

BEN AMI, CABERNET SAUVIGNON, 2008: Dark cherry toward garnet in color, a straight-forward Cabernet Sauvignon destined for entry-level drinkers. Soft, round and fruity, an easy-to-drink quaffer. Drink up. Score 82. K

BEN AMI, MERLOT, 2009: Dark cherry-red toward garnet, medium-bodied with soft tannins and showing red berry and cassis notes. A not at all complex, but appropriate, entry-level wine. Drink now. Score 83. K

Shel Segal

SHEL SEGAL, CABERNET SAUVIGNON, 2010: Ruby toward garnet, medium-bodied, with chunky tannins giving the wine a rustic nature. On the nose and palate blackberries, blueberries and notes of earthy herbaceousness. Drink now. Score 84. K

SHEL SEGAL, CABERNET SAUVIGNON, 2008: Dark ruby toward garnet, medium-bodied, with soft tannins and easy-to-take currant and wild berry fruits on a light peppermint background. Drink up. Score 84. K

SHEL SEGAL, MERLOT, 2010: Dark ruby in color, medium-bodied, with soft tannins and simple but appealing currant and wild berry fruits. An entry-level wine. Drink now. Score 84. K

SHEL SEGAL, MERLOT-CABERNET SAUVIGNON, 2009: Medium-dark garnet in color, a medium-bodied blend of 66% Merlot and 34% Cabernet Sauvignon with soft tannins complementing black cherry, wild berry and cassis fruits. No complexities here but a good entry-level wine. Drink up. Score 83. K

SHEL SEGAL, MERLOT-SHIRAZ, 2009: A blend of 66% Merlot and 34% Shiraz. Garnet red in color, medium-bodied, with gently gripping tannins and nice berry, black cherry and peppery notes. A simple entry-level wine with no complexities at all. Drink up. Score 80. κ

SHEL SEGAL, DRY RED WINE, 2009: A medium-bodied blend of Merlot, Argaman and Petite Sirah, its tannins barely felt, and showing a basic and straightforward berry-cherry personality. Drink up. Score 80. κ

SHEL SEGAL, EMERALD RIESLING, 2009: Light golden straw in color, a not at all complex half-dry white wine with citrus, pineapple and tropical fruits. An uncomplicated entry-level wine. Drink up. Score 80. κ

SHEL SEGAL, DRY WHITE WINE, 2010: Light in body, a dry blend of Sauvignon Blanc, French Colombard and Muscat. On the nose and palate basic citrus, pineapple and tropical fruits. A simple little white, pleasant enough for those just getting into wine. Drink up. Score 80. κ

SHEL SEGAL, SEMI-DRY WHITE WINE, 2010: A half-dry blend of what the label says is Riesling and French Colombard, but one wonders if that Riesling is not in fact Emerald Riesling. Some rather quiet citrus and citrus peel notes on a background that is just a bit too sweet and lacking the acidity that would have made it lively. Drink up. Score 78. κ

Shdema ✶

Set on Kibbutz Revivim in the Negev Desert, this artisanal winery released its first wines from the 2004 vintage. Relying on Cabernet Sauvignon, Merlot, Shiraz and Petit Verdot grapes, nearly all of which are purchased from other wineries, the winery is currently producing about 3,500 bottles annually.

SHDEMA, CABERNET SAUVIGNON, 2006: Garnet toward purple, medium- to full-bodied, with firm, astringent tannins and acidity that hide the fruits that are lurking here. Drink now. Score 74.

SHDEMA, CABERNET SAUVIGNON, 2005: Dark purple, medium-bodied, with high acidity and coarse, almost stinging tannins, and minimal berry and black cherry fruits that struggle to make themselves felt. Score 73.

SHDEMA, CABERNET SAUVIGNON, SDE BOKER, 2005: Dull, somewhat cloudy garnet, medium-bodied, with soft tannins. Showing muddy and bitter with only stingy black fruits. Score 70.

SHDEMA, MERLOT, 2007: Dark garnet, medium- to full-bodied with a fruit-rich nose. Oak-aged for 18 months and with a generous 15% alcohol content, showing appealing black fruits but those marred somewhat by high alcohol and glycerin content. Drink now. Score 79.

SHDEMA, MERLOT, 2006: Garnet, going to brown, medium- to full-bodied, with a whopping 16% alcohol and coarse tannins that give the wine the kind of power that makes you uncomfortably catch your breath. A few black fruits here but overall showing alcoholic and far too earthy barnyard notes. Score 65.

SHDEMA, MERLOT, SDE BOKER, 2005: Dark garnet, medium-bodied, with soft tannins, moderate wood influence and appealing currant and berry fruits accompanied by hints of pepper. Drink up. Score 83.

SHDEMA, SHIRAZ, 2006: Oak-aged for 28 months, showing super-dark garnet and full-bodied, with generous wood, sharp, almost biting tannins and an unwanted bitter note that tend to hide the black fruits that try hard to make themselves felt. Drink up. Score 72.

SHDEMA, PETIT VERDOT, 2006: Full-bodied, with soft tannins, dark garnet toward royal purple in color, showing a generous 15% alcohol content and equally generous wood, those thankfully making room for currant, cassis and blueberry fruits. Marred by alcoholic heat that rises on the finish. Drink up. Score 79.

SHDEMA, CARIGNAN, 2007: Dark garnet, full-bodied, with near-sweet tannins, reflecting its development with oak chips with a sweet cedar note. Opens to show ripe berry and plum fruits, those spoiled somewhat by a medicinal, near-iodine note that rises as the wine sits in the glass. Drink up. Score 74.

SHDEMA, SHIRAZ-CABERNET FRANC, 2007: Medium- to full-bodied, with soft tannins, a deep garnet blend of two-thirds Shiraz and one-third Cabernet Franc. Opens with raspberries and red plums, those yielding to notes of cassis and spices. Without complexities but an acceptable entry-level wine. Drink now. Score 84.

Shiloh ✶✶✶✶

Set in Shiloh in the Binyamin region of Judea and Samaria, this winery released its first wines from the 2005 vintage. Winemaker Amichai Lourie relies on Cabernet Sauvignon, Merlot, Cabernet Franc, Petit Verdot, Petite Sirah, Barbera and Chardonnay grapes, those largely from the winery's own vineyards. Production in 2007 was of 70,000 bottles, in 2008 (a *shmita* year) 40,000 and in 2009 about 60,000. In addition to a flagship wine named Mosaic, wines are released under three labels – Sod Reserve, Shor and Mor (sometimes on the labels as Mor'e).

Mosaic

MOSAIC, 2007: A blend from this vintage of Merlot, Cabernet Franc, Cabernet Sauvignon, Petit Verdot and Petite Sirah (60%, 20%, 7%, 7% and 6% respectively). Full-bodied, concentrated and intense at this stage but even now showing fine balance and structure, and thus avoids being an overpowering blockbuster. On first attack currants, blackberries and a note of cherry wood, those parting to make way for notes of ripe plums, saddle leather and earthy minerals. Long and generous. Approachable and enjoyable now but best 2013–2017, perhaps longer. Score 91. K

MOSAIC, 2006: Deep, almost impenetrable garnet with purple reflections, full-bodied, reflecting its 20 months in French oak with generous but not-overpowering spicy wood and gently mouth-coating tannins. A blend of 60% Merlot and 20% Cabernet Franc, those flushed out with Cabernet Sauvignon, Petite Sirah and Petit Verdot, opens to show a generous red- berry and chocolate personality, and on the long finish notes of dried herbs. Medium- to full-bodied, with good concentration, the wood and tannins parting from mid-palate and finishing on a velvety note. Drink now–2016. Score 91. K

Sod Reserve

SHILOH, CABERNET SAUVIGNON, SOD RESERVE, 2008: Dark garnet with purple reflections, full-bodied, with generous soft tannins that complement subdued notes of spicy oak and earthy minerals. Developed in French oak for 18 months, opens in the glass to reveal traditional blackcurrants, purple plums and crushed blackberries, those matched nicely by notes of licorice and mocha.

Long and mouth filling, moving toward elegance. Drink now–2017. Score 90. K

SHILOH, CABERNET SAUVIGNON, SOD RESERVE, 2007: Aged in 400 liter oak casks, showing full-bodied, with its once-gripping and somewhat chunky tannins now nicely subdued, opens to reveal blackcurrants and wild berries on a background of spicy oak. Mouth-filling and moderately long. Drink now–2013. Score 87. K

SHILOH, CABERNET SAUVIGNON, SOD RESERVE, 2006: Developed for 16 months in new and older French *barriques*, medium- to full-bodied, with soft, well-integrated tannins and notes of sweet cedarwood. Dark garnet, an aromatic wine, opening to reveal blackcurrants, blackberries and black cherries, those matched by notes of citrus peel, chocolate and freshly roasted herbs. Fine balance and a long and generous finish on which the tannins and fruits rise nicely. Drink now. Score 89. K

SHILOH, MERLOT, SOD RESERVE, 2008: My earlier tasting note holds firm. Dark, near-impenetrable garnet in color, a muscular Merlot, full-bodied, with gripping tannins and ample spicy oak, those parting slowly in the glass to reveal blackberry and wild berry fruits. In the background, playing nicely on the palate, notes of earthy minerals, bittersweet chocolate and roasted herbs. Drink now–2015. Score 89. K

SHILOH, SHIRAZ, SOD RESERVE, 2008: My earlier tasting note holds firm but with an extension of the drinking window. Dark enough so that one debates whether the wine is deep, near impenetrable garnet or out-and-out black. Full-bodied, reflecting its 20 months in primarily French oak with notes of sweet-and-spicy cedar and graphite, with still-gripping tannins, those needing a bit more time to integrate but already showing fine balance and structure. Opens with blackberries and purple plums, going on to aromas and flavors of wild berries and vanilla and, on the long, gently gripping finish, an appealing note of freshly cured cigar tobacco. Drink now–2016. Score 90. K

SHILOH, PETITE SIRAH, SOD RESERVE, 2007: Blended with 10% of Cabernet Sauvignon, dark, almost impenetrable garnet, full-bodied, with its firm tannins and somewhat pronounced spicy wood of its youth now settling in nicely. On opening attack blackberry and cassis, those yielding comfortably to a note of raspberries, all on a background that hints at one moment of licorice and at another of minted chocolate. Deep, full and rich. Drink now–2015. Score 89. K

Shor

SHOR, CABERNET SAUVIGNON, 2008: A round and well-structured wine, dark ruby-garnet, full-bodied with soft tannins and a gentle influence of dusty and spicy oak. On the nose and palate traditional Cabernet Sauvignon blackcurrants and blackberries, those parting to make way for notes of bitter-citrus peel and dark chocolate. Drink now–2016. Score 90. K

SHOR, CABERNET SAUVIGNON, 2007: Dark garnet toward royal purple, medium- to full-bodied, with soft tannins and reflecting its time in oak with a light spiciness that continues from first attack to the generous finish. Opens with red currants and blueberries, goes on to show traditional blackcurrant and blackberry fruits, those with hints of citrus peel and stony minerals. A mouth-filling wine that begs for fine cuts of lamb or beef. Drink now–2014. Score 88. K

SHOR, CABERNET SAUVIGNON, 2006: My earlier tasting note holds firm. Dark garnet toward royal purple, medium- to full-bodied, with soft tannins integrating well and a gentle hand with spicy wood. On the nose and palate lightly spicy blackcurrant, black cherry and blackberry fruits, those on a background of mint-tinged vanilla. Drinking nicely but starting to slide past its peak. Drink up. Score 87. K

SHOR, MERLOT, 2008: Dark ruby toward garnet, a soft, round and generous wine, anything but the internationalized Merlot, showing near-sweet cedarwood, wild berries and plentiful hints of milk chocolate. Generous fruit and tannins all come together nicely in a thoroughly hedonistic wine that calls to mind the better Merlots of Tuscany. Drink now–2015. Score 90. K

SHOR, BARBERA, 2008: Dark, glistening garnet in color, medium- to full-bodied, a juicy and rich wine. On the nose citrus and blackberries and on the palate raspberries, licorice, minerals and hints of cracked white pepper. A distinctly Mediterranean Barbera. Drink now–2015. Score 90. K

SHOR, BARBERA, 2007: Dark garnet, a concentrated Barbera opening with a somewhat medicinal whiff that blows off quickly to reveal clean, fresh aromas and flavors of violets, raisins, cassis and tobacco. Fine balance between wood, soft tannins and fruits, a distinctly Mediterranean wine with fine structure. Drink now–2014. Score 89. K

SHOR, CABERNET SAUVIGNON-MERLOT, 2007: Dark garnet with purple and orange reflections, full-bodied, with spicy oak in fine balance with fruits and acidity. Opens with red fruits on the nose and palate, those shifting comfortably in the glass to blackberries, blackcurrants and wild berries. Drink now–2014. Score 89. K

SHOR, CABERNET SAUVIGNON-MERLOT, 2006: Showing better than at an earlier tasting, its elements more fully integrated now. Dark garnet, medium- to full-bodied, with soft tannins, a blend of 50% Cabernet Sauvignon, 47% Merlot and 3% of Petite Sirah. Oak-aged for 15 months, opens to reveal blackcurrants and wild berries, those on a background that hints at one moment of roasted herbs and at another of dried tobacco leaf, the tannins and fruits rising nicely on the finish. Drink now. Score 87. K

SHOR, MERLOT-SHIRAZ, 2006: A blend of 65% Merlot and 35% Shiraz, oak-aged for 14 months. Dark garnet, medium-bodied, a bit quiet on the opening nose but after time in the glass shows appealing aromas of blackberries and smoky oak, its once-gripping tannins now integrated well with the wood, acidity and fruits. On the palate a light overlay of sweet and spicy cedarwood (call that cigar box if you like), that going on to show abundant black fruits and, on the moderately long finish, a note of bittersweet chocolate. Round and generous. Drink now. Score 87. K

SHOR, SHIRAZ-MERLOT, 2007: Deep royal purple toward garnet, medium- to full-bodied, with gently caressing tannins, reflecting its development in oak with a light spicy note. Generously aromatic, opens to reveal aromas and flavors of purple plums, wild berries and black currants, those supported by hints of saddle leather and minted chocolate, all lingering nicely. Drink now–2013. Score 88. K

Mor/Mor'e

MOR, 2008: Dark ruby toward garnet, a medium- to full-bodied blend of Cabernet Sauvignon, Merlot and Barbera. Oak-aged for 14 months, showing soft, caressing tannins and an appealing hint of spicy oak, on first attack revealing red currants and wild berries, those yielding to notes of blackberries. Round and generous. Drink now–2014. Score 89. K

MOR'E, 2007: A deep-garnet, medium- to full-bodied blend of Cabernet Sauvignon, Merlot and Barbera, reflecting its 14 months in oak with notes of dusty oak and gently gripping tannins. On the nose and palate a generous array of blackberries, currants and exotic spices and, from mid-palate on, a note of ripe purple plums. Opens nicely in the glass and finishes long and generous. Drink now. Score 87. K

Shiloh

SHILOH, CHARDONNAY, 2009: Fermented and developed in new 400 liter oak barrels for ten months, showing shining, lightly burnished gold in color and medium-bodied. On the nose and palate pears, white peaches, tropical fruits and an appealing hint of cedarwood, those on a lightly spicy background. Somewhat subdued on its own but blossoms nicely with food. Drink now. Score 87. K

SHILOH, CHARDONNAY, 2008: Bright golden straw in color, with light notes of spicy oak parting to make way for citrus and citrus peel notes. Oak-aged in 400 liter barrels, showing lively acidity. Not a complex wine but a very appealing one, at its best with fish kebabs and grilled fish. Drink now. Score 86. K

SHILOH, CHARDONNAY, 2007: Showing a light medicinal aroma, that giving the clue that the wine is oxidizing, the citrus and tropical fruits still lively but now with growing oaky and herbal overtones. Past its peak. Drink up. Score 84. K

SHILOH, ROSÉ, 2008: Barbera and Cabernet Franc come together nicely in a light- to medium-bodied blushing pink toward salmon color. Abundant raspberries and red currants here making the wine fruity enough that some will mistake this for a tantalizing hint of sweetness. Opens nicely in the glass, the red fruits complemented by a note of blueberries. Drink up. Score 88. K

Shvo Vineyards (Kerem Shvo) ✱✱✱✱

Unusual perhaps to write about a winery that to date has released only two wines (one a white and the other a rosé), and the rest of the wines a year or two from release, but when the winemaker involved is Gaby Sadan, not writing would be a sin, as Sadan is one of the most talented winemakers in the country. After a formal education at the University of Dijon, and garnering experience in Bordeaux, Burgundy, California and Australia, Sadan returned to his native Israel, first for a prolonged period as one of the winemaking team at the Golan Heights Winery and then as the founding winemaker at the then newly opened Galil Mountain Winery.

Several years ago Sadan struck out on his own, planting vineyards at the Shvo Vineyards, at an altitude of 800 meters (2,650 feet) in the Upper Galilee. With vineyards planted with Syrah, Grenache, Mourvedre, Petit Verdot, Barbera, Sauvignon Blanc, Chenin Blanc and Muscat Canelli, the winery is temporarily using a rented facility in Gush Halav (Jish). The winery is named Kerem Shvo after the vineyard and Sadan is relying on trellising methods yet unused in Israel as well as on the use of wild yeasts whenever possible. Plans are to release approximately 20,000 bottles from the 2009 vintage, that jumping to about 40,000 bottles from the 2010 vintage.. Future plans will take the winery to production of 100,000 bottles annually.

SHVO VINEYARDS, BLENDED RED, UPPER GALILEE, 2009: My tasting based entirely on components, this is scheduled to be a blend primarily of Grenache and Mourvedre with small percentages of Syrah and Barbera, the Barbera adding aroma and a sense of lightness, the Syrah adding a tempting herbal note, the whole coming together in ways that beguile and charm, framing its appealing red and black berries nicely. Full-bodied and generously but softly tannic, with fine balancing acidity, from mid-palate on notes of spicy wood, cherries and a hint of rhubarb. Simultaneously powerful and elegant. Drink from release–2019. Tentative Score 90–92.

SHVO VINEYARDS, ROSÉ, UPPER GALILEE, 2009: Made entirely from Barbera and then with fermentation relying entirely on wild yeasts. Light salmon pink in color, light- to medium-bodied, a smooth, ripe and generous wine, remarkably well balanced with appealing plum, cherry, berry and raspberry notes and even a light hint of tannins, all leading to a long and supple finish. Drink now. Not many rosé wines earn scores of 90 or higher but this is one of the best I have ever tasted and comfortably earns its Score of 91.

SHVO VINEYARDS, SAUVIGNON BLANC, UPPER GALILEE, 2009: Light gold with orange and purple reflections, full-bodied, a bold wine with light notes of persimmon and chamomile that float through from first attack to the long finish. Slowly fermented with indigenous yeasts, opens to show peach and apricot fruits, those supported by notes of roasted hazelnuts, brioche and paraffin. Crisply dry with fine balancing acidity, with notes of heather and Hymettus honey on the long, long finish. This one will age nicely. Not for everyone but those who do enjoy it will do so with gusto. Drink now–2015, perhaps longer. Score 92.

Sifsaf *

Founded by Arik Elbaz on Moshav Safsufa in the Upper Galilee, the winery's own vineyards contain Cabernet Sauvignon, Merlot, Cabernet Franc, Barbera, Nebbiolo, Sangiovese, Syrah, Chardonnay, Viognier and Sauvignon Blanc grapes. Production is about 15,000 bottles annually. Although the labels on the Sifsaf bottles state a given vintage year, the owner/winemaker acknowledges that because labels are expensive, he may at times use the same label for more than one year, which makes it impossible to know precisely which wine one is tasting or purchasing.

SIFSAF, CABERNET SAUVIGNON, 2008: Dark garnet, medium- to full-bodied, with still-firm tannins and generous spicy oak waiting to settle down, those somewhat hiding the black fruits that try hard to make themselves felt. Drink up. Score 78. K

SIFSAF, CABERNET SAUVIGNON, 2006: Oak-aged for about eight months, blended with 20% Syrah, remains as at a previous tasting, not so much fruity as it is dominated by aromas and flavors of sawdust, dill and apple vinegar. Score 50. K

SIFSAF, MERLOT, 2008: Medium-bodied, with chunky tannins, and opening to show spicy, near-sweet black fruits. A simple country-style wine. Drink up. Score 77. K

SIFSAF, CABERNET FRANC, 2008: Cloudy dark purple in color, medium- to full-bodied and even at this early stage dominated by mousy and metallic notes. Score 50. K

SIFSAF, CABERNET FRANC, 2006: Medium- to full-bodied, with chunky, almost coarse country-style tannins. Shows jammy black fruits and hints of spices. Not typical of the variety and showing an unwanted note of sweetness as well as a not at all delicate touch of Brett. Score 68. K

SIFSAF, NEBBIOLO, 2007: Still in the barrel and already showing such a devastating quantity of Brettanomyces that whatever fruits are here are hidden by mousy and metallic aromas and flavors. Score 50. K

SIFSAF, SANGIOVESE, 2008: Dusty garnet in color, medium-bodied, with decided aromas and flavors of grape vinegar. Unapproachable. Score 50. K

Smadar ✶✶✶

Established by Moty Sela in 1998 and located in Zichron Ya'akov, this winery draws on grapes from nearby vineyards owned by the family, those containing Cabernet Sauvignon, Merlot, Cabernet Franc and Carignan grapes. Production is currently about 4,000 bottles annually.

SMADAR, CABERNET SAUVIGNON, 2007: Somewhat astringent at this stage of its development, but showing overall balance and structure that should make this an easy-drinking Cabernet with black cherry and blackberry notes on a background of green olives. Drink now. Score 85.

SMADAR, CABERNET SAUVIGNON, 2006: Firm and ripe, medium- to full-bodied with an appealing earthy-mineral streak that runs through berry, cherry and anise aromas and flavors. Drink up. Score 85.

SMADAR, MERLOT, 2007: Almost inky-black at this stage of its development, showing gripping tannins and spicy wood needing time to settle in. Good black fruits here but a chocolate, licorice and spice-rich wine. Drink now. Score 87.

SMADAR, MERLOT, 2006: Dark royal purple in color, medium-bodied, with soft tannins. A round wine opening to show a gentle hand with spicy wood and appealing black fruits. On the finish look for hints of chocolate and vanilla that play nicely on the palate. Drink now. Score 86.

SMADAR, CARIGNAN, 2007: Medium- to full-bodied, dark garnet in color, with firm tannins and generous acidity needing time to integrate but already showing appealing red fruits, spices and earthy minerals, all with a hint of black pepper on the finish. Drink now. Score 86.

SMADAR, CARIGNAN, 2006: Medium- to full-bodied, with concentrated aromas and flavors of black cherries, raspberries, minerals and spices, all backed up by just-firm-enough tannins and peppery oak. Drink now. Score 85.

SMADAR, CABERNET FRANC, 2007: Dark royal purple, medium-bodied with still-tight tannins. On the nose and palate dried cherries and cranberries along with generous overlays of sage and green olives. Drink now. Score 85.

Snir **

Founded in 2002 by Danny Stein and located on Kibbutz Snir in the Upper Galilee, the winery relies on Cabernet Sauvignon and Merlot grapes from the Sha'al vineyards and has released wines in two series, Nimrod and Snir. Initial production was of 1,200 bottles and production for 2007 was about 5,000 bottles. No wines were released from the 2008 or 2009 vintages.

Nimrod

NIMROD, CABERNET SAUVIGNON, 2005: Dark ruby toward purple, medium-bodied, with soft tannins integrating nicely with gently spicy wood. On the nose and palate red currants, wild berries and spices. Flawed by a note of volatile acidity. Drink up. Score 82.

NIMROD, CABERNET SAUVIGNON, 2004: Oak-aged for 12 months, dark, but not fully clear royal purple, aged in oak for one year, medium-bodied, with soft, well-integrating tannins and plum and blackberry fruits on a lightly spicy background. Sliding past its peak. Drink up. Score 80.

NIMROD, CABERNET SAUVIGNON-MERLOT, 2006: Garnet toward royal purple, medium-bodied with somewhat chunky tannins, a pleasant little country-style wine with red and black berry, cherry and cassis fruits. A good quaffer. Drink now. Score 84.

NIMROD, CABERNET SAUVIGNON-MERLOT, 2005: Ruby toward garnet in color, medium-bodied, an oak-aged blend of 66% Cabernet Sauvignon and 34% Merlot showing red berries and cassis on a light background of minerals. Not complex but a good quaffer. Drink up. Score 84.

Snir

SNIR, CABERNET SAUVIGNON, 2006: Dark ruby toward garnet, medium- to full-bodied with near-sweet tannins, a round, soft and easy-to-drink wine with generous black fruits. Drink now. Score 84.

SNIR, CABERNET SAUVIGNON, 2005: Dark royal purple, medium-bodied, with soft tannins and lightly spicy wood. Shows currant, blackberry and raspberry fruits with a light spicy note that runs through to the finish. Drink now. Score 85.

SNIR, MERLOT, 2006: Ruby-red, medium-bodied, with soft tannins and forward berry, black cherry and currant fruits. A pleasant but somewhat internationalized Merlot. Drink up. Score 84.

SNIR, MERLOT, 2005: Garnet toward purple, medium-bodied, with soft tannins and an appealing array of spicy berries and black cherries. Not complex but a good quaffer. Drink up. Score 84.

Somek ***

Established by Australian-trained winemaker Hilla Ben Gera and vintner Barak Dahan in Zichron Ya'akov, the winery released its first wines from the 2003 vintage with 1,500 bottles. The winery is currently releasing about 7,000 bottles annually and relies on its own vineyards, those with Merlot, Syrah, Carignan, Petite Sirah and Chardonnay grapes. Coming on line in the near future will be Cabernet Franc, Malbec, Mourvedre and Petit Verdot grapes. The winery produces wines in a reserve and regular series.

Reserve

RESERVE, BIK'AT HANADIV, 2005: Dark, almost inky-garnet in color, medium- to full-bodied, this 24-months oak-aged blend of Cabernet Sauvignon, Merlot, Carignan and Petite Sirah (40%, 40%, 15% and 5% respectively) opens with a rich crushed berry and spicy nose. Firmly tannic at this stage of its development, but with gently mouth-coating tannins and spicy wood integrating nicely, the wine opens to reveal blackberry and cassis fruits, those with overlays of tobacco and chocolate. Drink now. Score 90.

RESERVE, BIK'AT HANADIV, 2004: A generously oak-aged blend of 60% Cabernet Sauvignon, 35% Merlot and 5% Petite Sirah, showing good balance between spicy wood, firm tannins and fruits. On first attack purple plums and blueberries, those yielding to black fruits, chocolate and hints of espresso coffee all lingering nicely on the palate. Drink up. Score 88.

Somek

SOMEK, MERLOT, 2005: Garnet toward royal purple, medium-, perhaps medium- to full-bodied, with soft tannins and spicy cedarwood yielding comfortably to black cherry, currant and wild berry fruits. Tannins, fruits and a note of earthy minerals rise on the finish. Drink now. Score 87.

SOMEK, MERLOT, 2004: Deep ruby toward garnet, medium-bodied, with gently mouth-coating tannins. Showing spices and vanilla from its oak-aging, those parting to reveal a generous array of currant and wild berry fruits and, on the moderately long finish, an appealing hint of Mediterranean herbs. Drink up. Score 87.

SOMEK, SYRAH, 2005: Dark garnet, medium- to full-bodied, reflecting its development in French oak for 20 months with a generous overlay of spicy and dusty wood and gripping tannins. Needs time in the glass to open and reveal the near-sweet black fruits, chocolate and peppery notes. Drink now. Score 88.

SOMEK, SYRAH, 2004: Mediterranean Syrah, with peppery wild berry, black cherry and plum aromas and flavors, those matched nicely by chewy but yielding tannins, intimations of spicy wood and a beefy hint on the finish. Medium- to full-bodied, with the clear potential for elegance. Drink now. Score 89.

SOMEK, CARIGNAN, 2005: Dark garnet, full-bodied, showing firm tannins and generous spicy wood, those in good balance with fruits and acidity. On first attack wild berries, black pepper and spicy oak, yielding to aromas and flavors of currants, licorice and earthy minerals. Score 86.

SOMEK, CARIGNAN, 2004: Oak-aged for 20 months in French *barriques*, medium-bodied, with generous black fruits, spicy oak and vanilla, a softly tannic wine that opens nicely on the palate. Plenty of spicy wood here, but that well integrated and, on the long finish, hints of orange peel and chocolate. Drink up. Score 88.

SOMEK, ADOM, 2008: An aromatic, medium- to full-bodied potpourri of Syrah, Carignan, Malbec and Mourvedre (40%, 30%, 15% and 15% respectively). Medium- to full-bodied, with firm tannins that part slowly to make way for a basic black-fruit, licorice and citrus peel personality. Drink now. Score 85.

SOMEK, HANADIV VALLEY, 2005: A Bordeaux blend, this year of Cabernet Sauvignon, Merlot and Petit Verdot. Reflecting its development in *barriques* with generous but softly caressing tannins and notes of sweet-and-spicy cedar. On the nose and palate blackcurrants, black and red berries and a hint of the licorice that is found often in Somek's wines. Lingers nicely. Drink now–2013. Score 88.

Soreq ★★★

Founded in 1994 on Moshav Tal Shachar and situated at the foot of the Jerusalem Mountains, with Nir Shacham as winemaker, this boutique winery relies on Cabernet Sauvignon and Merlot grapes grown in its own vineyards as well as Petit Verdot, Grenache and Cabernet Sauvignon from contract vineyards in the Judean Hills and Galilee. The winery releases wines in Special Reserve and regular editions. Current production is about 7,500 bottles annually.

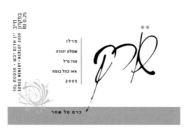

Special Reserve

SPECIAL RESERVE, CABERNET SAUVIGNON, 2004: Dark garnet toward royal purple, full-bodied, with generous, somewhat chunky tannins and dusty wood giving the wine a countrified personality. Generous currant, berry and black cherry fruits on a background of spicy oak and Mediterranean herbs. Sliding past its peak. Drink up. Score 87.

Soreq

SOREQ, CABERNET SAUVIGNON, KEREM YOSEF, 2008: Dark garnet, full-bodied, with still-gripping tannins and spicy oak that part in the glass to make way for traditional Cabernet Sauvignon aromas and flavors of blackcurrants and blackberries. From mid-palate on appealing notes of bittersweet chocolate and on the long finish a hint of roasted herbs. Very nice indeed. Drink now–2015. Score 90.

SOREQ, CABERNET SAUVIGNON, KEREM YOSEF, 2007: Dark garnet, full-bodied, with tannins and spicy oak in fine balance with fruits. On the nose and palate blackberries and cassis, those complemented nicely by notes of dark chocolate, green olives and Mediterranean herbs. Drink now–2014. Score 89.

SOREQ, CABERNET SAUVIGNON, TAL SHACHAR, 2006: Dark garnet toward purple in color, full-bodied, with firm tannins that need time to integrate but already showing appealing cassis, berry and black cherry fruits leading to a long minty finish. Drink up. Score 86.

SOREQ, MERLOT, KEREM YOSEF, 2007: Dark garnet toward royal purple, reflecting its 18 months in new oak with spices, vanilla and gently gripping tannins. Full-bodied, round and concentrated, opens to show black fruits and a note of black pepper, going on to reveal hints of citrus peel and dark chocolate. Drink now–2015. Score 90.

SOREQ, MERLOT, TAL SHACHAR, 2005: Made entirely from Merlot grapes, showing soft tannins and spicy wood integrated and revealing generous cedary blackberries and wild berries, those on a background of sage and minerals. Drink up. Score 89.

SOREQ, MERLOT, TAL SHACHAR, 2004: Dark garnet toward royal purple, full-bodied, with softly mouth-coating tannins and hints of vanilla and cinnamon. Opens to reveal currant and berry fruits, those on a lightly spicy background. Long and generous. Sliding past its peak. Drink up. Score 88.

SOREQ, GRENACHE, KEREM LATROUN, 2008: Dark garnet toward royal purple, full-bodied, with still-firm tannins needing a bit of time to integrate but already showing fine balance and structure. On the nose and palate black cherries and currants, those supported by notes of licorice and green olives. Drink now–2013. Score 86.

SOREQ, GRENACHE, 2007: Made from grapes from 26-year-old vines in the Latroun Vineyard, showing dark garnet, full-bodied and with still-intense tannins needing nothing more than a bit of time to settle in, and already showing an aroma and flavor profile that calls to mind the Southern Rhone and Coteaux de Provence. On the nose and palate kirsch and blackcurrants, those complemented nicely by notes of black tea and pepper, all lingering nicely on the palate. Only about 600 bottles were made. Worth hunting for. Drink now–2016. Score 91.

SOREQ, PETIT VERDOT, KEREM MATA, 2008: Medium- to full-bodied, with silky tannins parting to make way for well-focused boy-senberry, purple plum and floral notes, all lingering nicely on the finish. Drink now–2014. Score 87.

SOREQ, PETIT VERDOT, 2007: Dark garnet, opens generously aromatic and then shows medium- to full-bodied, with notes of cassis, briar and cigar tobacco, those supported by firm, slightly dusty tannins. Tannins and fruits rise on the finish as does a hint of not fully wanted acidity. Drink now–2013. Score 87.

Sraya **

Founded in 2002 by Sraya Ofer and set in the Jordan Valley, this small winery receives Cabernet Sauvignon, Merlot and Shiraz grapes from vineyards in Karmei Yosef and the Ella Valley. First releases were of under 1,000 bottles and currently the winery is releasing about 3,500 bottles annually.

SRAYA, CABERNET SAUVIGNON, 2005: Dark ruby, medium-bodied, with softly mouth-coating tannins and appealing currant, blackberry and blueberry fruits on a lightly spicy background. Drink up. Score 85.

SRAYA, CABERNET SAUVIGNON, 2004: Ruby toward garnet, medium-bodied, with soft tannins integrating nicely and showing red currant and cherry fruits on a spicy, herbal background. On the finish a hint of saddle leather. Past its peak. Drink up. Score 85.

SRAYA, MERLOT, 2005: Ruby toward garnet, medium-bodied, a soft, round wine with appealing wild berry, cherry and spicy notes. A good quaffer. Sliding past its peak. Drink up. Score 82.

SRAYA, MERLOT, 2004: A round, smooth and easy-going wine, medium-bodied, with soft tannins and forward berry, black cherry and spicy notes. Past its peak. Drink up. Score 80.

Srigim **

Founded by Uriel Harari and Moti Mordechai on Moshav Srigim in the Ella Valley, and with Harari acting as wine-maker, this small winery released its first wines from the 2002 harvest. Drawing on grapes from the Judean Mountains, the Ella Valley and Gush Etzion, current production is about 3,000 bottles annually. The winery relies on Cabernet Sauvignon, Cabernet Franc, Petit Verdot, Merlot and Shiraz from contract vineyards, and wines are developed largely in new American and French oak and are finished with only coarse filtration.

SRIGIM, CABERNET SAUVIGNON, 2007: Deep garnet toward royal purple, medium- to full-bodied with soft tannins and spicy wood integrating nicely and opening in the glass to reveal raspberry, cassis and fresh herbal notes. A blend of Cabernet Sauvignon, Petit Verdot and Cabernet Franc (85%, 10% and 5% respectively), with a long, lingering finish. Drink now. Score 86.

SRIGIM, CABERNET SAUVIGNON, BAR-RIQUE, 2006: Blended with 5% Petit Verdot, dark garnet in color and reflecting its 18 months in oak with spices and smoke. Once-firm tannins now integrating nicely and opening to reveal a generous black-fruit nose, and on the palate blackcurrants, black cherries and mint. On the finish an appealing hint of baking chocolate. Drink up. Score 87.

SRIGIM, CABERNET FRANC, 2007: Dark cherry-red toward garnet, a medium-bodied and softly tannic wine based on 85% Cabernet Franc and 15% Petit Verdot. On the nose and palate, red fruits on what many will consider a too-earthy background, with tannins rising dramatically on the finish. Drink now. Score 84.

SRIGIM, CABERNET FRANC, 2006: Deep royal purple in color, a medium-bodied blend of 85% Cabernet Franc 10% Cabernet Sauvignon and 5% Petit Verdot. Aged for 18 months in French and American *barriques*, with generous aromatic oak and chocolate on the nose and showing forward currant and blackberry fruits. Round, soft and caressing. Drink up. Score 85.

SRIGIM, CABERNET FRANC, 2005: A dark royal purple, medium- to full-bodied blend of 85% Cabernet Franc and 7.5% each of Cabernet Sauvignon and Petit Verdot. Oak-aged for 14 months, showing black fruits on an appealing earthy-mineral background. Tannins and a hint of unwanted acidity rise on the finish. Sliding past its peak. Drink up. Score 84.

SRIGIM, PETIT VERDOT, 2006: A blend of 85% Petit Verdot with 7.5% each of Cabernet Franc and Cabernet Sauvignon. Dark, bold and tannic, with aromas and flavors of blackberries, licorice and sweet cedar, all on a background of dusty wood. Drink up. Score 86.

SRIGIM, PETIT VERDOT, 2005: Dark garnet toward royal purple, medium- to full-bodied, this oak-aged blend of 85% Petit Verdot and 7.5% each Cabernet Sauvignon and Cabernet Franc shows fine balance between fruits, spicy wood and acidity. Aromatic, long and mouth-filling. Past its peak. Drink up. Score 84.

SRIGIM, BARRIQUE, 2007: Garnet toward royal purple, oak-aged for 16 months, with somewhat chunky tannins. A blend of 70% Cabernet Sauvignon, 20% Petit Verdot and 10% Cabernet Franc. Opens in the glass to reveal wild berry and plum fruits, those on an earthy and herbal background. Drink now. Score 85.

SRIGIM, BARRIQUE, 2006: A blend of 95% Cabernet Sauvignon, reflecting its 18 months in oak with notes of spices and vanilla. Medium-bodied, with a not-complex but appealing array of cherries, berries and red currants. Drink up. Score 85.

Stern ∗∗∗

Founded by Johnny Stern on Kibbutz Gadot in the Upper Galilee, first production from the 2004 harvest was of 1,100 bottles. In 2008 the winery released 7,000 bottles and production for 2009 is estimated at about 10,000 bottles. The winery, recently relocated on Kibbutz Toval, currently relies on Cabernet Sauvignon, Merlot, Cabernet Franc, Shiraz and Petit Verdot grapes from the Golan Heights, Upper Galilee and Karmei Yosef. Plans are to grow to annual production of about 20,000 bottles.

STERN, CABERNET SAUVIGNON, RE-SERVE, 2009: Made from grapes from Ramot Naftaly in the Upper Galilee and reflecting its aging in French oak for 15 months with caressing tannins and notes of spicy oak. Full-bodied and supple, with currant and purple-plum fruits on a background of earthy minerals and Mediterranean herbs. Best from mid-2012–2017. Score 91.

STERN, CABERNET SAUVIGNON, 2009: A blend of grapes from the Golan Heights and the Upper Galilee, oak-aged for 13 months, showing garnet toward royal purple. Medium- to full-bodied, leaning to the full, revealing soft, near-sweet tannins and hints of sweet-and-spicy cedar, opens in the glass to show a somewhat rustic wine, with its blackcurrants and blackberries complemented nicely with notes of roasted chestnuts, espresso coffee and sage. On the long finish, generous hints of tapenade and tar to grab our attention. Best from mid-2012–2017. Score 90.

STERN, CABERNET SAUVIGNON, 2008: Oak-aged for 14 months, ruby toward garnet in color, medium- to full-bodied with soft tannins and hints of sweet cedarwood. Round and gentle with appealing blackberry, currant and blueberry fruits supported by notes of freshly cut Mediterranean herbs leading to a medium-long finish. Drink now–2013. Score 87.

STERN, CABERNET SAUVIGNON, 2007: Dark garnet with purple reflections, showing full body, soft but mouth-coating tannins and traditional Cabernet aromas and flavors of blackberries and blackcurrants, those on a spicy background. Look as well for hints of licorice and dark chocolate. Drink now. Score 87.

STERN, CABERNET SAUVIGNON, 2006: Dark garnet toward royal purple, medium- to full-bodied, with soft, gently mouth-coating tannins and generous blackberry, currant and citrus peel notes supported nicely by hints of Mediterranean herbs. Lingers nicely. Drink up. Score 87.

STERN, MERLOT, 2007: Medium-bodied, dark garnet, with soft tannins and reflecting its 12 months in oak with spicy and toasty notes. On the nose and palate blackberries and black cherries, those accompanied by a hint of dark chocolate. Drink up. Score 86.

STERN, SHIRAZ, 2006: Medium-dark garnet in color, medium- to full-bodied, with silky tannins and generous wild berry and purple plum fruits on a spicy and earthy background. Well focused. Drink up. Score 86.

STERN, CABERNET FRANC, 2009: Full-bodied, reflecting its aging in French and American oak with comfortably subdued notes of cedarwood and spices. Deeply tannic and somewhat closed at this tasting, but showing the kind of balance and structure that bode well for the future. Opens slowly (after a first tasting I triple-decanted this one to let it blossom) to reveal a lithe and polished wine, with raspberry and cherry fruits on a background of tobacco and licorice notes. Destined to be a "tight" but long and well-focused wine. Best from mid-2012–2016, perhaps longer. Score 90.

STERN, CABERNET FRANC, 2008: Dark ruby toward garnet, full-bodied with firm tannins starting to integrate with notes of spicy oak. Reflecting its 14 months in *barriques* with a not-at-all exaggerated note of Brett which gives the wine a lightly funky aroma. On the nose and palate black fruits, earthy minerals and, on the long finish, notes of cinnamon and roasted herbs. Drink now–2013. Score 86.

STERN, CABERNET FRANC, 2007: Youthful royal purple in color, full-bodied, with gripping tannins that need time to settle down but already showing good balance and structure. Opens to reveal earthy, almost loamy flavors with dense berry, spicy oak and toast flavors. Drink now. Score 86.

STERN, CABERNET FRANC, 2006: Made entirely from Cabernet Franc grapes, aged in new *barriques* for 14 months, showing dark garnet, medium- to full-bodied, with soft tannins and appealing black fruits on a lightly leathery and earthy mineral background. Drink up. Score 87.

STERN, YONATAN, 2009: A medium- to full-bodied, oak-aged blend 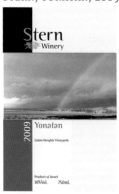 of 58% Cabernet Sauvignon, 33% Merlot and 9% Petit Verdot with a spicy red-fruit nose. Garnet toward royal purple, with soft tannins, opens with a wild berry nose, going on in the glass to reveal red and black berries, currants and spices, all on a background that hints of cigar tobacco and, on the generous finish, a note of eucalyptus. Give this one the time it needs for its elements to come completely together. Drink now–2016, perhaps longer. Score 89.

STERN, YONATAN, 2008: A blend of 48% Cabernet Sauvignon, 44% Merlot and 8% Petite Sirah, reflecting its 14 months in *barriques* with gently gripping tannins and spicy oak, opens to reveal a tempting array of wild berries, blackcurrants and fresh herbal notes. On the long finish appealing notes of black olives. Drink now. Score 87.

STERN, CABERNET SAUVIGNON-MERLOT, 2007: A blend of equal parts of Cabernet Sauvignon and Merlot, those oak-aged for 13 months. Medium- to full-bodied, with gently mouth-coating tannins and notes of near-sweet cedarwood, opens to reveal a distinct black fruit personality. Lacks complexity but a good option with small cuts of meat. Drink now. Score 85.

STERN, CABERNET SAUVIGNON-SHI-RAZ-MERLOT, 2009: Made from grapes harvested on the Golan Heights and Karmei Yosef (on the western slopes of the Judean Hills), a medium- to full-bodied blend of 40% each Cabernet Sauvignon and Shiraz and 20% Merlot. Reflecting its oak-aging for 13 months in French and American oak with tannins that open firmly but meld comfortably in the glass and hints of vanilla. On the nose and palate red and black berries, cassis and notes of citrus peel, those on a background that hints at one moment of sweet cedarwood and at another of mahogany. Long and generous. Drink now–2016. Score 89.

STERN, CABERNET SAUVIGNON-MERLOT-SHIRAZ, 2007: A blend of equal parts of Cabernet Sauvignon, Merlot and Shiraz, showing spicy oak and soft, gently mouth-coating tannins that part to reveal blackberry, blueberry and currant fruits, those matched nicely by notes of mocha, tobacco and freshly turned earth. Drink now, possibly longer. Drink now. Score 87.

STERN, ROTEM, 2009: Developed in French and American oak 13 months, a Bordeaux blend of Cabernet Sauvignon, Merlot, Cabernet Franc and Petit Verdot (64%, 21%, 11% and 4% respectively). Medium-dark garnet, medium- to full-bodied with gently gripping tannins, opens with a red-fruit nose, goes on to show blackcurrants and purple plums on a lightly spicy background, fruits and tannins rising on the medium-long finish. Drink now–2015. Score 88.

STERN, ROTEM, 2008: A blend this year of Cabernet Sauvignon, Merlot, Cabernet Franc and Petite Verdot (66%, 20%, 11% and 3% respectively). Garnet toward royal purple, reflecting its 14 months in oak with soft, near-sweet tannins and hints of cigar box, a rich, round wine. On first attack raspberries and cassis, those yielding to notes of wild berries and sweet herbs. Long and generous. Perhaps the best to date from the winery. Score 89.

STERN, ROTEM, 2006: A Bordeaux blend of Cabernet Sauvignon, Merlot and Cabernet Franc (65%, 22% and 13% respectively). Deep garnet toward royal purple in color, reflecting its 13 months in French oak with soft tannins and opening to reveal blackberry, blueberry and currant fruits, those highlighted by light earthy and herbal notes. Long and generous. Sliding past its peak. Drink up. Score 88.

Tabor ✶✶✶✶

Founded in 1999 by several grape-growing families in the village of Kfar Tabor in the Lower Galilee, this modern winery draws on white grapes largely from their own vineyards near Mount Tabor and on red grapes from the Upper Galilee. Initial production was of 20,000 bottles and current production is about 1 million bottles annually. With about 1,000 dunams (about 250 acres) of vineyards currently on line and new vineyards in the works, plans are to expand slowly until annual production will be between 3–6 million bottles annually. Among new grape varieties now being planted perhaps the most exciting is of Tannat, the grape so dark in color and so deeply concentrated that the Madiran region and the red wine that relies on this grape are often referred to as "the heart of darkness." With agronomist Michal Akerman now gaining full control of the winery's own and contract vineyards, European-trained winemaker Arieh Nesher is currently releasing wines in three series. The top-of-the-line label is Mes'cha, a blend of Cabernet Sauvignon, Merlot and Shiraz. Labels Adama and Adama II reflect the type of soils in the vineyards. In reading the Adama labels it may be useful to know that *adama* translates into soil; *gir* is chalky or limestone-rich soil; *terra rossa* is red earth; *charsit* is clay and *bazelet* refers to volcanic soil. There is also a more basic series released under the label Tabor.

Mes'cha

MES'CHA, CABERNET SAUVIGNON, 2009: By the time this one appears on the market (another year or two), its name may well have changed, but at this writing the wine is showing beautifully. Developed on fine lees, dark, almost impenetrable garnet in color, with its tannins showing almost intense at this stage but with balance and structure that bode well for the future. On the nose and palate blackcurrants, black cherries and crushed berries, those on a background of earthy minerals and roasted herbs, and from mid-palate on a tempting note of chocolate-covered citrus peel. Best from 2013–2018. Score 92. K

MES'CHA, 2008: A blend of Cabernet Sauvignon, Merlot and Shiraz (70%, 20% and 10% respectively), aged for 12 months in French oak. Dark, full-bodied, with gentle spicy, smoky and vanilla notes from the wood, opens in the glass to show blackberries, blackcurrants and bitter herbs, all in fine proportion to the caressing tannins that are here. Best from release (anticipated in 2013). Score 91. K

MES'CHA, 2007: A blend of approximately 75% Cabernet Sauvignon, 15% Merlot and 10% Syrah, oak-aged for 24 months and showing generous spicy and toasty notes and still-firm tannins waiting to integrate and settle down a bit. Opens slowly in the glass to reveal blackcurrants, purple plums and red and black berries, those on a background of citrus peel, cigar tobacco and baking chocolate. Drink now–2014. Score 92. K

MES'CHA, 2006: Good news...the bugle has sounded reveille, the wine has come out of a long sleep and is now showing beautifully. Developed partly in barriques and partly in 2,000 liter vats, a blend of 60% Cabernet Sauvignon, 30% Merlot and 10% Shiraz. On the nose, red fruits and a tantalizing hint of bitter-citrus peel, those making way in the glass for aromas and flavors of blackberries, currants, raspberries and cherries on a background that hints nicely of leather and earthy minerals. Medium- to full-bodied (leaning to the full) with gently chewy tannins. Perhaps the best to date from Tabor. Drink now–2016, perhaps longer. Score 93. K

MES'CHA, 2005: A blend of 75% Cabernet Sauvignon, 15% Shiraz and 10% Merlot, aged partly in 2000 liter casks and partly in 225 liter barriques for 24 months. Dark garnet with orange reflections, full-bodied, with its once-firm tannins and generous oak now integrating nicely. Concentrated and intense, with rich currant, wild berry and licorice notes supported by notes of Mediterranean herbs and cigar tobacco. Long, generous and elegant. Drink now–2014. Score 91. K

MES'CHA, 2003: A blend of Cabernet Sauvignon, Shiraz and Merlot (75%, 15% and 10% respectively), this deep garnet, medium- to full-bodied wine reflects its 18 months in oak with tannins and spicy wood integrating and opening to reveal blackcurrant, berry and plum fruits on a background of spicy wood and Mediterranean herbs. Generous, well balanced and long. Drink now. Score 90. K

MES'CHA, 2002: A blend of Cabernet Sauvignon and Merlot, this medium- to full-bodied red shows firm but well-integrated tannins with spicy oak and generous currant and blackberry fruits, those matched by hints of spices, earthiness and tobacco on the finish. Sliding past its peak. Drink up. Score 87. K

Adama II

ADAMA II, CABERNET SAUVIGNON, 2009: Generously aromatic with ample spicy black fruits on the nose, showing full-bodied with

אדמה II קברנה סוביניון - פטיט סירה 2008

soft, gently caressing tannins and bare hints of spicy cedarwood that give the wine a round persona. On the nose and palate red and black currants, black cherries and blackberries, those on a background of earthy minerals and freshly hung tobacco. Easy to drink but complex and long. Give this one the time it deserves. Best from 2013–2017, perhaps longer. Score 91. K

ADAMA II, MERLOT, 2009: Made entirely from Merlot grapes harvested at Ramot Naftaly, showing impenetrably dark royal purple in color. Opening with a spicy red-fruit nose, going on to reveal rich aromas and flavors of blackcurrants, black cherry and spicy oak, those with notes of roasted herbs, pepper and near-sweet cedarwood. Full-bodied but sleek and complex, with tannins and fruits rising nicely on the long finish. Drink from release–2016. Score 90. K

ADAMA II, MERLOT, 2008: Dark cherry red toward garnet, made entirely from Merlot grapes harvested on Kerem Ben Zimra in the Upper Galilee on volcanic soil, reflecting its 12 months in oak with full-body, soft tannins and light notes of smoky oak. On the nose and palate currants, red berries and notes of citrus peel all on a light note of white pepper. Round, long and generous. Drink now–2014. Score 90. K

ADAMA II, SYRAH, 2008: Dark garnet with a royal purple robe, made entirely from Syrah grapes harvested in the Galilee from vines culti-vated in red-earth soil, reflecting its 12 months in oak with full-body, gently gripping tannins and sweet and spicy wood, those parting to reveal aromas and flavors of purple plums, blackberries and blackcur-rants, all supported nicely by notes of bitter-sweet chocolate and cigar tobacco. Long and generous, with hints of black olives and earthy minerals on the finish. Drink now–2013, perhaps longer. Score 90. K

ADAMA II, CABERNET FRANC, 2009: Paraphrasing the name of the Richard Attenborough film, "Oh! what a lovely wine." Made entirely from Cabernet Franc grapes harvested from the Malkiya vineyard, super-dark garnet, opens with a red-fruit nose. Full-bodied, with still-generous chewy tannins and spicy oak but those in fine balance with fruits and acidity, destined to be a lithe wine, with a generous array of raspberries and cherries, those on a background of floral notes and, from mid-palate on, a hint of green pepper. Smooth and refined, picking up notes of spring flowers on the long finish. Best from mid-2012–2016, perhaps longer. Score 91. K

ADAMA II, PETITE SYRAH, 2008: Dark garnet toward youthful royal purple, made from grapes harvested in the Eastern Galilee and developed for 12 months in second- and third-year oak. Full-bodied, with firmly gripping tannins that yield nicely in the glass to reveal generous blackberry, blueberry and huckleberry fruits, those with overlays of peppery cedarwood. Mouth-filling, generous and well focused, promising a long future. Approachable and enjoyable now but best from mid-2012–2018. Score 91. K

ADAMA II, CABERNET SAUVIGNON-CABERNET FRANC, 2009: A dark-garnet blend of 70% Cabernet Sauvignon and 30% Cabernet Franc. With both varieties vinified before blending, reflecting its time in *barriques* with notes of spicy wood and ample but gently gripping tannins. On the nose and palate rich black fruits and spices, opens in the glass to show itself as medium- to full-bodied (leaning to the full). On the nose and palate blackberry, black cherry and currant fruits, those supported nicely by notes of violets and mocha, all going on to a long and generous finish. Drink from release–2016. Score 91. K

ADAMA II, CABERNET SAUVIGNON-PETITE SIRAH, 2008: Think of this as a Bordeaux blend plus, that is to say 60% Cabernet Sauvignon, 10% each of Cabernet Franc and Merlot plus 20% Petite Sirah. By whatever name, a fine effort, showing full-bodied, with notes of spicy cedar and generous, somewhat rustic tannins parting to reveal currants and juicy red and black berries. On the long finish an appealing hint of smokiness. Drink now–2017. Score 90. K

Adama

ADAMA, CABERNET SAUVIGNON, BAZELET, 2008: Deep garnet, with orange and purple reflections. Full-bodied, showing soft near-sweet tannins and generous spicy oak all in fine balance with blackcurrant, blackberry and purple plums. From mid-palate on an appealing spicy note and, on the long finish, tannins and fruits rise together. Drink now–2013. Score 90. K

ADAMA, CABERNET SAUVIGNON, BAZELET, 2007: Dark garnet toward royal purple, medium- to full-bodied, a rich, softly tannic wine showing dried currant, blackberry, sage and herbal notes and, on the finish, notes of minerals and dark chocolate. Drink now–2014. Score 90. K

ADAMA, CABERNET SAUVIGNON, BAZELET, 2006: Dark garnet, medium- to full-bodied, with fine-grained tannins integrating nicely. A ripe, supple and harmonious wine showing currant and black cherry fruits, those supported by hints of near-sweet cedarwood and dark chocolate. On the long finish an enchanting hint of licorice Drink now. Score 90. K

ADAMA, CABERNET SAUVIGNON, BAZELET, 2005: Medium-dark garnet toward purple, this medium- to full-bodied blend of 87% Cabernet Sauvignon and 13% Merlot was developed in 2000 liter wood casks and shows generous blackcurrant, blackberry, citrus peel and earthy-mineral aromas and flavors. On the long finish hints of sweet cedar, tobacco and eucalyptus. Drink now. Score 90. K

ADAMA, CABERNET SAUVIGNON, TERRA ROSSA, 2009: Precisely why this Cabernet Sauvignon calls to mind Tuscany is not certain. Also, I suppose not very important. Super-dark garnet in color, showing fine concentration and roundness, an opulent wine with black cherry, currant and plum fruits supported well by notes of sweet and bitter herbs and spices. From mid-palate on appealing notes of bittersweet chocolate and tobacco that carry over nicely to the long finish. Full-bodied, with chewy tannins at this stage. Drink now–2017. Score 91. K

ADAMA, CABERNET SAUVIGNON, TERRA ROSSA, 2008: Full-bodied, with tannins and spicy oak integrating nicely and opening to show generous black fruits, chocolate and tobacco. Long and round with a hint of black olives on the finish. Drink now–2013. Score 90. K

ADAMA, CABERNET SAUVIGNON, TERRA ROSSA, 2007: Super-dark garnet in color, an aromatic wine, opening with spicy wood and wild berries on the nose. Full-bodied, showing still-firm tannins that need a bit of time to settle in, but already revealing red currants, spices, licorice and notes of freshly roasted herbs. Drink now–2014. Score 90. K

ADAMA, CABERNET SAUVIGNON, TERRA ROSSA, 2006: Oak-aged for nine months, medium- to full-bodied, with soft tannins, hints of spicy wood and vanilla and mouth-coating tannins settling down nicely. Showing currant, blackberry and generous earthy minerals along with Mediterranean herbs. Round and generous. Drink now. Score 89. K

ADAMA, CABERNET SAUVIGNON, TERRA ROSSA, 2005: Dark garnet toward royal purple, medium- to full-bodied, with firm, near-sweet tannins integrating nicely. Aromatic and flavorful, with red plums, raspberries and currants matched by minerals and light hints of herbaceousness. Round, long and generous. Drink now. Score 89. K

ADAMA, MERLOT, BAZELET, 2009: Medium- to full-bodied, garnet to royal purple, based on grapes harvested at Ramot Naftaly in the Upper Galilee and reflecting its development in oak with gently caressing tannins and a note of sweet-and-spicy cedar. On the nose and palate currants, pomegranate and raspberries flavors, those on a background of red licorice and cigar tobacco, all lingering long and generously on the palate. Simultaneously lively and complex, supple and distinctive. Drink from release–2016, perhaps longer. Score 90. K

ADAMA, MERLOT, BAZELET, 2008: Made from grapes harvested in the Upper Galilee, medium- to full-bodied, leaning to the full, with soft tannins and showing dark cherry red toward garnet. On the opening nose spicy and smoky oak. Opens in the glass to reveal black and red cherries, red berries, cassis and peppery notes, all with a hint of citrus peel. Drink now–2013. Score 89. K

ADAMA, MERLOT, BAZELET, 2007: Dark ruby toward garnet, medium-bodied, with a sweet, almost jammy raspberry nose that goes on to show spicy plums, cherries and blackberries, those complemented nicely by spicy cedar notes, with fruits and tannins rising on the finish. Drink now. Score 89. K

ADAMA, MERLOT, BAZELET, 2006: Garnet toward royal purple, with light spicy wood on near-sweet tannins and opening to reveal currant, purple plum and blackberry fruits, those on a background of milk chocolate and, on the finish, nice hints of mint and white pepper. Drink now. Score 89. K

ADAMA, MERLOT, GIR, 2007: Developed in mostly French oak for 12 months, intensely dark garnet in color, opening with a rich mineral and black-fruit nose, going on to show firm but gently caressing tannins on a medium- to full-bodied frame. Opens in the glass to reveal currant, plum and licorice notes, and finishes with a generous hint of espresso. Drink now–2013. Score 90. K

ADAMA, MERLOT, GIR, 2006: Garnet toward youthful royal purple, medium-bodied, with soft tannins integrating nicely and showing blackberry, blueberry and cassis notes, those supported by a generous green and herbal overlay that may not please all. Drink now. Score 87. K

ADAMA, PETITE SIRAH, CHARSIT, SPECIAL EDITION, 2008: Super-dark garnet, well concentrated but ripe and round, with near-sweet tannins and a gentle spicy wood influence. On the nose and palate ripe spicy plums and wild berries, those matched nicely by notes of hazelnuts, dark chocolate and sweet chewing tobacco. Long and generous with a light herbal note rising on the finish. Drink now–2014, perhaps longer. Score 90. K

ADAMA, SYRAH, TERRA ROSSA, 2008: Dark ruby toward garnet, medium- to full-bodied, with soft tannins and a tempting hint of sweet cedarwood opening to reveal generous blackberry and black cherry fruits, those supported nicely by notes of dark chocolate and an appealing bittersweet herbal flavor that rises on the finish. Drink now–2013. Score 88. K

ADAMA, ROSÉ, CHARSIT, 2008: Ruby toward cherry-red, medium-bodied, a lovely rosé, fresh, crisp and full of life, with the most positive kinds of tutti-frutti aromas and flavors, those including strawberries, raspberries, red currants and just a tantalizing hint of bubble gum to tease our palates. Rosé as rosé should be. Drink now. Score 89. K

ADAMA, SAUVIGNON BLANC, GIR, 2010: Light gold, medium-bodied, with crisp acidity and an appealing array of citrus and ripe summer fruits, those complemented nicely by hints of flinty minerals. Not overly complex but absolutely delicious. Drink now. Score 90. K

ADAMA, SAUVIGNON BLANC, GIR, 2009: Pale straw in color, unoaked, and crisply fresh with aromas and flavors of citrus and kiwi fruits along with a note of freshly mown grass. Medium-bodied, lively and refreshing with just enough complexity to capture our imagination Drink now. Score 89. K

ADAMA, SAUVIGNON BLANC, GIR, 2008: Unoaked, a lovely and lively wine, showing light golden straw in color, medium-bodied and with crisp balancing acidity to highlight aromas and flavors of minerals, grapefruit, lime, anise and oyster shell notes. Tangy citrus and a grassy hint linger nicely. Drink up. Score 89. K

ADAMA, GEWURZTRAMINER, GIR, 2007: Light golden straw in color and medium-bodied, so sweet and lacking balancing acidity that one cannot distinguish any of the traditional fruits or spices of the Gewurztraminer grape. For reasons not fully clear, more than a bit *frizzante*. Drink up. Score 75. K

Tabor

TABOR, CABERNET SAUVIGNON, 2009: Garnet toward royal purple, medium-bodied, softly tannic, opening with blackberries, those yielding to currants and chocolate covered citrus peel. Drink now. Score 87. K

TABOR, CABERNET SAUVIGNON, 2008: Medium-dark garnet, medium- to full-bodied, with soft tannins and showing generous currant and wild berry fruits. Nothing complex here but fine on its own or with small cuts of beef, lamb or pork. Drink now. Score 86. K

TABOR, CABERNET SAUVIGNON, 2007: Garnet toward royal purple, with soft tannins integrating nicely with a light overlay of cedar (the wine was developed in stainless-steel tanks with oak staves). Opens with an appealing note of mint on the nose, that yielding to red currants, red berries and citrus. If the wine is faulted at all it is only by somewhat too-generous acidity. Drink up. Score 87. K

TABOR, MERLOT, 2009: Ruby toward garnet, medium-bodied, with gently caressing tannins and notes of eucalyptus (or is it licorice?) highlighting generous red fruits. A fine quaffer and a good match to Mediterranean dishes. Drink now. Score 87. K

TABOR, MERLOT, 2008: Youthful royal purple in color, medium-bodied, with soft tannins and a hint of spicy wood to complement cassis and milk chocolate notes. An easy-to-drink quaffer. Drink now. Score 86. K

TABOR, MERLOT, 2007: Garnet toward royal purple, medium-bodied, with light spicy and vanilla notes added by aging with oak staves. With soft tannins integrated well, a soft, round and fruit-forward wine showing raspberry and milk chocolate notes, all lingering nicely. Drink up. Score 87. K

TABOR, SHIRAZ, 2010: Medium-dark garnet, medium-bodied, with soft, gently caressing tannins and a hint of spicy wood. On the nose and palate a distinctly red fruit Shiraz, showing raspberries, red plums and red currants on a background of roasted herbs. Round, soft and easy to drink. Drink now. Score 86. K

TABOR, SHIRAZ, 2009: Dark garnet toward royal purple, medium-bodied, reflecting its development with oak staves reflecting gently spicy cedar notes and caressing tannins. Opens with aromas and flavors of red plums and raspberries, those going on to black cherries, all with a light and easy-going herbal note. Lingers nicely. Drink now. Score 87. K

TABOR, BLENDED RED, SPECIAL EDITION, 2008: A blend of 70% Cabernet Sauvignon, 20% Cabernet Franc and 10% Syrah. Made entirely from grapes from the Malkiya vineyard on the Lebanese border, deep garnet with near-sweet tannins and notes of vanilla from the oak in which it aged. Fruit forward, showing generous blackberry, cassis and citrus peel notes, those complemented by hints of bittersweet chocolate and, on the long finish, a note of cigar tobacco. Drink now–2015, perhaps longer. Score 91. K

TABOR, 562, ROUGE, 2010: Named (or numbered if you like) after the altitude at which the grapes were harvested. Made entirely from Barbera grapes this year, a deep-pink sparkling wine made by the Charmat method (secondary fermentation in stainless steel tanks), showing light- to medium-bodied, with an abundance of sharp bubbles and a long, long mousse, showing an appealing array of raspberry, strawberry and wild red berries that make you smile for pleasure. Not at all complex but great fun. Drink now. Score 85. K

TABOR, 562, BLANC, 2010: A blend of 80% Chardonnay and 20% *blanc de noirs* made from Cabernet Sauvignon, made by the Charmat method, that is to say with secondary fermentation in stainless steel tanks, a nearly colorless wine with a mousse that lingers on and on and on, looking something like soap bubbles but fortunately not at all tasting like that. Lots of bubbles here, with generous lemon and lime fruits, reminding me of a sophisticated version of the soft drink Sprite. Those who are going to like it will like it. Those who will not like it, won't. Drink now. Score 82. K

TABOR, PNINIM (PEARLS) WHITE, 2009: Made by the Charmat method, a moderately sweet blend of Gewurztraminer and Viognier, with notes of grapefruit and orange peel. Low in alcohol (about 10%) and lively, a simple but fun wine for summertime quaffing. Drink up. K

TABOR, PNINIM (PEARLS), RED, 2009: Cherry-red toward garnet in color, with moderate sweetness set off nicely by fresh acidity and showing appealing wild berry and cassis notes on the nose and palate. Made by the Charmat method entirely from Merlot grapes, a not at all complex but fun wine at its best at picnics, rooftop parties or at the beach. Serve well chilled. Drink up. K

TABOR, CHARDONNAY, 2010: Unoaked, showing light, shining gold, with fresh citrus aromas, opens in the glass to show green apple and tropical fruits on a crisply dry, mineral background. Fresh and vibrant, with a note of white peaches on the finish. Drink now–2014. Score 89. K

TABOR, CHARDONNAY, 2009: Damp golden straw in color, medium-bodied, mineral-rich with appealing pear, citrus and gooseberry notes. Clean, fresh and refreshing. Drink now. Score 88. K

TABOR, CHARDONNAY, 2008: Light gold in color, medium-bodied, a fresh and lively unoaked Chardonnay with citrus, melon and Anjou pears on a crisp mineral background. Just complex enough to grab our attention. Drink up. Score 88. K

TABOR, VIOGNIER, 2008: Light gold in color, medium-bodied, with fine acidity and spices to support rich pear, litchi and citrus. Long with a white pepper finish. Lovely. Drink up. Score 90. K

Tanya ✶✶✶✶

Located in the town of Ofra, north of Ramallah, this winery established by Yoram Cohen released its first wines in 2002. Drawing on Cabernet Sauvignon and Merlot grapes from Gush Etzion and the Golan Heights, the winery produced 6,500 bottles in 2004 and current production is about 30,000 bottles annually. The winery, showing marked quality improvement on a regular basis, produces three series, Enosh, Halel and Reserve. No wines were produced in 2008 because this was a Sabbatical year for the grapes.

Enosh

ENOSH, CABERNET SAUVIGNON, 2006: Deep garnet, full-bodied, with still-firm tannins and spicy wood needing time to integrate but showing fine balance and structure that bode well for the future. On the nose and tannins traditional Cabernet blackcurrant and blackberry fruits, those complemented by notes of black olives and earthy minerals. Perhaps the best to date from Tanya. Drink now–2015. Score 90. K

ENOSH, CABERNET SAUVIGNON, 2005: Dark garnet toward royal purple, full-bodied, with soft, gently mouth-coating tannins and spicy wood in fine balance with blackcurrant, blackberry and plum fruits all leading to a long, spicy finish. Drink up. Score 89. K

Halel

HALEL, CABERNET SAUVIGNON, 2009: Medium- to full-bodied, with notes of spicy oak and somewhat chunky tannins that give the wine a rustic character. On the nose and palate traditional Cabernet aromas and flavors of black fruits, those complemented by hints of licorice and black olives. Drink now–2013. Score 87. K

HALEL, CABERNET SAUVIGNON, 2007: Dark garnet, with notes of sweet cedarwood on the nose. Full-bodied, with soft, gently caressing tannins, opens to reveal an appealing array of blackcurrants, blackberries and purple plums, those on a background of Mediterranean herbs and earthy minerals. Tannins and fruits rise nicely on the long finish. Drink now–2014. Score 90. K

HALEL, CABERNET SAUVIGNON, 2006: Dark garnet toward royal purple, full-bodied, with soft, gently mouth-coating tannins and a gentle hand with spicy wood. Opens to show traditional Cabernet blackcurrant and blackberry fruits, those yielding to show hints of orange peel. Drink up. Score 88. K

HALEL, CABERNET SAUVIGNON, 2005: Deep and concentrated, almost impenetrable garnet in color and with firm tannins and generous wood still holding back the fruits here. No fear though, for this one shows fine balance and structure that bode well for the future. Oak-aged for 16 months, opening in the glass to reveal firm but elegant dried currants and blackberry aromas and flavors, those gaining complexity and depth on the long finish. Drink now. Score 90. K

HALEL, MERLOT, 2009: Dark garnet with a ruby robe, full-bodied, with soft, gently caressing tannins. On the nose and palate, black and red berries, dried currants and notes of minted chocolate. Round and generous. Drink now–2014. Score 88. K

HALEL, MERLOT, 2007: Aromatic, with jammy fruits and spices on the nose, but opening in the glass to be not at all jammy. Full-bodied with soft, near-sweet tannins and a gentle reflection of the oak in which the wine developed, showing an appealing array of plums, wild berries and spicy oak, all lingering nicely on the palate. Drink now–2013. Score 88. K

HALEL, MERLOT, 2006: With Tanya's signature of near-sweet tannins, a soft and generous medium- to full-bodied wine with a plush texture and its cherry, red berry fruits supported nicely by notes of tobacco, eucalyptus and smoke. Oak-aged for 14 months and with appealing spicy oak notes rising on the finish. Drink up. Score 89. K

HALEL, CABERNET FRANC, 2009: Full-bodied, dark garnet toward royal purple, with soft tannins and appealing notes of spicy cedar. On the nose and palate blackberries, plums and cassis, those on a background that hints at one moment of roasted herbs and at another of cigar tobacco. Drink now–2015. Score 90. K

HALEL, CABERNET FRANC, 2006: Dark garnet, medium- to full-bodied, with gently caressing near-sweet tannins. Opens with generous ripe berries, those yielding comfortably to purple plums and blackberries, all on an appealingly light herbal overtone. Long and mouth-filling. Drink now. Score 89. K

HALEL, BLENDED RED, 2009: Medium- to full-bodied, with chunky but gently gripping tannins and notes of spicy cedarwood. An appealing country-style wine opening to reveal aromas and flavors of blackberries, currants and earthy-herbal notes. Drink now–2013. Score 89. K

Reserve

RESERVE, CABERNET SAUVIGNON, ELIYA, 2006: Full and firm, almost muscular, with firm tannins that need time to integrate but already showing good balance and structure. Opens to reveal blackberry, currant and purple plum fruits, those with hints of mocha and black pepper. Drink now. Score 88. K

RESERVE, CABERNET SAUVIGNON, 2005: Dark ruby toward garnet, medium- to full-bodied, with firm tannins and spicy wood opening to reveal blackcurrant, blackberry and black cherry fruits, those with light overtones of fresh herbs. Drink up. Score 87. K

RESERVE, MERLOT, ELIYA, 2006: Deep ruby toward garnet, medium-bodied, with caressing soft tannins and hints of spices and vanilla from the *barriques* in which it developed. On first attack raspberries and cherries, those yielding to red plums and cassis, all on a light background of Mediterranean herbs. Drink up. Score 88. K

RESERVE, MERLOT, 2005: Aromatic, deep garnet in color, medium- to full-bodied with soft, mouth-coating tannins and a gentle wood influence. On the nose and palate blackberries and cassis fruits supported nicely by hints of chocolate and mint. Sliding past its peak. Drink up. Score 87. K

RESERVE, PINOT NOIR, 2007: Dark ruby in color, full-bodied and with near-chewy tannins waiting to settle down. Opens to reveal raspberry and cassis fruits on a generously herbal background. Drink now. Score 87. K

RESERVE, CABERNET FRANC, 2007: Garnet toward royal purple, medium- to full-bodied, with mouth-coating tannins. Opens to reveal traditional black fruits on a background of spring flowers and dark chocolate. Drink from release. Tentative Score 86–88. K

RESERVE, CABERNET FRANC, BRACHA, 2006: Made entirely from Cabernet Franc grapes, developed in *barriques* for 14 months, dark, almost impenetrable garnet in color, a medium- to full-bodied, softly tannic wine. On first attack notes of plums, tar and bittersweet chocolate, those yielding to aromas and flavors of blackcurrants and espresso coffee, all with a comfortable overlay of black pepper. Long and generous. Drink now. Score 90. K

RESERVE, CABERNET SAUVIGNON-MERLOT, ELIYA, 2006: A full-bodied blend of 70% Cabernet Sauvignon and 30% Merlot, the once-chunky tannins and generous wood now softening and falling into better balance. Still a somewhat country-style wine, but showing appealing black and red currants and berries, along with hints of licorice and chocolate. Drink now. Score 86. K

RESERVE, CABERNET SAUVIGNON-MERLOT, 2005: Developed in oak for ten months, now showing soft, round and generous with black fruits, strawberries and hints of bittersweet chocolate and, on the moderately long finish, an appealing hint of saddle leather. Drink up. Score 86. K

Tanya

TANYA, PORTO, 2005: An unlikely blend of Merlot and Chardonnay, those aged for 36 months in French oak. Medium-bodied, with its generous sweetness balanced nicely by fresh acidity, showing aromas and flavors of ripe plums, raisins and chocolate. Not Port but pleasant enough and, as President Lincoln said, this is the kind of thing that people who like this kind of thing will like. Drink now–2016. Score 85. K

Teperberg 1870 ***

Founded in 1870 by the Teperberg family in the Jewish quarter of the old city of Jerusalem, and then relocating outside of the walls, the winery moved to Motza, on the outskirts of the city, in 1964, and there took on the name of Efrat. For much of that time it produced primarily sacramental wines for the ultra-Orthodox community. During the 1990s it also started producing table wines. Starting in 2002, under the supervision of California-trained senior winemaker Shiki Rauchberger the winery began producing wines destined to appeal to a more sophisticated audience. Now relocated to their newly constructed winery on Kibbutz Tzora at the foothills of the Jerusalem Mountains, the winery has officially changed its name back to Teperberg. An important part of the winemaking team is French-born, French-trained winemaker Olivier Fratty.

More than a mere change in name and location, the new winery, still partly under construction, now boasts fully modern equipment, a new and very impressive barrel room and increasing control over its vineyards, and is currently producing about 4 million bottles annually. Wines of interest are in the Reserve, Terra and Silver series. The Efrat label has not fully disappeared and may now be considered a sub-label of the winery that includes an Efrat and an Israeli series. With the exception of the wines in the Reserve and Terra series, all of the wines are *mevushal*. As a rule of thumb, wines in the Silver series are oak-aged for six months; those in the Terra series for 12 months and those in the Reserve series for 18 months. More important, the wines are moving more and more toward elegance. Target production within the next five years is 7 million bottles annually.

Reserve

RESERVE, CABERNET SAUVIGNON, 2008: Dark garnet toward royal purple, full-bodied with its once-firm tannins now settling in nicely. On the nose and palate generous blackcurrants and figs, those highlighted by notes of espresso and cigar tobacco. Tannins and fruits rise appealingly on the long finish. Drink now–2016. Score 90. K

RESERVE, CABERNET SAUVIGNON, 2007: Dark, medium- to full-bodied (leaning toward the full) and intense with still-firm and gripping tannins needing a bit more time to integrate. Big and broad-shouldered, with blackberry, blackcurrant, fig and mocha notes backed up by hints of lead pencil and cocoa. Hints of licorice and bitter herbs here. Generous, with an appealing toasty sensation rising on the finish. The best to date from Teperberg. Drink now–2014. Score 91. K

RESERVE, CABERNET SAUVIGNON, 2006: Dark toward inky garnet, full-bodied, reflecting its 15 months in oak with gentle spices and a hint of smoke, with once-firm tannins now settling in and fine balance with wood and fruits. On the nose and palate an appealing array of spicy currant, blackberry, cedar and mineral notes, with light hints  of anise and cigar tobacco on the long and generous finish. Holds back a bit when first poured but opens very nicely in the glass. Drink now. Score 89. K

RESERVE, CABERNET SAUVIGNON, 2005: Dark garnet, medium- to full-bodied, with soft tannins and gentle smoky wood integrating nicely. Currant, blackberry and raspberry fruits complemented by hints of orange peel and light mocha aromas and flavors, all with a hint of Oriental spices rising on the finish. Drink up. Score 88. K

RESERVE, MERLOT, 2008: Almost inky black in color, full-bodied, with gripping tannins, a muscular Merlot opening slowly in the glass to reveal blackberries, cassis and dark chocolate. On the long, mouth-filling finish tannins rise with notes of red berries. Drink now–2014. Score 89. K

RESERVE, MERLOT, 2007: Super-dark garnet, full-bodied, with generous tannins settling in nicely to highlight abundant blackcurrant and blackberry fruits on first attack, those yielding to red berries and, on the long finish, hints of loamy earthy and sweet spices. Drink now–2013. Score 90. K

RESERVE, SHIRAZ, 2009: Almost impenetrably dark garnet with a rim of royal purple, full-bodied, with fine balance between wood, gently gripping tannins and fruits. On first attack blueberries and purple plums, those parting to make way for notes of cassis, earthy minerals and a generous meaty note, all lingering nicely. Drink now–2015. Score 90. K

RESERVE, SHIRAZ, 2008: Deep garnet in color, with notes of leather and licorice on the nose, opens to show still-firm tannins, those yielding slowly to reveal black fruits on a background of minted chocolate. Drink now–2015. Score 89. K

RESERVE, MERITAGE, 2007: A blend of Cabernet Sauvignon, Merlot and Cabernet Franc, medium- to full-bodied, with gently gripping tannins and hints of spicy oak to highlight blackcurrant, cherry and blueberry fruits. In the background notes of gently spicy wood and a hint of mocha. Lingers nicely. Drink now. Score 88. K

RESERVE, MERITAGE, 2006: A medium- to full-bodied blend of Cabernet Sauvignon, Merlot, Cabernet Franc and Petit Verdot, showing soft tannins and just the right notes of dusty oak, those in good balance with fruits. Opens with aromatic blueberries on the nose, goes on to aromas and flavors of currants, cherries and wild berries, those complemented by notes of tar and grilled beef. Drink up. Score 87. K

RESERVE, CHARDONNAY, 2010: Medium-bodied, with fine balance between spicy oak, acidity and fruits. Fermented in stainless steel before being transferred to barriques, showing citrus, tropical fruits and a bare but appealing note of bitter citrus pith from mid-palate on. Lively and refreshing with just enough complexity to grab the attention. Drink now. Score 87. K

RESERVE, CHARDONNAY, 2009: Deep gold, reflecting its development in French oak *barriques* with peppery and cinnamon notes. On the nose and palate citrus, melon, green apples and citrus peel. Lively, spicy and long, a generous wine. Drink now. Score 89. K

Terra

TERRA, CABERNET SAUVIGNON, 2008: Deep garnet toward royal purple, with firm, somewhat chunky tannins giving the wine a rustic note. On the nose and palate vanilla, spicy oak, blackcurrants and wild berries, those supported by notes of mocha and roasted herbs. Drink now–2013. Score 88. K

TERRA, CABERNET SAUVIGNON, 2007: Thoroughly traditional Cabernet. Super-dark garnet, with gripping, near-sweet tannins and spicy wood integrating nicely to show off blackcurrants and cassis, those with hints of mint and freshly roasted coffee. Somewhat quiet on the nose but with flavors that linger nicely. Drink now. Score 88. K

TERRA, CABERNET SAUVIGNON, 2006: Dark garnet, medium- to full-bodied, and reflecting its 14 months in French oak. Hints of toasty oak and moderately firm tannins, those in fine balance with acidity and fruits. With raspberry, cherry and cassis fruits complemented by notes of spices and a hint of what might be dried apricots, all leading to a long, gentle and near-elegant finish. Drink up. Score 88. K

TERRA, MERLOT, 2008: Garnet toward royal purple, medium- to full-bodied, with soft tannins and notes of spicy wood parting to reveal generous notes of raspberries and cassis, those on a background that hints nicely of earthy minerals and allspice. Drink now. Score 88. K

TERRA, MERLOT, 2007: Medium-bodied, dark garnet, with nicely gripping tannins, lively acidity and a gentle hand with the wood, those in fine balance with blackberry and blueberry. In the background, appealing hints of Oriental spices and earthy minerals. Drink up. Score 88. K

TERRA, MERLOT, 2006: Deep garnet toward royal purple, medium- to full-bodied with caressing tannins, reflecting its 14 months in *barriques* with sweet and dusty oak, gentle spices and a hint of smoke. On the nose and palate currant, blackberry and cranberry fruits, those backed up nicely by light earthy-herbal and dark chocolate overlays. Sliding past its peak. Drink up. Score 88. K

TERRA, MALBEC, 2009: As dark as a Malbec should be, medium- to full-bodied (leaning to the full), with generous, softly gripping tannins in fine balance with spicy cedarwood and fruits. On the nose and palate purple plums, black cherries and wild berries, those supported nicely by notes of cinnamon toast and, on the long finish, a comfortable note of espresso coffee. Drink now–2015. Score 90. K

TERRA, MALBEC, 2008: Dark garnet toward royal purple, with an appealing red-fruit nose, medium- to full-bodied and with generous, softly gripping tannins, a wine traditional to its variety. On the nose and palate reflecting its time in oak with white pepper and mixed spices, red plums and raspberries, those giving way nicely to crushed blackberries, a hint of milk chocolate and a spicy and mouth-filling finish. Drink now–2013. Score 89. K

TERRA, MALBEC, 2007: Made from grapes from the Jerusalem Hills, showing dark garnet in color, with firm tannins and notes of spicy wood in good balance with fruits and acidity. Reflecting its development in new French and American oak barriques for 12 months with notes of sweet toast and vanilla, opens in the glass to reveal black cherries, purple plums and bittersweet chocolate, all lingering nicely. Drink now. Score 88. K

TERRA, CABERNET SAUVIGNON-MERLOT, 2009: Garnet to royal purple in color, medium- to full-bodied, with soft tannins that caress gently. Opens in the glass to reveal raspberries, currants and appealing notes of mint. Round and generous. Drink now. Score 87. K

TERRA, CABERNET SAUVIGNON-MERLOT, 2008: A blend of 60% Cabernet Sauvignon and 40% Merlot. Medium-bodied, with silky tannins. Not much of a nose here but generous flavors of blackcurrants, blackberries and purple plums. Easy to drink. Drink now. Score 87. K

TERRA, CABERNET SAUVIGNON-MERLOT, 2007: A dark-garnet blend of Cabernet Sauvignon, Merlot, and Cabernet Franc (25%, 70% and 5% respectively). With light exposure to oak and showing medium-bodied, its once-chunky tannins now settled in comfortably and opening to show a blackberry-cherry personality. A very pleasant quaffer. Drink up. Score 87. K

TERRA, SAUVIGNON BLANC, 2010: Light straw colored with a green tint, light- to medium-bodied with fresh aromas of citrus and tropical fruits. Crisply dry with generous notes of citrus peel complemented nicely by hints of thyme and rosemary. Light, bright and eminently easy to drink. Drink now. Score 87. K

TERRA, SAUVIGNON BLANC, UNOAKED, 2009: Light golden straw in color, a crisply dry and aromatic, clean and refreshing wine with citrus, citrus peel and light grassy notes, all lingering nicely on the palate and with enough peppery complexity to grab our attention. Drink up. Score 88. K

TERRA, SAUVIGNON BLANC, 2009: Dark golden straw in color, think of this perhaps as the big brother of the unoaked version of the wine reviewed above, this one reflecting its six months in *barriques* with a surprisingly heavy oak influence that seems to mute the fruits somewhat. More complex than the unoaked version but because of the wood, less satisfying. Drink now. Score 86. K

554

TERRA, SAUVIGNON BLANC, 2008: Light gold, fresh and refreshing, with tangy acidity to highlight citrus, pear and tropical fruits, those matched nicely by notes of oyster shells and lemongrass. Drink up. Score 89. K

TERRA, GEWURZTRAMINER, 2010: Off-dry but with fine balancing acidity to keep it lively. On the nose and palate traditional Gewurztraminer rose petals and litchis, those fleshed out with notes of grapefruit, pineapple and white pepper. A fine choice with Indian or Chinese cuisine. Drink now. Score 86. K

TERRA, EMERALD RIESLING, 2010: Half-dry, light straw colored, with a floral nose, opens to show grapefruit and white peach aromas and flavors. Shows good acidity to balance the sweetness. A fine choice for those who enjoy Emerald Riesling. Drink now. Score 85. K

TERRA, EMERALD RIESLING, 2009: The color of damp straw, light- to medium-bodied with mild sweetness balanced nicely by acidity, showing citrus, apples and tropical fruits. A fine entry-level white. Drink up. Score 85. K

Silver

SILVER, CABERNET SAUVIGNON, 2009: Deeply extracted and almost impenetrably dark garnet in color, opens with aromas and flavors of raspberries, goes on to reveal blackcurrants and blackberries on a lightly spicy, gently tannic background. Medium- to full-bodied, round and generous. Drink now. Score 88. K

SILVER, CABERNET SAUVIGNON, 2008: Deep garnet in color, medium- to full-bodied, with somewhat flabby tannins that dull the black fruits and spices that are here. Drink up. Score 84. K

SILVER, MERLOT, 2009: Oak-aged for six months, showing very dark garnet toward royal purple, medium- to full-bodied with well-integrated tannins that make the wine soft, round and caressing. Fine balance between spicy cedarwood, plums and earthy minerals, those with hints of eucalyptus and tobacco on the generous finish. Drink now. Score 88. K

SILVER, MERLOT, 2008: A classic style of Merlot, soft, round and supple, with plums and spices on a background of red currants, freshly ground coffee and an appealing hint of bitterness on the finish. Drink now. Score 87. K

SILVER, MERLOT, 2007: Dark garnet, medium- to full-bodied, with gently mouth-coating tannins and vanilla notes. Opens to show berry, black cherry and purple plum fruits on a lightly spicy background with a hint of black olives coming in on the finish. Drink up. Score 86. K

SILVER, SYRAH, 2009: A fine traditional Syrah nose, showing hints of leather and grilled meat opening to real medium- to full-body with generous but soft tannins. Reflects its six months in oak with spices and a hint of vanilla and on the nose and palate purple and green-gage plums together with notes of currants. Drink now. Score 87.

SILVER, SYRAH, 2008: Dark royal purple in color, medium- to full-bodied, showing soft tannins that highlight the forward and ripe plum and black cherry fruits. Finishes with notes of spice and cedar. Drink up. Score 85. K

SILVER, SANGIOVESE, 2009: Dark cherry red toward garnet, medium-bodied, with soft, gently caressing tannins, and aromas and flavors of black cherries, wild berries and red currants, all with a hint of white pepper. Calls to mind a fun Chianti. Drink now. Score 87. K

SILVER, MERITAGE, 2009: A blend of 60% Cabernet Sauvignon and 25% Merlot, those fleshed out with Petit Verdot and Cabernet Franc. Medium- to full-bodied with soft tannins and fine balance between notes of spicy wood and fruits. On the nose and palate crushed berries, cassis and an appealing mineral note, all lingering nicely. Drink now–2013. Score 87. K

SILVER, MERITAGE, 2006: A deep, almost inky-garnet, lightly-oaked blend of Cabernet Sauvignon, Merlot and Cabernet Franc (70%, 25% and 5% respectively). Medium-bodied, opens with wild berries and hints of orange peel, those yielding to gentle overtones of vanilla and espresso coffee. Drink up. Score 86. K

SILVER, CHARDONNAY, 2010: Oak-aged for six months, showing light gold, with appealing hints of spicy cedarwood. On the nose and palate citrus, citrus peel and ripe summer fruits. Finishes crisp and lively. Drink now. Score 86. K

SILVER, CHARDONNAY, 2009: Light gold, reflecting its eight months in oak with spicy and cedar-like notes, opens with a fresh nose and then reveals apple, citrus and pineapple notes, those with good balancing acidity. Medium-bodied but mouth-filling and generous. Drink up. Score 87. K

SILVER, SAUVIGNON BLANC, 2010: Unoaked, light- to medium-bodied, the color of damp straw. Fresh and lively, opening with appealing

lemon and lime notes, those making way for hints of peaches and pineapple, all along with a hint of freshly cut grass. Drink now. Score 86. K

SILVER, WHITE RIESLING, LATE HARVEST, 2009: Light gold in color,
with honeyed guava, peach and nectarine fruits, those opening to notes
of sweet, stewed apples. Medium-bodied, with moderate-to-rich sweetness but with fine balancing acidity to keep the wine lively and fresh.
Fine as an aperitif, with goose liver dishes or with fruit-based desserts.
Drink now–2013, perhaps longer. Score 89. K

**SILVER, WHITE RIESLING, LATE HARVEST,
2008:** Opens with a burst of honeyed quince,
continues to nectarine and peach fruits and
finally to light notes of pepper and mint. Honeyed flavors throughout. Generously sweet
but with fine balancing acidity. Drink now.
Score 89. K

**SILVER, WHITE RIESLING, LATE HARVEST,
2007:** Shining gold in color, with moderate
sweetness offset by natural acidity. Opens
to show notes of honeysuckle, dried apricots
and honeyed apples, those complemented
nicely by hints of white pepper. Lively, fresh
and complex, as good an aperitif as it is a dessert wine. Drink up.
Score 88. K

Teperberg

TEPERBERG, RED, 2009: Dark royal purple in color, a medium-bodied
blend of 55% Cabernet Sauvignon and 45% Merlot. On the nose a hint
of raspberry-flavored bubble gum, that thankfully subsiding and giving
way to aromas and flavors of wild berries, cherries and cassis. A pleasant
enough entry-level wine, fruity enough that despite its dryness, some
will think it sweet. Drink now. Score 84. K

TEPERBERG, ROSÉ, 2009: Blush pink in color, light- to medium-
bodied, made from Cabernet Sauvignon grapes, with tutti-frutti aromas
and flavors. A pleasant little wine best served either quite well chilled
or with a few ice cubes added. Drink now. Score 85. K

TEPERBERG, WHITE, 2009: A blend of 80% Sauvignon Blanc and
20% Chardonnay, light gold in color, with pineapple, citrus and tropical
fruits on the nose and palate, those with just the barest hint of sweetness. Clean and refreshing, a fine entry-level wine. Drink up. Score 84. K

Terra Nova ✳✳✳

2007 קברנה סוביניון
Cabernet Sauvignon
כנף רמת הגולן

Located on Moshav Kanaf on the Golan Heights, the winery released its first wines from the 2007 vintage. With four partners, among them Gil Sharon acting as winemaker, the winery has its own vineyards at Tel Phares on the Golan, those with Cabernet Sauvignon, Merlot and Syrah grapes. Production has grown from 2,500 bottles in 2007 to 12,000 in 2010.

TERRA NOVA, CABERNET SAUVIGNON, 2007: Garnet, with purple reflections, medium-bodied, reflecting its 12 months in oak with caressing tannins and opening on the nose to show traditional Cabernet currant and blackberry fruits, those complemented by notes of fresh herbs. Drink now. Score 87.

TERRA NOVA, SYRAH, 2007: Oak-aged for 12 months, dark ruby toward garnet, medium-, perhaps medium- to full-bodied, opening with a chocolate and berry-rich nose, going on to reveal soft, gently gripping tannins in fine balance with light toasty oak and red currant and wild berry fruits all on a lightly spicy background. Drink now. Score 87.

TERRA NOVA, BREISHEIT, 2007: Dark garnet, a blend of 75% Merlot, 20% Cabernet Sauvignon and 5% Syrah. Oak-aged for 12 months, showing notes of near-sweet cedarwood, wild berries and currants. Soft, round and generous. Drink now. Score 88.

Three Vines ✳✳✳

Founded by Yossi Ben Barak and located on Moshav Ramot Naftaly in the Upper Galilee, this small winery (formerly known as Ben Barak Winery) draws on Cabernet Sauvignon, Merlot, Syrah, Cabernet Franc and Viognier grapes from its own vineyards. Now situated in a new winery, wines produced currently are in two series – Emek Kadesh and Kerem Naftaly. Production in 2007 was of 4,000 bottles, and production for 2009 and 2010 was of about 2,000 bottles, all being blends.

THREE VINES, CABERNET SAUVIGNON, 2007: Full-bodied, with still-firm tannins waiting to integrate but already opening to reveal an attractive array of blackberries, blackcurrants and licorice, all leading to a long and mouth-filling finish. Drink up. Score 86.

THREE VINES, CABERNET SAUVIGNON, 2006: Deep royal purple, medium- to full-bodied, showing still-firm tannins and dusty cedar, but those yielding well to currant, blackberry and spices, all lingering nicely. Drink up. Score 86.

THREE VINES, MERLOT, 2007: Barrel tasting showed medium- to full-bodied, with soft, mouth-coating tannins and hints of spicy oak. Opens to show forward berry and black cherry fruits, those complemented nicely by hints of earthy minerals and spices. Drink up. Score 85.

THREE VINES, MERLOT, 2006: Dark garnet, medium- to full-bodied, with soft tannins integrating nicely and showing spicy red plum, raspberry and currant aromas and flavors. Drink up. Score 85.

THREE VINES, EMEK KADESH, 2008: A blend of Cabernet Sauvignon, Merlot and Shiraz, deep royal purple in color, full-bodied, with gentle tannins and an appealing influence of spicy wood. On the nose and palate currants, wild berries and black cherries, those supported nicely by hints of spice. Moderately long. Drink now. Score 86.

THREE VINES, EMEK KADESH, 2007: A full-bodied blend of 75% Cabernet Sauvignon, 15% Merlot and 10% Shiraz. Reflecting its 21 months in oak with gripping, somewhat chunky tannins and spicy wood, a distinctly country-style wine, opening to show ripe berry, black cherry and currant fruits. Not complex but quite pleasant. Drink now. Score 85.

THREE VINES, EMEK KADESH, 2006: A blend of Cabernet Sauvignon, Merlot and Shiraz (77%, 16% and 7% respectively). Garnet toward inky-black, medium- to full-bodied with firm tannins integrating nicely and showing spicy and near-sweet cedar. Opens to reveal a generous array of currant, berry and plum fruits, those lingering to a rich and long finish. Drink up. Score 87.

THREE VINES, KEREM NAFTALY, 2007: Medium- to full-bodied, deep garnet in color, an oak-aged blend of 53% Cabernet Sauvignon and 47% Merlot. Smooth, soft and round, opening to show berry, black cherry and cassis aromas and flavors, those on a lightly spicy background. Drink now. Score 85.

THREE VINES, KEREM NAFTALY, 2006: A blend of near-equal parts of Cabernet Sauvignon and Merlot. Dark garnet, medium- to full-bodied, with soft tannins and gentle spicy wood influences integrating nicely. On the nose and palate primarily ripe red fruits. Not complex but an appealing quaffer. Drink now. Score 85.

Tishbi ✳✳✳

Following the initiatives of Baron Edmond de Rothschild, the Tishbi family started to plant vineyards in 1882 on the slopes of Mount Carmel near the town of Zichron Ya'akov and continued to cultivate vines throughout the next hundred years. In 1985, Jonathan Tishbi, a fourth-generation member of the family, launched this family-owned winery in the nearby town of Binyamina, initially named Habaron as homage to Baron Rothschild, and later renamed Tishbi.

With Jonathan's son, Golan Tishbi, serving as senior winemaker, the winery is currently producing about one million bottles annually. Drawing on grapes from their own nearby vineyards as well as from vineyards in the Jerusalem region, the Upper Galilee and Golan and the Negev, the winery produces wines in several series. The top-of-the-line, age-worthy, varietal Special Reserve series and the varietal Estate series, those followed by wines in the Tishbi series which are meant for youthful consumption. The winery also occasionally produces a sparkling wine.

Special Reserve

SPECIAL RESERVE, SDE BOKER, 2007: Oak-aged for 24 months, a full-bodied blend of Merlot, Cabernet Sauvignon, Cabernet Franc, Petit Verdot and Shiraz (48.4%, 35.9%, 5.1%, 6.8% and 3.8% respectively). Dark garnet, full-bodied, with its once-gripping tannins now integrating nicely with smoky oak and fruits. On the nose and palate blackberries, currants, purple plums and wild berries, those on a background of bittersweet chocolate and Mediterranean herbs. Drink now–2015. Score 90. K

SPECIAL RESERVE, 2004: A Bordeaux blend of Cabernet Sauvignon, Merlot and Cabernet Franc (50%, 40% and 10% respectively), the grapes from the Negev vineyards at Kibbutz Sde Boker. Developed in new French oak for 24 months, showing soft tannins and a generous wood influence, the wood in fine balance with fruits and acidity. On first attack blackberries, blackcurrants and baking chocolate, those followed by appealing hints of raspberries and earthy minerals. Drink now–2014. Score 90. K

SPECIAL RESERVE, CABERNET SAUVIGNON, BEN ZIMRA, 2002: Deep purple in color, ripe, bold and concentrated, the wine has solid and chewy tannins, those well balanced by notes of sweet-cedarwood. Oak-aged for 18 months, On the nose and palate spicy currant and berry fruits. Showing age. Drink up. Score 85. K

SPECIAL RESERVE, CABERNET SAUVIGNON, GUSH ETZION, 2002: Medium- to full-bodied, oak-aged for 18 months, well balanced, with soft tannins and aromas and flavors of currant, cherry, plum and wild berry fruits, just the right hints of spicy wood and anise on the medium-long finish. Showing age. Drink up. Score 86. K

SPECIAL RESERVE, CABERNET SAUVIGNON, SDE BOKER, 1999: Garnet, showing a good deal of clearing at the rim now. Made from grapes grown in the Negev Desert, the wine is not so much earthy or herbal but instead is marked by distinct flavors of green olives and spices. Full-bodied, now fully mature, with well-integrated tannins, it shows ripe and well-focused black cherry and currant flavors along with an appealing, long finish. Well past its peak. Drink up. Score 84. K

SPECIAL RESERVE, CABERNET SAUVIGNON, KFAR YUVAL, 1999: With earthy currant and cherry flavors emerging through firm tannins, this rich and concentrated wine is now fully mature and showing the smooth and supple texture promised in its youth. Showing age. Drink up. Score 85. K

SPECIAL RESERVE, CHARDONNAY, 2008: Dark golden straw in color, full-bodied and reflecting generous oak-aging with a buttery and light bitter note. On the nose and palate appealing tropical and citrus fruits, those supported by hints of vanilla and cinnamon. Drink now or in the next year or two. Score 88. K

SPECIAL RESERVE, CHARDONNAY, 2007: Reflecting spicy and vanilla notes from its oak-aging, medium-bodied, with generous pineapple, citrus and pear notes leading to a long finish. Drink up. Score 88. K

SPECIAL RESERVE, BRUT, 2009: Made entirely from French Colombard grapes, a sparkling wine made in the *Methode Champenoise*, that is to say with first fermentation in stainless steel and second fermentation in the bottle. From a technical point of view the wine is crisply dry, but because it shows all of the flowery traits of the variety and is generously fruit forward with summer fruits, many will mistake the wine for off-dry (confusion between fruitiness and sweetness being quite common). A short mousse but fine bubbles that linger nicely. Drink now. Score 84. K

SPECIAL RESERVE, BRUT, 2008: A sparkling wine, made by the *Methode Champenoise* and continuing to surprise by being made entirely from French Colombard grapes. Light golden in color, medium-bodied, with aromas and flavors that hint nicely of toasted white bread and white pepper on a background of peach and apple fruits. Not a long mousse but sharp bubbles that last nicely. A pleasant bubbly. Drink now or in the next few years. Score 86. K

SPECIAL RESERVE, MUSCAT, DESSERT WINE, 2007: Made from Muscat Hamburg grapes and fortified with grape alcohol, a sweet dessert wine. Not so much full-bodied as it is cloying, with blueberry, raspberry and wild berries, lacking the acidity that might have made it complex or refreshing. Drink now–2014. Score 84. K

SPECIAL RESERVE, BARBERA-ZINFANDEL, DESSERT WINE, 2006: A blend of 50% each of Barbera and Zinfandel, those reinforced with Red Muscat Brandy. Full-bodied, generously sweet, showing notes of wild berries, cherries, licorice and bittersweet chocolate. Oak-aged in the sun for 18 months, showing a Port-like nature but faulted by the lack of acidity. One to adore or not depending on personal taste. Drink now–2013. Score 85. K

Estate

ESTATE, CABERNET SAUVIGNON, LIMITED EDITION, 2007: A bit of confusion here, for the label of the wine states that this full-bodied Bordeaux is a blend of 92% Cabernet Sauvignon, that fleshed out with 4% Petit Verdot and 2% each of Cabernet Franc and Merlot, while the winery's Internet site states it to be a blend of 93% Cabernet Sauvignon and 7% Petit Verdot. Whatever, dark garnet, medium-to full-bodied, with soft tannins and spicy oak, showing a nose rich with black fruits and an appealing hint of tar. Opens in the glass to reveal blackcurrants, wild red and black berries and notes of nutmeg and freshly picked Mediterranean herbs. On the long and mouth-filling finish, black olives and bittersweet chocolate. Drink now–2014. Score 90. K

ESTATE, CABERNET SAUVIGNON, 2006: Blended with 7% of Petit Verdot, dark ruby toward garnet, medium-bodied, with soft tannins and a gentle wood influence from its 12 months in *barriques*. On the nose and palate blackberry, blueberry and currant fruits complemented by notes of spices. Drink now. Score 87. K

ESTATE, CABERNET SAUVIGNON, 2005: Deep garnet with violet and orange reflections, medium- to full-bodied, with still-firm tannins but those in fine balance with acidity, wood and fruits. A blend of 90% Cabernet Sauvignon, 7% Cabernet Franc and 3% Petit Verdot, oak-aged for about 13 months, showing an appealing layer of spiciness together with currant and blackberry fruits. Drink up. Score 88. K

ESTATE, MERLOT, LIMITED EDITION, 2007: Garnet toward royal purple, a medium- to full-bodied blend of 88% Merlot, 8.5% Cabernet Sauvignon and 3.5% Ruby Cabernet. Reflecting its development in oak with notes of both spices and vanilla and gently caressing tannins, opens in the glass to reveal blackberries and cassis, those complemented nicely by hints of black licorice and earthy minerals. Drink now–2013, perhaps longer. Score 88. K

ESTATE, MERLOT, 2006: Opens with blackberries, spices and a hint of tar, goes on to reveal black and red berries and hints of chocolate. Medium- to full-bodied, with soft tannins and reflecting its brief aging in oak with hints of spicy wood. Long and generous. Drink now. Score 88. K

ESTATE, SYRAH, ORGANIC, LIMITED EDITION, 2007: Garnet with a robe of royal purple, reflecting its five months in oak with medium body and soft tannins, opens with berry and cherry flavors, those parting to make way for red plums and light overlays of mocha and cinnamon that linger nicely. Lively acidity makes this an easy wine to pair with food. Drink now–2013. Score 89. K

ESTATE, SHIRAZ, 2007: Developed in oak for 12 months, medium- to full-bodied, garnet-red toward royal purple, an aromatic wine opening to show traditional black fruits, leathery and earthy mineral notes. Major bottle variation here: some round, well balanced and long and earning a Score of 89, others with a hint of volatile acidity and earning only 85 points. Drink now. K

ESTATE, SHIRAZ, 2006: A once-strong whiff of alcohol now blowing off and letting the wine open. Medium- to full-bodied, with black cherry, blackcurrant and plums all with a somewhat earthy edge. Drink up. Score 84. K

ESTATE, PINOT NOIR, 2007: Developed in 300 liter French oak barrels for four months, showing dark garnet with a perhaps too-distinct note of brown creeping in. Medium-bodied, with light tannins, showing berry and cherry fruits. A good quaffer but faulted somewhat by a light "off" aroma that develops as the wine sits in the glass. Sliding past its peak. Drink up. Score 85. K

ESTATE, PINOT NOIR, 2006: Light- to medium-bodied, with a somewhat muddy garnet color, showing too much volatile acidity and, on the nose and palate, forward red berry and strawberry fruits, the kind that one expects from a red lollipop. Past its peak. Drink up. Score 80. K

ESTATE, CABERNET FRANC, 2006: Dark garnet in color, full-bodied and with chewy tannins, a well-focused wine, its spicy (almost peppery) wood settling down nicely to show a fine array of currant and blackberry fruits, those with an appealing leathery overtone. Long and satisfying. Sliding past its peak. Drink up. Score 89. K

ESTATE, PETITE SIRAH, 2007: Deep garnet, with a blackfruit nose and still-firm tannins and wood just starting to settle in. Oak-aged for 12 months, and on the nose and palate showing appealing cassis, red berries and spices. Drink now–2013. Score 87. K

ESTATE, CHARDONNAY, 2009: Partly oak-aged, light gold in color, medium-bodied with summer fruits, citrus and hints of tropical fruits that play nicely on the palate. Drink up. Score 87. K

ESTATE, CHARDONNAY, 2008: An unoaked white blended with 10% of Viognier. Golden straw in color, medium-bodied with green apple, orange, summer fruits and pineapple notes. Fresh and refreshing. Drink up. Score 87. K

ESTATE, SAUVIGNON BLANC, 2009: Blended with 4% of Viognier, light- to medium-bodied, almost clear in color, showing pineapple, citrus and tropical fruits on a lightly grassy background. Refreshing and lively. Drink now. Score 85. K

ESTATE, SAUVIGNON BLANC, 2008: Unoaked, light- to medium-bodied, light straw colored, showing apple and citrus fruits on a light grassy background. Drink up. Score 86. K

ESTATE, LATE HARVEST RIESLING, 2005: Made from Emerald Riesling grapes, light- to medium-bodied, with generous sweetness and appealing floral and summer fruits. Best with fruit-based desserts. Drink up. Score 84. K

ESTATE, LATE HARVEST RIESLING, 2004: Made from Emerald Riesling grapes. Floral on the nose, with ripe peach and apricot fruits. Moderate sweetness set off nicely by acidity makes for a pleasant quaffer. Drink up. Score 85. K

Tishbi

TISHBI, CABERNET SAUVIGNON, 2009: Garnet toward royal purple, medium-bodied, with soft, gently caressing tannins and an appealing array of berry, black cherry and cassis fruits. Round, fruity and easy to drink. Drink now. Score 86. K

TISHBI, CABERNET SAUVIGNON, 2008: Going along with their 2008 policy of releasing several unoaked wines, this deep purple, medium-bodied wine proves without complexities but quite pleasant, its light tannins and black fruits making for a fresh and appealing quaffer. Drink now. Score 85. K

TISHBI, MERLOT, 2008: A very nice unoaked quaffer, medium-bodied, soft and round, with strawberry and cranberry fruits yielding to blueberries and a hint of milk chocolate. A fun wine. Drink now. Score 86. K

TISHBI, SHIRAZ, 2009: Garnet toward royal purple, medium-bodied, with soft tannins. On the nose and palate black cherries, raspberries and wild berry fruits, those matched nicely by hints of black pepper and earthy minerals. Drink now. Score 85. K

TISHBI, SHIRAZ, GUSH ETZION, 2008: A light- to medium-bodied red, unoaked, showing dark cherry-red in color and opening to reveal generous raspberry and cherry fruits along with a hint of spices. A good and refreshing quaffer, best served lightly chilled. Drink now. Score 86. K

TISHBI, SYRAH, ORGANIC, 2007: A limited edition, dark garnet in color, reflecting its 12 months in new *barriques* with sweet-and-spicy wood. Full-bodied, with caressing tannins, opens to reveal a tempting array of plum, black cherry and currant fruits, those supported nicely by notes of Mediterranean herbs and earthy minerals. Long and generous. Drink now. Score 90. K

TISHBI, PINOT NOIR, JUDEAN HILLS, ESTATE, 2007: Ruby toward garnet, medium-bodied, somewhat on the acidic side, with cherry and berry fruits leading to a pleasant near-sweet finish. A good summertime quaffer. Drink now. Score 85. K

TISHBI, CABERNET SAUVIGNON-PETITE SIRAH, 2009: Garnet toward royal purple, medium-bodied, with soft tannins and simple but clean berry, cherry and currant fruits. An appropriate entry-level wine. Drink up. Score 84. K

TISHBI, CABERNET SAUVIGNON-SYRAH, 2009: Garnet toward royal purple and medium-bodied, an unoaked wine showing fresh and lively with tempting aromas and flavors of red berries and strawberries, and notes of Mediterranean herbs. Nothing complex here but a very pleasant quaffer. Drink now. Score 85. K

TISHBI, CABERNET SAUVIGNON-PETITE SIRAH, 2008: Ruby toward garnet, medium-bodied, with soft tannins and appealing raspberry and red currant fruits supported by notes of spices and a hint of chocolate. Not at all complex but fresh, lively and refreshing, especially when served lightly chilled. Drink now. Score 85. K

TISHBI, CABERNET SAUVIGNON-PETITE SIRAH, 2007: Garnet toward royal purple, with soft tannins and showing a basic berry-cherry personality, the fruits on a light earthy-herbal background. An entry-level wine. Drink up. Score 83. K

TISHBI, CABERNET SAUVIGNON-PETITE SIRAH, 2006: Deep garnet, with soft tannins, a round wine showing red and black berries and black cherries on a lightly spicy background. Easy to drink. Drink up. Score 85. K

TISHBI, BARBERA-ZINFANDEL, 2006: A blend of 50% each Barbera and Zinfandel, those "sun-aged" for 18 months and fortified with brandy to bring it to an 18% alcohol level. Full-bodied, generously sweet, with caressing tannins and showing blackberry and raspberry fruits, those highlighted by notes of spicy dates and prunes. Thickly textured and finishing with a note of candied walnuts. Best not with dessert but as dessert. Drink now. Score 87. K

TISHBI, GEWURZTRAMINER, 2010: Light gold in color, medium-bodied with light sweetness set off comfortably by refreshing acidity. Opens in the glass to show aromas and flavors of citrus, litchis and Granny Smith apples. Drink now. Score 85. K

TISHBI, GEWURZTRAMINER, 2009: Off-dry, light- to medium-bodied, showing a floral nose and, on the palate, appealing green apple, citrus and litchi fruits. Good balancing acidity keeps the wine lively. Drink now. Score 85. K

TISHBI, FRENCH-RIESLING, 2009: Light- to medium-bodied, as always an off-dry blend of French Colombard and Emerald Riesling. Clean and fresh but one-dimensional. An entry-level wine. Drink up. Score 82. K

TISHBI, FRENCH-RIESLING, 2008: Light golden straw in color, light- to medium-bodied, an off-dry blend of French Colombard and Emerald Riesling with fine acidity to show its citrus and tropical fruits. A pleasant quaffer. Drink up. Score 84. K

Trio ★★★★

Founded by Oran, Tal and Kobi Shaked, with Oran as winemaker and located in Ramat Gan, this small winery released its first wines from the 2006 vintage. The winery sources Cabernet Sauvignon, Shiraz and Merlot grapes from the Jerusalem Hills and from the Upper Galilee. Releases from 2006 were of 4,000 bottles and current production is about 20,000 bottles. Wines

are released under three labels, Special Cuvée, The Secret and The Spirit of Jerusalem Heights.

TRIO, SPECIAL CUVÉE, 2008: Dark garnet toward royal purple, a full-bodied and generously oaked and firmly tannic blend of Cabernet Sauvignon and Syrah in equal parts. Opens slowly in the glass to reveal blackcurrants and black and red berries, those supported nicely by notes of spices and saddle leather. Drink now–2016. Score 91.

TRIO, SPECIAL CUVÉE, 2007: Made entirely from Syrah grapes, developed in partly new and partly one-year-old *barriques* for 14 months, showing medium- to full-bodied (leaning toward the full), with gently gripping tannins settling in nicely with notes of spicy wood. Opens to reveal wild berry, blackberry and raspberry fruits. Still tight and needs a bit of time to show its zest, that matched by a long and persistent finish. Drink now–2013. Score 91.

TRIO, THE SECRET, 2009: A blend of Cabernet Sauvignon Merlot and Syrah, oak-aged for 12 months. Dark garnet, full-bodied, soft and round, opening to reveal aromas and flavors of currants, blackberries and purple plums, those supported by notes of spicy cedar, figs and roasted herbs. Long and generous. As the wine continues to develop in the bottle look as well for hints of baking chocolate. Best 2013–2017. Score 90.

TRIO, THE SECRET, 2008: An oak-aged blend of Cabernet Sauvignon and Syrah, showing full-bodied, with notes of near-sweet cedarwood and soft, gently caressing tannins that yield comfortably to blackberry, currant and red-plum fruits. In the background, hints of bittersweet chocolate and saddle soap (not to fear, a very positive descriptor reminding one of freshly polished leather). Tannins and fruits rise together on the moderately long finish. Drink now–2016. Score 91.

TRIO, THE SECRET, 2007: Medium- to full-bodied, reflecting its 12 months in *barriques* with notes of spicy and vanilla-rich wood. Silky tannins part to reveal a generous array of wild berry, currant and bitter citrus peel notes all in fine balance with spicy hints that run through the medium-long finish. Drink now–2013. Score 90.

TRIO, THE SECRET, 2006: Dark, almost impenetrable garnet in color, full-bodied, made entirely from Cabernet Sauvignon grapes, with firm tannins that yield and show just the right dose of spicy and vanilla-rich oak. On first attack blackberries, those yielding in the glass to red currants and raspberry fruits, all with appealing overlays of black pepper, cigar tobacco and a note of freshly turned truffles. Drink now. Score 92.

TRIO, THE SPIRIT OF JERUSALEM HEIGHTS, 2009: A dark-garnet, medium- to full-bodied blend of 86% Cabernet Sauvignon and 14% Merlot. Gently caressing tannins and notes of spicy oak complement blackberry, cassis and licorice notes. Long and mouth-filling. Drink now–2014. Score 89.

TRIO, THE SPIRIT OF JERUSALEM HEIGHTS, 2008: Cabernet Sauvignon with the addition of 3% Petite Verdot. Dark, almost inky garnet in color, with gently gripping tannins, generous alcohol (14.5%) and appealing hints of spicy cedarwood, those now integrating very nicely indeed. Developed in stainless-steel vats with oak staves for six months, now showing appealing blackberries, raspberries and notes of cassis liqueur, those yielding in the glass to notes of blueberries and spices. Drink now. Score 88.

TRIO, THE SPIRIT OF JERUSALEM HEIGHTS, 2007: A blend of 84% Cabernet Sauvignon, 14% Merlot and 2% Petit Verdot. Showing generous berry aromatics, medium- to full-bodied, developed with oak staves in stainless-steel vats, with gently mouth-coating tannins and notes of spicy wood parting to reveal generous blackberry, cassis and blueberry fruits, those hinting nicely of fresh Mediterranean herbs. Drink now. Score 88.

TRIO, THE SPIRIT OF JERUSALEM HEIGHTS, 2006: Made entirely from Cabernet Sauvignon grapes, with a light hint of spicy wood and gently mouth-coating tannins integrating nicely and parting to show the fruits. Medium- to full-bodied, dark garnet in color and opening in the glass to reveal red currant, blackberry and raspberry fruits along with gentle hints of white chocolate, all of which linger nicely on the long finish. Simultaneously elegant and easy to drink. Drink now. Score 90.

Tulip ✶✶✶✶

Located near the town of Kiryat Tivon, not far from Haifa, this winery is an effort of the Yitzhaki family. The winery currently draws on Cabernet Sauvignon and Syrah grapes from the Alma vineyard and other locations in the Upper Galilee, as well as Cabernet Sauvignon, Merlot, Cabernet Franc and Petit Verdot from the Karmei Yosef and Mata vineyards near Jerusalem. Currently in development are vineyards planted in red varieties near Mount Meron.

The winery is currently releasing about 120,000 bottles annually, those in four series: the top-of-the-line Black Tulip; Reserve; blended wines in the Mostly series; and single-variety wines in the Just series. Also periodically released is a Port-style reinforced red wine.

A special word of praise for the Yitzhaki family, whose winery sits on Kfar Tikva, a residential community in which people with disabilities and special needs can live, develop and realize their potential. The winery considers these people as an integral part of their effort. Not long ago, when the Yitzhaki family considered "going kosher," they were told that this would be no problem so long as the community members would no longer work there. Itzhak Yitzhaki, the acknowledged leader of the clan, replied with his head held high that "you should live so long until these people will no longer be part of the winery." For which, indeed, a rousing "Bravo." Happily, that problem has been resolved and the wines will be kosher from the 2010 vintage.

Grand Reserve

GRAND RESERVE, 2004: This blend of Cabernet Sauvignon and Merlot reflects its 30 months in oak with notably heavy, somewhat sweetish wood and firm, chunky country-style tannins that seem to not want to integrate. Beneath those and making their way slowly to the surface are blackberry, kirsch and dark chocolate aromas and flavors. A good wine but lacking the fine-tuned balance or depth that might have made it more interesting. Drink now. Score 86.

GRAND RESERVE, CABERNET SAUVIGNON, 2003: Oak-aged for 30 months, but with the once-heavy wood now integrating with soft tannins and opening to reveal appealing blackcurrant and berry fruits, those with overlays of dark chocolate and sweet herbs. Drink up. Score 88.

Black Tulip, White Tulip and White Franc

BLACK TULIP, 2007: Close to but not yet a final blend at this tasting, showing youthful deep royal purple in color, with generous near-sweet tannins and spicy oak, those parting to make way for blackberries and blueberries on a generously spicy background and then, from mid-palate on, clear notes of currants, black pepper and grilled herbs. Look as well for a light meaty note here. Drink now–2014. Score 88.

BLACK TULIP, 2006: A distinctly Bordeaux blend, this year of Cabernet Sauvignon, Merlot, Cabernet Franc and Petit Verdot (60% 20%, 13% and 7% respectively). Developed in *barriques* for an extended period of 30 months, and at this stage of its development showing full-bodied, the tannins still gripping and the wood rather pronounced but with structure and balance that bode well for the future. On first attack aromas and flavors of cigar box, blueberries and black pepper, those yielding to clear, clean notes of currants and wild berries. Long, mouth-filling and with the kind of complexity that gives comfortable pause for reflection. Drink now–2014. Score 91.

BLACK TULIP, 2005: A Bordeaux blend of Cabernet Sauvignon, Merlot, Cabernet Franc and Petit Verdot (66%, 14%, 14% and 6%, respectively), that given a distinct California touch by being aged in new oak for somewhat over 24 months. Full-bodied, with firm tannins and reflecting generous vanilla, smoky and spicy oak, those parting slowly in the glass to reveal black fruits and notes of Oriental spices. Primarily for those who thrive on the flavor of oak. Drink now. Score 86.

WHITE FRANC, 2010: Medium-bodied, off-dry, a partly *blanc de noirs* wine, a blend of 65% Cabernet Franc and 35% Sauvignon Blanc. Shows an aromatic nose and opens in the glass to reveal aromas and flavors of citrus, red berries and earthy minerals. Lacks the balancing acidity that might have made the wine more lively. Best served "on the rocks." Drink now. Score 84. K

WHITE TULIP, 2009: Similar to the 2008 blend, being composed of 70% Gewurztraminer and 30% Sauvignon Blanc, but not nearly as successful, this year's release showing none of the traits of either variety. Generously acidic on the palate, light straw colored, with un-complicated citrus and pineapple notes, a quite simple little white. Drink now. Score 84.

WHITE TULIP, 2008: A somewhat odd but quite successful unoaked blend of 60% Gewurztraminer and 40% Sauvignon Blanc. Golden straw toward lemon-lime in color, medium-bodied and deeply aromatic, reflecting an array of aromas and flavors, those including freshly mown grass, litchis, grapefruit and peppermint. Not complex but plenty of fresh acidity to keep the wine refreshing. Drink up. Score 87.

Reserve

RESERVE, CABERNET SAUVIGNON, 2008: Not yet a final blend but already showing both dark and concentrated with a special note added by a graphite background that supports generous currant and cherry fruits. Full-bodied, perhaps even a bit chunky, but needing only time for the elements to come together as a truly Mediterranean wine with hints of olives, roasted herbs and tobacco always in the background. Drink now–2015. Score 89.

RESERVE, CABERNET SAUVIGNON, 2007: Full-bodied, with still-gripping tannins and reflecting spicy wood from its 18 months in *barriques*, those in fine balance with fruits and acidity. Dark garnet, opening with red fruits (red currants and raspberries), going in the glass to both blackcurrants and blackberries, all on a background of Mediterranean herbs and, along with tannins rising on the finish, a note of earthy minerals. Drink now–2014. Score 91.

RESERVE, CABERNET SAUVIGNON, 2006: Blended with 5% Petit Verdot and oak-aged for 18 months in new French *barriques*, show-ing an abundance of spicy oak and a more than generous 15% alcohol content. Full-bodied, with firm tannins only now starting to integrate and opening slowly to reveal spicy blackcurrant and blackberry fruits on a background of cigar tobacco. Drink now. Score 88.

RESERVE, CABERNET SAUVIGNON, 2005: Dark garnet, full-bodied, showing still-youthful firm tannins that need time to integrate. A blend of 90% Cabernet Sauvignon with equal parts of Petit Verdot and Cabernet Franc, aged in new French oak *barriques*, showing fine balance between spicy wood and fruits. Opens to reveal blackberry, currant and light leathery notes, all on a generously peppery and vanilla-rich background. Long and juicy. Drink up. Score 88.

RESERVE, SYRAH, 2008: Blended with 10% Cabernet Sauvignon, reflecting its development in *barriques* with notes of spicy cedarwood and a hint of cinnamon, the oak generous but in fine balance with fruits. Full-bodied, with its chewy tannins integrating nicely and opening in the glass to reveal wild berries, blueberries, minerals and spices. On the long finish tannins rise together with an appealing note of sage. Drink now–2015. Score 90.

RESERVE, SYRAH, 2007: Blended with 10% Cabernet Sauvignon and oak-aged for 16 months, dark and full-bodied, with spicy wood and softly gripping tannins in fine balance and integrating nicely with rich blackberry, wild berry and black cherry fruits. New World Syrah that almost gives you the feeling that you could eat it with a spoon rather than from a wine glass. Sumptuous, deep and long. Drink now–2014. Score 91.

RESERVE, SYRAH, 2006: Dark garnet with orange and violet reflections, this full-bodied red is lithe and well focused. Opens with a surprising but pleasing root beer note which holds through the long finish as a background to plum, blackberry and leathery notes. Well balanced, long and generous. Drink now. Score 88.

Mostly

MOSTLY, SHIRAZ, 2008: 85% Shiraz blended with 15% Cabernet Sauvignon, a country-style wine showing spicy wood and gripping tannins, those parting to make way for blackberry, plum and herbal aromas and flavors. One-dimensional and lacking complexity. Drink now. Score 84.

MOSTLY, SHIRAZ, 2007: Deep garnet, reflecting its 14 months in primarily new oak, a blend, as the name of the series implies, mostly of Shiraz, that flushed out by Cabernet Franc and Petit Verdot (65%, 30% and 5% respectively). Full-bodied, with still-firm tannins and a generous spicy oak influence in fine balance with fruits and acidity but needing a bit of time for the elements to integrate. On the nose and palate blackberries, blackcurrants and notes of mint and, on the generous finish, a note of leather. Drink now–2014. Score 90.

MOSTLY, SHIRAZ, 2006: Dark garnet, medium- to full-bodied, a blend of 65% Shiraz, 30% Cabernet Sauvignon and 5% Petit Verdot. Firm tannins dominate when first poured, but those yield nicely in the glass to reveal generous currant and purple plum fruits, those supported nicely by hints of Oriental spices and saddle leather. Tannins and fruits rise simultaneously on the finish. Drink now. Score 89.

MOSTLY, SHIRAZ, 2005: Dark garnet, this blend of 60% Shiraz and 20% each of Cabernet Sauvignon and Merlot shows medium-bodied, soft, round and well balanced, filling the mouth nicely. On the nose and palate blackberries, plums and gently spicy oak from its 14 months in *barriques*. Look for hints of Mediterranean herbs and freshly turned earth on the moderately long finish. Drink now. Score 87.

MOSTLY, CABERNET FRANC, 2008: Dark garnet, a medium- to full-bodied blend of 85% Cabernet Franc and 15% Merlot. Reflecting its 15 months in French and American oak with chunky, gripping tannins and generous wood parting slowly to make way for aromas and flavors of purple plums, currants and black cherries, all on a generously spicy background. Drink now–2013. Score 85.

MOSTLY, CABERNET FRANC, 2007: Cabernet Franc blended with 15% Cabernet Sauvignon. Dark, almost impenetrable garnet, developed in French oak *barriques* for 14 months, showing generous spicy wood and firm tannins, those yielding slowly in the glass to a nose rich in sweet herbs and, on the palate, blackberries, blueberries and green peppers on a light earthy-mineral background. Give this one some time for its elements to come together. Drink now. Score 88.

MOSTLY, CABERNET FRANC, 2006: A blend of 86% Cabernet Franc and 7% each of Merlot and Cabernet Sauvignon. Showing spicy oak and firm tannins now integrating well. Opens to show red and black berries, green pepper and earthy aromas and flavors. On the moderately long finish appealing hints of licorice and mint. Drink now. Score 88.

Just

JUST, CABERNET SAUVIGNON, 2008: Made entirely from Cabernet Sauvignon grapes, dark garnet with violet and orange reflections, showing surprisingly generous wood after only eight months in oak but that in good balance with tannins and fruits. On the nose and palate traditional Cabernet blackcurrant, blackberry and spices, those with an appealing earthy-herbal overlay that lingers nicely on the palate. Drink now. Score 88.

JUST, CABERNET SAUVIGNON, 2006: Dark, almost impenetrable garnet, full-bodied and concentrated, with generous, soft tannins yet maintaining the roundness that has come to typify the Tulip wines. Opens slowly in the glass to reveal blackcurrant, wild berry and kirsch, those backed up by spicy wood and appealing hints of herbaceousness on the long finish. Drink up. Score 88.

JUST, CABERNET SAUVIGNON, 2005: Dark garnet, this medium-bodied wine's soft tannins are integrating nicely with hints of the oak in which it was aged for six months. On the nose and palate plums, cassis and berries along with intimations of vanilla and tobacco on a moderately long finish. Past its peak. Drink up. Score 85.

JUST, MERLOT, 2008: Reflecting its eight months in French oak with notes of near-sweet cedarwood and soft tannins. Dark garnet toward royal purple, medium- to full-bodied, with generous wild berry and currant fruits. Not long but soft, round and generous. Drink now. Score 87.

JUST, MERLOT, 2007: Medium-bodied, with somewhat chunky, country-style tannins. A subdued nose but with appealing flavors of blueberries, cherries, blackberries and currants on a background of spicy oak and minted chocolate. A pleasant country-style wine. Drink now. Score 85.

JUST, MERLOT, 2006: Medium-bodied, with gentle, near-sweet tannins, this soft, round aromatic red shows appealing berry, black cherry and currant fruits on a light background of spicy oak and eucalyptus. Drink up. Score 87.

Special Edition

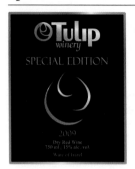

SPECIAL EDITION, CABERNET SAUVI-GNON-SHIRAZ, 2009: A medium-bodied, lightly oaked blend of 80% Cabernet Sauvignon and 20% Shiraz. On first attack red fruits, those yielding in the glass to currants, purple plums and earthy minerals, all with a tantalizing hint of spicy wood. Drink now–2013. Score 88.

SPECIAL EDITION, WHITE BLEND, 2010: A blend of equal amounts of Gewurztraminer and Sauvignon Blanc. Light gold, medium-bodied, with just a bare, tantalizing hint of sweetness, showing a generous array of litchi, citrus and tropical fruits, all lingering nicely on the palate. Drink now. Score 88. K

Tura **

Founded in 2003 as Erez Winery by Erez Sadon and renamed in 2005 as Tura, this boutique winery uses the facilities of the Asif service winery for making their wines. The winery is currently producing about 12,000 bottles annually, those primarily from Cabernet Sauvignon, Merlot and Chardonnay grapes. Several of the wines are available under both the Erez and Tura labels but large bottle variation indicates that these might be separate editions.

TURA, CABERNET SAUVIGNON, 2008: Oak-aged for 22 months, with a whopping 15.3% alcohol content – a hot wine. Full-bodied, dark garnet in color, with generous oak that tends to hide the red fruits that struggle to make themselves felt. Not a well-balanced wine. Drink up. Score 82. K

TURA, CABERNET SAUVIGNON, 2007: Dark cherry-red toward garnet, with a generous 14.9% alcohol content and reflecting its oak-aging for 21 months with gripping tannins and unconstrained notes of spicy oak. Opens slowly in the glass to reveal black and red currants and dried berries, alas, with the alcohol adding a too-generous bite on the finish. Drink now. Score 83. K

TURA, CABERNET SAUVIGNON, 2006: Showing vastly different than at an earlier tasting, different enough in fact that I might easily think I was drinking two different wines. Deep, almost impenetrably dark garnet in color, medium- to full-bodied, with what were only two months ago chunky country-style tannins now settling in and softening nicely. Generous currant and blackberry fruits here but continuing to reflect its 21 months in oak with sawdust-like notes on the nose and a light medicinal aroma that rises as an aftertaste. Drink up. Score 83. K

TURA, MERLOT, 2008: Dark garnet, softly tannic but with a bit of heat reflecting its 15.1% alcohol content. Oak-aged for 22 months, showing generous sweet-oak flavors, those parting in the glass to reveal tempting blackberry, cassis and candied citrus peel, all lingering nicely. Drink now. Score 84. K

TURA, MERLOT, 2006: My fourth tasting of this wine and once again, showing so differently from my earlier tastings that I might think I was tasting completely different wines. Oak-aged for 22 months. Instead of ruby toward garnet as at my original tasting, now showing dark garnet; not so much medium-bodied as closer to full-bodied; distinct notes of sawdust on the nose and skimpy black-fruit and floral notes. Acidity rises on the finish as do hints of licorice and a not-totally-wanted note of iodine. Drink up. Score 80. K

TURA, BLENDED RED, 2008: An oak-aged blend of Merlot, Cabernet Sauvignon, and Cabernet Franc, medium-dark garnet in color, medium- to full-bodied with gently gripping chunky tannins. On the nose and palate wild berries, black cherries and currants on a background of earthy minerals. An appealing rustic wine. Drink now. Score 85. K

TURA, MERLOT-CABERNET SAUVIGNON, 2008: Oak-aged for 22 months, reflecting that and its 14.7% alcohol content with notes of spicy wood and a hint of unwanted heat. Opens in the glass to show redcur- rants, raspberries and crushed wild berries. Drink now. Score 84. K

TURA, PORTURA, 2007: Said to be Port-like but with no resemblance whatever to true Port. Made entirely from Cabernet Sauvignon grapes, the fermentation halted by the addition of alcohol and aged in old oak for 32 months. Best way to describe the wine is as a sweet Cabernet Sauvignon. As Mr. Lincoln put it so nicely: "This is the kind of thing that people who like this kind of thing will like." Drink now–2014. Score 82. K

Tzora Vineyards ✶✶✶✶✶

Set on Kibbutz Tzora at the foothills of the Jerusalem Mountains and overlooking the Soreq Valley, this formerly kibbutz-owned winery released its first 1,500 bottles from the 1993 vintage. Production is currently about 80,000 bottles annually.

The winery was founded as a one-man enterprise by Ronnie James, a visionary viticulturist who was dedicated to the influence of *terroir* on his wines. James, who earned a high level of respect throughout the local wine industry, passed away in 2008, but not before bringing aboard winemaker Eran Pick who had experience in California, Bordeaux and Australia. Pick has maintained the winery's devotion to *terroir* and is currently releasing five wines, three of those named after the single vineyards from which the grapes were harvested (Giv'at Hachalukim, Shoresh and Neve Ilan), one a Judean Hills blend made from two vineyards, and Misty Hills, a flagship wine released only from selected vintages.

Private investment has added state-of-the-art equipment to the winery. The winery has full control over its own vineyards, those yielding Cabernet Sauvignon, Merlot, Syrah, Chardonnay and Gewurztraminer. The Tzora wines have been kosher since the 2002 vintage. Construction of a new winery in the Shoresh vineyards is currently in the planning stage.

Misty Hills

MISTY HILLS, 2009: A blend of equal parts of Cabernet Sauvignon and Syrah, showing dark garnet, medium- to full-bodied (leaning toward the full). Destined for 18 months in oak, opens with notes of dusty oak and blackberries, a softly tannic wine that goes on to reveal aromas and flavors of blackcurrants and figs, those on a gently spicy background. Long and elegant, the fruits rising on a long finish to reveal a tempting note of freshly roasted herbs. Drink now–2018. Score 90. K

MISTY HILLS

2006

Grown, Produced, & Bottled by
TZORA VINEYARDS · JUDEAN HILLS

MISTY HILLS, 2007: A blend of 70% Cabernet Sauvignon and 30% Syrah, full-bodied, with a nose rich with Oriental spices and black fruits. Deep, almost impenetrable garnet toward royal purple, full-bodied and concentrated, with generous tannins that grip gently. On first attack wild berries, those making way for blackberries, blackcurrants and finally raspberries, all on a background that hints of baking chocolate. Long and generous. A firm and intense wine that avoids becoming a blockbuster by maintaining its elegance. Drink now–2015, perhaps longer. Score 92. K

MISTY HILLS, 2006: A blend of equal parts of Cabernet Sauvignon and Syrah, those aged for 18 months in *barriques*. Deep garnet, full-bodied, concentrated and intense, showing generous mouth-coating tannins and a judicious hand with the oak, all in fine balance with fruits. On first attack strawberries and red currants, those going to black fruits on a background of earthy minerals and Oriental spices. Now showing tempting hints of saddle leather and freshly hung cigar tobacco. Long, mouth-filling and elegant. Drink now–2016. Score 92. K

Giv'at Hachalukim

GIV'AT HACHALUKIM, CABERNET SAUVIGNON, 2008: Dark garnet, oak-aged for 12 months, made entirely from Cabernet Sauvignon, with a generous but comfortable level of spicy, vanilla-rich oak and tannins that build comfortably as the wine sits on the palate. On opening attack a floral and light tobacco note complementing the black-currant, blackberry and purple plum fruits that are here. Long, round and generous. Drink now–2015, perhaps longer. Score 91. K

GIV'AT HACHALUKIM, CABERNET SAUVIGNON, 2007: Dark garnet in color, generously aromatic and opening to reveal a medium- to full-bodied red with soft tannins integrating nicely with spicy wood and fruits. On the nose and palate opens with raspberries, those going to blackberries, currants and hints of orange peel. Firm but yielding, generous and long. Drink now. Score 90. K

GIV'AT HACHALUKIM, CABERNET SAUVIGNON, 2006: Made entirely from Cabernet Sauvignon grapes, with softly caressing tannins and reflecting a gentle hand with oak. Medium- to full-bodied, with generous currant and wild berry fruits, those matched nicely by hints of anise and white pepper. Finishes moderately long with a note of minted chocolate. Drink now. Score 88. K

GIV'AT HACHALUKIM, CABERNET SAUVIGNON, 2005: Dark ruby toward garnet, medium- to full-bodied, with soft tannins and generous spicy wood. Opens to show generous red and black fruits, those supported nicely by hints of freshly turned earth and tobacco. Drink now. Score 90. K

Shoresh

SHORESH, 2009: As the name implies, made from grapes harvested exclusively in the Shoresh vineyard, a blend of 46% Syrah, 35% Cabernet Sauvignon and 19% Merlot. Deep garnet toward royal purple with orange reflections, opens to a distinctly red-fruit nose. Destined for 18 months in oak, on first attack blackberries, currants and spicy wood, those parting to make way for ripe red plums, black pepper and appealing hints of leather and bitter herbs, all promising to come together as a coherent whole.

SHORESH
2008

Grown, Produced, & Bottled by
TZORA VINEYARDS · JUDEAN HILLS, ISRAEL

Long and mouth-filling and on its way to elegance. Best from 2013–2017. Tentative Score 90–92. K

SHORESH, 2008: Aged in French oak for 18 months, a deep-garnet blend of 90% Cabernet Sauvignon and 10% Syrah. Full-bodied, concentrated and with its once-gripping tannins now settling in nicely together and an overlay of spicy cedarwood, but at the same time elegant and round. Peppery black fruits and notes of Oriental spices, those backed up by a comfortable hint of dark chocolate. On the long finish an appealing appearance of tar. As this one develops look as well for a hint of mint that will creep in softly. Drink now–2017, perhaps longer. Score 92. K

SHORESH, 2007: Cabernet Sauvignon blended with 15% Syrah, dark royal purple in color, opens with a deep nose of plums and freshly turned earth. Full-bodied, showing spicy oak and gently caressing tannins in fine balance with blackcurrants and blackberries and notes of bittersweet chocolate and tar. On the long finish, the tannins rise comfortably with an appealing note of saddle leather. Drink now–2015. Score 90. K

SHORESH, 2006: Made entirely from Cabernet Sauvignon grapes, showing dark garnet and medium- to full-bodied, reflecting its 18 months in oak with a sweet cedar nose. Soft tannins integrating nicely with the oak and opening to show a tempting array of currants, wild berries and purple plums, those matched by notes of minerality and cocoa. Drink now–2014. Score 90. K

SHORESH, MERLOT, 2005: Dark garnet toward royal purple, medium- to full-bodied, with soft, mouth-coating tannins and spicy wood integrating nicely. Opens to show a fine array of berry, black cherry and citrus peel, those leading to a moderately long finish. Drink up. Score 89. K

SHORESH, BLANC, 2010: Wisely developed entirely in stainless steel vats to guard the freshness and flavors of the grapes, a blend as it was in 2009 of 85% Gewurztraminer and 15% Chardonnay. Light golden straw with green tints and fine aromatics, medium-bodied, with lively but not at all exaggerated acidity, opening to reveal aromas and flavors of white peaches, pink grapefruit and what at one moment seems like litchis and another like mango, the fruits on a tantalizingly light spicy background. A tempting wine, both lively and complex, with a surprisingly long finish for an unoaked wine. Drink now–2013, perhaps a bit longer. Score 90. K

SHORESH, SHORESH BLANC, 2009: An unoaked blend of 85% Gewurztraminer and 15% Chardonnay from a low-yield vineyard. Light gold with a distinct tint of green, aromatic with floral and spicy notes on the nose but showing crisply dry. On first attack a clear lemon-lime note, that going to tangerines and spices, all lingering nicely on the palate. Simultaneously refreshing and complex. Drink now. Score 90. K

Neve Ilan

NEVE ILAN, CABERNET SAUVIGNON, 2005: Made entirely from Cabernet Sauvignon grapes, dark ruby toward garnet in color, full-bodied with tannins showing more gripping, and with somewhat earthy and herbal aromas and flavors rising, the fruits are more subdued than at an earlier tasting. Continuing to show black fruits and hints of licorice. Drink up. Score 87. K

NEVE ILAN, CABERNET SAUVIGNON-MERLOT, 2006: Medium- to full-bodied, deep garnet toward royal purple, with tannins integrated with notes of spicy oak and fruits. A blend of 70% Cabernet Sauvignon and 30% Merlot, oak-aged for 18 months, opening with raspberries and red currants, those yielding to red plums, spices and earthy minerals. Soft, round and generous. Drink now. Score 90. K

NEVE ILAN, NEVE ILAN BLANC, 2010: Made entirely from Chardonnay grapes, one-third developed in new oak, one-third in second-year oak and one-third in stainless steel. Light gold with green and orange tints, medium-bodied, with an appealing array of citrus and summer fruits, those supported by notes of orange blossoms and flinty minerals. Simultaneously lively and complex, calls to mind a fine Chablis. Drink now–2014 Score 91. K

NEVE ILAN, NEVE ILAN BLANC, 2009: 100% Chardonnay, 65% of which developing in French *barriques*, with no malolactic fermentation to allow the clean, pleasingly sharp aromas and flavors to best make themselves felt. Aromatic, with light and tantalizing notes of spicy oak on both the nose and palate and opening in the glass to reveal green melon and summer fruits, those on a lightly spicy mineral-rich background. Concentrated and deep and crisply elegant. Drink now–2013. Score 91. K

NEVE ILAN, NEVE ILAN BLANC, 2008: Made entirely from Chardonnay grapes, developed in French oak, 40% of which were new, and partly in stainless-steel vats, drinking quite nicely. Showing medium-bodied, with fine acidity and minerality. On first attack tropical and summer fruits, those followed by notes of citrus, all on a lightly spicy background. Fresh, lively and complex, lingering nicely on the palate, an intriguing Chardonnay wine. Drink up. Score 91. K

Judean Hills

JUDEAN HILLS, 2009: A blend this year of Cabernet Sauvignon, Merlot and Syrah (72%, 18% and 10% respectively) from grapes from the Neve Ilan and Shoresh vineyards. Garnet to royal purple, medium- to full-bodied, and with still-gripping tannins that need a bit more time to settle in but already showing good structure and fine-tuning between the tannins, oak and fruit. Opens in

the glass to reveal red and black berries and black currants, those on a background of minted chocolate. Drink from release–2014. Tentative Score 88–90. K

JUDEAN HILLS, 2008: Cabernet Sauvignon with 8% of Syrah to flesh the wine out. Medium- to full-bodied, with soft, gently gripping tannins and gentle spicy wood influences. Royal purple toward garnet, opens with raspberry notes, those going to blackberries and ripe purple plums, an easy-to-drink red with just enough spicy complexity to grab our attention. Drink now–2013. Score 89. K

JUDEAN HILLS, 2007: Cabernet Sauvignon, dark garnet in color, medium- to full-bodied with still-gripping tannins needing a bit of time to settle in. Reflects its 12 months in French oak with notes of spices and cedarwood those followed by traditional black fruits and a light hint of cinnamon all on a mineral-rich background. Drink now–2013. Score 88. K

JUDEAN HILLS, MERLOT-CABERNET SAUVIGNON, 2006: Garnet toward royal purple, medium- to full-bodied, with soft tannins and reflecting its 12 months in oak with a gentle spiciness. A blend of 65% Merlot and 35% Cabernet Sauvignon with aromas and flavors of cassis, blackberries and an appealing hint of vanilla. Easy to drink but with just enough complexity to catch our attention. Drink now. Score 87. K

JUDEAN HILLS, GEWURZTRAMINER, DESSERT WINE, OR, 2008: Finely tuned balance between sweetness and acidity highlight guava, pineapple and pear fruits, those with hints of ripe peaches and a generous note of peppery quince jam, all on a light mineral background. Drink now–2015. Score 90. K

JUDEAN HILLS, GEWURZTRAMINER, DESSERT WINE, OR, 2006: Light, sweet and silky, almost calling to mind an ice wine, with distinct honeyed pineapple and pear fruits and a hint of kumquat marmalade on the finish. A low 8% alcohol content and good balancing acidity to make the wine both lively and tempting. Drink now. Score 89. K

Tzuba ✴✴✴✴

Set on Kibbutz Tzuba in the Jerusalem Hills, the winery's first releases from the 2005 vintage were of 30,000 bottles. South African-born and trained winemaker Paul Dubb currently issues wines in two series: the top-of-the-line HaMetsuda, to be produced only in selected years, and Tel Tzuba, of varietal wines. The winery also produces a red dessert wine. The winery's grapes all come from the kibbutz's own vineyards, those containing Cabernet Sauvignon, Cabernet Franc, Merlot, Petit Verdot, Shiraz, Malbec, Sangiovese and Pinot Noir grapes as well as the white Viognier, Chardonnay and Sauvignon Blanc. Current annual production is about 40,000 bottles and plans are to increase to about 50,000.

HaMetsuda

HAMETSUDA, 2009: A blend this year of 50% Cabernet Sauvignon, 30% Merlot and 20% Cabernet Franc. Dark, almost impenetrable garnet in color, full-bodied, with generous notes of spicy oak but those in fine balance with gently caressing tannins and fruits. Blackcurrant, blackberry and black cherry fruits complemented by notes of earthy minerals and, on the long finish, a hint of bittersweet chocolate. Drink from release–2016. Tentative Score 89–91. K

HAMETSUDA, 2008: A very different blend than at a barrel tasting a year ago. Deep, dark garnet, a full-bodied blend of 60% Cabernet Sauvignon, 30% Merlot and 10% Cabernet Franc. Oak-aged for 16 months in new and used barriques, showing fine balance between soft tannins, sweet cedarwood and fruits. On first attack black currants and spices, those parting to make way for red berries and notes of Mediterranean herbs. Long, round and generous. The best to date from Tzuba. Drink now–2016. Score 92. K

HAMETSUDA, 2007: Dark garnet with purple and orange reflections, a full-bodied blend of Cabernet Sauvignon, Cabernet Franc and Malbec (60%, 25% and 15% respectively). Full-bodied and concentrated, with still-firm tannins and generous wood waiting to settle in but already showing balance and structure that bode well for the future. On first attack purple plums and notes of mocha, those yielding comfortably to an array of blackberry, cassis and orange peel, and, on the long finish, notes of red cherries and red licorice. Long, generous and mouth-filling. Drink now–2015. Score 92. K

HAMETSUDA, SHIRAZ, 2007: Made entirely from Shiraz grapes, gently oak-aged and with generous but gently mouth-coating tannins. On first attack huckleberries and blueberries, those parting to make way for blackberries and a temptingly peppery background. Full-bodied, well focused and concentrated. Tempting now but has the structure and balance for cellaring. Drink now–2014. Score 90. K

HAMETSUDA, 2006: A blend of 75% Cabernet Sauvignon, 20% Cabernet Franc and 5% Malbec. Deep purple, medium- to full-bodied, reflecting its 24 months in oak with soft tannins and light notes of spicy wood, those coming together with notes of sweet herbs and opening to show blackcurrants, red and black berries and notes of espresso coffee and red licorice. Long and generous. Drink now–2014. Score 90. K

HAMETSUDA, 2005: A blend of 75% Merlot and 25% Cabernet Sauvignon, oak-aged for 24 months. Medium-dark garnet, full-bodied, with near-sweet tannins now integrating nicely to show an appealing array of blackberry, cherry and herbal notes. A gentle spicy wood influence and a hint of licorice on the long finish add to the charms of the wine. Drink up. Score 88. K

Tel Tzuba

TEL TZUBA, CABERNET SAUVIGNON, 2010: Deep royal purple, with a nose rich in red fruits and cocoa. On first attack raspberries, wild berries and spices, those followed by notes of cassis and an appealing earthy-herbal overlay. Drink from release–2016. Tentative Score 88–90. K

TEL TZUBA, CABERNET SAUVIGNON, 2009: Dark, almost impenetrable garnet in color, with soft tannins and gentle notes of spicy wood. A generous wine, with red fruits on the first attack yielding in the glass to blackberries and currants, those on a background that hints of cherries, sassafras and dried herbs. Stylish and tempting. Drink now–2017. Score 88. K

TEL TZUBA, CABERNET SAUVIGNON, 2008: Oak-aged for 14 months, showing garnet toward brick red. Generously aromatic with notes of berries and spicy sawdust on the nose, showing medium- to full-bodied and still-firm tannins, those needing just a bit of time to settle in. On the nose and palate generous black fruits and notes of bittersweet chocolate carrying on to a generous finish. Drink now–2013. Score 89. K

TEL TZUBA, CABERNET SAUVIGNON, 2007: Medium- to full-bodied, with gently gripping tannins. Dark garnet with purple and orange reflections, opening with red berries, those yielding comfortably to currants and wild berries on a gently spicy background. Fruits and tannins rise on the finish. Drink now. Score 89. K

TEL TZUBA, CABERNET SAUVIGNON, 2006: Reflecting spices and near-sweet tannins from its 14 months in French oak, a medium- to full-bodied red with good concentration, soft tannins and a gentle wood influence. On the nose and palate, starts off with blackcurrants and blackberries, those yielding to a pleasing red berry-cherry character and finally, on the long finish, notes of Mediterranean herbs. Drink up. Score 90. K

TEL TZUBA, CABERNET SAUVIGNON, 2005: A blend of 85% Cabernet Sauvignon, 9% Cabernet Franc and 6% Merlot, aged in French oak for 14 months. Ruby to purple, medium- to full-bodied, with soft tannins and gentle wood. Showing clean red fruits on a lightly spicy, moderately long finish. Sliding rapidly past its peak. Drink up. Score 85. K

TEL TZUBA, MERLOT, 2010: Dark garnet, almost black in color, full-bodied, still firmly tannic and concentrated, needing only time for the wine to come into its own. On the nose and palate blackcurrants and wild berries, those on a background of earthy minerals, the fruits going to notes of raspberries as the wine lingers on the palate. Long and generous with a hint of red licorice on the finish. Drink from release–2016. Tentative Score 89–91 K

TEL TZUBA, MERLOT, 2009: Super-dark garnet in color, medium- to full-bodied (leaning toward the full), with crisp acidity. On the nose and palate red and black berries with overlays of tobacco, cloves and freshly turned damp earth. Tannins are still gripping now but those will settle down in time. Best from release–2015. Tentative Score 86–88. K

TEL TZUBA, MERLOT, 2008: Garnet toward royal purple with orange reflections, full-bodied with soft, gently mouth-coating tannins and showing fine concentration and balance. On first attack red currants and raspberries, those yielding to blackberries and an appealing hint of bitter herbs. Drink now–2014. Score 90. K

TEL TZUBA, MERLOT, 2007: Medium-deep garnet in color, generously aromatic, medium- to full-bodied and with soft tannins. On the nose and palate wild berries, red currants and spices, and on the moderately long finish a hint of espresso coffee. Marred somewhat by a slight bitter streak that runs through. Drink now. Score 87. K

TEL TZUBA, MERLOT, 2006: Dark garnet with violet reflections, medium-bodied, with soft, gently mouth-coating tannins. Opens to reveal blackberry, currant and purple plum fruits, those supported nicely by hints of mint, licorice and, on the finish, a hint of bittersweet chocolate. Drink up. Score 88. K

TEL TZUBA, SHIRAZ, 2010: Dark garnet with notes of royal purple, medium- to full bodied (leaning to the full), with still-firm tannins just starting to integrate with notes of spicy oak. On the nose and palate plums, wild berries and cassis, those matched nicely by hints of saddle leather, all leading to a long, bittersweet-chocolate-rich finish. Drink now–2015. Score 88. K

TEL TZUBA, SHIRAZ, 2009: Dark garnet, medium- to full-bodied, with gently caressing tannins and notes of vanilla and spices from oak-aging. Opens with a subdued nose but that comes around nicely with time in the glass and then goes on to reveal generous red currant, wild berry and Oriental spices, those set off nicely by notes of saddle leather and dark chocolate that come in on the finish. Tempting. Best from 2013–2016. Score 89. K

TEL TZUBA, SHIRAZ, 2008: Oak-aged for 14 months, inescapably Shiraz, showing appealing notes of plums and red berries, those complemented nicely by notes of smoky and spicy oak. Medium- to full-bodied with tannins that grip gently, all leading to a generous and mouth-filling finish. Drink now–2014. Score 89. K

TEL TZUBA, SHIRAZ, 2007: Dark garnet toward royal purple, medium- to full-bodied, with generous but not overpowering spicy oak and vanilla, those parting to reveal raspberry, cherry and red plum fruits in fine harmony with spices and notes of leather. Polished, long and well focused. Drink now–2013. Score 89. K

TEL TZUBA, SHIRAZ, 2006: Garnet toward royal purple, medium- to full-bodied, with good concentration and balance. Firm tannins are settling in nicely now and part to reveal cherry, blueberry and cassis notes, those with hints of spices and saddle leather. Drink now. Score 89. K

TEL TZUBA, PINOT NOIR, 2009: Opens with appealing earthy and red-fruit aromatics, medium- to full-bodied, with gently caressing tannins, a soft, round red showing blackberries, red berries, cassis and orange peel. From mid-palate on, notes of dried berries and sage. Destined to be a lithe and polished wine with a long finish. Drink now–2018. Score 90. K

TEL TZUBA, PINOT NOIR, 2008: Deep garnet, with a wood-rich nose, medium- to full-bodied, with generous tannins and resembling Cabernet Sauvignon or Merlot more than Pinot Noir. On the nose and palate raspberries, ripe red plums and cassis. Drink now. Score 87. K

TEL TZUBA, PINOT NOIR, 2007: Pinot with a distinctly Mediterranean flavor. Dark ruby in color, medium- to full-bodied, with generously caressing soft tannins. On first attack shows floral, mineral and raspberry fruits and then to black cherries, green tea and notes of both licorice and saddle leather. A multi-layered wine. Drink now. Score 89. K

TEL TZUBA, CABERNET FRANC, 2009: Made from grapes in a high-density, low-yield vineyard, opens with notes of freshly hung tobacco leaves, those parting to make way for currant, black cherry, briar and mineral notes. On the long finish a clean flavor of dried herbs. A fine effort that will remind many of a Bordeaux red. Best from 2013. Tentative Score 89–91. K

TEL TZUBA, SANGIOVESE, 2009: Deep garnet toward royal purple, with fresh, fruity aromatics. Medium- to full-bodied, a round wine with soft tannins and just the right notes of spicy wood. Opens to show blackberries and blackcurrants on a background of minted chocolate. Leads to a long, juicy finish. Drink from release–2014. Tentative Score 88–90. K

TEL TZUBA, SANGIOVESE, 2008: Reflecting its development in *barriques* with soft, gently caressing tannins and spicy oak, garnet toward royal purple and, medium-body. On the nose and palate black cherries, wild berries and hints of exotic spices. Drink now. Score 87. K

TEL TZUBA, SANGIOVESE, 2007: Oak-aged for 14 months, showing dark cherry-red toward garnet, medium-bodied, soft and round, with fine-grain tannins and floral, blackberry and black cherry fruits. Not a complex wine but an appealing one. Drink up. Score 86. K

TEL TZUBA, CHARDONNAY, 2010: Developing *sur lie* in French oak, bright, lively gold in color, medium-bodied with fresh citrus, peach and mango fruits complemented nicely by stony minerals. Drink from release–2013. Tentative Score 87–89. K

TEL TZUBA, CHARDONNAY, 2009: Light bright gold in color, developed partly in stainless steel, partly in *barriques* (50% of which were new), and with no malolactic fermentation. Opens a bit flat but don't let that put you off, for all this needs is a few minutes in the glass to reveal aromas and flavors of green apples, peaches and nectarines. Medium-bodied, with appealing notes of Anjou pears that come in on the finish. Drink now. Score 88. K

TEL TZUBA, CHARDONNAY, 2008: Light gold in color, with an appealing hint of spicy wood, and opening to show tempting citrus, apple and Anjou pears. Medium-bodied and lively. Drink up. Score 86. K

TEL TZUBA, CHARDONNAY DESSERT WINE, N.V.: Intentionally harvested late, almost at the point where the grapes had raisined and then fortified to a 14.5% alcohol level. Generous sweetness balanced nicely by acidity makes this a lively wine, showing honeyed apricot and peach notes. Sweet and spicy but not at all syrupy, a comfortable and refined wine with a clear hint of Anjou pears coming in on the finish. Drink now. Score 89. K

Hama'ayan

HAMA'AYAN, SANGIOVESE, 2006: Not much in common with its Italian cousins made from the same grape. Medium-bodied, with somewhat chunky tannins and showing basic berry and red plum notes. Drink up. Score 84. K

HAMA'AYAN, SANGIOVESE, 2005: Made entirely from Sangiovese grapes, oak-aged for 14 months, this red is showing soft, well-integrating tannins, a moderate overlay of spicy wood and appealing berry, cherry and plum fruits. A good quaffer. Drink up. Score 85. K

HAMA'AYAN, BELMONT RED, 2006: A somewhat unusual blend of 55% Pinot Noir and 45% Merlot, those developed in new French *barriques* for 14 months. Medium-bodied, soft and round, opens with a generous red-fruit and flowery nose, goes on to show berries, red cherries, cassis and a hint of currants. Not overly complex but a very good quaffer and a fine accompaniment to food. Drink up. Score 88. K

HAMA'AYAN, SEMILLON, 2006: An unoaked blend of 88% Semillon and 12% Sauvignon Blanc, with grapefruit, mandarin orange and citrus peel aromas and flavors. Drink up. Score 82. K

HAMA'AYAN, BELMONT WHITE, 2008: Light straw in color, categorized as semi-sweet, a blend of 55% Semillon and 45% Sauvignon Blanc. Summer and tropical fruits on the nose and palate but lacking the acidity to keep it lively. Drink up. Score 82. K

HAMA'AYAN, BELMONT WHITE, 2007: A light gold, unoaked blend of 55% Sauvignon Blanc and 45% Semillon. Showing appealing pineapple and peach fruits, a fresh, round and lively wine that opens nicely on the palate. Drink up. Score 87. K

Tzuba

TZUBA, BLEND T (TENTATIVE NAME), 2009: A blend of Cabernet Sauvignon, Merlot, Shiraz and Sangiovese (20%, 30%, 15% and 35% respectively), winemaker Paul Dubb likes to think of this one as a Super–Judean Hills wine. Garnet in color, medium- to full-bodied and softly tannic, showing generous red fruits, on a background of chocolate and saddle leather. On the finish an appealing hint of grilled meat. A mini-cuvée, perhaps to be released, perhaps just to be shared with friends and, because of the winemaker's insistence on hands-on contact with the wine, not kosher. Drink from release. Tentative Score 89–91.

Vanhotzker **

Founded by Eli Vanhotzker in 2003 on Moshav Meron, the winery has its own vineyards with Cabernet Sauvignon and Merlot grapes on the slopes of Mount Meron in the Upper Galilee. Releases, entirely of Cabernet Sauvignon from the 2004 and 2005 vintages, were of 1,500 bottles, and production from the 2006 vintage was 3,000 bottles, that including the winery's first Merlot.

VANHOTZKER, CABERNET SAUVIGNON, 2007: Garnet toward royal purple, medium-bodied, with somewhat chunky tannins that grip firmly. Opens in the glass to reveal a basic cherry-berry personality, the fruits complemented by notes of spicy wood and Mediterranean herbs. Drink now. Score 84. K

VANHOTZKER, CABERNET SAUVIGNON, 2006: Ruby toward garnet, medium-bodied, with gently mouth-coating tannins. On the nose and palate currant and berry fruits along with notes of dark chocolate and Mediterranean herbs. Drink now. Score 85. K

VANHOTZKER, CABERNET SAUVIGNON, 2005: Dark garnet, medium- to full-bodied, with firm tannins and ripe and juicy currant, black cherry and kirsch aromas and flavors. On the finish herbal and vanilla notes. Drink up. Score 84. K

VANHOTZKER, CABERNET SAUVIGNON, 2004: Medium- to full-bodied, with generous soft tannins and spicy oak already integrating nicely and showing good balance with blackcurrant, plum and blackberry fruits. Generous and moderately long. Drink up. Score 85. K

VANHOTZKER, MERLOT, 2007: Medium-bodied with soft tannins and notes of spicy oak. On the nose and palate plum, black cherry and currant notes. Not complex but a good quaffer. Drink now. Score 85. K

VANHOTZKER, MERLOT, 2006: Medium- to full-bodied, with still-firm tannins waiting to settle down. Opens in the glass to reveal purple plum and cassis notes. Drink now. Score 84. K

Villa Wilhelma ✶✶

Founded in 2003 by Motti Goldman and
Amram Sourasky and located on Moshav
Bnei Atarot not far from Ben Gurion Airport
on the central plain, the winery draws its
red grapes from the vineyards of the Upper
Galilee and from Karmei Yosef at the foothills of the Jerusalem Mountains. Wines
are released in three series, Grand Reserve,
Timeless and Villa Wilhelma, and the winery has grown from production of 3,500
bottles from the 2003 vintage to 18,000
bottles in 2007.

Grand Reserve

GRAND RESERVE, CABERNET SAUVIGNON, 2006: Tasted as components and at this stage showing medium- to full-bodied, with so-far
gentle oak influences and soft tannins. Opens to show traditional
Cabernet blackcurrant and blackberry fruits along with hints of Mediterranean herbs. Drink from release. Tentative Score 84–86.

GRAND RESERVE, CABERNET SAUVIGNON, 2005: Vastly differing
from an earlier tasting. Deep garnet in color, medium- to full-bodied
with once-firm tannins and generous toasty wood now integrating
nicely. Oak-aged for 30 months, showing an interesting mélange of
red and black fruits, spices and hints of licorice. Drink now. Score 88.

GRAND RESERVE, MERLOT, 2006: Showing a super-generous dose
of near-burned toasted white bread, chunky country-style tannins and
a few fruits that struggle but never quite make their way to the fore.
Drink up. Score 78.

GRAND RESERVE, MERLOT, 2005: Ruby toward garnet in color,
medium-bodied, with soft, near-sweet tannins and showing appealing
red fruits. A simple country-style wine. Drink up. Score 83.

GRAND RESERVE, MEDOCABERNET, 2005: Named after Bordeaux's
Medoc wines, a medium- to full-bodied blend of 75% Cabernet Sauvignon and 25% Merlot. Oak-aged for 21 months in medium- to heavy-
toasted oak and showing generous smoke and firm tannins, those
parting slowly in the glass to reveal blackberry, raspberry and cassis

fruits on a generously spicy background. Straightforward and lacking depth. Drink up. Score 84.

GRAND RESERVE, MEDOCABERNET, VERSION 1, 2004: This medium- to full-bodied blend of Cabernet Sauvignon and Merlot shows generous spicy and smoky wood after having spent 18 months in oak, along with aromas and flavors of wild berries, cassis and Mediterranean herbs. Drink up. Score 85.

GRAND RESERVE, MEDOCABERNET, VERSION 2, 2004: Dark garnet in color, full-bodied, with once-searing tannins now receding but continuing to reflect its 30 months in oak with a far-too-smoky, nearly burned woody overlay that makes it difficult to find the fruits that lie underneath and never quite make themselves felt. Showing signs of age. Drink up. Score 76.

Timeless

TIMELESS, 780 DAYS, 2007: A blend of 75% Cabernet Sauvignon and 25% Merlot, the grapes from Kerem Ben Zimra in the Upper Galilee. Developed in new French and partly American oak for 780 days (26 months). Deep garnet in color, on the nose spicy oak and hints of black fruits, those parting in the glass to make way for raspberries and cassis. From mid-palate on blackcurrants, spices and a hint of espresso coffee. Generously but not overpoweringly oaky. Drink now–2013, perhaps longer. Score 87.

TIMELESS, 929 DAYS, 2006: A blend made from the same grapes from the same vineyards, harvested one year later and made precisely in the same manner as the wine reviewed above, but this cuvée aged in oak for 929 days (31 months). On the nose more than generous spicy and smoky notes of oak and cedarwood, and what strikes at one moment as sur-ripe black fruits and at another of cigar box and tobacco. Be there no question that this is a "blockbuster" of a wine, concentrated and intense, showing a far too generous oaky overlay, that parting only slowly in the glass to let the fruits make themselves felt. Primarily for those who enjoy their wines on the distinctly oaky side. Drink now–2013. Score 85.

TIMELESS, 1120 DAYS, 2006: A blend made from precisely the same grapes and blend as the wine reviewed above, but this one allowed to develop in new oak for a whopping 1120 days (37 months). Dark garnet in color, full-bodied and with firm tannins and very generous oak that seem not to want to yield. Think of this as an oak-bomb if you like, the sweet and smoky oak so dominant that the purple plum and cassis flavors seem far too jam-like. Drink now–2013. Score 82.

TIMELESS, 633 DAYS, 2005: Precisely the same wine released (at a considerably more reasonable price it should be noted) as the winery's MedoCabernet 2005 but now relabeled and repriced as part of this new "series." A medium- to full-bodied blend of 75% Cabernet Sauvignon and 25% Merlot. Oak-aged for 21 months in medium- to heavy-toasted oak and showing very generous smoke and firm tannins, those parting slowly in the glass to reveal blackberry, raspberry and cassis fruits on a generously spicy background. Straightforward and lacking depth. Drink now. Score 84.

TIMELESS, 917 DAYS , 2005: An identical blend to the Timeless 633 but oak-aged for 917 days (31 months) in medium- to heavy-toasted oak barriques. Abundant smoky wood that adds notes of bitter burnt toast and generously gripping tannins. Indeed there are black fruits and wild berries here and possibly some roasted herbs and perhaps even a touch of licorice, but the aromas and flavors of the wood keep those fairly well hidden. Drink now. Score 84.

TIMELESS, 1243 DAYS, 2005: A blend a tad different than the 633 and 917 wines, this one of 72% Cabernet Sauvignon and 28% Merlot, developed for 30 months in new oak and then transferred to completely new barrels for an additional 12 months. Perhaps a noble experiment but one that yields a wine so firmly dominated by its smoky and bitter wood that whatever fruits are here seem to evade bringing themselves to consciousness. Dark and intense, I suppose those who like chewing on charred wooden toothpicks may find some charm here. Drink now. Score 78.

Villa Wilhelma

VILLA WILHELMA, FLORAL BLANC, 2009: A generously aromatic blend of 40% each Sauvignon Blanc and Riesling with 20% of Semillon, opening to show aromas and flavors of green melon, apples and citrus, those with a light petrol overlay. Not complex but a good quaffer. Drink up. Score 85.

Vitkin ★★★★★

Established by Doron and Sharona Belogolovsky on Moshav Kfar Vitkin on the central Coastal Plain, this winery released its first wines from the 2002 vintage. Bordeaux-trained wine-maker Assaf Paz relies on Carignan, Cabernet Franc, Syrah, Pinot Noir, Tempranillo, Petit Verdot, Petite Sirah, Viognier, French Colombard, Johannisberg Riesling, Gewurztraminer and Muscat grapes, some from their own vineyards and others from vintners in the Jerusalem hills as well as several other parts of the country. This exciting winery, specializing in creative blends and producing several varietal wines, is currently producing about 65,000 bottles annually. The Vitkin series is of age-worthy wines, and the Israeli Journey wines are meant for relatively early drinking. The latest entry from the winery is their flagship wine, "Shorashim" (Roots).

Shorashim (Roots)

SHORASHIM, 2007: As it was in 2006, a super-dark blend of Carignan, Petite Sirah, Syrah and Petit Verdot, this year again blended with a small amount of French Colombard (adding a small quantity of white grapes to a red wine has the tendency to intensify the color and to add a bit of aging potential). Developed for 20 months in new French oak, showing generous soft tannins and notes of sweet and spicy cedarwood. Opens to reveal a fine array of red and black berries, cassis and notes of mocha. On the long finish, a generously spicy note. Drink now–2017. Score 92.

SHORASHIM, 2006: Vitkin's new flagship wine, a super-dark garnet, full-bodied blend of Carignan, Petite Sirah, Syrah and Petit Verdot. Somewhere in style between Bordeaux, the Rhone and the Mediterranean, aged for 20 months in all, first in new 350 liter French oak and then in smaller used barrels, and showing spicy oak and near-sweet tannins in fine balance with fruits. Opens with crushed red fruits, white pepper and coffee, goes on to plums, mocha and minerals, all backed up by plenty of acidity and tannins. As this one develops look as well for notes of dark chocolate. Drink now–2016. Score 91.

Vitkin

VITKIN, SYRAH, 2009: The first varietal Syrah from the winery. Aging in large, new French oak and still tightly wound and firm but already showing fine focus and balance. On the nose and palate Mediterranean herbs and minerals to support blueberries, blackberries, and spices and, on the long, long finish a note of near-sweet cedarwood. Approachable on release but best 2013–2019. Tentative Score 91–93.

VITKIN, PINOT NOIR, 2010: A very happy surprise from a difficult vintage. Ripe, firm and concentrated, showing medium-dark cherry red toward garnet, medium- to full-bodied, with soft tannins that grip gently. On the nose and palate blackberries, blueberries and raspberries, those on a background of lightly bitter citrus peel and, from mid-palate on, notes of nutmeg and cloves. Drink from release–2018. Tentative Score 90–92.

VITKIN, PINOT NOIR, 2009: Dark cherry red toward garnet, medium-bodied, with silky tannins that grip gently and a hint of polished mahogany wood on the nose. Ripe and rich, opening with blackberries and spices, those going on to notes that at one moment call to mind plum pudding and another black tea. On the long finish, following the general wont of the winemaker, a tempting hint of bitterness. Highly stylized, a distinctly Mediterranean Pinot Noir. Best from mid-2012–2016. Score 90.

VITKIN, PINOT NOIR, 2008: Medium-dark garnet in color, medium- to full-bodied and generously aromatic, reflecting its ten months in oak that had been previously used to develop Viognier, with gently gripping tannins and light spices. Made by a double selection of the grapes – half early-harvested and half moderately late-harvested, showing black cherry, spiced mushrooms and light earthy-mineral overtones. On the long finish notes of near-sweet cedar and roasted nuts. Drink now–2015. Score 91.

VITKIN, PINOT NOIR, 2007: Made from low-yield vines and harvested early, oaked for ten months, with silky tannins with just enough of a grip to catch our attention. Dark in color for a Pinot but showing fine varietal traits, opening with black cherry, red plums and raspberries, those supported nicely by notes of spices, cedarwood and minerals. Supple, fresh and rewarding. Drink now. Score 90.

VITKIN, PINOT NOIR, 2006: Developed for ten months partly in new and recycled 250 liter barrels formerly used with Viognier. Medium-bodied, with soft tannins integrating nicely, showing gentle, spicy mushroom forest-floor notes, those supporting cassis and fine red and black berries. From mid-palate on, hints of roasted cashew nuts and smoke along with an appealing hint of bitter almonds on the finish. Drink up. Score 89.

VITKIN, CARIGNAN, 2008: Made entirely from Carignan grapes, opens with a note of iodine on the nose, that quickly going to mint. Dark, almost impenetrable garnet, full-bodied with firm tannins and spicy wood in fine proportion to fruits. On first attack, raspberries and cherries, those followed by blackberries and purple plums. On the long finish, tannins and fruits rise together. Concentrated and muscular but simultaneously gentle and elegant, showing fine potential for cellaring. Drink now–2018. Score 91.

VITKIN, CARIGNAN, 2007: Super-dark garnet, medium- to full-bodied, with gentle notes of spices and vanilla from the oak in which it aged for 15 months and tannins that are now yielding comfortably. On the nose and palate raspberries, blackberries and blueberries, those with a light peppery note that lingers nicely. On the long finish tempting notes of minerals and licorice. Drink now–2013. Score 90.

VITKIN, CARIGNAN, 2006: Made entirely from Carignan grapes and developed in new 360 liter French oak casks for 15 months. Intensely dark garnet in color, full-bodied, with deep, firm tannins just starting to settle in, and showing fine extraction. On first attack, shows primarily spicy black fruits, those yielding to "let loose" notes of mint and freshly turned earth. Simultaneously concentrated and intense while warm and generous, with fruits and tannins rising on the long finish. Drink now. Score 91.

VITKIN, CARIGNAN, 2005: Made from grapes of 30–40-year-old vines, this full-bodied red offers up generous oak and tannins, those integrating well and showing fine balance with purple plums, blackberries and spices. Light meaty and mineral overlays. Drink up. Score 91.

VITKIN, CARIGNAN, 2004: Deep purple, medium- to full-bodied, with firm tannins that are now integrating nicely to reveal spicy wood, earthy minerals and blackberry and plum fruits, those overlaid nicely with a pleasing gamey sweetness that lingers on the long finish. Drink up. Score 90.

VITKIN, CABERNET FRANC, 2010: Full-bodied, round and generous, with supple tannins, fresh acidity and an appealing floral note. 80-90% Cabernet Franc fleshed out with Petit Verdot, with fresh acidity and generous notes of ripe plums and cherries, those with appealing hints of tobacco and espresso. As this one develops look as well for a note of dark chocolate that comes in toward the finish. Best from 2013–2018. Tentative Score 90–92.

VITKIN, CABERNET FRANC, 2008: Aged in 40% new oak for 15 months, dark royal purple in color, full-bodied, with still-firm tannins and generous wood but those settling down nicely and integrating with blackberry, currant and black cherry fruits, supported comfortably by notes of rye, figs and cigar tobacco. Given the time it deserves this one will show long and generous. Drink now–2018. Score 92.

VITKIN, CABERNET FRANC, 2007: Dark garnet toward royal purple, full-bodied, and with generous but silky tannins integrating beautifully. Oak-aged for 15 months but showing a gentle hand with spicy oak and cigar tobacco notes. On the nose and palate blackberries, black cherry and roasted herbs, all leading to a long, stylishly aromatic finish. Drink now–2014. Score 92.

VITKIN, CABERNET FRANC, 2006: Ripe and polished, a blend of 86% Cabernet Franc and 14% Petit Verdot. Aged in new French oak for 15 months and showing gentle near-sweet cedar notes along with soft tannins that are integrating nicely. On the nose and palate currants and black cherries, those parting to reveal notes of toasted white bread, figs and tobacco. On the long and mouth-filling finish floral and mocha hints. Drink now–2013. Score 91.

VITKIN, CABERNET FRANC, 2005: Deep garnet toward royal purple, oak-aged for 16 months and blended with 12% Petit Verdot, the wine offers up generous tannins integrating nicely with the wood. Already showing an abundant array of spicy black cherries and currants, those with overtones of Madagascar green peppercorns, herbs and smoked meat. Long and satisfying. Drink now. Score 90.

VITKIN, CABERNET FRANC, 2004: Deep, almost impenetrable royal purple in color, this blend of 90% Cabernet Franc and 10% Petit Verdot shows fine balance between wood, moderately firm tannins and vegetal-fruity characteristics. On first attack pepper and spicy wood, that followed by blackcurrants, plum and blackberry fruits, all supported by hints of cloves, Oriental spices and, on the long and mouth-filling finish, Mediterranean herbs. Drink up. Score 90.

VITKIN, PETITE SIRAH, 2009: Deep, dark and mysterious but remarkably rich with notes of teak and sandalwood coming together with blackberry, cassis and huckleberry fruits. Firm tannins and already generous wood here, but those in fine balance and highlighting and not at all hiding the flavors. Long and generous. Drink from release–2018. Tentative Score 91–93.

VITKIN, PETITE SIRAH, 2007: Made from old vine grapes (30–40 years old), a super-dark garnet wine with fine balance between spicy wood, acidity and fruits. Opens with the traditional rich huckleberry, boysenberry and blackberry notes that we have come to associate with the better wines of this variety, those matched nicely by notes of minerals, dark chocolate. Once-firm and somewhat chunky tannins now settling in nicely to produce a powerful but round and elegant wine. Drink now–2013. Score 90.

VITKIN, PETITE SIRAH, 2006: Dark royal purple, medium- to full-bodied, with fine extraction and with lively notes of spices, white pepper, tobacco and cedar-wood supporting generous blackberry and huckleberry fruits. Chewy tannins rise on the finish along with hints of hazelnuts and grilled beef. Drink now–2013. Score 90.

VITKIN, PETITE SIRAH, 2005: Made from old-vine grapes and oak-aged for 16 months. Full-bodied, impenetrably dark purple-black, with deep spicy overlays and firm tannins all coming together beautifully. On the nose and palate blackberry and blueberries, those matched nicely by notes of white pepper, peppermint, chocolate and cedarwood, and on the long finish enchanting hints of raspberry jam. Drink now. Score 91.

VITKIN, BLENDED RED, AS YET UNNAMED, 2006: Not only un-named but unidentified, in that the winery is holding the blend close to its chest, not to be disclosed until the wine's release. Aged in new French oak for about 20 months, showing generous wood but that in fine balance with equally generous but gently mouth-coating tannins. Dark royal purple and full-bodied, opens with a burst of blueberry and purple plum notes, those yielding in the glass to black fruits that are simultaneously spicy and jammy and, on the remarkably long finish, notes of nutmeg and bittersweet chocolate. A wine headed for elegance. Drink now–2015. Score 93.

VITKIN, RED DESSERT WINE, N.V.: Primarily Petite Sirah and Carignan with a small amount of Cabernet Sauvignon (that from the 2002 vintage), a blend made from eight different vintage years, the blend reinforced to 18% with white brandy (that is to say, unoaked brandy). Somewhere in style between a Ruby and Late Bottled Vintage Port, with a spicy overlay on plum and black cherry fruits. Well balanced and not overly sweet with an appealing dusty oak finish. Drink now–2013. Score 88.

VITKIN, GEWURZTRAMINER, LIMITED EDITION, 2007: Light- to medium-bodied, light golden in color, so crispy dry that if this were a Champagne you would categorize it as "extra brut." On first attack a floral (look especially for rose petals) and spicy nose, and on the palate litchis, peaches and peach pits, those supported nicely by a vague but tantalizing near-bitter overtone. Crisp, clean and refreshing. Drink up. Score 88.

VITKIN, JOHANNISBERG RIESLING, 2010: Light gold with green tints, medium-bodied, crisp and dry with fine acidity and even at this early stage already giving a hint of the petrol aromas that it will develop. An appealing light floral nose, and boasting aromas and flavors of grapefruit and mango, one might think of this as a somewhat "tropical Riesling," but that's fine, for the elements come together in a rich, long and mouth-filling wine. Drink from release–2014, perhaps longer. Score 89.

VITKIN, JOHANNISBERG RIESLING, 2009: Light, bright gold in color, with a typical floral Riesling nose and showing appealing red grapefruit, ripe peach and green apples on a spicy background. Fine acidity here along with notes of Oriental spices on the background. Drink now–2014. Score 90.

VITKIN, JOHANNISBERG RIESLING, 2008: Somewhere in style between the Rhine and Alsace, light gold in color, medium-bodied and with finely tuned balance between fruits and acidity. On the nose and palate generous spices to add charm to white peach, grapefruit and white mulberries. Taking on an appealing light Riesling petrol note. Drink now. Score 90.

VITKIN, JOHANNISBERG RIESLING, 2006: Light gold in color, opens with a floral nose and goes on to reveal apricot, grapefruit, bitter orange peel and notes of green apples. Since release has come to show traditional Riesling traits. Spicy and long, with the flowers of Alsace and the petrol note of the Rhine. Drink now. Score 90.

VITKIN, RIESLING, LATE HARVEST, 2006: Based on 90% Johannisberg Riesling, with a bit of French Colombard and Viognier blended in, light golden, showing generous sweetness and concentration set off nicely by balancing acidity. Opens to show citrus and dried apricots, those lightly honeyed and on a background of heather and spring flowers. Good intensity and length. Drink now–2016. Score 89.

VITKIN, RIESLING, LATE HARVEST, 2005: Pale gold, medium-bodied, with lightly honeyed summer and tropical fruits and an appealing floral-citrus finish. Drink up. Score 89.

Israeli Journey

ISRAELI JOURNEY, RED, 2009: Deep garnet toward royal purple, a medium- to full-bodied blend of 55% Carignan, 35% Syrah and 10% Cabernet Franc. Reflecting its ten months in American and French oak, of which 10% was new, showing soft tannins and a tantalizing note of spicy oak. On the nose and palate opens with red and black berries, those going on to reveal notes of eucalyptus, garrigue and stony minerals. Red fruits rise comfortably on the finish. Drink now–2014. Score 89.

ISRAELI JOURNEY, RED, 2008: Deep ruby toward garnet, with a rich floral and berry nose, showing medium- to full-bodied with gently gripping tannins and equally gentle notes of spicy wood. A blend of 60% Carignan, 30% Syrah and 10% Cabernet Franc, oak-aged for ten months in mostly used barrels, opening to show ripe berries and plums, going on to reveal notes of roasted herbs, black pepper and, on the long finish, vanilla. Round and generous. Drink now. Score 88.

ISRAELI JOURNEY, RED 2007: Medium- to full-bodied with soft tannins and gentle wood influences, a round and generous deep garnet blend of Carignan, Syrah and Cabernet Franc. Opens with a light floral note, goes on to red plums, currants and berries on a light peppery and earthy-mineral background, all leading to a tempting near-sweet finish. Drink up. Score 87.

ISRAELI JOURNEY, PINK, 2010: A blend primarily of Tempranillo and Carignan with a tad of Shiraz. Baby pink in color (think of those pink blankets one buys for baby girls), and bone dry, with crisp acidity and showing generous raspberry, cranberry and strawberry fruits. Adding complexity to the wine is a bare trace of bitter herbs that sneaks nicely in from mid-palate on. Drink now. Score 89.

ISRAELI JOURNEY, PINK, 2009: A blend of about 50% Tempranillo, the balance of Syrah and Carignan. Off-dry, with fine balancing acidity, fresh and refreshing showing raspberries and red and black cherries on the nose and palate. Rose-petal pink in color, medium-bodied and lingering nicely on the palate. Drink up. Score 88.

ויתקין

חסם
ע
י׳
אראל
י׳

ISRAELI JOURNEY, WHITE, 2010: A blend of Viognier, French Colombard and Gewurztraminer (50%, 30% and 20% respectively). Light, bright gold, medium-bodied, partly oak-aged and partly aged in stainless steel, opens to reveal citrus and citrus peel, lemon grass and litchis, all on a mineral-rich background. On the long finish an appealing hint of bitter almonds. Drink now–2013. Score 89.

ISRAELI JOURNEY, WHITE, 2009: A blend of 55% Viognier, 35% French Colombard and 10% Gewurztraminer, the Viognier aged in new French oak, the others *sur lie* in stainless-steel tanks. Flowery on both the nose and palate, comfortably supported by its crisp and refreshing acidity, and opening to reveal generous ripe summer fruits. Lively and refreshing. Drink now. Score 88.

לבן
2008

Vortman ✶✶✶✶

With his winery literally in his Haifa home, Hai Vortman is a dedicated *garagiste*. Relying entirely on grapes grown on Mt. Carmel, Vortman has planted two vineyards – Netiv Ofakim (planted in 2003, literally in front of his home) and one planted in Shfeya. Grapes include Cabernet Sauvignon, Merlot, Cabernet Franc, Petit Verdot, Mourvedre, Petite Sirah, Pinotage and Carignan. First production, from the 2007 vintage, was of 1,000 bottles and 2008 production was about 2,000 bottles. Releases from 2009 and 2010 will be of 4,000 and 6,000 bottles respectively.

VORTMAN, PETITE SIRAH, 2008: Petite Sirah blended with 25% Merlot, reflecting its 16 months in French oak with chewy tannins and notes of smoky mahogany, those in fine balance with fruits and acidity. Medium- to full-bodied (leaning to the full), and on the nose and palate purple plums, cassis and blackberries, those supported comfortably by notes of tobacco and spices. A long and appealing, almost charred finish. Drink now–2014. Score 89.

VORTMAN, MOURVEDRE-CARIGNAN, 2010: Garnet toward royal purple, medium- to full-bodied with soft tannins, a hint of spicy oak and a perhaps too-generous acidity. A spicy red-fruit nose and then opens in the glass to reveal blackberry and black cherry fruits, those with an appealing hint of mint that linger nicely on the finish. The acidity may well settle down with additional time in the oak. Drink from release. Tentative Score 88–90.

VORTMAN, GRENACHE-MOURVEDRE, 2010: A blend of 87% Grenache and 13% Mourvedre. Dark ruby toward garnet, medium- to full-bodied, a plush wine with gently caressing tannins and a bare hint of spicy wood parting to reveal aromas and flavors of cherries, blueberries, exotic spices and earthy minerals. Complex and round, potentially the best to date from Vortman. Drink from release–2015, perhaps longer. Tentative Score 89–91.

VORTMAN, NETIV OFAKIM, 2009: Garnet toward royal purple, a blend of 54% Carignan, 30% Merlot and 13% Cabernet Sauvignon, those fleshed out with Cabernet Franc and Petit Verdot. Medium- to full-bodied, with gentle wood influences and silky, gently caressing tannins, those parting to reveal an appealing array of wild berry, cassis and citrus peel notes all on a background of dark cocoa and earthy minerals. Drink from release–2014. Tentative Score 88–90.

VORTMAN, NETIV OFAKIM, 2008: Developed in French oak for 12 months, a blend of 38% Carignan, 31% Malbec, 22% Merlot and 3% each of Cabernet Sauvignon, Cabernet Franc and Petit Verdot. A super-dark potpourri of just about everything in the vineyard if you like, but one that comes together very nicely indeed. Ripe and floral, with caressing tannins and generous minerals and herbs to support currants and berries on a background of earthy minerals. An impressive effort. Drink now–2013. Score 89.

VORTMAN, NETIV OFAKIM, 2007: Medium- to full-bodied, a deep garnet blend of 70% Carignan and 20% Merlot, the rest made up of small parts of Cabernet Sauvignon, Cabernet Franc, Malbec and Petit Verdot (note that each of the five traditional red Bordeaux grapes are found here). Medium- to full-bodied, developed in French oak for ten months, showing soft, gently caressing tannins and opening to reveal generous currant, blackberry and ripe purple plum fruits, all on a lightly spicy background. Drink now. Score 88.

VORTMAN, SHAMBOUR, 2010: A blend this year of 45% each of Cabernet Sauvignon and Carignan with 10% Merlot. Dark garnet toward royal purple, full-bodied, with gently caressing tannins and an appealing note of spicy oak. On the nose and palate currants, blackberries and purple plums, those on a background that hints of roasted herbs and earthy minerals. Generous and mouth-filling. Drink from release–2015, perhaps longer. Tentative Score 87–89.

VORTMAN, SHAMBOUR, 2009: Ruby toward garnet, medium- to full-bodied, a blend of Cabernet Sauvignon, Merlot and Carignan (54%, 35% and 11% respectively), reflecting its eight months in French oak with soft tannins that open to reveal red and black berries and cassis, those supported nicely by notes of chocolate and tobacco. Fine balance between fruits, tannins, wood and acidity. Drink now–2014, perhaps longer. Score 90.

VORTMAN, SHAMBOUR, 2008: Dark garnet with orange and purple reflections, a blend of Merlot, Mourvedre and Petite Sirah (68%, 30% and 2% respectively). Aged in French oak *barriques* for six months, medium-bodied, with gently mouth-coating tannins and hints of spicy wood, opening in the glass to show appealing currants and ripe plums, those on a background that hints comfortably of tobacco and dark chocolate. Drink now. Score 88.

VORTMAN, SHAMBOUR, 2007: Somewhat of an "oddball blend" of 50% Merlot and 25% each of Petite Sirah and Pinotage. Medium-dark garnet, reflecting its ten months in oak with a nose that is quiet when the wine is first poured but opens to show floral and earthy aromas and then goes on to show generous blackberries and purple plums, those supported by notes of roasted herbs and green olives, all with the tannins and fruits rising nicely on the moderately long finish. Drink up. Score 88.

Yaffo ★★★

Founded in 1998 by Moshe and Anne Celniker and with their son Stephan now acting as winemaker, the winery, located in the Jerusalem Hills, is currently producing about 25,000 bottles annually and has plans to grow to 40,000. Grapes, primarily Cabernet Sauvignon, Merlot, Shiraz, Cabernet Franc, Carignan and Chardonnay, come from the winery's own vineyards on Moshav Neve Micha'el in the Jerusalem Hills and from the Upper Galilee.

YAFFO, CABERNET SAUVIGNON, 2008: Oak-aged for 12 months and blended with 10% Merlot, showing medium-dark ruby toward garnet. Medium-bodied with soft tannins and a moderate hand with spicy oak, opens to show raspberry, cherry and cassis fruits, those supported nicely by notes of stony minerals. Drink now. Score 87.

YAFFO, CABERNET SAUVIGNON, 2007: Blended with 15% Merlot, medium- to full-bodied, dark garnet with purple and orange reflections, with soft tannins and gentle wood integrating nicely. Opens in the glass to reveal traditional Cabernet blackberry, blackcurrant and spicy notes. Lingers nicely. Drink up. Score 89.

YAFFO, MERLOT, AUTHENTIQUE, 2007: Developed in French and American *barriques* for 12 months, deep garnet in color, with soft, gently gripping tannins and notes of spicy wood highlighting red currant and wild berry fruits, those complemented by notes of freshly picked herbs and earthy minerals. Long and generous. Drink up. Score 88.

YAFFO, SYRAH, SPECIAL EDITION, 2009: Dark royal purple, medium- to full-bodied, with soft tannins. On the nose and palate purple plums, blackberries and appealing notes of cigar tobacco and licorice, all lingering comfortably. Drink now–2013. Score 88.

YAFFO, CARIGNAN, 2009: Deep garnet toward royal purple, medium-bodied, with somewhat chunky tannins giving the wine an appealing rustic note. On the nose and palate plums, blackberries, cigar tobacco and a hint of white pepper, all lingering nicely on the palate. Drink now–2013. Score 89.

YAFFO, HERITAGE, 2006: A blend of 78% Cabernet Sauvignon and 22% Merlot, reflecting its oak-aging with spices and cinnamon notes, those highlighting black fruits, tobacco and a hint of licorice that comes in on the finish. Long, round and generous. Drink now. Score 89.

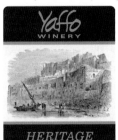

YAFFO, HERITAGE, 2005: A Bordeaux blend of 78% Cabernet Sauvignon and 22% Merlot, but with a distinctly fruit-forward New World personality. Full-bodied, with generous plum and blackcurrant fruits supported very nicely indeed by hints of dark chocolate. Reflects its 18 months in French *barriques* with notes of spices and vanilla. Well balanced and long, the best wine to date from this small winery. Drink up. Score 89.

YAFFO, MERLOT-SYRAH, 2008: A blend of 70% Merlot and 30% Syrah, oak-aged in a combination of new and older *barriques* for 12 months. Garnet toward royal purple, opens with raspberries and then goes to blackberries and currants, all with gentle hints of spices and leather. Generous and long. Drink now. Score 88.

YAFFO, CHARDONNAY, 2009: Developed on its lees in stainless steel together with oak staves for two months, light, bright gold in color, with generous but not excessive acidity to support aromas and flavors of white peaches and citrus, a crisply clean and refreshing wine. Not complex but a good quaffer. Drink up. Score 86.

Special Edition

SPECIAL EDITION, SYRAH, 2009: Dark royal purple, medium- to full-bodied, with soft tannins. On the nose and palate purple plums, blackberries and appealing notes of cigar tobacco and licorice, all lingering comfortably. Drink now–2013. Score 88.

Yatir ✴✴✴✴✴

Set in a state-of-the-art winery near the archaeological digs of Tel Arad at the foot of the Judean Hills, this boutique winery draws its name from the Yatir Forest. Although the winery is owned solely by Carmel it maintains complete autonomy under the supervision of Australian-trained wine-maker Eran Goldwasser. The winery, which releases wines under the Yatir Forest and Yatir labels, cultivates their own vineyards, those with Cabernet Sauvignon, Merlot, Petit Verdot, Shiraz, Sauvignon Blanc, and Viognier grapes. Also currently under cultivation are Tempranillo, Cabernet Franc and Malbec, those at this stage destined primarily as blending agents. The first wines were from the 2001 vintage, and current production is about 150,000 bottles annually.

Yatir Forest

YATIR FOREST, 2009: Deep garnet toward royal purple, a full-bodied blend of Cabernet Sauvignon, Petit Verdot and Malbec (50%, 41% and 9% respectively). Showing fine balance between firm but comfortably yielding tannins, spicy wood and fruits, an elegant wine, opening to reveal blackcurrants, crushed blackberries and eucalyptus notes. From mid-palate on hints of tobacco and a light note of earthiness that lingers nicely on the long finish. Elegance on the grand scale. Best from 2013–2018, perhaps longer. Tentative Score 92–94. K

YATIR FOREST, 2008: An "Oh, wow!" wine. Dark, almost impenetrable garnet, full-bodied, with soft, gently gripping tannins and notes of sweet-and-spicy cedar. On first attack traditional currant and blackberry fruits, those followed by purple plums, bittersweet chocolate, espresso coffee and, on the finish that goes on and on, seemingly without end, tempting notes of anise and black olives. Approachable now but best 2013–2022. Perhaps the best yet from Yatir. Score 95. K

YATIR FOREST, 2007: Dark garnet toward royal purple, a full-bodied, softly tannic blend of 50% Cabernet Sauvignon, 36% Petit Verdot and 7% each of Malbec and Merlot, those reflecting 16 months development in *barriques* with notes of spicy cedarwood and of roasted almonds. On first attack blackcurrants and blackberries, those making way for purple plums, bittersweet chocolate and licorice. On the long and generous finish tannins and fruits rise comfortably together. Drink now–2021. Score 93. K

YATIR FOREST, 2006: Deep garnet in color, with orange and purple reflections, a Bordeaux blend of Cabernet Sauvignon, Petit Verdot and Merlot (50%, 38% and 12% respectively), oak-aged for 16 months in French oak (of which one-third were new). Ripe, round and generous, with caressing tannins and a gentle spicy wood influence, opens to reveal layer after layer of currant, plum, blackberry, mocha and floral notes, all of which linger on a superbly long and mouth-filling finish. A wine that boasts intensity together with grace and elegance. One of Israel's very best. Approachable and thoroughly enjoyable now, but this is one for aging. Drink now–2020. Score 94. K

YATIR FOREST, 2005: A full-bodied Bordeaux blend of 77% Cabernet Sauvignon, 13% Petit Verdot and 10% Merlot. A third aged in new and two-thirds aged in old wood *barriques* for 15 months, this deep royal purple wine casts intense orange and green reflections. Soft tannins integrating beautifully and the intentionally gentle hand with the wood come together nicely to let the wine open with spicy berry and cassis aromas and flavors, those going on to show blackberries and an underlying and fascinating mélange of bitter herbs. Long, generous and elegant. Drink now–2014. Score 94. K

YATIR FOREST, 2004: Almost inky in its deep garnet color, this full-bodied blend of Cabernet Sauvignon, Merlot and Syrah (80%, 14% and 6% respectively) is showing elegant and solid, with soft tannins, smoky wood and vanilla, all in fine balance with ripe blueberry, blackcurrant and plum flavors. Look as well for an appealing, earthy undercurrent leading to a long, deep, broad and generous finish. Drink now–2014. Score 93. K

YATIR FOREST, 2003: This blend of 85% Cabernet Sauvignon and 15% Merlot reflects its 12 months in *barriques* with gentle spices and lightly dusty wood and is showing fine balance between tannins, wood and acidity. On the palate light herbal and white pepper traits underlying rich blueberry and blackcurrant fruits. Well focused, long and elegant. Drink now. Score 93. K

YATIR FOREST, 2002: Made from 100% Cabernet Sauvignon grapes, this dark garnet toward purple, full-bodied wine is now showing still-firm tannins, gentle and well-integrated smoky oak and sweet cedar aromas, those coming together very nicely with aromas and flavors of ripe currant and purple plum fruits as well as generous hints of chocolate and mint. Throwing sediment and worth decanting. Drink up. Score 90. K

YATIR FOREST, 2001: Dark ruby toward garnet, this medium- to full-bodied blend of 85% Cabernet Sauvignon and 15% Merlot shows good balance between soft tannins and oak. Rich aromas and flavors of currants, wild berries and cherries integrating nicely with spicy oak and generous minerals. A luxurious and elegant wine. Worth decanting because some bottles are throwing sediment. Showing age so drink up. Score 90. K

Yatir

YATIR, CABERNET SAUVIGNON, 2010: Dark, almost impenetrable garnet, a deeply extracted, full-bodied wine opening slowly in the glass at this stage but then opening very nicely indeed. On the nose crushed berries, vanilla and a gentle hint of spicy cedarwood, those yielding to aromas and flavors of blackcurrants, blackberries and bitter herbs, with tannins and fruits rising on the finish. Well balanced and with structure that bodes well for development in the bottle. Best 2013–2018. Tentative Score 90–92. K

YATIR, CABERNET SAUVIGNON, 2009: Blended with 10% Malbec and 5% Shiraz, showing dark garnet, with generous, softly caressing tannins and toasty oak in fine balance with fruits. On first attack blueberries and baking chocolate, those parting to make way for blackcurrant and black cherry fruits on a background of freshly picked mushrooms, vanilla and Mediterranean herbs. Long, round and generous, the elements coming together nicely. Best from 2013–2018, perhaps longer. Tentative Score 89–91. K

YATIR, CABERNET SAUVIGNON, 2008: Blended with 11% Shiraz, showing dark garnet with a royal purple rim. Medium- to full-bodied (leaning to the full) with still-gripping tannins needing only time to integrate, opens with rich, near-sweet raspberries and plums, unfolds to show blackberries and spices. Developed in one-year-old barriques, concentrated and deep, long, round and generous. Best 2013–2018. Score 92. K

YATIR, CABERNET SAUVIGNON, 2007: Impenetrably dark garnet in color, full-bodied, with firm tannins and gentle wood influence integrating nicely. On first attack black fruits and spices, those parting to show notes of fresh herbs, black olives and bittersweet chocolate. Drink now–2015. Score 91. K

YATIR, CABERNET SAUVIGNON, 2006: Despite a difficult harvest year, a rich, round and deeply extracted wine. Blended with 15% Petit Verdot, oak-aged for 12 months, on opening attack traditional blackberry, blackcurrant and black cherry fruits, those with notes of mocha, vanilla and cedarwood that play nicely on the palate and, on the long finish, a tantalizing note of greenness that creeps quietly in. Drink now–2015. Score 92. K

YATIR, CABERNET SAUVIGNON, 2005: Blended with 15% of Shiraz, dark garnet with purple and orange reflections, showing fine balance between gentle spicy wood and mouth-coating tannins that are now well integrated. On first attack blackberries and currants, those yielding to raspberries, spices and light overlays of earthiness and leather, all with a hint of what at one moment feels like lead pencil and the next like cigar box. Long, generous and elegant. Drink now–2015. Score 93. K

YATIR, MERLOT, 2006: Dark and dense but even at this early stage showing admirable depth, length and complexity. On the nose and palate layer after layer of currants, black cherries, chocolate and mocha all backed up by tannins that are simultaneously soft and powerful. Drink now–2014. Score 92. K

YATIR, MERLOT, 2005: Medium- to full-bodied, with generous near-sweet tannins, this seductive wine is already showing delicious blueberry, blackberry, mocha and vanilla flavors. Plush and round, on the way to becoming a delicious, complex and concentrated wine. Drink now. Score 90. K

YATIR, SHIRAZ, 2010: Intensely dark royal purple in color, full-bodied and, despite deep extraction, showing soft, round tannins. Complex enough to intrigue. On first attack spicy blackberries and crushed wild berries those making way in the glass for aromas and flavors that I can describe only as those of a raspberry mousse. From mid-palate on, notes of saddle leather, earthy minerals and Mediterranean herbs. Makes me want to hum the lyrics of "parsley, sage, rosemary and thyme." Long, generous and mouth-filling. Best from 2013–2020. Tentative Score 91–93. K

YATIR, SHIRAZ, 2009: Dark royal purple, full-bodied, with tannins that grip nicely together with notes of spicy cedarwood, those integrating well now. On first attack a meaty note to highlight red-currant and raspberry fruits, those making way in the glass for notes of blackberries and figs. On the long finish notes of roasted herbs, with fruits and tannins rising along with appealing hints of licorice and loam. Best 2013–2018, perhaps longer. Tentative Score 91-93. K

YATIR, SHIRAZ, 2008: Blended, as is the winemaker's wont, with a small amount of Viognier (1% this year) and developed partly in used barriques for 12 months, partly in 3,600 liter vats. Super-dark garnet with a royal purple robe, full-bodied and with generous tannins now integrating nicely with wood and fruits. Look for the traditional leathery, licorice, blackberry and plum aromas and flavors that we have come to associate with this grape, but then stand back as clear and pronounced notes of raspberries, citrus peel and roasted herbs make themselves felt. This one will always be a firm and muscular wine but through that there is a clear sense of elegance. Approachable now but best from 2013–2018. Score 92. K

YATIR, SHIRAZ, 2007: Showing even more intense than at an earlier tasting. Dark, almost impenetrable garnet, with gripping tannins and generous but not at all imposing spicy wood integrating nicely now. On first attack almost peppery plums and blackberries, those followed by red fruits, dark chocolate and a note of sweet chewing tobacco. Give this one the time it needs. Drink now–2017. Score 93. K

YATIR, SHIRAZ, 2006: Blended with 15% Malbec, aged in *barriques* for 12 months, showing full-bodied and concentrated with still-firm tannins that need time to settle in. Showing fine balance and structure, the tannins integrating nicely now with a gentle spicy wood influence and opening in the glass to show blackberry, black cherry and prune notes, those on a background that hints of grilled beef and dark chocolate. Drink now–2017. Score 93. K

YATIR, SHIRAZ, 2005: Dark, almost impenetrable garnet in color, intentionally aged in second- and third-year *barriques* in order to highlight the typical characteristics of the variety but still showing generous wood, the wine opens with meaty and herbal aromas, those yielding nicely to cherry, red currant and berry fruits and finally, creeping in comfortably, an agreeable hint of saddle leather. Opens beautifully in the glass. Long, generous and elegant. Drink now–2014. Score 93. K

YATIR, PETIT VERDOT, 2010: Deeply aromatic, almost impenetrably dark royal purple in color, full-bodied, firm and concentrated. On first attack blackcurrants and blackberries, those yielding in the glass to purple plums and raspberries, the tannins firm but seeming almost to melt on the palate to a muscular roundness. On the long finish notes of cigar tobacco, eucalyptus and a fine balancing acidity. Complex and generous. Best from 2014–2020. Tentative Score 92–94. K

YATIR, PETIT VERDOT, 2009: Super-dark garnet, deeply extracted, full-bodied and with still-gripping tannins that need only a bit of time to settle in. On first attack cassis, raspberries and cola aromas and flavors, those yielding to purple plums and earthy minerals. From first sip to the long finish an appealing loamy note that adds to the complexity of the wine. Best from 2013. Tentative Score 89–91. K

YATIR, PETIT VERDOT, 2008: A blend of 85% Petit Verdot and 15% Cabernet Franc, the varieties developed separately in one-year-old oak. Dark, almost impenetrable garnet, full-bodied, with still-gripping tannins waiting to settle down but already showing fine balance and structure. Opens with aromas and flavors of black fruits, those yielding to notes of bittersweet chocolate and roasted herbs. On the long, long finish notes of what at one moment seem like black olives and another like eucalyptus. Perhaps or perhaps not to be released as a varietal wine. Fascinating and, for my two cents, delicious. Best 2013–2018. Score 93. K

YATIR, PETIT VERDOT, 2007: Inky-dark and dense in color, with firm, still-gripping tannins that need nothing more than time to show the wine's elegance. On the nose and palate a generous array of black cherries, red and blackcurrants along with notes of mint, chocolate and tar, all coming together in a long and generous finish. Drink now–2014. Tentative Score 89–91. K

YATIR, PETIT VERDOT, 2006: Deep purple, a powerful wine with intense tannins, concentration and complexity. On the nose and palate layers of plum, blackberry, pomegranate, coffee and earth, those with appealing hints of smoky oak. Drink now–2013. Score 92. K

YATIR, BLENDED RED, 2009: A dark-garnet, full-bodied blend of 28% Merlot, 45% Shiraz and 27% Cabernet Sauvignon. Full-bodied, with gently gripping tannins and hints of spices that linger nicely from first attack to the long finish. On the nose and palate showing blackcurrants, black cherries and blackberries and, from mid-palate on to the long finish, appealing hints of blueberries. A muscular wine but one that shows its muscles in a quiet and dignified manner. Long, complex and generous. Best from 2013–2018. Tentative Score 90–92. K

YATIR, BLENDED RED, 2007: In addition to 33% Merlot and 21% each of Shiraz and Cabernet Sauvignon, this blend also contains 10% of Petit Verdot, 8% Malbec and 7% Cabernet Franc. Medium- to full-bodied (leaning toward the full), with gently gripping tannins and fine balance between wood, acidity and fruits. On opening attack purple plums and wild berries, those yielding to currants and blackberries, all on a tempting background that hints nicely of roasted cashew nuts. Long and generous. Drink now–2014, perhaps longer. Score 90. K

YATIR, BLENDED RED, 2006: A complex blend of Merlot, Shiraz, Cabernet Sauvignon, Malbec, Cabernet Franc and Petit Verdot (35%, 24%, 20%, 10%, 8% and 3% respectively). Not showing any specific varietal traits (but with such a blend one would not expect that) but indeed showing full-bodied, with soft, gently gripping tannins and reflecting its 12 months in oak with near-sweet cedarwood notes. On the nose and palate a potpourri of black fruits, those supported nicely by notes of spices and espresso coffee. Drink now–2014. Score 91 K

YATIR, BLENDED RED, 2005: A blend of Merlot, Shiraz, Cabernet Franc and Petit Verdot (37%, 36%, 15% and 12% respectively). Aged in oak for 12 months, this still-young wine shows firm tannins nicely balanced with lightly spicy wood. Starts with a rich blackberry nose and then goes on to aromas and flavors of wild berries, currants and anise, all on a gently herbal background. Drink now. Score 90. K

YATIR, CABERNET SAUVIGNON-MERLOT-SHIRAZ, 2004: A blend of 40% each Cabernet Sauvignon and Merlot and 20% Shiraz, this full-bodied red shows depth and concentration but never loses sight of elegance. Deep royal purple in color, with near-sweet tannins and appealing smoky and light vegetable overlays highlighting aromas and flavors of ripe plums, blackberries, cherry and licorice. On the long finish a tantalizing hint of spicy oak. Drink now. Score 91. K

YATIR, CABERNET SAUVIGNON-MERLOT-SHIRAZ, 2003: A blend of 56% Cabernet Sauvignon, 33% Merlot and 11% Shiraz. Aged in oak for one year, this medium- to full-bodied wine shows ripe berry, cherry and currant fruits, those with just a hint of toasted oak, all backed up with vanilla and spicy aromas and flavors. Long and caressing. Drink now. Score 90. K

YATIR, FORTIFIED RED WINE, 2005: Made entirely from Cabernet Sauvignon grapes, those allowed a short period of fermentation before being fortified by the addition of grape brandy and then being allowed to develop for 18 months in older oak barrels. Deep enough in color that one might describe it as "near-black," with a moderate level of sweetness set off nicely by balancing acidity. On the nose and palate lightly oxidized (quite intentionally) notes of sweet red and black berries, violets, prunes and a hint of coffee beans. Full-bodied, with well-focused fruits and chewy tannins leading to a long finish, some will compare this to a Late Bottled Vintage Port. Not I, for this is a distinctly Mediterranean wine, as good with Stilton, Gorgonzola or other blue cheeses as with a rich fruitcake, or, if it is "your thing," a good cigar. Not a "great" wine but an excellent one that certainly captures and deserves the attention. Drink now–2018. Score 90. K

YATIR, SAUVIGNON BLANC, 2010: Fermented in stainless steel and then transferred to primarily older oak for two months, dark golden straw with a green tint and just a bare – and thus tantalizing – hint of the oak. Light- to medium-bodied, as fresh and lively on the nose as on the palate, showing aromas and flavors of citrus, pear, melon and apples, those along with notes of guava and minerals that arise from mid-palate on. A fine balance between ripeness and finely tuned acidity. Drink now. Score 90. K

YATIR, SAUVIGNON BLANC, 2009: With half of the wine developed in used *barriques* for three months and the remainder in stainless steel, a wine that is simultaneously crisply refreshing and complex, with just the barest hint of the wood to add to its charm. Light golden in color, with fine aromatics and delicious balancing acidity to highlight grapefruit, kiwi, green apple and melon notes all on a background of sea shells and flint. Drink now. Score 91. K

YATIR, SAUVIGNON BLANC, 2008: Developing beautifully. Light golden straw with a green tint, developed primarily in stainless steel, partly in older *barriques* for three to four months. Fresh and crisp with citrus, kiwi and gooseberry fruits, those with a tantalizing hint of almonds that have been soaked in seawater. Delicious and attention-catching. Drink up. Score 90. K

YATIR, VIOGNIER, 2010: Made entirely from Viognier grapes, uno-aked, thus maintaining its fresh-fruit character and crisp nature. Light golden straw with a tint of glistening green. Light- to medium-bodied, opening with floral and nutty aromas and flavors, going on to show a generous mouthful of pear, apricot and litchi fruits, all on a background that hints of spices and, on the finish, a note of kiwi. Round, lively and generous. Drink now–2014. Score 91. K

YATIR, VIOGNIER, 2009: Light gold with orange and green reflections, medium-bodied but with remarkable mouth-filling abilities. A luxurious, rich and ripe wine with notes of guava, butter, pear and peach fruits all with a tempting floral overtone and a tantalizing hint of bitter almonds on the long finish. Wisely unoaked to highlight the juicy fruits and to keep them in fine balance. Drink now. Score 92. K

YATIR, VIOGNIER, 2008: An unoaked, juicy wine, its once-youthful pear and peach flavors and aromas still showing nicely but the green-gage plums now replaced by notes of tropical fruits. In the background continues to show fine balancing acidity that highlights notes of cara-way seeds and peach pits. Long, round and with a near-creamy finish. Drink up. Score 91. K

YATIR, VIOGNIER, 2007: Made entirely from Viognier grapes, some intentionally harvested early, some quite late and wisely unoaked to maintain the fruity and aromatic nature of the variety. Rich, ripe and crispy dry, a generous mouthful of pear, green apple, melon and sum-mer fruits, those backed up by crisp acidity and a hint of cream. Drink up. Score 92. K

Ye'arim ✶✶✶✶

Located in the village of Givat Ye'arim near Jerusalem, this small winery is owned by Sasson Ben-Aharon, who is also the senior winemaker for Binyamina Wineries. With vineyards in the Judean Mountains, the winery produced 1,000 bottles from the 2000 vintage and is currently releasing about 3,000 bottles annually.

YE'ARIM, CABERNET SAUVIGNON, SASSON'S WINE, 2009: Potentially the best yet from the winery. Dark garnet, full-bodied with soft tannins that caress gently and appealing notes of sweet-and-spicy cedarwood. On the nose and palate blackcurrants and wild berries supported nicely by notes of cigar tobacco and tar. Drink from release–2015, perhaps longer. Tentative Score 90–92.

YE'ARIM, CABERNET SAUVIGNON, SASSON'S WINE, 2006: Dark ruby toward garnet, full-bodied, with firm tannins and gentle wood integrating nicely, those in fine balance with fruits and natural acidity. On the nose and palate blackberries, currants and blueberries, all on a lightly spicy background. On the long finish an appealing hint of tar. Drink now–2013. Score 90.

YE'ARIM, CABERNET SAUVIGNON, SASSON'S WINE, 2005: Garnet toward royal purple, medium- to full-bodied, with caressing tannins and gentle wood parting to reveal blackberry, blueberry and cassis notes, those on a background of Oriental spices and a note of red licorice. Drink now. Score 90.

YE'ARIM, CABERNET SAUVIGNON, SASSON'S WINE, 2004: Dark garnet, medium- to full-bodied, with silky smooth tannins and a gentle hand with spicy wood, opening to show generous red currant, berry and cherry fruits, those matched nicely by spices and hints of licorice that come in on the long finish. Drink up. Score 89.

YE'ARIM, CABERNET SAUVIGNON, SASSON'S WINE, 2002: Out of a dumb period and showing surprisingly youthful and holding its own very nicely. Full-bodied, reflecting its development in oak with now gently caressing tannins and a tantalizing hint of cigar-box aromas. Opens in the glass to reveal itself as soft and round, with aromas and flavors of blackcurrants, blackberries, spices and a tantalizing hint of earthy minerals. Long and generous but about to slide past its peak. Drink up. Score 90.

YE'ARIM, MERLOT, SASSON'S WINE, 2005: Medium- to full-bodied, with soft, caressing tannins and a moderate hand with spicy and vanilla-rich wood. Opens to show black cherry, red and black berries, and a generous minty note on the finish. Drink now. Score 89.

YE'ARIM, MERLOT, SASSON'S WINE, 2003: Merlot blended with 10% Cabernet Sauvignon grapes, garnet toward purple in color, well balanced and medium-bodied. With soft tannins, and reflecting 16 months in French oak with a gentle touch of spicy wood, the wine shows aromas and flavors of cherries, wild berries and tobacco as well as an appealing hint of minty-chocolate on the finish. Sliding past its peak. Drink up. Score 87.

Yehuda *

Located on Moshav Shoresh in the Jerusalem Mountains, this winery was founded by Avi Yehuda in 1998. Cabernet Sauvignon, Merlot and Sauvignon Blanc grapes come from the winery's own nearby vineyards as well as from Moshav Shoresh. Current production is about 6,000 bottles annually.

YEHUDA, CABERNET SAUVIGNON, RESERVE, 2007: Dark garnet in color, with aromas and flavors too strongly influenced by Brettanomyces, that giving the wine an unwanted note of wet fur and hiding the fruits that fail to make themselves felt. Score 70.

YEHUDA, CABERNET SAUVIGNON, HILA, 2007: Aged for 24 months in new oak, showing dusty-dark garnet in color, with chunky tannins and skimpy berry and currant fruits. A simple, country-style wine. Drink up. Score 75.

YEHUDA, CABERNET SAUVIGNON, RESERVE, 2006: Dark but not completely clear garnet in color, medium-bodied, with chunky country-style tannins but turning smoother as it develops in the glass. Reflecting its 24 months in *barriques* with generous spicy cedar on the nose and palate and showing berry and black cherry fruits. One-dimensional, an acceptable entry-level quaffer. Past its peak. Drink up. Score 79.

YEHUDA, CABERNET SAUVIGNON, HILAH HASHIRAZ, 2005: Blended with 12% Shiraz and oak-aged for 18 months, a dark garnet, medium- to full-bodied wine with firm tannins integrating nicely with spicy wood. Opens to show appealing black fruits on a light leathery and earthy background. Past its peak. Drink up. Score 79.

YEHUDA, MERLOT, RESERVE, 2007: Medium- to full-bodied, dark but not fully clear garnet in color, with distinctly chunky tannins that seem not to want to yield. Aromas and flavors of overripe plums and cherries on a background of herbs and, from mid-palate on, a note of damp cardboard. Drink up. Score 74.

YEHUDA, MERLOT, NEVE ILAN, 2007: Deep royal purple, showing firm tannins and spicy oak, those parting to reveal black cherry and wild berry fruits. A simple little country-style wine. Drink now. Score 78.

YEHUDA, MERLOT, 2005: Dark royal purple in color, medium- to full-bodied, with firm tannins that seem to not want to integrate and a few berry, cherry and cola notes. Past its peak. Drink up. Score 75.

YEHUDA, CABERNET SAUVIGNON-MERLOT, 2006: Garnet toward royal purple, medium-bodied, with gently caressing tannins and a light spicy wood influence. On the palate blackberries, blueberries and currants supported nicely by hints of freshly roasted herbs. Not complex but easy to drink and appealing. Drink up. Score 84.

YEHUDA, SHIRAZ-ARGAMAN, 2007: Dark garnet toward royal purple, reflecting its 36 months in oak with firm, chunky tannins and a generous overlay of spicy wood. On the nose and palate notes of overripe plums and blue cheese. Drink up. Score 68.

Yiftah'el ∗∗

Founded in 1999 in the community of Alon Hagalil in the Upper Galilee, owner-vintners Tzvika Ofir and Avner Sofer rely on Cabernet Sauvignon, Merlot, Petite Sirah, Shiraz, Mourvedre and Sangiovese grapes from their own vineyards. Current production is about 8,000 bottles annually.

YIFTAH'EL, CABERNET SAUVIGNON, 2006: Dark ruby, medium- to full-bodied, with chunky tannins and moderate spicy oak. On the nose and palate blackberries and blueberries with overlays of roasted herbs. Not complex but a pleasant little country-style wine. Drink up. Score 84.

YIFTAH'EL, CABERNET SAUVIGNON, 2005: Ruby toward garnet, medium-bodied, reflecting its 12 months in American oak with soft tannins and hints of vanilla. Opens to show blackberry and currant fruits along with notes of Mediterranean herbs and minerals. Round, soft and with good length. Past its peak. Drink up. Score 86.

YIFTAH'EL, MERLOT, 2006: Medium-dark garnet in color, medium-bodied, with chunky tannins and spicy oak, opens to show blackberries, blueberries and earthy-herbal notes. Drink up. Score 83.

YIFTAH'EL, SHIRAZ, 2006: Dark, almost inky-garnet, full-bodied, and with soft, mouth-coating tannins. Opens to show black fruits, and goes on to reveal black pepper, licorice and spicy wood, all coming together and lingering nicely. Drink up. Score 86.

YIFTAH'EL, SHIRAZ, 2005: Dark garnet, medium- to full-bodied, with chunky, country-style tannins and appealing plum, herbal and earthy minerals that linger nicely. Drink now. Score 85.

YIFTAH'EL, YOUNG SANGIOVESE, 2010: Young and fresh, unoaked and medium-bodied with tannins soft enough that they go almost unnoticed. Look for flavors and aromas of raspberries, blueberries and cassis. A fine picnic wine. Drink up. Score 84.

YIFTAH'EL, SANGIOVESE, 2007: Oak-aged for 12 months, a lively country-style wine that will call to mind the kind of Chianti that used to come in *fiaschi* (woven straw baskets). Medium-bodied, with soft tannins and plenty of berry, black cherry and light, earthy notes. Drink now. Score 85.

YIFTAH'EL, SANGIOVESE, 2006: Dark royal purple in color, with soft tannins and showing berries, prunes, freshly picked mushrooms and spices on a background of citrus-flavored chocolate. Drink up. Score 84.

YIFTAH'EL, PETITE SIRAH, LIMITED RESERVE, 2007: Deep garnet, reflecting its time in oak with spicy and vanilla notes, and showing somewhat chunky tannins that give the wine a countryesque nature. Full-bodied, and on the nose and palate wild berry, cassis and herbal notes. Drink now. Score 86.

YIFTAH'EL, PETITE SIRAH, LIMITED RESERVE, 2006: Developed in *barriques* for 12 months, ruby toward garnet in color, medium-bodied, with soft tannins and showing appealing plum, cherry and cassis fruits, those supported by light spicy notes. Somewhat light and acidic for a Petite Sirah but a good quaffer. Sliding past its peak. Drink up. Score 83.

YIFTAH'EL, SANGIOVESE-SHIRAZ, LIMITED RESERVE, 2007: Medium-dark garnet, a medium- to full-bodied blend of 40% Sangiovese and 60% Shiraz, with chunky, country-style tannins and smoky wood parting to reveal wild berry and cassis fruits. Not complex but an acceptable quaffer. Drink up. Score 84.

Zafririm ✶✶

Founded by Lori and Shaike Lender in 2002 and set on Moshav Zafririm in the Judean Hills, this boutique winery is currently producing about 5,000 bottles annually. Grapes from their own and contract vineyards include Cabernet Sauvignon, Shiraz, Merlot, Cabernet Franc and Petit Verdot. The winery relies on French and American oak barriques.

ZAFRIRIM, CABERNET SAUVIGNON, 2008: Medium-dark garnet, medium- to full-bodied, with soft, gently caressing tannins and notes of spicy wood. Developed with oak staves, showing traditional Cabernet fruits of blackberries and blackcurrants, those on a background that hints of spices and cigar tobacco. Drink now. Score 86.

ZAFRIRIM, CABERNET SAUVIGNON-MERLOT, 2009: A blend of 55% Cabernet Sauvignon and 45% Merlot. Developed in older French *barriques* for 15 months, dark cherry red in color, medium-, perhaps medium- to full-bodied, with soft tannins and a generous array of red fruits all lingering nicely. Drink now. Score 85.

ZAFRIRIM, CABERNET SAUVIGNON-MERLOT, 2008: Oak-aged for 15 months in two-year-old *barriques*, this dark-garnet, medium-bodied blend of equal parts of Cabernet Sauvignon and Merlot shows appealing aromas and flavors of dusty oak, raspberries and red plums. On the clean nose dusty oak and red fruits, those supported by a hint of Mediterranean herbs, all leading to a long, near-sweet finish. Drink now. Score 86.

ZAFRIRIM, CABERNET SAUVIGNON-SHIRAZ, 2009: Deep royal purple in color, medium-bodied, with soft tannins integrating nicely with notes of spicy cedarwood and fruits. On the nose and palate red and black berries, cassis and notes of bittersweet chocolate and tobacco. Fruits and tannins rise nicely on a long finish. Drink now–2013. Score 87.

ZAFRIRIM, SHIRAZ-CABERNET SAUVIGNON, 2009: Medium- to full-bodied, with silky, near-sweet tannins, a blend of 70% Shiraz and 30% Cabernet Sauvignon. Opens with aromas and flavors of purple plums, those parting to reveal notes of cassis, dark chocolate and spiced beef. Drink now. Score 85.

Zauberman ✴✴✴✴

Founded in 1999 by Itzik Zauberman and located in the town of Gedera in the Southern Plains, this small winery draws on organically raised grapes from its own nearby vineyards as well as grapes from Karmei Yosef. Current production is about 3,000 bottles annually.

ZAUBERMAN, LIMITED EDITION, 2005: Cabernet Sauvignon made in the system of Italian Amarone. With a whopping 15.4% alcohol content, reflecting generous sweet and spicy cedar from its aging in *barriques* for 22 months. Almost chewy, with raspberries, dried cherries and blackberry jam on the nose and palate, those supported by hints of black tea and licorice on the finish. Missing the deep bitterness of true Amarone, but an "interesting" wine and one of the most expensive on-release prices in the country. Drink now–2015. Score 90.

ZAUBERMAN, CABERNET SAUVIGNON, LIMITED EDITION, 2004: Deep royal purple, full-bodied, intense and concentrated, with generous soft tannins, moderate spicy oak and showing raspberry, blackcurrant, chocolate and light earthy herbaceousness. Drink up. Score 91.

ZAUBERMAN, CABERNET SAUVIGNON, LIMITED EDITION, GOLD, 2004: A wine so intense, potent and wood-dominated that you might mistake it for a liqueur. Oak-aged for 36 months (for two periods of 18 months, each time in new *barriques*). With a whopping 17.2% alcohol content so powerful that it does not even let you feel the tannins, opens slowly in the glass but when it does reveals jammy blackberry, blueberry and fried banana notes (yes, fried bananas, think even Chinese-style if you like). A style popular in some quarters, so have no fear, for with spicy, almost peppery wood dominating and a hot opening and equally hot finish, this one will find its special audience. Drink now. Score 85.

ZAUBERMAN, CABERNET SAUVIGNON, LIMITED EDITION, 2003: Dark garnet, full-bodied, with generous tannins starting to integrate and equally generous spicy wood. Showing blackberry, plum and cassis fruits, all leading to a long, intense finish. Drink now. Score 91.

ZAUBERMAN, CABERNET SAUVIGNON, LIMITED EDITION, 2002: Deep garnet red, full-bodied, with intense tannins and generous, almost powerful wood integrated nicely with plum, raspberry and currant fruits along with spicy and earthy aromas and flavors. On the long finish generous hints of well-roasted nuts. Consider decanting before drinking. Drink now. Score 90.

ZAUBERMAN, MERLOT, 2007: As are many of the Zauberman wines, a blockbuster, full-bodied, alcoholic, tannic and dense with generous oak and sur-ripe fruits. On the nose and palate black and red fruits on a background of espresso coffee, those and the tannins coating the mouth and lingering on and on. A New World wine if ever there was one but a well-crafted and interesting wine. Drink now–2014. Score 90.

ZAUBERMAN, MERLOT, SPECIAL EDITION, 2006: Full-bodied, dense and concentrated, with a more than generous 15.2% alcohol content and an almost intense presence of spicy wood. A wine so tightly wound that it opens very slowly even after decanting, and then goes on to show aromas and flavors of plums, red currants, mocha, anise and espresso coffee. Starts and finishes with muscular tannins. A well-crafted wine, but one primarily for those who prefer to chew their wines. Drink now–2015. Score 90.

ZAUBERMAN, MERLOT, 2004: Dark, almost impenetrable garnet, full-bodied, with soft tannins, spicy oak, and plum, currant and berry fruits. Long and generous. Drink up. Score 89.

Zion ✱✱✱

Founded in the old city of Jerusalem in 1848 by the Shor family, until recently this winery produced primarily wines for sacramental purposes. Managed by the ninth generation of the family, starting four years ago the winery began to release dry, more upscale wines aimed at a more sophisticated market. Now located in Mishor Adumim, not far from Jerusalem, the winery produces about 2,200,000 bottles annually. Many are still considered Kiddush wines but some 350,000 are now dry table wines, those in three series, Armon, Tidhar and Erez being of primary interest to sophisticated wine consumers. The winery's better wines rely on Cabernet Sauvignon, Merlot, Carignan, Petite Sirah and Emerald Riesling grapes from the Galilee, the Judean Hills and the Central Plain. Vineyards with Chardonnay, Sauvignon Blanc and Viognier are under development.

Armon

ARMON, CABERNET SAUVIGNON, 2006: Dark, almost inky-garnet in color, full-bodied and generously tannic, and at this early stage opening with a somewhat medicinal aroma that blows off after a few moments in the glass. On the nose and palate traditional blackcurrant, blackberry and spices followed by a hint of vanilla. Drink now. Score 85. K

ARMON, RESERVE, 2007: A medium- to full-bodied blend of 62% Cabernet Sauvignon, 31% Merlot and 7% Petite Sirah, each variety developed for ten months in barriques before a final blend was made and then developed for 12 months longer in second- and third-year barriques. Deep garnet, with soft, near-sweet tannins and a gentle note of spicy cedarwood, showing a distinctly red-fruit nose. Opens in the glass to reveal appealing aromas and flavors of blackcurrants, wild berries and chocolate-coated citrus peel. Tannins and fruits rise together on the long finish. Drink now. Score 89. K

ARMON, 2005: Aged in partly new and partly one- and two-year-old American *barriques* for 24 months, a medium- to full-bodied blend of 65% Cabernet Sauvignon, 30% Merlot and 5% Petite Sirah. On the nose and palate generous currant, blackberry and purple plums, those supported nicely by notes of spices, espresso coffee and earthy minerals. Drink up. Score 90. K

ARMON, CHARDONNAY, 2010: Made entirely from Chardonnay grapes from a very low-yield vineyard and developed in second-year 400 liter oak casks for ten months, showing light gold with an orange tint. Medium-bodied, its generous 14.5% alcohol content set off nicely by lively acidity (the wine did not undergo malolactic fermentation), showing an appealing array of summer and citrus fruits, those supported by hints of pineapple and flinty minerals that linger nicely. Drink now–2013. Score 90. K

ARMON, CHARDONNAY, 2009: As is the winemaker's wont, developed in 400 liter oak casks with no malolactic fermentation, showing glistening gold with green and orange reflections. Medium- to full-bodied, not so much a lively wine as a deep one, its generous wood in fine balance with acidity and giving the wine a creamy nature. On the nose and palate, white peaches, melon and pears, those supported nicely by notes of spices and spring flowers. Long and mouth-filling. Drink now or in the next year or so. Score 90. K

Tidhar

TIDHAR, CABERNET SAUVIGNON, 2007: An unoaked blend of 85% Cabernet Sauvignon and 15% petite Sirah. Light- to medium-bodied, ruby toward garnet in color, opens with a distinct note of acidity but that settles down nicely in the glass to yield a smooth wine with generous currant and wild berry fruits. Not complex but a good quaffer. Drink now. Score 84. K

TIDHAR, CABERNET SAUVIGNON, 2006: A medium- to full-bodied blend of 85% Cabernet Sauvignon, 10% Merlot and 5% Petite Sirah. Shows silky tannins and opens in the glass to reveal aromas and flavors of blackberries, black cherries and plums. Not overly complex but a good quaffer. Drink now. Score 86. K

TIDHAR, CABERNET SAUVIGNON, 2005: A garnet-red, lightly oaked, medium-bodied and softly tannic blend of 85% Cabernet Sauvignon, 10% Merlot and 5% Petite Sirah. Black and red berries, ripe purple plums and light spices that run throughout. Drink now. Score 85. K

TIDHAR, MERLOT, 2006: Medium-bodied, dark ruby toward black cherry in color, an unoaked red with soft tannins and showing notes of berry, black cherry and wild strawberry notes, those on a lightly spicy background. A blend of 90% Merlot and 5% each of Cabernet Sauvignon and Petite Sirah. Soft, round and easy to drink. Drink now. Score 85. K

TIDHAR, CARIGNAN-MERLOT, 2006: An unoaked blend of 70% Carignan, 25% Merlot and 5% Cabernet Sauvignon. Dark royal purple in color, with soft tannins and generous blackberry and raspberry fruits, those on a lightly spicy and earthy-mineral background. Drink now. Score 85. K

TIDHAR, CARIGNAN-MERLOT-CABERNET SAUVIGNON, 2005: Dark ruby-red in color, this lightly oaked, light- to medium-bodied wine shows soft tannins and opens with light minty aromas and flavors going on to raspberry and plums. A refreshing quaffer. Drink up. Score 84. K

Erez

EREZ, CABERNET SAUVIGNON, VINEYARD'S SELECTION, 2007: 88% Cabernet Sauvignon and 12% Merlot, both varieties developed for 16 months in barriques before the blend was made. Ruby toward garnet, medium- to full-bodied, with gently chewy tannins and a distinct note of red cherries on the nose. Opens in the glass to reveal blackberry and black cherry fruits, those on a background of stony minerals, and from mid-palate on, tempting notes of bitter almonds and anise. Drink now–2013, perhaps longer. Score 88. K

EREZ, CABERNET SAUVIGNON, 2007: Dark garnet, medium- to full-bodied, with gently gripping tannins and notes of vanilla from the wood in which it aged. A blend of 85% Cabernet Sauvignon, 10% Merlot and 5% Petite Sirah, opening in the glass to show aromas and flavors of black and red berries and cassis, those on a background that hints nicely of minted chocolate. Good balance and moderately long. Drink now. Score 87. K

EREZ, CABERNET SAUVIGNON, 2006: Dark garnet toward royal purple, medium-, perhaps medium- to full-bodied, with somewhat chunky country-style tannins, but those yielding in the glass to show blackberry, black cherry and purple-plum fruits on a background of nutmeg-flavored dark chocolate. Drink now. Score 86. K

EREZ, MERLOT, 2007: Medium- to full-bodied, dark garnet in color and with soft tannins and spicy wood. Opens with a lightly off aroma but that passes in the glass and the wine shows a basic berry and plum personality. Some may not appreciate the generous acidity here. Drink now. Score 83. K

EREZ, PETITE SIRAH, 2007: Dark royal purple, full-bodied, showing the onset of spicy wood influence and with gripping tannins just starting to settle in. Opens to show black and red berries along with black pepper, anise and hints of Mediterranean herbs. Drink up. Score 84. K

EREZ, CABERNET SAUVIGNON-MERLOT, 2007: A blend of 55% Cabernet Sauvignon, 40% Merlot and 5% Petite Sirah. Garnet in color, medium- to full-bodied, with soft tannins integrating nicely with hints of smoky wood. Aromatic and flavorful, showing appealing wild berry, cassis and orange-peel notes. Drink now. Score 86. K

EREZ, CABERNET SAUVIGNON-MER-LOT, 2006: Dark garnet toward royal purple, medium- to full-bodied, a blend of 50% Cabernet Sauvignon, 45% Merlot and 5% Petite Sirah. Reflecting 12 months of development in *barriques* with gently spicy wood, and opening on the nose and palate to show an array of currant, blackberry, citrus peel and red licorice. Turns a bit astringent on the finish. Drink up. Score 85. K

EREZ, PETITE SIRAH-MERLOT, 2007: Reflecting its ten months in oak with gently gripping tannins and a moderate spicy wood influence, a medium- to full-bodied blend of 60% Petite Sirah and 40% Merlot. Dark royal purple in color, with appealing blackberry and currant fruits, those supported nicely by notes of Oriental spices and chocolate. Drink now. Score 86. K

EREZ, PETITE SIRAH-MERLOT, 2006: Developed partly in new, partly in 1–2-year-old *barriques*, a blend of 60% Petite Sirah and 40% Merlot. Dark royal purple, medium- to full-bodied, with softly caressing tannins parting to show plums, wild berries and currants, all on a lightly spicy background. Turns a bit astringent on the finish. Drink up. Score 85. K

EREZ, PETITE SIRAH-MERLOT, 2005: Petite Sirah and Merlot in equal parts. Ruby to garnet, clean and fresh, with soft tannins, a hint of spicy wood and generous red fruits. Not complex but an acceptable entry-level wine. Drink up. Score 83. K

EREZ, FUMÉ BLANC, VINEYARD'S SELECTION, 2009: One usually associates fumé blanc with Sauvignon grapes and at least a gentle smoky oak overlay. This one, however, is made from Chenin Blanc grapes and lacks that smoke. All of which is forgivable other than the choice of names, a nice wine indeed with acidity and fruits in fine balance. Light gold, having spent eight months in 400 liter oak casks, showing medium-bodied with a bare hint of spicy oak and appealing white peach and chamomile flavors, those supported by a note of lime on the long finish. Drink now. Score 87. K

EREZ, CHARDONNAY-CHENIN BLANC, 2007: An unoaked blend of equal parts of Chardonnay and Chenin Blanc. Light gold with green and orange tints, medium-bodied, with summer fruits and melon highlighted by floral and apple notes. Just enough complexity to get our attention. Drink now. Score 86. K

Special Edition

SPECIAL EDITION, CABERNET SAUVIGNON, 2009: Garnet toward royal purple, medium-bodied, with gently caressing tannins and a hint of spicy oak. Opens in the glass to reveal traditional Cabernet aromas and flavors of blackcurrants and blackberries, those complemented by hints of chocolate-coated citrus peel. Drink now. Score 87. K

Zohar ***

Founded by the Zohar family, who have been vintners for many years, and Dr. Carlos Cozacov, the Zohar winery released its first commercial wines from the 2008 vintage. With Doobie Zohar acting as winemaker, this mini-winery, currently producing about 3,000 bottles annually, is located on Moshav Kidmat Zvi on the Golan Heights, with vineyards containing Cabernet Sauvignon, Merlot, Cabernet Franc, Syrah and Petit Verdot. For the 2008 and 2009 vintages the winery relied largely on oak chips and staves, but has now acquired barriques in which to develop their wines.

ZOHAR, CABERNET SAUVIGNON, 2009: Medium- to full-bodied, dark but somewhat dull garnet in color, with rather chunky tannins and notes of dusty wood that give the wine a rustic note. On the nose and palate blackcurrant and blueberry notes that linger nicely. An appealing country-style wine. Drink now. Score 86.

ZOHAR, CABERNET SAUVIGNON, 2008: Dark garnet, medium-bodied, with slightly chunky tannins that give the wine a rustic note, but don't let that hold you back. With generous blackcurrants, blackberries and notes of tobacco and roasted herbs this is wine made for osso bucco and veal or lamb chops and stews. Drink now. Score 86.

ZOHAR, MERLOT, 2009: Dark garnet, medium- to full-bodied, with gently gripping tannins and a bare kiss of the oak, opens in the glass to reveal aromas and flavors of blackberries, currants and an appealing earthy herbaceousness, those lingering nicely, the tannins and fruits rising on the finish. Drink now–2013. Score 88.

ZOHAR, MERLOT, 2008: Garnet toward royal purple, medium- to full-bodied, with tannins that grip gently and notes of spicy wood. Opens to reveal blackcurrants, blueberries and dark chocolate. Tannins and fruits rise comfortably together on a long finish. Drink now. Score 87.

ZOHAR, PETIT VERDOT, 2009: A wine that was made in small quantities, as much as an "experiment" as with anything commercial in mind. Impenetrably dark garnet, full-bodied, with abundant but gently gripping tannins and opening to reveal generous black fruits, those on a background that hints simultaneously of Mediterranean herbs, spices and bitter chocolate. Long and generous. Drink now–2013. Score 88.

ZOHAR, EVA, 2009: A dark-garnet, medium-to full-bodied blend of Cabernet Sauvignon, Merlot and Petit Verdot (70%, 25% and 5% respectively). Just the right notes of spicy oak to highlight aromas and flavors of blackberries, blueberries and cassis on first attack, those parting from mid-palate on to reveal notes of peppery dark chocolate. Very nice indeed. Drink now. Score 88.

1848 Winery ✶✶✶

Owned by Yossi Shor and with Tzvika Shor as winemaker, both part of the Shor dynasty, which is now in its ninth generation in Israeli winemaking, the family is no stranger the local wine scene. The very first commercial winery in Israel was founded in 1848 by Rabbi Itzhak Shor. Preceding the days when the Baron de Rothschild provided massive input to the local wine industry, the inspiration of Rabbi Shor was Sir Moses Montefiore, who visited the Holy Land on numerous occasions and while here encouraged the Jews to work the land and plant vines.

Originally set in the Old City of Jerusalem, so close to the Western Wall of the Temple that barrels of wine were often seen lining the lower part of the wall, the winery later shifted location to other parts of Jerusalem and today is set in Mishor Adumim, not far from the city. The family today owns four wineries – Zion, Arza, HaCormim and now, with the latest addition, 1848 – each of which has its own senior winemaker but all sharing the same physical plant.

The winery has set out to present a fully upswing and prestigious set of wines. Grapes are drawn largely from the Tel Shachar vineyards not far from Jerusalem, as well as from the vineyards of Mount Tabor in the Galilee and include Cabernet Sauvignon, Merlot, Petit Verdot, Shiraz, Petite Sirah, Cabernet Franc, Malbec and Chardonnay.

1848 WINERY, SPECIAL RESERVE, 2006: A full-bodied, super-dark garnet blend of 78% Cabernet Sauvignon and 22% Petite Sirah. Reflecting its 30 months in primarily French oak with firm tannins and generous but not overpowering notes of spices and smoke, those parting comfortably to make way for purple plums, blackcurrants, blueberries and black licorice. Firm and concentrated with grainy tannins and a note of raspberries rising nicely on the finish. Drink now–2014, perhaps longer. Score 89. K

1848 WINERY, RESERVE, 2007: Dark, almost impenetrable garnet, a full-bodied blend of 87% Cabernet Sauvignon, 10% Merlot and 3% Petite Sirah, each component aged in oak for 12 months before the final blend was made and then returned to oak for an additional 3 months. A distinctly black-fruit nose, that surprising somewhat because the aromas and flavors are primarily of red fruits – raspberries, red currants and cherries that make themselves felt nicely through the oak, tannins and acidity. Somewhat tight when first poured but opens very nicely in the glass. Finishes long and generous with an appealing note of roasted herbs. Drink now–2015. Score 90. K

1848 WINERY, CHARDONNAY, 2010: Light gold in color, medium-bodied, not having undergone malolactic fermentation to keep its crispness intact. Good acidity here to complement aromas and flavors of grapefruit, tangerines and green apples, those on a mineral-rich and spicy background. Bright and fresh, with fine balance that leads to a long mouth-filling finish. Drink now. Score 88. K

Afterword

A Guide to Tasting Wines

Wine tasting is not a complex or difficult task. All that is required is the use of one's senses of sight, smell and taste. Before setting out to taste wines, try to eliminate as many distractions as possible. During the actual tasting, for example, extraneous aromas (e.g., food, perfume and aftershave lotion) should be avoided as they interfere with the ability to appreciate the aromas and bouquet of the wine. Also, during a tasting, try as hard as possible to ignore the comments by others in order not to be influenced by their opinions. Be sure to use high-quality glasses (ideally of thin crystal) as this enhances the flavors and aromas of wines. A separate glass should be provided for each wine, this allowing the taster to return to earlier tasted wines in order to make comparisons. The glasses should be, of course, perfectly clean, without any aroma of soap or detergent. Glasses should be filled to no more than 20% of their capacity as this will give ample room for swirling the wine, that process serving to aerate and release the more subtle aromas and flavors of the wine being tasted.

Basic Rules for Tasting Wines

Professionals can sample fifty or more wines at a single sitting, but it is widely agreed that in a private tasting, alone at home or at a friendly gathering, the number of wines for tasting should not exceed eight.

White wines should be tasted before reds, and within each group wines that are light in body should be tasted before fuller-bodied wines. When tasting wines of the same variety, such as Cabernet Sauvignon or Merlot, always start with the youngest wines and end with the most mature.

Wines should be served at their proper temperatures. Young reds should be opened about fifteen or twenty minutes before the tasting, and more mature reds about half an hour before they are poured.

You can either place the bottles on the table with the labels exposed or place each bottle in a paper bag, each bag identified only by a number, for a blind tasting. I prefer blind tastings, for the power of suggestion is strong and it is difficult to be entirely objective vis-à-vis a label of a prestigious Chateau.

Wines should be arranged on the table in the order they are to be tasted. I suggest using a felt-tipped pen to put a number on each bottle and then to mark the correspond-ing number on the base of each glass in order to avoid any confusion.

Professional wine tasters spit the wine in order to avoid intoxication, but there is no need to spit at a home tasting where much of the pleasure comes from drinking the wine. For those who choose to spit, prepare adequate receptacles (clay jugs, low vases and Champagne buckets are ideal).

Allow half a bottle per person. That is to say, for eight people you will need four bottles. When pouring during the tasting, remember that the average sampling should be small enough to allow room for swirling the wine in the glass. Whatever wines are left over after the actual tasting can be served with the meal or snacks afterward.

Use a tasting form, such as that on the inside of the dust jacket of this book, or record your impressions on a piece of paper. Making notes helps people make up their minds before they commit themselves.

Food should be served after a wine tasting and never before or during because food changes the taste of wine. If you must have something on the table, use unsalted and sugar-free white bread.

Wine Appreciation

1. VISUAL APPEARANCE

In order to best see the color and clarity of a wine, hold your glass against a white background (a white tablecloth or even a blank sheet of white paper will do) and tilt the glass away from yourself slightly so that the exposed surface is larger. Red wines can be anywhere from bright cherry-red in color to dark and opaque, in fact almost black. Although most white wines will have a light golden-straw color, they can range from almost colorless to deep golden, and rosé or blush wines are only rarely true pink and can vary from purple-pink to orange or even bright ruby-red. Whatever the color, the wine should be perfectly clear. Wines that have thrown a sediment will become clear as the sediment settles.

Consider whether the color is deep or pale and whether it is vivid and youthful or browning and perhaps showing age. While the glass is tilted look as well at the rim (that point where the wine meets the glass), for it is not generally a positive sign if the color at the rim fades to an almost watery consistency. After noting the qualities of the color, swirl the wine in the glass gently and then hold it up to see the legs or tears – these are the threads of wine that appear and linger on the inside of the glass. These are an accurate indicator of the alcohol level in the wine; the broader and more viscous the legs, the greater the alcohol content and, according to many, a good indicator of the wine's ability to age. At the same time, note whether the wine is *frizzante*, that is to say, whether it has tiny little bubbles in it. Although this is acceptable in some white wines (e.g., Muscadet de Sevres et Maine Sur Lie, Vinho Verde, Moscato d'Asti), and occurs in many white wines when they have been overly chilled, such bubbles indicate a fault in nearly all red wines. When evaluating Champagnes or other sparkling wines, the bubbles should be sharp, small and long lasting, rising from a central point in the glass.

A hint: Never taste wines under fluorescent light as this makes all red wines appear brown.

2. SMELL

It surprises many to realize that people with a normal sense of smell can identify more than 1,000 different aromas. That should not be daunting, however, as the process of identifying aromas is a largely automatic one, and, although we may sometimes "struggle" to distinguish between the aroma of a blackberry or raspberry, our associations with aromas are quite strong. In order to best evaluate and appreciate the aromas of a wine, swirl the glass rapidly for a few seconds, place your nose well into the glass and inhale deeply through your nostrils.

One of the first sensations to be evaluated is the alcohol content of the wine. If the wine appears to be highly alcoholic, ask yourself whether it is a fortified wine (e.g. Sherry, Port, Madeira) or whether the strong alcoholic aromas reflect a fault. After that, consider whether the wine smells as youthful or as mature as it appears to the eye, whether the aromas are smooth and harmonious, whether they are distinctive, bland or reticent, and whether they are simple or complex. Consider as well whether there is a creamy, spicy or vanilla note to the aromas as this may give a hint about whether the wine was aged in oak. Also consider whether the wine has any "off" aromas that may indicate a fault. With a bit of practice it becomes possible for many to identify from aroma alone the variety of the grape used and even the region in which the wine was made.

A hint: A slight musky aroma can add great charm, but when exaggerated almost always reveals a fault in the wine.

3. TASTE

When actually setting out to taste the wine, take a good mouthful, close the lips firmly and swirl the wine vigorously in order to coat the entire mouth. This is important because different taste sensations are perceived by different parts of the mouth (sweetness on the tip of the tongue, sourness on the sides, bitterness on the back and the roof of the mouth, saltiness on the front and sides of the tongue). Some tasters also draw a bit of air into the mouth, believing this will accentuate the flavors.

The first thing to be noted is whether the flavors are in accord with the aromas of the wines. Then, with the wine lingering in the mouth, identify the various taste sensations imparted. Ask yourself: Are the flavors pronounced and easily identifiable or somewhat confused; is the wine clean or muddy; are the tannins, acidity, wood and fruits in balance; are the tannins and wood in good proportion to the fruits; is the level of sweetness appropriate for the wine?

Keep in mind that the major goal of tasting is not only to evaluate a wine but to determine whether it is to your taste. Wine tasting is not a guessing game but with increased practice and repeated tastings, many come to the point where they can identify and discuss the grape variety, area of origin and age and quality of the wines they are tasting.

A hint: A wine dominated by a single flavor is one-dimensional and thus lacking excitement.

Among the fruit aromas and flavors to be sought in white wines: citrus (especially lemon, grapefruit, lime and citrus peel), apple, melon, pear, peach, apricot, grapes, figs and, especially in sweet dessert wines, dried fruits. Also in white wines look for hints of grassiness, herbaceousness, honey and a creamy sensation. Fruits to be found in red wines include, among others, black and red currants (sometimes referred to as cassis), plums and a variety of berries. Other taste sensations that may be imparted by red wines are chocolate, coffee and tobacco. In both reds and whites look for aromas and flavors imparted by oak-aging, those including spicy or smoky oak, sweet cedar, asphalt and vanilla. Be aware that some of the aromas and flavors traditionally found in a red may appear in a white and vice versa.

TASTING FORMS

Because few of us have perfect memories, one of the very best aids in tasting wines is to use an organized sheet for keeping notes. Such sheets, used by professional wine tasters as well as amateurs, help to organize our thoughts and to leave a permanent record for future reference with which to compare the same wine or similar wines. The act of writing our reactions down also serves to implant our thoughts in long-term memory.

The tasting form that appears on the inside of the dust jacket of this book is meant for those purposes. Readers may feel free to reproduce this form for their own use or for the use of friends, and should the original be lost, a download-able and printable copy can be found at: www.tobypress.com/rogov/tasting.pdf

Elegance and the Spittoon

The question of spitting at wine tastings is one that haunts both professionals and amateurs. Let's start off with one given – spitting is never and can never be elegant, but if you are going to be tasting more wine than you would normally drink, it is a way of maintaining one's sanity, sobriety and dignity. For professionals who sometimes taste 40, 50 or even 100 wines at a sitting, it is also a way of assuring that their livers, kidneys and brains will continue to function with some sense of normalcy until they reach a ripe old age. There are several ways in which you can maintain, if not elegance, at least a sense of dignity while spitting:

1. Those just learning to spit will do well to practice at home before trying it in public. Perhaps the best way to practice is to start with wine glasses filled first with water, then with white wine and only after that with red wine. In this way you can become comfortable with the idea, learn how to spit without dribbling on your clothing and how to spit with just the right amount of force to clear the lips and chin but without so much force that the liquid will spatter back at you.

2. Despite a great many jokes, there is no saving grace whatsoever in being able to spit long distances, even if one does it with great accuracy. That kind of behavior is simply vulgar and is in place primarily with fresh-men and sophomores in college fraternity or sorority houses or in old Western movies for those heroes or villains who spit tobacco juice.

3. It is safe to generalize that there are three kinds of spit-ting vessels – large buckets (sometimes Champagne buckets) that are shared by three, four or even five people; smaller vessels, sometimes of metal, some-times of plastic and sometimes of clay, that are shared

by two or three people; and individual spitting buckets, generally of stainless steel and plastic. When using shared buckets, never linger too long over the bucket because this will prevent others from reaching it when they need it. Also, with large buckets be careful not to spit with too much force for these tend to splatter rather badly. With individual buckets, many (including myself) prefer to move them fairly close to (but not in contact with) the lips in order to allow for discrete spitting

3a. Some spitting buckets come to the table with sawdust or wood shavings in the bottom. This is done in order to avoiding the liquid splashing out. Of course as the bucket fills, those shavings are of little help

3b. If you are going to a tasting and are not sure that spittoons will be provided, bring your own. Many wine accessory shops sell small, attractively designed personal spittoons and these are a good investment. If during the tasting your small spittoon becomes too full, simply go to the kitchen or the washroom there to clean and refresh it.

4. Be sure to have either a handkerchief or paper napkins on hand for dabbing the lips and when necessary to gently dab off the few drops that may make their way to the chin. My own habit is to take at least two perfectly clean handkerchiefs and quite a few paper napkins with me to tastings.

5. If your spitting vessel becomes too full, either from spitting or from rinsing glasses in between tastings, ask that it be refreshed or that a new one be brought to you. Your request will be seen as a sign of intelligent behavior.

6. If you encounter a situation where reaching the spitting bucket is difficult, spit gently into the water glass that has been provided for you and from time to time simply dump that into the larger bucket.

7. Keep in mind that no-one is a "perfect spitter" and a bit of dribbling happens to everyone from time to time.

When this does happen, or if you happen to drop a bit of wine on your clothing, do not make a public issue of it. With white wine simply dab it dry with a clean handkerchief or napkin; with red, simply sprinkle the stain with salt and rub the salt in gently, as that will probably allow the stain to come out easily in the next laundry. Another possibility is to carry a few small "wet napkins" with you. Those are remarkably effective at removing red wine stains. There is no need to apologize or to declare aloud how clumsy you are. The probability is that no one noticed anyhow and if they did they really don't care for they know full well it happens to them as well.

8. If there is a television crew nearby, let them photograph you while spitting only if you have a passion for making a fool of yourself in public. Believe me, you will not enjoy seeing yourself that way. If the crew insists on photographing, simply turn your back to the camera as you spit.

    There is probably no professional who has not encountered questions dealing with what happens when the wines we are tasting are "so great that it is a sin to spit them." Not that long ago, for example, I attended a tasting of the wines of the Domaine de la Romanee-Conti in which all but two of the wines received scores of 95 or higher! Simple enough – if tasting more wine than you would normally drink, spit regardless of the quality of the wine. As you do that you pray to whatever God or gods in whom you may believe that there will be at least some of the one you enjoyed the most left over at the end of the tasting.

Several Words about Scores

A great many people walk into wine stores and order this or that wine entirely on the basis of its high score. This is a mistake. A Score is nothing more than a critic's attempt to sum up in digits the overall quality of a wine. Scores can provide a valid tool, especially when awarded by experienced critics, but they should not be separated from the tasting notes that precede them; for although a Score may be a convenient summary, it says nothing about the style, personality or other important traits of the wine in question and therefore cannot give the consumer a valid basis for choice.

There are, however, three major advantages to scores. First of all, scores can serve as initial guides for the overall impression of the wine in question. Second, scores also give an immediate basis for comparison of that wine to others in its category and to the same wine of the same winery from earlier years. Finally, such scores give valuable hints as to whether the wine in question is available at a reasonable value for one's money.

The scores awarded in this book should be taken as merely one part of the overall evaluation of the wine, the most important parts of which are the tasting notes that give details about the body, color, aromas, flavors, length and overall style of the wine. It is also important to keep in mind that scores are not absolute. The Score earned by a light and hyper-fruity wine made from Gamay grapes, a wine meant to be consumed in its youth, cannot be compared to that given to a deep, full-bodied wine made from a blend of Cabernet Sauvignon, Merlot and Cabernet Franc, the peak of drinking for which may come only five, ten or even thirty years later on. Numerical comparisons between the wines of the great Chateaux of Bordeaux and those meant to be consumed within weeks or months of the harvest is akin to comparing, by means of a single number, the qualities of a 1998 Rolls Royce and a 1965 Volkswagen Beetle.

Even if there was a perfect system for rating wines (and I do not believe such a system exists), no two critics, no matter how professional or well intentioned they may be, can be expected to use precisely the same criteria for every facet of every wine they evaluate. Even when similar scoring systems are used by different critics, readers should expect to find a certain variation between them. The trick is not in finding the critics with whom you always agree, but those whose tasting notes and scores give you direction in finding the wines that you most enjoy.

My own scoring system is based on a maximum of 100 points, interpreted as follows:

95–100	Truly Great Wines, My Highest Recommendation
90–94	Exceptional in Every Way, Highly Recommended
85–89	Good to Very Good and Recommended
80–84	Average and Not Exciting, Recommended Primarily as Entry-Level Wines
75–79	Mediocre and At Least Somewhat Faulted, Not Recommended
70–74	Drinkable But with a Major Fault and Not Recommended
Under 70	Seriously Faulted and Most Definitely Not Recommended

Glossary of Wine Terminology

ACIDIC: A wine whose level of acidity is so high that it imparts a sharp feel or sour taste in the mouth.

ACIDITY: An important component of wine. A modicum of acidity adds liveliness to wine, too little makes it flat and dull, and too much imparts a sour taste. The acids most often present in wines are tartaric, malic and lactic acids.

AFTERTASTE: The flavors and aromas left in the mouth after the wine has been swallowed.

AGGRESSIVE: Refers to the strong, assertive character of a young and powerful wine. Aggressive wines are too high in acidity, have harsh tannins, or both, and often lack charm and grace.

ALCOHOL CONTENT: Percent by volume of alcohol in a wine. Table wines usually have between 11.5–13.5% in alcohol content but there is an increasing demand for wines as high as 15–16%.

ALCOHOLIC: A negative term, referring to wines that have too much alcohol and are thus hot and out of balance.

AROMA: Technically, this term applies to the smells that come directly from the grapes, whereas bouquet applies to the smells that come from the winemaking process. In practice, the two terms are used interchangeably.

ASTRINGENT: A puckering sensation imparted to the wine by its tannins. At a moderate level, astringency is a positive trait. When a wine is too astringent it is unpleasant.

ATTACK: The first sensations imparted by a wine.

ATYPICAL: A wine that does not conform to its traditional character or style.

AUSTERE: A wine that lacks fruits or is overly tannic or acidic.

BACKWARD: Describes a wine that is not yet ready to drink, or a wine that has not yet developed its maximum potential.

BALANCED: The term used to describe a wine in which the acids, alcohol, fruits, tannins and influence of the wood in which the wine was aged are in harmony.

BARNYARD: Aromas and flavors that call to mind the barnyard, and when present in excess impart dirty sensations, but when in moderation can be pleasant.

BARREL: The wood containers used to ferment and hold wine. The wood used in such barrels is most often French or American oak but other woods can be used as well.

BARREL AGING: The process in which wines mature in barrels after fermentation.

BARRIQUE: French for "barrel" but specifically referring to oak barrels of 225 liter capacity, in which many wines are fermented and/or aged.

BIG: A term used to describe a wine that is powerful in flavor, body or alcohol.

BLANC DE BLANCS: White wines made entirely from white grapes.

BLANC DE NOIRS: White wines made from grapes usually associated with red wines.

BLEND: A wine made from more than one grape variety or from grapes from different vintages. Some of the best wines in the world, including most of the Bordeaux wines, are blends of different grapes selected to complement each other.

BLUSH WINE: A wine that has a pale pink color imparted by very short contact with the skins of red grapes.

BODY: The impression of weight or fullness on the palate. Results from a combination of fruits, alcohol and glycerin. Wines range from light- to full-bodied.

BOTRYTIS CINEREA: Sometimes known as "noble rot," this is one of the few fungi that is welcomed by winemakers, for as it attacks the grapes it shrivels them, drains the water and concentrates the sugar, thus allowing for the making of many of the world's greatest sweet wines.

BOTTLE AGING: The process of allowing wine to mature in its bottle.

BOUQUET: Technically, the aromas that result from the winemaking process, but the term is used interchangeably with aroma.

BRETTANOMYCES: Often referred to simply as Brett, a side effect of yeast that causes a metallic or wet-fur note to develop in a wine. In small amounts Brett can add charm, but in large amounts it is a serious fault.

BRILLIANT: A wine whose color is clear and has no cloudiness.

BROWNING: When a red wine starts to develop a brown edge or a brownish color. Such wines are generally fully mature and will almost surely not improve.

BRUT: Bone dry. A term used almost exclusively to describe sparkling wines.

BURGUNDY BARRELS: The major differences in size between Bordeaux barrels, generally called barriques, and the Burgundy-style barrel are that the head of the barrique measures 54.6 cm (21.5″) and that of the Burgundy barrel 58.4 cm (23″), and the barrique holds 225 liters while the Burgundy barrel holds 228 liters. As is well known, however, size itself does not matter. Because of the difference in interior surface dimensions, the Burgundy-style barrel can have a less dramatic and profound impact on the wine, some feeling that this gives even Bordeaux-style blends a softer, rounder palate-feel.

BUTTERY: A positive term for rich white wines, especially those that have undergone malolactic fermentation.

CARAMELIZED: A wine that has taken on a brown color, and sweet and sour aromas and flavors, often due to exposure to oxygen as the wine ages.

CARBONIC MACERATION: Method of fermenting red wine without crushing the grapes first. Whole clusters of grapes are put in a closed vat together with carbon dioxide, and the fermentation takes place within the grape berries, which then burst.

CHARACTER: Balance, assertiveness, finesse and other positive qualities combine to create character. The term is used only in the positive sense. Charmat Method: The production of sparkling wine with secondary fermentation in stainless steel tanks (as opposed to the *Methode Champenoise* in which secondary fermentation takes place in the bottles)

CHEWY: Descriptive of the texture, body and intensity of a good red wine. A chewy wine will be mouth-filling and complex.

CLONE: A vine derived by vegetative propagation from cuttings, or buds from a single vine called the mother vine.

CLOSED: A wine that is not showing its potential and is holding back on its flavors and aromas.

CLOYING: A wine that has sticky, heavy or unclean aromas or flavors.

COARSE: A wine that is rough or overly alcoholic. Appropriate in some country-style wines but not in fine wines.

CONCENTRATED: Wines with intense flavors, depth and richness. Synonymous with deep.

CORKED: A wine that has been tainted by TCA (2, 4, 6–Trichloroanisole), increasingly caused by faulty corks. TCA imparts aromas of damp, moldy and decomposing cardboard to a wine. Sometimes only barely detectable, at other times making a wine unapproachable.

COUNTRY-STYLE/RUSTIC: A simple wine that is somewhat coarse but not necessarily unpleasant.

CREAMY: A soft, silky texture.

CRISP: A clean wine with good acidity.

CUVÉE: A wine selected by a winemaker as special, and separated out for bottling under a special label.

DELICATE: Wines that are valued for their lightness and subtlety.

DENSE: Full in flavor and body.

DEPTH: Refers to complexity and intensity of flavor.

DESSERT WINE: A sweet wine. Often served as an accompaniment to goose liver dishes at the start of a meal.

DIRTY: A wine typified by off aromas or flavors resulting from either poor vinification practices or a faulty bottling process.

DRINKING WINDOW: The predicted period during which a wine will be at its best.

DRY: The absence of sugar or sweetness.

DUMB: A wine that has gone into a dumb period is one that has closed down and is holding back on its aromas and flavors. A natural process in many red wines 12–18 months after bottling.

EARTHY: Clean sensations of freshly turned soil, minerals, damp leaves and mushrooms. Can be a very positive trait.

ELEGANT: A wine showing finesse or style.

EVERYDAY WINES: Inexpensive, readily available and easy-to-drink wines, lacking sophistication, but at their best pleasant accompaniments to food.

FAT: A full-bodied wine that is high in alcohol or glycerin but in which the flavor overshadows the acidity, giving it a heavy, sweetish sensation. A negative term.

FERMENTATION: A process by which yeast reacts with sugar in the must, resulting in the creation of alcohol.

FILTRATION: Usually done just prior to bottling, the process of filtering of the wine in order to remove large particles of sediment and other impurities. Over-filtration tends to rob wines of their aromas and flavors.

FINESSE: Showing great harmony. Among the best qualities of a good wine.

FINISH: The aromas and flavors that linger on the palate after the wine has been swallowed.

FIRMNESS: The grip of a wine, determined by its tannins and acidity.

FLABBY: The opposite of crisp, often a trait of wines that lack acidity and are thus dull and weak.

FLAT: Synonymous with flabby.

FLINTY: A slightly metallic taste, sometimes found in white wines such as Chardonnays. A positive quality.

FORTIFIED WINE: A wine whose alcoholic strength has been intensified by the addition of spirits.

FORWARD: Can be used in three ways – wines that border on being flamboyant; wines that have matured quickly; or wines that are delicious and well developed.

FRIZZANTE: Lightly sparkling.

GARAGISTE: The smallest of wineries, sometimes located in one's garage. Generally produces under 5,000 bottles annually.

GARRIGUE: A wine that hints of scrub brush, Provençal herbs and light earthy notes. A positive term.

GRASSY: A term often used to describe white wines made from Sauvignon Blanc and Gewurztraminer grapes.

GREEN: In the positive sense, wines that are tart and youthful but have the potential to develop. In the negative sense, a wine that is unripe and sour.

HARD: A sense of austerity usually found in young, tannic red wines before they mellow and develop with age.

HARSH: Always a negative term, even more derogatory than "coarse."

HERBACEOUS: Implies aromas and flavors of grass, hay, herbs, leather and tobacco.

HOT: The unpleasant, sometimes burning sensation left on the palate by an overly alcoholic wine.

ICE WINE: From the German *eiswein*, a dessert wine made by a special method in which the grapes are left on the vine until frozen and then pressed while still frozen. Only the water in the grape freezes and this can be removed, leaving the must concentrated and very sweet. In warm weather areas the freezing process may be done in the winery.

INTENSE: A strong, concentrated flavor and aroma.

INTERNATIONALIZED WINES: Reds or whites that are blended to please any palate. At their best such wines are pleasant, at their worst simply boring.

LATE HARVEST: In such a harvest, grapes are left on the vines until very late in the harvest season, the purpose being to obtain sweeter grapes that will be used to make dessert wines.

LEES: Sediments that accumulate in the bottom of the barrel or vat as a wine ferments.

LEGS: The "tears" or stream of wine that clings to a glass after the wine has been swirled.

LENGTH: The period of time in which the flavors and aromas of a wine linger after it has been swallowed.

LIGHT: Low in alcohol or body. Also used to describe a wine low in flavor.

LIVELY: Clean and refreshing.

LONG: A wine that offers aromas and flavors that linger for a long time after it has been swallowed.

LONGEVITY: The aging potential of a wine, dependent on balance and structure.

MALOLACTIC FERMENTATION: A second fermentation that can occur naturally or be induced, the purpose of which is to convert harsh malic acid to softer lactic acid.

MATURE: A wine that has reached its peak after developing in the bottle.

MELLOW: A wine that is at or very close to its peak.

METHODE CHAMPENOISE: The classic method for making Champagne by inducing a second fermentation in the bottle.

MID-PALATE: Those aroma and taste sensations felt after the first attack.

MOUSSE: The foam and bubbles of sparkling wines. A good mousse will show long-lasting foam and sharp, small, concentrated bubbles.

MOUTH-FILLING: A rich, concentrated wine that fills the mouth with satisfying flavors.

MUST: The pre-fermentation mixture of grape juice, stem fragments, skins, seeds and pulp, that results from the grape-crushing process.

NOSE: Synonymous with bouquet.

NOUVEAU: Term that originated in Beaujolais to describe very young, fruity and light red wines, often made from Gamay grapes and by the method of carbonic maceration. Such wines are always meant to be consumed very young.

N.V.: A non-vintage wine; a term most often used for sparkling wines or blends of grapes of different vintage years.

OAK: The wood most often used to make the barrels in which wines are fermented or aged. The impact of such barrels is reflected in the level of tannins and in its contribution to flavors of smoke, spices and vanilla to the wines.

OAKED: A wine that has been fermented and/or aged in oak barrels.

OFF: A wine that is spoiled or flawed.

OXIDIZED: A wine that has gone off because it has been exposed to oxygen or to high temperatures.

PEAK: The optimal point of maturity of a given wine.

PERSONALITY: The overall impression made by an individual wine.

RESIDUAL SUGAR: The sugar that remains in a wine after fermentation has been completed.

RICH: A wine with full flavors and aromas.

RIPASSO: A second fermentation that is induced on the lees of a wine made earlier.

ROBUST: Assertive, full-bodied and characteristic of good red wines at a young age, or country-style wines that are pleasingly coarse.

ROTTEN EGGS: Describes the smell of hydrogen sulfide (H_2S). Always an undesirable trait.

ROUND: A wine that has become smooth as its tannins, acids and wood have integrated.

RUSTIC: Synonymous with country-style.

SHARP: Overly acidic.

SHORT: A wine whose aromas and flavors fail to linger or to make an impression after the wine has been swallowed.

SILKY: Synonymous for lush or velvety. Silky wines are never hard or angular on the palate.

SIMPLE: A wine that has no nuances or complexity.

SMOKY: A flavor imparted to a wine from oak casks, most often found in unfiltered wines.

SMOOTH: A wine that sits comfortably on the palate.

SOFT: A wine that is round and fruity, relatively low in acidity and is not aggressive.

SPICY: A wine that imparts a light peppery sensation.

STALE: A wine that has lost its freshness, liveliness or fruitiness.

STEWED: The sensation of cooked, overripe or soggy fruit.

STINGY: A wine that holds back on its aromas or flavors.

SULFITES: Usually sulfur dioxide that is added to wine to prevent oxidation.

SUR LIE: French for "on the lees." A term used to describe the process in which a wine is left in contact with its lees during fermentation and barrel aging.

TANNIC: A wine still marked by firm tannins. In their youth, many red wines tend to be tannic and need time for the tannins to integrate.

TANNINS: Phenolic substances that exist naturally in wines and are extracted from the skins, pips and stalks of the grapes, as well as from development in new oak barrels. Tannins are vital for the longevity of red wines. In young wines, tannins can sometimes be harsh, but if the wine is well balanced they will blend with other substances in the wine over time, making the wine smoother and more approachable as it ages.

TASTED FROM COMPONENTS: A barrel tasting done before the final blend was made.

TCA: 2, 4, 6–Trichloroanisole. See "corked."

TERROIR: The reflection of a vineyard's soil, altitude, microclimate, prevailing winds, and other natural factors that impact on the quality of the grapes, and consequently on the wines produced from them.

THIN: Lacking in body or fruit.

TOASTING: Searing the inside of barrels with an open flame when making the barrels. Heavy toasting can impart caramel-like flavors to a wine; medium toasting and light toasting can add vanilla, spices or smokiness to the wine, all positive attributes when present in moderation.

VANILLA: Aroma and flavor imparted to wines from the oak barrels in which they age.

VARIETAL TRAITS: The specific colors, aromas and flavors traditionally imparted by a specific grape variety.

VARIETAL WINE: A wine that contains at least 85% of the grape named on the label.

VEGETAL: An often-positive term used for a bouquet of rounded wines, in particular those made from Pinot Noir and Chardonnay grapes, whose aromas and flavors often call to mind vegetables rather than fruits.

VINTAGE: (a) Synonymous with harvest; (b) A wine made from grapes of a single harvest. In accordance with EU standards, a vintage wine must contain at least 85% grapes from the noted year.

VOLATILE ACIDITY: Acetic acid in a wine. Most often a by-product of fermentation, this is a serious fault in a wine, giving it a vinegar-like aroma and flavor.

WATERY: A wine so thin that it feels diluted.

WOOD: Refers either to the wood barrels in which the wine ages or to a specific aroma and flavor imparted by the barrels.

YEAST: A kind of fungus, vital to the process of fermentation.

Contacting the Wineries

Abaya Winery
Kfar Clil 235233
Tel: 052 7282977
yossiyodfat@gmail.com
www.abayawinery.com

Achziv Winery
Rehov Rokach 5/11A
Kiryat Motzkin 26376
Tel: 050 7713687   Fax: 04 8772112
gmark5@bezeqint.net
www.guberman.net

Adir Winery
Moshav Kerem Ben Zimra 13815
Tel: 04 6991039 Fax: 04 6991045
avir@adir-winery.co.il

Agmon Winery
Tel: 050 8866268
yekevagmon@gmail.com
www.yekevagmon.co.il

Agur Winery
Moshav Agur 99840
Tel/Fax: 02 9910483
shukiya@017.net.il
www.agurwines.com

Alexander Winery
POB 8151
Moshav Beit Yitzhak 42970
Tel: 09 8822956   Fax: 09 8872076
 yoram@alexander-winery.com
www.alexander-winery.com

Aligote Winery
Moshav Gan Yoshiya 38850
Tel/Fax: 04 6258492
aligote@aviv-flowers.co.il
www.aligote.co.il

Alon Wineries
Moshav Alonei Aba 36005
Tel: 04 9535251 Fax: 04 9800727
alonwinery@walla.co.il

Alona Winery
Moshav Givat Nili 37825
Tel: 052 2425657
ap_azoulay@hotmail.com

Amphorae Vineyard
Makura Ranch
POB 133
Zichron Ya'akov
Tel: 04 9840702 Fax: 04 6540756
info@amphorae-v.com
www.amphorae-v.com

Amram's Winery
Moshav Ramot Naftaly 13830
Tel/Fax: 04 6940039
amramswine@gmail.com
www.amramwinery.com

Anatot Winery
POB 3390
Givat Ze'ev 90917
Tel: 02 5860187 Fax: 02 5362565
 info@anatotwinery.co.il
www.anatotwinery.co.il

Aneva Winery
Tel: 052 3902611
aneva.winery@gmail.com

Argov Winery
Tel: 054 6689905
amir@argovwinery.com
www.argovwinery.com

Arza Winery
POB 91181
Jerusalem
Tel: 02 5351442   Fax: 02 5352128
eshor@arza.biz

Asif Winery
8 Sadan St.
Artists Quarter, Arad
Tel: 052 5931100   Fax: 08 6326322
oryah@zahav.net.il
www.asifwinery.co.il

Assaf Winery
Moshav Kidmat Tzvi 12421
Tel/Fax: 04 6820292
assaf@assafwinery.com
www.assafwinery.com

Avidan Winery
Kibbutz Eyal 45840
Tel: 09 7719382   Fax: 09 7712679
avidanwine@walla.com
www.avidanwinery.com

Bar Winery
22 Ha'avoda St.
Binyamina 30500
Tel: 04 9806504
alanbar@zahav.net.il

Baram Winery
Kibbutz Baram 13860
Tel: 052 8313208
baram.winery@gmail.com

Bar Giora Winery
Tel: 052 3822221
s_avitan@walla.com

Barkai Vineyards
Moshav Neve Michael 99865
Tel/Fax: 02 9993281
barkaimi@bezeqint.net

Barkan Wine Cellars
POB 146
Kibbutz Hulda 76842
Tel: 08 9355858 Fax: 08 9355859
winery@barkan-winery.co.il
www.barkan-winery.co.il

Bashan Winery
Moshav Avnei Eitan
Golan Heights 12925
Tel: 054 8238880 Fax: 04 6764418
bashanwinery@013.net

Bazelet Hagolan Winery
POB 77
Moshav Kidmat Tzvi 12421
Tel: 04 6965010 Fax: 04 6965020
bazelet@netvision.net.il
www.bazelet-hagolan.co.il

Beit-El Winery
Beit-El 90628
Tel/Fax: 02 9971158
hmanne@netvision.net.il

Benhaim Winery
Sderot Ben Zvi 34
Ramat-Gan 52247
Tel: 03 6762656 Fax: 03 5741089
benhaim@benhaim.co.il
www.benhaim.co.il

Ben Hanna Winery
Moshav Gefen 99820
Tel: 052 5434253
shlomi@ben-hanna.com
www.ben-hanna.com

Ben-Shoshan Winery
Kibbutz Bror-Hail 79152
Tel: 054 6744161   Fax: 08 6203201
yuval_b@brorhail.orgil

Ben-Zimra Winery
Moshav Kerem Ben-Zimra 13815
Tel/Fax: 04 6980056
ashk_y@netvision.net.il
www.yekev-benzimra.com

Binyamina Wine Cellars
POB 34
Binyamina 30550
Tel: 04 6388643   Fax: 04 6389021
info@binyaminawines.co.il
www.binyaminawines.com

Birya Winery
Birya 13805
Tel/Fax: 04 6923815
drporat@zahav.net.il

Bustan Winery
POB 55
Moshav Sharei Tikva 44860
Tel: 054 4892757
bustanwinery@yahoo.com

Bustan Hameshusheem Winery
Moshav Had Ness 12950
Tel: 052 4358407

Carmel Winery
Rishon Letzion
Tel: 03 9488888
Zichron Ya'akov
Tel: 04 6390105
www.carmelwines.co.il

Carmey Avdat Winery
Midreshet Ben Gurion 84990
Tel: 08 6535177 Fax: 08 6535188
Carmey-avdat@bezeqint.net
www.carmey-avdat.co.il

The Cave
POB 34
Binyamina 30550
Tel: 04 6388643 Fax: 04 6389021
thecave@zahav.net.il

Chateau Golan Winery
Moshav Eliad 12927
Tel: 04 6600026 Fax: 04 6600274
winery@chateaugolan.com
www.chateaugolan.com

Chemla Winery
29 Topaz St.
Shoam
Tel: 052 6093802
chemla_wine@yahoo.com
www.chemla-wine.com

Chillag Winery
12 Shabazi St.
Yehud 56231
Tel: 03 62032290 Fax: 03 6325473
chillag@netvision.net.il
www.chillagwinery.com

Chotem HaCarmel Winery
Tel: 052 7398087
hotemhacarmel@gmail.com

Clos de Gat
Kibbutz Har'el 99740
Tel: 02 9993505 Fax: 02 9993350
harelca@netvision.net.il
www.closdegat.com

Dadah Winery
Havat Makura
Tel: 04 6262112
www.dadah.co.il
dadahwinery@gmail.com

Dalton Winery
Dalton Industrial Park
Merom Hagalil 13815
Tel: 04 6987683 Fax: 04 6987684
info@dalton-winery.com
www.dalton-winery.com

Domaine de Latroun
Latroun Monastery 99762
Tel: 08 9220065

Domaine du Castel
Moshav Ramat Raziel 90974
Tel: 02 5342249 Fax: 02 5700995
castel@castel.co.il
www.castel.co.il

Domaine Herzberg
Hagafen 1
Sitrya 76834
Tel: 08 9410647 Fax: 08 9400647
max@herzbergwine.com
www.herzbergwine.com

Domaine Netofa
Mitzpe Netofa 15295
Tel: 052 4313706
netofa@gmail.com

Domaine Ventura
Industrial Area
Efrat 90627
Tel/Fax: 02 9979094
dventura@013.net
www.domaineventura.com

Dror Winery
Kfar Shamai 55
Tel: 054 2129932
drorwinery@gmail.com
www.drorwines.co.il

Ein Nashut Winery
Moshav Kidmat Tzvi
Tel: 052 27991457
www.bellofri.co.il

Ein Teina Winery
Moshav Givat Yoav 12946
Tel: 050 8217554 Fax: 02 6920414
Yotam76@yahoo.com
www.ein-teina.com

Ella Valley Vineyards
Kibbutz Netiv Halamed Hey 99855
Tel: 02 9994885 Fax: 02 9994876
ella@ellavalley.com
www.ellavalley.com

Erez Winery
Rechalim 44830
Tel: 02 9409026 Fax: 02 9400402
yekev-erez@barak.net.il

Erle Family Winery
Moshav Givat Nili
www.erlefamilywinery.com

Essence Winery
Ma'aleh Tsvia 20129
Tel: 04 6619058 Fax: 04 6619054
essencewines@zvia.org.il

Eyal Winery
Moshav Givat Nili
Tel: 057 7744135
eyalwinery@gmail.com

Flam Winery
Dvorah Baron 3/4
Rishon Letzion 75285
Tel: 02 9929923 Fax: 02 9929926
info@flamwinery.com

Flegmann Wines
robertofl@juno.com
Tel: 001-516-695-1953

Gad Winery
Moshav Sdot Micha 99810
Tel: 050 5601886
ohad1478@walla.com

Galai Winery
Moshav Nir Akiva 85365
Tel: 08 9933713 Fax: 08 9933622
info@galai-winery.co.il
www. galai-winery.com

Galil Mountain Winery
Kibbutz Yiron 13855
Tel: 04 6868740 Fax: 04 6868506
winery@galilmountain.co.il
www.galilmountain.co.il

Gat Shomron Winery
Karnei Shomron 44855
Tel: 052 4643810
sharonaa@zahav.net.il

Gesher Damia Winery
2 Hatavor St.
Pardes Hannah-Karkur 37011
Tel/Fax: 04 6377451
damiya@walla.co.il

Ginaton Winery
Moshav Ginaton 73110
Tel/Fax: 08 9254841
ginaton1999@walla.co.il

Givon Winery
POB 140
Givon Hachadasha 90901
Tel: 02 5362966
info@givonwine.com
www.givonwine.com

Gizo Winery
Moshav Gizo
Tel: 052-5342228
yoavalongizo@gmail.com

Golan Heights Winery
POB 183
Katzrin 12900
Tel: 04 6968420   Fax: 04 6962220
ghwinery@golanwines.co.il
www.golanwines.co.il

Greenberg Winery
51 Hameginim St.
Herzliya 46686
Tel: 052 3237689
elegant@netvision.net.il

Gush Etzion Winery
POB 1415
Efrat 90435
Tel: 02 9309220 Fax: 02 9309156
winery@actcom.co.il
www.gushetzion-winery.com

Gustavo & Jo Winery
19 Marvah St.
Kfar Vradim 25147
Tel: 04 9972190
boia@netvision.net.il

Gvaot Winery
POB 393
Kedumim 44856
Tel: 09 7921292 Fax: 09 7921086
info@gvaot-winery.com
www.gvaot-winery.com

Hakerem Winery
POB 645
Qiryat Arba 90100
Tel: 052 4621390

Hamasrek Winery
Moshav Beit Meir 90865
Tel: 02 5701759 Fax: 02 5336592
hamasrek@netvision.net.il
www.hamasrek.com

Hans Sternbach Winery
Moshav Givat Yeshayahu 99825
Tel: 02 9990162 Fax: 02 9911703
sk-Gadi@zahav.net.il

Hatabor Winery
POB 22
Kfar Tavor 15241
Tel: 04 6767889
ssiecodo@zahav.net.il

Hevron Heights Winery
Moshav Geulim 42820
Tel: 09 8943711 Fax: 09 8943006
mm@churchill.fr

Jascala Winery
Gish (Gush Halav) 13872
Tel: 052 3833261
www.jascala.com

Kadesh Barnea Winery
Moshav Kadesh Barnea 85513
Tel: 08 6555849 Fax: 08 6571323
winerykb@012.net.il
www.kbw.co.il

Kadita Winery
POB 1052
Safed
Tel: 050 6933219
winery@kadita.co.il
www.kadita.co.il

Kahanov Vineyards
PO Box 423
Gedera 70700
Tel: 052 3936999 Fax: 08 8566588
info@kahanov.co.il
www.kahanov.co.il

Karmei Yosef Winery
Karmei Yosef 99797
Tel: 08 9286098
bravdo@bravdo.co.il
www.bravdo.com

Karmei Ziv Winery
Tel: 054 4869677
benji@reginatours.com

Katamon Winery
Tel: 054 6334206

Katlav Winery
Moshav Nes Harim 99885
Tel/Fax: 02 5703575
 info@katlav.co.il
www.katlavwinery.com

Katz Winery
Moshav Mesilat Tzion 99770
Tel: 050 2573950   Fax: 02 5855356
jossi@katz-winery.com
www.katz-winery.com

Kella David Winery
Meshek 61
Givat Yeshayahu
Tel: 02-9994848
keladavidwinery@gmail.com

Kfir Winery
POB 4125
Gan Yavne 70800
Tel: 08 8570354 Fax: 08 8673708
meirkfir@gmail.com
www.kfir-winery.co.il

Kitron Winery
Kibbutz Ma'abarot 17915
Tel/Fax: 09 8669006
kitronwinery@gmail.com
www.kitrone.com

Kleins Winery
19 Tchelet Mordechai St.
Jerusalem 94396
Tel: 02 5022946 Fax: 02 5022947
yomtov@kleins1.com

Lagziel Winery
Moshav Abu Menachem 22860
Tel: 050 4861405
www.hayain.co.il

La Terra Promessa Winery
Moshav Shachar 79335
Tel: 08 6849093 Fax: 050 5684775
laterrapromessa@bezeqint.net

Lachish Winery
Moshav Lachish 79360
Tel: 054 7920151
galiam@bezeqint.net

Lavie Winery
15 Zeit Shemen St.
Ephrata 90435
Tel: 02 9938520

Levron Winery
10 Orbach St.
Haifa 34985
Tel: 04 8344837 Fax: 04 8246724

Lewinsohn Winery
Hod HaSharon 45287
Tel: 054 2444018
amnonlewinsohn@gmail.com
www.l-wines.com

Livni Winery
POB 1736
Kiryat Arba 90100
Tel: 052-4214426
zipi@livni-wine.com

Lueria Winery
Moshav Safsufa 15875
Tel: 050 2249557
contact@lueriawinery.com
www.lueriawinery.com

Maccabim Winery
Maccabim-Re'ut 71908
Tel: 050 8503362
info@maccabimwinery.com

Maor Winery
Moshav Ramot 12948
Tel: 052 8515079
danny@maorwinery.com
www.maorwinery.com

Margalit Winery
POB 4055
Caesarea 38900
Tel: 050 5334433 Fax: 04 6262058
a_m_n_l@netvision.net.il
www.margalit-winery.com

Meishar Winery
Moshav Meishar 76850
Tel: 08 8594759
winery@meishar.co.il
www.meishar.co.il

Meister Winery
33 Schunat Hashalom,
Rosh Pina 12000
Tel: 054 4976940
meister@bezeqint.net
www.ruth-meister.co.il

Miles Winery
Moshav Kerem Ben-Zimra 13815
Tel: 04 6980623
miles013@013.net.il
www.miles-winery.com

Miller Winery
114 Ya'alom St.
Sha'arei Tikva 44810
Tel: 050 5211079 Fax: 09 7687761
yekev@gomiller.co.il

Mond Winery
Moshav Mishmeret 40695
Tel: 09 7968297
www.mond-winery.co.il
herzelkeren@walla.com

Mony Winery
Dir Rafat Monastery
POB 275
Beit Shemesh 99000
Tel: 02 9916629 Fax: 02 9910366
monywines@walla.co.il
www.monywinery.co.il

Na'aman Winery
Moshav Ramot Naftaly 13830
Tel: 04 6944463 Fax: 04 6950062
rami@naamanwine.co.il
www.naamanwine.co.il

Nachshon Winery
Kibbutz Nachshon 99760
Tel: 08 9278641 Fax: 08 9278607
winery@nachshon.co.il
http://winery.nachshon.org.il

Nahal Amud
Moshav Kfar Shamai 20125
Tel: 04 6989825

Nashashibi Winery
Kfar Eehbelin 30012
Tel: 054 6387191
nash_win@hotmail.com

Natuf Winery
Kfar Truman 73150
Tel: 052 2608199
natuf@012.net.il

Neot Smadar Winery
Kibbutz Neot Smadar 88860
Tel: 08 6358111

Nevo Winery
Moshav Mata 58
Harei Yehuda
Tel: 052-6071780
Yekev.nevo@012.net.il

Noga Winery
POB 111
Gedera 70700
Tel: 08 8690253
nogawinery@bezeqint.net

Odem Mountain Winery
Moshav Odem 12473
Tel: 04 6871122 Fax: 04 6871120
me_golan@012.net.il
www.odem-mountain-winery.com

Or HaGanuz Winery
D.N. Marom HaGalil 13909
Tel: 04 6990836 Fax: 04 6987306
yekev@orhaganuz.com

Pelter Winery
POB 136
Kibbutz Ein Zivan
Golan Heights
Tel: 052 8666384 Fax: 04 6993709
tal@pelterwinery.co.il
www.pelterwinery.co.il

Poizner Winery
71 Hameyasdim St.
Zichron Ya'akov
Tel: 052 3202323
poizner.winery@gmail.com
www.poiznerwinery.wordpress.com

Psagot Winery
Psagot 90624
Tel/Fax: 02 9978222
info@psagotwines.com
www.psagotwines.com

Ra'anan Winery
Moshav Ganei Yochanan 76922
Tel: 08 9350668
orsss@zahav.net.il

Ramim Winery
Moshav Shachar 79335
Tel: 054 4608080 Fax: 08 6849122
enrade@multinet.net.il

Ramot Naftaly Winery
Moshav Ramot Naftaly 13830
Tel: 04 6940371 Fax: 04 6962220
Yitzhak3@012.net.il

Recanati Winery
POB 12050
Industrial Zone
Emek Hefer
Tel: 04 6222288 Fax: 04 6222882
info@recanati-winery.com
www.recanati-winery.com

Red Boat Winery
Rehov Gefen 3
Karmei Yosef
Tel: 054 4825777
omernegev@gmail.com

Red Poetry Winery
Havat Tal
Karmei Yosef 99797
Tel: 08 9210352 Fax: 08 9210353
talfarm@bezeqint.net

Rosh Pina Winery
Rosh Pina 12000
Tel: 04 6827062
bloom_r@walla.com

Rota Winery
Havat Rota 85515
Tel: 054 4968703 Fax: 03 9732278
rotawinery@walla.com

Rozenbaum Winery
Kibbutz Malkiya 13845
Tel: 050 5423046 Fax: 09 8996316
aviroz@bezeqint.net

Ruth Winery
Tel: 08 9761800 Fax: 08 9761833
info@ruth-vineyard.co.il
www.ruth-vineyard.co.il

Safed Winery
Simtat Beit Yosef 29
Tsfat 13210
Tel: 050 3480883
paul@safed-winery.co.il

Salomon Winery
Moshav Amikam 37830
Tel: 04 6380475

Sarig Winery
Moshav Merchavia 19105
Tel: 050 5415554 Fax: 04 6420594
33sarig@gmail.com

Saslove Winery
POB 10581
Tel Aviv 69085
Tel: 09 7492697 Fax: 03 6492712
info@saslove.com
www.saslove.com

Sassy Winery
24 Ha'atzmaut Ave.
Bat Yam 59378
Tel: 052 2552012

Savion Winery
41 Bareket St.
Mevaseret Zion 90805
Tel: 02 5336162

Sde Boker Winery
Kibbutz Sde Boker 84993
Tel: 050 7579212 Fax: 08 6560118
winery@sde-boker.org.il
www.sde-boker.org.il/winery

Sea Horse Winery
Moshav Bar Giora 99880
Tel: 050 7283216 Fax: 02 5709834
info@seahorsewines.com
www.seahorsewines.com

Segal Wines
Kibbutz Hulda 76842
Tel: 08 9358860 Fax: 08 9241222
segal@segalwines.co.il
www.segalwines.co.il

Shdema Winery
Kibbutz Revivim 85515
Tel: 050 5255128 Fax: 08 6562397
motis@revivim.org.il

Shiloh Winery
Ma'aleh Levona
Efraim 44825
Tel: 02 9400736 Fax: 02 9942312
ykveyshilo@bezeqint.net
www.shiloh-winery.com

Shvo Winery
POB 1188
Rosh Pina 12000
Tel: 054 6700891 Fax: 04 6800414
gaby@shvo.co.il

Sifsaf Winery
Moshav Safsufa 13875
Tel: 06 7498928
eazywine@bezeqint.net

Smadar Winery
31 Hameyasdim St.
Zichron Ya'akov 30900
Tel: 04 6390777

Snir Winery
Kibbutz Snir 12250
Tel: 04 6952500 Fax: 04 6951765

Somek Winery
16 Herzl St.
Zichron Ya'akov 30900
Tel: 04 6397982 Fax: 04 6391194
barakdhn@netvision.net.il

Soreq Winery
Moshav Tal Shachar 78805
Tel: 08 9450844 Fax: 08 9370385
soreq@barak.net.il
www.soreq.co.il

Sraya Winery
Moshav Tomer 90680
Tel: 02 9944704 Fax: 02 9944705
brosho1@netvision.net.il

Srigim Winery
POB 174
Moshav Srigim 99835
Tel: 050 6991398 Fax: 02 9991512
srigim@srigimwinery.co.il
www.srigimwinery.co.il

Stern Winery
Kibbutz Gadot 12325
Tel: 054 6737423 Fax: 04 6939144
johnnys@stern-winery.co.il
www.stern-winery.co.il

Tabor Winery
POB 422
Kfar Tavor 15241
Tel: 04 6760444 Fax: 04 6772061
twc@twc.co.il
www.taborwinery.co.il

Tanya Winery
Ofra 90627
Tel: 050 9974949
yoram5733@walla.co.il
www.tanyawinery.co.il

Teperberg 1870
POB 609
Kibbutz Tzora 99803
Tel: 02 9908080 Fax: 02 5340760
www.teperberg1870.co.il

Terra Nova Winery
Moshav Kanaf
Golan Heights
Tel: 054 6700827
terranova-winery@gmail.com
www.terranova-winery.co.il

Three Vines
Moshav Ramot Naftaly 13830
Tel: 052 2660933 Fax: 04 6940462
ybarak@gmail.com

Tishbi Estate Winery
33 Hameyasdim St.
Zichron Ya'akov 30900
Tel: 04 6389434 Fax: 04 6280223
tishbi_w@netvision.net.il
www.tishbi.com

Trio Winery
Tel: 050 5333765 Fax: 03 5748861
triowinery@gmail.com

Tulip Winery
Rehov HaCarmel 24
Kiryat Tivon 36081
Tel/Fax: 04 9830573
tulip@tulip-winery.co.il
www.tulip-winery.co.il

Tura Estate Winery
Har Bracha 44839
Tel: 03 3128000 Fax: 03 5716266
www.turawinery.com
info@turawinery.com

Tzora Vineyards
Kibbutz Tzora 99803
Tel: 02 9908261 Fax: 02 9915479
info@tzoravineyards.com
www.tzoravineyards.com

Tzuba Winery
Kibbutz Tzuba 90870
Tel: 02 5347678 Fax: 02 5347999
winery@tzuba.org.il
www.tzubawinery.co.il

Vanhotzker Winery
Moshav Meron 13910
Tel/Fax: 04 6989063
Elivan1@bezeqint.net

Villa Wilhelma Winery
Moshav Bnei Atarot 60991
Tel: 054 4564526 Fax: 03 9721988
motti_goldman@yahoo.com
www.villawilhelma.co.il

Vitkin Winery
POB 267
Kfar Vitkin 40200
Tel: 09 8663505 Fax: 09 8664179
info@vitkin-winery.co.il
www.vitkin-winery.co.il

Vortman Winery
23 Netiv Ofakim St.
Haifa 34467
Tel: 054 7522221
hvortman@gmail.com
www.vortmanwinery.com

Yaffo Winery
Moshav Neve Micha'el
Emek Ha'Ella
Tel: 03 6474834 Fax: 03 6472059
info@yaffowinery.com
www.yaffowinery.com

Yatir Winery
POB 5210
Arad
Tel: 08 9959090 Fax: 08 9959050
y_yatir@zahav.net.il
www.yatir.net

Ye'arim Winery
Moshav Givat Ye'arim 90970
Tel: 052 5791080
sassons_wine@hotmail.co.il

Yehuda Winery
Moshav Shoresh 90860
Tel: 054 4638544 Fax: 02 5348100
yekev_yehuda@neve-ilan.co.il

Yiftah'el Winery
Alon Hagalil 17920
Tel: 052 2824644 Fax: 04 9501350
Habikta2@bezeqint.net
www.yfw.co.il

Zafririm Winery
Moshav Zafririm
Adulam
Tel: 052 4493042
lenderis@gmail.com

Zauberman Winery
50 Piness St.
Gedera 70700
Tel: 08 8594680
www.zaubermanwines.com

Zion Winery
45 Charuvit St.
Mishor Adumim
Tel: 02 5352540 Fax: 02 5355535
yossi@zionfinewines.co.il
www.zionfinewines.co.il

Zohar Winery
Moshav Kidmat Tzvi 12421
Tel: 04 6964234 Fax: 03 7254932
zoharwine@013net.net

1848 Winery
Tel: 800 801848
office@1848-winery.co.il
www.1848-winery.co.il

Index of Wineries

About the Author

Daniel Rogov is Israel's most influential and preeminent wine critic. He writes weekly wine and restaurant columns in the respected newspaper Haaretz, and contributes regularly to two prestigious international wine books – Hugh Johnson's Pocket Wine Book and Tom Stevenson's Wine Report. Rogov also maintains a wine and food forum, which can be found at www.tobypress.com/rogov.

The fonts used in the book are from the Chaparral family

Other works by Daniel Rogov
available from *The* Toby Press

Rogov's Guide to Kosher Wines

Rogues, Writers & Whores:
Dining with the Rich and Infamous

The Toby Press publishes fine writing,
available at bookstores everywhere. For more information,
please contact *The* Toby Press at www.tobypress.com